Soldier-Statesmen of the Constitution

by

Robert K. Wright, Jr.
and
Morris J. MacGregor, Jr.

Center of Military History
United States Army
Washington, D.C., 1992

Michael P. W. Stone, Secretary of the Army

U.S. Army Center of Military History

Brig. Gen. Harold W. Nelson, Chief of Military History

Chief Historian	Jeffrey J. Clarke
Chief, Histories Division	Col. Robert H. Sholly
Editor in Chief	John W. Elsberg

Library of Congress Cataloging in Publication Data

Wright, Robert K., 1946–
Soldier-statesmen of the Constitution.

(Army historical series)
Bibliography: p.
1. United States—Constitution—Signers—Biography.
2. Statesmen—United States—Biography. 3. United
States. Army—Biography. 4. Soldiers—United States—
Biography. 5. United States—Politics and government—
1783–1789. I. MacGregor, Morris J., 1931–
II. Title. III. Series
E302.5.W85 1987 973.3'092'2 87–1353

First Printed 1987—CMH Pub 71–25

For sale by the U.S. Government Printing Office
Superintendent of Documents, Mail Stop: SSOP, Washington, DC 20402-9328
ISBN 0-16-035959-7

Foreword

This volume represents an important part of the U.S. Army Center of Military History's contribution to the celebration of the Bicentennial of the Constitution. This Bicentennial, like the anniversary of the Declaration of Independence, produced a resurgence of interest on the part of the Army, the scholarly community, and the general public in understanding the formation of our republic and the principles on which it is based.

The mission of the Center of Military History is very explicit in such matters. In part we are to "serve the Army and the nation by ensuring the complete and appropriate use of military historical experience relevant to professional issues of today and tomorrow." To mark the Bicentennial of the Declaration of Independence, we produced five volumes on the role of the Army in the Revolution. In 1986 and 1987, through a series of historical brochures and the first printing of this volume, we took a systematic look at the role of the U.S. military as defined by the Constitution, focusing in particular on the individual parts played by Revolutionary War veterans—the Soldier-Statesmen—in the shaping of that role. In 1987 the Center also sponsored the Bicentennial Lecture Series—initiated by Secretary of the Army John O. Marsh, Jr.—at Fort Lesley J. McNair in Washington, D.C.; those lectures, plus several additional papers, were collected in *Papers on the Constitution*, a volume published by the Center in 1990.

Since 1987, reflecting the continuing interest and encouragement of Secretary Marsh and Secretary of the Army Michael P. W. Stone, we have continued our efforts to commemorate the enduring legacy of the Constitution by publishing four additional historical studies, one per year, on the ratification of the Constitution, on the Presidents, on the Judiciary, and on the Bill of Rights. In response to Secretary Stone's concern to preserve these studies, this second printing of *Soldier-Statesmen of the Constitution* incorporates them as natural extensions of the story of the creation of the Constitution.

That living document is revered by all of us, but it takes on a particular meaning for men and women in uniform when they give their solemn oath to "defend the Constitution against all enemies, foreign and domestic." For them, these words, crafted at the inception of our national government, are still very real. And to them especially we dedicate this book, with the hope that it will increase their understanding of the contributions made by their military forebears, not only to independence and freedom but also to the art of governance.

Washington, D.C.
20 September 1991

HAROLD W. NELSON
Brigadier General, USA
Chief of Military History

Preface

This book was written to explore the contribution of Revolutionary War veterans to the founding of the American republic. By veterans, we mean all those who served in the Continental and state forces, on land or sea. Twenty-three of those veterans were among the men who signed the Constitution in Philadelphia on 17 September 1787. That document, as the eminent American historian Samuel Eliot Morison put it, is "a work of genius, since it set up what every earlier political scientist had thought impossible, a sovereign union of sovereign states. This reconciling of unity with diversity, this practical application of the federal principle, is undoubtedly the most original contribution of the United States to the history and technique of human liberty."

We fully agree with Admiral Morison's eloquent assessment, and the following pages attempt to demonstrate how the Founding Fathers, especially those who had fought to gain the nation's independence, produced this singular work of genius. A central element of that genius was evident in the Constitution's careful delineation of the functions of the military in a democratic republic. In stark contrast to the actions of soldiers in many other revolutions, America's military leadership never sought to usurp power. We hope that this volume sheds some light on that phenomenon.

The creation of a new government did not end with the ratification of the Constitution. Most of the twenty-three veterans who signed that document, along with hundreds of their comrades, went on to serve their country and states at the highest political levels. Their careers provided us with the general thesis of our work: that the veterans of the Revolutionary War formed a human bridge between the promise of independence and the realization of representative government.

At the heart of this book are biographical studies of the twenty-three Soldier-Statesmen of the Constitution. Twenty-two signed as delegates; the twenty-third was the secretary of the Convention. Previously published in separate brochures by the Center of Military History as part of the Army's celebration of the Bicentennial, these brief biographies are included here with only minor editorial change. They are preceded by a general narrative survey of the period and are followed by summaries of the careers of the other signers of the Constitution. Obviously, no survey of the early republic would be complete without an account of the equally critical contributions of men such as James Madison, Benjamin Franklin, and William Paterson, but we must leave a fuller study of their role to others. We have in addition included a selection of documents, many from the pens of our Soldier-Statesmen, that outline the formation of America's military establishment, an unfolding event of singular interest and concern to the Founding Fathers. Except for minor deletions, as indicated, because of space limitations, these documents appear without any historical editing on our part. For those specialists who desire to consult the complete texts, we have included a list of the printed primary sources we used.

We have appended an account of the important Annapolis Convention of 1786. This study was also previously published as a separate Army contribution to the Bicentennial. This account is followed by a number of items, including charts and tables, that provide specific information on the political careers of the Revolutionary veterans.

Although two names appear on the spine of this volume, the work was more accurately a collaborative effort that used the special talents of four others as well. We want to acknowledge the important contribution of John W. Elsberg, Editor in Chief, who edited and coordinated the design of the volume; Lt. Col. Richard O. Perry, Chief, Histories Division, who supervised the project and served as a most exacting reader; Arthur S. Hardyman, senior Visual Information Specialist, who selected and placed the art work; and Ricardo Padron, Junior Fellow, who researched and drafted a significant part of the Other Signers section. We want to thank Joycelyn M. Canery, Barbara H. Gilbert, Catherine A. Heerin, Cheryl A. Morai, Rae T. Panella, Linda M. Cajka, and Marshall T. Williams for their careful assistance. The final draft of this work was read and critiqued by two renowned students of the period, and we acknowledge our debt and gratitude to Dr. Richard H. Kohn, the Chief of Air Force History, and Dr. Robert W. Coakley, the former Deputy Chief Historian of the Army. Finally, we want to add a special thanks to Col. Patrick Holland, Deputy Chief of Military History, for his unflagging support during the months this volume was aborning.

Washington, D.C.
5 February 1987

ROBERT K. WRIGHT, JR.
MORRIS J. MACGREGOR, JR.

Contents

Page

Page

The Constitutional Convention

Ratification

The Early Republic

Illustrations

Page

Page

The following illustrations appear between pages 256 and 263:

THE U.S. ARMY AND THE FOUNDING OF THE REPUBLIC

The U.S. Army and the Founding of the Republic

During the summer of 1787, fifty-five men assembled in the Pennsylvania State House (as Philadelphia's Independence Hall was then called) to hammer out a new form of government for the United States of America. The Constitution they produced has proved to be one of the most influential documents ever penned, a flexible instrument that has guided the nation through two hundred years of profound change and has served as a model for emerging democracies around the world.

The Framers sought to preserve and improve upon a way of life that had evolved in America over the preceding century and a half, but in so doing they also made a bold leap of faith. Advancing an idea considered radical in their time, they expressed their belief in the fundamental right of the people to govern themselves. They fashioned a republic carefully balanced so that the rights of the individual were protected, but one sufficiently powerful to prevent internal chaos and deter external attack. Even two centuries ago this singular notion had great popular appeal, but both the authors of the Constitution and its critics were well aware of the pitfalls. History could boast of no prior successful establishment of such a system.

The delegates were a diverse lot. Among them could be counted socially elite planters and merchants, along with lawyers, educators, and farmers. Like all humans, they were driven by complex motives and sought to protect the special interests of their family and class as well as their state and local community. What set them apart was their sense of statesmanship. Time and again they transcended regional concerns and economic self-interest to compromise for the general good. Historians have long sought to explain the capacity for growth and understanding that emerged during the Philadelphia meetings. One factor often overlooked, however, is that 23 of the 40 men (to include the secretary of the Convention) who signed the Constitution had served in uniform during the Revolutionary War. While the war had helped focus the attention of all the delegates on areas of mutual concern, the separate, shared experiences of those who had served under arms undoubtedly acted as a catalyst in moving the majority toward final compromise and action on national problems.

These 23 signers had volunteered to fight for independence, had sacrificed and suffered to win the war, and then, with their fellow Patriots, had shed their uniforms to resume civilian careers. Many of them would go on to lead the new government established under the Constitution. In a certain sense their work in Philadelphia was not only a continuation and culmination of the Revolution they had served in uniform, but also a preamble to the important role they would play in the governing of the new republic.

The Colonial Heritage

On the morning of 15 June 1775, as he had for the past month, George Washington entered Independence Hall and took his seat with the rest of the Virginia delegation to the Continental Congress. He was an imposing presence. At 43, he stood six feet four inches, weighed over 225 pounds, and was renowned for his military bearing and astonishing feats of physical strength. But he had also captured the attention of his colleagues in more important ways. The quiet planter was universally respected as a judicious Patriot with a natural dignity and an intense sense of personal honor. He was also known for an iron will that kept a passionate nature firmly in control. In short, he was gifted with all the essential ingredients of leadership, and now, in an act destined to alter the course of American history, he would be chosen to command his country's armed forces.

Congress had already agreed to accept responsibility for the improvised army that had set siege to General Thomas Gage's British regulars in Boston in the aftermath of the fighting at Lexington and Concord. New Englanders had responded to that first bloodshed by taking up arms, but, unaided, they could not hope to withstand the full might of the British. When Congress convened in mid-May, the New England delegates, supported by New Yorkers worried about an invasion from

George Washington (1732–99) as a colonel of Virginia Provincials. *(Oil, by Charles Willson Peale, 1772; Washington/Curtis/Lee Collection, Washington and Lee University, Virginia.)*

Canada down the Hudson River–Lake Champlain corridor, pleaded for united military action. Colonel Washington's military experience (he had commanded Virginia's troops in the French and Indian War) naturally led his fellow delegates to listen closely to his views. Acting on his advice, Congress adopted all existing forces as "the American continental army."

On the 15th the delegates turned to the delicate task of selecting a general who could be trusted to lead these men. They needed an individual with military experience, but also one who shared their fundamental political values and therefore posed no threat to the Patriot cause. Washington, the highest-ranking native-born American veteran, appeared the ideal choice. He had served in Virginia's House of Burgesses and in both Continental Congresses, where he had impressed his peers as a man who could be trusted with authority. The fact that he came from Virginia would help convince London that Americans from all sections were united in resistance. Although outwardly modest, his habit of wearing a uniform to the sessions indicated clearly his interest in the assignment. His election as commander of "all the continental forces raised, or to be raised, for the defense of American liberty" was unanimous. A score of the delegates, including Thomas Jefferson, Benjamin Franklin, and John Langdon, treated their new general to dinner that evening to celebrate the occasion.

It took the Commander in Chief a week to complete his preparations. In the interim four other delegates also agreed to serve in the Army: New York's Philip Schuyler and New Hampshire's John Sullivan as generals; Thomas Mifflin and Joseph Reed, both from Pennsylvania, as members of Washington's personal staff, or "family," as they came to be called. Finally, on 23 June, a cavalcade consisting of Washington and Schuyler, Charles Lee and Horatio Gates (two former British officers also appointed as generals), assorted aides and servants, and an escort of militia cavalrymen (the Philadelphia City Troop) departed Philadelphia.

The entourage drew crowds at every village as it crossed through New Jersey, New York, Connecticut, and Massachusetts. In New York City, where Schuyler remained to begin organizing a separate subordinate command, the generals encountered perplexed local officials who wished to extend them the proper courtesies without offending the colony's Royal governor. During these hectic days Washington received his first exposure to the burden of serving as a symbol for the Revolution and, in effect, for the emerging nation. The cavalcade finally reached headquarters in Cambridge, Massachusetts, on 3 July. After paying a brief call on officials from the colony's Provincial Convention, Washington quietly took command. The next morning the Virginian began the difficult task of learning more about these New Englanders and transforming the assembled ragtag military units into a true eighteenth-century army.

Although sharing a common heritage, the opposing forces outside Boston were profoundly different, reflecting the development of separate military and political traditions in the New World during the century and a half of colonial history. Ideas carried from England had clearly shaped both colonial society and its military institutions. One of the English notions incorporated into fundamental American thinking involved a belief that the individual had an obligation to society at large. Translated into military terms by the medieval Anglo-Saxons, this belief required every free able-bodied male to own weapons and turn out under local leaders to defend the realm. The militia, as this military force was called, ensured in a rough way that everyone participated in the country's defense in proportion to the benefits he received from it.

But these ideas concerning military obligation had developed differently in the colonies and the mother country. Taking advantage of its island geography, England had come to rely primarily on its navy for defense. Although a loosely controlled militia was assigned the task of protecting against the unlikely event of invasion,

"First Muster" depicts typical training by colonial militia musketeers and pikemen in the seventeenth century. *(Oil on hardboard, by Don Troiani, 1985; National Guard Heritage Painting, Department of the Army, National Guard Bureau.)*

military expeditions overseas were handled by raising temporary armies of paid soldiers. This arrangement pleased both the Crown and influential elements of society because it kept costs to a minimum and avoided major disruptions in everyday life. Eventually, two categories of militia emerged: the theoretical general militia of all able-bodied men available in event of general mobilization, and a smaller contingent of volunteers formed into "trained bands" that held periodic musters, or meetings, to practice military skills needed for temporary military contingencies. In time even these trained bands were allowed to deteriorate in favor of a small permanent, or standing, army controlled by Parliament.

The need to defend the relatively poor and sparsely settled colonies against both Indian tribes and European powers led to a different military arrangement in America. Defense played a major role in colonial life. Although the Royal Navy, supported by a few fortifications equipped with cannon, defended the coastline, the colonies themselves bore the major burden of their own defense. No colony could afford to maintain enough troops to meet all contingencies, so all relied on the concept of the citizen-soldier to defend the community. Within two years of its founding in 1607, for example, Jamestown had organized itself into a virtual regimental garrison complete with companies and squads. Plymouth, on the advice of Miles Standish, formed four companies of militia within a comparable period. The Massachusetts Bay Colony profited from the experience of the earlier settlements. By 1629 it had a militia company, equipped with the latest weapons, at Salem; by 1636 it had formed three permanent regiments throughout the colony.

Since the colonies could ill afford the luxury of exempting the majority of the population from regular training requirements, they expanded the trained-band concept to encompass all settlers. Only Pennsylvania remained an exception to the general pattern. Settled by Quakers, it did not pass a law establishing a mandatory militia until 1777. In fact, well into the eighteenth century few adult Americans were exempted by law from actual training. In the early fighting between settlers and Indians, citizen-soldiers actually fought in defense of their homes. Later, when more elaborate retaliatory offensive operations were launched against the tribes, the colonists tried to minimize the economic dislocation by using detachments temporarily organized for the occasion. Although the immediate military danger subsided as the frontier moved westward, the colonial standing militia remained as the means to train young men in the rudiments of war, as a law-enforcement agency, and as a source of recruits or draftees for short-lived military ex-

"Braddock's Defeat" captures both the confusion of combat and the difficulty of using regulars in the wilderness. *(Oil, by Edwin W. Deming, 19th century; State Historical Society of Wisconsin Museum Collection.)*

peditions on the frontier.

Eventually, supplemental military institutions emerged for frontier defense. Hired military volunteers began to range the wilderness throughout colonial America, patrolling outposts and giving early warning of Indian attack. Other volunteers combined with friendly Indians for offensive operations deep in the wilderness where European tactics were ineffective. This volunteer concept matured during the colonial wars. Regiments completely separated from the militia were raised for specific campaigns. These units, called Provincials, were patterned after regiments in the regular British Army and were recruited from the militia, often during normal drill assemblies. In 1754, for example, Royal Governor Robert Dinwiddie of Virginia raised a Provincial regiment to secure the colony's claims to the Ohio Valley against French encroachment. Major George Washington led the vanguard of the regiment toward the forks of the Allegheny and Monongahela rivers (now Pittsburgh, Pennsylvania) with instructions to force a French withdrawal. After some initial success, he surrendered to superior numbers, thus setting off the French and Indian War, the last and greatest of the colonial wars between France and England.

This colonial military system, with extensive responsibilities even in prolonged periods of peace, was profoundly important in shaping American politics. Except for slaves, just about every adult male served in the militia at some point in his life, making it perhaps the single most persuasive political institution affecting the daily lives of Americans. Even individuals technically denied the franchise in local elections participated in the process by which junior officers were elected for the units, and many political leaders gained their first responsible position in government as company commanders in the militia. When war threatened, Provincial service provided other opportunities. The widespread use of grants of land as recruiting bounties provided propertyless laborers and younger sons the chance to gain a homestead and therefore to rise in the social structure. Military skill also opened the door for individual officers to raise their economic standing and join the social elite. A clear understanding that the militia and Provincial units had an important function in protecting society also made Americans of all political views read contemporary political philosophers in a special way. These citizen-soldiers passionately believed that defense of life and liberty was an integral part of the citizen's duties, not something that could be left to a professional force responsible to a distant government.

The evolution of separate military institutions in the colonies and mother country paralleled a colonial elaboration of the English political model. During the seventeenth century, England not only planted colonies in the New World but also underwent a series of dramatic domestic changes. The period of early colonial growth witnessed an intense struggle for power between monarchy and Parliament that twice split the mother country apart. Accumulated grievances, coupled with religious differences, triggered a civil war in 1642 that pitted the Crown against a Parliamentary majority. The war cost King Charles I his life, and the remnant of the House of Commons abolished the monarchy and the House of Lords before being forced in turn to relinquish power to General Oliver Cromwell and the army. For a decade, England witnessed a virtual military dictatorship under Cromwell as "Lord Protector." A newly elected Parliament restored the Crown after Cromwell's death, but not before exacting major concessions, in particular limiting the size of the military establishment that the King might maintain. This traumatic period also had far-reaching consequences in the colonies, where Cromwell's dictatorship engendered an abiding suspicion of standing armies and an active opposition to the use of professional soldiers.

In 1688 King James II provoked a second constitutional crisis that ended in a nearly bloodless coup by his daughter Mary and her husband, William of Orange. As a price for supporting the "Glorious Revolution" and William's European military ambitions, the House of Commons extracted still more concessions, making it a full partner in most governmental affairs. Parliament further consolidated its power in 1714 when a Hanoverian prince, George I, succeeded Queen Anne. Henceforth kings ruled through ministers who sat in a Parliament that represented the interests of the landed and mercantile classes, a sequence of events that helped shape political institutions in the colonies.

The colonies had come into being largely as the result of individual initiative with a minimum of external control, thus paving the way for them to adopt and expand English models of representative government. By the start of the eighteenth century a basic pattern had emerged in the colonies; regardless of formal arrangement, all colonial governments functioned in essentially the same way. They had a governor, normally a Briton who returned home at the end of his term and who performed executive functions with the assistance of a small staff. Accountable to London, he had to juggle often-conflicting demands of the colonists and use patronage and persuasion to forge compromises. The colonial legislatures consisted, like Parliament, of two houses. The upper chamber, most commonly called the council, usually consisted of about a dozen members chosen from the colony's most powerful families. They advised the governor and exercised certain executive and judicial functions, although their influence waned as that of the lower house rose. The more powerful lower house was an elective body. Regardless of formal rules, the franchise in America came to be exercised by a very broad segment of society. Virtually every free, Protestant, adult male could vote as long as he met minimal property-owning restrictions. Members of the lower house, or assembly, were not compensated for their service. Because of this fact, and because colonists expected those with a greater stake in society to work actively for society's benefit, members of the assembly were largely drawn from the landowning and merchant classes. Most of these legislatures consciously adopted Parliament's procedures and precedents as a guide. They controlled their colony's finances and used this power to gain dominance in the government, much as the House of Commons had in England.

Despite these basic similarities in government, the quarter-million colonists in North America in 1700, although still thinking of themselves as Englishmen living abroad, had already begun to emerge as a separate people. The most conspicuous difference came from the fact that while individuals in their daily lives continued to show respect to those who stood above them in the social order, the rigid stratification of the Old World had disintegrated in the New under the impact of enhanced economic opportunity. In America self-sustaining farmers quickly replaced a tenant yeomanry, while talent and ambition allowed families to rise in social status in a brief period. A form of equality, based on economic self-sufficiency and reflected in the broad franchise, came to exist throughout society, which, although Americans did not realize it at the time, set it apart from its European counterparts. Poverty and slavery continued, but throughout most layers of society there existed an openness to change and a common perception that one could improve one's lot through personal effort. People who thought this way paid close attention to the concessions William and Mary made to Parliament and considered that they too had been guaranteed the "traditional" liberties of Englishmen.

This perception of traditional rights matured during the first half of the eighteenth century and set off a storm of protest when, after the Seven Years War, Parlia-

George III (1738–1820). *(Oil, from the studio of W. Beechey, c. 1800; courtesy of the National Portrait Gallery, London.)*

ment tried to increase its control over the colonies. This effort began with a scheme to raise money to retire the war debt and to garrison Royal regiments in the newly acquired colonies of Canada and Florida. Parliament decided that the colonies would pay for the defense and administration of North America, allowing Britain to concentrate on the war debt. At the same time, the economy of the mother country would be stimulated by a determined, and unprecedented, effort to enforce trade regulations.

The colonists resented the change, and over the course of the next decade became increasingly vocal in their objections. Their first protests came when, just eight months after the war ended, King George III signed the Proclamation of 1763, limiting settlers from the thirteen colonies from moving west of the Appalachian Mountains. The King's ministers had hoped thereby to minimize expenses by preventing clashes between the colonists and the Indians. To this end, they decreed the creation of an unoccupied zone that would be policed by regular British regiments under the direct authority of the London government and not answerable to any colonial governor. Most colonists saw the proclamation as an unwarranted intrusion into their internal affairs. Their charters allowed westward expansion, and the possibility of acquiring western land was the reason many of them had supported the French and Indian War. They especially resented the fact that the Redcoats stationed in North America were supported by taxes on the colonies voted in England, not in North America. On those rare occasions in the past when companies of regulars had been stationed in their midst, funding had been provided by the colonial assemblies which thereby retained considerable say in how they were employed.

The assemblies challenged this erosion of their "rights," using the same arguments that Englishmen had used against their Kings during the seventeenth century. Americans asserted that for a century and a half their own militia, supplemented as needed by Provincial units, had been more than adequate for defense. At the same time, London tried to reduce expenses further by ordering many of the British regiments from the frontiers to coastal cities, thereby simplifying logistical problems. The similarity of this move to events in the English Civil War and the Glorious Revolution raised colonial suspicions. Already convinced that these troops served no useful military purpose, the colonists increasingly felt that the regulars were a standing army stationed in their midst to enforce unpopular new revenue measures. In 1765 Parliament had passed the Stamp Act, which taxed paper products, including newspapers. In an effort to make the law acceptable, it appointed prominent Americans to serve as the collectors. Local opposition quickly forced those nominated to refuse appointment, and the Massachusetts legislature issued a call for a congress or general meeting of all the colonies to assemble in New York City in October to prepare a unified response. Nine colonies attended the Stamp Act Congress, the first such national meeting convened at the colonists' initiative, and drew up a petition of grievance. The delegates stated that one of the basic rights guaranteed to all Englishmen involved having taxes voted by an assembly of their own representatives. The Stamp Act, they argued, was improper because Americans were not represented in Parliament. They voted to impose a voluntary boycott of British goods until such time as the measure was repealed.

An angry Parliament reasserted its right to pass laws governing the colonies in "all cases whatsoever," but it decided that a different approach to raising taxes would be more practical. It rescinded the Stamp Act in 1766 and went on in the following year to enact the so-called Townshend Duties in an effort to raise monies in ways less objectionable to Americans. These new duties sought to impose a series of small "external" taxes on imports and exports, as an exercise of Parliament's unquestioned power to control trade, rather than the Stamp Act's single large "internal" tax, and specified

Patrick Henry (1736–99). *(Oil, by Thomas Sully, 1851; Virginia Historical Society.)*

John Hancock (1737–93). *(Oil, by John Singleton Copley, 1765; deposited by the City of Boston, courtesy of Museum of Fine Arts, Boston.)*

that all monies thus raised would be spent in America to boost the local economy. Americans rejected the argument, but the new round of protest took the form of pamphlets and newspaper articles. The most significant of these works was a series of *Letters from a Farmer in Pennsylvania* by a young leader of that colony's legislature, John Dickinson.

Incidents continued to multiply. In 1768 zealous British customs officials seized a ship belonging to John Hancock, a leading Boston merchant and prominent member of the Massachusetts assembly. Mob violence provoked by this incident provided London with an opportunity to show Americans that the Empire's authority could not be flaunted, and four regiments of regulars were ordered to Boston to make a show of force. The Boston town meeting, charging that the regiments were a "standing army," called on the colony's other towns to meet to devise plans for another economic boycott. The subsequent gathering reinforced the precedent set by the Stamp Act Congress for convening extralegal assemblies to bypass legislatures subject to a Royal governor's veto.

Compromise still seemed possible. Parliament withdrew most of the troops and rescinded the Townshend Duties, except for a purely symbolic one on the importation of tea. Unfortunately these concessions coincided with a clash between a Boston crowd and Captain Thomas Preston's detachment of the 29th Regiment of Foot guarding the Boston Customs House. When the crowd grew threatening, Preston ordered his men to fire, killing five civilians. News of the "Boston Massacre" sped through the colonies, but cool heads prevailed and further bloodshed was avoided. Preston and his men were placed on trial, but, defended by a rising young lawyer named John Adams, were acquitted on the grounds of self-defense. The remaining soldiers were subsequently withdrawn from the town in an effort to avoid further troubles.

The calm proved short-lived. In an effort to relieve some of the pressure on its Royal governor, the government in London announced in 1772 that hereafter it, not the Massachusetts assembly, would pay the salaries of both the governor and the colony's judiciary. Boston's town government immediately established a Committee of Correspondence to communicate with other localities on a regular basis as a way of combating what it considered to be this further erosion of self-government. The idea rapidly spread across North America. The following year these committees proved invaluable in organizing resistance to the Tea Act of 1773 when Parliament sought to solve the economic problems of the East India

"Stand Your Ground" depicts the first fighting of the Revolution on Lexington Common, 19 April 1775. *(Oil on hardboard, by Don Troiani, 1985; National Guard Heritage Painting, Department of the Army, National Guard Bureau.)*

Company by giving it a monopoly on that commodity in the American market through the enforcement of import duties. Carefully orchestrated resistance throughout the colonies resurrected the protest tactics of the Stamp Act. Local agents were forced to resign, and most governors chose not to let shipments of tea land in order to prevent trouble. In Boston, however, Royal authorities tried to enforce the law. In response, a small group of men, vaguely disguised as Indians, threw forty-five tons of tea into the harbor. Town authorities refused to prosecute them.

News of the Boston Tea Party shocked British authorities. The King, his ministers, and an overwhelming majority in Parliament agreed that an example had to be made of the town or the entire structure of imperial authority would be undermined. Between March and June of 1774 a series of laws, known in America as the Intolerable Acts, closed the port of Boston until restitution was made to the East India Company and suspended the civil government of Massachusetts, replacing it with a military regime backed by a large garrison. The colony's legislature immediately issued a call for another meeting of all the colonies.

The Continental Congress met in Philadelphia's Carpenter's Hall between 5 September and 26 October 1774 and created a fundamental shift in the focus of the crisis. Every colony except Georgia appointed delegates, sending their most respected leaders. These men realized that should Parliament succeed in bringing Massachusetts to its knees by employing such unprecedented measures, similar force might be used against any other colony in the future. They issued a Declaration of Rights and Resolves setting forth the view that colonists were entitled to the same rights as any other Englishmen, approved a boycott (the Association) of imports from and exports to Great Britain, and set plans to reconvene on 10 May 1775.

This Second Continental Congress, like its predecessor, was intended to serve as a temporary forum for debate, but in the end it became the governing body that directed the Revolution for the thirteen states. This ad hoc arrangement was echoed in the individual colonies, which, with the exception of Connecticut and Rhode Island, could not use existing governmental structures because they were controlled by the British. To fill the void, Patriots in each colony mobilized public opinion to establish new, extralegal governing bodies, called Provincial Conventions or Congresses, and local Committees of Safety. In every case their argument was the same, stemming directly from what they perceived as outside interference by Parliament. Embued with the political philosophy of the Enlightenment, the colonists believed that a social contract existed between them and their sovereign, who had granted their Royal charters, and not with Parliament, in which they were not represented. In 1775 the colonists rose up to oppose a "ministerial army" sent, in their eyes, by Parliament, rather than the King, to deprive them of their rights as Englishmen. But when King George III later sided openly with his ministers in what the majority of colonists considered Parliament's usurpation of powers properly reserved to the colonial governments, the social contract was broken and revolution became inevitable. From its outset, therefore, the Revolutionary War was a fight to preserve existing norms of local self-government.

From the start of the crisis local politicians had seen a military dimension to their political problems. Militia assemblies provided convenient gatherings to marshal public opinion and in some cases in 1765 furnished both the leaders and manpower when Sons of Liberty organized to intimidate tax collectors. If a strong militia could remove the need for British troops to protect North America against French or Spanish aggression, thereby eliminating any justification of the odious taxes, a strong militia could also directly oppose arbitrary power exercised by British troops. As the crisis deepened, many leaders began agitating for serious militia reforms on that very ground. Working closely with the Committees of Safety, militiamen purged their ranks of British sympathizers and provided enforcement machinery for the acts of the extralegal assemblies, a process expedited by the fact that many of the elected representatives were also officers in the militia. The political impact of the militia cannot be overestimated in the critical process of mobilizing public support for the Revolution, although reliance on the militia did create some military problems, just as it had in the French and Indian War. Militia forces, organized locally, were ideal for use in short tours of service in defense of nearby areas, but were impractical for duty covering either extended periods of time or great distances. Communities simply could not sustain the resulting economic disruption. To fill the immediate void, the colonists turned to the Provincial precedent—a full-time military force recruited for a limited term of service (therefore not a "standing army") and directly under the control of popularly elected authorities.

Some Patriot leaders, including George Washington, began to organize voluntary military companies for extra training. But in this area, as in political ones, Massachusetts took the lead. In October 1774 a convention of representatives from across the colony, acting in place of the suspended legislature, passed resolutions calling for a reorganization of the militia under Patriot officers, began assembling depots of weapons and military supplies, and established the Minutemen, a select force ready to turn out quickly in an emergency. Other colonies followed this precedent, and early in 1775 New Englanders began planning for a regional defensive army patterned after the Provincial regiments of earlier wars.

On 18 April 1775 a British column of some 600 men set out in the dark from Boston with orders to proceed to Concord, where the Massachusetts Provincial Congress was accumulating military stores, and to seize any materiel found there. Early the next morning the column encountered Lexington's company of militia drawn up near their route of march. Neither side wished to provoke trouble, but both needed to make a political statement. The British deployed to confront the militiamen, and ordered them to disperse. Just as the colonists were beginning to comply, a shot rang out. Seconds later the British line opened fire, leaving a number of Americans lying dead and wounded. No one knows for sure who fired the "shot heard round the world," although it probably was a junior British officer simply trying to gain the attention of a milling crowd. This incident and a later engagement just outside Concord touched off a general battle when the small British column began to withdraw, having failed in its mission to destroy military stores. Several hundred British soldiers died or suffered wounds during the long march back to Boston as the militia forces of eastern Massachusetts converged to harass them. Only the appearance of a relief column with artillery, and the lack of central control among the Patriots, enabled the force to escape total annihilation.

The colony quickly set about collecting testimony from participants to prove that British troops were the aggressors and then turned to other colonies for assistance. Within two months four separate armies—one from each New England colony—emerged, enlisted for service through the end of the year and patterned on the Provincial model. They relieved the Minutemen and militia who had begun the siege of Boston, drawing heavily on those organizations for both an officer corps and for trained soldiers. Danger of British raids on the coastline led to new laws that raised the militia's strength to a level not seen for more than a century.

The Revolutionary Experience

The military situation that greeted General Washington at Cambridge in July 1775 might well have given him pause. To be sure, the strategic realities favored the Americans in drawn-out military operations. With the militia firmly controlled by the Patriots, and with Committees of Correspondence and other extralegal bodies acting effectively in place of the old colonial governments, the British faced armed and organized opposition in each colony. Reestablishing Royal control, either through occupation or intimidation of a vast and hostile region stretching from New England to Georgia, presented formidable, if not insurmountable, difficulties. Only fools would ignore Britain's military might, based on a large and professional army, vast wealth that permitted hiring of foreign auxiliaries, and the world's largest navy, which guaranteed control of the seas. These obvious advantages prompted most politicians and military leaders in London, along with their Loyalist supporters in America, to predict a speedy Redcoat victory over the "upstart rabble." In so doing, however, they ignored Britain's need to balance offensive operations in North America against its defensive responsibilities in other parts of the globe and the many practical handicaps implicit in communicating with and supplying large forces across 3,000 miles of ocean in the era of sailing vessels.

Despite strategic advantages accruing from geography and self-reliance, the colonies, too, faced formidable problems. The ability of the Continental Congress to lead the thirteen independent states in war and, more specifically, to adopt a national military policy, organize an effective military force, and support its commander, was questionable. In fact, Washington's problems were rooted less in military matters than in the fears, divisions, and inhibitions of the new national government. Congressional delegates had emerged from a political

"The Battle of Bunker Hill" illustrates the precision needed for linear combat. *(Oil, by Howard Pyle, c. 1898; Howard Pyle Collection, Delaware Art Museum.)*

tradition that viewed central authority, even that exercised at the level of individual colonies, with strong suspicion. Their rejection of the concept of a standing army was well known. By European standards, their view of the conduct of military affairs would have been considered naive. They adopted the Continental Army only reluctantly as a minimal response to the presence of Royal troops in their cities and ordered the Army to operate strictly as a defensive force. In the days that followed Lexington and Concord, few delegates contemplated the likelihood of extended military operations; they meant their military initiatives as merely a signal to London that Americans were united in their willingness to defend their rights. To underscore this sense of unity, their resolution that turned the troops in New England into the national Army on 14 June also requested Pennsylvania, Maryland, and Virginia to raise a force of riflemen to serve as light infantry during the siege of Boston. By the same token, they liked to stress as another evidence of unity the fact that the commander appointed to lead the troops in New England was a Virginian.

But old fears die slowly, and for every supportive step Congress took in military affairs, the delegates seemed impelled to impose yet another limitation on their commander. While they recognized, for example, the need for an efficient Army led by competent generals, they feared creating another Oliver Cromwell. By adopting units raised by the individual colonies, Congress obtained a sizable body of men in short order, but the result was a haphazard collection of units led by locally appointed commanders selected first for their political reliability and only secondly for their military experience. Congress, moreover, allowed Washington no direct voice in selecting his major subordinates. Although nearly all of the first thirteen generals it appointed were veterans of the French and Indian War, most of these men were also from legislative backgrounds, and sectional balance was a paramount consideration in their choice. Congress left to Washington the task of sorting out the problems attendant on conducting operations with leaders whose politics were above reproach, but whose military competence was not. Furthermore, Congress' fear of standing armies meant that the units of the new Continental Army were enlisted for only limited periods. The men Washington was sent to train and organize into a unified fighting force, those expected to match the British regiments, would be going home at the end of the year when their enlistments ran out.

Evidence of his Army's strengths and weakness was readily apparent to the new commander, since it had fought its first engagement just before his arrival. A council of local Patriot leaders had decided to occupy the hills on Charlestown Peninsula, which dominated both Boston and the warships in the harbor. Unfortunately, the amateur planners failed to establish a clear chain of command and committed units piecemeal during the night. The local commanders compounded this mistake by selecting Breed's Hill, instead of the safer Bunker Hill, as the site for their fieldworks. The British then committed their own error by opting for a massive show of force to convince the Americans that armed resistance to the Crown was doomed. General Sir William Howe landed 2,200 regulars on the tip of the peninsula and launched them in a European-style frontal assault. Twice the 2,000-odd defenders, under the cover of hastily erected fortifications, used close-range volleys to drive Howe back. But Howe's third try with fixed bayonets carried the hills when most of the front-line New England units ran out of ammunition. Howe's victory cost him 42 percent of his effectives and made him realize that he had to force the Americans to fight battles in the open where superior British training and discipline would be most effective. For their part, the Patriots took great pride in the performance of the raw troops, but they misread the lesson taught by the battle. They mistakenly assumed that the courage and marksmanship displayed under these special circumstances meant that citizen-soldiers would always be equal to trained professionals. Their new commander suffered

Sir William Howe (1729–1814). *(Mezzotint, by C. Corbett, 1777; Anne S. K. Brown Military Collection, Brown University Library.)*

"Sir Peter Parker's Attack Against Fort Moultrie." The failure of this assault against Charleston, South Carolina, in the summer of 1776 ended British threats to the southern states for several years. *(Oil, by James Peale, c. 1782; Colonial Williamsburg Foundation.)*

from no such illusion.

By the end of the summer control over the war had clearly passed from the individual colonies to the Continental Congress. Washington's main contingent adopted a minimum-risk strategy of encircling Boston to keep the largest British force neutralized. Going beyond purely defensive operations, Washington sent a second field force, under Major General Schuyler, to launch a preemptive invasion of Canada in late fall, hoping to win over that colony to the Revolutionary cause and to prevent the British garrisons stationed there from harassing the frontiers. Despite a series of successes, the campaign ground to a halt in the winter snows when a night attack on Quebec, the last major British strongpoint, was repulsed. At the same time, the enlistments of the 1775 continentals expired on the last day of the year, forcing Washington and the Congress to rebuild the Army.

With overall conditions largely unchanged, the Americans followed a similar military policy at the start of 1776, employing a force balanced between short-term militia and Provincial-style units enlisted in the various states for one year's Continental service. The politicians and generals knew that militiamen were most useful in roles compatible with their historic functions: conducting local security, defending their homes from invasion, and providing select groups of men for specific operations of limited duration. Under the supervision of local Committees of Safety, these militia troops prevented the Loyalists (probably about one colonist in ten) from organizing, guarded coastal communities, and kept an eye on Indians along the frontier. Regulars, with more time to train and learn discipline, were needed to fight formal European-style battles, and the continentals, as these troops were now called, appeared capable of carrying out this mission. The only new military initiative in early 1776 was a slight expansion of the Army to include units from all thirteen colonies, plus two from Canada.

London faced a clear-cut choice in early 1776: make political concessions or launch an offensive war to crush the rebellion. The King's advisers decided for war. They rejected Congress' last attempt at reconciliation, the so-called Olive Branch Petition, and set about expanding the military and naval forces stationed in North America to include over 30,000 auxiliaries (the Hessians), whose services were acquired through treaties with various German states. Lord George Germain, who as Secretary of State for America had primary responsibility for devising British strategy, decided to avoid directly challenging Patriot control in New England and to apply resources against especially vulnerable targets. His plan for the campaign of 1776 called for three separate operations. A relatively small expedition under General Sir Henry Clinton would try to regain the southern colonies by rallying Loyalists, who London erroneously presumed were in the majority. Other units would proceed to Canada to turn back the American invasion and to apply pressure on the frontiers of New York and New England. An even larger force would be sent to join Howe, who had evacuated Boston on 17 March. Thus reinforced, Howe would capture New York City and would then use that port as a naval base and as the center of operations to regain control over the middle colonies.

By summer, two of the three operations had ended. A combination of militia and continentals defeated the British southern thrust rather easily. Virginia expelled its Royal governor and his small army and fleet. North Carolina crushed a premature uprising by local Loyalists. Finally, an invasion force sent from England was repulsed at Charleston, South Carolina, on 28 June. Again, Patriots misread these early sucesses. Given the role of Minutemen and militia forces in defeating the governors, their Loyalist supporters, and Indians on the frontier, they came to assume that the militia could carry the major burden of defense. This misjudgment would cost the Americans dearly in later clashes in the south. In the far north, operations ended in a stalemate. The Americans were driven out of Canada in May 1776, but the British had to stop to reorganize their supply lines and to build a fleet on Lake Champlain before they could mount their own offensive. Clearly, the great military test would occur around New York City, where Congress had concentrated about 31,000 men under Washington. Over half were militia and state troops, who had even less training than the main force Washington had rebuilt after Boston. The Americans faced 32,000 British and German regulars under General Howe, supported by a fleet of 73 warships, 370 transports, and 13,000 seamen under his brother, Admiral Sir Richard Howe—the largest transoceanic force ever dispatched before the twentieth century.

As battle lines were forming for New York, Congress weighed a momentous decision. Washington's soldiers, facing the realities of the battlefield, had been talking for some time about the need to sever all connections with the Crown. Public opinion had been galvanized by Thomas Paine's stirring call for independence in *Common Sense*. And now news of the King's declaration that the colonists were in rebellion and of the decision to send Hessians to America finally convinced a majority in Congress that the British government was united in its refusal to make concessions. On 7 June Richard Henry Lee introduced a resolution in Congress, drafted by the Virginia Convention, that called upon Congress to declare independence, create a formal national government, and seek foreign allies.

The more outspoken Patriots led by John and Samuel Adams of Massachusetts argued that these measures were necessary to win the war. John Dickinson of Pennsylvania and other moderates supported defensive measures required to carry out military operations, but still considered independence premature; they wanted to make one last attempt at a negotiated settlement. Congress decided to appoint two committees: one under Dickinson to develop specific proposals for a confederation of the colonies (now called states) and one under Thomas Jefferson of Virginia to prepare a statement of independence. As chairman, Jefferson wrote most of the draft Declaration. He was assisted by Benjamin Franklin of Pennsylvania, John Adams, Roger Sherman of Connecticut, and Robert R. Livingston of New York.

On 4 July, after three days of debate, Congress declared the United States of America to be a free and

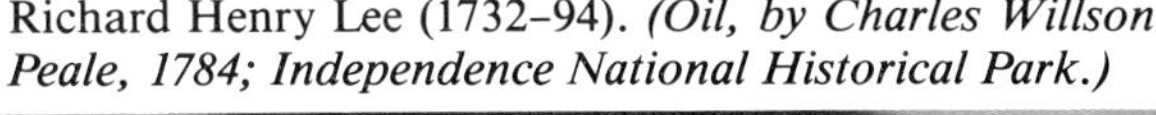

Richard Henry Lee (1732–94). *(Oil, by Charles Willson Peale, 1784; Independence National Historical Park.)*

"The Signing of the Declaration of Independence," completed between 1786–97, was based on detailed research as well as interviews with Jefferson. *(Oil, by John Trumbull; copyright Yale University Art Gallery.)*

independent nation. Jefferson's elegant words, amended by the other delegates, provided a concise statement of purpose both to the inhabitants of the colonies and to foreign governments. The Declaration also justified independence in terms familiar to Enlightenment philosophers, charging King George with a list of actions that had "broken" the social compact between Americans and the British Crown. Significantly, a third of this list related to military actions, including assertions that "He has kept among us, in Times of Peace, Standing Armies, without the consent of our Legislatures" and that "He has affected to render the Military independent of and superior to the Civil Power." On 9 July Washington assembled his troops and had Congress' Declaration of Independence read to the men to help motivate them for the coming battle.

Howe also understood the important interrelationship between military action and political loyalty. He knew that Congress had mobilized large numbers of militiamen to strengthen the continentals, and he reasoned that an overwhelming blow could break the Patriots' current strong will to resist. On 27 August his army badly mauled a large American contingent on Long Island, forcing Washington to undertake a risky night evacuation, and followed it up with a crushing blow on 15 September that captured New York City. During the next two months, although Washington won a few skirmishes, Howe drove him out of Manhattan Island and the nearby mainland.

The American defeat at New York marked a turning point for the Continental Army. Now committed to independence, the Americans had to prepare for a long war to outlast the British, and Washington was able to convince Congress that militia and short-term regulars alone could not meet British and German regulars on equal terms. Since most of the existing enlistments would expire on 31 December, Congress used that opportunity to draft its first comprehensive military program. Central to its new approach were the recruitment of men for the duration of the war rather than for the customary single campaign, and expansion of the regular Army to about 120 regiments, including artillery and light dragoons, capable of facing the British in open battle. The plan called for an Army of 90,000 officers and men, but since only a small proportion of that number was ever recruited, militiamen remained an important source of reinforcements. That teamwork would prove its worth before the full plan could even begin to be implemented.

On 16 November Fort Washington and its important garrison of 2,800 men, the last American toehold on Manhattan, fell to a sudden attack by Howe, unhinging

Philip Schuyler (1733–1804). *(Miniature, by John Trumbull, 1792; copyright Yale University Art Gallery.)*

Arthur St. Clair (1736–1818). *(Oil, by Charles Willson Peale, 1782; Independence National Historical Park.)*

the American defensive array just as the summer's militia contingents were leaving for home. Howe promptly exploited the situation by driving across New Jersey toward Philadelphia, the American capital. Washington had to retreat all the way to the Pennsylvania side of the Delaware River before Howe called off operations and settled down in winter quarters. Washington knew that he had to end the year on a positive note to encourage recruiting and sustain the will to resist. Using militia reinforcements from Pennsylvania and Delaware, he decided to strike at several isolated garrisons. It was a risky gamble, for defeat would probably bring the Revolution to an end. But Washington won a brilliant victory on 26 December in a snowstorm at Trenton and another on 3 January at Princeton, recovering in one swift and daring operation most of New Jersey.

When campaigning resumed in 1777, the logic of British strategy called for their two main armies in Canada and New York, working in unison, to sever New England from the rest of the country. The authorities in London, however, failed to ensure that the two commanders coordinated their operations. For his part, General Howe planned to continue his previous year's effort to break American will by now moving south to capture Philadelphia. He reasoned that this move would cause Washington to follow him with the main Continental force. General John Burgoyne in Canada could then deal with the American garrison at Fort Ticonderoga and drive south to the Hudson River. When events failed to work out this way, the scene was set for a major American victory.

Burgoyne's expedition enjoyed immediate success. American engineers had left one key hill mass at Ticonderoga unprotected because they incorrectly assumed that it was impassable for artillery. As soon as Burgoyne's cannoneers placed guns on it, the badly outnumbered Americans under Major General Arthur St. Clair were forced to evacuate the fort. The garrison retreated south until it made contact with General Schuyler's forces in New York. Although St. Clair saved most of his men, the defeat of his rear-guard regiments in several delaying actions and the loss of the fort, which had been a vital defensive position in the colonial era, started a movement in Congress to replace the Northern Department's senior officers.

Burgoyne was unable to take advantage of his early success. He spent weeks reorganizing at Ticonderoga to secure his lines of communication back to Canada, to establish a forward supply base, and to organize transportation to continue south. In the interim, a supporting column, headed down the Mohawk Valley, ran into unexpected trouble. The small Continental garrison at

Ford Stanwix stubbornly refused to surrender. Then a relief force of New York militiamen, although defeated in a bloody battle at Oriskany, managed to punish Burgoyne's Indian allies in the region so badly that those valuable auxiliaries began withdrawing their support, eventually forcing the British flanking column to retreat to Niagara. Burgoyne also lost a large foraging force of Germans at Bennington, to Brigadier General John Stark's militiamen, reinforced by a regiment of continentals.

By the time Burgoyne began his advance in earnest, work parties of militiamen and continentals had torn up the roads and bridges and had obstructed the creeks and streams stretching south from Lake Champlain. Schuyler, a veteran of logistical operations in the wilderness during the French and Indian War, had recognized that transportation would be Burgoyne's achilles heel, and that time would be the Americans' most valuable ally. The successful delaying tactics allowed the movement of additional continentals up from the lower Hudson Valley and the mobilization of masses of militia from New England.

Schuyler never benefited from the strategy he devised. Major General Horatio Gates replaced him as commander of the Northern Department in mid-August. Gates placed his five Continental brigades in an entrenched position on Bemis Heights, near Saratoga, New York, to bar Burgoyne's route to Albany. The masses of militia took up positions outflanking Burgoyne's line of march and threatening his rear. Raiding parties penetrated as far as the outer lines at Ticonderoga, fatally disrupting British supplies. By early September Burgoyne was in an untenable situation. Rather than retreat, he pushed on in the hope of reaching Albany and safety. On 19 September he fought with Gates' men, led in combat by Colonel Daniel Morgan and Major General Benedict Arnold, in the fields and woods in front of the American lines on the heights above. This first battle at Freeman's Farm ended with the British, badly bloodied, stopped cold and forced to dig in.

On 7 October, his supply situation now critical, Burgoyne gambled one last time. He sent forward most of his effective troops in a reconnaissance in force, hoping to find a weakness in Gates' fortifications. American skirmishers quickly discovered the British, and once again the continentals led by Morgan and Arnold sallied out to meet the enemy in the woods and scattered fields of Freeman's Farm. They stopped the British, and a wounded Arnold succeeded in leading his men into the outlying British earthworks before the onset of darkness. Burgoyne, incapable of movement in any direction, accepted a conditional surrender. On 17 October "Gentleman Johnny" and his 6,000 troops marched out to lay down their arms at Saratoga, the most stinging defeat suffered to date in America by the Crown.

Howe, never anticipating that Burgoyne would run into problems, completed his own planning for the 1777 campaign without any intention of direct coordination with the army in the north. He had selected Philadelphia as his target to help erase the sting of Trenton and Princeton and to eliminate the largest American logistical base. Occupation of the American capital would also serve as an important political victory and allow the Crown to rally the middle states' Loyalists, mistakenly believed to be a substantial proportion of the population. To avoid the problems encountered in New Jersey in 1776, especially the difficult terrain and the danger implicit in Washington's ability to rally large numbers of militiamen to reinforce his continentals, Howe decided to attack Philadelphia from the sea. The transports and accompanying warships left New York in late July.

Howe's original choice was to approach the city by way of the Delaware River, but naval experts quickly convinced him that the forts and American ships based below Philadelphia rendered that route impractical. Instead, he sailed up the Chesapeake Bay and landed at Head of Elk (now Elkton), Maryland, in late August. Washington had been mystified by the illogic of the British movements, believing that Howe's only reasonable plan was to use the Hudson to link with Burgoyne. Once Howe's true intentions were confirmed, the American commander set out rapidly for Philadelphia. The continentals concentrated on defending the main route between Head of Elk and the capital while hastily mobilized militia guarded the flanks in Delaware, Maryland, and Pennsylvania.

Howe organized a base area to support his operations, and in early September started northeast toward his target. On 11 September he brilliantly outmaneuvered Washington to secure a crossing over Brandywine Creek, the major natural obstacle in the area, although several of Washington's brigades gave a very respectable account of themselves in the afternoon's fighting. Howe, although unable to pursue Washington, occupied Philadelphia on the 27th. Congress managed to escape, and most of the Army's important supplies were saved from the defeat.

Although the British now held the American capital, the approach of winter and the massing of American militia left their control of the region tenuous. Overland supply from Head of Elk could not sustain an occupying garrison, and Howe had to turn his attention to the task of clearing the forts and obstructions along the Delaware River in order to communicate with the British fleet. In the interim, Washington regrouped his forces and launched a sharp counterattack. He selected the primary British camp area at Germantown, some six miles outside the city, as his target, attempting to dupli-

"Attack on the Chew House." *(Oil, by Howard Pyle, 1898; Howard Pyle Collection, Delaware Art Museum.)*

cate the tactics that brought victory at Trenton and Princeton.

During the night of 3–4 October, the Americans, marching in multiple columns, began a twelve-mile approach. According to the plan, the continentals in two bodies would strike at dawn along the two main routes into town while militiamen and small flanking parties would provide deception by simultaneously engaging the extreme ends of the cantonment area. But the long approach march proved to be too difficult for the troops to execute with precision, and the columns struck piecemeal. The vanguards of both Continental columns enjoyed initial success, overrunning the camps of Howe's elite light infantry battalions, even penetrating into the village of Germantown. Alert action by the commander of the 40th Foot, however, enabled six of his companies to occupy the Chew House, a stone structure that commanded one of the roads.

Washington's advancing columns began to flag, their commanders confused in the fog and musket smoke that had begun to hang over the battlefield. Meanwhile Howe stabilized his lines, brought up reinforcements, and counterattacked. His units cut off the 9th Virginia Regiment inside Germantown and took most of its men prisoners. Several American units mistook each other for enemy and opened fire, throwing both columns into further confusion. Finally, although the leading American brigades had bypassed the Chew House, the reserve units became preoccupied in a futile attempt to storm the structure and, consequently, were not on hand to help keep the American advance moving. Washington reluctantly concluded that prolonging the attack was too risky and ordered a withdrawal. Howe, shaken by the close call, made only a halfhearted attempt at pursuit (easily checked by a rear guard under Maryland's Lieutenant Colonel John Eager Howard) before settling back down to the long, hard job of clearing the river of American forces.

The lesson of Germantown was not lost on Washington, who used the winter pause in operations to train his troops in professional, European-style tactics. Amid the cold and deprivations of the camp at Valley Forge, he adopted changes in doctrine and organization, beginning with the preparation of a standard drill by Major

Sir Henry Clinton (c. 1738–95). *(Miniature, by John Smart, c. 1777; National Army Museum, London.)*

General Frederick von Steuben for use by both the continentals and militia. Steuben displayed a genius for developing a simple and efficient system for maneuvering on the battlefield that drew on many American and European precedents. The result, published in 1779 as *Regulations for the Order and Discipline of the Troops of the United States, Part I,* became the first official Continental Army field manual, and was distributed to the militia as well as the regulars. The effort to provide similar training to both militia and regulars, however, implied no change in the strategic use of the militia. The fundamental commitment to a policy of blending the separate talents and skills of regulars and citizen-soldiers remained the same.

A measure of American success in 1777 was the fact that France decided the following February to enter into an alliance against Britain. The war in America eventually assumed even larger global implications as first Spain and then the Netherlands also declared war on their old enemy. The addition of traditional European adversaries into the war forced Britain in turn to change its strategy. New requirements for ships and men to protect possessions in Europe, Africa, Asia, and the Caribbean turned North America into a secondary theater. With resources limited, Sir Henry Clinton, who replaced Howe as the British commander in May 1778, received orders to develop a new strategy. He began by evacuating Philadelphia, just in time to avoid being trapped by a French fleet sent to work with Washington. Washington's continentals and New Jersey militiamen caught up with the British rear guard at Monmouth, but the resulting battle ended in a draw and the British escaped. Action then shifted to the British outpost at Newport, Rhode Island, where large contingents of New England militia turned out to assist continentals and the French fleet in besieging the town. The operation ended prematurely when damage from a storm and an inconclusive sea battle caused the French to withdraw and left the British still in control of this northern outpost.

Clinton used this reprieve to implement a new "southern strategy." He consolidated a defensive position in New York where a portion of his army could tie down Washington's main force. Orders went to Canada to use Indians and Loyalists to raid the frontiers of Virginia, Pennsylvania, and New York in an effort to force Congress to divert regiments to protect those regions. The rest of the British troops were to be used in the south to defeat local Continental forces and disperse the militia. At that point the Loyalists, whose numbers the Crown still grossly overestimated, would be formed into units and used to secure the newly regained area. The British regulars could then move north against the next state and repeat the process. On 23 December 1778 Savannah fell to an invading force from New York and Florida. The following year a Franco-American counterattack, supported by militia units from Georgia and South Carolina, ended in a bloody fiasco—a Bunker Hill in reverse. Clinton then mounted another invasion, this time aimed at Charleston, South Carolina. On 12 May 1780, after a 42-day siege and gallant defense, Major General Benjamin Lincoln's 5,000 continentals and militia were forced to surrender in America's worst defeat in the war.

A second disaster of colossal proportions followed almost at once. A crack division of Maryland and Delaware continentals marched south to serve as a nucleus for a new field army. Congress sent Gates to take command, assuming that he would repeat his Saratoga success by rallying the militia to augment his regulars. Gates impetuously called out a large force and launched an offensive without rebuilding his army's supply system. On 16 August 1780 near Camden, South Carolina, his troops collided with General Charles Cornwallis, now the senior British officer in the south. Gates placed all of his militia on the left flank, his continentals on the right. The two wings promptly lost sight of each other in the smoke of battle. Cornwallis routed the militia, who were unfamiliar with linear combat, then wheeled on the continentals and shattered them. For the second time in a matter of months the Southern Department found itself without a field army.

Daniel Morgan (1736–1802), left, and John Eager Howard (1752–1827), heroes of the battle of Cowpens. *(Both oils, by Charles Willson Peale, Morgan in 1794, Howard in 1782; Independence National Historical Park.)*

By the end of the year, however, American fortunes shifted again. Major General Nathanael Greene, who had replaced Gates, emerged as a first-rate strategist. He used irregular Patriot units in Georgia and the Carolinas, many under former continentals like Francis Marion and Thomas Sumter, to harass British rear areas, forcing the enemy to shift attention further north in an effort to cut supply lines sustaining the partisans' operations. Cornwallis marched his main body through the more populous low country while light forces covered the interior. Unfortunately for the Crown, the flanking parties ran into immediate trouble at the hands of backcountry militiamen, most notably on 7 October, when a force of 900 frontiersmen captured the Loyalist units screening Cornwallis' left flank at King's Mountain, South Carolina.

Cornwallis soon suffered a much more devastating blow. Contrary to conventional wisdom, Greene did not keep his outnumbered force concentrated. He recognized that local militia, if supported by continentals, could inflict considerable damage on the vulnerable British rear. Exploiting the opening created by King's Mountain, Greene concentrated his light troops, both infantry and dragoons, under Daniel Morgan, now a brigadier general. From a vantage point well inland from the Southern Department's main body, Morgan could slip behind Cornwallis, rally militiamen, and begin offensive operations against British supply trains and bases.

Cornwallis, on the other hand, was determined to push the main Continental force back in order to gain time to pacify South Carolina. At the same time, he concentrated his remaining light troops under his best junior leader, Lieutenant Colonel Banastre Tarleton. They were ordered inland to neutralize the threat to his flank by finding and crushing Morgan. On the evening of 16 January 1781 Tarleton began closing in on his quarry, who had halted at Cowpens, South Carolina.

Morgan, well trained by Washington, spent that evening preparing for the forthcoming battle. He had selected a battlefield in the open woodland, relatively free of undergrowth, with large patches of open pasture dominated by a small hill. After carefully studying the strengths and weaknesses of his troops, he positioned them to take maximum advantage of the terrain and to play on Tarleton's known impetuosity. The most reliable part of his force consisted of veterans of Steuben's rigorous Valley Forge training — a battalion of Maryland and Delaware infantry under Lieutenant Colonel John Eager Howard and two companies of Virginia volunteer militia, all ex-continentals. He placed these troops as a main line of resistance on the hill. He sent the militiamen from the Carolinas and Georgia to form a line about 150 yards in front of the continentals, and a smaller skirmish line another 150 yards further forward. Morgan's military genius was revealed in this use of his militia. Realizing that they lacked the training to stand and slug it out with the Redcoats, Morgan told them merely to wait for the enemy to get in range, fire two well-aimed shots per man, and then retreat. He was able to instill confidence by his homespun style of leadership and by taking time to visit each small group before the battle began. By telling the militia in advance that retreat was expected, he avoided the danger of panic and rout. He positioned them in such a way that the effect of their fire would disrupt Tarleton's advance and force him to commit his reserves before his troops closed with the main line of continentals.

On 17 January the trap was sprung. Tired British and Loyalist soldiers reached Cowpens and were quickly ordered into a line, supported by two small field guns. As they advanced, the American skirmish line fired its two volleys and withdrew, as did the second line of militia. The casualties they inflicted, and the sudden shift in their lines, led Tarleton, as Morgan had predicted, to commit his reserves. The British continued their advance, confident of victory because they had so easily swept the first two American elements from the battlefield. But there was to be no duplication of Camden. The British ground to a halt when they collided with Howard's regulars. Tarleton committed his cavalry on the flank in an effort to turn the American line, but it was driven back by the Continental dragoons in heavy hand-to-hand fighting. Howard, meanwhile, slowly retreated, drawing the British infantry forward and increasing their disarray. As soon as he judged the confusion sufficient, Howard ordered his veterans to counterattack with bayonets. The shock of the sudden charge, coupled with the reappearance of the American militiamen on the flanks where Tarleton's exhausted men expected to see their own cavalry, proved too much. The British line collapsed, and Morgan's men took over 600 prisoners, overran the two artillery pieces, and captured Tarleton's wagon train. In less than an hour, Cornwallis' light infantry, some of his best soldiers, had been lost.

Cornwallis immediately attempted to counteract the Cowpens defeat by chasing Greene all the way to Virginia. The British became so exhausted by this futile effort that they had to withdraw to the coast, where Cornwallis could establish a base and refit his regiments. Greene then seized the initiative. By concentrating on quality and mobility, he turned the small size of his army into a logistical advantage. Large militia contingents were called out only on the eve of a battle and used as they had been at Cowpens. Greene began his offensive with a battle at Guilford Court House, North Carolina, on 15 March 1781. North Carolina and Virginia militia brigades opened the engagement by delaying and disrupting the British advance. The continentals then punished Cornwallis' regiments with accurate musket fire and a bayonet charge, and when Greene began to lose control, he carefully broke off the action, knowing that as long as his main body remained intact, the British could never disperse to deal with the irregulars. By September a repetition of these tactics, coordinated with attacks on depots and outposts, left the British isolated in Charleston and Savannah.

Meanwhile, Washington's main army in the north had been reinforced by a division of French troops under Lieutenant General le comte de Rochambeau in the summer of 1780. Washington immediately began planning a joint land-sea assault on New York City. A victory against this British stronghold, he reasoned, would have a decisive impact on the war, depriving the enemy of his major naval base and breaking the will of the English people to support further hostilities. The French, however, were reluctant to strike against the heavily defended British position. Washington was forced to abandon his plan, and he spent the year inconclusively in a wide defensive arc around the city.

By the summer of 1781 Cornwallis had moved into Virginia in an effort to cut Greene off from reinforcements and supplies. This tactic failed to achieve the desired results, as continentals under Major General le marquis de Lafayette and Brigadier General Anthony Wayne, reinforced by Virginia militiamen, prevented the British from permanently occupying any important inland city. General Clinton finally ordered Cornwallis to terminate his offensive operations and find a site for a naval base on the Chesapeake Bay. Ships operating from such a base, under the protection of a reasonably small garrison, could effectively disrupt the American tobacco trade, the primary source of the Continental Congress' hard currency. Cornwallis was then to send the rest of his men to reinforce New York. On 1 August, on the advice of naval and engineer experts, he selected Yorktown, Virginia, as his base.

Washington's plan for the 1781 campaign again depended on the cooperation of the French for an attack on New York City. In early July, in anticipation of that event, Rochambeau's troops moved to the vicinity of New York City from their winter quarters in Rhode Island, and the allied staffs began reconnoitering the approaches to Manhattan. In mid-August dispatches arrived from Admiral le comte de Grasse, however, announcing that he did not wish to risk his warships at New York and that his fleet would sail instead to the Chesapeake, bringing a force of French troops with him from Santo Domingo.

Washington and Rochambeau immediately changed

their plans. Instead of striking at Clinton, they now decided to capture Cornwallis. On 20 August they led the vanguard of an allied army across the Hudson on a rapid march south, covered by an elaborate deception plan to lull Clinton. Six days later de Grasse's ships entered the Chesapeake and on 2 September began landing French troops near Williamsburg to join forces with Lafayette and Wayne. A British relief force engaged de Grasse's ships three days later off the Virginia Capes, but was unable to break through to Cornwallis. Its retreat to New York sealed any chance the British at Yorktown had of escaping by sea.

On 14 September Washington and Rochambeau arrived at Williamsburg, joined over the following days by their regiments. The consolidated force, with a logistical base firmly established at Williamsburg and with the French fleet in control of the Chesapeake, set out on 28 September to bring Cornwallis to battle. Militiamen, reinforced by French light troops, blocked any retreat across the York River at Gloucester. The main body forced Cornwallis' outposts to withdraw and on the night of 30 September began digging the trenches for a formal European-style siege of Yorktown. Morale among the allies soared, the two contingents engaging in competitions to demonstrate which was more efficient and professional.

"They Scrambled Up the Parapet" portrays the capture of Redoubt 10 at Yorktown. *(Oil, by Howard Pyle, c. 1898; Howard Pyle Collection, Delaware Art Museum.)*

As the siege progressed, heavy guns were moved ever closer to the defenders' earthworks. Two isolated outworks, known as Redoubts 9 and 10, presented the last obstacle. On 14 October, Washington ordered a night bayonet attack to capture them. Elite French troops under le vicomte de Noailles, Lafayette's brother-in-law, were assigned Redoubt 9; Lafayette's light infantrymen under Lieutenant Colonel Alexander Hamilton were to assault Redoubt 10. Each attacking column marched with unloaded muskets to prevent accidental discovery. Number 10 fell after a quarter of an hour's fighting; Number 9, a few minutes later. Engineers immediately began incorporating the positions into the allied siege lines, and a few days later, as heavy guns pounded his final positions, Cornwallis was forced to ask for terms. The surrender took place on 19 October amid pomp and circumstance. Although no one realized it at the time, Yorktown would be the last major battle of the war.

On 19 April 1783, eight years to the day after the first shots at Lexington, an armistice halted the fighting. Almost immediately Congress began disbanding the Continental Army. The Treaty of Paris ending the war and recognizing American independence followed on 3 September. Washington returned his commission as Commander in Chief to the nation's civilian leaders, then meeting in Annapolis, Maryland, on 23 December; the soldiers of his last regiment received their discharges at West Point, New York, on 20 June 1784.

America's victory surprised many European observers. Some attributed it to the effect of the frontier; others, to British blunders. Actually, a key factor in the victory came from the successful innovations Washington and his generals made in the traditional colonial approach to warfare. The Americans created a unique mix of militia and regulars, each with clearly defined functions, and employed a conservative defensive strategy combined with selective offensive blows against targets created by British mistakes. The militia served as the enforcement arm of Revolutionary government and carried out the traditional function of local defense with renewed vigor. In essence, the existence of the militia restricted British authority to those areas physically occupied by Royal troops. The continentals, improving on the Provincial model of earlier wars, performed missions requiring a main battle force able to operate for extended periods and in any geographical location. Their strengths, particularly their offensive capabilities, complemented the militia's and prevented British commanders from dispersing their troops to crush local resistance.

"The Surrender of Cornwallis at Yorktown" was painted by the Continental veteran, John Trumbull. *(Oil, 1797; copyright Yale University Art Gallery.)*

Achieving these results was not a simple task. Politicians frequently bristled over any hint of challenge to their authority, while military leaders grumbled about inefficient civilian administration and critical deficiencies in logistical support. In fact, there was little military threat to congressional authority. Even in the two most celebrated cases of unrest, the mutinies in 1781 by enlisted men from Pennsylvania and New Jersey and an officers' protest in 1783 known as the Newburgh Conspiracy, the continentals accepted the ultimate authority of Congress and the state governments. In the end, it was not any challenge to congressional authority that threatened the Revolution, but rather the weakness of the central government. Washington and his staff faced almost insurmountable difficulties in the day-to-day conduct of the war because of the frustrations involved in dealing with an ineffectual Congress.

Washington's personal example of unparalleled devotion to duty clearly played a critical role in victory. To most Americans he, rather than the Continental Congress, became the symbol of the Revolution. He took great pains constantly to remind the soldiers that they were engaged in a common struggle for liberty, and he used his officers, especially chaplains like Abraham Baldwin of Connecticut, to turn the Army into a school devoted to the civic obligations of the American citizen-soldier. Military service, either in a contingent of mobilized militia or as a regular in the Continental Army, thus became an important formative influence on men from every state. By serving side by side, they came to understand that a unified country had greater potential and strength than any single state or loose confederation of states, and many came to identify themselves first as Americans and as Virginians or New Yorkers only in a secondary sense. Washington and his fellow military leaders also formed ties of mutual respect and friendship with the politicians who supported them in Congress and in the state governments—ties that would survive the war. When these citizen-soldiers of the Revolution returned to civilian life, they did so as experienced leaders, confident about assuming new duties in their communities and eager to build a new nation.

The Articles of Confederation

The Treaty of Paris ended the Revolution, established the United States as a member of the community of nations, and fixed its boundaries. But it also left formidable tasks in its wake. Americans still had to convince a sceptical world that their new nation could maintain an effective government for its people, assert control over its new lands, and protect national interests beyond its borders. In trying to solve these problems during the first years of independence, the nation faced fundamental questions both about the relationship between the states and the central government and about the nature and role of military forces in a free society.

When Richard Henry Lee had introduced Virginia's resolution in 1776 calling on Congress to vote for independence, he had also urged the delegates to draw up an instrument to govern national affairs. Even as Jefferson's committee began drafting the Declaration of Independence, a second group headed by Pennsylvania's John Dickinson had taken up the task of fashioning Articles of Confederation—the nation's first constitution.

Dickinson proceeded to write the basic draft himself. An eminent lawyer, he believed that the Articles should preserve the familiar organization of American society and restore the liberties lately threatened by Parliament. At the same time, Dickinson was a pragmatic politician who realized that the nation's first and most important task was to ensure its survival in a war against a vastly more powerful enemy. His Articles, therefore, were designed primarily to deal with the war emergency, providing the Continental Congress with the specific powers needed to meet Washington's military needs. A militiaman himself, Dickinson counted on the states to maintain local forces adequate to local defense—the "well-regulated" (well-trained, well-organized, and well-equipped) militias that had played so important a role in the ideology of the colonial days. But, as the presence of a British army in New York City made clear, situations could arise that no single state or region could handle. He planned, therefore, to turn Congress into a national government with strong central powers, especially in the military arena, and provide after-the-fact justification for the creation of the Continental Army (see Selected Documents). Congress debated Dickinson's Articles in the summer of 1776, focusing on powers to be retained by the states, but then put the revised draft aside to deal with other matters.

In the interim, individual states organized their governments on a formal basis, replacing their extralegal conventions with governors and legislatures established under state constitutions. By early 1777 ten states had completed this process. Connecticut and Rhode Island simply dropped references to the King from their colonial charters and continued business as usual. Massachusetts did not finish writing its new document until 1780. These new governments were largely moderate in nature; most called for a two-house legislature, with the interests of property owners represented in one and the concerns of the population at large in the other. The constitutions also provided for elected governors, although with less power than previously held by the departed Royal appointees, and for new state court systems. The most common innovation in these state constitutions was the inclusion of a formal bill of rights. Virginia's Bill of Rights, drawn up by George Mason, was the first and served as a model for most of the others. Turning the new state governments into functioning entities absorbed the energies of many able leaders as they assumed the demanding work of such positions as governor, judge, and state legislator. In this critical time in the nation's history, talented men like New Jersey's William Livingston, who in the past had served simultaneously in his colony's legislature and in the Continental Congress, now became absorbed in purely

John Dickinson (1732–1808). *(Oil, by Charles Willson Peale, 1770; Historical Society of Pennsylvania.)*

state affairs.

Meanwhile, the Continental Congress turned its attention to General Washington's requests for help. In retrospect, the national legislature proved to be an impediment to the progress of the war. Established primarily as the instrument to develop a joint defense effort, the Congress was responsible for enlisting a Continental Army, obtaining reinforcements when needed from the state militias, paying and supplying the troops, and conducting a foreign policy that supported the independence movement. But even Dickinson's original draft of the Articles, calling for a far stronger centralization than provided by subsequent versions of the document, had envisioned supporting no more than the basic military machinery as it existed in the summer of 1776: a small body of regulars enlisted annually and backed by large numbers of militiamen.

The loss of New York City in September 1776 had led a reluctant Congress to accept Washington's advice and create a much larger regular Army—one raised for the duration of the war and trained to meet European troops in open battle—but Congress was never able adequately to sustain this expanded version of a national defense system. It left Washington to wrestle with the problems of organizing and fielding an expanded force. He did this by coordinating with the various state governments to ensure that a sufficient number of regiments were mobilized and positioned in time to counter the Howe-Burgoyne offensive. Congress, meanwhile, faced the perhaps even more daunting problem of finding the necessary weapons, equipment, medicines, and food for the American forces, a logistical operation on a scale never before attempted in North America. Given the weakness of the congressional system, failure was predictable. By the time Washington's main army moved into Valley Forge in December 1777, Quartermaster General Thomas Mifflin's supply system had collapsed from the strain.

During the next year Washington and his staff pressed for more immediate and responsive congressional support, but politicians with a residual aversion to standing armies incorrectly interpreted Gates' victory at Saratoga in October 1777 as vindication for a return to the older defense model. These delegates, working with a minority of Army officers, including Mifflin and Gates, pressed for a reduction in the number of continentals and a return to the earlier militia ideal of the yeoman farmer. Washington, most of his senior officers, and other delegates fought this movement, and early in 1778 the issue came to a head in an ill-defined confrontation known to history as the Conway Cabal.

Pushed by Mifflin, Congress in October 1777 had reorganized the Board of War, its committee that exercised general oversight over defense, by adding outside experts and in other ways attempting to transform the group into a true executive arm for military affairs. Gates was named the Board's presiding officer in a manner that implied that Washington would lose overall control of the war effort. This implication was reinforced when Congress then attempted to launch an invasion of Canada without coordinating its plan with the Commander in Chief. Meanwhile, Gates and Mifflin schemed to get Lafayette, a member of Washington's staff and considered by many congressmen as the key to alliance with France, to serve as a stalking horse for Major General Thomas Conway, the Board of War's Inspector General and their real choice to lead the expedition. The young, politically sophisticated Frenchman, however, refused to cooperate. His adherence to the military chain of command, Conway's own intemperate remarks, and the emergence of strong congressional backing for Washington in the form of a "Committee to Camp" were sufficient to turn back this challenge. Although Congress, led in this instance by Gouverneur Morris, supported Washington by preserving the basic military structure intact, it again failed to make any fundamental improvements in the administrative machinery to support the war effort. Piecemeal reforms would allow the Army merely to stagger along until final victory.

Washington paid a heavy cost in time and energy because of this inability of a weak Congress to support the Army adequately. The Commander in Chief often had to put aside questions of strategy, tactics, and morale in order to try to convince thirteen separate state governments of the need to provide supplies and money. And despite the national importance of his military needs, his was merely one voice among many vying for the attention of state leaders. Governors, even those deeply committed to the welfare of the Continental Army such as William Livingston, George Clinton, and Jonathan Trumbull, possessed only limited powers under the new state constitutions, and they had to submit Washington's pleas for men and supplies to their legislatures, where approval was often tied to local political concerns. As the war progressed and the needs of the Army multiplied, the lack of strong national government one step removed from local and state concerns increasingly frustrated or hobbled Washington's ability to conduct the war.

When Congress had resumed its consideration of the Articles of Confederation in 1777, the concentration on state interests by important leaders was reflected in a renewed effort to dilute the powers given to the central government by Dickinson's proposed Articles. Led by North Carolina's Thomas Burke, Congress further amended the draft Articles, shifting more power back to the states. On 17 November the new draft was forwarded to the states for approval. Twelve quickly agreed, but

Marie-Paul-Joseph-Roch-Yves-Gilbert du Motier, marquis de Lafayette (1757–1834). *(Oil, by Charles Willson Peale, 1781; Independence National Historical Park.)*

Connecticut Governor Jonathan Trumbull (1710–85). *(Miniature, by John Trumbull, 1793; copyright Yale University Art Gallery.)*

implementation was blocked by Maryland. Taking advantage of the requirement for unanimous consent—the same condition imposed on the vote for independence—Maryland insisted that states with claims to the vast unsettled regions of the west transfer jurisdiction of these lands to the national government as the price for its support. Finally, after Virginia promised to make this concession, Maryland's delegates signed the document on 1 March 1781 and the Articles took effect.

Actually, the Articles merely formalized a national government that in most essentials remained severely restricted. Under their terms, the United States remained a "firm league of friendship" that bound together thirteen independent entities. No provision existed for a national executive or judicial organization, and the one-state, one-vote procedure rule in the old Continental Congress continued to frustrate the political process. The national legislature lacked authority to impose taxes, and therefore could not provide for its own revenue. It could only ask the states to make contributions "for the general good." The Continental Army was responsible to the Congress, but it consisted of troops raised and sustained by the individual states. Congress could not enforce the quotas it set for each state, and control of the purse strings allowed the state legislatures to retain a final say in many areas of military matters. In foreign affairs, although Congress could enter into treaties and conduct diplomacy, it did so only as an agent of the states, and the states technically were free to pursue independent agreements with other nations or Indian tribes. In a related area, Congress could not control international trade, or even trade between the states.

These were precisely the weaknesses in government that were being attacked by many Americans, especially those in uniform, who were witnessing firsthand the problems they caused in times of crisis. The signing of the Articles only seemed to energize an emerging nationalist element in Congress which became more outspoken in calling for a stronger central government. In 1781 the group won a small victory when three executive departments—military affairs, finance, and foreign affairs, all approved by and responsible to the Congress—were added to the government. The nationalists, however, failed when they pushed for substantial change in the vital area of taxation. To achieve any semblance of national authority, they argued, Congress required an independent source of income, and to that end they proposed an import duty known as the Impost. Twelve states reluctantly supported the idea, but it died when Rhode Island, fearing disruption of its economy which

Secretary at War Benjamin Lincoln (1733–1810), left, and Secretary of Foreign Affairs Robert R. Livingston (1746–1813). During the winter of 1781–82, Charles Willson Peale painted these two department heads who served under the Articles of Confederation. *(Both oils; Independence National Historical Park.)*

depended heavily on commerce, adamantly refused to approve the idea.

As the Revolution drew to a close the nationalists were defeated on a second critical issue. Shifts in congressional membership and a revival of old ideological objections to a standing army in the traditional European sense resulted in strong opposition to the work of a congressional committee established in April 1783 under Alexander Hamilton to explore the idea of a peacetime army. The committee requested General Washington's views, and he in turn solicited the opinions of his most trusted subordinates before transmitting his "Sentiments on a Peace Establishment," in effect an official Continental Army position, to Hamilton on 2 May. To these officers the Revolution had underscored the need for a peacetime military establishment consisting of a small regular Army, a uniformly trained and organized militia, a system of arsenals, and a military academy to train the Army's artillery and engineer officers.

The most original part of Washington's "Sentiments," echoed by Generals Steuben and Knox in later pamphlets, called for institutional change in the militia. The generals never questioned the basic premise that every individual owed society military service. On the contrary, they argued that the lessons of the Revolutionary campaigns showed that national defense depended heavily on the contribution of the citizen-soldier and that a "well-regulated" militia would eliminate the need for a large peacetime force. At the same time they considered the existing system defective and proposed reforms to enable the militia to serve more effectively with the regulars on the battlefield. Specifically, they called for the establishment of uniform organization and training, and the creation of a select force, composed of men between the ages of 18 and 25 who would receive special advanced training beyond that received by the average militiaman. This was not a radical change; it simply formalized the old idea of the Minutemen, bringing them under supervision of the national government rather than the individual states.

Washington's proposal was a reasoned attempt to match resources to the realities of the American situation, both militarily and politically. Hamilton's committee modified these proposals somewhat and recommended their adoption. But the opposition was too strong. Buoyed by the prospect of peace and dubious of the need for a comprehensive program, Congress voted down the original plan in May and again in October 1783. The following April it rejected a further scaled-down version, in part because New York feared that the four proposed battalions of regulars, continentals primarily from Massachusetts, might take sides in a land dispute between the two states. Finally, on 3 June, one day after ordering the discharge of the last Continental regiment, Congress created a peace establishment, a single regiment under Lieutenant Colonel Josiah Harmar. The First American Regiment consisted of eight companies of infantry and two of artillery (perpetuated by today's 3d Infantry and 1st Battalion, 5th Field Artillery). It was enlisted for a single year and ordered to oversee the occupation of the western lands, chiefly by creating a buffer zone in the wilderness between settlers and Indians. Other military duties were left to the militias of the individual states. These militias, which had absorbed many of the ex-continentals upon their discharge, were expected to maintain combat readiness.

Demobilization of the Continental Army did not end the network of associations that had developed among its veterans, the militiamen who had served with them, and those nationalist political leaders who had supported the Army in Congress and the states. All returned to peacetime civilian life with shared memories of the inadequacies of the Articles of Confederation. The fellowship forged during the war remained particularly strong among ex-Continental officers. Some, like Washington, had been Masons before the war, and many more joined that order during the struggle. When they returned home, they promptly organized chapters among fellow veterans to preserve contacts made during the war. Some officers helped establish the first national veterans' organization, the Society of the Cincinnati. The group's name was a deliberate attempt to evoke the classical ideal of the citizen-soldier as personified by Lucius Quintus Cincinnatus, who returned to the life of a simple farmer after leading the armies of Rome to victory. Although Washington served as the organization's first president-general, the society was not without its critics, who saw it as an effort to establish a form of hereditary artistocracy.

A third, more popular, postwar association evolved from efforts by veterans to improve their economic status by settling new lands on the nation's frontiers. Groups like the Ohio Company, organized by former Brigadier General Rufus Putnam of Massachusetts, copied another Roman idea, seeking to stabilize the frontier by establishing towns populated by discharged soldiers and their families at the limits of civilization. Used to discipline, these settlers, who would form the basis of the region's postwar militia, were considered less prone to start trouble with the Indians and would, therefore, help eliminate the need for a large regular army. (Included among the more notable settlements founded in the Ohio territory under this scheme were Cincinnati, named for the veterans' order, Dayton, named for Constitution signer Jonathan Dayton, and Marietta, named for Putnam's wife.)

This approach to settlement attracted considerable support as Congress began to wrestle with the responsibility it had gained under the Articles for the western territories. On 23 April 1784 it approved a plan, originally drafted by Jefferson, providing for an orderly transition to self-government in the Northwest Territory. A second resolution, the Land Ordinance of 1785, established procedures for the surveying and settling of the west. Ironically, Congress sought to accomplish these tasks through a process very similar to George III's infamous Proclamation of 1763. Finally, on 13 July 1787 Congress passed the Northwest Ordinance, which established a territorial government to rule the area until settlement reached a density sufficient to form states.

Congress' weakness actually complicated western settlement because the limited ability to conduct negotiations and to field military forces left the nation's frontier vulnerable. Congress could only stand by, for example, when the British refused to evacuate those western forts ceded to the United States under the terms of the Treaty of Paris. From these bases, British merchants involved in the fur trade worked to encourage tribal resistance to the American government, thus contributing indirectly to sporadic Indian raids on settlers pushing westward into the trans-Appalachian area. Most significantly, in December 1786 British officials in Detroit hosted a meeting of Indians from ten tribes in an attempt to organize opposition to the American advance into the Ohio Valley. To make matters worse, individual state governments began to prepare for independent military action to meet the danger, prompting Henry Knox, who had been appointed Secretary at War in 1785, to warn Colonel Harmar that as commander of the First American Regiment he was an official of the United States and therefore not responsible to any governor.

The financial restrictions on Congress created even more complex problems. The postwar depression had hit small farmers and small merchants particularly hard. Elimination of traditional British markets coincided with a period of rampant inflation in the United States, and Congress lacked the power to impose a retaliatory tariff to force open foreign markets. At the same time it was unable to standardize currency or set financial policies to reduce the impact of the inflation. Shortages in hard cash coupled with business failures and farm foreclosures created unrest throughout the nation, but especially in western counties, which traditionally had been underrepresented in state legislatures.

Washington quickly emerged as the leader most concerned with the postwar development of the west. His understanding of the region's potential dated to his participation in the Fort Necessity campaign of 1754. As a private citizen, he later invested heavily in the region. Washington feared that without positive government action, western settlers inevitably would begin to use either the Mississippi River or the Great Lakes as trade routes and drift away from the union. He wanted to develop east-west lines of communications. New roads and improvements in river navigation, he reasoned, could be used both to supply military posts and to support economic development. He urged elected officials to pursue this idea, and in the fall of 1784 he made a 640-mile trip through Virginia's frontier regions to assess their potential for development. This expedition strengthened his conviction that the Potomac and James rivers, in particular, could be improved and tied in to the Ohio River basin to bind the western settlements to the nation.

Washington's great personal prestige and his active interest in the economy of the west provided an essential catalyst to the process that eventually led to an effective solution to the nation's economic and political stalemate. While some delegates continued to push in Congress for action, Washington joined with James Madison and others who looked to the states to break the deadlock. Although a grateful public would later dub Madison the Father of the Constitution, in fact nothing that he later did would outshine his contribution to the constitutional process in the mid 1780s. Pursuing a carefully thought-out plan to strengthen the national government, he had asked Virginia's General Assembly in the summer of 1784 to send representatives to Maryland to resolve tariff disagreements over the use of the Potomac River. Seizing upon Washington's interest in the river's development, Madison broadened the agenda of the meeting to include issues relating to the area's economic development and persuaded the general to serve on Virginia's delegation. The presence of the nation's premier war hero, the common interests of lead-

Gouverneur Morris (1752–1816), left, and Robert Morris (1734–1806) held the Continental Congress' finances together during the later years of the Revolution. *(Oil, by Charles Willson Peale, c. 1783; courtesy of the Pennsylvania Academy of Fine Arts.)*

ing figures on both sides of the river, and the fact that the individuals knew each other on a personal basis all contributed to the meeting's success.

The representatives agreed to form a quasi-public corporation, the Patowmack Company, to carry out improvements to the waterway and collect tolls to finance them, with each state purchasing a block of stock to provide seed money. The agreement eliminated all jurisdictional and customs issues for that part of the river above the Great Falls. Both states approved the agreement, but Washington was dissatisfied. He and Madison believed that although progress on the Potomac issue represented a first step toward the long-range goal of securing the west, other states, especially Pennsylvania, needed to become involved. Washington's personal financial involvement in the new Patowmack Company forced him to relinquish public leadership of the drive, but Madison quickly assumed command.

Madison won agreement to a second Virginia-Maryland conference, which in the end was held at Washington's home after some confusion caused by Virginia's failure to notify its delegates of the meeting. On 28 March 1785 Virginia and Maryland signed the Mount Vernon Compact, which granted reciprocal rights to seamen of each state in using the Chesapeake Bay and its tributaries, settled criminal jurisdiction and safety responsibilities, and recommended solutions to the more complex issues of import-export duties and currency exchange. The delegates forwarded the draft compact to their legislatures for approval with the recommendation that yet another meeting be held, this time with other states present and with an agenda that included the Ohio River system.

The success of the Mount Vernon meeting encouraged Madison to proceed with his long-range plan to discuss broader constitutional issues on the state level. He had been repeatedly frustrated in his efforts to persuade the Virginia General Assembly to send instructions to its delegates in the Continental Congress to push the states to grant Congress expanded powers to deal with the regulation of interstate and international trade. Now, after winning approval for the Mount Vernon Compact, he changed his tactics and introduced a proposal in the Virginia Assembly to act on the suggestion of the Compact commissioners. On 21 January 1786, after a week of debate, Virginia issued an invitation to all the states to attend a special meeting on commercial issues in Annapolis, Maryland, in the first week of September. Washington, with strong support from Madison and others interested in strengthening the national government, immediately began lobbying among the continental veterans throughout the country to persuade the other states to name delegations.

Eventually twelve representatives from five states met at George Mann's Tavern, which became the site of the Annapolis Convention.[1] Four other states (New Hampshire, Massachusetts, Rhode Island, and North Carolina) named delegations, but none of their representatives arrived in time for the meeting. The remaining four states (Connecticut, South Carolina, Georgia, and Maryland) decided against participation.

Informal discussions among the delegates, most of whom were old friends from Congress or the Continental Army, preceded the opening session on 11 September, when Delaware's John Dickinson, the senior statesman of the group, was chosen chairman. The delegates agreed immediately that they could not proceed with the stated purpose of the meeting because so many states were unrepresented and because the states with delegates in attendance had each given their representatives different powers. At the same time, the delegates, all strong nationalists, decided that some positive action should result from the abortive meeting, and they appointed a committee to draft a report to the individual state legislatures and Congress.

The delegates agreed that the question of trade regulation could not be divorced from larger political issues relating to the weaknesses of the Articles of Confederation, but this opened a subject they had no authority to discuss. Apparently Abraham Clark of New Jersey suggested that the report recommend a second meeting explicitly empowered to frame measures to strengthen the Articles. Alexander Hamilton drafted a report along these lines, but other members of the committee considered his proposals too strong, so he, Madison, and Edmund Randolph reworked it. The full convention spent two days amending the final report, which summarized their instructions and activities, pointed out the need for a broader mandate, and issued a call for a meeting to be held in Philadelphia on the second Monday in May of 1787. Dickinson signed the finished report, and the meeting broke up on the afternoon of the 14th.

The delegations each carried a copy of the report back to their state legislatures. Dickinson took a copy to the Continental Congress where he introduced it on 20 September. On 21 February, after consideration by a committee containing representatives of each state, Congress concurred and endorsed the call for a convention at Philadelphia. By that time seven states had already voted to send delegations, and five more soon followed suit. Only Rhode Island decided not to participate.

During the summer and fall of 1786 a wave of spontaneous, grassroots protests spread across states from Maryland to New England and imparted a sense of urgency to plans for the Philadelphia meeting. Again, eco-

[1] For an extended discussion of the Annapolis Convention, see Appendix A.

Annapolis as it looked about 1794, shortly after the Annapolis Convention. *(Detail from a watercolor, attributed to C. Milburn, c. 1794; courtesy of Hammond-Harwood House Association.)*

nomic problems were the catalyst, as the nation's debtor farmers became frustrated with the indifference to their plight shown by the mercantile interests who dominated most state governments. Threats gave way to occasional violence as farmers blocked court sessions to prevent foreclosures. In Massachusetts' westernmost counties, mobs shut down the county courts; their actions earned a stinging denunciation from Governor James Bowdoin and criminal indictments for the suspected ringleaders from the state supreme court. The wave of protest crested in late September when a group of armed men, informally led by Daniel Shays, a 40-year-old former Continental Army captain, blocked the court's sessions in Springfield. The outnumbered local militiamen under Major General William Shepard, another Continental veteran, offered no resistance. The following month a letter signed by Shays and other ringleaders circulated in the western counties, calling on the citizens to organize and take up arms in opposition to the state government.

The legislature immediately reacted to the challenge. It passed several bills designed to address the protesters' grievances, but it also invoked the riot act, suspending certain civil liberties, and ordered elements of its militia into active service. Secretary at War Knox, observing events from the site of the United States Arsenal at Springfield, also reacted with alarm. Since no national troops were stationed at the facility, which housed a significant number of small arms and artillery pieces, he asked Congress to raise a national force to protect national property. Congress, citing a larger need to reinforce the frontier, authorized adding over 2,000 men to the Army, although only two artillery companies (perpetuated by today's 1st Battalions of the 4th Air Defense Artillery and 5th Field Artillery) were actually formed, and they arrived in Springfield long after the troubles had ended.

State rather than national troops quelled the civil disturbance. When Shays at the head of some 1,500 men actually moved against the arsenal on 25 January 1787, he was met by 900 militiamen from eastern Massachusetts under Shephard. In the skirmish that ensued, three of Shays' men were killed and another was mortally wounded by artillery fire. The rest scattered, and by March the militiamen had ended the abortive uprising. About a dozen ringleaders were subsequently sentenced to death, although none was ever executed.

Shays' Rebellion, as the incident was immediately dubbed, had repercussions far beyond the state's borders. The rioting in western Massachusetts further undermined confidence in the Articles of Confederation in its existing form. Supporters of the British before and during the Revolutionary War had forecast such a collapse of law and order. Newspapers around the nation now reinforced that prediction, circulating dire warnings that the union was coming apart and that liberties won on the battlefield were about to be lost. Washington himself was severely upset by the incident. Many Americans agreed with Massachusetts' Fisher Ames when he wrote (under the pen name "Camillus"), "If we fall, we fall by our folly, not our fate." The Articles of Confederation depended for success to an unnatural extent upon mutual trust and confidence among the people living in thirteen separate and independent states; Shays showed that more was needed.

The scene was set for the nationalists to take the center stage. Their demand for the creation of a central government powerful enough to transcend the individual interests of states and sections to ensure order and to protect the liberties won in the Revolution was beginning to attract widespread support. In September 1786 the *Maryland Journal* had printed the first public notice of the Annapolis Convention and its recommendations. In the course of the article, the editor commented, "Should this Address have its Effect, we may hope to see the Federal Union of these States established upon Principles, which will secure the Dignity, Harmony, and Felicity of these confederated Republics; and not only rescue them from their present Difficulties, but from that insolent Hauteur and contemptuous Neglect, which they have experienced as a Nation." The meeting scheduled for Philadelphia in 1787 would decide if such hopes could be fulfilled.

The Constitution

The Constitutional Convention is a major transition point in American history between the Revolutionary era and the birth of national republican government. The delegates who met in Philadelphia in 1787 not only fashioned a new form of government to replace the Articles of Confederation, but also submitted their handiwork to the citizens of the individual states for ratification. Long debates marked both stages of this process. On one side were ranged those who argued that survival depended on increasing the efficiency and strength of central government; their opponents, worried more about potential abuses, sought to reserve as much power as possible to the states, where government was closer to the people. The question of military force, in the form of an army, navy, and militia, was a central topic in these debates. In the end, compromise produced a uniquely American solution derived from colonial modifications of a European heritage: a federal system of checks and balances that divided responsibility between the states and the national government, a separation of the latter's powers into executive, legislative, and judicial branches, and a clear subordination of the military to the elected government.

Although the delegates who assembled in Philadelphia were acutely aware of the immediate threat raised by Shays' Rebellion, they were determined to lay the foundations for a government that could endure over time. They understood that their work would be judged in the light of history, and used that discipline as a guide. More importantly, however, they understood the nature of American society and took a remarkably pragmatic approach to resolving problems. During the Convention, John Dickinson typified this approach when he warned his colleagues that "Experience must be our only guide; Reason may mislead us." Specifically, the delegates' study of history indicated that each of the three "pure" systems of government—monarchy, aristocracy, and democracy—when allowed to operate by itself had revealed serious flaws. By drawing on their English heritage and colonial experience, however, the delegates concluded that a mixture of the three, supported by a large and economically secure middle class, might provide a workable solution. As South Carolina's Pierce Butler later pointed out, the Founding Fathers set about developing a government that was practical, not one designed for discussion in Europe's philosophical circles.

The representatives met in Independence Hall, in the room where the Declaration of Independence had been signed. The Convention was slated to open on 14 May 1787, but for various reasons a quorum was not achieved until the 25th. The intervening time was not wasted. The Virginia delegation, under the leadership of James Madison and Governor Edmund Randolph, used the delay to hold daily meetings and prepare a draft document known to history as the Virginia Plan. By 25 May the delegations from New York, New Jersey, Pennsylvania, Delaware, Virginia, North Carolina, and South Carolina had arrived, along with individual representatives from Massachusetts and Georgia. Other delegates continued to trickle in until 23 July, when New Hampshire's elected representatives took their seats. Only Rhode Is-

"The Birch View of Philadelphia in 1800" portrays the city much as it must have appeared to the Framers. *(Watercolor, 1800; Independence National Historical Park.)*

land failed to send delegates. On 10 July two of the three delegates from New York departed, leaving Hamilton alone and technically unable to cast a ballot for the state. During the course of the Convention there were two recesses (3–4 July and 26 July–6 August). For the rest, the delegates met six days a week, usually working from ten in the morning until three in the afternoon. Given the fact that so many were old friends, much of the more important work of compromise and persuasion tended to occur in social meetings apart from formal Convention sessions.

The Convention used most of the first week to organize. On the 25th the delegates unanimously chose Washington as president. During his career Washington won unanimous election to three offices, the other two as Commander in Chief of the Continental Army and as President of the United States. He was somewhat dubious of the honor now bestowed by the Convention since the presiding officer could not participate actively in the debates. Yet despite his reservations, Washington played an exceptionally important role, setting the tone of the proceedings and guiding the body through periods of tense discussion. On Hamilton's recommendation, the delegates next hired William Jackson, a former Army staff officer, as the Convention's secretary. Completing arrangements, a committee on rules and procedures adapted those used in the Continental Congress, including the provisions that each state delegation cast a single ballot and that the states vote in geographical order from north to south, the same order the Continental Army had used for parade-ground formations. The delegates insisted on maintaining secrecy over their deliberations, reasoning that only within a completely free atmosphere could they speak their minds honestly and without fear of outside pressure. Secrecy would also allow them to change their votes and conduct the bargains necessary for compromise and unity.

On 29–30 May the Virginians presented their Plan in the form of fifteen resolutions. This tactic, Madison's handiwork, gave the nationalists an important advantage by setting out an agenda for discussion. Instead of merely amending the Articles of Confederation, the stated purpose of the Convention, the Virginians proposed a completely new system. Their plan called for a national government of three branches (executive, legislative, and judicial) with a bicameral (two-house) legislature. It vested strong power in the national government and required that state officials take an oath to uphold the new Constitution. To ensure that the final form of the Constitution expressed the will of the people, the Virginians also called for ratification by state conventions chosen by special elections.

Immediately following submission of the Virginia Plan, South Carolina's Charles Pinckney submitted a plan of his own. Developed along the lines of the Virginia proposal, Pinckney's plan called for a less rigidly centralized national government. The Convention, following the same tactics used by the Continental Congress in debating Richard Henry Lee's independence resolution in 1776, promptly voted to refer both plans to a Committee of the Whole. This standard parliamentary technique provided a more open forum for debate under the less formal committee rules. When Washington turned the gavel over to the committee chairman, Nathaniel Gorham of Massachusetts, the president was free to join in the discussion. The Committee of the Whole spent most of the time until 13 June debating these proposals, agreeing by majority vote on the first day to devise a new national government containing three separate branches.

The first indication of a division appeared when the delegates considered how to apportion representation in the new legislature. The more outspoken nationalists, frequently those representing the larger states, wanted to change the provision of one vote per state, allowing population to control the number of seats, and the number of votes per state, in each house. The smaller states objected so strenuously to this proposal that by 13 June it was clear to all that some sort of compromise was needed. On that date the Committee of the Whole reported out a series of nineteen resolutions embodying an amended version of the Virginia Plan. This report indicated that despite serious disagreements, a majority in the Convention accepted the notion of a new national government, and that an increasing number were beginning to accept the idea that power should be invested in the people at large, through more proportional representation.

On 14 June William Paterson of New Jersey asked for a day's delay to present an alternative plan drawn up by himself, Connecticut's Roger Sherman, and other delegates from small states. This proposal, known later as the New Jersey Plan, took the form of nine resolutions designed to strengthen the Articles without abandoning the essential character of the United States as a league of separate and equal states. Although the national legislature's powers would be expanded significantly, each state would still retain a single vote. Although proposing a less radical solution than the Virginia Plan, the small-state proposal nevertheless did significantly alter the balance of power within the nation in favor of the central government.

The Convention promptly committed the New Jersey Plan, along with the amended Virginia Plan, to the Committee of the Whole so that the two could be compared. Debate in committee lasted until 19 June. On the 18th Hamilton made one of his rare speeches. He deliberately outlined an extreme position (a national government totally dominant over the states) to establish the boundaries of the debate. As expected, his notion was promptly rejected, but the next day, by a vote of seven states to three, with Maryland divided, the Committee of the Whole accepted Virginia's modified plan over New Jersey's.

The Convention then debated the same issues in regular sessions during the third week of June. It reached a number of compromises about the mechanics of the representation process, but no consensus on fundamental issues. Tempers began to flare in the early summer heat as debate centered on representation and the powers vested in the legislature under the Virginia Plan. As early as 29 June a majority of states agreed to proportional representation in the lower house, but a deadlock occurred on 2 July over the upper house. To break the impasse, the Convention established a new committee with membership drawn from each of the eleven states in official attendance.[1] On 5 July that committee reached a compromise. The basic idea of the compromise had been suggested as early as 2 June by Dickinson, and repeated by others in the weeks that followed. It based representation in the lower house on population (including three-fifths of the slaves) while giving each state an equal vote in the upper house. This suggestion provided a way to break the deadlock, although much additional work was required to arrive at specific numbers acceptable to all.

On 11 July discussion turned to slavery, introducing the second major representational issue. The heat engendered by this point should have been expected, since in 1776 an argument over Jefferson's condemnation of slavery had nearly doomed the Declaration of Independence. On 12 July Gouverneur Morris of Pennsylvania suggested tying representation to taxation, while deferring consideration of the institution of slavery until a later date. This solution proved acceptable and allowed discussion to shift to the details of apportioning the lower house. The Great Compromise, begun on 5 July, held on 16 July in a final vote by a tally of five states to four, with Massachusetts split.

Although a consensus had been achieved on key issues, many minor points of contention remained. At the same time, the balanced federal organization outlined in the Great Compromise now allowed the delegates from

[1] For membership on this and all Convention committees, see Appendix B.

James Madison (1751–1836). *(Oil, by Gilbert Stuart, 1804; courtesy of Colonial Williamsburg Foundation.)*

Edmund Jennings Randolph (1753–1833). *(Oil, by Flavius J. Fisher after unknown artist 19th century; courtesy of Virginia State Library.)*

the smaller states to express their own nationalist sentiments more vocally without fearing that they might jeopardize the interest of their state. So much progress was achieved that on 26 July a select Committee of Detail began preparing a draft document incorporating the results of the sessions held thus far while the delegates took a recess to escape the city's heat and humidity. The results of this committee's effort was a seven-page document consisting of a preamble and twenty-three articles drawn liberally from various state constitutions, the Articles of Confederation, and the Pinckney Plan, and incorporating the basic text of the amended Virginia Plan. It assigned names to the offices and branches of the national government (President, Congress, House of Representatives, Senate, Speaker, Supreme Court) and coined many of the phrases, such as "We the People," made famous in the final document. The committee also recommended that a favorable vote of nine states in ratification conventions would be sufficient to put the new Constitution into effect. This in itself represented a major break from previous arrangements. Both the Articles and the Constitutional Convention required unanimity for approval, as had the vote for independence. During these discussions in late July those favoring a strong central government, relying on the leadership of Madison, James Wilson of Pennsylvania, and Gouverneur Morris, proved the dominant voice, while Elbridge Gerry emerged as the leader of the opposition.

When the Convention reconvened on 6 August, copies of the committee's work, printed with wide margins for notes, awaited the delegates. The number and scope of the changes wrought by the committee triggered five weeks of detailed, line-by-line debate. Given the sheer number of issues, speeches became shorter and the spirit of compromise gained strength, although the delegates also displayed a tendency to lose patience with minority objections. Most potentially explosive issues were resolved through compromises, including national control over the militia and explicit restrictions on the states in areas such as maintaining their own armies and navies, issuing money, entering into treaties, and granting titles of nobility. Sometimes compromise merely postponed a decision that would eventually require a constitutional amendment. In the case of slavery, the failure to achieve a just solution at the Convention would lead, after many further attempts at compromise in succeeding years, to resolution only through a bloody civil war.

On 31 August a few remaining issues were officially turned over to the Committee on Postponed Matters, consisting of one representative from each state. It refined much of the previous draft, in the process providing a means for electing the President that made him

Roger Sherman (1721-93). *(Oil, by Ralph Earl, c. 1777; copyright Yale University Art Gallery.)*

William Paterson (1745–1806). *(Oil, by James Sharples, Sr., 1794; United States Supreme Court.)*

more independent of the legislature and, in consequence, increased his powers.

By the close of business on 8 September the review of the draft prepared by the Committee on Postponed Matters was essentially completed, and the amended draft document was turned over to the Committee on Style. The five members of that committee spent from 8 until 12 September reworking the language of the draft (in the process cutting the twenty-three articles in the earlier draft to seven), with Gouverneur Morris playing the role of chief stylist, much as Jefferson had shaped the Declaration and Dickinson the first draft of the Articles. Morris followed their precedent and used his literary license in subtle rewordings that strengthened the document's nationalist sentiments. For example, he dropped a listing of the states at the beginning of the Preamble, and inserted after "We the People" the words, "of the United States in order to form a more perfect Union." This terminology made it clear that the authority behind the new government would be derived directly from the people, not from the states as separate entities, as had been the case under the Articles.

One last matter of business remained. By a vote of ten to zero the delegates agreed to omit a bill of rights. This decision proved to be a costly liability during the ratification process that was about to begin, for much criticism would focus on the lack of such an explicit list of popular liberties. The remaining days of the Convention's sessions were devoted to minor editorial corrections in the final wording of the document.

The system of checks and balances forged on the anvil of political compromise at the Convention came into focus most significantly when the delegates turned their attention to military affairs. Most shared the views expressed by the three men who exercised direct national responsibility for military matters under the Articles: Secretary at War Knox, Colonel Harmar, and Arthur St. Clair, the former Continental general now serving as president of Congress. Informed opinion in 1787 identified three threats to national security: civil insurrections like the one that had occurred in western Massachusetts during the previous year, Indian attacks aided and abetted by the British on the frontier, and, more remotely, invasion by European powers. The delegates in Philadelphia set about providing the new national government with means to face these three possible threats.

Like Knox, Harmar, and St. Clair, a majority of the delegates had been involved in the prosecution of the War of Independence, either on the battlefield, in Congress, or in state governments. That formative influence provided a crucial frame of reference during the discussion of military affairs. Delegates were not dealing in

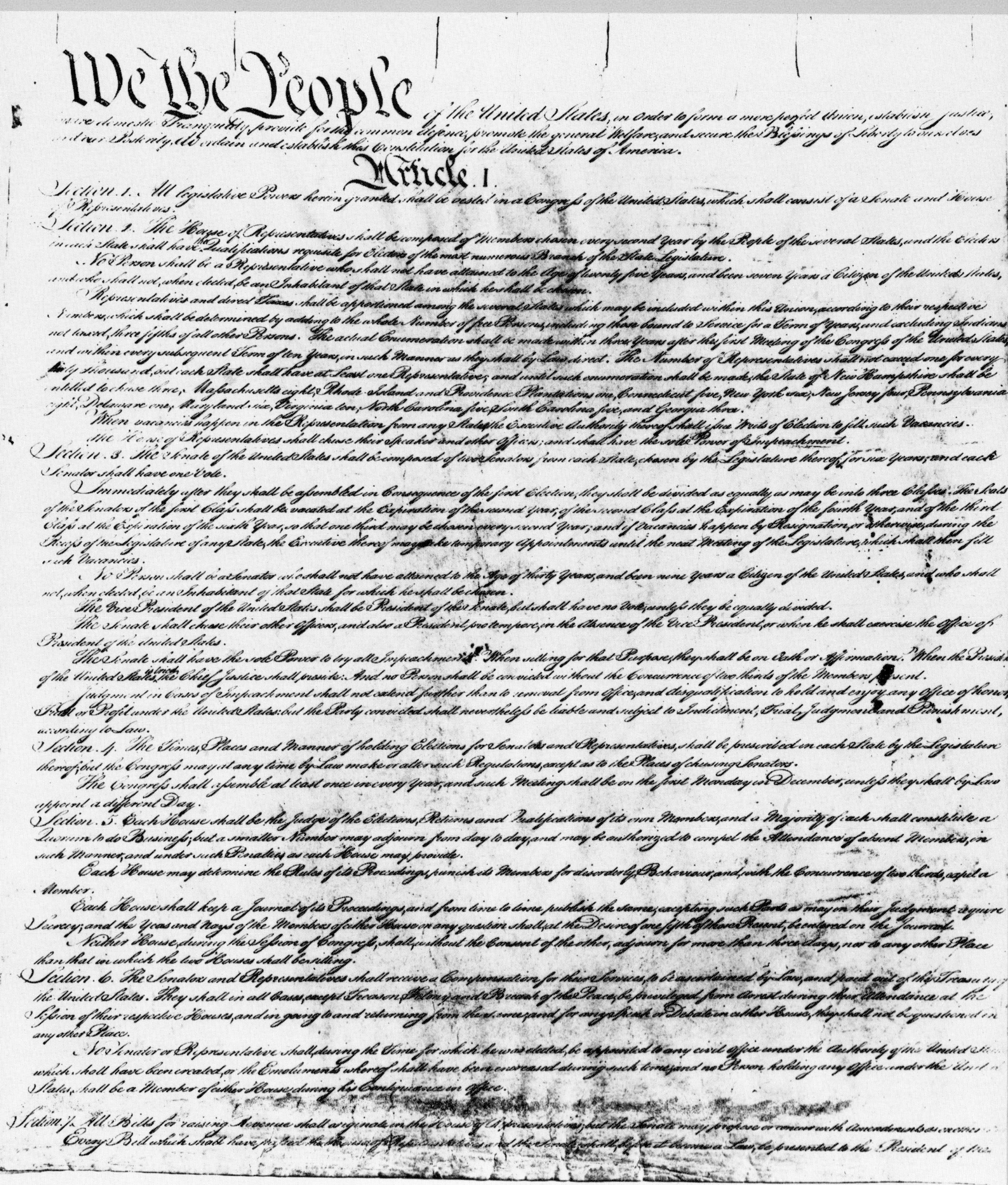

We the People of the United States, in Order to form a more perfect Union, establish Justice, insure domestic Tranquility, provide for the common defence, promote the general Welfare, and secure the Blessings of Liberty to ourselves and our Posterity, do ordain and establish this Constitution for the United States of America.

Article. I

Section. 1. All legislative Powers herein granted shall be vested in a Congress of the United States, which shall consist of a Senate and House of Representatives.

Section. 2. The House of Representatives shall be composed of Members chosen every second Year by the People of the several States, and the Electors in each State shall have the Qualifications requisite for Electors of the most numerous Branch of the State Legislature.

No Person shall be a Representative who shall not have attained to the Age of twenty five Years, and been seven Years a Citizen of the United States, and who shall not, when elected, be an Inhabitant of that State in which he shall be chosen.

Representatives and direct Taxes shall be apportioned among the several States which may be included within this Union, according to their respective Numbers, which shall be determined by adding to the whole Number of free Persons, including those bound to Service for a Term of Years, and excluding Indians not taxed, three fifths of all other Persons. The actual Enumeration shall be made within three Years after the first Meeting of the Congress of the United States, and within every subsequent Term of ten Years, in such Manner as they shall by Law direct. The Number of Representatives shall not exceed one for every thirty Thousand, but each State shall have at Least one Representative; and until such enumeration shall be made, the State of New Hampshire shall be entitled to chuse three, Massachusetts eight, Rhode Island and Providence Plantations one, Connecticut five, New York six, New Jersey four, Pennsylvania eight, Delaware one, Maryland six, Virginia ten, North Carolina five, South Carolina five, and Georgia three.

When vacancies happen in the Representation from any State, the Executive Authority thereof shall issue Writs of Election to fill such Vacancies.

The House of Representatives shall chuse their Speaker and other Officers; and shall have the sole Power of Impeachment.

Section. 3. The Senate of the United States shall be composed of two Senators from each State, chosen by the Legislature thereof for six Years; and each Senator shall have one Vote.

Immediately after they shall be assembled in Consequence of the first Election, they shall be divided as equally as may be into three Classes. The Seats of the Senators of the first Class shall be vacated at the Expiration of the second Year, of the second Class at the Expiration of the fourth Year, and of the third Class at the Expiration of the sixth Year, so that one third may be chosen every second Year; and if Vacancies happen by Resignation, or otherwise, during the Recess of the Legislature of any State, the Executive thereof may make temporary Appointments until the next Meeting of the Legislature, which shall then fill such Vacancies.

No Person shall be a Senator who shall not have attained to the Age of thirty Years, and been nine Years a Citizen of the United States, and who shall not, when elected, be an Inhabitant of that State for which he shall be chosen.

The Vice President of the United States shall be President of the Senate, but shall have no Vote, unless they be equally divided.

The Senate shall chuse their other Officers, and also a President pro tempore, in the Absence of the Vice President, or when he shall exercise the Office of President of the United States.

The Senate shall have the sole Power to try all Impeachments. When sitting for that Purpose, they shall be on Oath or Affirmation. When the President of the United States is tried, the Chief Justice shall preside: And no Person shall be convicted without the Concurrence of two thirds of the Members present.

Judgment in Cases of Impeachment shall not extend further than to removal from Office, and disqualification to hold and enjoy any Office of honor, Trust or Profit under the United States: but the Party convicted shall nevertheless be liable and subject to Indictment, Trial, Judgment and Punishment, according to Law.

Section. 4. The Times, Places and Manner of holding Elections for Senators and Representatives, shall be prescribed in each State by the Legislature thereof; but the Congress may at any time by Law make or alter such Regulations, except as to the Places of chusing Senators.

The Congress shall assemble at least once in every Year, and such Meeting shall be on the first Monday in December, unless they shall by Law appoint a different Day.

Section. 5. Each House shall be the Judge of the Elections, Returns and Qualifications of its own Members, and a Majority of each shall constitute a Quorum to do Business; but a smaller Number may adjourn from day to day, and may be authorized to compel the Attendance of absent Members, in such Manner, and under such Penalties as each House may provide.

Each House may determine the Rules of its Proceedings, punish its Members for disorderly Behaviour, and, with the Concurrence of two thirds, expel a Member.

Each House shall keep a Journal of its Proceedings, and from time to time publish the same, excepting such Parts as may in their Judgment require Secrecy; and the Yeas and Nays of the Members of either House on any question shall, at the Desire of one fifth of those Present, be entered on the Journal.

Neither House, during the Session of Congress, shall, without the Consent of the other, adjourn for more than three days, nor to any other Place than that in which the two Houses shall be sitting.

Section. 6. The Senators and Representatives shall receive a Compensation for their Services, to be ascertained by Law, and paid out of the Treasury of the United States. They shall in all Cases, except Treason, Felony and Breach of the Peace, be privileged from Arrest during their Attendance at the Session of their respective Houses, and in going to and returning from the same; and for any Speech or Debate in either House, they shall not be questioned in any other Place.

No Senator or Representative shall, during the Time for which he was elected, be appointed to any civil Office under the Authority of the United States, which shall have been created, or the Emoluments whereof shall have been encreased during such time; and no Person holding any Office under the United States, shall be a Member of either House during his Continuance in Office.

Section. 7. All Bills for raising Revenue shall originate in the House of Representatives; but the Senate may propose or concur with Amendments as on other Bills.

Every Bill which shall have passed the House of Representatives and the Senate, shall, before it become a Law, be presented to the President of the

First page of the Constitution. *(Photograph, National Archives and Records Administration.)*

Congress may by general Laws prescribe the Manner in which such Acts, Records and Proceedings shall be proved, and the Effect thereof.

Section. 2. The Citizens of each State shall be entitled to all Privileges and Immunities of Citizens in the several States.

A Person charged in any State with Treason, Felony, or other Crime, who shall flee from Justice, and be found in another State, shall on Demand of the executive Authority of the State from which he fled, be delivered up, to be removed to the State having Jurisdiction of the Crime.

No Person held to Service or Labour in one State, under the Laws thereof, escaping into another, shall, in Consequence of any Law or Regulation therein, be discharged from such Service or Labour, but shall be delivered up on Claim of the Party to whom such Service or Labour may be due.

Section. 3. New States may be admitted by the Congress into this Union; but no new State shall be formed or erected within the Jurisdiction of any other State; nor any State be formed by the Junction of two or more States, or Parts of States, without the Consent of the Legislatures of the States concerned as well as of the Congress.

The Congress shall have Power to dispose of and make all needful Rules and Regulations respecting the Territory or other Property belonging to the United States; and nothing in this Constitution shall be so construed as to Prejudice any Claims of the United States, or of any particular State.

Section. 4. The United States shall guarantee to every State in this Union a Republican Form of Government, and shall protect each of them against Invasion; and on Application of the Legislature, or of the Executive (when the Legislature cannot be convened) against domestic Violence.

Article. V.

The Congress, whenever two thirds of both Houses shall deem it necessary, shall propose Amendments to this Constitution, or, on the Application of the Legislatures of two thirds of the several States, shall call a Convention for proposing Amendments, which, in either Case, shall be valid to all Intents and Purposes, as Part of this Constitution, when ratified by the Legislatures of three fourths of the several States, or by Conventions in three fourths thereof, as the one or the other Mode of Ratification may be proposed by the Congress; Provided that no Amendment which may be made prior to the Year One thousand eight hundred and eight shall in any Manner affect the first and fourth Clauses in the Ninth Section of the first Article; and that no State, without its Consent, shall be deprived of its equal Suffrage in the Senate.

Article. VI.

All Debts contracted and Engagements entered into, before the Adoption of this Constitution, shall be as valid against the United States under this Constitution, as under the Confederation.

This Constitution, and the Laws of the United States which shall be made in Pursuance thereof; and all Treaties made, or which shall be made, under the Authority of the United States, shall be the supreme Law of the Land; and the Judges in every State shall be bound thereby, any Thing in the Constitution or Laws of any State to the Contrary notwithstanding.

The Senators and Representatives before mentioned, and the Members of the several State Legislatures, and all executive and judicial Officers, both of the United States and of the several States, shall be bound by Oath or Affirmation, to support this Constitution; but no religious Test shall ever be required as a Qualification to any Office or public Trust under the United States.

Article. VII.

The Ratification of the Conventions of nine States, shall be sufficient for the Establishment of this Constitution between the States so ratifying the Same.

The Word, "the," being interlined between the seventh and eighth Lines of the first Page, The Word "Thirty" being partly written on an Erazure in the fifteenth Line of the first Page, The Words "is tried" being interlined between the thirty second and thirty third Lines of the first Page and the Word "the" being interlined between the forty third and forty fourth Lines of the second Page.

Attest William Jackson Secretary

done in Convention by the Unanimous Consent of the States present the Seventeenth Day of September in the Year of our Lord one thousand seven hundred and Eighty seven and of the Independance of the United States of America the Twelfth In witness whereof We have hereunto subscribed our Names,

G°. Washington—Presidt and deputy from Virginia

Delaware: Geo: Read, Gunning Bedford jun, John Dickinson, Richard Bassett, Jaco: Broom

Maryland: James McHenry, Dan of St Thos. Jenifer, Danl Carroll

Virginia: John Blair—, James Madison Jr.

North Carolina: Wm Blount, Richd Dobbs Spaight, Hu Williamson

South Carolina: J. Rutledge, Charles Cotesworth Pinckney, Charles Pinckney, Pierce Butler

Georgia: William Few, Abr Baldwin

New Hampshire: John Langdon, Nicholas Gilman

Massachusetts: Nathaniel Gorham, Rufus King

Connecticut: Wm Saml Johnson, Roger Sherman

New York: Alexander Hamilton

New Jersey: Wil: Livingston, David Brearley, Wm Paterson, Jona: Dayton

Pensylvania: B Franklin, Thomas Mifflin, Robt Morris, Geo. Clymer, Thos FitzSimons, Jared Ingersoll, James Wilson, Gouv Morris

Last page of the Constitution showing the forty signatures. *(Photograph, National Archives and Records Administration.)*

Elbridge Gerry (1744–1814). *(Oil, by James Bogle after John Vanderlyn, 1861; Independence National Historical Park.)*

theory but reflecting personal experiences. They assumed that security in its broadest context provided the fundamental reason for any government's existence; they feared military dictatorship; and they recognized that a more effective governmental system than the one used between 1775 and 1783 had to be found. Given the precedents of American history, however, the delegates had to consider two different approaches to the development of military forces. One, reflecting the experiences of the Continental Army, held that the nation needed a trained, full-time military force capable of defeating an organized enemy on the battlefield; the other emphasized the traditional role of the citizen-soldier militiaman defending his home and region during short-lived emergencies. Seeking as broad a consensus as possible, the Convention chose to employ elements of both.

The Virginia and Pinckney Plans introduced on 29 May had cited the need for explicit national authority over the means for defense against both external and internal threats. Randolph cited Revolutionary experiences to prove that the Articles denied the central government both the ability to deter war and the authority to prosecute war efficiently. He argued that the Revolution had demonstrated conclusively that a regular army was needed to defend the nation without the economic disruption brought about by large-scale mobilization of the militia. Most of the delegates agreed with Randolph, a Continental Army veteran then serving as Virginia's governor (and therefore as commander of its militia). The New Jersey Plan, introduced on 15 June, did not challenge Randolph's assumptions and also vested broad powers over military operations in the national government. The general consensus on military issues held until the Convention began the line-by-line analysis of the work of the Committee of Detail.

Arguments surfaced on 17 August when Elbridge Gerry challenged the clauses enumerating the powers of the national government. The committee's draft had allowed the government to "subdue rebellion" when a state legislature called upon it for assistance. Charles Pinckney, Gouverneur Morris, and John Langdon argued that the federal government should be able to act unilaterally in domestic disturbances since circumstances could easily arise when a state was unable or unwilling to issue the required call. Objections to this proposed change as an excessive concentration of power came from Luther Martin, John Francis Mercer, and Gerry, with the latter warning of the dangers of "letting loose the myrmidons of the United States on a state without its own consent." Oliver Ellsworth then proposed a modification which suggested that the state legislature issue the appeal "when possible." This wording passed, a majority of the delegates apparently agreeing with Morris that the national legislature, as the representative of the people, could safely be trusted with "such a power to preserve the public tranquility."

A second debate on the same day related to the power "to make war." Charles Pinckney objected to vesting that responsibility in the legislative branch, arguing that it moved too slowly and did not always stay in session. If the power were to be placed there, he argued, it should be in the hands of the Senate, where action could be swifter and where each state would have an equal voice so that the bigger states could not drag the smaller ones into a war they did not support. Pierce Butler, Madison, Roger Sherman, and Gerry all pursued Pinckney's ideas, but they drew a distinction between declaring war and conducting actual operations. At their suggestion, the wording was changed to emphasize that the legislature would deal only with the former. By a vote of seven states to two, the words "declare war" were substituted for "make war."

One last discussion took place the following day when Gerry and Martin sought to insert an explicit limit on the number of regular troops that could be maintained in peacetime, using once again the rhetoric about the dangers of a "standing army." Judging by accounts left by several of the delegates, Washington glowered at Gerry, sparking a rush by veterans to object to the amendment. Charles Cotesworth Pinckney, Hugh Williamson, John Langdon, and Jonathan Dayton all restated the need to deter war by preparing for it in peacetime and argued that the proposed Constitution contained more than enough safeguards to prevent military despotism. The full Convention then rejected the amendment by a unanimous vote of eleven states to none.

These minor debates constituted the entire substantive discussion of the "Army Clause." Even Gerry, probably the most extreme anticentralist in attendance, did not object to the premise that the central government could establish a small peacetime military force. The precedent set by the Continental Congress three years earlier when it had created Harmar's regiment clearly served as a factor in this consensus. More importantly, the aggressive nationalist leadership within the Convention had emerged from the Revolution with such a goal firmly in mind, as reflected in the attempt by Washington and Hamilton to have a military peace establishment enacted into law as early as 1783.

On 18 August the discussion shifted to the "Militia Clause," a much more emotional issue. George Mason, himself a militia officer, although never on active duty, pushed for federal regulation of the militia. Citing a key lesson from the Revolution's campaigns, he pointed to the need to standardize the militia's weapons, organization, and tactics so that they could operate effectively in combat. Mason also stressed that an effective militia force would reduce the requirement for a large regular army.

In the opening round of debate only Gerry and Martin, repeating their view about a standing army, opposed the basic concept of some central control. Others, mostly veterans with a nationalist background, simply explored various approaches to shared control of the militia. The first possibility discussed was the proposals advanced by Washington, Steuben, and Knox for a national, select militia force. Ellsworth and Sherman both raised objections, the former arguing that creation of such a body would inevitably lead to the erosion of the common militia, the latter pointing out that in addition to their federal missions the militias also had state responsibilities. Mason then proposed a modification of his motion that would make explicit reference to the dual missions. The whole issue was then referred to committee for further study.

On 21 August this committee reported out with a wording for the militia clause that reflected the basic federalism of the draft Constitution as a whole, splitting authority between the central government and the states in a system of checks and balances. It gave the national body the power to pass "laws for organizing, arming, and disciplining the militia, and for governing such part of them as may be employed in the service of the United States, reserving to the states respectively the appointment of officers and the authority of training the militia according to the discipline prescribed by the United States." Two days later the Convention began consideration of this proposal. The veterans, led by Rufus King, took great pains to explain the meanings of three key terms used in the clause. "Organizing" related only to the technical matter of specifying how many men would form each type of unit and what their ranks would be; "arming" related to specifying types and calibers of weapons, not their issuance; and "disciplining" referred to the establishment of drill manuals and other doctrinal materials, not to courts martial or related procedures. Once again Martin and Gerry raised objections. They charged that surrendering any authority over the militia would fatally undermine state rights. Madison, Randolph, Charles Cotesworth Pinckney, Dayton, and Langdon answered with charges that the existing system, which Gerry wanted to keep, had proven itself ineffectual, and they refuted the notion that a federally monitored militia posed a threat. The only way that a militia of citizen-soldiers could be corrupted would be if the militiamen themselves, as citizens, willingly sacrificed their own liberties. If this condition came to pass,

Benjamin Franklin (1706–90) played a key role in creating compromises. *(Oil, by Charles Willson Peale, 1772; courtesy of American Philosophical Society.)*

Gerry's opponents reasoned, no document could prevent disaster. Two minor word changes were considered in an attempt to mollify Gerry, but both were rejected by a majority grown increasingly impatient with constantly rehashed arguments. The delegates then voted on the original committee motion in three parts. The first, covering the right to make laws regarding the militia, passed nine states to two, with only Connecticut and Maryland opposing. The second, relating to the appointment of officers, required two separate votes. First an amendment offered by Madison, which attempted to reserve the power to appoint general officers to the Congress, was defeated after Sherman pointed out that this undermined the basic compromise, and then the original wording passed unanimously. The third gained the approval of seven states; Delaware, Virginia, South Carolina and Georgia voted against it because they objected to granting training responsibility to state governments.

The votes of 23 August ended discussion of military matters. As finally written and ratified, the Constitution raises military issues in five sections located in Articles I (legislative branch) and II (executive branch), mostly in the former. Sections 6 and 7 of Article I prevent regular officers from serving in Congress while retaining their commissions and assign responsibility for initiating military revenue bills to the House of Representatives. Section 10 of the same article prohibits any state from maintaining troops or warships in peacetime without the consent of Congress, or from waging war unless that state is actually invaded or in imminent danger of invasion. Section 2 of Article II makes the President the Commander in Chief of the Army and Navy and of militiamen while in federal service. The heart of the Constitution's military provisions rests in the enumerated powers given to Congress in Section 8, Article I, including the key right to "provide for the common Defense." The actual wording follows rather closely on the August debates over the military clauses.

In its totality, the Convention arrived at a very important set of decisions concerning military matters with relatively little disagreement. The delegates were able to resolve the thorny issue of potential abuses of power by inserting the Army, Navy, and militia into the same carefully structured set of checks and balances that applied throughout the Constitution. To promote efficiency, it placed the regulars under the national government, at the same time providing for a dual system of defense by dividing responsibility over the much larger militia establishment with the states. While the national government might employ the militia for the common defense, that authority was checked by the states, which retained authority to appoint their militia officers and to supervise the peacetime training of citizen-soldiers. The Founders were able to create a standing army, the hobgoblin of the Anglo-Saxon world for more than a century, by establishing much tighter civilian control over the armed forces than existed in any contemporary European country. A civilian President served as Commander in Chief; the Senate had to concur in the appointment of all senior officers; and the House of Representatives controlled financial resources. Furthermore, Mason's inclusion of a provision for limiting appropriations for the military to two years made the legislature a full partner with the executive in military matters.

Late in the afternoon on 15 September the draft Constitution received the unanimous approval of the state delegations. On Monday, 17 September, the Convention, with forty-one of the fifty-five members present, reassembled one last time for the formal signing. Secretary Jackson probably read the finished document, then a speech by Benjamin Franklin was read urging any doubters to sign on behalf of their states, not themselves, to make approval unanimous. In the end thirty-eight of those present signed; only Randolph, Mason, and Gerry did not. Dickinson, who was ill and not present, had his name affixed by George Read of Delaware. Washington, as president of the Convention, signed first, just as Hancock, the president of the Continental Congress, had signed the Declaration of Independence. The remaining delegates then signed in strict congressional voting order, under Washington. Washington, however, had signed in the middle of the page, and when the delegates ran out of space they began a second column of signatures at the left margin. Hamilton signed as only an individual, for he was not empowered to sign for his state. About four in the afternoon the last signatures were affixed, including that of Secretary Jackson, who authenticated the document. The papers of the body were then turned over to Washington for safekeeping, and the Convention adjourned *sine die* (indefinitely).

Secretary Jackson transmitted the signed document to Charles Thomson, the secretary of the Continental Congress, on 20 September. Six days later that body, which included about a dozen delegates recently returned from the Philadelphia Convention, began debate. A majority decided on 28 September to forward it to the states for ratification with a noncommittal letter of transmittal. In deliberate contrast to the adoption of the Articles, approval—as provided by the Convention—could come only through the action of special conventions, thus justifying the Preamble's claim that the people of the United States, not simply the states, had created the new government. The delegates, however, had little assurance that their work would be well received at home. These tough, pragmatic politicians had shied away from abstract philosophy. Their work, built upon a century and

"George Washington Addressing the Constitutional Convention." *(Oil, by Junius Brutus Stearns, c. 1856; Virginia Museum of Fine Arts.)*

a half of colonial experience, was a blueprint for a federalism that represented a compromise solution to a host of government problems.

Attention quickly focused on the state-by-state struggle between proponents (the Federalists) and opponents of the new system. Once again the nationalists, those proposing a change in government, had the initiative. Their opponents, who came to be called the Antifederalists, were more loosely organized. They could count on the leadership of only a handful of Convention delegates (Luther Martin and John Francis Mercer of Maryland, Robert Yates and John Lansing of New York, George Mason of Virginia, and Elbridge Gerry of Massachusetts) and few other figures of national stature: Patrick Henry and Richard Henry Lee in Virginia, Samuel Chase of Maryland, and Governor George Clinton in New York. These men called on the voters to reject the Constitution because of its "defects," but they offered no comprehensive alternative. They tended to be inherently suspicious of any concentration of power. They feared a stronger national government because it was further removed from the people than the state governments and because of the potential they saw for abuse of power. Following the same logic, the Antifederalists also opposed the creation of a peacetime army and sought to limit the nation's military to the existing state-controlled militias. Their arguments were couched in terms used a century earlier in England against the Stuarts and in the American Revolutionary era against Parliament.

Working under the leadership of those delegates who had signed the Constitution, the Federalists quickly established a network to coordinate the strategy for the ratification effort. Washington, still the hero of the Revolution to a grateful public, lent his considerable prestige and played a key behind-the-scenes role. Others contributed pamphlets and speeches and acted as floor managers for the Constitution in the state conventions. Federalist leaders devised a two-part strategy. To respond to the public's legitimate concerns over the new government, they embarked on a long-range public education program, emphasizing issues on which consensus was possible. Three themes with broad public appeal were quickly identified: national security, poor economic conditions under the Articles, and national pride. As experienced politicians, the Federalist leaders also knew that supporters of the Constitution already formed a majority in some states. By taking advantage of that situation and of their ability to delay votes in states with strong initial opposition to the Constitution, the Federalists planned to create a sense of momentum to swing undecided voters. Furthermore, they concentrated their efforts in the four states whose approval was deemed essential to the viability of the new nation because of their size, population, and wealth: Pennsylvania, Virginia, Massachusetts, and New York.

Initiative and excellent leadership in the middle states enabled the Federalists to establish the desired momentum. Delaware's signers, especially Dickinson and Bassett, were the first to deliver. On 7 December 1787 their state's convention ratified by unanimous vote. New Jersey (18 December) and Georgia (2 January) provided two more clean sweeps within a month. Pennsylvania (46–23, on 12 December) and Connecticut (128–40, on 9 January), although not unanimous, ratified by wide margins. These five states proved relatively easy; the remaining ones tested the Federalists' tactical skills.

Massachusetts posed the first major test. Gerry, although not a member of the ratification convention, led the opposition. Skillful maneuvering by Rufus King and Nathaniel Gorham of Massachusetts won the popular John Hancock and Samuel Adams over, and on 6 February the Federalists were able to eke out a narrow margin of victory (187–168). Focusing on the importance of the general issue, they defused specific objections by proposing an innovative compromise. With their support, Massachusetts' approval of the Constitution included a request for the swift adoption of amendments, including a bill of rights. All of the remaining states, except Maryland, would follow a similar path.

Maryland (on 28 April) and South Carolina (on 23 May) became the seventh and eighth states to ratify, both by wide margins. The stage was now set for the crucial ninth state that would turn the Constitution into the official law of the land. During June of 1788 three state conventions were in session: New Hampshire, Virginia, and New York. The New Englanders (57–47) approved on the 21st; the Old Dominion (89–79) five days later. Neither knew of the other's decision when the votes were taken, and each thought that it had become the deciding vote. Both Federalist victories were narrow ones, and each was obtained only after promises to support amendments to the Constitution were made.

New York, where Governor Clinton was an immensely popular figure, had long been recognized as a bastion of Antifederalist strength. Although the Constitutional Convention had set only a nine-state requirement for ratification, New York's support was clearly indispensable to the survival of the new federal government, and the Federalists regarded their effort to educate the public in that state as critical. Hamilton, with the assistance of Madison and to a lesser extent John Jay, set about writing a series of eighty-five essays, under the pen name "Publius," for publication in various New York City newspapers. These articles were intended to be a point-by-point refutation of Antifederalist arguments about the Constitution, extolling the positive potential of a federal government while reminding readers of the weaknesses of the Articles. Known collectively as *The Federalist Papers,* they remain one of America's greatest works of political theory. "Publius" paid particular attention to security issues, defending both the army and militia clauses by demonstrating that the military under the Constitution was a servant and protector of the people, not a European standing army. Thanks to the impact of the essays and skillful parliamentary maneuver, the Federalists won a narrow (30–27) ratification vote on 26 July, but only after agreeing to support thirty-two requests for amendments.

John Jay (1745–1829). *(Oil, by Gilbert Stuart, 1795; National Gallery of Art.)*

The last two states to ratify followed much later. North Carolina approved by a lopsided 194–77 on 21 November 1789 after the First Congress had already introduced a bill of rights. It actually took two separate conventions to achieve this approval. When the vote in the first convention seemed ready to defeat ratification by a wide majority, the Federalists maneuvered to have the convention adjourn without a formal vote to gain time to win over the electorate. The last of the thirteen states, Rhode Island, finally accepted the federal system on 29 May 1790 on the closest vote of all (34-32). It took the threat of secession by the largest towns and economic pressure from the national government to achieve this grudging concession.

Federalist tactics succeeded. When the First Congress assembled in 1789, the winners, in keeping with promises made during the ratification process, set about adding a bill of rights to the Constitution. As leader in the House of Representatives, Madison initiated the legislation as specified by Article V, and by September Congress had approved a set of twelve amendments and sent them to the states for ratification. Ten survived the process, and the Bill of Rights was added to the Constitution on 15 December 1791. Most defined specific liberties, such as freedom of religion, speech, press, and other traditional Anglo-American concepts widely discussed in the eighteenth century, including a prohibition on quartering troops in private homes (Third Amendment).

Only the Second Amendment contained any substantial statement relating to military power. Its reference was quite specific: "A well regulated Militia, being necessary to the security of a free State, the right of the people to keep and bear Arms, shall not be infringed." Eighteenth-century Americans understood the precise meaning of those few words and tied them directly to the basic militia clause in Article I of the Constitution. Creating a "well regulated" militia—that is, one with adequate organization, weapons, and training, uniform across the nation—ensured that, when mobilized, the militiamen could effectively carry out combat functions. This point had been fully articulated during the drafting of Article I. Mason and other advocates of the Second Amendment knew that during the last years of the Revolution many militia units had virtually disintegrated because they lacked sufficient arms. The amendment reinforced the original militia clause by stating this fact explicitly.

Over the years historians have been fascinated with the question of how the Constitution came to be written and ratified. An early, somewhat simplistic, explanation presented the Founding Fathers as a group of wise and virtuous men concerned only with providing greater freedom to their fellow Americans. Early in the twentieth century some scholars began to challenge this popular view. Concentrating on economic issues, they painted a picture of men of property devising a charter that protected their interests. Over the past several decades this view has proved unsatisfactory. Today's more complex interpretation attempts to correlate ideological background with local issues, economics, relative ages, and the formative experience of the participants. Antifederalists as a group tended to be somewhat older men, first exposed to high-level civic affairs during the decades prior to Lexington, and committed to a more literal interpretation of Enlightenment texts. The Federalists, on the other hand, had often first entered political life during the Revolution itself. In the late 1780s most of these men were just reaching full maturity. A basic tenet of this latest interpretation suggests strongly that ex-continentals were particularly prone to become Federalists while militiamen often sided with the opposition. A study of the men who went to Philadelphia in May 1787, and especially of the signers, indicates that this idea too needs further refinement.

Actually more than seventy individuals were nominated as delegates by the state legislatures. Some stayed away for personal reasons; others, because they did not wish to change the Articles. Actual delegations ranged in size from New Hampshire's two men to Pennsylvania's eight. Not all of the fifty-five who attended remained throughout the deliberations. Twenty-nine had nearly perfect attendance records and ten others missed relatively short stretches. Of the remaining sixteen, four put in only token appearances.

Although Jefferson's depiction of the Convention as an "assembly of demigods" may be overblown, the Founding Fathers were in fact a distinguished group and not atypical of the top leadership available in the nation. As could be expected in a deferential society, wealthy and well-educated men dominated the membership of the Convention. Forty-four had been, or were still, members of the Continental Congress. Most had been active in the Revolutionary movement: eight had signed the Declaration of Independence, and thirty had served on active military duty. Of the latter, seventeen were Continental Army veterans, while thirteen had taken to the field with militia units. Virtually every member had served in state or local offices. This commonality of experience allowed these men to understand each other's motives and viewpoints, a factor that enabled the Convention to survive the heated debates that ensued. Despite wide differences in background, temperament, and age (that ranged from Jonathan Dayton's 26 to Benjamin Franklin's 81 years), they shared a basic commitment to the concept of a single, unified nation. Their common experience also made them keenly aware of the weaknesses in the Articles of Confederation and determined to improve upon them.

Distinctions between service in the Continental Army or militia are deceptive. For example, George Mason, who held high rank in the Virginia militia but never participated in active campaigns, expressed sentiments on constitutional issues that closely paralleled those of delegates Edmund Randolph and John Lansing, men with very brief service as Continental staff officers. They all refused to sign the Constitution. John Langdon, William Few, and Charles Pinckney, on the other hand, were militiamen with extensive combat records. In 1787 they could be found espousing ideas very similar to those of long-term Continental officers and fellow signers such as Hamilton, Dayton, and Charles Cotesworth Pinckney. In short, the length and nature of a man's service, not simply the type of commission he held, influenced his attitude toward government. Those who had experienced the trauma of campaigning alongside men from other states in a hard war were likely to draw the same pointed lessons from those days and to view the Constitution in a similar light. It was these same veterans who would help guide the new republic.

Federalists and Jeffersonians

To secure passage of the Constitution, the Framers resorted to wholesale compromise. But by deliberately avoiding divisive details that might frustrate agreement, they only postponed the formidable task of fashioning the workaday policies and procedures of the new federal structure. Their task, then, did not conclude with the ratification of the Constitution, and many of the architects of that document would remain to lead the nation as it came to grips with the complex issues of representative government. In so doing, they passed laws and established precedents, many of which endure to this day.

Among those signers of the Constitution and others who stepped forward to lead the new nation were numerous veterans of the Revolution. In fact, in the debates that surrounded the creation and implementation of the new government, the wartime experiences of this large group of men created a special bond and a commonality of purpose. Although often masked by the overblown partisan rhetoric of the era, this element of a shared personal experience undoubtedly contributed to their record of accomplishment in a special time of national testing. Eventually the Revolution's aging citizen-soldiers would turn over leadership to a new generation of political leaders—but not before they had produced the first political parties, formulated the basic domestic policies that increased the size and economic strength of the country, and made the United States a full-fledged member of the family of nations. Carefully adhering to the letter and spirit of the Constitution, they also created an effective military force to protect the frontiers, meet domestic disturbances, and wage general war, all while adhering strictly to the cherished principle of civilian supremacy.

The First Congress under the new Constitution convened in New York City on 4 March 1789 with only eight senators and thirteen representatives in attendance. The lower chamber finally achieved a quorum on 1 April and began its work by electing Frederick A. C. Muhlenberg of Pennsylvania as the first Speaker of the House. Five days later the Senate followed suit, choosing New Hampshire's John Langdon, a signer, as its first President Pro Tempore. As soon as these formalities were completed, Congress convened the joint session specified in Section 1, Article II, of the Constitution to open and count the ballots of the Electoral College, which had voted on 4 February. To no one's surprise, the College had unanimously chosen George Washington as the first President of the United States. John Adams was elected Vice President. Robert R. Livingston, New York's state chancellor, administered the oath of office to the former general on the balcony of Federal Hall (located at the corner of Broad and Wall Streets) on 30 April 1789.

Washington's enormous personal popularity and prestige had made him the obvious choice for President in an era of strong political controversy. His wealth of administrative and political experience, gained in large measure during his years as Commander in Chief of the Continental Army, qualified him as no other to handle the complex duties of an office that combined the European roles of head of state and head of government. Above all, and to the immense good luck of the new nation, he possessed the common sense to judge accurately the mood of his fellow citizens and the temperament to avoid overly ambitious schemes. He retained a clear vision of the nation's future—one based on liberty and justice for all citizens, strength through union, and economic prosperity through commercial expansion and westward migration.

Washington shared the difficult task of creating a new government with the First Congress (1789–91). Among the 29 senators and 66 representatives who served in that body, 59, including 17 signers of the Constitution, had seen active military service during the Revolution. These veterans provided the new government with a substantial pool of common experience, a decisive factor when Congress passed the implementing legislation that launched the new government.

Its first task was to establish the structure of the other two branches. The Constitution gave Congress the authority to create departments within the executive branch to assist the President in carrying out his responsibilities and to organize a system of federal courts. Accordingly, it created a Department of Foreign Affairs on 27 July 1789, a War Department on 7 August, and a Treasury on 2 September. The office of Postmaster General followed on 22 September. Two days later it passed the Federal Judiciary Act, which established the position of Attorney General and organized a federal judiciary with three circuit and thirteen district courts below the Supreme Court. The Supreme Court, consisting of Chief Justice John Jay and five other justices, opened its first session on 2 February 1790.

This spate of legislation was quickly passed, and by

1790 the center of political initiative had shifted to the executive branch. Washington relied on a Cabinet composed of the heads of the departments to help develop an agenda for both domestic issues and foreign policy. Naturally enough, he turned to Revolutionary veterans to fill his Cabinet and many of the positions in the new federal civil service. With the exception of Secretary of State Thomas Jefferson, every member of the Cabinet had served in the Continental Army—Attorney General Edmund Randolph, Secretary of War Henry Knox, Secretary of the Treasury Alexander Hamilton, and Postmaster General Samuel Osgood. Washington used these men like a council of war. During meetings he encouraged them to speak their minds and discuss issues freely. The President's quiet demeanor led his fellow citizens, and most historians ever since, to focus on the roles of his subordinates, rather than on his decisive voice, in the events of his administration. True, Washington always sought consensus before embarking on a policy, but he always felt free to disregard his Cabinet's advice. In fact, Washington proved singularly successful in imposing his personality, first on the Continental Army and later on the office of President. Many of the traditions and customs of both the Army and the Cabinet draw directly on the precedents he set.

Washington turned first to the national security and the economy. He believed that by pursuing a program based on safeguarding the nation's boundaries he could encourage prosperity and cement the bonds of union. He also believed that international affairs had to be subordinated to nation building, which required supporting and protecting the expansion of American trade to new markets. Specifically, he looked to the nation's frontiers, where he worked for a withdrawal of British forces from their bases on American soil, for peace with the Indians, and for the opening of western rivers, especially the Mississippi, to American commerce. He tended to agree with Hamilton on these issues, believing that the Treasury Secretary's programs to broaden the economy and strengthen the national government were essential for national growth. His administration's two major international agreements, the Treaty of London (Jay's Treaty) in 1794 and the Treaty of San Lorenzo (Pinckney's Treaty) in 1795, attempted, among other goals, to neutralize British and Spanish influence in the trans-Appalachian west. A measure of his success in these areas was the fact that during his term of office he presided over the admission of three new states to the union—Vermont in 1791, Kentucky in 1792, and Tennessee in 1796.

His Cabinet figured prominently in the development of these policies. But given the brilliance and aggressive

John Adams (1735–1826). *(Oil, by Charles Willson Peale, 1791; Independence National Historical Park.)*

Henry Knox (1750–1806). *(Oil, by Charles Willson Peale, c. 1783; Independence National Historical Park.)*

Thomas Jefferson (1743–1826). *(Oil, by Charles Willson Peale, 1791; Independence National Historical Park.)*

Aaron Burr (1756–1836). *(Oil, by John Vanderlyn, c. 1802; copyright Yale University Art Gallery.)*

personalities of Jefferson and Hamilton, it was not surprising that the two disagreed over the proper course of action to pursue in both domestic and foreign arenas. Hamilton, concerned with developing the material resources necessary for the advancement of prosperity and the influence of the government both internally and diplomatically, proposed a far-reaching economic policy to render the nation self-sufficient. He tended to favor Great Britain in foreign affairs. Jefferson, more attuned to the old fears of concentrated power and to the ideal of an agrarian society of yeoman farmers, was more cautious about enhancing the powers of the federal government. He also sympathized with the French, who were in the early years of their own revolution, triggered in part by the debt engendered during the recent war. Each man attracted supporters. Given the era's depth of political passion, these national-level disagreements naturally became grafted onto local issues, providing the nucleus of political parties.

Washington sought to preserve a consensus throughout his eight years in office, but his treaties with Britain and Spain became issues of contention between the nascent parties, as did his attempt to keep America neutral in the resurgent conflict between France and Britain, a policy that initially appeared to favor the latter. No longer able to accept these policies, Jefferson left the Cabinet in 1793. His followers, led in Congress by James Madison and James Monroe, and known as Democratic-Republicans (or, more commonly, as Jeffersonians) gathered round him. Supporters of the administration, ranging in viewpoint from Hamilton's outspoken followers to moderates like John Adams, who succeeded Washington as President in 1797, became known as Federalists.

The Founding Fathers, who viewed any internal division as a threat to the republic, had left the Constitution mute on the subject of political parties. The significant factor behind the emergence of the parties, however, was not their obvious disagreements over policies and programs, but rather their mutual, steadfast support of the Constitution and the principles of government it enshrined. The peaceful transfer of political power from the Federalists to the Democratic-Republicans in 1801 marked an important step in the nation's political evolution.

In defeating Adams in the election of 1800, Jefferson profited from a division in the Federalist party between the followers of Adams and Hamilton. The Virginian and his running mate, Aaron Burr, a former Continental lieutenant colonel, each garnered an equal number of votes in the Electoral College, throwing the election for the first time into the House of Representatives. Ironically, Jefferson would owe his victory to Hamilton, who advised his followers to vote for his old rival. The bitterness engendered by this election led directly to the adoption of the Twelfth Amendment, which in effect bestowed constitutional recognition on political parties in the American system of government. More significantly, however, this election underscored the widespread acceptance of the new Constitution and the union it had created. Despite the unprecedented partisan rivalry, compromise remained essential to the operation of government, and parties, then as now, were actually broad-based coalitions. Even important state leaders such as South Carolina's Charles Pinckney could shift back and forth between the parties according to specific issues. During his inauguration that year, the first held in the new capital on the banks of the Potomac, Jefferson said, "We are all Republicans, we are all Federalists." In this declaration, he accurately reflected how widely most of the five million Americans agreed on basic goals and forecast how readily he and the new leadership could adjust, rather than rescind, their predecessors' policies.

Under Jefferson and Madison, who became President in 1809, American foreign and domestic policy continued to pursue with only minor adjustments the course set by Washington. As could be expected given the relative power of nations, American diplomacy still had to react to events in Europe, where the Napoleonic Wars were the dominant fact of life. Washington had been able to avoid entanglement. Adams had become embroiled in limited hostilities with France for a time, but he also had sought diplomatic rather than military solutions to outstanding differences. Jefferson and Madison in turn attempted to place primary reliance on diplomacy. To back up their efforts, however, they relied more on economic leverage than on the military preparedness favored by the Federalists, drawing particularly on the boycott tactics of the decade before the Revolutionary War for a precedent. The logical extension of this policy came during the period of the Embargo Act (22 December 1807–1 March 1809) when American commerce with both France and Britain was halted to eliminate friction and preserve neutrality. Federalists, especially in New England and other regions heavily dependent upon foreign trade, complained bitterly that their interests were being ruined by the government.

Jefferson's domestic policy also retained the essence of many Federalist initiatives, to include Hamilton's economic program. In particular he continued Washington's focus on western expansion and development, underscored by the admission of Ohio to statehood in 1802 and by his greatest triumph, the Louisiana Purchase. As soon as he learned of the transfer of the Louisiana territories from Spain to France, Jefferson instructed Monroe and Robert R. Livingston to try to purchase the area around New Orleans. Westerners depended upon the Mississippi River to move their produce to market and were anxious to secure unfettered use of the river's sole port. To the Americans' surprise, Napoleon eventually offered them the entire region, and in April 1803 the territories were transferred to the United States for the sum of $15 million. The purchase proved immediately popular, but the irony of the situation was not overlooked. Here was Jefferson, the leader of those dedicated to a strict interpretation of presidential powers under the Constitution, abrogating to himself alone the nationalistic decision to seize the unique opportunity of doubling the size of the nation. Continuing in the spirit of Washington's nation-building policy, Jefferson immediately sent out a series of military expeditions—the most famous being led by Meriwether Lewis and William Clark—to explore the vast region. In 1812 Louisiana became the first state admitted to the union from the former French region.

One of the most critical issues facing the first generation of federal leaders was the formulation of a national military policy. Washington's administration and Congress set important precedents in this area as they filled in the outline of military forces sketched by the Constitution. Working together, they determined the size and role of the Regular Army and then resolved the relationship between the states and the national government in dealing with the militia. These decisions had to be made in the context of foreign and domestic policy objectives. They also had to be based on the realities of increasing partisan political activity, since the Constitution explicitly gave the final say to the people, speaking through their elected representatives in Congress, in appropriating the funds to pay for troops, guns, and ships.

When Washington took office he inherited a situation verging on open warfare in the west. Along with the Congress, he quickly came under intense pressure from interest groups to provide the settlers with better protection. The delicate issue of the role of the military thus received its first airing within that highly charged specific context. Josiah Harmar's small regiment had been created by the Continental Congress in 1784 to serve as a frontier constabulary, but the westward movement had accelerated with the establishment of the Northwest Territory in 1787 and the organization in 1790 of the Territory South of the Ohio River, or Southwest Territory, under Governor William Blount. Indian tribes, encouraged by British garrisons and traders, began sporadic attacks, and as early as 1788 the Army began taking casualties.

The President hoped to avoid war and set in motion a series of interim measures even before the new War Department was organized. He ordered Harmar's men fur-

William Clark (1770–1838). *(Oil, by Charles Willson Peale, 1810; Independence National Historical Park.)*

ther west and asked Henry Knox and Arthur St. Clair to begin gathering information in case operations had to be mounted. In the meantime the creation of the War Department on 7 August 1789 provided for an orderly transfer of responsibility to the new government. Secretary of War Knox exercised oversight for Indian diplomacy in addition to his other duties. The following month Congress imposed on the officers and men of Harmar's regiment the requirement to take an oath to "support the constitution of the United States." Hidden as a rider in this law was authorization empowering the President to mobilize frontier militia under federal pay and control if the situation warranted. Conditions continued to worsen as Washington pursued a policy of trying to negotiate a settlement while at the same time preparing for possible fighting.

To placate settlers in the Kentucky region, Washington successfully persuaded Congress in early 1790 to provide a modest (four company) increase in the size of the Army. In June he ordered Harmar into the field. Washington and Knox envisioned a raid deep into the Indian heartland by a small, hard-hitting party to demonstrate the federal government's power, followed by a negotiated treaty. Unfortunately, the slow-moving Harmar did not start until late fall, burned a few Indian villages, and then lost most of his rear guard during the withdrawal. Knox and Washington ordered St. Clair, who replaced Harmar as the commander of the Army, to try again the next year. In the interim, the administration persuaded Congress to raise a second regular regiment and to authorize several thousand Provincial-style short-term levies. St. Clair not only repeated all of Harmar's errors, he also violated one of the cardinal rules of frontier warfare by ignoring adequate security and reconnaissance. At dawn on 4 November 1791 about 1,000 Indians overran his camp. More than 600 soldiers and militiamen died in the ensuing rout.

Although St. Clair's defeat marked the second major setback in less than two years, Washington and Knox decided that their basic policy of combining diplomacy with regular troops constituted the correct approach to the western problem, and they redoubled efforts to raise a proper force to carry it out. Congress eventually conducted a full investigation into the Army's conduct of the 1791 campaign, establishing thereby an important precedent for congressional oversight of the executive branch, one not specifically authorized by the Constitution. But it also continued to support the administration's military policy. In January 1792, Washington requested that the military budget be tripled to a million dollars a year to support a 5,000-man Army. When neither Gerry, the most outspoken foe of a large military, nor Madison, the leading Jeffersonian in Congress, opposed the request, a bill to that effect became law in March. Revolutionary War hero "Mad" Anthony Wayne resigned his seat in the House of Representatives to replace St. Clair, with a commission as major general.

The Second Congress also passed the first comprehensive militia law. Washington and other nationalists ended the Revolutionary War convinced that militia forces needed to be highly trained and capable of close coordination with the regulars on the battlefield. Their proposals for a peace establishment in 1783 had advanced the notion of a select militia force to achieve this goal, backed up by the general militia. In succeeding years both Steuben and Knox published pamphlets refining this idea, which included paying this "advanced corps" for their days of extra training. Many others believed that the highly motivated militias of the 1770s had been the key to success in the Revolution, and they were highly suspicious of any reforms that might weaken the close ties to local government inherent in the old colonial militia system.

Washington had been unable to push a federal militia bill through Congress in either 1789 or 1790. In February 1792, while debate over the expanded Regular Army continued, Congress finally began detailed consideration of two bills which, known collectively as the Militia Act of 1792, passed in early May. This legislation rejected separating militiamen into two distinct classes.

The reformers had clearly failed to convince a majority that the current situation warranted either the expense or the political risk of such tight federal control. Instead, the Militia Act compromised, allowing the President to mobilize the citizen-soldiers when necessary and to set national, but nonbinding, standards for organization and training. This arrangement, identical to the one discussed during the writing of the Constitution's militia clause, was accepted because it still left the individual states with major control over their militia. The reformers might lament the fact that the efficiency of the citizen-soldiers would continue to depend ultimately on local rather than national initiatives, but they could read progress in the general acceptance of the notion of a national standard and in the new law's provision for the organization of volunteer groups who purchased their own uniforms and underwent extra military training to become elite "flank" companies in the militia regiments. Everyone understood that under normal circumstances only these men would be mobilized. Despite some minor modifications, this law would remain in force until the creation of the modern National Guard in 1903.

The first test of the new militia act came on the frontier. Wayne, like Harmar and St. Clair, was a veteran who had served in Washington's main army and in Nathanael Greene's Southern Army during the Revolution. Unlike his predecessors, however, he remembered the important lessons about the need for adequate training, proper organization and logistics, and blending regulars and militia into a combat team that made use of their separate skills. He worked closely with Knox to adapt those ideas to the task of wilderness fighting. The regulars were regrouped into the Legion of the United States, a special combined-arms arrangement, based on European ideas, that already had been used in the later stages of the Revolution. After two years of careful preparation, the Legion, reinforced by nearly 3,000 frontier militiamen, penetrated into the heart of Indian territory in the Ohio Valley. On 20 August 1794, at Fallen Timbers, Wayne's hard work paid off. His regular infantry used their bayonets to drive the Indians into the open where the mounted frontiersmen rode them down. The battle and resulting destruction of neighboring villages and crops broke the tribes' resistance. On 3 August 1795 in the Treaty of Greenville a dozen tribes ceded their claims to disputed lands and moved farther west. At about the same time, Jay's Treaty brought British agreement to withdraw from all forts within the boundaries of the United States.

Anthony Wayne (1745–1796). *(Pastel, by James Sharples, Sr., c. 1795; Independence National Historical Park.)*

James Wilkinson (1757–1825). *(Oil, by Charles Willson Peale, c. 1797; Independence National Historical Park.)*

These treaties eliminated much of the Army's preoccupation with the old Northwest Territory, freeing the troops for service in the Southwest Territory, where settlement was beginning to accelerate. This frontier was noted for the spirit and independence of the settlers in Kentucky and Tennessee. Controlling the area had been a challenging assignment for Governor William Blount, a signer of the Constitution, and would prove equally troublesome for the Army officers assigned to duty in the region.

Southwesterners had a reputation for independent military action. This tradition had proved beneficial during the Revolution, particularly at King's Mountain and during George Rogers Clark's epic struggles, but it would pose serious difficulties for both Federalist and Jeffersonian officials. Free access to the river systems feeding into the Mississippi, as Washington had foreseen during the 1780s, remained essential to the region's economic prosperity, and westerners were tempted to take direct action against Spanish-controlled Louisiana. English agents encouraged such actions because of the Napoleonic Wars, believing that any action harmful to Spain, France's ally, could only benefit England. In fact, national leaders of both parties regarded the southwest as an area that might try to break away from the union and sought to preclude such a disaster, even to the point of expelling Blount from the Senate—to which he had been elected when Tennessee became a state in 1796—when they suspected that he might have been involved with British agents in such a plot. Others, notably General James Wilkinson, who had succeeded Wayne as commanding general, and Aaron Burr, were also later charged with plotting with foreign agents to separate the region from the United States. The Army played an important role in defusing the situation. Garrisons of regulars steadfastly preserved law and order and guaranteed that any attempt to create an independent republic in the southwest never progressed beyond the realm of dreams. With adequate military protection, the frontier remained calm for a generation.

The military had faced a different and more difficult mission in the summer of 1794 when farmers in western Pennsylvania, who bitterly resented Hamilton's 1791 excise taxes on liquor since it was manufactured from their only cash crop, rebelled. The new government's response to the so-called Whiskey Rebellion stood in sharp contrast to the Continental Congress' reaction to the rioting led by Daniel Shays. When Washington learned that Governor Thomas Mifflin had refused to use state militia against the rioters because he feared the political consequence, the President exercised his powers under the Constitution and the 1792 Militia Act. In August 1794 he called out a force of some 15,000 militiamen from nearby states under Governor Henry Lee of Virginia, an ex-Continental. The overwhelming display of strength ended the "revolt" without serious incident. This success, coupled with Wayne's victory at Fallen Timbers, greatly enhanced the prestige of the central government. Washington and most other leaders accepted the use of force in each of these cases only as a last resort; a small element of the Federalist party, however, drew a different lesson. Led by Hamilton, they pressed for a larger Regular Army as a means of expanding the power of the national government, an aim central to their political thinking.

International circumstances seemed to support their scheme. The Federalists had originally justified the need for a peacetime army to cope with Indian harassment on the frontier. Raids by North Africa's Barbary States on American shipping and the growing threat of peripheral entanglement in the war in Europe provided the rationale for an expansion of this military force in 1794. After some debate, Congress created a modest six-frigate Navy, approved a plan for federally funded harbor defenses at selected ports, and increased the size of the Army by forming a Corps of Artillerists and Engineers. The latter would provide small regular garrisons for the new fortifications, which could easily be reinforced in an emergency by the militia from the surrounding area. This political compromise, acceptable to both parties, reflected the lesson learned in the Revolution that effective defense required full-time troops that only the national government could train and support, but also relied, for reasons of cost, on the abilities of the militia to turn out in mass. A month after approving the coast defense program, Congress authorized the establishment of federal arsenal and armory facilities at Springfield, Massachusetts, and Harpers Ferry, West Virginia, for government production of arms and equipment.

With tensions on both the frontier and high seas defused during the winter of 1795–96, the Jeffersonians pressured Washington's administration to cut military expenses as a way of reducing taxes. They cited the successful use of federalized militia, rather than regulars, in the Whiskey Rebellion to strengthen their arguments. The resulting legislation, passed in May 1796, reflected a broad bipartisan consensus on defense issues. Although cuts were made in spending, establishing a precedent of congressional review of line items in a defense budget, the Army and Navy were accepted as permanent institutions, not just temporary expedients to meet specific crises. The Army, reduced in size, used the ensuing years of peace to consolidate its internal organization and sense of identity. James McHenry, the third consecutive Continental veteran to serve as Secretary of War, introduced a variety of administrative reforms to improve Army efficiency. He issued the first comprehensive

"Washington Reviewing the Western Army at Fort Cumberland, Maryland." These militia troops ended the "Whiskey Rebellion" without bloodshed. *(Oil, by Frederick Kemmelmeyer, c. 1794; Metropolitan Museum of Art, gift of Edgar William and Bernice Chrysler Garbisch.)*

peacetime Army Regulations in 1798 and took actions to reinforce the concept of civilian control over the Army's officer corps.

Rising tensions between France and the United States in 1797 once more favored Hamilton's plans for military expansion. Adams dispatched three diplomats, Gerry, Charles Cotesworth Pinckney, and John Marshall (the latter two, Continental veterans), to Paris to try to resolve differences, but in what has come to be known as the XYZ Affair, their French counterparts demanded bribes as a condition for holding meetings, an affront that triggered popular outrage across the United States. The Federalists believed that the best way to avoid open warfare would be to demonstrate that the country was prepared to fight, and as membership in the volunteer militia surged, the Adams administration introduced a modest request for additional regular forces.

The more extreme wing of the Federalist party, spearheaded by Hamilton, had much more ambitious goals. It pushed a series of bills through Congress between May 1798 and March 1799 that created, on paper at least, an elaborate military array: an expanded force of regulars, a 10,000-man Provisional Army, and an even larger "Eventual Army." Hamilton and his followers persuaded Washington to lend his prestige and popularity to the cause. Commissioned a lieutenant general, the retired President became commander of this "Grand Army," while other Revolutionary veterans (including Charles Cotesworth Pinckney) filled the remaining senior positions. Hamilton himself became the Inspector General and assumed the burden of day-to-day administration. Reality lagged far behind these grandiose plans, and less than 4,000 men actually joined an Army that never saw action in this "Quasi-War." On the other hand, naval vessels successfully fought in the Caribbean and Atlantic, and Congress established a separate Navy Department on 30 April 1798 under ex-Continental Benjamin Stoddert to manage the rapid growth of the fleet.

The size of the Army during the Quasi-War soon became a sensitive political issue. The Jeffersonians were convinced that France was not about to fight in North America, and in the same sense used by the colonists in the decade before the Revolution, they came to consider the underutilized regulars a "standing army." They feared that Hamilton and his allies planned to use it to crush domestic opposition. At each step of the expansion process they raised this issue. While Federalist spokesmen in Congress such as Connecticut's Uriah Tracy, a Revolutionary militiaman, stressed the notion of preparing for war with a well-trained regular force and then negotiating from strength, Jeffersonian military experts like Thomas Sumter, Daniel Morgan, and William Shepard, also veterans of the Revolution, claimed that the militia provided an adequate force for the purpose. President Adams sided with the Jeffersonians against the extremists in his own party. He had always preferred diplomacy, and when he resolved the outstanding issues with France, he quickly persuaded Congress to trim the military back to peacetime levels. Federalist leaders, aware that they lacked support for an extensive defense establishment, led the planning for demobilization in the hope that in doing so they could preserve a minimal regular force. Three Revolutionary veterans in Congress, John Marshall, Samuel Smith, and Theodore Sedgewick, representing, respectively, the moderate Federalists, the Jeffersonians, and the extreme Federalists, worked out a series of compromises that led to reductions in the Army in May 1800 and in the Navy early the following year.

Jefferson's administration took office determined to reduce federal expenses, especially military ones, but with no intention of dismantling the remaining Regular Army. Although he and his service Secretaries, Revolutionary veterans Henry Dearborn (Army) and Robert Smith (Navy), placed great faith in the prowess of the militia to defend the nation from invasion, they pragmatically accepted the need for a limited force of full-time soldiers and sailors. Beginning in 1802 they used the annual appropriations process to tailor the armed forces to more limited defensive roles. Their reorganization of the Army in 1802, for example, called for drastic cuts, but actually eliminated few enlisted men. Instead, units and the staff were manipulated to force out most of the more partisan Federalist senior officers, who were replaced with Jeffersonians or moderate Federalists.

Jefferson also seized upon a reform originally proposed by the Federalists but transformed it to meet his own needs. Since the Revolution, the Army had suffered from a lack of native-born engineers and technical specialists. Proposals to establish a European-style military academy to train such individuals had failed in Congress, although it did authorize training for a group of cadets in the Corps of Artillerists and Engineers during the Quasi-War period. The Federalists had hoped to expand this nucleus into separate courses of formal instruction for artillery, engineer, infantry, cavalry, and naval officers. Jefferson recognized that many Federalists enjoyed a competitive edge when they applied for commissions because, generally, they came from families that could afford good educations. To obtain equal opportunity for others, he altered the Federalist proposal and won congressional approval for the establishment of a military academy at West Point where cadets would receive a basic civilian and military education; their technical, branch-related training would occur after graduation.

Henry Dearborn (1751–1829). *(Oil, by Charles Willson Peale, c. 1796; Independence National Historical Park.)*

Jeffersonian hopes of further naval reductions were shelved when the Barbary States resumed raids on American shipping. Washington and Adams both had chosen to pay tribute to halt these piratical acts, but Jefferson, believing that fundamental issues of justice and honor were at stake, refused to follow suit. He also believed direct action in this instance would be more cost-effective than bribery. With Congress in recess, he dispatched a small Navy squadron to Tripoli on his own authority. Even his Cabinet questioned the legality of such an action, but Jefferson justified it, and provided a new interpretation of the Constitution in so doing by claiming that as Commander in Chief he could respond to aggression without prior congressional approval. In fact, when Congress reconvened in November 1801, it approved the naval expedition. Operations dragged on until 1805 when bombardment, close blockade, and an internal revolt finally forced the Pasha of Tripoli to sue for peace. Similar aggressive tactics were also employed by both Jefferson and Madison to neutralize the remaining Barbary States.

These operations combined with political pressure from commercial interests to force Jefferson to retain a larger blue-water Navy than members of his party would have liked. The latter argued that the large frigates and ships of the line favored by the Federalists could provoke trouble by appearing to Europeans to be a threat against their colonies in the Caribbean and in Latin America. On the other hand, they pointed out, a combination of fortifications and small boats mounting one or more heavy cannon had effectively protected most of the coastline during the Revolution. Jefferson came in time to agree that reverting to this purely defensive system could guarantee American interests in a cost-effective way and avoid the risk of antagonizing the Europeans. But in June 1807 a major international incident in American territorial waters caused a *volte face*. The British frigate *Leopard* fired on the United States Navy's *Chesapeake* just off the Virginia coast when the American vessel refused to submit to being searched. An indignant population called for a declaration of war, but the administration remained committed to diplomatic measures. At the same time, the Jeffersonians were pragmatic enough to realize that stronger defenses would add leverage, and in 1808 and 1809 they persuaded Congress to fund a new round of coastal fortifications and once again to expand the Regular Army to man the new forts and to garrison the Louisiana Territory more effectively.

When Jefferson's party first came to power, its military and foreign policies, reminiscent of the pre-Revolutionary days, appeared strongly at odds with those of the Federalists. It preached the importance of the militia as the bulwark of freedom, the dangers of standing armies, the sufficiency of economic persuasion in international relations, and the need to reduce government expenses and taxes. But once in power, the Jeffersonians developed pragmatic policies not all that different from Federalist precedents. This similarity actually should have come as no surprise, since many of the Jeffersonians had served in the Revolution alongside their Federalist counterparts and had absorbed the same lessons. In retrospect, the basic defense program initiated under Washington and Adams survived and prospered under Jefferson and Madison because both sides saw it as a natural evolution from two centuries of experience that met the needs of the new nation. Passionate political speeches aside, the difference between the two parties came to be more a matter of emphasis than a fundamental division over principles.

The military policies fashioned by the first generation of federal leaders had their final test when the country went to war against Britain in 1812. Americans called the War of 1812 a "Second War of Independence," and, indeed, the war did reaffirm the victory of 1783. But in a larger sense, the War of 1812 was really one small phase of the last of the eighteenth century's global struggles. Once again the British considered fighting in North America less important than the struggle against Napoleon in Europe. In many ways, the conduct of the war was conditioned by and mirrored the Revolution, particularly the phase after 1778. The Madison administration divided military responsibilities for the war along traditional lines. The regulars, like Washington's continentals, formed the main battle forces, first to carry the attack to Canada and thereafter to defend against the main British Army. The militia retained its customary local functions, reinforcing the coast defense forts and Navy gunboats and supporting the regulars in major engagements.

Between 1812 and 1815 the American military system, created by the Soldier-Statesmen of the Revolutionary generation and in part still commanded by veterans of the War for Independence, was tested again. If the war did not noticeably enhance the international reputation of America's military forces, it nevertheless proved them sufficient to the task of stalemating a powerful enemy. In a number of key engagements, the nation watched able young generals, whose careers would continue well into the nation's coming of age, assume the mantle of leadership from the aging veterans of the Revolution. The youthful Andrew Jackson's victory at New Orleans, for example, mirrored that of Samuel Smith of Revolutionary War renown in the successful repulse of the British before Baltimore just months before. Both proved once again that regulars and militia could be effectively combined in combat, just as they had been at Cowpens, when they were employed in a team effort that did not require either to carry out tasks alien to its own capabilities. Their achievements in this "second War for Independence" demonstrated that the Founding Fathers, ever suspicious of standing armies in the European sense, had created a workable alternative for the new nation.

The contribution of the Soldier-Statesmen to the foundation of the republic is often dominated by a discussion of numbers. As might be expected, former soldiers, who had developed strong leadership and organizational skills during the war, gravitated to similar positions in the peacetime government. As a result, Revolutionary veterans clearly dominated government in the early years of the new republic.[1] A majority of the men who signed the Constitution were veterans. A similar ratio of veterans to nonveterans existed in the First Congress. Successive Congresses would continue to include a significant number of veterans down through the end of the Thirteenth Congress in 1815, and in fact veterans would control the leadership in both houses of Congress long after their total numbers dwindled to a minority. Veterans also dominated the executive branch of the na-

[1] For a comprehensive statistical breakdown of soldier-statesmen and their subsequent service in government, see Appendix D.

"Battle of New Orleans." *(Oil, by Jean Hyacinthe de Laclotte, 1815; New Orleans Museum of Art, gift of Edgar William and Bernice Chrysler Garbisch.)*

tional government well into the nineteenth century. Two, Washington and Monroe, served as President, and their colleagues in arms constituted a majority in every presidential Cabinet through 1816, thirty-five years after the battle of Yorktown. They also held office in great numbers at every level of the civil service, from senior diplomats serving in delicate international negotiations to customs officials, postmasters, and those unheralded workers who managed the day-to-day functions of the commonweal. While the number of veterans in the federal judiciary was considerably less imposing, a former Continental Army captain, John Marshall of Virginia, presided as Chief Justice for thirty-four years and did as much to shape the future of the nation as any figure of his time. Veterans also held a host of positions in state and local government where, allied with their comrades in the federal system, they would exercise a major influence on the direction of government for many generations.

More important than sheer numbers was the common sense of purpose of this group of leaders. Most wanted to institute a powerful federal republic, yet one embodying a system of checks and balances that would prevent any single element of government from overriding the common good. They also wanted to create a military establishment that was always subordinate to the elected civilian leaders. If they sometimes seemed to pay excessive attention to the size and roles of that establishment, it should be remembered that the Founding Fathers had clear precedents—both colonial and European—for regarding the Army as a potential source of mischief. The system they devised—a carefully circumscribed regular military force supplemented by a well-regulated militia—has remained in force for two hundred years. The success of this system owes much to the first President and Commander in Chief. Washington's wise military advice, clearly articulated in his "Sentiments on a Peace Establishment" and his "Farewell Address," has been a guidepost for the American military establishment. Above all, he demanded that the American soldier is first and foremost a citizen, with all the duties and rights that others enjoy, not someone outside the mainstream of society.

As rationalists, the Founding Fathers had a profound respect for the appeal of personal civic duty and responsibility. In the early days of the new republic, they reinforced the subordination of the military establishment to the civilian government in an individual way. In 1789 they called on every officer, noncommissioned officer, and private soldier "who are, or shall be, in the service of the United States" to take an oath, which with only minor modification in wording has remained an integral part of the life of every serviceman and woman. In a special way they become partners of the Founding Fathers when, at the beginning of their military careers, each repeats the familiar words:

> I do solemnly swear (or affirm) that I will
> support the Constitution of the United States
> against all enemies, foreign and domestic;
> that I will bear true faith and allegiance
> to the same.

In taking this oath, they not only underscore the nation's continuing dedication to the Constitution, but reflect the central place of that document in the unfolding history of the republic.

SOLDIER-STATESMEN OF THE CONSTITUTION

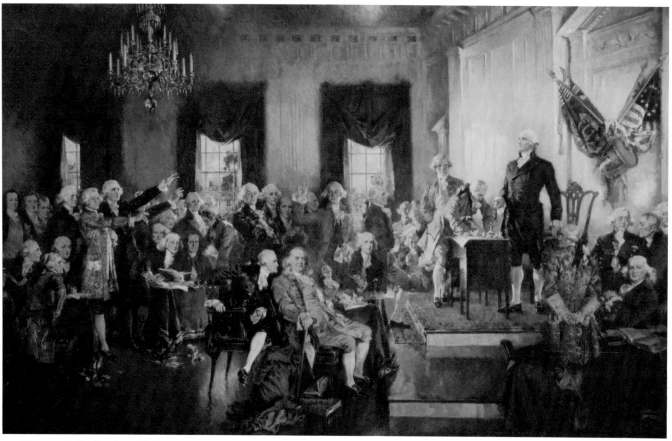

"Scene of the Signing of the Constitution of the United States." *(Oil, by Howard Chandler Christy, 1940; courtesy of the Architect of the Capitol.)*

1. Washington, George, Va.
2. Franklin, Benjamin, Pa.
3. Madison, James, Va.
4. Hamilton, Alexander, N.Y.
5. Morris, Gouverneur, Pa.
6. Morris, Robert, Pa.
7. Wilson, James, Pa.
8. Pinckney, Chas. Cotesworth, S.C.
9. Pinckney, Chas., S.C.
10. Rutledge, John, S.C.
11. Butler, Pierce, S.C.
12. Sherman, Roger, Conn.
13. Johnson, William Samuel, Conn.
14. McHenry, James, Md.
15. Read, George, Del.
16. Bassett, Richard, Del.
17. Spaight, Richard Dobbs, N.C.
18. Blount, William, N.C.
19. Williamson, Hugh, N.C.
20. Jenifer, Daniel of St. Thomas, Md.
21. King, Rufus, Mass.
22. Gorham, Nathaniel, Mass.
23. Dayton, Jonathan, N.J.
24. Carroll, Daniel, Md.
25. Few, William, Ga.
26. Baldwin, Abraham, Ga.
27. Langdon, John, N.H.
28. Gilman, Nicholas, N.H.
29. Livingston, William, N.J.
30. Paterson, William, N.J.
31. Mifflin, Thomas, Pa.
32. Clymer, George, Pa.
33. Fitzsimons, Thomas, Pa.
34. Ingersoll, Jared, Pa.
35. Bedford, Gunning, Jr., Del.
36. Brearly, David, N.J.
37. Dickinson, John, Del.
38. Blair, John, Va.
39. Broom, Jacob, Del.
40. Jackson, William, Secretary

George Washington

Among the Founding Fathers, the man who presided over the Constitutional Convention most clearly embodies the classic concept of the soldier-statesman. Just as George Washington was the architect of victory in the Revolution, so too, as the first President, he was the key figure in establishing essential political precedents to ensure the success of the new republic. Even to his contemporaries, Washington seemed larger than life. Possessed of an extraordinary strength of character and a wealth of public virtues, he exhibited an integrity, self-discipline, and devotion to duty that made him the natural leader in the task of nation building.

Rising above the interests of class and section, Washington made a strong, viable union his goal. In a very real sense, he personified the emerging spirit of nationhood in the newly independent colonies. His support for a strong central government undoubtedly reflected his military experience, both as an officer in the Virginia militia and as the commanding general of the Continental Army. Indeed, the thirteen years that Washington spent on active service—more than a quarter of his adult life—were a singular devotion to public duty by a prosperous, eighteenth-century landowner. The practical experiences provided by this lengthy military career furnished Washington with a sure grasp of the political, economic, and military advantages to be gained from an effective central government. His unwavering support of this concept, and his understanding of the importance of political compromise, were essential to the success of the Constitutional Convention.

The Patriot

A younger son in a family of the landed gentry, Washington appeared destined by birth and education to a career as farmer and land surveyor. But the death of his older brother in 1752 abruptly changed his life. It opened the way to his obtaining Mount Vernon, a large plantation on the Potomac, and to his succeeding his brother as one of Virginia's four adjutants responsible for militia training. Sworn in as a major of militia in February 1753, at the age of 21, he volunteered for active duty some ten months later.

Washington entered military service just as the lengthy rivalry for empire between England and France was reaching its climax in America. If the colonists had appeared indifferent to some of the larger aspects of this conflict between traditional European enemies, their desire for expansion and their fear of alliances between the French and the Indians made them increasingly opposed to a continued French presence in North America. Virginia in particular was incensed when the French established a series of forts in the west. Reacting to this threat, Lieutenant Governor Robert Dinwiddie sent the young Washington to deliver an ultimatum to the intruders. When diplomacy failed, Dinwiddie ordered out a force of 300 colonials under Washington to defend English claims to the "Forks of the Ohio," where the Allegheny and Monongahela rivers join to form the Ohio (now Pittsburgh). Washington promptly led his men into what would become the first engagement of the French and Indian War. He won a preliminary skirmish before being captured by superior French forces some 50 miles south of his objective.

Widespread criticism, especially among the English after his release, only seemed to strengthen Washington's resolve. He served as a volunteer aide in 1755 to Major General Edward Braddock when the British sent a large force of regulars to capture Fort Duquesne, the French stronghold recently erected at the Forks of the Ohio. Although the Braddock expedition met defeat on the banks of the Monongahela, Washington's display of courage and tactical skills in battle caused his personal reputation to soar. A grateful Dinwiddie subsequently placed him in charge of Virginia's frontier defenses. He commanded the colony's regiments and separate ranger companies (both perpetuated in today's 116th Infantry, Virginia Army National Guard), as well as its mobilized militiamen. In 1758 Washington became a brigade commander, the only American to achieve that rank during the war.

The French and Indian War served as a training ground for the leaders of the American Revolution. From his experiences in the field Washington came to understand the key role played by discipline, "the soul of an army," as he later called it. He also learned that tactics and formations had to be adapted to terrain. Perhaps most important for his future, he came to realize that the able leader pays close attention to administrative detail, learns how to make do with limited resources, and seeks to foster the welfare of his men.

Resigning his commission in 1758, Washington de-

GEORGE WASHINGTON
Virginia

Birth: 22 February 1732, at "Wakefield," Westmoreland County, Virginia
Death: 14 December 1799, at "Mount Vernon," Fairfax County, Virginia
Interment: Mount Vernon

All dates appearing in this and the following biographies of the Framers of the Constitution are rendered in New Style. In 1752 the English-speaking world adopted the Gregorian calendar, thereby adding 11 days to the date and officially moving back New Year's Day from 25 March to 1 January. Thus Washington's date of birth, for example, was recorded originally as 11 February.

Oil on canvas, by Gilbert Stuart (c. 1795-96); National Gallery of Art.

voted the next fifteen years to his expanding agricultural enterprises. He also began to acquire political skills, emerging as a moderate leader of the opposition to English colonial policy. By 1774, however, Virginia's opposition to the mother country had hardened, and Washington, always loyal to his colony, joined in supporting the revolutionaries. He accepted the leadership of the volunteer militia and represented Virginia in the Continental Congress.

The Soldier

The Continental Congress quickly took advantage of Washington's military experience. Following the fighting at Lexington and Concord, it appointed him to various committees handling military matters, and on 15 June 1775 his fellow delegates unanimously elected him "General and Commander in Chief" of all Continental forces. Washington accepted the assignment only out of a profound sense of duty, refusing any salary. For eight years, the longest American war before Vietnam, he led the main elements of the Continental Army in combat while also carrying out the broader responsibilities of the Revolution's senior military officer.

The two sides adopted different strategies in the war. The English concentrated on occupying urban centers and seeking set battles. Washington put his emphasis on preserving his forces, believing the Revolution could succeed only if he kept his Army intact. He therefore bided his time, avoiding major defeats and acting decisively when the chance for surprise arose. Trenton and Princeton, in the winter of 1776, were memorable victories in a bleak campaign. In 1777 General Horatio Gates won the battle of Saratoga, and France entered the war on the American side, thus offering Washington the prospect of an allied offensive. In the interim, he employed his main force to neutralize the English army in New York, while nibbling away at the enemy's strength and resolve in other areas, principally in the south. When French naval superiority off the Virginia Capes offered the opportunity for victory, Washington struck swiftly, defeating the British at Yorktown in 1781.

Washington had overcome massive obstacles in pursuing this strategy. After organizing and training the Army, he had met the challenge of holding it together as a professional fighting force during the dark days of defeat. At the same time, he had to placate a demanding Congress and jealous state governments, improvise to offset shortages in material support, curb his sometimes impulsive subordinate commanders, and deal with allies. Only a soldier endowed with extraordinary foresight, personal integrity, and self-discipline could have provided the necessary leadership. The claim can be made that without Washington the Revolution would not have succeeded.

At war's end, Washington promptly dismantled his victorious Army and once again became a private citizen. These actions astounded European observers, who fully expected the victorious general to seize power in the independent but unorganized colonies. Such assessments overlooked Washington's strong belief in the subordination of the military to civilian authority. He had made his position clear in March 1783 when a petition urging the Army to force Congress to restore back pay had circulated among the officers at Newburgh, New York. Washington recalled his own sacrifices in the service of his country and reminded his officers that their loyalty should be to their country, not to the Army. To dramatize the point, he fumbled through the first paragraph of his prepared remarks, donned glasses, and commented that not only had he grown gray in the service of his country but now he was also going blind. He then proceeded to denounce the petition as treason. The chastised officers meekly dispersed.

The Statesman

Washington, his personal finances in shambles, returned to Mount Vernon in 1783 to resume his agricultural and business interests. But his absence from public life proved brief. The course of government under the Articles of Confederation convinced him that a stronger central authority was essential if the political and economic promises of independence were to be realized. His active participation in the drive for a stronger union of the thirteen states sprang in part from his fascination with the potential of the west, an interest born during his youthful days as a surveyor in the Shenandoah Valley and as an officer in the French and Indian War. To promote the development of the Potomac River Valley, he hosted a conference between officials from Virginia and Maryland at Mount Vernon in 1785. This meeting led to a convention in Annapolis the next year and, finally, to the Constitutional Convention in Philadelphia in 1787.

The delegates unanimously elected Washington president of the Constitutional Convention. He proved uniquely suited to the task, his presence lending prestige and dignity to the proceedings. He also served as an important unifying force in the deliberations. Under his judicious guidance the Convention reached the many compromises necessary to achieve a more perfect union and wrote the provisions that would provide for a strong central government. Ratification of the Constitution led in time to Washington's inauguration as President in New York City in April 1789.

Once in office, Washington tried to transform the promises of the Revolution and the Constitution into realities. Applying experiences gained in commanding the Continental Army, he set about the task of organizing and molding a new central government. With quiet authority, he balanced the competing factions coalescing around two of his subordinates, Thomas Jefferson and Alexander Hamilton. He dealt with the demands of the Congress with typical restraint, respecting its legislative prerogatives but never hesitating to exercise his presidential powers. In foreign affairs he insisted on strict neutrality in the continuing Anglo-French conflict; in economic matters he supported measures to strengthen the stability of the new nation. He secured the west through military actions and international treaties. He also jealously defended the authority of the federal government, quickly calling forth state militia forces to suppress the Whiskey Rebellion, a flouting of the excise tax laws by farmers in western Pennsylvania. Always a precedent-setting leader, he established a critical final one when he refused to accept a third term.

Washington's stirring Farewell Address to the country not only cautioned against sectional differences and foreign entanglements but also encapsulated his philosophy of government. In relinquishing the reins of power for the last time, he reminded his fellow citizens that "the Unity of Government which constitutes you one people is also now dear to you. It is justly so; for it is a main Pillar in the Edifice of your real independence, the support of your tranquility at home; your peace abroad; of your safety; of your prosperity; of that very Liberty which you so highly prize."

Abraham Baldwin

Abraham Baldwin, who represented Georgia at the Constitutional Convention, was a fervent missionary of public education. Throughout his career he combined a faith in democratic institutions with a belief that an informed citizenry was essential to the continuing well-being of those institutions. The son of an unlettered Connecticut blacksmith, Baldwin through distinguished public service clearly demonstrated how academic achievement could open opportunities in early American society. Educated primarily for a position in the church, he served in the Continental Army during the climactic years of the Revolution. There, close contact with men of widely varying economic and social backgrounds broadened his outlook and experience and convinced him that public leadership in America included a duty to instill in the electorate the tenets of civic responsibility.

Baldwin also displayed a strong sense of nationalism. Experiences during the war as well as his subsequent work in public education convinced him that the future well-being of an older, more prosperous state like Connecticut was closely linked to developments in newer frontier states like Georgia, where political institutions were largely unformed and provisions for education remained primitive. His later political career was animated by the conviction that only a strong central government dedicated to promoting the welfare of the citizens of all the states could guarantee the fulfillment of the ideals and promises of the Revolution.

The Patriot

The Baldwins were numbered among the earliest New England settlers. Arriving in Connecticut in 1639, the family produced succeeding generations of hard-working farmers, small-town tradesmen, and minor government officials. Abraham Baldwin's father plied his trade in Guilford, where he eventually rose to the rank of lieutenant in the local unit of the Connecticut militia. A resourceful man with an overriding faith in the advantages of higher education, he moved his family to New Haven where he borrowed heavily to finance his sons' attendance at Yale College (now Yale University). Abraham Baldwin never married, but he made a similar sacrifice, for after his father's death he assumed many family debts and personally financed the education of the family's next generation.

Baldwin graduated from Yale in 1772, but, intending to become a Congregationalist minister, he remained at the school as a graduate student studying theology. In 1775 he received a license to preach, but he decided to defer full-time clerical duties in order to accept a position as tutor at his alma mater. For the next three years he continued in this dual capacity, becoming increasingly well known both for his piety and modesty and for his skill as an educator with a special knack for directing and motivating the young men of the college.

The Soldier

Baldwin's continuing association with Yale College contributed directly to his entry into military service. The college, which had produced a major share of Connecticut's clergy for nearly a century, now became the major source of chaplains for the state's Continental Army contingent. Baldwin apparently served as a chaplain with Connecticut forces on a part-time basis during the early stages of the war, and finally in February 1779 he succeeded the Reverend Timothy Dwight, another Yale tutor, as one of the two brigade chaplains allotted to Connecticut's forces. He was appointed as chaplain in Brigadier General Samuel H. Parsons' brigade, remaining with the unit until the general demobilization of the Army that followed the announcement of the preliminary treaty of peace in June 1783.

The duties of a Revolutionary War chaplain were quite extensive, varying considerably from the modern concept of a clergyman's military role. In addition to caring for the spiritual needs of the 1,500 or so soldiers of differing denominations in the brigade, Baldwin assumed a major responsibility for maintaining the morale of the men and for guarding their physical welfare. He was also assigned certain educational duties, serving as a political adviser to the brigade commander and subordinate regimental commanders. In his sermons and in less formal conversations with the officers and men he was expected to help the soldiers understand the basis for the conflict with the mother country and thereby to heighten their sense of mission and dedication to the Patriot cause.

Although Baldwin's unit did not participate in combat during the last four years of the war, it still played a

ABRAHAM BALDWIN
Georgia

Birth: 23 November 1754, at Guilford, Connecticut
Death: 4 March 1807, at Washington, D.C.
Interment: Rock Creek Cemetery, Washington, D.C.

Pencil drawing, by Robert Fulton (early nineteenth century); National Portrait Gallery.

major role in Washington's defensive strategy. The Connecticut brigades were assigned to garrison duty near West Point. There they helped secure vital communications along the Hudson River and guard this critical base area against British invasions. They performed their mission well; the Continental brigades in the Hudson Valley formed the bedrock of Washington's main army against which no British general was likely to attack. With his center thus secured, Washington was free to launch successful offensive operations against smaller enemy forces in other parts of the country. The soldiers in Baldwin's brigade eventually trained for an amphibious attack on the British stronghold at New York City late in the war, but the plan was never put into effect.

Baldwin had little to do with these purely military matters, but his service as a chaplain proved vital to the Patriot cause. Along with the rest of the main Continental line units from the New England and middle states, Baldwin's Connecticut brigade had weathered the darkest days of the war. During 1778 these units had received rigorous training under Washington's famed Inspector General, Frederick von Steuben, and they had emerged as seasoned professionals, the equal of Britain's famous Redcoats. Nevertheless, the deprivations of such a long war exacted a toll on morale, leading to desertions and occasional mutinies in the 1780s. The Connecticut units, however, remained among the most reliable. Thanks in great part to the success of leaders like Baldwin, the troops had been thoroughly educated as to the nation's war aims and the need for extended service by the Continental units. As a result, Connecticut stood firm.

Military service in turn had a profound influence on Baldwin's future. During these years he became friends with many of the Continental Army's senior officers, including Washington and General Nathanael Greene, who would take command in the south in late 1780. He was also a witness to Major General Benedict Arnold's betrayal of his country. These associations moved the somewhat cloistered New England teacher and theology student toward a broader political outlook and a strong moral commitment to the emerging nation.

The Statesman

In 1783 Baldwin returned to civilian life and to a change in career. He rejected opportunities to serve as a minister and to assume the prestigious post as Yale's Professor of Divinity. While still in the Army he had studied law and had been admitted to the Connecticut bar. Now, after settling his family's affairs, he left New England for the frontier regions of Georgia, where he established a legal practice in Wilkes County near Augusta. Two men probably influenced this decision. Nathanael Greene had announced his intention to move to the state he had so recently freed from British occupation and was encouraging other veterans to join him in settling along the frontier. More importantly, Governor Lyman Hall, himself a Yale graduate, was interested in finding a man of letters to assist in developing a comprehensive educational system for Georgia. He apparently asked Yale's president, Ezra Stiles, to help him in the search, and Baldwin was persuaded to accept the responsibility.

Baldwin decided that the legislature was the proper place in which to formulate plans for the education of Georgia's citizens. A year after moving to the state, he won a seat in the lower house, one he would continue to hold until 1789. During his first session in office he drew up a comprehensive plan for secondary and higher education in the state that was gradually implemented over succeeding decades. This plan included setting aside land grants to fund the establishment of Franklin College (today's University of Georgia), which he patterned after Yale.

Baldwin quickly emerged as one of the leaders in the Georgia legislature. In addition to sponsoring his educational initiatives, he served as the chairman of numerous committees and drafted many of the state's first laws. His role reflected not only an exceptional political astuteness, but also an ability to deal with a wide variety of men and situations. As the son of a blacksmith, Baldwin exhibited a natural affinity for the rough men of the Georgia frontier; as the graduate of one of the nation's finest schools, he also related easily to the wealthy and cultured planters of the coast. This dual facility enabled him to mediate differences that arose among the various social and economic groups coalescing in the new state. As a result, he exercised a leadership role in the legislature by devising compromises necessary for the adoption of essential administrative and legal programs.

Baldwin's exceptional work in the legislative arena prompted political leaders in his adopted state to assign him even greater responsibilities. In early 1785 Georgia elected him to the Continental Congress, initiating a career in national government that would end only with his death. Although he had moved to Georgia to serve as a "missionary in the cause of education," as he put it, he nevertheless willingly assumed the burdens associated with national politics in the cause of effective government. In 1787 Georgia called on Baldwin to serve in the Constitutional Convention where, avoiding the limelight, he earned the respect of his colleagues both for his diligence as a delegate and his effectiveness as a compromiser.

Baldwin was an active participant in the deliberations over representation that were at the heart of the constitutional process. He had originally supported the idea of representation in the national legislature based on property qualifications, which he saw as a way to bond together the traditional leadership elements and the new sources of political and economic power. When delegates from his native state convinced him that small states like Connecticut would withdraw from the Convention if the Constitution did not somehow guarantee the equality of state representation, he changed his stand. His action tied the vote on the issue and paved the way for consideration of the question by a committee. Baldwin eventually helped draw up the Great Compromise, whereby a national legislature gave equal voice to all thirteen states in a Senate composed of two representatives from each, but respected the rights of the majority in a House of Representatives based on population. His role in this compromise was widely recognized, and Baldwin himself considered his work in drafting the Constitution as his most important public service.

After the adoption of the Constitution, Baldwin continued to serve in the last days of the old Continental Congress and then went on to serve five terms in the House of Representatives and two terms in the Senate, including one session as the President Pro Tem of that body. His political instincts prompted him to support the more limited nationalist policies associated with James Madison, and he was widely recognized as a leader of the moderate wing of the Democratic-Republican party. Throughout his years of congressional service, Baldwin remained an effective molder of legislative opinion, working in committees as well as in informal political circles to develop the laws that fleshed out the skeletal framework provided by the Constitution.

Baldwin's political philosophy was encapsulated in his often quoted formula for representative governments: "Take care, hold the wagon back; there is more danger of its running too fast than of its going too slow." A man of principle, who had learned much from his service in the Continental Army, Baldwin demonstrated throughout a lengthy public career the value of accommodation between competing political interests, the critical need of national unity, and the importance of education to a democratic society.

Richard Bassett

Richard Bassett, who represented Delaware at the Constitutional Convention, devoted most of his career to the service of his county and state. Reflecting the particular interests and needs of his region, he concentrated on agricultural matters, local military organization, and religious and charitable affairs. Only rarely and for the briefest periods during his adult life did he even travel outside the boundaries of Kent County. Yet at a key moment in his country's history, Bassett assumed an important role in advancing the cause of a strong central government. He led the fight for ratification of the Constitution in Delaware, an effort crowned on 7 December 1787 when his state became the first to approve the new instrument of government.

Bassett's experiences as a politician and soldier during the Revolution broadened his political horizons. The war had demonstrated, even to a man whose concerns had seldom transcended the confines of his state, the need for greater regional and national cooperation for the mutual interest of every community and section. In Bassett's case, the war transformed him into an effective proponent of a truly cohesive union of all the states.

The Patriot

Bassett's life illustrates the economic and social opportunities that existed in colonial America. He was born in Cecil County, Maryland. His father, a part-time tavern keeper and farmer, abandoned his family when Bassett was a child. The young man had to depend on the assistance of his maternal relations, but with their help, he eventually became a lawyer and acquired a small plantation. In 1770 he moved to Dover, Delaware, where he practiced law and pursued his agricultural interests. He quickly became a man of property, and began to move with ease in the social world of the local gentry, among whom he developed a reputation for hospitality and philanthropy.

Bassett's legal and charitable activities led naturally to politics. In 1774 he was elected by the voters of Kent County to serve as a member of its Boston Relief Committee. In this role Bassett helped to collect contributions for those suffering hardship as a result of the Coercive Acts, a series of political and economic measures that Parliament had enacted to reassert its control over the colonies, but which the colonists interpreted as a blow to their liberties. The committee brought Bassett into close working relationship with the leaders of the local Patriot movement: Caesar Rodney (who would later sign the Declaration of Independence), his brother Thomas, and John Haslet, the future commander of Delaware's Continental Army regiment. This association led to further political responsibilities during the Revolution, when Bassett represented the citizens of his county in a variety of offices. He participated in the convention that drafted Delaware's constitution and served three terms in the state senate and one in the lower house of the state legislature. As a member of both the Delaware and Kent County Councils of Safety, which functioned as the executive arms of those political bodies, Bassett also had the opportunity to help manage the day-to-day fortunes of his state during the crucial years of the Revolution.

The Soldier

Bassett's close association with military affairs began early in 1776 when he helped plan the mobilization of Delaware's forces for service in the Revolution. He developed plans for the organization of Haslet's regiment (perpetuated by today's 198th Signal Battalion, Delaware Army National Guard), the only unit of Continental regulars recruited in the state. Relying on his legal and political skills, he coordinated the all-important task of selecting officers for the regiment, measuring nominees against the military criteria of the day: patriotism, sufficient popularity to attract recruits, and military competence. Bassett's selections were clearly a success; Haslet's regiment was later judged among the very best combat units in Washington's command.

Bassett was instrumental in raising a militia unit to serve as Delaware's contribution to the Flying Camp, a mobile reserve that provided Washington with some 10,000 men who could be called forward to join the continentals holding New York City. He also helped organize Captain Thomas Rodney's Dover Light Infantry, a company of volunteer militia which served in the Trenton-Princeton campaign late in 1776.

Later emergencies allowed Bassett to learn firsthand the responsibilities of the citizen-soldier. During the

RICHARD BASSETT
Delaware

Birth: 2 April 1745, at "Bohemia Manor," Cecil County, Maryland
Death: 15 August 1815, in Kent County, Delaware
Interment: Wilmington and Brandywine Cemetery, Wilmington, Delaware

Engraving, by Charles B. J. Fevret de Saint-Memin (1802); National Portrait Gallery, Smithsonian Institution, Washington, D.C.; gift of Mr. & Mrs. Paul Mellon.

summer of 1777 the British entered the upper Chesapeake Bay with the objective of capturing Philadelphia, the American capital. Under Washington's defense plan, Delaware mobilized its militia force under the command of General Caesar Rodney; its mission was to maintain a sector of the cordon thrown up between the approaching British and the capital by combined troops from the middle states. Rodney's units were also expected to delay any possible British drive south toward Baltimore until Washington's continentals could arrive on the scene. Although legally exempted from militia service because of his legislative position, Bassett nevertheless appears to have joined his friend Rodney in the field as a volunteer. The Delaware militia returned home after the British retired from the area, but Bassett continued as a part-time soldier, assuming command of the Dover Light Horse, Kent County's militia cavalry unit.

Bassett gained a great deal of practical experience and insight during his service in the Revolution. On one hand, he learned how to raise troops and supply them in the field so well that his state repeatedly called on him to manage its mobilizations. But as events propelled him from local leadership to a major role in state affairs, Bassett also came to appreciate the more general point that cooperation between the states was vital. Planning for the common defense against the British in 1777 required him to coordinate frequently with military leaders in Pennsylvania and Maryland as well as with the strategists in Washington's Continental Army. At the same time, his milita service demonstrated to him that sacrifices would be required from citizens of every economic and social level if the concept of the citizen-soldier was to remain effective. The war even seemed to have a profound effect on Bassett's personality, prompting him to adopt a simpler lifestyle. Gone was the ambitious social leader of the local gentry. Instead a quiet, serious, and "most efficient" public servant emerged to deal with the state's postwar problems.

The Statesman

Designing a new national government for the victorious colonies posed a dilemma for politicians like Bassett who represented a small state. A strong central government might well promote economic prosperity and guarantee civil liberties, but it might also subordinate the local interests of the smaller states to the overriding concerns of their larger, more populous neighbors. Bassett's wartime experiences, however, convinced him that the weak government created by the Articles of Confederation had to be strengthened. In 1786 he agreed to represent Delaware at the Annapolis Convention, a meeting called to discuss closer economic cooperation among the states. The Annapolis gathering resulted in a call to the states to meet in Philadelphia the next year to design a new government. Bassett again represented Delaware. Although he rarely addressed the Constitutional Convention, Bassett strongly supported the Great Compromise advanced by his colleague John Dickinson and others. Designed to protect the rights of the small states, the compromise called for a national legislature that gave an equal voice to all thirteen states in a Senate composed of two representatives from each, but which respected the rights of the majority in a House of Representatives based on population.

Actually, Bassett's major contribution to the cause of strong government was made after the Convention. The work of the Founding Fathers would clearly have come to naught if the new Constitution had failed to receive the approval of the states, and historians agree that Bassett was the most important leader in the fight to win ratification in Delaware. Here the political skills and personal alliances that he had forged during the Revolution came to the fore, enabling Bassett to convince his colleagues that a strong central government indeed supported the interests of the smaller states. He won their unanimous agreement just five months after the document had been drawn up in Philadelphia.

Bassett's growing popularity in his state was then rewarded by his election to the new United States Senate. While he continued to support strong government, he allied himself with the moderate wing of the Federalist party that had gathered around Vice President John Adams. As a senator, for example, he supported President Washington's right to control the internal workings of the executive branch through the power of dismissing appointed officials, but he opposed some of Secretary of the Treasury Alexander Hamilton's more extreme proposals for advancing the powers of the presidency. Reflecting the continuing concerns of the small states, Bassett was the first to vote for locating the new national capital away from New York and Pennsylvania in an independent federal enclave on the banks of the Potomac River. Bassett's political interests had never strayed far from the affairs of his state. Even before ending his Senate service, he played a principal role, along with John Dickinson, in drafting a new constitution for Delaware. In 1793 he began a six-year term as first chief justice of Delaware's court of common pleas, and in 1796 he served as a member of the Electoral College in the presidential election. Bassett followed his previous Federalist loyalties by casting his electoral vote for John Adams. In 1799 he was elected governor. Bearing in mind the lessons he had learned during the Revolution, Governor Bassett actively executed his responsibilities as commander in chief of the Delaware militia, working with veterans of the Continental Army to improve its organization. He was particularly conscious of the importance of leadership in a military unit and devoted much care to the selection and commissioning of militia officers as a means of ensuring the revitalization of his state's military forces.

Bassett's tenure as governor of Delaware was the natural culmination of a public life spent in service to his state. Although his remarkable contribution to the cause of strong national government epitomized the breadth of his vision, his active promotion of an effective union of the states was always motivated by concerns for the interests, welfare, and liberties of his own home state.

William Blount

William Blount, who represented North Carolina at the Constitutional Convention, personified America's enduring fascination with its frontier. Raised in the aristocratic tradition of the seaboard planter society, Blount faithfully served his native state in elective office and under arms during the Revolution. But like George Washington, Blount also foresaw the boundless opportunities and potential of the west. Drawn to the trans-Allegheny territories, he eventually played a major role in the founding of the state of Tennessee.

Blount's journey from the drawing rooms of the east to the rude frontier cabins of his adopted state not only illustrates the lure of the region to a man of business and political acumen but also underscores the fact that the creation of a strong central government that could protect and foster westward expansion was a critical factor in America's growth as a nation. Indeed, Blount had led the fight in North Carolina for ratification of the new Constitution because he, like many of his fellow veterans, had already come to realize that the various political and economic promises of independence could be fulfilled only by a strong, effective union of all the states.

The Patriot

Blount was born into a world of wealth and privilege. The oldest son in a family of distinguished merchants and planters who owned extensive properties along the banks of the Pamlico River, he was educated by private tutors, and with his brothers he moved with ease into a career managing some of his father's mercantile interests. At this stage of his life, Blount showed little sympathy for the aspirations of the roughhewn settlers in the western regions of the colony. Influenced by the Whig planter class, he opposed the demands of the Regulators, a loose organization of western populists who sought greater economic and political parity with the eastern planters through reform of the colony's election laws, tax and land regulations, and judicial system. When these demands turned to physical confrontation, Blount joined a force of militia loyal to the governor, which in May 1771 confronted some 2,000 mostly unarmed Regulators on the banks of the Alamance River. Although the largely bloodless battle that followed saw the defeat of the Regulators and the execution of their leaders, many of their reforms were eventually adopted by the North Carolina assembly.

The Whig leaders responsible for defeating the Regulators would later ally themselves with their old western foes in the fight for independence in North Carolina. The former Regulators turned against Britain when a Royal proclamation in 1774 closed off western expansion; the Whigs, representing the interests of the eastern seaboard, opposed the efforts of the Royal governor to reassert British control over local affairs, which for nearly a century had been exercised by the colonial assembly. Both groups were represented in the assembly, and the growing political tension between that body and an increasingly autocratic Royal governor led the colony to cast its lot with the Patriot cause. As leading members of the moderate faction of North Carolina's Whig party, the Blounts played an important role in the move toward independence.

The Soldier

When differences with the Royal governor moved beyond any hope of reconciliation, the North Carolina assembly began recruiting troops in the summer of 1775, ultimately contributing ten regiments of infantry and several separate companies of artillery and cavalry to the Continental Army. This mobilization attracted many prominent citizens to the colors, including six members of the Blount family. As part of a general reorganization of the state's military units in December 1776, William Blount accepted appointment as the regimental paymaster for the 3d North Carolina Regiment. Although a regimental paymaster was not a commissioned officer with command responsibility on the battlefield, Blount served under a warrant on the regimental staff and drew the same pay and allowances as a captain. He also participated in the regiment's march north in the late spring of 1777 when it joined Washington's main army in defense of Philadelphia against Sir William Howe's Royal forces.

Washington planned to defend the American capital from behind a series of fortifications along the Delaware River. When Howe chose instead to land at the head of the Chesapeake Bay and move overland, Washington quickly drew up new defensive positions along the Brandywine River, but when Howe outmaneuvered him in a

WILLIAM BLOUNT
North Carolina

Birth: 6 April 1749, at "Rosefield," Bertie County, North Carolina
Death: 21 March 1800, at Knoxville, Tennessee
Interment: First Presbyterian Church Cemetery, Knoxville, Tennessee

Oil on canvas, by Washington Cooper (c. 1850); courtesy of Tennessee State Museum, Tennessee Historical Society Collection.

battle on 11 September, he was forced to withdraw. Less than a month later, Washington went on the offensive, counterattacking at Germantown, near Philadelphia. Repeating surprise tactics used at Trenton, the continentals enjoyed initial success, smashing several battalions of British light infantry before coordination broke down between the assault columns. Rather than risk defeat, Washington called off the attack and safely withdrew. The North Carolina forces, although reduced by disease and other causes to an understrength brigade, served as the reserve force, successfully screening the retreating continentals. Blount and his comrades had participated in one of the key battles of the war. By demonstrating Washington's willingness to fight and the Continental Army's recuperative powers, the battle convinced France that the Americans were in the war to the end and directly influenced France's decision to support the Revolution openly.

Following its first major campaign, the greatly weakened North Carolina Line began a series of reorganizations to recoup its fighting strength. Blount returned home to become chief paymaster of state forces and later deputy paymaster general for North Carolina. For the next three years he remained intimately involved in the demanding task of recruiting and reequipping forces to be used in support both of Washington's main army in the north and of separate military operations in defense of the southern tier of states.

The fall of Charleston, South Carolina, to British forces under Sir Henry Clinton in May 1780 was a major defeat for the Patriot cause. During that battle the last of North Carolina's continentals were captured, exposing the state to invasion. Once again the state was forced to join its neighbors in the difficult task of raising new units, this time to counter a force of British, Hessian, and Loyalist troops under General Charles Cornwallis. Blount not only helped organize these citizen-soldiers but also took to the field with them. His North Carolina unit served under General Horatio Gates, who hastily engaged Cornwallis in a bloody battle at Camden, South Carolina. On August 16 Gates deployed his units—his continentals to the right, the North Carolina and Virginia militia on his left flank—and ordered an advance. The American soldiers were exhausted from weeks of marching and insufficient rations. Furthermore, the militia elements had only recently joined with the regulars, and disciplined teamwork between the two components had not yet been achieved. Such teamwork was especially necessary before hastily assembled militia units could be expected to perform the intricate infantry maneuvers of eighteenth-century linear warfare. While the continentals easily advanced against the enemy, the militia quickly lost their cohesion in the smoke and confusion, and their lines crumbled before the counterattacking British. Cornwallis then shifted all his forces against the continentals. In less than an hour Gates' army had been lost to the Patriot cause. This second defeat in the south, the result of inadequate preparations, provided the young Blount a lesson that would stand him in good stead in later years. It also marked the end of Blount's active military career.

The Statesman

Following the defeat at Camden, Blount resigned his military responsibilities to accept a seat in the North Carolina assembly. During the next six years he served in both houses of the legislature, including one term as speaker of its lower house, and represented his state in the Continental Congress. He also served North Carolina as its negotiator with the powerful Indian tribes on its western frontier. Like many of his fellow veterans during this period, Blount had become an investor and speculator in western lands. His developing interest in the economic potential of western expansion as well as his exposure to national issues both as a soldier and as a member of the Continental Congress completed the transformation of this tidewater Whig into an exponent of a strong, stable central government.

Blount expressed these related interests most clearly when he accepted the invitation to represent North Carolina at the Constitutional Convention in 1787. Although he did not actively participate in the Convention debates and even expressed reservations about some sections of the final document, Blount signed the Constitution because, as he explained, in a democracy the will of the people, expressed through their elected delegates, should be heard. He actively supported ratification of the Constitution when North Carolina debated the issue in 1789.

In 1790 President Washington chose his old comrade in arms to serve as territorial governor of the trans-Allegheny lands ceded by North Carolina to the new nation. He also appointed Blount to the post of superintendent of Indian affairs for the Southern Department. These dual responsibilities tested Blount's political abilities to the utmost, forcing him to balance the expansionist interests of the frontier settlers against the protectionist policies of the national government toward the Indian tribes. He performed a wide array of tasks extraordinarily well. He negotiated a series of treaties with the powerful tribes of the southern frontier—the Creeks, Cherokees, Choctaws, and Chickasaws. Drawing on his experience in the Revolution, and mindful of the losses that had resulted from poorly prepared militia in that war, he organized the territorial militia, supervising its training and deploying it in conjunction with the militias of neighboring states to protect settlements and punish roving bands of hostile Indians. This combination of diplomacy and force preserved the peace during a period when the Regular Army's single regiment was fully committed to operations in the Northwest Territory. It also won Blount the respect and support of the settlers pouring into the region. After he led Tennessee to full statehood in 1796, serving as chairman of its constitutional convention, he was elected as one of the new state's first United States senators.

Blount's new career proved short-lived. In less than a year his colleagues expelled him from the Senate on charges of conspiring with an agent of the British government. These charges, unconfirmed to this day, connected Blount with a plot to seize control of Spain's possessions in Louisiana and Florida. There was certainly a widespread frustration in the frontier states, and especially in Tennessee, over Spain's continued control of the Mississippi River, on which the economic survival of the region depended. Whatever his connection with the affair, Blount's popularity in Tennessee remained undiminished. In 1798 he was elected to the state legislature, where he served with honor as speaker of the senate until his death.

Like many men of his generation, Blount was transformed by his experiences in the War for Independence. It caused him to moderate his initial sense of loyalty to one class and section, allowing him to become a leader in the westward expansion of the nation. It also transformed him into a strong nationalist by convincing him that only a strong central government could harness the potential for nationhood that he saw around him.

David Brearly

David Brearly, who represented New Jersey at the Constitutional Convention, was an important spokesman for the proposition that law has primacy over governments and social institutions. A student of the Enlightenment philosophers and English jurists, he adopted their idea that a contract existed between the individual and the state. He held that the citizen possessed basic rights that had been encapsulated in the Common Law and customs of England, and that neither the will of Parliament nor the immediate needs of local society should take precedence over these fundamental rights. He defended these beliefs on the battlefield during the Revolution and later, as an eminent American jurist, from the bench. Brearly then helped frame the Constitution, with its careful definition of the rights of citizens and the obligations of government, and became one of the first federal judges to serve under this new supreme law of the land.

Brearly's experiences during the Revolution did much to clarify his attitudes toward government. He came to realize in the tumult of the civil war that raged through his home state that without the protection of a strong government the individual citizen's rights would always be hostage to the whims of popular prejudice. A soldier with ties to both militia and regulars, he concluded that only a constitutionally based government could guarantee that the nation's military forces would remain properly subordinated to its elected civilian leaders. From his wartime experience, he also recalled the confusion and chaos that had accompanied a government that was only a weak confederation of the states. A future under such a confederation seemed especially dangerous for small states like New Jersey. He sought a stronger government that would recognize and protect the rights of all the states under a rule of law.

The Patriot

The Brearly family emigrated from Yorkshire in the north of England in 1680, settling in "West Jersey," an area of the colony that looked toward Philadelphia rather than New York for leadership. Brearly grew up near Trenton and attended the College of New Jersey (now Princeton University). He left college before graduating (Princeton would later award its eminent son an honorary degree) to take up the study of the law. He was eventually accepted by the bar and opened a practice in Allentown, a flourishing community at the western end of Monmouth County near Trenton.

Brearly's student years set the course of his subsequent political interests. Princeton's curriculum exposed him to the intellectual ferment of the Enlightenment, especially its notions of individual rights, while his legal training required a thorough grounding in treatises on the Common Law. Brearly's studies formed him into a young Patriot, one of Monmouth County's outspoken opponents of Parliamentary absolutism. His biting criticism of the government provoked the ire of Royal Governor William Franklin, who threatened to arrest the popular lawyer for high treason.

Brearly's career took a new turn in the summer of 1776 when New Jersey openly supported the call for independence. His neighbors had elected him to serve as a colonel in the county militia. During this period the Patriots used the militia as the vehicle to implement the decisions of the as yet unofficial government of New Jersey and to prevent opponents from obstructing the move toward independence. Working under the supervision of the local Committee of Safety and the legislature, Brearly recruited, organized, and trained his unit and used it to disarm local Loyalists. Brearly would later come to realize the risks inherent in this kind of extralegal action, but at the time his efforts contributed directly to smoothing the transition to a new state government.

The Soldier

While New Jersey was taking its final steps toward independence, a massive British armada appeared off New York harbor. These forces clearly outnumbered Washington's continentals, and Congress called on nearby states to mobilize their citizen-soldiers to resist the coming assault. Included in New Jersey's 3,300-man quota was Colonel Philip Van Cortlandt's regiment, in which Brearly was second in command. The regiment spent part of its active duty guarding New Jersey's shoreline before transferring to Manhattan for the closing phases of the fight for New York City.

Despite the efforts of Washington's regulars and the massed militia, New York and its strategic harbor fell to the enemy in September 1776. This defeat provided an

DAVID BREARLY
New Jersey

Birth: 11 June 1745, at Spring Grove, New Jersey
Death: 16 August 1790, at Trenton, New Jersey
Interment: St. Michael's Episcopal Church Cemetery, Trenton, New Jersey

Portrait by unknown artist; courtesy of Grand Lodge of the Most Ancient and Honorable Society of Free and Accepted Masons for the State of New Jersey.

important lesson that Washington and his senior officers pressed on the Continental Congress: it would take full-time soldiers to engage British and Hessian regiments successfully in open battle. While militia units could play an important role in local defense and flank security, the Continental Army required men who could serve long enough to learn the complex tactics involved in eighteenth-century linear warfare. Congress accepted this argument, authorizing a large increase in the Army and directing that it serve for the duration of the war instead of one year at a time.

New Jersey's quota of Continental regiments under the new legislation increased by one, and the state's political and military leaders conferred over the choice of the additional senior officers required to form it. Brearly's militia record attracted their attention, and they commissioned him as lieutenant colonel of the 4th New Jersey Regiment, although resignations and promotions almost immediately led to his transfer to the state's senior unit, the 1st, which had just returned to the state from a year of duty on the Canadian front.

Brearly assisted the regiment's commander, Colonel Matthias Ogden, in reenlisting the men, replacing losses, and reequipping the unit. At the same time, the regiment had to help defend the northern part of the state in the aftermath of the battles of Trenton and Princeton. This latter activity involved constant patrols and frequent skirmishes with British troops based around New Brunswick and Amboy. Beginning in May 1777 the New Jersey Brigade under Brigadier General William Maxwell joined the main army in a series of marches and countermarches across the middle of the state while Washington puzzled over whether Philadelphia or Albany would be the enemy's next target.

General Sir William Howe's Redcoats eventually boarded ships and, sailing by way of Chesapeake Bay, attacked Philadelphia from the rear. Washington hastily redeployed his units to face the new danger, eventually establishing a defensive line along Brandywine Creek. On the morning of 11 September Hessians and some British light troops appeared before Chad's Ford and immediately engaged the New Jersey Brigade. Hard skirmishing lasted all morning as the outnumbered continentals appeared to be holding their own; in the afternoon Howe's main force, which had crossed far upstream at an unguarded ford, appeared on Washington's flank and eventually forced the Americans to retreat. Brearly and the rest of Maxwell's men helped cover the withdrawal as Philadelphia fell to the enemy. When the Americans counterattacked at Germantown three weeks later, the New Jersey Brigade formed the reserve of one of the two assault columns. The American units were engaged in hard fighting when fog and confusion forced Washington to break off the battle.

Although participating in these two defeats, Brearly's regiment remained highly motivated. During the following winter the men's confidence increased when they were trained by Frederick von Steuben at Valley Forge. In June 1778 the regiment joined in a pursuit of British forces across New Jersey, forming part of the American advance guard and acquitting itself with honor at the battle of Monmouth.

Unable to mass the strength required to take on Washington's full force, the British adopted a new strategy in 1778, concentrating their military effort on the conquest of the southern states. With operations drawing down in the northern theater, and facing a reorganization caused by reduced strength, New Jersey surveyed the senior officers of the state line to determine which were willing to retire. Brearly volunteered, retiring in August 1779 to resume his legal career. In his three years with the militia and continentals, Brearly had gained valuable insights into the political dimension of the age-old issue of civilian control over the military. He remained in touch with military affairs by resuming his old militia command in Monmouth County's 2d Regiment, and later serving as a vice president of the Society of the Cincinnati, the famous veterans' organization.

The Statesman

In the summer of 1779 New Jersey appointed Brearly to succeed Robert Morris as the state's chief justice. Despite his relative youth, he immediately made his mark in American legal history when his court decided the famous case of *Holmes vs. Walton*. The case evolved out of the state's effort to curb contraband trade with the British. Trading with the enemy was popular since the British could buy food and supplies with hard cash or scarce imported items while the American forces most often depended on depreciated paper money or promissory notes. In 1778 New Jersey passed a law that allowed Patriots to seize goods being brought into the state by Loyalists or enemy troops. Suspects were to be tried in a civilian court before juries of six men, instead of the customary twelve dictated by Common Law.

Caught smuggling goods to the British, John Holmes and a companion were duly tried and convicted by a six-man jury. They appealed the conviction to the state supreme court, and after lengthy deliberation, Judge Brearly overturned the conviction, declaring the law null and void because it violated the state's constitution that guaranteed trial by jury under customary English Common Law. For the first time in American history a court asserted the concept of judicial review, including the right to declare laws passed by a legislature unconstitutional. The decision provoked a public outrage. Although Brearly, a famous veteran, clearly sympathized with the intent of the legislature, he decided in favor of the higher principle involved. His decision was cited in courts in other states and was incorporated into the Constitution of the United States.

In 1787 the New Jersey legislature appointed Brearly to represent the state at the Constitutional Convention in Philadelphia. Although no orator, Brearly quickly won the respect of his fellow delegates for his legal wisdom and his willingness to work for essential compromises. In addition to his labor on the judicial provisions of the new instrument of government, he served as a spokesman for a group that sought to defend the rights of the small states. He also presided over the important Committee on Postponed Matters that developed many of the compromises needed to achieve final agreement. After signing the Constitution, he returned to New Jersey to preside over the state's ratification convention.

Brearly served as a member of the first Electoral College, which chose his old commander, George Washington, President. At the start of his first administration, Washington nominated Brearly as federal district judge for New Jersey, but the noted jurist lived to serve just one year before his death shortly after his forty-fifth birthday.

Brearly was willing to risk his life and reputation in the cause of the rule of law. He donned uniform, first as a citizen-soldier and later as a regular, because he sought to defend fundamental individual rights. This same dedication to the idea of basic rights continued in his later career when as a jurist he took a very unpopular stand so that the citizen's basic freedoms could be preserved, even when they carried short-term costs in efficiency to the state. His dedication to the concept of a supreme law to which all other laws must comply found its most noted expression in the Constitution he helped devise.

Pierce Butler

Pierce Butler, who represented South Carolina at the Constitutional Convention, was a man of startling contrasts. As late as 1772 he was a ranking officer in those British units charged with suppressing the growing colonial resistance to Parliament. In fact, a detachment from his unit, the 29th Regiment of Foot, had fired the shots in the "Boston Massacre" of 1770, thereby dramatically intensifying the confrontation between the colonies and England. But by 1779 Butler, now an officer in South Carolina's militia and a man with a price on his head, was organizing American forces to fight the invading Redcoats. Butler lost his considerable estates and fortune during the British occupation of South Carolina, but at the end of the Revolutionary War he was among the first to call for reconciliation with the Loyalists and a renewal of friendly relations with the former enemy. Although an aristocrat to the manor born, Butler became a leading spokesman for the frontiersmen and impoverished western settlers. Finally, this Patriot, always a forceful and eloquent advocate of the rights of the common man during the debate over the Constitution, was also the proud owner of a sizable number of slaves.

The unifying force in this fascinating career was Butler's strong and enduring sense of nationalism. An Irish nobleman, he severed his ties with the old world to embrace the concept of a permanent union of the thirteen states. His own military and political experiences then led him to the conviction that a strong central government, as the bedrock of political and economic security, was essential to protect the rights not only of his own social class and adopted state but also of all classes of citizens and all the states.

The Patriot

Pierce Butler was the third son of Sir Richard Butler, the fifth Baronet of Cloughgrenan and a member of the Irish Parliament. Traditionally British aristocrats directed younger sons into the military or the church, and Butler's father was no exception. In the honored fashion of the times, he bought his son a commission in the 22d Regiment of Foot (today's Cheshire Regiment). Butler demonstrated both military skill and the advantages of powerful and wealthy parents in his subsequent career in the British Army. His regiment came to North America in 1758 to participate in the French and Indian War and served in the campaigns that resulted in the capture of Canada from the French. Butler later transferred to the 29th Foot (today's Worcestershire and Sherwood Foresters Regiment), before returning to Ireland in 1762.

The overwhelming success of the forces of the British Empire and its allies ended French territorial claims in North America and brought about profound changes in the nature of the mother country's relationship with its American colonies. To occupy Canada and other new lands won during the war, Parliament for the first time ordered the permanent stationing of large British garrisons in North America. Because the government had incurred heavy war debts, Parliament chose to support these troops by levying new taxes on the colonists. Americans generally disagreed with Parliament over the need for the garrisons, arguing that their local militias could handle the defense of the colonies. They also opposed the new taxes that began with the Stamp Act of 1765.

Butler's regiment was serving on garrison duty in Nova Scotia at the time, but he could not long escape becoming embroiled in the growing controversy. In 1768 the intensity of protests over Parliament's taxes in Massachusetts led London to order the 29th Foot, along with a second infantry regiment, to Boston to maintain the King's peace. In 1771, the year after the "Massacre," Butler, now a major, married Mary Middleton, the daughter of a wealthy South Carolina planter and colonial leader. Marriage led him to seek new directions, for when the 29th received orders to return to Great Britain in 1773, he decided to leave the army. He sold his commission and used the proceeds to purchase a plantation in the coastal region of South Carolina, adapting to the lifestyle of a southern landowner with apparent ease. Management skills learned in the military undoubtedly proved useful as he increased his land holdings to over 10,000 acres. He also began to accumulate a small fleet of coastal vessels to support his expanding business ventures.

When war broke out between Great Britain and the colonies in 1775, Butler joined several other former British officers (including the future generals Horatio Gates, Charles Lee, and Richard Montgomery) in casting his lot with the American cause. In Butler's case the success of his business interests as well as the important role played by the Middleton family in the Patriot movement

PIERCE BUTLER
South Carolina

Birth: 11 July 1744, in County Carlow, Ireland
Death: 15 February 1822, at Philadelphia, Pennsylvania
Interment: Christ Churchyard, Philadelphia

Miniature by unknown artist, unknown date; National Archives and Records Administration.

in South Carolina clearly influenced his decision. Butler's father-in-law had been the president of the First Continental Congress, and a brother-in-law would soon sign the Declaration of Independence. Butler himself lost little time in expressing his patriotic sentiments by standing for local election. He began his public service in 1776 when his neighbors elected him to a seat in the South Carolina legislature, a post that he continued to hold until 1789.

The Soldier

Although bad health prevented Butler from assuming an active combat role, he offered his military talents to his state, and in early 1779 Governor John Rutledge turned to the former Redcoat to help reorganize South Carolina's defenses. Butler assumed the post of the state's adjutant general, a position that carried the rank of brigadier general, although he continued to prefer to be addressed as major, his highest combat rank.

The decision to reorganize South Carolina's defenses followed in the wake of a shift in Britain's war strategy. By 1778 the King and his ministers found themselves faced with a new military situation. Their forces in the northern and middle states had reached a stalemate with Washington's continentals, now more adequately supplied and better trained after Valley Forge. The British also faced the prospect of France's entering the war as an active partner of the Americans. In response, they adopted a "southern strategy." Assuming that the many Loyalists in the southern states would rally to the Crown if supported by regular troops, they planned a conquest of the rebellious colonies one at a time, moving north from Georgia. They launched their new strategy with the capture of Savannah in December 1778.

Butler joined in the effort to mobilize South Carolina's citizen-soldiers to repulse the threatened British invasion and later helped prepare the state units used in the counterattack designed to drive the enemy from Georgia. During the operation, which climaxed with an attempted investiture of Savannah, Butler served as a volunteer aide to General Lachlan McIntosh. The hastily raised and poorly prepared militia troops were no match for the well-trained British defenders, and the effort to relieve Savannah ended in failure.

In 1780 the British captured Charleston, and with it most of South Carolina's civil government and military forces. Butler, as part of a command group deliberately left outside the city, escaped. During the next two years he employed his considerable military talents in developing a counterstrategy to defeat the enemy's southern operations. He and his fellow South Carolinians, along with their neighbors in occupied portions of Georgia and North Carolina, refused to submit to London's demand that they surrender. Instead, they organized a resistance movement. Butler, as adjutant general, worked with former members of the militia and Continental Army veterans such as Francis Marion and Thomas Sumter to integrate their various partisan efforts into a unified campaign, in conjunction with the operations of the Southern Army under the command of Horatio Gates and later Nathanael Greene.

These partisan tactics involved considerable expense and personal risk for Butler who, as a former Royal officer, remained a special target for the British occupation forces. Several times he barely avoided capture. Once, surprised by the sudden arrival of enemy dragoons in the middle of the night, he escaped by sneaking from his home dressed only in his nightshirt. On another occasion, a British regiment, repeatedly denounced by Butler for plundering civilian properties—he called it a "band of jailbirds"—placed a bounty on his head. Throughout the closing phases of the southern campaign he personally contributed cash and supplies to help sustain the American forces and also assisted in the administration of prisoner-of-war facilities.

The Statesman

Military operations in the latter months of the Revolution left Butler a poor man. Many of his plantations and ships were destroyed, and the international trade on which the majority of his income depended was in shambles. These economic realities forced him to travel to Europe when the war ended in an effort to secure loans and establish new markets. Betraying a singular tolerance for a foe who had caused him much personal harm, Butler took the occasion to enroll his son in a London school and to engage a new minister from among the British clergy for his church in South Carolina. In late 1785 he returned home, where he became an especially outspoken advocate of reconciliation with former Loyalists and equal representation for the residents of the backcountry. Testifying to his growing political influence, the South Carolina legislature asked Butler to represent the state at the Constitutional Convention that met in Philadelphia in 1787.

Butler's experiences as a soldier and planter-legislator influenced his forceful support for a strong union of the states at the Convention. As a military leader during the campaigns in the south he had come to appreciate the need for a national approach to defense. As a planter and merchant, especially after his trip to Europe, he came to understand that economic growth and international respect depended upon a strong central government. At the same time, he energetically supported the special interests of his region.

This dual emphasis on national and state concerns puzzled his fellow delegates, just as other apparent inconsistencies would bother associates throughout the rest of his political career. For example, Butler favored ratification of the Constitution, yet absented himself from the South Carolina convention that approved it. Later, he would serve three separate terms in the United States Senate, but this service was marked by several abrupt changes in party allegiance. Beginning as a Federalist, he switched to the Jeffersonian party in 1795, only to become a political independent in 1804. These changes confused the voters of his state, who rejected his subsequent bids for high public offices, although they did elect him three more times to the state legislature as an easterner who spoke on behalf of the west.

Butler retired from politics in 1805 and spent much time in Philadelphia where he had previously established a summer home. He continued his business ventures, becoming one of the wealthiest men in America with huge land holdings in several states. Like other Founding Fathers from his region, Butler also continued to support the institution of slavery. But unlike Washington or Thomas Jefferson, for example, Butler never acknowledged or grasped the fundamental inconsistency in simultaneously defending the rights of the poor and supporting slavery.

The contradictions in this fascinating man led associates to label him an "eccentric" and an "enigma." Within his own lights, however, he followed a steady path along lines which were intended to produce the maximum of liberty and respect for those individuals whom he classed as citizens. His later political maneuverings were animated by his desire to maintain a strong central government, but a government that could never ride roughshod over the rights of the private citizen. He opposed the policies of the Federalists under Alexander Hamilton because he decided that they had sacrificed the interests of westerners and had sought to force their policies on the opposition; he later split with Jefferson and the Democrats for the same reason. Butler never wavered from his central emphasis on the role of the common man. Late in life he summarized his view: "Our System is little better than [a] matter of Experiment, . . . much must depend on the morals and manners of the people at large." This was certainly an interesting view, coming as it did from a former member of the British hereditary aristocracy.

Jonathan Dayton

Jonathan Dayton, who represented New Jersey at the Constitutional Convention, believed that government should defend individual freedoms, but within the framework of an established social hierarchy. He held to this traditional concept of government well into the nineteenth century. Even when the social distinctions that had guided the leaders of the Revolutionary generation had long faded, he retained the manners, customs, and political philosophy of his youth. His insistence on the old ways won him the title "the last of the cocked hats." But if Dayton insisted on outmoded social distinctions, he also possessed a healthy political realism that contributed in full measure to the creation of the new American republic.

Dayton's practical approach to government evolved out of his experiences as a unit commander during the Revolution. Eight years' service in the Continental Army provided him with first hand evidence of the consequences of weak political leadership. He became convinced that a strong central government was needed to guide and protect the new nation, and was in fact the only means by which organizations essential to future prosperity—including a professional army—could operate efficiently while remaining securely under the people's control. He also realized that the rights of small states like New Jersey needed special protection, and that a powerful government, grounded in law, provided the best guarantee of such protection.

The Patriot

Dayton was born in Elizabethtown (now Elizabeth), the focal point of "East Jersey," as the northern part of the colony was commonly known. The town traditionally supplied a major portion of the colony's leaders. Dayton's father, Elias, for example, was a militia officer in the French and Indian War who returned home to prosper as a merchant and colonial official. Dayton was clearly influenced by his family's position in the community and his father's ideas about government. Both men, like most Americans of their day, believed that the average citizen should defer to the views of his "betters," while prominent citizens, those with the largest stake in society, had an obligation to lead the community, sacrificing their own interests if necessary for the common good. These beliefs moved the family by natural steps into local leadership of the Patriot cause.

Elizabethtown had a reputation for educational excellence. The local academy, which prepared young men for college with a classical liberal arts curriculum, emerged in the decade and a half prior to the Revolution as one of the leading schools in the colonies under the famous educator Tapping Reeve and his protege, Francis Barber. After graduating from Reeve's school, where two of his schoolmates were Alexander Hamilton and Aaron Burr, Dayton attended the nearby College of New Jersey (today's Princeton University).

In late 1774 the First Continental Congress called on the colonies to resist Parliament's recent tax policy by joining in an association to boycott goods imported from the mother country. Both Daytons served on Elizabethtown's enforcement committee and quickly allied themselves with the local Revolutionary movement. When New Jersey turned irrevocably against Royal Governor William Franklin in 1775, the state's Provincial Congress, an extralegal legislative body established by the Patriots, set about raising regular troops and reorganizing the militia. It chose the senior Dayton to lead the 3d New Jersey Regiment. The new commander promptly arranged for his fifteen-year-old son, then in the midst of his final year in college, to join the unit as an ensign. Although Dayton was absent with the regiment for the entire war, he still received his diploma with the rest of his class. Later, Princeton granted its distinguished son an honorary Doctor of Laws degree.

The Soldier

The colonel and the ensign marched off with their regiment in the spring of 1776 to support the Patriot army invading Canada. Buffeted by a reinforced enemy and a serious outbreak of smallpox, the American force had already begun to disintegrate, and the fresh troops from New Jersey were diverted to the Mohawk Valley region of upstate New York to prevent an insurrection by Loyalists and Indians. The regiment spent the rest of the campaign on detached duty along the frontier, constructing Forts Schuyler (later Stanwix) and Dayton. These defensive strongpoints remained centers for the protection of Patriots in this important grain-producing region throughout the rest of the war.

In early 1777, the 3d New Jersey returned home to

JONATHAN DAYTON
New Jersey

Birth: 16 October 1760, at Elizabethtown (now Elizabeth), New Jersey
Death: 9 October 1824, at "Boxwood Hall," Elizabethtown, New Jersey
Interment: St. John's Episcopal Church Cemetery, Elizabeth, New Jersey

Engraving, by Charles B. J. Fevret de Saint-Memin (1798); National Portrait Gallery, Smithsonian Institution, Washington, D.C.

reorganize. Dayton, now a lieutenant, soon found himself engaged in the heavy skirmishing that took place between Washington's main army and British forces threatening Philadelphia, the American capital. When General Sir William Howe decided instead on a flank attack by sea, Dayton's 3d New Jersey accompanied Washington in a rapid march to Pennsylvania and saw action in the subsequent battles at Brandywine Creek and Germantown.

Philadelphia fell to the British in October 1777. While Howe's men enjoyed the comfort of winter quarters, Washington's continentals passed through the trial of Valley Forge. The Daytons endured the cold and hunger, but more importantly, they also received superb training under Frederick von Steuben. In June, when the British retreated across New Jersey to the safety of New York City, the 3d New Jersey played an important role in the Continental Army's pursuit. Knowledge of the terrain, plus an excellent combat record, ensured that the regiment was in the heart of the fighting near Monmouth Court House, when the well-trained American regulars caught up with their British and Hessian opponents. Although the battle ended in a draw, the continentals finally proved themselves capable of standing toe-to-toe with the enemy in a formal European-style battle.

While Washington maintained his main force in a cordon stretching from New Jersey to Connecticut, the British shifted their attention to the southern states. The 3d New Jersey remained near home, forming part of Washington's line that separated the British garrison in New York City from the region's farms and towns. In 1779 the New Jersey unit returned to the Mohawk Valley as part of Major General John Sullivan's effort to relieve enemy pressure on New York's frontier farmers. Here the continentals, supplemented by local militiamen, demonstrated their capacity for operating successfully in a wilderness, before rejoining Washington around New York City. Dayton's service as the commanding general's aide during this campaign gave him a new appreciation for the importance of organization and discipline and led him to recognize the frontier's economic potential.

By 1780 skirmishes between Loyalists and Patriots had reduced New Jersey to a state of civil war pitting neighbor against neighbor. In October Dayton and his uncle, Lieutenant Colonel Matthias Ogden, were captured by a Loyalist raiding party led by Elizabethtown Tories. The two spent the winter as prisoners in New York; when they were finally released in the new year, they returned to duty with a reorganized New Jersey Brigade. The unit consisted of two regiments under Colonel Elias Dayton (soon to be promoted to brigadier general). The younger Dayton, promoted to captain, transferred to the 2d New Jersey and took his company to Virginia in the fall of 1781 when Washington's main army converged for the decisive Yorktown campaign. During the siege, he led his company in the crucial nighttime bayonet attack on Redoubt 10, under the command of his old schoolmate Alexander Hamilton and their teacher Lieutenant Colonel Francis Barber.

After the British surrendered, the main army returned to the New York area. The Daytons remained in service near their homes until the Continental Army was discharged in 1783.

The Statesman

Dayton came home from the war to assume important responsibilities in the family's mercantile business and to study law. Although a political neophyte, his prominence in the community, his war record, and his father's influential connections led quickly to a role in state government. When his father left to represent New Jersey in the Continental Congress, Dayton stepped up to represent Elizabethtown in the legislature. When New Jersey was selecting delegates to the Constitutional Convention in Philadelphia in 1787, it again turned to Elias Dayton, but the old general declined the appointment in favor of his son.

As one of the youngest members of the Convention, Dayton prudently maintained a low profile as the delegates set out to devise a new system of government. He limited his participation to supporting the initiatives proposed by the senior delegates from New Jersey, who concentrated on securing guarantees for the rights of the smaller states. In the end Dayton was part of the group that devised a federal approach to national government, creating an Electoral College to select the President and a legislature of two houses: a Senate that gave equal voice to the separate states, and a House of Representatives that, based on population, more closely reflected the views of the citizens.

Dayton's performance in Philadelphia enhanced his political reputation at home. The New Jersey legislature promptly elected him to the closing session of the Continental Congress. Following this brief assignment he returned to serve as speaker of the lower house of the state legislature, and, in 1791, to begin the first of four terms in the House of Representatives.

Legislative skills honed at the state level allowed Dayton to play a leading role in national government. Personal ties with Federalist leaders developed during the war led Dayton naturally to that political party. He worked closely with Hamilton, his former schoolmate, on financial policy. He also was instrumental in organizing Congress' response to the threat posed by the 1794 Whiskey Rebellion, and he marshaled the votes needed to approve the Jay Treaty that settled with Britain issues left over from the Revolution. He spent his last four years in Congress as Speaker of the House. There his constant support for a strong standing army, but one clearly responsible to the people through congressional appropriations and review, led President John Adams to nominate him for an important position in the force hastily organized during the 1798–1800 "Quasi-War" with France. Dayton declined appointment as commanding officer of the Corps of Artillerists and Engineers, preferring to remain in Congress. Beginning in 1799 he served a single term in the United States Senate, part of the moderate segment of the Federalist party. His pragmatic approach allowed him, for example, to cross party lines and support President Thomas Jefferson's purchase of the Louisiana Territory.

Dayton's interests in the west, first stimulated during the 1779 Sullivan Expedition, contributed to his political demise. He had invested heavily in land speculation in the Ohio region, owning claims to nearly a quarter of a million acres (a town in Ohio would be named for him). This involvement led him to loan money to his other old classmate, Aaron Burr. When illegal activities by Burr were unveiled in 1807, Dayton also fell under suspicion. Although exonerated by a grand jury, Dayton suffered from a guilt by association that effectively ended his political career. He served once again briefly in the New Jersey legislature, but he largely confined his activities during his remaining years to business and farming.

Dayton exemplifies the best in the Revolutionary generation's philosophy of political deference. Like Washington, he enjoyed describing himself as a "simple farmer," but like the Virginia aristocrat, he enjoyed the benefits of a family with strong political and financial connections. He prospered from this arrangement, but he also willingly accepted the obligation to serve his fellow citizens. To that end he risked his life and fortune on the battlefield and his reputation in the political arena.

John Dickinson

John Dickinson represented both Delaware and Pennsylvania at the founding of the republic. A man of the Enlightenment, he believed that government was a solemn social contract between the people and their sovereign. Like most colonial leaders, Dickinson considered himself an Englishman with all the ancient rights and privileges such citizenship conferred, and he was quick to oppose any abridgment of those rights by Parliament. But when others carried such opposition to the point of rebellion with the Declaration of Independence, Dickinson refused to sign. His reasoning set him apart from most of his colleagues. He understood the contract to be with the King, not with Parliament, and to be mutual as well as permanent. He hoped that an appeal to reason might remind the King of that contractual obligation to his American subjects and thereby restore good relations. Only when King George publicly sided with his ministers and ordered a Royal army to New York did Dickinson consider the social contract dissolved. Although he refused to sign the Declaration, Dickinson was among the first to don uniform to defend the new nation.

The Patriot

Dickinson's view of government evolved naturally. Born into a family of wealth and privilege, he elected to follow his father, a judge in the Delaware courts, into the law. He began his training in Philadelphia and then spent four years studying at the Inns of Court in London. His time there provided the young colonial with an opportunity to hear the leading legal minds of the day argue the fine points of Enlightenment philosophy and the rights of English citizens. Returning in 1757 to practice law in Philadelphia, Dickinson through industry and ability quickly earned a reputation as one of America's finest lawyers. His interest in politics grew apace. In 1760 he was elected to the Delaware legislature. During the next fifteen years he would serve both in that body and in the Pennsylvania legislature, a dual service made possible because of his property holdings and residency in both colonies.

Dickinson's entry into politics coincided with the rise of colonial opposition to the government in London. In debt from the Seven Years War and obliged to maintain an army in America, Parliament now ended a century of "salutary neglect" in regard to the financial and political affairs of the colonies by instituting measures to raise revenue and provide for the quartering of British troops. One of these Parliamentary measures, the Stamp Act of 1765, was the first attempt to impose a direct tax on the colonies, and it provoked a strong and united opposition. Jealous of the rights and privileges of their own legislatures, the colonies retaliated by refusing to pay the tax and by boycotting English goods.

Dickinson played a major but restraining role in this opposition. Sympathetic to colonial complaints, he nevertheless sought to avoid violence. He urged Americans to rely primarily on economic pressure, and he enlisted the help of the powerful British merchants in the colonists' cause. His diplomatic approach coupled with his commitment to the colonial side led the Pennsylvania legislature to appoint him to represent the colony at the Stamp Act Congress in 1765. There he eloquently defended the proposition that reconciliation was possible if King and Parliament could be brought to see colonial opposition as an expression of the time-honored English principles of political liberty. His arguments were encapsulated in his *Letters from a Farmer in Pennsylvania,* a series of essays that gained its author international recognition as a man of reason and principle.

Later Dickinson organized Philadelphia's protest over the Coercive Acts, a series of political and economic measures that Parliament enacted in 1774 to demonstrate its control over the colonies, but which the Americans interpreted as a blow to their liberties. In keeping with his support of the colonial protest movement, Dickinson also figured prominently in the convening of the Continental Congress. Elected to that assembly, he played a critical role, drafting two key documents: a petition for redress of grievances, and a message urging the inhabitants of Canada to join the thirteen colonies in opposition. He returned to serve in the Second Continental Congress, but after the clashes at Lexington and Concord changed the attitudes of many members, Dickinson's continuing stand for reconciliation cast him in the role of a conservative when compared to such firebrands as John Adams and Benjamin Franklin. In July 1775 he drafted Congress' last attempt at compromise, the "Olive Branch Petition." Against ever-increasing odds, Dickinson continued into July 1776 to work for one further appeal to King George. But bowing to what

JOHN DICKINSON
Delaware

Birth: 19 November 1732, at "Crosiadore," Talbot County, Maryland
Death: 14 February 1808, at Wilmington, Delaware
Interment: Friends Burial Ground, Wilmington, Delaware

Oil on canvas, by Charles Willson Peale (1780); Independence National Historical Park.

had become inevitable, he absented himself on July 4 so that the vote for independence could be unanimous.

The Soldier

Dickinson saw no contradiction in his decision to volunteer immediately for militia service. In his "Declaration of Causes for Taking Up Arms," he actively supported the right of free citizens to defend themselves from direct attack, and he preached the concept of military preparedness to his fellow Pennsylvanians. Since June 1775 he had been chairman of Pennsylvania's Committee of Safety and Defense. He also had organized the first battalion of troops raised in Philadelphia, the so-called Associators (today's 111th Infantry, Pennsylvania Army National Guard). Lacking a militia organization, Pennsylvania traditionally had relied on volunteer units such as Dickinson's Associators for military support. When a large British invasion force appeared in New York harbor in July 1776, Pennsylvania called the Associators into active duty as a part of the general mobilization of militia to defend New York City, and Dickinson absented himself from Congress to assume command. His unit was assigned to the Flying Camp, a mobile reserve that provided Washington with some 10,000 men who could be called forward to join the continentals holding New York City. Dickinson commanded a major garrison point at Elizabeth, New Jersey, in the defense against any attempt by British forces on Staten Island to cross the New Jersey countryside to attack Philadelphia.

Turned out of Congress after refusing to sign the Declaration, Dickinson resigned his commission in the Associators and retired to his home in Delaware. During the summer of 1777, however, he once more enlisted for active duty, this time to serve as a private in Captain Stephen Lewis' company of Delaware volunteers. The mobilization of Delaware units was in response to the appearance of a British force under General Sir William Howe at Elkton, Maryland, at the headwaters of the Chesapeake Bay. From there Howe planned to attack Philadelphia, the American capital. General Washington's hastily organized defense called for the mobilization of Delaware's militia under the command of General Caesar Rodney; its mission was to maintain a sector of the cordon thrown up between the approaching British and the capital by combined troops from the middle states. Rodney's units were also expected to delay any possible British drive south toward Baltimore until Washington's continentals could arrive on the scene. During the defensive action, Dickinson's company guarded the approaches to the Brandywine River. His unit, along with the rest of Delaware's forces, returned home after the British retired from the area, but Dickinson continued as a part-time soldier. In October 1777 General Rodney issued him a commission as a brigadier general of militia. His resignation the following year would usher in his later political career, which began when Delaware appointed him to serve in the Continental Congress from 1779 to 1781.

The Statesman

During that term Dickinson signed the Articles of Confederation, which he had drafted while representing Pennsylvania in the Congress in 1776. Like most Americans, he had assumed at first that the political and economic liberties being defended on the battlefield could best be preserved by state governments and military forces created by state governments. In adopting the Articles after much debate, Congress thereby endorsed his plan for a limited national organization of independent and sovereign states.

Military and political experiences during the course of the war, however, served to modify Dickinson's views, and the once strong proponent of a loose confederation of states was gradually transformed into a leader of the cause of strong central government. Dickinson's active duty had demonstrated to this observant citizen-soldier that the country needed a strong national defense, but that dependency on temporary and often inexperienced state units imposed many limitations. Later service as governor of both Delaware and Pennsylvania in the early 1780s reinforced his growing belief that many problems rising at the local level could be resolved only by national action. His executive experience also convinced him that the citizen's basic rights were best safeguarded by a national government that represented all the citizens.

Setting aside his wish to retire, Dickinson accepted Delaware's call to represent it at a convention in Annapolis in 1786 to discuss economic problems affecting Delaware and its neighboring states. There he supported the idea of creating a new national government, and in 1787 he went on to represent Delaware at the Philadelphia Convention, where his experience and skills made a significant contribution to the foundation of the new republic. In particular, Dickinson was a major architect of the Great Compromise that reconciled the differences among delegates over representation in the new government. Designed to protect the rights of both the small and more populous states, the compromise called for a national legislature that gave equal voice to all thirteen states in a Senate composed of two representatives from each, but which respected the rights of the majority in a House of Representatives based on population. The Great Compromise ushered in a series of other compromises on lesser subjects and was critical to the final approval of the Constitution. Ironically, Dickinson again failed to sign one of history's most important documents. This time illness, not a lack of ardent support, was the cause; his name was penned to the new instrument of government by a colleague.

Before finally retiring to the pleasures of his library and estates, Dickinson made one last contribution to the nation. Signing himself "Fabius," he again addressed a series of open letters to his fellow citizens, this time in defense of the new Constitution. His concern for liberty was at the heart of his arguments. "The power of the people pervading the proposed system, together with the strong confederation of the states," he contended, "forms an adequate security against every danger that has been apprehended." With compelling examples drawn from history and the Enlightenment philosophers, Dickinson explained how the Constitution's system of checks and balances—among the branches of government and between the new government and the individual states—would safeguard the civil rights of the people while it promoted the liberty of the nation.

His reasoned appeal bore fruit. In December 1787 Delaware became the first state to ratify the Constitution.

William Few

William Few, who represented Georgia at the Constitutional Convention, was a self-made man. Born into a family struggling against the poverty and hardships that were the common lot of the small yeoman farmer, Few achieved both social prominence and political power. Exhibiting those characteristics of self-reliance vital for survival on the American frontier, he became an intimate of the nation's political and military elite. The idea of a rude frontiersman providing the democratic leaven within an association of the rich and powerful has always excited the American imagination, nurtured on stories of Davy Crockett and Abe Lincoln. In the case of the self-educated Few, that image was largely accurate.

Few's inherent gifts for leadership and organization, as well as his sense of public service, were brought out by his experience in the Revolutionary War. Important in any theater of military operations, leadership and organizational ability were particularly needed in the campaigns in the south where a dangerous and protracted struggle against a determined British invader intimately touched the lives of many settlers. Few's dedication to the common good and his natural military acumen quickly brought him to the attention of the leaders of the Patriot cause, who eventually invested him with important political responsibilities as well.

The war also profoundly affected Few's attitude toward the political future of the new nation, transforming the rugged frontier individualist into a forceful exponent of a permanent union of the states. Men of his stripe came to realize during the years of military conflict that the rights of the individual, so jealously prized on the frontier, could be nurtured and protected only by a strong central government accountable to the people. This belief became the hallmark of his long public service.

The Patriot

The Few family might well serve as the prototype of those mobile Americans forever seeking better times down the road. Descendents of Quaker farmers who emigrated to Pennsylvania in the 1680s, the Fews lived in northern Maryland, where they eked out a modest living raising tobacco on small holdings. When a series of droughts struck the region in the 1750s, the Fews and their neighbors—actually a sort of extended family consisting of cousins and distant relations—found themselves on the brink of ruin. The whole community decided to abandon its farms and try its luck among the more fertile lands on the southern frontier.

The group ultimately selected new homesites along the banks of the Eno River in Orange County, North Carolina. Here young Few developed the skills expected of the eighteenth-century farmer. Such a life left little time for formal schooling, although the community hired an itinerant teacher for a brief time in the 1760s. From this experience Few obtained a rudimentary education that led to a lifelong love of reading. Essentially a self-educated man, Few also found time to read law and qualify as an attorney despite a full-time commitment to the unrelenting demands of agricultural toil.

In time the Few family achieved a measure of prosperity, emerging as political leaders in rural Orange County. Like many other western settlers, however, the family became involved with the Regulators, a populist movement that grew up in reaction to the political and economic restrictions imposed on the frontier farmers by the merchants and planters of the tidewater area. By 1771 protest had become confrontation, and a large group of mostly unarmed westerners gathered to clash with North Carolina militia units at the "battle" of the Alamance. The uneven fight ended in total victory for the militia, although most of the frontiersmen's demands for political representation and economic relief eventually would be met by the state legislature. More immediately, one of Few's brothers was hanged for his part in the uprising. The rest of the family fled to western Georgia, leaving Few behind to settle their affairs and sell their property.

These antagonisms within North Carolina began to evaporate as American opinion turned against the imperial measures instituted by Great Britain in the 1770s. Both the eastern planters and the new settlers found repressive new taxes and restrictions on western expansion at odds with their idea of self-government, and Patriot leaders were able to unite the state against what they could portray as a threat to the liberties of all parties. By the time open warfare erupted in Massachusetts in 1775, North Carolina had begun to revitalize its militia formations, hastily training them in the linear tactics used by British regulars as well as in the techniques of frontier warfare employed by their traditional Indian foes.

WILLIAM FEW
Georgia

Birth: 8 June 1748, in Baltimore County, Maryland
Death: 16 July 1828, at Beacon-on-Hudson, New York
Interment: St. Paul's Church, Augusta, Georgia

Oil on canvas, attributed to James Sharples, Sr. (no date); Independence National Historical Park.

Few participated in this training as one of the first men to enlist in the volunteer militia company formed by Patriot leaders in Hillsborough. Typically, Few's unit received its tactical instruction from a veteran of the colonial wars, in this case a former corporal in the British Army who was hired by the company as its drill sergeant. Citing the press of family business, Few rejected the offer of a captaincy in one of the first units North Carolina raised for the Continental Army in the summer of 1775. But when he finally settled the family's accounts the next year and joined his relatives in Augusta, Georgia, where he opened a law office, he quickly placed his newly acquired military knowledge at the service of the Patriot cause in his new state.

The Soldier

Georgia organized its citizen-soldiers on a geographical basis, forming local companies into a regiment in each county. Few joined the Richmond County Regiment, which his older brother commanded. For the next two years Few's military duties consisted of attending military assemblies where he instructed his friends and neighbors in the skills he had acquired in the North Carolina militia. Only in 1778, when Georgia faced the threat of invasion by a force of Loyalist militia and British regulars based in Florida, was Few finally called to active duty.

The Georgians' first military campaign ended in disaster. A force of state and Continental units successfully combined to repulse an enemy raid on Sunbury near the state's southeastern border, but a counterattack orchestrated by Major General Robert Howe of the Continental Army and Governor John Houston bogged down before the Patriots could reach St. Augustine. Few, now in command of a company of Georgia militia, watched the collapse of the campaign's logistical support and then the disintegration of the force itself, as senior officers bickered among themselves and as disease began to decimate the units. Only half of the American soldiers survived to return home. At the end of the year a sudden amphibious invasion by British forces resulted in the capture of Savannah and the destruction of the rest of the Continental units under Howe and most of the eastern militia formations. Armed resistance to the British continued in the western part of the state, led by the Richmond County Regiment. Throughout 1779 the regiment, with Few now second in command, frequently turned out to skirmish with probing British units, eventually forcing the enemy to abandon Augusta, which the British had captured soon after the fall of Savannah.

The success of the citizen-soldiers in defending their own homes began to reverse the fortunes of war in Georgia, prompting the new Continental commander in the region, Major General Benjamin Lincoln, to take the offensive. Lincoln combined his continentals and militia units from Georgia and South Carolina with a French force newly arrived from the Caribbean to lay siege to Savannah. He immediately encountered difficulty, however, in coordinating the efforts of his diverse forces. The French, under pressure to terminate operations quickly in order to move on to other assignments, persuaded Lincoln to launch a full frontal attack. The result was a bloody defeat, but Few's militiamen participated in a successful rear-guard action that shielded the retreat of the American units. In the aftermath of the battle his regiment was posted to the frontier where the Creek Indians, interpreting the defeat before Savannah as proof of the Georgians' weakness, had taken to the field in support of British forces.

Enemy operations in Georgia in 1779 were part of a new "southern strategy" by which the British planned to use the state as a base for conquering the rebellious colonies in a sweep up from the south. Few's military service in the later years of the war proved critical both in frustrating this strategy and in enhancing his credentials as a state leader. The western forces, in which Few's regiment played a prominent role, kept the British from consolidating their position. The area never developed into a secure Loyalist base, and British troops needed for subsequent operations against the Carolinas and Virginia had to be diverted to counter the threat posed by the frontier militia units. Few emerged as a gifted administrator and logistician in this demanding and difficult effort to maintain a viable military force in Georgia. He also turned into a bold, innovative partisan commander. Experience and innate common sense enabled him to develop patience, preserve his forces for key attacks, and then pick his time and place to defeat small enemy parties without unduly risking the safety of his men. Most important, he displayed the raw physical stamina required to survive the serious hardships of guerrilla warfare.

The Statesman

Military success went hand in hand with political service. During the late 1770s Few also won election to the Georgia Assembly, sat on the state's Executive Council, acted as state surveyor-general, represented Georgia in negotiations with the Indians that succeeded in minimizing the danger of frontier attacks, and served as Richmond County's senior magistrate. Few's growing political prominence and undisputed talent for leadership prompted the state legislature in 1780 to appoint him to represent Georgia in the Continental Congress.

Few served in Congress less than a year when, in the wake of General Nathanael Greene's successful effort to drive the British out of most of Georgia, Congress sent him home to help reassemble Georgia's scattered government. This task accomplished, Few returned to Congress in 1782, where he remained to serve throughout most of the decade. While a member of that body, Few was asked by his state to serve concurrently in the Constitutional Convention that met in Philadelphia in 1787. This dual responsibility caused him to split his time between the two bodies and therefore to miss portions of the constitutional proceedings. Nevertheless, Few firmly supported the effort to create a strong national union and worked hard to secure the Continental Congress' approval of the new instrument of government. He also participated in the Georgia convention in 1788 that ratified the document.

Georgia promptly selected Few to serve as one of its original United States senators. Planning to retire from politics at the expiration of his term in 1793, he bowed instead to the wishes of his neighbors and served yet another term in the state legislature. In 1796 the Georgia Assembly appointed him as a circuit court judge. During this three-year appointment he not only consolidated his reputation as a practical, fair jurist but became a prominent supporter of public education. His efforts to establish a state university indicated the importance this self-educated man gave to formal instruction.

At the urging of his wife, a native New Yorker, Few left Georgia in 1799 and moved to Manhattan. There, he embarked on yet another career of public service, while supporting his family through banking and the occasional practice of law. His new neighbors promptly elected him to represent them in the state legislature and later as a city alderman. He also served for nine years as New York's inspector of prisons and one year as a federal commissioner of loans before finally retiring to his country home in Dutchess County, New York.

Few's career clearly demonstrates the potential for economic and social advancement that existed for men of ability in colonial society. More importantly, it revealed the willingness, common among many of these self-made men, to place their talents at the service of the nation in war and in peace.

Thomas Fitzsimons

Thomas Fitzsimons, who represented Pennsylvania in the Constitutional Convention, viewed government as a logical extension of the relationship that existed among families, ethnic communities, and business groups. His own immigrant family, Philadelphia's Irish-Catholic community, and the city's fraternity of merchants all figured prominently in Fitzsimons' rise to wealth and status, and he sought a government strong enough to protect and foster the natural interplay of these elements in a healthy society.

Experiences in the Revolution reinforced Fitzsimons' nationalist sympathies. Like many immigrants, he demonstrated his devotion to his adopted land by springing to its defense. Participation at the battle of Trenton and the later defense of Philadelphia convinced him of the need for central control of the nation's military forces. Similarly, his wartime association with Robert Morris and the other fiscal architects of the nation convinced him that an effective national government was essential for the prosperity of the country. Though his talents brought him great wealth, Fitzsimons never lost sight of the aspirations and concerns of the common people. He retained their respect and affection because his career reflected not only a sense of civic duty but also a profound honesty. He judged each political issue on ethical grounds. "I conceive it to be a duty," he said, "to contend for what is right, be the issue as it may." Using this standard, he concluded with justifiable pride that the Constitution he helped devise was a "treasure to posterity."

The Patriot

Fitzsimons' family came to Philadelphia from Ireland in the mid-1750s. His father died soon after settling in the New World, but not before providing an adequate education for his five children. Both Thomas and his twin sister Ann married into the city's growing community of Irish merchants. In 1763 Thomas went into business with his new brother-in-law, George Meade (the grandfather of the Civil War general), specializing in trade with the West Indies.

The new firm's emergence coincided with Parliament's attempt to restructure the British Empire in the aftermath of the Seven Years War. Old laws designed to regulate commerce were supplemented by new revenue measures such as a Stamp Act in 1765 to fund troops stationed in the colonies. Merchants felt the burden directly and emerged as leaders of the resulting storm of protest. When Parliament reacted to the 1773 Boston Tea Party with punitive measures, which the Americans called the Coercive Acts, Philadelphia merchants, including the partners in the prosperous George Meade & Co., were infuriated. They felt that if British warships could close the port of Boston, no city in America was truly safe.

Such economic concerns thrust the young Fitzsimons into politics and the Patriot cause. In 1771 the city's merchants and tradesmen of Irish heritage had elected him as the first vice president of the Friendly Sons of St. Patrick, a politically powerful fraternal association. Popular respect for his political judgment and economic acumen led in 1774 to his election to a steering committee organized to direct the protest over the Coercive Acts and to the city's Committee of Correspondence, the Patriots' shadow government. In choosing him for these posts, the voters ignored a law that barred Catholics from elective office. Fitzsimons went on to represent the city in a special colony-wide convention held to discuss the crisis. Its deliberations led Pennsylvania to issue a call for a meeting of all the colonies—the First Continental Congress, which met in Philadelphia in September 1774.

The Soldier

Pennsylvania's Quaker pacifist traditions had resulted in a unique military situation on the eve of the Revolution. Lacking a militia, the local Patriots had to organize a military force from the ground up by forming volunteer units, called Associators. Thanks to his wealth and wide-ranging connections in the community, Fitzsimons contributed significantly to this speedy mobilization. When Philadelphia's contingent of infantry (today's 111th Infantry, Pennsylvania Army National Guard) was organized, Fitzsimons, as a captain, raised and commanded a company in Colonel John Cadwalader's 3d Battalion.

During the summer of 1776 these citizen-soldiers faced their first crisis. A large British army, supported by the Royal Navy, attacked New York City, and Congress asked the nearby states to reinforce Washington's

THOMAS FITZSIMONS
Pennsylvania

Birth: In 1741, in Ireland (exact date and place unknown)
Death: 26 August 1811, at Philadelphia, Pennsylvania
Interment: St. Mary's Roman Catholic Church Cemetery, Philadelphia, Pennsylvania

Pen and ink drawing, by Marshall Williams, after ca. 1802 oil. Documentary evidence indicates the oil is a likeness of Fitzsimons painted by Gilbert Stuart.

outnumbered Continental Army regulars. Pennsylvania sent the Associators to the Flying Camp, a mobile reserve stationed in northern New Jersey to prevent any sudden diversion of Redcoats toward Phildelphia, the national capital. Fitzsimons' company served in the cordon of outposts that under Colonel John Dickinson guarded the New Jersey shoreline. Although a month of active duty passed without incident, the assignment provided Fitzsimons valuable time in which to train his men.

In November, with New York secured, the British suddenly invaded New Jersey. This move caught the Americans with their forces geographically divided and badly outnumbered. While Washington began a slow withdrawal of his main force to safe positions on the Pennsylvania side of the Delaware River, Congress again called on the state for reinforcements. Fitzsimons' company went on duty on 5 December to cover the continentals' retreat. For the remainder of the month it guarded the river's Pennsylvania shore. Complaining in his diary of the hardships the company was enduring in the bitter cold of that famous winter campaign, a company sergeant noted that Captain Fitzsimons was "very kind to our men." Concern for the well-being of others, a hallmark of Fitzsimons' military career that echoed through his later life, formed the basis of his broad political appeal.

Aware that a symbolic victory was needed to bolster civilian morale, Washington launched a counterattack on Christmas night. He chose Trenton, the winter quarters for a Hessian brigade, as his target. Plans called for a three-pronged dawn attack, with a large body of militia under Cadwalader crossing downstream to cut British reinforcement routes. Fitzsimons' company was in Cadwalader's column, but like most of the militia force, was unable to cross the river because of deteriorating weather. It thus did not share in Washington's great surprise victory, but it joined Washington several days later, in time to deal with a British counterattack. When General Charles Cornwallis reached Trenton on 2 January, the Americans slipped away in the dark and at dawn struck the enemy's rear guard at Princeton, smashing a second British brigade. Cadwalader's militiamen played a key role in the engagement, although Fitzsimons' company appears to have served in a reserve force. Washington moved on to northern New Jersey, forcing the British to abandon most of the state. Fitzsimons finally retired from active duty at the end of the month.

Pennsylvania authorities then asked him to serve on an eleven-member board to oversee the Pennsylvania navy, which formed the primary defense of Delaware Bay and the river approaches to Philadelphia. In this role Fitzsimons not only helped plan the capital's defenses, but organized logistics, coordinated defense with neighboring states, and negotiated with a sometimes reluctant Continental Congress over regional strategy. The assignment also provided him with an important lesson when the British captured Philadelphia. Finding Pennsylvania's defenses too formidable along the river approaches to the city, the enemy sailed up the Chesapeake Bay, and, marching through poorly defended sections of Maryland and Delaware, attacked the capital from the south. Even then, the defenses Fitzsimons had worked so hard to create held out for several months. With Philadelphia, along with his home and business, in enemy hands, Fitzsimons came to understand that no matter how well organized and defended one state might be, its safety depended ultimately on the united strength of all the states.

When France entered the war on the American side in 1778, British strategy changed. The field commander, Sir Henry Clinton, evacuated Pennsylvania and turned his attention to the conquest of the southern states, thus ending Pennsylvania's need for frequent militia mobilizations. Although Fitzsimons was involved in supplying the French naval forces that occasionally called at Philadelphia, he was now free to concentrate on politics.

The Statesman

Fitzsimons was concerned about the inflation and other serious economic problems that marked the latter years of the Revolution. Pennsylvania, burdened with a weak government, was unable to cope with these issues. Fitzsimons' experiences both in uniform and on the state's Navy Board convinced him that stronger central authority did not pose a threat to liberty and was in fact the only solution to the new crisis. Many leaders who felt this way were unpopular in Philadelphia because of their wealth, but Fitzsimons' reputation as a caring officer, as well as his work for the poor on numerous local relief committees, sustained his popularity. At this time he also became associated with the Patriot financier Robert Morris, helping to organize the banking facilities that Morris used to support the Continental Army and Navy in the last years of the war. In fact, Fitzsimons served as a director of the Bank of North America from its founding in 1781 until 1803.

Pennsylvania sent Fitzsimons to the Continental Congress in 1782. There he concentrated on financial and commercial matters, working closely with Morris and the nationalist faction led by Hamilton and Madison on developing a centralized economy. He supported the growth of domestic industry and the payment of the nation's debts, particularly those owed to the soldiers of the Continental Army, but he argued that it was essential "that the weight of the taxes fall not too heavily upon any particular part of the community." Although his integrity impressed Madison, his political evenhandedness did not sit so well with the voters, who began to criticize his stand on fiscal matters. Chagrined by the criticism and distracted by business obligations, Fitzsimons resigned in 1783.

But Fitzsimons could not abandon politics. He accepted election to Pennsylvania's Council of Censors, a unique group that reviewed the constitutionality of executive and legislative actions. In 1786 he began the first of three terms in the state legislature, where he was a floor leader of the more conservative forces. He also represented Pennsylvania in a commission that met in 1785 with Delaware and Maryland to try to work out interstate commerce issues.

In 1787 the state selected Fitzsimons to represent it at the Constitutional Convention. There he spoke often on issues relating to commerce and finance, arguing that the central government should have the right to tax both exports and imports to raise revenue and regulate commerce—reiterating a position that he had advocated with little success in the Continental Congress. Following the completion of the Convention's work, Fitzsimons resumed his seat in the Pennsylvania legislature, where he led the fight for a special convention to ratify the Constitution, arguing that since the document derived its power from the people, the people must approve it through representatives elected solely for that purpose.

Fitzsimons sat for six years as a Federalist in the new House of Representatives. He served on several important committees and was chairman of the Ways and Means Committee. He also chaired the committee that organized the government of the Northwest Territory, and, in the aftermath of the Army's defeat by Indians in 1791, presided over a select committee that investigated the matter. That committee set an important precedent by asserting that the Congress, under the powers vested in the first article of the Constitution, had the right to oversee the President's handling of military affairs.

Defeated in 1794, Fitzsimons devoted the rest of his life to business and charitable affairs. Financial reverses in old age did not shake his faith in the common man, nor his sense of obligation to those less fortunate than himself. In a fitting tribute to Fitzsimons' abiding sense of civic duty, a contemporary noted the fact that "he died in the esteem, affection and gratitude of all classes of his fellow citizens."

Nicholas Gilman

Nicholas Gilman, New Hampshire Patriot and Revolutionary War veteran, was among those assembled in Philadelphia in the summer of 1787 to devise a new instrument of government for the independent American states. Gilman realized that the resulting Constitution was less than perfect, leaving certain viewpoints and interests largely unsatisfied. It was, in fact, an amalgam of regional ambitions and citizen safeguards forged in the spirit of political compromise. But Gilman was among the Constitution's most ardent supporters, believing that there was no alternative to the strong, viable union created by such a Constitution except a drift into political and economic chaos. Imbued with the emerging spirit of nationhood, he entered the struggle for ratification in his own state. At least nine favorable votes from the states were needed to install the new Constitution. Thanks to the work of Gilman and others, New Hampshire cast the crucial ninth aye vote.

Gilman's fervor for national unity flowed naturally from his experiences during the Revolution. An officer in the Continental Army, he served on George Washington's staff through the dark days of Valley Forge to the final victory at Yorktown. From this vantage point he came to appreciate the need for a government capable of preserving those personal liberties for which Americans had sacrificed so much. Daily contact with military and civilian officials representing a wide spectrum of economic interests made it obvious to this businessman-turned-soldier from a small New England state that the cost of a strong, permanent union was political compromise. During his long public career, Gilman worked hard to conciliate the differences between the various factions. He lived to see this course of action vindicated in a flourishing republic.

The Patriot

Gilman could trace his roots in America to the earliest days of New Hampshire. The family had settled in Exeter, a substantial town in the eastern part of the colony. Here the Gilmans engaged in ship construction as well as in the profitable mercantile trade that linked the growing frontier settlements, the rest of the American colonies, and the West Indies. The Gilman family also performed the traditional public services expected of men of substance in eighteenth-century America. Its sons, for example, served as militia officers in the 1745 campaign against the French stronghold at Louisbourg, Canada, and ten years later they were among those soldiers New Hampshire mobilized to fight in the French and Indian War. Gilman's father was both a prosperous local merchant and the commander of the town's militia regiment.

Gilman was the second son in a family of eight children. Born during the French and Indian War, he was soon aware of the military responsibilities that went with citizenship in a New England colony. After attending local public schools, he became a clerk in his father's trading house, but the growing rift between the colonies and Great Britain quickly thrust Gilman into the struggle for independence. New England merchants in particular resented Parliament's attempt to end its "salutary neglect" of the financial and political affairs of the colonies by instituting measures to raise and to enforce the raising of revenue—measures that many Americans considered violations of their rights as British citizens. Gilman's father, along with Nathaniel Folsom and Enoch Poor, emerged as a leader of the Patriot cause in Exeter. He represented his community in the New Hampshire Provincial Congresses, which met just after hostilities broke out at Lexington and Concord in 1775 and which later drafted the first state constitution. During the Revolution he served as the state's treasurer. His oldest son, John, was a sergeant in Exeter's company of militia that marched to fight the Redcoats around Boston. Nicholas remained behind, but already an ardent supporter of the Patriot cause, he likely trained with the local militia regiment.

The Soldier

In November 1776 a committee of the state legislature appointed young Nicholas Gilman to serve as adjutant, or administrative officer, of the 3d New Hampshire Regiment. That unit was in the process of a complete reorganization under the direction of its commander, Colonel Alexander Scammell. A superb combat officer, Scammell made good use of Gilman's administrative talents in the task of creating a potent fighting force out of the limited manpower resources at hand—a combination of raw recruits from around the state and ragged veterans of the Trenton-Princeton campaign. In time the

NICHOLAS GILMAN
New Hampshire

Birth: 3 August 1755, at Exeter, New Hampshire
Death: 2 May 1814, at Philadelphia, Pennsylvania
Interment: Winter Street Cemetery, Exeter, New Hampshire

Oil, by Albert Rosenthal (no date); Independence National Historical Park.

3d New Hampshire would be recognized as one of the mainstays of General Washington's Continental Army.

Because New Hampshire lay along the major invasion route from Canada to New York, Washington assigned its regiments a key role in the strategic defense of the northern states. In the spring of 1777 Gilman and the rest of the officers and men of the 3d New Hampshire marched to Fort Ticonderoga on Lake Champlain to participate in an attempt by American forces to halt the advance of a powerful army of British and German regulars and Indian auxiliaries under General John Burgoyne. Difficulties in coordinating the efforts of several different states turned Gilman's first military experience into one of defeat. The veteran British troops outflanked the fort, and only at the last minute did the garrison, including the 3d New Hampshire, escape capture by making a dangerous night withdrawal.

The Patriots' grudging retreat lasted through the early summer, until a combination of British transportation difficulties and delaying tactics employed by the continentals finally slowed the enemy advance. This delay allowed time for a mass mobilization of New England militia, including a New Hampshire company of volunteers led by John Langdon and Gilman's father. It also provided Major General Horatio Gates with time to establish new positions near Saratoga, New York, to block Burgoyne's further advance, and then, once Gates had a numerical advantage, to cut off the British line of withdrawl to Canada. During this campaign Gilman was busily employed in supervising the training and readiness of Scammell's men. He participated with his unit in two important battles at Freeman's Farm, where Burgoyne's units were so pummelled that "Gentleman Johnny" was eventually forced to surrender his whole army.

Neither Gilman nor Scammell was granted a respite after this great victory. Less than a week after the British surrender, the 3d New Hampshire set out to reinforce Washington's main army near Philadelphia. The American capital had recently fallen to a larger British force, and the New Englanders had to spend a harsh winter in the snows of Valley Forge. That winter encampment put the units of the Continental Army to their supreme test, a time of suffering and deprivation from which they emerged as a tough, professional combat team. Gilman's administrative skills came to the fore at this time. When Washington selected Colonel Scammell to serve as the Continental Army's Adjutant General,

Scammell made Gilman his assistant. Promotion to the rank of captain followed in June 1778.

For the remainder of the war Gilman found himself in close proximity to the military leaders of the Continental Army. His duties in carrying out the myriad tasks necessary to keep a force in the field placed him in daily contact with Washington, Steuben, Knox, Greene, and others. He personally saw action in the remaining battles fought by Washington's main army, including Monmouth and Yorktown, while continuing to hold his captain's commission in the New Hampshire Line. The death of Colonel Scammell, however, during the preliminary skirmishing before Yorktown robbed him of much of the joy of that great victory. Following the death of his father in late 1783, he retired from military service and returned to Exeter to assume control of the family's business.

The Statesman

Gilman's career as a merchant proved short-lived. His service as a Continental Army officer had exposed him to many of the ideas of such prominent nationalists as Washington and Alexander Hamilton. Their influence, his family's own tradition of service, and his special skill at organization all combined to divert the young veteran into a political career. In 1786 the New Hampshire legislature appointed Gilman to the Continental Congress. He was also selected in 1786 to represent the state at the Annapolis Convention. Although he was unable to attend, his selection recognized Gilman's emergence as a nationalist spokesman, since the convention had been called specifically to address the country's serious economic problems and the inability of the separate states or Congress to solve them.

The outbreak of unrest and latent insurrection in western Massachusetts in late 1786 further strengthened Gilman's commitment to changing the Articles of Confederation. He was pleased to serve his state as a representative at the Constitutional Convention that met in July 1787. Although he and fellow New Hampshire delegate John Langdon, his father's former commanding officer, reached Philadelphia after the proceedings were well under way, they both immediately joined in the debates and helped hammer out the compromises needed to produce a document that might win approval in every state and region.

During the subsequent struggle to secure New Hampshire's ratification of the Constitution, Gilman remained in New York as a member of the Continental Congress, but he kept in close touch with his brother, John, who was one of the leaders of the state's ratification forces. Working in tandem, the brothers used all of their considerable political influence to engineer a narrow 57–47 margin of victory in the final vote.

When the First Congress of the new United States of America convened in New York in 1789, Gilman was in attendance as a member of the House of Representatives, a seat he filled for four terms. During this period the Gilman brothers became a feature of New Hampshire politics. John Gilman became governor, a post he would hold for fourteen terms, while a younger brother embarked on a career in the state legislature. After returning to Exeter, Nicholas Gilman resumed his own political career in 1800, serving a term as state senator.

During this time Gilman's political loyalties began to change. Ever a staunch nationalist, he had supported the Federalists while that party led the fight for a more binding union of the states. But once that concept was firmly established, Gilman became increasingly concerned with the need to protect the common man from abuses of power by government. As a consequence, he gave his support to the Democratic-Republican party that was beginning to form around Thomas Jefferson. In 1801 he accepted appointment from Jefferson as a federal bankruptcy commissioner. Following one unsuccessful attempt, he was then elected to the United States Senate in 1804 as a Jeffersonian. Although the New Hampshire Yankee rarely spoke at length in legislative debate, his peers recognized his political prowess. He remained an influential member of the Senate until his death in 1814, which occured while he was returning home from Washington during a recess.

Gilman summarized his belief in the importance of a strong national government on the day after he signed the Constitution. He called the new supreme law of the land "the best that could meet the unanimous concurrence of the States in Convention; it was done by bargain and Compromise, yet, notwithstanding its imperfections, on the adoption of it depends (in my feeble judgment) whether we shall become a respectable nation, or a people torn to pieces . . . and rendered contemptible for ages." These modest words typified this eminently practical Soldier-Statesman. Yet his modesty failed to mask the justifiable pride he obviously felt in the accomplishment of the Founding Fathers. Gilman himself had played no small part. He was one of those rare figures who successfully combined an eminently pragmatic approach to government with an unwavering vision of future greatness for his nation.

Alexander Hamilton

Alexander Hamilton, who represented New York at the Constitutional Convention, was a brilliant political theorist and a leading advocate of centralized government. As an immigrant, Hamilton was able to transcend loyalty to any single state or region and think in terms of nationhood. He combined a natural affinity for aristocratic values with a generally pessimistic view of human nature and concluded that successful government must be strong and must win the support of men of property and social standing. Hamilton was among the most intellectually gifted of the Founding Fathers, rivaling in ability his arch foe, Thomas Jefferson, but he lacked practical political experience and failed to win support for many of his most cherished ideas. A blunt, practical man, he never understood the role that idealists like Jefferson played in shaping society. Ironically, his major contributions to the political life of the nation occurred only when his specific policies were adopted and carried forward by others with broader vision.

Hamilton was a master of financial planning and central organization. Many of his ideas about government matured during a youth spent in the uniform of the Continental Army. The fact that Hamilton's lifetime was dominated by a series of global wars between Great Britain and France colored his thinking about politics. He came to believe that the survival of the United States depended on its ability to provide for its self-defense, and his plans to strengthen the political union, eloquently expressed during the fight to ratify the Constitution, were directly linked to his ideas on military matters.

The Patriot

Hamilton's original prospects were very limited. His parents never married and separated while he was still a child. His father, a younger son of a minor Scottish noble, had drifted to the West Indies where he eked out a living as an occasional clerk and minor merchant while dreaming of glory; his mother died when Hamilton was eleven, leaving him to fend largely for himself. Hamilton's childhood was spent on the edge of poverty first on Nevis, the smallest of Britain's Leeward Islands, and later on St. Croix in the Danish Virgin Islands.

This background produced a boy older than his years, suspicious of human motives, and obsessed with a highly idealistic concept of nobility. It also created a youth consumed by an ambition to conquer the world that had dealt him such a poor hand. Fortunately, he found employment on St. Croix as an apprentice in tiny Christiansted, then very much a frontier "boom town." By the time he was fourteen, his employer, a New York-born merchant trading with the American mainland, recognized Hamilton's intelligence, honesty, and gift for finances and gave him considerable responsibility. Others encouraged his voracious reading and made it possible for him to go to New York City to obtain a formal education.

His patrons back in St. Croix provided him with letters of introduction to a circle of influential men in that city and nearby New Jersey, men who also happened to be among the most important leaders of the mounting opposition to Great Britain. He used their contacts to gain admission to Francis Barber's preparatory school in Elizabethtown, New Jersey. Hamilton also lived for a year with William Livingston, later a fellow signer of the Constitution. During these years, Hamilton met a number of men who would become lifelong friends and political allies. He entered King's College (now Columbia University), and he also became active in the city's Patriot movement. He gained some local notoriety by writing two pamphlets which attacked one of New York's leading Tories, the Reverend Samuel Seabury. Hamilton never graduated from college; the rush of outside events intervened.

The Soldier

Hamilton's first experience with the military came during the heady days of the summer of 1775, after the outbreak of fighting at Boston. Along with a group of other students from King's, he joined a volunteer militia company, the Hearts of Oak. They adopted distinctive uniforms, complete with the words "Liberty or Death" on their hatbands, and drilled under the watchful eye of a former British officer. Hamilton's political connections with the Patriot leadership soon led him into full-time service. In March 1776 the state government commissioned him as a captain, with instructions to raise the New York Provincial Company of Artillery (today the Regular Army's 1st Battalion, 5th Field Artillery) to protect Manhattan Island.

ALEXANDER HAMILTON
New York

Birth: 11 January 1757, on Nevis, British West Indies
Death: 12 July 1804, at New York City
Interment: Trinity Episcopal Church Cemetery, New York City

Oil, by John Trumbull (1792); National Gallery of Art.

In the same month that Hamilton received his commission, George Washington's Continental Army troops forced the British to evacuate Boston. Conceding that opposition was too strong in New England, the King's ministers ordered their forces to occupy New York City, with its superb harbor, as a new base. While the Continental Congress in Philadelphia declared independence, the largest trans-Atlantic invasion force assembled prior to the twentieth century began concentrating offshore.

Congress and Washington assembled continentals, militia, and state units like the Provincial Company to defend the city. Hamilton dutifully reported for orders to Washington's Chief of Artillery, Colonel (later Major General) Henry Knox, and his men served alongside Knox's gunners throughout the fall campaign. They stayed with the rear guard of Washington's main army during the retreat across New Jersey after the city fell. One of Hamilton's finest moments as an officer came during the dramatic two weeks of the Trenton-Princeton campaign. Knox's fieldpieces crossed the ice-choked Delaware River on Christmas Night, 1776, and supported Major General Nathanael Greene's division through the snowstorm. In a dawn attack on the Hessian garrison at Trenton, their cannon balls and grapeshot contributed directly to one of the most lopsided victories of the war. At Princeton they then set up outside the college's Nassau Hall and "persuaded" the better part of a British regiment to surrender.

Impressed by Hamilton's abilities, Knox and Greene recommended the young officer to Washington's personal attention. In March he received appointment as an aide to the Commander in Chief, along with a promotion to lieutenant colonel. Hamilton had been an excellent combat leader; he now had a chance to try his hand at staff work, for Washington used his staff "family" as the center of his military administration. These handpicked young men acted as messengers and prepared Washington's voluminous official correspondence. Hamilton's workaholic habits made him an instant success and a key member of the close-knit team. From the Philadelphia campaign of 1777 through Monmouth and on into the dark years of virtual stalemate, he stayed with the main army, learning many important lessons about the need for central government to deal with crises. When he eventually came to resent the limits of his role, he seized upon a minor reprimand as a reason to resign in April 1781.

The preceding December he had married a daughter

of Major General Philip Schuyler, a powerful conservative political leader in New York and one of Washington's closest supporters. Schuyler sought to heal the breach between Washington and Hamilton. Although not recalled to the staff, Hamilton was given the command of a battalion of elite light infantry for the 1781 campaign. At the subsequent siege of Yorktown Hamilton's battalion openly taunted the British by performing close order drill on the parapet of the entrenchments. Hamilton then led his own battalion and two others in the decisive engagement of the siege, a bayonet assault on Redoubt 10 on the evening of 14 October. Five days later Cornwallis surrendered.

There is no question that military service shaped Hamilton's thinking. Years of combat and, even more importantly, the administrative and logistical struggle to keep men from all over the nation working together made him an ardent nationalist and exponent of strong central government. One biographer has even gone so far as to claim that "Hamilton's wartime . . . aideship was, in other words, his postgraduate education."

The Statesman

Hamilton took up the study of the law in early 1782. He completed a program of apprenticeship which normally took three years in as many months, and was admitted to the bar in July. Within six months he found himself representing New York in the Continental Congress, where he quickly joined a young Virginian, James Madison, as a leading exponent of stronger national government. By August of the following year frustration with his failure to persuade a majority to support his ideas led him to return to New York, where he rapidly built a thriving law practice and gained fame as a legal theorist.

Hamilton, however, could not long remain out of the public arena. In 1787 he spent a term in the New York legislature. More importantly, he played an essential role in the movement which resulted in the adoption of the Constitution. He had attended the Annapolis Convention the previous year when representatives from the middle states met to discuss economic problems of mutual interest. In 1787 he was included in the New York delegation to the Constitutional Convention. His influence was most pronounced, however, during the ratification battles that followed the meeting in Philadelphia. In an effort to win popular support for the Constitution in New York, Hamilton persuaded Madison and John Jay (a future Chief Justice of the Supreme Court) to join him in publishing a series of essays, *The Federalist Papers,* which still serve as one of the most fundamental statements of American political philosophy. The authors successfully argued that strong central government was not an inevitable step toward tyranny. Their efforts not only swung public opinion in other states, but helped pave the way for New York's ratification in July 1788, an event that had appeared extremely unlikely the previous fall. Hamilton's performance as floor manager during the ratification convention provided the margin of victory.

In 1789 when Washington began the task of organizing the new federal government, he asked his old aide to become the nation's first Secretary of the Treasury. For nearly six years Hamilton worked out a comprehensive fiscal and economic program for the national government that remains in place two centuries later. He persuaded Congress to establish a national coinage, a national banking system, a revenue program to provide for the repayment of the national debt, and measures to encourage industrial and commercial development. His goal was a vigorous, diversified economy that would also provide the nation with the means to defend itself.

Such an ambitious economic program was bound to create opposition, especially when Hamilton's strong personality clashed in cabinet meetings with that of Secretary of State Thomas Jefferson. Frustrated by the political rivalry and exhausted by hard work and personal financial sacrifice, Hamilton retired in the summer of 1795 to resume his law practice. He was back in federal service three years later when the nation expanded the Army to prepare for a possible war with France, serving as a major general with the additional duty of Inspector General until 1800.

Although Hamilton was a great innovator and statesman, his lack of legislative experience and of faith in the common man made him a poor politician. His tactical failures as a leader of the Federalists on both the state and national level fractured the party into competing groups and contributed directly to the election of Jefferson as President in 1800. Both Jefferson and his running mate Aaron Burr received the same number of electoral votes. To Hamilton's credit, he refused to back a plan by some members of the party to cast votes for Burr to deny Jefferson a victory. Burr's bitterness over that decision, coupled with his long-standing rivalry with Hamilton in local politics, led inexorably to tragedy. On 11 July 1804 the two men met at dawn at Weehawken Heights, New Jersey. Hamilton, who detested dueling, participated because he felt that his honor had been impugned. Mortally wounded, he was carried back to New York City where he died the next day.

Rufus King

Rufus King, who represented Massachusetts in the Constitutional Convention, was a political realist. The lessons of a classical education and certain tragic events in his family's history combined to convince him that idealism had to be tempered with vigilance and that a fledgling nation would need a strong government to protect the rights of its citizens while defending its interests in a hostile world. Throughout a lengthy public career he employed his considerable diplomatic and oratorical skills to promote the twin causes of nationalism and civil liberty, fighting in the last decade of his life to extend those liberties to the nation's enslaved minority.

The Revolutionary War marked a watershed in King's life. Like other major social and political upheavals, the Revolution was accompanied by local breakdowns of justice and public order. The King family was the victim of one such breakdown, and the incident turned the young Patriot into a passionate advocate of the rule of law and the rights of the individual. King's military experience would also make him a leading exponent of strong national defense, but one who always demanded that the nation's military forces remain subordinated to the needs and purposes of the civilian government. King also served as an important transitional figure, passing on to a new generation of leaders the ideals that had animated the Revolution. The last of the Founding Fathers to pass from the scene, he served in various political and diplomatic offices until 1826.

The Patriot

King was born in Scarboro, in that part of Massachusetts which subsequently became Maine. His father had served as a citizen-soldier during the early stages of Britain's contest for North America, participating in the successful assault on the French fortress at Louisbourg, Canada, in 1745. Shortly after that victory he left the Boston area to settle on the northern frontier of Massachusetts, where he quickly rose to prominence as a well-to-do farmer and merchant. His ability to dominate affairs in Scarboro provoked considerable envy, an emotion that turned ugly as the rift between the colony and the mother country widened. A strong supporter of Royal authority, the elder King defended the unpopular Stamp Act, a measure enacted by Parliament to raise revenues in the colonies to defray the cost of the French and Indian War. In retaliation the local Patriots, dubbed Sons of Liberty, ransacked the family's home in 1766. Unintimidated, the father retained his Loyalist sympathies, provoking yet another confrontation in 1774. This time a force of local militia visited the King home and demanded a public recanting. The humiliation and strain caused by this incident led directly to the old captain's death and instilled in his son a lifelong passion for law and order and for a society controlled by rational men.

Rufus King was the first member of his family to benefit from a formal education. Thanks in great part to the persistence of his stepmother, he attended a boarding school, where he received the rudiments of a classical education, and then Harvard College. There he graduated first in his class in 1777 before moving on to Newburyport to study law under Theophilus Parsons, who later became Massachusetts' chief justice and one of the most important Federalist theoreticians and philosophers. King also joined a men's club in Boston whose members would form the nucleus of what eventually became the state's Federalist party.

Traditionally, young men in Massachusetts deferred military service until completing their education. King was no exception. In addition to his scholastic obligations, King faced severe financial problems. His father's sudden death left the family's affairs in shambles, and King was forced to support his stepmother and the younger children. He organized the estate and invested his share in the Massachusetts lumber trade. But his failure to enlist caused tongues to wag. Scarboro's local Patriots continued to harbor doubts about the family's loyalties. Given the father's outspoken support for the old regime, they especially questioned the son's commitment to the cause. King, who had become an ardent Patriot during his years at Harvard, was particularly incensed when charges of disloyalty were leveled against him in the summer of 1777, but he allowed the talk to continue a full year before he suspended his legal training and donned uniform. This steadfastness in settling matters in an orderly fashion marked the measure of the young scholar, just as it would come to characterize his later political career.

RUFUS KING
Massachusetts

Birth: 24 March 1755, at Scarboro, Massachusetts*
Death: 29 April 1827, at New York City
Interment: Grace Episcopal Church Cemetery, Jamaica, New York

*Now Scarborough, Maine. Maine achieved statehood in 1820; prior to that time it was a part of Massachusetts.

Oil, by Charles Willson Peale (1818); Independence National Historical Park.

The Soldier

Actually, during this period King considered himself first and foremost a New Englander. He stood ready to sacrifice all for his native region, but he felt no nationalistic commitment to rush to the defense of the other colonies. Although the Revolution began in New England in 1775, events and strategic decisions had shifted the military action to other locations relatively early in the war. Strategists in London decided that opposition to the Crown was strongest in the four New England states and concentrated instead on trying to regain control of the middle colonies, where they believed loyalties were more evenly divided. The British evacuated Boston in March 1776 and captured New York in the summer, intending to use that important port city as their main base. New England was left to endure the economic hardships caused by a naval blockade and frequent raids on coastal cities.

When the chance arose in 1778 to drive the last of the enemy from New England, King quickly volunteered. The military picture now had changed considerably. The American victory at Saratoga in the fall of 1777 had freed New England from the threat of attack from Canada. France's entry into the war led the British to withdraw from Philadelphia, allowing Washington to concentrate most of the Continental Army near New York. Several of his regular brigades were now available to reinforce New England's citizen-soldiers, and the appearance of a French naval squadron off the American coast provided the occasion to attack the British at Newport. Massachusetts mobilized its militia for a campaign organized by Major General John Sullivan. King and other members of his Boston club volunteered their services to Governor John Hancock. On reaching Rhode Island, King received a commission as major of infantry and appointment as aide to Brigadier General John Glover of Marblehead. Glover, commander of the regiment of Massachusetts seamen (today's 101st Engineer Battalion, Massachusetts Army National Guard) who had ferried Washington's men across the Delaware before the Battle of Trenton, was now in command of an infantry brigade. The brigade crossed from the Rhode Island mainland to Newport, where it joined other militia and Continental units in constructing redoubts and preliminary siege lines.

At this point, American fortunes turned sour. British reinforcements arrived, and the French fleet, after suffering severe damage during an inconclusive battle with a British squadron and from a sudden tropical storm, withdrew. Faced with the prospect of entrapment on the island, Sullivan had no choice but to retreat. As one of the best trained and equipped units on the scene, Glover's brigade covered the withdrawal. During that successful exercise King narrowly escaped death at the hands of the Redcoats.

Following the aborted Newport campaign, King returned to the study of law. He was admitted to the bar in 1780 and opened a practice in Newburyport. Although short-lived, his military career was important to his development as a national leader. It enlarged his political outlook, introducing him to conditions outside his native state and providing him the opportunity to serve with soldiers from far-flung areas of the nation. It also taught him the importance of interstate cooperation in major defensive endeavors. Finally, and most important on a practical level, it helped him cement relations with a group of men who would become future leaders of the Federalist party.

The Statesman

King's legal practice in Newburyport thrived and in 1783 his fellow citizens elected him to the state legislature. The following year his colleagues in the legislature selected him to serve as a delegate to the Continental Congress, which moved to New York City shortly after King took his seat. There, exposure to the cosmopolitan atmosphere of the metropolis and to the company of distinguished men broadened the young New Englander's political vision. He became close friends with Secretary at War Henry Knox and with such delegates as John Jay and Robert Livingston as a result of his diligent day-to-day activities in Congress, where he took a particular interest in commercial, financial, diplomatic, and military issues.

Unrest among debt-ridden farmers in western Massachusetts, culminating in Shays' Rebellion, marked a final assault on the nation's confidence in the Articles of Confederation. For King, the abortive uprising not only proved the inherent weakness of the existing government, but completed his conversion to the cause of strong central government. He clearly demonstrated these sentiments when he joined other delegates as a representative of Massachusetts at the Constitutional Convention in 1787. He was the first delegate from New England to reach Philadelphia, and he quickly joined James Madison in leading the fight for national union on the Convention floor. His brilliant oratory and clear pragmatism helped win over wavering delegates. After the document was signed, he returned to the Continental Congress, where he worked to secure that body's approval of the new Constitution. He then returned to Massachusetts to act as floor leader in the state's ratification convention. To effect the compromise needed to win approval in that meeting, he helped organize the first formal call for a bill of rights.

In 1789 King married and moved permanently to New York City. He was elected to the state legislature and then, just ten days into the legislative session, to the United States Senate. He represented New York in the Senate for two terms, serving as a leader of the Federalists and demonstrating a rare understanding of military issues. When war with France threatened, he fought to establish the national government's responsibility for coastal defense, to reestablish the Navy, and to impose a tax to fund these projects.

King declined President Washington's offer of a Cabinet post, but he agreed in 1796 to serve as ambassador to Great Britain, a position he would hold under three presidents. Demonstrating singular tact and foresight, he negotiated a settlement of Revolutionary War issues and initiated discussions on European interests in Latin America that would find fruition in the Monroe Doctrine.

King retired in 1803, but he remained closely involved in politics. During the next decade he ran unsuccessfully as Federalist candidate for various offices including the vice presidency. Reelected to the Senate in 1813, he quickly became a leader of the small group of Federalists who supported the administration in the War of 1812, arguing "when the efforts for peace were rejected and a barbarous warfare proclaimed against us, it became the duty of all to resist, and thereby preserve the country from ruin." Deeply admired by men of differing political persuasions, King won 34 electoral votes for President in 1816. During his final years in the Senate he continued to defend his political ideals in an age of rigid partisan attitudes. In particular, he denounced slavery as anathema to the principles underlying the Declaration of Independence and the Constitution. In the greatest speech of his career, he fervently opposed admitting Missouri as a slave state in 1820. In 1825 President John Quincy Adams asked him to return once again to London. He remained at his post for a year before his declining health forced him to return home.

Among the Founding Fathers, King probably traveled the longest philosophical distance. Beginning his career as an isolated, provincial scholar, he matured into a unionist of broad vision. This transformation left him optimistic about the nation's future. The United States, he claimed, "on account of the freedom of their government, and the vigor and enterprise of their People, have the Right as well as the Power to take the lead in whatever may affect or concern the new world."

John Langdon

John Langdon, who represented New Hampshire at the Constitutional Convention, was a wealthy international trader. Thrust by his widespread commercial interests into the forefront of the Patriot cause, Langdon contributed his highly developed business acumen during the Revolution to the problems of supplying the Continental Navy. As a citizen-soldier, he also participated under arms in the American victory, on several occasions using his personal fortune to ensure the success of his militia command.

Langdon's various political and military experiences in the Revolution led him to believe that the well-being of his country demanded a binding union of the states. A citizen of one of the smaller and less influential states, he realized in particular that only a strong central government could ensure that the rights and privileges of all citizens would be equally protected. His business background also convinced him of the need for a government that could guarantee economic stability and growth. At the same time, his experiences in the militia and in the Continental Congress made him an articulate exponent of the idea that a well-regulated militia force, subordinate to civilian authority, was an important ingredient of any new government. During a long political career at both the state and national level, Langdon would continue to extol and explain the unique blending of the advantages and responsibilities bestowed upon the republic by the Constitution.

The Patriot

The Langdon family was among the first to settle near the mouth of New Hampshire's Piscataqua River, a settlement which in time became Portsmouth, one of New England's major seaports. The son of a substantial farmer and local politician, John Langdon was educated at a local school run by a veteran of New England's 1745 expedition against the French at Louisbourg, Canada. Langdon and his older brother Woodbury both rejected the opportunity to join in their father's successful agricultural pursuits, succumbing instead to the lure of the thriving port. With the idea of entering the Yankee sea trade, they apprenticed themselves to local merchants.

John Langdon did not remain long in the counting house. By the age of twenty-two he was captain of a cargo ship sailing to the West Indies, and four years later he owned his first merchantman. Over time he would acquire a small fleet of vessels, which engaged in the triangular trade between Portsmouth, the Caribbean, and London. His older brother was even more successful in international trade, and by 1770 both young men could be counted among Portsmouth's wealthiest citizens.

The brothers entered local politics on the eve of the Revolution. Despite similar educations and business careers, however, they represented opposite ends of Portsmouth's political spectrum. While Woodbury Langdon rapidly rose to become a leader of the conservative merchants, John served on the town committees elected to protest the tax Parliament enacted on the tea trade and to enforce the Continental Association, a boycott of British goods organized throughout the colonies. Illustrating divided political opinion in the colony, both brothers were elected in 1774 to represent Portsmouth in the New Hampshire legislature. But John Langdon soon grew impatient with the political process. He joined a group of militiamen who removed the gunpowder stored at the local fort before it could be seized by the Royal governor. In 1775 New Hampshire selected him and another leader of the gunpowder raid, John Sullivan, to attend the Second Continental Congress. Langdon immediately cast his lot with those calling for independence.

Langdon made an important contribution to the war effort during his year in the Continental Congress. In November 1775 he traveled to the northern front as part of a three-man committee to confer with Major General Philip Schuyler on preparations for the coming campaign. He stopped en route to investigate the situation along the Hudson River and approved the organization of the first regiment of Canadian volunteers in the Continental Army. More significantly, Congress, recognizing Langdon's maritime experiences, appointed him to the committee that oversaw the establishment of the Continental Navy.

In early 1776 Langdon resigned to accept appointment as the Marine Agent for New Hampshire, the national government's primary official within the state. Employing his local contacts, he established a shipyard in Portsmouth and began work on one of the first Continental frigates, the *Raleigh*. While he operated his own

JOHN LANGDON
New Hampshire

Birth: 26 June 1741, at Portsmouth, New Hampshire
Death: 18 September 1819, at Portsmouth, New Hampshire
Interment: Old North Cemetery, Portsmouth, New Hampshire

Pastel, attributed to James Sharples, Sr. (c. 1795); Independence National Historical Park.

fleet of privateers, he also supervised construction of the Navy's first major warship, the 74-gun *America.* The most ambitious shipbuilding project in the country to that time, the *America* was launched near the end of the war. Another of Langdon's major responsibilities as marine agent involved supervising the importation and distribution of arms. Shipped from France to ports in New England, and especially Portsmouth, these vital weapons were disguised in a complicated trade deal to maintain the appearance of French neutrality. Thanks in part to Langdon's efforts they reached the regiments of the Continental Army in time for the crucial campaigns of 1777.

Langdon's efforts as marine agent made it clear to him that the lack of an efficient central administration was an impediment to the success of the war effort. To equip his warships, he had to spend much time persuading the various states to contribute precious resources to projects that did not promise any immediate return. Even the distribution of weapons taxed his diplomatic skills to the utmost, for he had to weigh and assign priorities to the competing claims of the various New England governments, at the risk of losing their vital support for other projects.

The Soldier

In 1777 Langdon assumed a more direct role in the defense of the country. Serving as speaker of the lower house of New Hampshire's legislature—a position he would hold for the rest of the war—he devoted much energy to reorganizing the state militia. Under Washington's strategic concept, the citizen-soldiers were expected to provide for local security against sudden raids and to reinforce the Continental Army during specific campaigns. Langdon and his colleagues now formed the New Hampshire militiamen into two brigades. One was based in the east to protect the coast from attack by the Royal Navy and to support the other New England states. A second brigade was organized in the west to guard the frontier against attack from Canada. Langdon himself took command of an elite company of light infantry in General William Whipple's eastern brigade. Langdon's unit, often called a "silk-stocking" outfit by his contemporaries because it was composed of wealthy citizens who all held officer commissions in their own local militia units, was in fact a highly trained combat formation.

British strategy for the summer campaign of 1777 called for a major attack to cut New England off from the other states. While the main British army moved out of New York City against Philadelphia, drawing Washington's soldiers south, a second army under Lieutenant General John Burgoyne was to move down from Canada, capture Fort Ticonderoga, and then follow the Hudson River at least as far as Albany. Ticonderoga fell in early July, suddenly exposing the full length of New Hampshire's frontier. The state mobilized its western brigade under Brigadier General John Stark to deal with this emergency. These troops played a major role in the victory at Bennington in August, and then started attacking Burgoyne's lines of communications.

By September, Burgoyne's army had been halted near Saratoga, New York, by the combined efforts of continentals and various militias from New York and New England. To help break the stalemate, additional militia units were called up, including Langdon's company. They arrived in time to surround the British, cutting off retreat to Canada. On 17 October 1777 "Gentleman Johnny" Burgoyne and his entire army surrendered. Langdon witnessed this "grand scene," as he called it, the result of the cooperative efforts of the regulars and the militia of four separate states. He also took considerable satisfaction in the fact that he had paid out of his own pocket for much of the equipment used by his militia company, saying, "If we defend our homes and our firesides, I may get my pay; if we do not defend them, the property will be of no value to me."

In 1778 it was the turn of the eastern brigade to be mustered first. General Whipple planned a march to Rhode Island to join in an effort to oust the British from Newport, their last foothold in New England. Langdon's company, reorganized as a cavalry troop, again at its commander's personal expense, volunteered for duty. Whipple's men combined with other militia units and a force of continentals for the ambitious campaign. Timing their attack to the arrival of a French fleet off Newport, the Americans crossed from the mainland to the northern end of the island containing the city and began cautiously pushing south. Before Newport could be brought under effective siege, however, the appearance of a Royal Navy squadron and an unexpected storm forced the French to withdraw. Too weak to operate without naval support, the Americans had to retreat.

The Statesman

The Rhode Island campaign marked the end of Langdon's active duty. At the conclusion of the war he declined further service in the Continental Congress, but retained his seat in the state legislature. In 1785 he became president of the state, the title New Hampshire bestowed on its governors. Defeated for reelection in 1786, he returned to the legislature. During this period Langdon became increasingly concerned with the financial health of the newly independent nation. As a merchant, he realized that the slide of the states and Congress toward bankruptcy hurt America's international economic standing. He strongly supported the efforts of Washington, Madison, and others who were calling for the creation of a new government.

Langdon joined this effort when in 1787 New Hampshire appointed him to represent the state in the Constitutional Convention. In fact, so anxious was he to participate that when the legislature failed to provide funds for its delegation, Langdon personally paid his own way and that of fellow delegate Nicholas Gilman. Langdon and Gilman missed the early sessions of the Convention, but Langdon was soon noted for his strong support of measures to strengthen the national government. As to be expected from one with his wartime experiences, Langdon was particularly forceful in advocating centralized authority for the regulation of commerce, taxation, and military matters.

Following the Convention, Langdon served briefly in the Continental Congress, returning to New Hampshire later in the year to participate in the state's ratification convention. In these meetings Langdon exercised his considerable political skills, devising the strategy that ultimately won the state's approval. Although many feared the new instrument of government would be rejected nationally, New Hampshire's ratification, as the ninth state to do so, put the Constitution into effect.

Langdon went on to serve another term as governor before resigning in 1789 to become one of the first United States senators. He presided over the Senate's first session in which the electoral votes that made George Washington President were counted. Initially, Langdon supported Hamilton's economic policies, but over the years he grew disenchanted with the Federalists, becoming one of New England's earliest supporters of the political party forming around Thomas Jefferson. Retiring from the Senate in 1801, Langdon rejected Jefferson's offer to become Secretary of the Navy. Instead he returned to his business interests in New Hampshire and further service as legislator and as governor, retiring finally in 1812. Throughout his long political career, Langdon had espoused a simple philosophy of government: The people must grant government sufficient authority to promote their interests, but must impose sufficient controls to protect their liberties. He lived to see these ideas perpetuated in a living Constitution.

William Livingston

William Livingston, who represented New Jersey at the Constitutional Convention, was one of the new nation's authentic renaissance figures. An accomplished man of letters, linguist, agronomist, and charter member of the American Philosophical Society, he was also a notable man of action, as attorney, soldier, and state governor. The many facets of his personality combined to form a complex public figure who stood at the forefront of those fighting for independence and the creation of a strong national government. His was not a career eagerly sought. In fact, Livingston sincerely desired the quiet life of a country gentleman, but his exceptional organizational skills and dedication to popular causes repeatedly thrust him into the hurly-burly of politics.

The strong sense of public service that animated his long career also led him to champion the rights of the common man. For Livingston, freedom of religion and freedom of the press, for example, were no idle speculations, but rather living causes to which he devoted his considerable legal and literary talents. His experiences during the Revolutionary War, both as soldier and as governor of New Jersey, convinced him that weak government and unchecked local interests posed a threat to citizens equal to that endured under the Crown. An ardent republican, he considered the new Constitution an ideal instrument for guaranteeing that the rights of the individual and the aspirations of the nation would exist together in harmony under a rule of law.

The Patriot

The Livingstons stood at the pinnacle of colonial New York society, controlling a vast estate along the Hudson River near Albany. Their wealth and an interlocking series of marriages with other major families gave them great political and economic influence in the colony. William Livingston received his primary education in local schools and from private tutors, but his horizons were considerably expanded at the age of fourteen when his family sent him to live for a year with a missionary among the Iroquois Indians in the wilds of the Mohawk Valley. In 1738 he enrolled at Yale College, where he developed a lifelong interest in political satire.

Graduating in 1741, Livingston resisted pressure to enter the family fur business and moved to New York City to study law. He clerked under James Alexander and William Smith, both champions of civil rights and among the best legal minds of the day. In 1748 Livingston was admitted to the bar and opened a practice in the city, a year after marrying the daughter of a wealthy New Jersey landowner. The couple became a glittering fixture in the city's social whirl, but Livingston still found time to pursue his interest in art, languages, and poetry.

The young attorney quickly achieved prominence in the colony's legal circles. His progressive views on legal matters led naturally to a political career. In 1752 he launched the *Independent Reflector,* a weekly newspaper which, like his law practice, allied him with critics of the political status quo. Through the publication of essays and satiric pieces, he developed a consistent position on important local and national issues. He forcefully argued, for example, that King's College (now Columbia University) should be nonsectarian, with its trustees and faculty free from any religious or political tests. His reasoned appeals for a separation of church and state attracted many allies.

Such activities led to Livingston's election to the New York legislature, where his attention turned increasingly to what he considered the mother country's interference with the political and economic rights of her American subjects. Through incessant criticism of the entrenched political elite, he sought to promote an alliance between powerful, more progressive landowners and the tradesmen and mechanics of the city. But Livingston still believed that control over public affairs was best exercised by men of property and education, and he was concerned about the growing intensity of popular uprisings against Parliament's increased efforts to control the colonies. When his efforts to moderate the activities of the Sons of Liberty and other radical groups in New York failed in 1769, he and his allies lost control of the legislature. Out of political favor and burdened with raising a large family, Livingston retired from politics to pursue the life of a gentleman farmer.

Livingston turned his considerable energies to creating an estate near Elizabethtown (now Elizabeth), New Jersey. He constructed elaborate plans to turn "Liberty Hall," as he called his new home, into a showpiece of modern scientific agriculture. But this pleasant bucolic existence proved short-lived. When relations between the

WILLIAM LIVINGSTON
New Jersey

Birth: 30 November 1723, at Albany, New York
Death: 25 July 1790, at Liberty Hall, Elizabethtown, New Jersey
Interment: Greenwood Cemetery, Brooklyn, New York

Oil, by John Wollaston (ca. 1750); courtesy of Fraunces Tavern Museum, New York City.

colonies and Great Britain collapsed in 1774, Livingston's new neighbors promptly elected him to Essex County's Committee of Correspondence. He also joined New Jersey's delegation in the Continental Congress, where his legal and literary abilities made him an effective shaper of public opinion. In a particularly crucial moment in the fortunes of the Patriot cause, he won popular support for the declarations and decisions of these revolutionary bodies.

The Soldier

Livingston brought to the Revolution—in his capacity as both militia officer and state governor—the same boundless energy that characterized his earlier career as lawyer and Patriot politician. When New Jersey began organizing its defenses in late 1775, he joined the militia as brigadier general, the state's ranking officer. Livingston, however, insisted that the first regiments raised for Washington's Continental Army be commanded by more experienced men, while he concentrated on the less glamorous tasks of raising, organizing, and training the state's citizen-soldiers. These efforts contributed significantly to the later combat effectiveness of New Jersey's units.

On the eve of independence, Livingston left his seat in the Continental Congress to assume full-time military duties. When a massive buildup of British ships and troops in New York harbor indicated that a major invasion was imminent, Congress called on the states to reinforce Washington's outnumbered continentals. Livingston took to the field with New Jersey's militia contingent to secure the state's northern shoreline against any sudden enemy landing, break communication between the British and local Loyalists, and hunt for deserters. With the militia's headquarters located in nearby Elizabethtown, General Livingston used his own beloved Liberty Hall as a barracks for some of his men.

Livingston's political gifts led to his assuming a wider role in the war. In August 1776 he resigned his military commission to become the first governor elected under the new state constitution. In his inaugural speech Livingston called on the people to show "a spirit of economy, industry and patriotism, and that public integrity and righteousness that cannot fail to exalt a nation, setting our faces like flint against that dissoluteness of manner and political corruptness that will ever be a reproach to any people." A delighted public immediately nicknamed the new governor "Doctor Flint."

Wartime governors, especially committed men like Livingston who enjoyed political longevity (he was annually reelected to the position until his death) and who had good relations with General Washington, provided a link between the Continental Congress and the states. In many respects they served as local administrators for the national government. Livingston proved especially effective in providing vital support for New Jersey's contingent of regulars. His cooperation in sustaining the Continental Army during the critical middle years of the Revolution was an important factor in its survival.

Governor Livingston did not shy from politically unpopular decisions. His insistence on treating those who remained loyal to the Crown with justice and moderation, for example, was resented by many Patriots. Actually his forbearance was quite remarkable, considering that his home was pillaged in 1776 and that a bounty was put on his head by the Loyalists. That bounty, and the widespread recognition of Livington's importance to the war effort, led to a number of dangerous personal encounters. The most dramatic occurred in February 1779 when a thousand British troops, guided by local Tories, landed in the predawn darkness near Elizabethtown to capture Livingston and surprise the Continental brigade stationed nearby. Alert sentries detected the approaching British columns, and Livingston managed to escape just twenty minutes ahead of the enemy. Two of his daughters remained behind to mislead the British and hide official state papers. Confronted with a brigade of fully alerted continentals, the raiders quickly withdrew. Throughout these trying months Livingston's force of character prevented widespread public bitterness over constant enemy harassment from diluting the state's commitment to the cause of liberty.

The Statesman

Governor Livingston's greatest contribution to the future republic may well have been his work with the state militia. Livingston saw militia membership as a right, not a duty. He also knew that an effective body of citizen-soldiers eliminated the need for a large standing army, thus keeping the military under the firm control of the civilian government. To that end, he sought to upgrade the quality of state forces, providing them with the best available equipment and training them according to the manuals issued by General von Steuben, Washington's drillmaster. "Our militia," he told von Steuben, "is composed of materials capable of being formed into as good Soldiers as any part of the World can produce; and disciplined upon your plan, would certainly constitute the best & most natural Defense of a republican state, against all hostile Invasion." His clear understanding of the different but equally important roles to be played by militia and regulars was translated through the new Constitution into the nation's laws.

Livingston's wartime experiences convinced him that the Articles of Confederation were inadequate to guide the new nation. In the postwar years he spoke out strongly and repeatedly for the need to grant greater powers to the central government. In 1787 he led his state's delegation to the Constitutional Convention at Philadelphia. Livingston supported the efforts of the assembled delegates to create a new and stronger government despite the likelihood that the result would prove unpopular in a small state like New Jersey that feared domination by its larger neighbors. He put his trust in the belief that reasonable and patriotic men could eventually create a compromise that would protect everyone's interests.

At first committed to the New Jersey Plan, that gave each state an equal voice in the new government, Livingston eventually accepted the Great Compromise, whereby the rights of the states were protected in a Senate that gave equal weight to each while the rights of the majority were recognized in a House of Representatives that reflected the relative population of the states. His own greatest personal compromise came as chairman of the committee that handled the explosive issue of slavery. Bitterly opposed to slavery himself, Livingston nevertheless subordinated his own feelings and hammered out a compromise that assured the Constitution's acceptance by the slave states. He was convinced that the Constitution would make possible the political and legislative processes by which slavery in the longer term could be peacefully eradicated.

After the Convention, Livingston returned home to muster support for the critically important ratification vote. He led that battle, and was gratified by the speed with which his state registered its approval. In 1788, just two years before his death, his alma mater awarded him an honorary doctorate in recognition of his great service.

Livingston was, in the words of a contemporary, "a man of first rate talents, . . . equal to anything, from the extensiveness of his education and genius." In his case, he combined talent with the highest sense of public duty. By heritage an aristocrat, Livingston nevertheless fought with brilliance and selflessness for the rights of his fellow citizens. His career reached its culmination at the Constitutional Convention, where he helped translate the revolutionary idea that power should rest with the people into an enduring reality.

James McHenry

James McHenry, who represented Maryland at the Constitutional Convention, was a recent immigrant to America. Like many of those who would come after, he quickly developed a strong sense of patriotism, which he then demonstrated by volunteering to defend his new homeland. Less than five years after first landing in Philadelphia, McHenry, who included himself among those he called the "sons of freedom," was serving with the Continental forces surrounding Boston. The young Irish immigrant proved to be a strong nationalist, focusing more on the concept of a united America than on loyalty to any one of the three colonies in which he had lived before the Revolution. From the beginning, this nationalistic outlook led him to see "absolute independency" as the goal of the true Patriot. His experiences in the Army, including service on General George Washington's personal staff, convinced him that the only obstacles to nationhood were timidity among the citizenry and "disunion" among the states. Throughout a career of public service that lasted into the second decade of the new republic, he would forcefully and consistently uphold the ideal of a strong central government as embodied in the Constitution as the best guarantee against any such disunity or loss of national purpose in the future.

The Patriot

McHenry was born into a Scots-Irish family in the province of Ulster. Son of a prosperous merchant, he received a classical education in Dublin, an education continued in the New World at the Newark Academy (later the University of Delaware). McHenry, at eighteen, had been the first of his family to immigrate. While his relatives then went about establishing a prosperous import business in the expanding port of Baltimore, McHenry maintained his independent course by turning to the study of medicine. He spent two years in Philadelphia as an apprentice to one of America's foremost physicians, Dr. Benjamin Rush. The young student quickly acquired the skills and knowledge expected of an eighteenth-century doctor, but more important for the Revolutionary cause, he also received an important political education from Rush, one of Pennsylvania's leading opponents of British rule and a future signer of the Declaration of Independence.

McHenry came to accept the proposition that the breach between colonies and mother country could not be healed, and he offered his services to his adopted land when hostilities broke out in New England in 1775. McHenry, still a civilian, joined the American forces participating in the siege of Boston. He worked in the military hospital in Cambridge as a volunteer assistant surgeon, but before long he was asked to accept the demanding assignment of surgeon in one of the hospitals being established in northern New York to care for the wounded in the wake of an abortive American attack on Canada. Before reporting for duty, however, McHenry returned to Philadelphia to collect additional medical supplies.

The Soldier

Before the Continental Congress could confirm McHenry's appointment as an officer in the Hospital Department, Pennsylvania officials, probably at the suggestion of Dr. Rush, selected him to serve instead as the surgeon of a regiment recently raised in the eastern part of that colony by Colonel Robert Magaw. Once again McHenry left Philadelphia for the front, this time as a regular member of the 5th Pennsylvania Battalion.

Unlike other Pennsylvania units that were assigned to the Flying Camp, Washington's mobile reserve force stationed in the northern New Jersey area, the 5th Pennsylvania, as a regular Continental unit, reported directly to New York City. Its mission was to construct and defend Fort Washington, an American outpost near the northern end of Manhattan Island. According to plans developed in Washington's headquarters, this stronghold was to deny the British full access to the city and to the Hudson River. The plans went awry. Overwhelming British and Hessian forces under General William Howe attacked the fort from three directions on the morning of 16 November 1776. Pushing forward despite fierce resistance by the outnumbered garrison, they forced Magaw to surrender. This defeat marked the beginning of a British campaign that would drive Washington back to the Delaware River, and to Valley Forge, the lowest ebb of the Continental Army's military fortunes during the war.

McHenry missed the dramatic American victories at Trenton and Princeton that saved the Patriot cause. He

JAMES McHENRY
Maryland

Birth: 16 November 1753, at Ballymena, County Antrim, Ireland
Death: 3 May 1816, at "Fayetteville," Baltimore County, Maryland
Interment: Westminster Presbyterian Churchyard, Baltimore, Maryland

Pastel, by James Sharples, Sr. (c. 1795); Independence National Historical Park.

was one of five physicians and some 2,000 soldiers who were captured by the British at Fort Washington. After spending some time caring for sick and wounded prisoners of war, he was paroled, in accord with the rules of eighteenth-century warfare, to his home while awaiting exchange. Only in March 1778 was he free to join the Continental Army again, at Valley Forge. There McHenry temporarily served with the Flying Hospital (a kind of Revolutionary War MASH) before coming to General Washington's personal attention. In May 1778 the Commander in Chief selected him to serve as assistant secretary on his staff. McHenry remained on Washington's staff as a volunteer without rank or pay for two and a half years. During that period he saw action in the battles of Monmouth and Springfield, New Jersey, and became a valued member of Washington's immediate "military family," along with men like Henry Knox, Alexander Hamilton, and the Marquis de Lafayette.

McHenry's lifelong friendship with the dynamic Lafayette dated from this experience. Near the end of 1780 he transferred to the Frenchman's staff, a change that led to a commission as a major. He served at Lafayette's side during the climactic campaign of the war. During the winter of 1780 Washington sent his light infantry units under Lafayette south on a forced march to Virginia. Their arrival was to coincide with that of a French fleet from Rhode Island in order to surprise British forces that were disrupting logistical bases established for General Nathanael Greene's Southern Army. Although the British eluded capture, Virginia became a new theater of war when Washington left Lafayette's units in the state to reinforce local militia and sent an additional force of Pennsylvania regulars under General Anthony Wayne.

The stage was set for a major confrontation when Royal troops under General Charles Cornwallis marched north into Virginia. Throughout the summer Lafayette's militia and continentals shadowed Cornwallis and, although greatly outnumbered, engaged the British in minor disruptive actions. In July, for example, McHenry participated in a skirmish at Green Springs, near Jamestown. During this period McHenry's close personal friendship with Governor Thomas Sim Lee of Maryland also paid important dividends, for Lafayette's forces relied heavily on Maryland for logistical support, and McHenry's intercession with Lee ensured prompt delivery of materials to the Frenchman's units.

When the British established a defensive position at

Yorktown, Washington saw an opportunity to win a decisive victory. He quickly moved his main army from New York, as a French fleet from the West Indies arrived to block any British escape by sea. Washington's brilliant concentration of forces trapped Cornwallis. A formal siege of Yorktown culminated with a bayonet attack on British positions during the night of 14 October. Cornwallis' surrender brought the active military phase of the war to an end.

The Statesman

McHenry resigned his commission at the end of 1781 to enter Maryland politics. Elected to the state legislature, he served for thirteen years, using this forum to argue the cause of federalism. Between 1783 and 1786 he sat in the Continental Congress, and in the following year he represented Maryland at the Constitutional Convention in Philadelphia. Although he played no leading part in the deliberations of the Convention, McHenry continued to support the call for a strong central government. His military staff training was reflected in his meticulous notes of the Convention's proceedings—notes that have proved invaluable for generations of American historians.

In 1796 President Washington once again called on his old wartime aide, this time to assume the duties of Secretary of War. McHenry, who would preside over the Army under both Washington and John Adams, was the third of seven Continental soldiers to hold that position. His immediate goal was to transform the isolated western military garrisons into an efficient and economical fighting force capable of protecting the new nation's frontiers against the Indian tribes. During the next two years he largely succeeded in regularizing military procedures, organizing the chaotic military supply system, and subordinating the military establishment to his authority as the civilian Secretary.

In 1798, however, the possibility of war with France brought the Army to a critical period in its history, when the question of establishing a permanently organized fighting force became a topic of much debate in Congress. McHenry took the lead in defending the need to establish a 20,000-man Army to meet the immediate threat. The opposition saw this "provisional" force as nothing less than a large standing army, which they considered inimical to the interests of a free people. A man of McHenry's political and military experience saw the situation differently. To refuse to take adequate military measures, he warned a generally reluctant Congress, "would be to offer up the United States a certain prey to France." His arguments prevailed, and Congress eventually approved the creation of twelve new regiments of regulars.

Although inexperienced in the administration of large military organizations, McHenry struggled valiantly with the task of building a disciplined, professional Army, a task complicated by a separate controversy in regard to civilian control of military affairs. McHenry's dedication to strong central government led him to advocate civilian leadership, a democratic ideal held by many of the citizen-soldiers of the Revolution, including most notably George Washington. But in McHenry's case the concept was put to the practical test as newly appointed generals, including his friend Hamilton and the controversial James Wilkinson, vied to control military appointments and organizational plans for the provisional Army. His own military experience had taught McHenry the importance of the dedicated professional officer, and as Secretary he added his voice to those demanding a military academy to train officers. But his experiences in the Continental Army had also convinced him of the danger of soldiers meddling in the decisions of a democratic government. His forthright stand against his impetuous generals and their political allies not only enhanced the powers of the civilian Secretary of War but also marked McHenry's most important service to his country.

McHenry continued in office for some months after the threat of war with France ended in 1800, but disputes with Adams over the future of the Federalist party finally made his presence in the cabinet untenable. His last years were spent in quiet retirement at his Maryland estate, "Fayetteville," named after his general at Yorktown. As a staunch Federalist, he opposed America's slide into war in 1812, although he lived to see his son follow in his footsteps as a wartime volunteer. Ironically, the son participated in the 1814 defense of the Baltimore fort named for his father, the battle which inspired Francis Scott Key to write the "Star-Spangled Banner."

Thomas Mifflin

Thomas Mifflin, who represented Pennsylvania at the Constitutional Convention, seemed full of contradictions. Although he chose to become a businessman and twice served as the chief logistical officer of the Revolutionary armies, he never mastered his personal finances. A Quaker with strong pacifist beliefs, he helped organize Pennsylvania's military forces at the outset of the Revolution and rose to the rank of major general in the Continental Army. Despite his generally judicious deportment, contemporaries noted his "warm temperament" that led to frequent quarrels, including one with George Washington that had national consequences.

Throughout the twists and turns of a checkered career Mifflin remained true to ideas formulated in his youth. Believing mankind an imperfect species composed of weak and selfish individuals, he placed his trust on the collective judgment of the citizenry. As he noted in his schoolbooks, "There can be no Right to Power, except what is either founded upon, or speedily obtains the hearty Consent of the Body of the People." Mifflin's service—during the Revolution, in the Constitutional Convention, and, more importantly, as governor during the time when the federal partnership between the states and the national government was being worked out—can only be understood in the context of his commitment to these basic principles and his impatience with those who failed to live up to them.

The Patriot

Mifflin was among the fourth generation of his family to live in Philadelphia, where his Quaker forebears had attained high rank. His father served as a city alderman, on the Governor's Council, and as a trustee of the College of Philadelphia (today's University of Pennsylvania). Mifflin attended local grammar schools and graduated in 1760 from the College. Following in his father's footsteps, he then apprenticed himself to an important local merchant, completing his training with a year-long trip to Europe to gain a better insight into markets and trading patterns. In 1765 he formed a partnership in the import and export business with a younger brother.

Mifflin married a distant cousin, and the young couple—witty, intelligent, and wealthy—soon became an ornament in Philadelphia's highest social circles. In 1768 Mifflin joined the American Philosophical Society, serving for two years as its secretary. Membership in other fraternal and charitable organizations soon followed. Associations formed in this manner quickly brought young Mifflin to the attention of Pennsylvania's most important politicians, and led to his first venture into politics. In 1771 he won election as a city warden, and a year later he began the first of four consecutive terms in the colonial legislature.

Mifflin's business experiences colored his political ideas. He was particularly concerned with Parliament's taxation policy and as early as 1765 was speaking out against London's attempt to levy taxes on the colonies. A summer vacation in New England in 1773 brought him in contact with Samuel Adams and other Patriot leaders in Massachusetts, who channeled his thoughts toward open resistance. Parliament's passage of the Coercive Acts in 1774, designed to punish Boston's merchant community for the Tea Party, provoked a storm of protest in Philadelphia. Merchants as well as the common workers who depended on the port's trade for their jobs recognized that punitive acts against one city could be repeated against another. Mifflin helped to organize the town meetings that led to a call for a conference of all the colonies to prepare a unified position.

In the summer of 1774 Mifflin was elected by the legislature to the First Continental Congress. There, his work in the committee that drafted the Continental Association, an organized boycott of English goods adopted by Congress, spread his reputation across America. It also led to his election to the Second Continental Congress, which convened in Philadelphia in the aftermath of the fighting at Lexington and Concord.

The Soldier

Mifflin was prepared to defend his views under arms, and he played a major role in the creation of Philadelphia's military forces. Since the colony lacked a militia, its Patriots turned to volunteers. John Dickinson and Mifflin resurrected the so-called Associators (a volunteer force in the colonial wars, perpetuated by today's 111th Infantry, Pennsylvania Army National Guard). Despite a lack of previous military experience, Mifflin was elected senior major in the city's 3d Battalion, a commission that led to his expulsion from his Quaker

THOMAS MIFFLIN
Pennsylvania

Birth: 10 January 1744, at Philadelphia, Pennsylvania
Death: 20 January 1800, at Lancaster, Pennsylvania
Interment: Trinity Lutheran Church Cemetery, Lancaster, Pennsylvania

Oil, by Charles Willson Peale (1784); Independence National Historical Park.

church.

Mifflin's service in the Second Continental Congress proved short-lived. When Congress created the Continental Army as the national armed force on 14 June 1775, he resigned, along with George Washington, Philip Schuyler, and others, to go on active duty with the regulars. Washington, the Commander in Chief, selected Mifflin, now a major, to serve as one of his aides, but Mifflin's talents and mercantile background led almost immediately to a more challenging assignment. In August, Washington appointed him Quartermaster General of the Continental Army. Washington believed that Mifflin's personal integrity would protect the Army from the fraud and corruption that too often characterized eighteenth-century procurement efforts. Mifflin, in fact, never used his position for personal profit, but rather struggled to eliminate those abuses that did exist in the supply system.

As the Army grew, so did Mifflin's responsibilities. He arranged the transportation required to place heavy artillery on Dorchester Heights, a tactical move that ended the siege of Boston. He also managed the complex logistics of moving troops to meet a British thrust at New York City. Promoted to brigadier general in recognition of his service, Mifflin nevertheless increasingly longed for a field command. In 1776 he persuaded Washington and Congress to transfer him to the infantry. Mifflin led a brigade of Pennsylvania continentals during the early part of the New York City campaign, covering Washington's difficult nighttime evacuation of Brooklyn. Troubles in the Quartermaster's Department demanded his return to his old assignment shortly afterwards, a move which bitterly disappointed him. He also brooded over Nathanael Greene's emergence as Washington's principal adviser, a role which Mifflin coveted.

Mifflin's last military action came during the Trenton-Princeton campaign. As the Army's position in northern New Jersey started to crumble in late November 1776, Washington sent him to Philadelphia to lay the groundwork for a restoration of American fortunes. Mifflin played a vital, though often overlooked, role in mobilizing the Associators to reinforce the continentals and in orchestrating the complex resupply of the tattered American forces once they reached safety on the Pennsylvania side of the Delaware River. These measures gave Washington the resources to counterattack. Mifflin saw action with the Associators at Princeton. His service in the campaign resulted in his promotion to major general.

Mifflin tried to cope with the massive logistical workload caused by Congress' decision in 1777 to expand the Continental Army. Congress also approved a new organization of the Quartermaster's Department, but Mifflin had not fully implemented the reforms and changes before Philadelphia fell. Dispirited by the loss of his home and suffering from poor health, Mifflin now attempted to resign. He also openly criticized Greene's advice to Washington. These ill-timed actions created a perception among the staff at Valley Forge that Mifflin was no longer loyal to Washington.

The feuding among Washington's staff and a debate in Congress over war policy led to the so-called Conway Cabal. A strong faction in Congress insisted that success in the Revolution could come only through heavy reliance on the militia. Washington and most of the Army's leaders believed that victory depended on perfecting the training and organization of the continentals so that they could best the British at traditional European warfare. This debate came to a head during the winter of 1777–78, and centered around the reorganization of the Board of War, Congress' administrative arm for dealing with the Army. Mifflin was appointed to the Board because of his technical expertise, but his political ties embroiled him in an unsuccessful effort to use the Board to dismiss Washington. This incident ended Mifflin's influence in military affairs and brought about his own resignation in 1779.

The Statesman

Mifflin lost little time in resuming his political career. While still on active duty in late 1778 he won reelection to the state legislature. In 1780 Pennsylvania again sent him to the Continental Congress, and that body elected him its president in 1783. In an ironic moment, "President" Mifflin accepted Washington's formal resignation as Commander in Chief. He also presided over the ratification of the Treaty of Paris, which ended the Revolution. Mifflin returned to the state legislature in 1784, where he served as speaker. In 1788 he began the first of two one-year terms as Pennsylvania's president of council, or governor.

Although Mifflin's fundamental view of government changed little during these years of intense political activity, his war experiences made him more sensitive to the need for order and control. As Quartermaster General, he had witnessed firsthand the weakness of Congress in dealing with feuding state governments over vitally needed supplies, and he concluded that it was impractical to try to govern through a loose confederation. Pennsylvania's constitution, adopted in 1776, very narrowly defined the powers conceded to Congress, and during the next decade Mifflin emerged as one of the leaders calling for changes in those limitations in order to strike a balanced apportionment of political power between the states and the national government.

Such a system was clearly impossible under the Articles of Confederation, and Mifflin had the opportunity to press his arguments when he represented Pennsylvania at the Constitutional Convention in 1787. Although his dedication to Federalist principles never wavered during the deliberations in Philadelphia, his greatest service to the Constitution came later when, as the nationalists' primary tactician, he helped convince his fellow Pennsylvanians to ratify it.

Elected governor under the new state constitution in 1790, Mifflin served for nine years, a period highlighted by his constant effort to minimize partisan politics in order to build a consensus. Although disagreeing with the federal government's position on several issues, Mifflin fully supported Washington's efforts to maintain the national government's primacy. He used militia, for example, to control French privateers who were trying to use Philadelphia as a base in violation of American neutrality. He also commanded Pennsylvania's contingent called out in 1794 to deal with the so-called Whiskey Rebellion, even though he was in sympathy with the economic plight of the aroused western farmers.

In these incidents Mifflin regarded the principle of the common good as more important than transitory issues or local concerns. This same sense of nationalism led him to urge the national government to adopt policies designed to strengthen the country both economically and politically. He led a drive for internal improvements to open the west to eastern ports. He prodded the government to promote "National felicity and opulence . . . by encouraging industry, disseminating knowledge, and raising our social compact upon the permanent foundations of liberty and virtue." In his own state he devised a financial system to fund such programs. He also took very seriously his role as commander of the state militia, devoting considerable time to its training so that it would be able to reinforce the Regular Army.

Mifflin retired in 1799, his health debilitated and his personal finances in disarray. In a gesture both apt and kind, the commander of the Philadelphia militia (perpetuated by today's 111th Infantry and 103d Engineer Battalion, Pennsylvania Army National Guard) resigned so that the new governor might commission Mifflin as the major general commanding the state's senior contingent. Voters also returned him one more time to the state legislature. He died during the session and was buried at state expense, since his estate was too small to cover funeral costs.

Gouverneur Morris

Gouverneur Morris, who represented Pennsylvania at the Convention in Philadelphia in 1787, was the author of much of the Constitution. The noble phrases of that document's Preamble—"We the People of the United States, in order to form a more perfect Union"—sprang from his gifted mind, and, like the finely wrought clauses that followed, clearly mirrored his personal political philosophy. Morris was perhaps the most outspoken nationalist among the Founding Fathers. Although born into a world of wealth and aristocratic values, he had come to champion the concept of a free citizenry united in an independent nation. In an age when most still thought of themselves as citizens of their sovereign and separate states, Morris was able to articulate a clear vision of a new and powerful union. He was, as Theodore Roosevelt later put it, "emphatically an American first."

Morris witnessed two of history's greatest revolutions, and both had a profound influence on his idea of government. His service as a soldier and as a key member of the Continental Congress during the American Revolution convinced him that a strong central government was needed to preserve and enhance the liberties and boundless opportunities won in the war. As ambassador to Paris during the cataclysmic French Revolution, he came to fear the excesses of power that could be perpetrated in the name of liberty. Influenced by these events, he would later reject what he saw as unjustified assertions of authority by his own government.

Morris was an indifferent politician. His career suffered repeatedly from his frankness and impulsive and caustic tongue. Nevertheless, his personal contribution to the cause of union exceeded that of many of his colleagues. Devoted to the ideal of a united country, he fought wholeheartedly for it despite his certainty that the new political and social order he was helping to shape would have little use for patricians like himself.

The Patriot

The Morris family of New York, descended from Welsh soldiers, represented the closest thing to an aristocracy that could be found in colonial America. Morris' father had inherited a large manor in Westchester County, but his economic and political interests extended to nearby colonies as well. He raised two families. Gouverneur, the only son of the second marriage, knew that he would inherit only a small share of the estate and would have to work to retain the comforts and privileges of his forebears.

Morris attended local preparatory schools, and then enrolled at King's College (now Columbia University) in New York City at the age of twelve. Here the young scholar, displaying flashes of academic brilliance, along with a streak of laziness, graduated in 1768. His speech on receiving a master's degree in 1771 reflected the ideals of his Enlightenment education as well as his own emerging political philosophy when he asserted that "love of country, for a British subject, is based on the solid foundation of liberty."

Morris was admitted to the bar after three years of study with William Smith, one of New York's leading legal minds and a strong opponent of British policies toward the colonies. The new lawyer's social status, combined with his natural wit and aristocratic grace, gave him ready access to the colony's leaders. His mentor, who had successfully instilled in Morris a greater sense of mental discipline, urged him to exploit these contacts and introduced him to rising young Patriots like John Jay and Alexander Hamilton.

Morris' political career began in 1775 when he was elected to represent the family manor in New York's Provincial Congress, an extralegal assembly organized by the Patriots to direct the transition to independence. He soon discovered that the cauldron of revolutionary events imposed a personal choice from which there could be no drawing back. Class identity and family ties should have inclined him away from revolution. Morris' half-brother was a senior officer in the British Army, his mother remained a staunch Loyalist, and Smith, now with almost a father's influence, has precipitously abandoned the Patriot cause when he saw it heading toward independence. Like many of his contemporaries, however, Morris adhered to the principle that, as he put it, "in every society the members have a right to the utmost liberty that can be enjoyed consistent with the general safety."

The Soldier

Morris could have avoided military service. He was physically handicapped—scalding water had badly dam-

GOUVERNEUR MORRIS
Pennsylvania

Birth: 31 January 1752, at "Morrisania," Westchester County, New York
Death: 6 November 1816, at Morrisania, New York
Interment: St. Anne's Episcopal Church Cemetery, The Bronx, New York

Pastel, by James Sharples, Sr. (1810); Independence National Historical Park.

aged his right arm in a childhood accident—and as a legislator he was automatically exempted from militia duty. But he viewed active service as a moral obligation and joined one of the special militia companies proliferating in New York City. These units, predecessors of the modern National Guard, trained in uniforms the members purchased themselves and acted as the city's Minutemen. By early 1776 they formed two complete regiments. Morris was asked to serve as second in command in his regiment, but withdrew when it declined transfer to the Continental Army.

Morris' major contribution to the Patriot cause lay in the political realm. As a member of the Provincial Congress, he concentrated on the formidable task of transforming the colony into an independent state. The new state's constitution was largely his work. He also displayed hitherto unsuspected financial skills, emerging as chairman of the legislature's Ways and Means Committee, which was charged with funding the state's war effort. This newfound interest in detail and his willingness to undertake hard work led to numerous other assignments, including revitalizing the militia and restraining suspected Loyalists. His knack for providing a political solution to military problems led to a series of special missions. In May 1776 the state picked him to coordinate defense measures with both George Washington's main army and the Continental Congress. When the British invaded New York City and overran much of Westchester County in the fall, Morris found himself a refugee. His mother, whom he would not see for seven years, turned the family estate over to the enemy for military use. During this campaign his old regiment saw duty, and Morris probably rejoined it as a volunteer.

In 1777 he served as a member of the New York Committee of Safety. In this capacity Morris visited the northern front in the aftermath of the British capture of Fort Ticonderoga to coordinate state support of the continentals operating in that area, and then journeyed to Washington's headquarters to plead for reinforcements. In October he again took to the field as a militia volunteer, serving as an aide to Governor George Clinton during the unsuccessful American defense of the strategic Hudson Highlands fortifications.

Since his home was in enemy-occupied territory, Morris was ineligible to seek election to the new legislature. He rejected appointment to that body as an undemocratic procedure, but agreed to serve as a delegate to the Continental Congress. His major contribution to the

American military effort began on 20 January 1778, the day he took his seat in Congress, when he was selected to serve on a committee being sent to Valley Forge to coordinate military reforms with Washington. The sight of the troops in the snow—he called them "an army of skeletons . . . naked, starved, sick, discouraged"—shocked him, for he considered the continentals "the heart of America." Morris threw himself into this organizational work, serving as the Continental Army's spokesman in Congress. His support for Washington, Nathanael Greene, and Frederick von Steuben contributed directly to the success of the training and structural reforms thrashed out in the snows of Valley Forge and in the meeting rooms of Congress.

Other assignments quickly established him as a leading proponent of stronger central authority, but these nationalist views were more advanced than the thinking of most of his New York constituents. This growing estrangement, compounded by his often unstatesmanlike frankness and sarcasm, cost him reelection to Congress in 1779. Political rejection led him to resettle in Philadelphia, where he took up the life of lawyer and merchant. His interest in financial matters led to an association with the noted Patriot financier Robert Morris (no relation), and when the latter was appointed in 1781 as Minister of Finance—a sort of treasury secretary under the Articles of Confederation—Gouverneur Morris became his assistant. Together the two men participated in the informal cabinet system that arose during the closing years of the war. Through their efforts, Congress' finances were stabilized and logistical arrangements were successfully made for the crucial Yorktown campaign. In 1782 Morris introduced the idea of decimal coinage (he invented the word "cent") that later became the basis of the nation's currency.

The Statesman

During the years immediately following the Revolution, Morris continued to live and work in Philadelphia, although he visited the family estate and reconciled with his mother. In fact, he made a special effort to encourage former Loyalists to participate in political affairs, arguing that as Americans they should cast their lot with the new nation. Although he remained a leading spokesman for nationalist issues, he seemed genuinely surprised when the Pennsylvania legislature selected him to represent the state at the Constitutional Convention.

The sessions of the Convention held in Philadelphia during the summer and early fall of 1787 represented the high point of Morris' public career. He went to the Convention viewing himself not just as a delegate from a particular state or even as an American, but, in his own words, "in some degree as a representative of the whole human race." For once in his life he avoided the bluntness and sarcasm that so often had diluted his usefulness to the cause of nationalism. He employed his considerable social and verbal skills to help smooth over issues that threatened to divide the delegates, and then subtly used his position as primary draftsman to strengthen the final version of the Constitution (much as Jefferson had done as author of the Declaration of Independence). During the Convention debates, he defended ideas that had been associated with him ever since he had helped write the New York constitution in 1776: religious liberty, opposition to slavery, the right of property as the foundation of society, the rule of law, and the consent of the governed as the basis of government. His aims were ambitious and reflected his vision of a government that would serve as an example to the rest of the world.

Morris' later career never matched the level attained at the Convention. In 1789 he left for Europe on business, where he remained for a decade. During that time he twice served the new government. In 1790 he acted as a diplomatic agent for President Washington in London to resolve issues left unsettled by the peace treaty. He later replaced Jefferson as ambassador to France, then in the throes of its own revolution. Neither mission proved successful, although he did display great personal courage as the only diplomat who refused to flee Paris during the bloody Reign of Terror.

Morris returned to New York in 1798, settling in the family manor that he had purchased from an older brother. He became active in the Federalist party, allying himself with his friend Alexander Hamilton. The party secured his appointment to fill an unexpired term in the United States Senate, but he lacked the political popularity to win the position in his own right at the next election. Once again a private citizen, he helped lead the effort to create the Erie Canal, a project that dramatically altered the history of western development.

During the last decade of his life Morris became increasingly disenchanted with the policies of President Jefferson and his successors. Although he supported the purchase of the vast Louisiana Territory, he was particularly virulent in his condemnation of the government's restrictive economic policies and controls during the War of 1812. But no matter how angry he became with the new generation of political leaders, he never lost sight of the values of nationhood. In 1802 Morris summarized his best sentiments in a letter to fellow signer John Dickinson: "In adopting a republican form of government, I not only took it as a man does his wife, for better for worse, but what few men do with their wives, I took it knowing all its bad qualities."

Charles Pinckney

Charles Pinckney, who represented South Carolina at the Constitutional Convention, was an ardent apostle of the rights of man. He dedicated his considerable political and legal talents to the establishment of a strong national government so that, as he put it to his fellow South Carolinians, "the effects of the Revolution may never cease to operate," but continue to serve as an example to others "until they have unshackled all the nations that have firmness to resist the fetters of despotism."

These ringing sentiments, perhaps easily explained as the idealism of a youthful veteran of the Revolution, nonetheless represented a very serious concern on Pinckney's part that his fellow citizens were growing complacent since their victory over Britain. While many politicians, enjoying the fruits of independence, celebrated the sovereignty of the individual states, Pinckney was among those who perceived a clear and present danger in allowing a weak confederation of the states to lead the new nation that had emerged from the Revolutionary War. He worked unceasingly for an effective and permanent union of the states because his own experiences in the Revolution and as a member of the Continental Congress had reinforced his conviction that only a strong central government could provide the economic and military strength essential to prosperity and security. Unlike some of his prominent colleagues, Pinckney saw little to fear in a powerful government. He agreed with the Federalists that the rights of the citizen would be protected under the Constitution since it recognized that the government's power came from the people and that the government remained in all things accountable to the people.

The Patriot

The Pinckneys were one of South Carolina's oldest and most distinguished families, and successive generations made a significant contribution to the development of the new nation. The family had arrived in America in 1692, and Pinckney's great-grandfather, a wealthy English gentleman, quickly established an enduring base of political and economic power. Pinckney's father, a rich planter and lawyer with an extensive practice in Charleston, rose to the rank of colonel in the state militia and was a prominent leader within the colonial assembly.

Unlike his famous cousins—and fellow Patriots—Charles Cotesworth and Thomas Pinckney, Charles Pinckney was not educated abroad. Instead, his parents arranged for his private tutoring under the direction of a noted South Carolina scholar and author, Dr. David Oliphant. Through Oliphant's instruction, the new political currents circulating around Pinckney's cousins at Oxford and at the Inns of Court also touched the young man in Charleston. Oliphant was among those Enlightenment scholars who were successfully and eloquently instilling in their students a political philosophy that viewed government as a solemn social contract between the people and their sovereign, with each possessing certain inalienable rights that government was obliged to protect. If government failed to fulfill the contract, the people had a right to form a new government.

Oliphant also imparted to Pinckney a love of scholarship that led over the years to a mastery of five languages, the accumulation of a personal library of over two thousand volumes, and, at the age of thirty, to an honorary degree from the College of New Jersey (now Princeton University). When Pinckney left Oliphant's care, he concluded his formal education by studying law under his father's personal direction. He was admitted to the South Carolina bar in 1779 while still in his twenty-first year.

Pinckney, however, never saw a career in the law as his major vocation. Coming of age in the midst of the Revolution, the gifted young scholar turned naturally to politics. His neighbors obliged by electing him to a seat in the South Carolina legislature. But where the elder Pinckney had been a cautious and somewhat hesitant member of various legislative and administrative bodies that led South Carolina into the Revolution, the son was a wholehearted Patriot. Again unlike his father, who would later repudiate the Revolution and seek a Royal pardon, Pinckney never wavered in his dedication to the cause.

The Soldier

By late 1778 the King's ministers found themselves facing new difficulties in North America. George Washington's main force of increasingly well trained and well supplied continentals had frustrated a series of British

CHARLES PINCKNEY
South Carolina

Birth: 26 October 1757, at Charleston, South Carolina
Death: 29 October 1824, at Charleston, South Carolina
Interment: St. Philip's Episcopal Churchyard, Charleston, South Carolina

Oil on canvas, attributed to Gilbert Stuart (1786); New York State Office of Parks, Recreation and Historic Preservation.

generals to produce a virtual military stalemate. France's entry into the war on the colonial side had also forced the Royal Army to stretch resources to meet contingencies in other areas, not just in North America.

British leaders were forced to adopt a new plan of action, their "southern strategy." They proposed to attack northward from a base of operations in Florida, while continuing to tie down Washington's main force around Philadelphia. They would conquer the southern states one at a time, using local Loyalists to garrison newly captured areas as the Royal forces pushed ever further north. The first phase in this new plan began with a lightning attack on Savannah, which British forces captured in December 1778.

With the enemy approaching, Pinckney lost no time in taking up arms. In 1779 he accepted election as a lieutenant in the Charleston Regiment of South Carolina's militia and quickly learned the responsibilities that went with serving as a citizen-soldier. His regiment turned out with other state units to meet and repulse the first tentative British move up from Georgia that summer, and then joined in a counterattack. It was an international campaign. French warships and troops under the command of the Comte d'Estaing sailed north from operations in the Caribbean in the early fall of 1779 to link up with a combined force of Continental regulars and mobilized militiamen under the command of Major General Benjamin Lincoln. These forces met outside Savannah and began a formal siege of the surrounded British garrison. Unlike the later victory at Yorktown, time ran out on the allies at Savannah. Under pressure to return to France, d'Estaing persuaded Lincoln to launch a direct assault on the enemy's earthworks. Pinckney was in the heart of the doomed attack and witnessed the heavy casualties that resulted.

The British soon reinforced the garrison, and by early 1780 Lincoln's men had been pushed back to Charleston. Redcoats, Hessians, and Loyalists then began a siege of their own, pounding the city with heavy artillery and choking off its food supply. On 12 May, Lincoln's army surrendered in what was the single worst defeat suffered by Americans in the Revolution. Unlike the continentals, who were imprisoned in a disease-ridden camp in Charleston harbor, Pinckney and his fellow citizen-soldiers were allowed to return home after promising not to fight again until they were formally exchanged. Because of his family's prominence and his own political importance, Pinckney came under intense pressure from the British, who hoped to induce him to renounce the Patriot cause. But the young officer resisted the British propaganda, and with the tide of war turning against them in 1781, his captors revoked his parole and incarcerated him—and other militia officers who refused to swear allegiance to King George—with the Continental officers. A general exchange of prisoners finally secured his repatriation.

The Statesman

Though retaining his position in the militia, Pinckney retired from active service to resume his duties in the South Carolina legislature, where he continued to represent various districts until 1796. Meanwhile, his colleagues called on him in 1784 to represent the state in the Continental Congress, a post he held for three successive terms. Pinckney's service in the postwar Continental Congress served to reinforce the lessons he had learned as a militiaman during the Revolution—that the problems facing America were too large to be met by the states individually but demanded the close cooperation of all the states if they were to be overcome. He pressed for measures that would strengthen the central government, traveling widely to preach the need for concerted action, especially in regard to commerce and the discharge of war debts. In 1786 he was among those in Congress to call for a strengthening of the federal authority to raise revenues, and in 1787 he led the fight for the appointment of a "general committee" to amend the Articles of Confederation, a move that led directly to the Constitutional Convention.

Chosen to represent South Carolina at the Convention, Pinckney arrived in Philadelphia with many specific proposals in hand. In fact, he was one of several members who submitted draft constitutions for the Convention's deliberation. Although the second youngest of those who would sign the Constitution, Pinckney stood out as one of the most active members of the Convention—in formulating working procedures, in attending committee sessions, and in speaking frequently and convincingly during the long process of hammering out compromises. Over thirty of the Constitution's provisions can be traced directly to his pen, and his personal experience in the Revolution clearly influenced his support of others. Among the more important issues for which he fought was the subordination of the military to civil authority. This principle was made explicit in the provision that declared the President Commander in Chief and retained for Congress, the branch of government most directly representing the will of the people, the power to declare war and maintain military forces. Defending his position on this sensitive subject, Pinckney once expressed to South Carolina's voters his inability to understand how anyone, considering the nation's recent experiences, could fail to perceive the need for "regular military forces." Only the timid would oppose it, he concluded, for although the Constitution made the President the Commander in Chief, it also guaranteed that "he can neither raise nor support forces by his own authority." Pinckney also tried, unsuccessfully, to include in the Constitution some explicit guarantees concerning trial by jury and freedom of the press—measures that would later be enshrined in the Bill of Rights.

Pinckney returned to South Carolina to serve as the floor manager for the nationalist forces in the state's convention that ratified the Constitution in 1788, and then chaired a second assembly that drafted a new state constitution along the lines laid out in Philadelphia. In between, he won the first of several terms as governor.

Although Pinckney associated in Philadelphia with many future leaders of the Federalist party, his nationalist sentiments were more compatible with those expressed by Thomas Jefferson and James Madison. As a result, he served as the manager in South Carolina of Jefferson's successful campaign for President in 1800 and supported Jefferson's program during a brief term in the United States Senate before resigning in 1801 to become ambassador to Spain, where he helped negotiate the Louisiana Purchase.

Pinckney returned home in 1804 to resume an active political career in the state legislature and, in 1806, as governor for a fourth term. As governor he supported an amendment to the state constitution to increase representation from the frontier regions and pressed for measures that would eventually lead to universal white male suffrage. Pinckney retired from politics in 1814 to attend to his personal finances, which had been eroded by years of absence on public service, and to promote a number of educational and charitable endeavors. But in 1818 he responded to the pleas of his political allies and ran for office one last time, winning a seat in the House of Representatives.

Few Founding Fathers could match Pinckney's record of service to the nation and his state. Nor were many driven by so strong and clear a political philosophy. "We have already taught some of the oldest and wisest nations to explore their rights as men," he once told his fellow citizens. The idea that a free citizenry should control its own destiny through a strong, elected government had served as the consistent guiding principle in the long and fruitful career of this citizen-soldier and statesman.

Charles Cotesworth Pinckney

Charles Cotesworth Pinckney, who represented South Carolina at the Constitutional Convention, was an American aristocrat. Like other first families of South Carolina, whose wealth and social prominence could be traced to the seventeenth century, the Pinckneys maintained close ties with the mother country and actively participated in the Royal colonial government. Nevertheless, when armed conflict threatened, Pinckney rejected Loyalist appeals and embraced the Patriot cause. Pragmatically, his decision represented an act of allegiance to the mercantile-planter class of South Carolina's seaboard, which deeply resented Parliament's attempt to institute political and economic control over the colonies. Yet Pinckney's choice also had a philosophical dimension. It placed him among a small group of wealthy and powerful southerners whose profound sense of public duty obliged them to risk everything in defense of their state and the rights of its citizens. In Pinckney's case this sense of public responsibility was intensified by his determination to assume the mantle of political and military leadership traditionally worn by members of his family.

Balancing this allegiance to his native state, Pinckney also became a forceful exponent of nationalism during the Revolutionary War. Unlike many of his contemporaries, who generously responded only when their own states were in danger, Pinckney quickly came to grasp the necessity for military cooperation on a national scale. No state was truly safe, he reasoned, unless all the states were made safe. This belief, the product of his service in the Continental Army, easily translated into a spirited defense of strong national government after the war.

The Patriot

As a boy, Pinckney witnessed firsthand the close relationship between the colonial elite and the British. His father was the colony's chief justice and also served as a member of its Royal Council; his mother was famous in her own right for introducing the cultivation of indigo, which rapidly became a major cash crop in South Carolina. In 1753 the family moved to London where the elder Pinckney served as the colony's agent, in effect, as a lobbyist protecting colonial interests in political and commercial matters. Charles Cotesworth Pinckney enrolled in the famous Westminster preparatory school, and he—with his brother Thomas—remained in England to complete his education when the family returned to America in 1758. After graduating from Christ Church College at Oxford, he studied law at London's famous Middle Temple. He was admitted to the English bar in 1769, but he continued his education for another year, studying botany and chemistry in France and briefly attending the famous French military academy at Caen.

Returning to South Carolina after an absence of sixteen years, Pinckney quickly threw himself into the commercial and political life of the colony. To supplement an income derived from plantations, he launched a successful career as a lawyer. He became a vestryman and warden in the Episcopal church and joined the socially elite 1st Regiment of South Carolina militia, which promptly elected him as lieutenant. In 1770 he won a seat for the first time in the state legislature, and in 1773 he served briefly as a regional attorney general. During this period he married Sarah Middleton, the daughter and sister of South Carolina political leaders who, respectively, would serve in the Continental Congress and sign the Declaration of Independence.

When war between the colonies and the mother country finally erupted in 1775, Pinckney cast aside his close ties with England and South Carolina's Royal colonial government to stand with the Patriots. He served in the Provincial Congresses that transformed South Carolina from Royal colony to independent state and in the Council of Safety that supervised affairs when the legislature was not in session. During this period Pinckney played an especially important role in those legislative committees that organized the state's military defenses.

The Soldier

Directing the organization of military units from the relative safety of the state legislature did not satisfy Pinckney's sense of public obligation. Going beyond his previous militia service, he now volunteered as a full-time regular officer in the first Continental Army unit organized in South Carolina. As a senior company commander, Pinckney raised and led the elite Grenadiers of the 1st South Carolina Regiment. He participated in the successful defense of Charleston in June 1776, when

CHARLES COTESWORTH PINCKNEY
South Carolina

Birth: 25 February 1746, at Charleston, South Carolina
Death: 16 August 1825, at Charleston, South Carolina
Interment: St. Michael's Episcopal Church Cemetery, Charleston, South Carolina

Oil on canvas, by Henry Benbridge (c. 1773), in uniform of a militia lieutenant; National Portrait Gallery.

British forces under General Sir Henry Clinton staged an amphibious attack on the state capital. Later in 1776 Pinckney took command of the regiment, with the rank of full colonel, a position he retained to the end of the war. A strong disciplinarian, he also understood the importance of troop motivation, especially when his men were forced to serve for long periods under dangerous and stressful conditions.

Following the successful repulse of General Clinton's forces in 1776, the southern states enjoyed a hiatus in the fighting while the British Army concentrated on operations in the northern and middle states. Dissatisfied with remaining in what had become a backwater of the war, Pinckney set out to join Washington near Philadelphia. He arrived in 1777, just in time to participate in the important military operations centering around Brandywine and Germantown. Pinckney's sojourn on Washington's staff was especially significant to his development as a national leader after the war. It allowed him to associate with key officers of the Continental Army, men like Alexander Hamilton and James McHenry, who, beginning as military comrades, would become important political allies in the later fight for a strong national government. The opportunity to form such far-reaching political alliances seldom occurred for other Continental officers from the deep south.

In 1778 Pinckney returned to South Carolina to resume command of his own regiment just as the state experienced a new threat from the British. Pinckney's 1st South Carolina joined with other Continental and militia units from several states in a successful repulse of an invasion by a force of Loyalist militia and British regulars based in Florida. But disaster ensued when a counterattack bogged down before the Patriots could reach St. Augustine. The American Army suffered severe logistical problems and then a disintegration of the force itself, as senior officers bickered among themselves while disease decimated the units. Only half of the American soldiers survived to return home.

At the end of 1778 the British shifted their attention to the southern theater of operations. Their new strategy called for their regular troops to sweep north, while Loyalist units remained behind to serve as occupying forces. To frustrate this plan, the Continental Congress dispatched Major General Benjamin Lincoln to South Carolina to reorganize the army in the Southern Department. Lincoln placed Pinckney in command of one of his Continental brigades. In that capacity Pinckney participated in the unsuccessful assault on Savannah by the Americans and their French allies in October 1779, and then in a gallant but equally unsuccessful defense of Charleston in 1780. The capture of Charleston gave the British their greatest victory, and in May Pinckney, along with the rest of Lincoln's army, became a prisoner of war.

The victors made a distinction in the treatment of prisoners. They allowed the militiamen to go home on parole while they imprisoned the continentals. Pinckney was one of the ranking officers in the prison camp established by Clinton on Haddrell's Point in Charleston Harbor. There he played a key role in frustrating British efforts to subvert the loyalty of the captured troops, who suffered terribly from disease and privation. When an effort was made to wean Pinckney himself from the Patriot cause, he scornfully turned on his captors with words that became widely quoted throughout the country: "If I had a vein that did not beat with the love of my Country, I myself would open it. If I had a drop of blood that could flow dishonourable, I myself would let it out."

Pinckney was finally freed in 1782 under a general exchange of prisoners. By that time the fighting had ended, but he remained on active duty until the southern regiments were disbanded in November 1783, receiving a brevet promotion to brigadier general in recognition of his long and faithful service to the Continental Army.

The Statesman

Pinckney turned his attention to his law practice and plantations at the end of the Revolution, seeking to recover from serious financial losses suffered during his period of active service. He continued to represent the citizens of the Charleston area in the lower house of the legislature, however, a task he willingly carried out until 1790. Once again he became active in the state militia, rising to the rank of major general and commanding one of South Carolina's two militia divisions. During these years he also endured personal tragedy: his wife died in 1784, and he was wounded the following year in a duel with Daniel Huger, an event that would later lead him to advocate laws against dueling.

Pinckney made no secret of his concern over what he saw as a dangerous drift in national affairs. Freed of the threat of British invasion, the states appeared content to pursue their own parochial concerns. Pinckney was one of those leaders of national vision who preached that the promises of the Revolution could never be realized unless the states banded together for their mutual political, economic, and military well-being. In recognition of his forceful leadership, South Carolina chose him to represent the state at the Constitutional Convention that met in Philadelphia in 1787. There he joined Washington and other nationalist leaders whom he had met during the Pennsylvania campaign. Pinckney agreed with them that the nation needed a strong central government, but he also worked for a carefully designed system of checks and balances to protect the citizen from the tyranny so often encountered in Europe. When he returned to Charleston, he worked diligently to secure South Carolina's ratification of the new instrument of government. In 1790 he then participated in a convention that drafted a new state constitution modeled on the work accomplished in Philadelphia.

Retiring from politics in 1790, Pinckney devoted himself to various religious and charitable works, including the establishment of a state university, strengthening of Charleston's library system, and the promotion of scientific agriculture. He repeatedly declined President Washington's offer of high political office, but in 1796 he finally agreed to serve as ambassador to France.

Pinckney's appointment signaled the beginning of one of the new nation's first international crises. The French government rejected his credentials, and then—in the so-called XYZ Affair—the leaders of the French Revolution demanded a bribe before agreeing to open negotiations about French interference with American shipping. Exploding at this affront to America's national honor, Pinckney broke off all discussion and returned home, where President John Adams appointed him to one of the highest posts in the new Provisional Army which Congress had voted to raise in response to the diplomatic rupture with France. As a major general, Pinckney commanded all forces south of Maryland, but his active military service abruptly ended in the summer of 1800 when a peaceful solution to the "Quasi-War" between France and the United States was successfully negotiated.

Despite his earlier intention to retire, Pinckney once again became deeply involved in national and state politics. He ran unsuccessfully for Vice President on the Federalist ticket in 1800 and was later defeated in presidential races won by Thomas Jefferson and James Madison. He also served for two terms in the South Carolina senate. Until the end Pinckney remained a Federalist of the moderate stamp, seeking to preserve a balance between state and national powers and responsibilities. His tomb bears an inscription that captures the essence of his loyalty to the highest national aspirations and standards of his period: "One of the founders of the American Republic. In war he was a companion in arms and friend of Washington. In peace he enjoyed his unchanging confidence."

Richard Dobbs Spaight

Throughout his short life Richard Dobbs Spaight, who represented North Carolina in the Constitutional Convention, exhibited a marked devotion to the ideals heralded by the Revolution. The nephew of a Royal governor, possessed of all the advantages that accompanied such rank and political access, Spaight nevertheless fought for the political and economic rights of his fellow citizens, first on the battlefield against the forces of an authoritarian Parliament and later in state and national legislatures against those who he felt sought excessive government control over the lives of the people. The preservation of liberty was his political lodestar.

Always an ardent nationalist, Spaight firmly supported the cause of effective central government. In this, he reflected a viewpoint common among veterans of the Revolution: that only a close union of all the states could preserve the liberties won by the cooperation of all the colonies. At the same time, Spaight believed that to guarantee the free exercise of these liberties, the powers of the state must be both limited and strictly defined. He therefore advocated constitutional provisions at the Convention that would protect the rights of the small states against the political power of their more populous neighbors, just as he later would fight for a constitutionally defined bill of rights to defend the individual citizen against the powers of government.

The Patriot

Spaight's political ideas were formed during a youth spent outside his native North Carolina. Following the death of his parents in 1767, the boy sailed to Ireland to be raised and educated among his Anglo-Irish relatives. This experience, which would include matriculation at the University of Glasgow, thrust the young colonial into the intellectual ferment swirling around the philosophers of the Enlightenment. These men taught that government was a solemn social contract between the people and their sovereign, with each party possessing certain inalienable rights. Like many of their American counterparts, the Anglo-Irish politicians considered themselves Englishmen with all the ancient rights and privileges such citizenship conferred and were quick to oppose any abridgment of those rights by Parliament. But while the Irish had been able to retain home rule, the American colonies were finding the power of their popular assemblies increasingly curtailed by a Parliament anxious to end an era of "salutary neglect." The contrast was not lost on young Spaight. The Declaration of Independence found a sympathetic audience in Ireland, and Spaight's loyalty to the Patriot cause only increased with the news in 1777 that North Carolina units had participated in the battle of Brandywine.

In his twentieth year Spaight made his own private declaration of independence from the British sovereign. He traveled to the Continent to secure passage for the dangerous trip to America. Successfully evading the blockading British fleet, he arrived back in North Carolina in early 1778 and promptly offered his services to Governor Richard Caswell. Caswell, who under the state constitution also served as commander in chief of the militia, appointed the well-educated, socially prominent patriot as his aide-de-camp. In this capacity Spaight helped organize the mobilization of North Carolina's militia in 1778 and again in 1779.

Despite the increasingly democratic inclinations of the age, family and fortune still counted heavily in the political life of the North Carolina seaboard. Spaight's uncle, Arthur Dobbs, whose name Spaight proudly and conspicuously bore, had been a highly popular Royal governor. His father, a popular Royal official in his own right, was North Carolina's treasurer and later a member of the Royal Governor's Council, the executive committee that directed the affairs of the colony. The Spaight family enjoyed extensive properties in the mercantile-planter region of Pamlico Sound. These advantages brought with them a traditional deference, especially when combined with young Spaight's patriotic ardor, and made the newly returned native son a natural choice for hometown voters. In 1779 the citizens of Newbern elected him to the state legislature, where he would remain for nearly a decade, including one term as speaker. As a legislator the young man quickly won a reputation for conscientiousness and industry, especially for his work in committees that dealt with militia and financial matters. Although he lacked the oratorical gifts in an age that set great store on such abilities, Spaight quickly developed a facility in the equally valuable art of compromise. This knack of reconciling the political differences of his colleagues would later stand him in good stead in the national political arena.

RICHARD DOBBS SPAIGHT
North Carolina

Birth: 25 March 1758, at Newbern, North Carolina
Death: 6 September 1802, at Newbern, North Carolina
Interment: "Clermont," near Newbern, North Carolina

Pastel, attributed to James Sharples, Sr. (c. 1798–1800); Independence National Historical Park.

The Soldier

Although a member of the North Carolina legislature, Spaight remained active in the militia, eventually rising to the rank of lieutenant colonel in command of an artillery regiment. Under General George Washington's strategy for the conduct of the Revolutionary War, militia forces had an exact and important role. Washington planned for a main force of regulars to serve as a Continental Army in opposition to major British forces while the militia protected isolated areas, conducted security missions on the frontiers and against Loyalist units, and reinforced the continentals in major campaigns. Accordingly, North Carolina supplied units for the Continental Army in defense of Philadelphia in 1777 and New York in 1778 and 1779 before the war shifted south. At the same time, it used its militia to defend its western frontiers and to suppress a Loyalist uprising in South Carolina.

The fall of Charleston, South Carolina, to the British in 1780 was a crushing blow to American fortunes. Most of the region's continentals became prisoners of war, opening the whole southern tier of states to invasion. In hastily devising a defense strategy, the Continental Congress called on Governor Caswell to recruit 4,000 militiamen to take to the field under his command. Spaight wrestled with the mechanics of mobilization and helped train the recruits who began trickling into central camps. These units were to be combined with a similar militia force raised in Virginia by Governor Thomas Jefferson and a division of continentals sent to the region by Washington. This force, under the command of Major General Horatio Gates, the hero of Saratoga, was expected to counter the British army under the command of General Charles Cornwallis that had established a base at Camden, South Carolina. In early July Spaight donned uniform and marched with the state militia units into South Carolina.

On 16 August Gates' army moved forward to attack the British at Camden. Deploying his continentals to the right and the militia on his left flank, Gates advanced. His soldiers were exhausted from weeks of marching and insufficient rations. Furthermore, the militia had only recently joined with the regulars, and the disciplined teamwork between the two components, especially necessary before hastily assembled militia units could be expected to perform the intricate maneuvers of eighteenth-century linear warfare, had not yet been achieved.

Although the continentals easily advanced against the enemy, the militia lost its cohesion in the smoke and confusion, and its lines crumbled. Cornwallis then shifted all his forces against the continentals. In less than an hour Gates' army had been lost to the Patriot cause.

Spaight remained on active duty during the aftermath of the defeat. Once more he was involved with his state's efforts to raise forces to cope with an invasion. But during these months he also witnessed Major General Nathanael Greene's successful effort to restore American control over the south. Avoiding Gates' mistakes, Greene delayed mobilization of the militia units until he had a clear need for them in roles that matched their particular abilities. His success in blending the talents of citizen-soldiers with his continentals created an effective force that divided and isolated the British into small, ineffective groups, and then drove them back to the coast.

The Statesman

Spaight's participation in the mobilization of two American armies and his experiences in the state legislature reinforced the young Patriot's nationalist sentiments. Coordinating the contribution and duties of forces from various states convinced him of the need for close and binding interstate cooperation. In pursuing the interests of his constituents, Spaight concluded that the economic potential of the new nation, in particular that of its mercantile interests, could only be realized under a strong national government. This nationalism was further strengthened in 1783 when North Carolina elected Spaight to serve in the Continental Congress and when it chose him in 1787 as one of its representatives at the Constitutional Convention.

Spaight attended every session of the Convention and supported the Great Compromise. Designed to protect the rights of both the small and the more populous states, this compromise called for a national legislature that gave equal voice to all thirteen states in a Senate composed of two members from each, but which respected the rights of the majority in a House of Representatives based on population.

Spaight's major contribution to constitutional government took place not in Philadelphia but in his native state, where the fight for ratification proved exceptionally difficult. The Anti-Federalists were in the majority when the ratifying convention met at Hillsboro in 1788. They did not plan to reject the Constitution outright, preferring to recommend a series of amendments, specifically a bill of rights, and adjourn. When the Federalists forced the issue, the Constitution went down to defeat.

The Federalists bided their time. They kept closely informed about the ratification progress in other parts of the country through Spaight's contacts with George Washington. By 1791 the Constitution had been approved by eleven states and the new national Congress had submitted a bill of rights to the states in the form of ten amendments to the Constitution. With Anti-Federalist power in North Carolina eroding, Spaight and his colleagues called for a new ratifying convention. Their strategy worked. Even the traditionally Anti-Federalist western counties now elected Federalist delegates, and North Carolina quickly approved the Constitution.

Spaight retired from public life in early 1792, but he was again returned to the state legislature later that same year. In 1793 he became governor, the first native-born North Carolinian to win that position. Here his leadership abilities were evident when he organized the politically difficult movement of the state capital to Raleigh. He was also instrumental in establishing a state university, a project that this European-trained scholar considered of first importance to the future of North Carolina. Using skills developed during the Revolution, he organized the mobilization of the state militia to cope with Indian unrest and, at President Washington's request, prepared for a massive mobilization in 1794 to deal with potential conflict with French privateers.

Often in poor health, Spaight retired from public life several more times. He was elected to the House of Representatives in 1798 and served slightly more than one term before health problems forced his resignation. While in Congress Spaight's increasing concern with states' rights led him to abandon the Federalist cause and join the Democratic-Republican party forming around Thomas Jefferson. He emerged from retirement one last time in 1801 to run for the state senate. A bitter argument with his Federalist rival, John Stanley, ended in a pistol duel on the outskirts of Newbern. After each party missed three successive shots, Spaight was hit and fell mortally wounded.

Hugh Williamson

Hugh Williamson, who represented North Carolina at the Constitutional Convention, was a scholar of international renown. His erudition had brought him into contact with some of the leading intellectuals of the Patriot cause and, in turn, with the ferment of political ideas that eventually found expression in the Constitution. During the Revolution, Williamson contributed his considerable talents as physician and natural scientist to the American war effort. His experiences in that preeminent event of his generation transformed the genial scholar into an adroit politician and a determined leader in the campaign for effective national government. This leadership was evident not only at the Convention in Philadelphia but also, with telling effect, during the ratification debates in North Carolina.

Williamson's career demonstrates the rootlessness that characterized the lives of many Americans even in the eighteenth century. Born on the frontier, he lived for significant periods of his long life in three different regions of the country. This mobility undoubtedly contributed to the development of his nationalistic outlook, an outlook strengthened by wartime service with interstate military forces and reinforced by the interests of the planters and merchants that formed his North Carolina constituency. These experiences convinced him that only a strong central government could adequately protect and foster the political, economic, and intellectual future of the new nation.

The Patriot

Williamson was born in Chester County in what was then the frontier region of Pennsylvania. His fragile health as a youth weighed against his beginning a career in the family's clothier business. His parents instead sent him to a private academy and then to the College of Philadelphia (today's University of Pennsylvania). A member of the college's first graduating class, Williamson obtained a license to preach in Connecticut, but factional disputes among the local clergy and a resurgence of ill health led him to abandon a career in the ministry. Further study and a master's degree led to employment in 1760 as a professor of mathematics at his alma mater.

In another career shift four years later, Williamson turned to the study of medicine. Armed with a degree from the prestigious University of Utrecht in the Netherlands, he returned to Philadelphia to open a private practice. At the same time, he pursued a number of independent scientific and educational projects, and his work in these areas eventually led to membership in the American Philosophical Society as well as acclaim in Europe's intellectual circles.

Interest in science and education indirectly led Williamson to politics and the Patriot cause. Sailing for England in 1773 to raise funds for a local educational project, Williamson stopped en route at Boston. There he witnessed the famous Tea Party, in which Patriots dressed as Indians destroyed a cargo of tea in protest over a newly enforced Parliamentary tax on imported commodities. On reaching London he was summoned before the Privy Council to testify on this act of rebellion and on colonial affairs in general.

Williamson came of age politically during this encounter. In response to questions by Council members, who were in the process of formulating punitive measures against Massachusetts, he bluntly warned that repression would provoke rebellion. He then went on to express the argument that was becoming the core of the Patriot position: Americans were entitled to the full rights of Englishmen, including representation in the decisions of the English government. This testimony brought him to the attention of other Americans in London. A mutual interest in scientific matters cemented a solid working relationship with Benjamin Franklin, and Williamson soon found himself joined with the famous American scientist and others in appealing for support among those Englishmen who, in opposition to their own government, sympathized with American claims.

Williamson continued on to the Netherlands where, taking advantage of the cover afforded by his attendance at meetings on scientific and educational subjects, he organized the publication of pamphlets and other papers that supported the Patriot cause. While there he learned that the colonies had declared their independence. Narrowly avoiding capture at sea, he rushed back to Philadelphia in early 1777 and volunteered for service in the Medical Department of the Continental Army. The Department had no opening at that time, so Williamson decided to form a partnership with a younger brother to import medicines and other scarce items from the West Indies through the British blockade. Believing

HUGH WILLIAMSON
North Carolina

Birth: 5 December 1735, in West Nottingham Township, Chester County, Pennsylvania
Death: 22 May 1819, at New York, New York
Interment: Apthorp Tomb, Trinity Churchyard, New York City

Etching by Albert Rosenthal (1888) after Painting by John Trumbull; North Carolina Division of Archives and History.

that he could best contribute to the war effort by using his contacts and reputation in this manner, Williamson made Edenton, North Carolina, his base of operations. Settlement in North Carolina soon led to his establishing a medical practice to serve the planters and merchants of the region.

The Soldier

These various activities brought Williamson to the attention of North Carolina's political leaders. Facing the threat of a British invasion of the region from the sea and bases in Florida, the state legislature voted to raise a force of 4,000 men to assist South Carolina. When Governor Richard Caswell, with the rank of major general, took to the field at the head of these citizen-soldiers, he named Williamson to serve as the state's Physician and Surgeon General, a post Williamson held until the end of the war.

The capture of Charleston in 1780 not only marked a stunning defeat for American forces, but also signaled the end of the first phase in a new British war strategy. Under this strategy British forces would continue to tie down Washington's main army in the north while a Royal army under General Charles Cornwallis would advance northward. Using Savannah and Charleston as their bases of operations, the British expected their regular units to push through North Carolina and Virginia while a militia composed of local Loyalists secured areas captured by the regular forces. If successful, this strategy would have led to the conquest of the colonies from the south. To counter Cornwallis' efforts, the Continental Congress sent Horatio Gates, the hero of Saratoga, to command a small force composed of a division of continentals, Caswell's units from North Carolina, and a group of hastily assembled Virginia militia units.

Gates attempted to attack the British advance base near Camden, South Carolina, but his tired militia units, which were still forming when the battle began, were easily routed, and the Americans suffered another defeat. Williamson, who witnessed the disaster, volunteered to pass behind enemy lines to care for the American wounded. He spent two months on this mercy mission. When smallpox threatened the prison camp, he argued strenuously with Cornwallis and other British officers over the proper method to combat the disease. His perseverance and scientific reputation paid off. The British followed his advice, and an epidemic was averted.

In the fall of 1780 Williamson returned to the field. Major General Nathanael Greene, Gates' replacement, had begun his brilliant campaign to recover the south through the joint efforts of continentals and militia. While his main force engaged the British in a series of battles, the militiamen concentrated on picking off small outposts and isolated enemy parties. Francis ("Swamp Fox") Marion and others who operated mainly in South Carolina are most remembered for this type of guerrilla warfare, but North Carolina units also adopted these tactics. Williamson was attached to a force under Brigadier General Isaac Gregory whose mission was to limit British activity in eastern North Carolina. Gregory established his base in the vast reaches of the Dismal Swamp where he could pin the British down in Wilmington without jeopardizing his small force. Williamson's bold innovations in preventive medicine, especially his strenuous efforts to indoctrinate raw troops in the importance of sanitation and diet, kept the command virtually free of disease during the six months that it inhabited the swamp—a rare feat in eighteenth-century warfare.

The Statesman

In 1782 Williamson's neighbors elected him to the lower house of the North Carolina legislature, where he served for several terms. He sat on numerous committees, including those formed to regulate veterans' rights, and he authored the state's copyright law. His fellow legislators also chose Williamson to serve in the Continental Congress in 1782. Appointment to this national body represented a natural political progression for Williamson, who was evolving into a champion of federalism. His experiences during the Revolution, especially his exposure to the pressing need for interstate cooperation during the 1780 and 1781 campaigns in the Carolinas, had convinced him of the military importance of strong national government. This interest increased when he came to realize the economic benefits that might accrue from binding interstate association. In 1786 North Carolina chose Williamson to attend the Annapolis Convention, a meeting called to settle economic questions affecting the middle Atlantic states. Although he arrived too late to play a role in the Maryland proceedings, he was prepared to discuss interstate issues the following year when his state appointed him as a representative at the Constitutional Convention in Philadelphia.

Williamson, a faithful attendee at Convention sessions, lodged with Alexander Hamilton and James Madison, two of the country's best-known nationalist leaders. His intellectual stature and international background also propelled him into a leadership role in the North Carolina delegation. A capacity for hard work and his innate good humor made him invaluable to the Federalists as they worked out the many political compromises necessary for consensus on the new instrument of government.

Shortly before the Convention adjourned, Williamson wrote a series of public letters in defense of a strong federal system. These "Letters of Sylvius" addressed many of the practical concerns of his state, where the rural and frequently debt-ridden farmers favored minimal government regulations, while the mercantile-planter group from the seaboard region wanted an economy strictly regulated by a central government. Using simple examples, Williamson explained to both groups the dual dangers of inflationary finances and of taxes that would stunt the growth of domestic manufacture. He exhorted North Carolinians to support the Constitution as the basis for their future prosperity. The ratification process, he explained, would decide whether the United States would remain a "system of patchwork and a series of expedients" or become "the most flourishing, independent, and happy nation on the face of the earth."

Following adjournment in Philadelphia, Williamson returned to New York to participate in the closing sessions of the Continental Congress and to serve as one of the agents settling North Carolina's accounts with that body. These duties caused him to miss the Hillsboro Convention, where North Carolina first considered and rejected the Constitution, but he played a major role at a second convention that met in Fayetteville in 1789. Here he participated in a successful effort to rally support for the Constitution.

Williamson's neighbors elected him to represent them in the first federal Congress. He served two terms before retiring and settling in New York City, where he continued to pursue a wide range of scholarly interests. He wrote extensively about his research, joined numerous learned societies, and contributed to many charities. He also served as one of the original trustees of the University of North Carolina.

Thomas Jefferson described Williamson's role at the Philadelphia Convention in the following terms: "he was a useful member, of an acute mind, attentive to business, and of an high degree of erudition." As these words suggest, the American people were well served during a critical period in their history when a scientist of international renown volunteered to defend the principles of democracy both on the battlefield and in the government.

William Jackson

In all, thirty-nine delegates, designated the Founding Fathers by a grateful nation, signed the Constitution in September 1787. But in fact a fortieth name appears on that historic document, that of William Jackson, the secretary of the Convention, whose signature authenticated the results of the sessions in Philadelphia. Although Jackson lacked the delegates' right to debate and vote on the issues, he was clearly at one with those who manifested a strong dissatisfaction with the weakness of the central government under the Articles of Confederation. His own experiences in the Revolution—as a line officer in some of the war's most frustrating campaigns and as a staff officer who worked with both the country's allies and the Continental Congress—led him to identify completely with the ideals of the nationalists. He became convinced that only a strong government, responsive to the collective will of the electorate, could regulate the country's foreign trade, organize its westward expansion, and defend its institutions. This conviction animated both his work at the Convention and his service to the nation during the presidency of George Washington.

Jackson became the quintessential civil servant. A gifted writer and orator, he employed his considerable organizational talents in the service of the new republic, competently and unobtrusively managing the flow of official business as President Washington's private secretary. His loyalty to the President, his self-effacement before the luminaries of Washington's Cabinet, his "faithfullness and integrity," as General Benjamin Lincoln put it, established a model of professional behavior for succeeding government employees.

The Patriot

Jackson's youth was one of dramatic contrasts. The son of an Englishman of some local standing in the region along the Scottish border, he received the rudimentary education typical of the area. But his limited and sheltered world was suddenly changed when his parents died and neighbors arranged for the orphan's emigration to Charleston, South Carolina, to be reared by Owen Roberts, a prominent merchant and family friend. Roberts rapidly became a formative influence on his ward, just as he was on his neighbors. A veteran of the French and Indian War, he introduced the boy to the colonial idea of the citizen-soldier by bringing Jackson along to the musters of the Charleston Battalion of Artillery (today's 263d Air Defense Artillery, South Carolina Army National Guard), which Roberts commanded. Roberts also represented Charleston's merchants and artisans in various legislative bodies.

Although criticism of the King's government was considerably muted in the southern colonies, a majority of the people joined their northern neighbors in opposing British taxation policies and attempts to interfere in local affairs. Roberts' standing as a leader in this movement helped shape Jackson's emerging interest in the Patriot cause. In the summer of 1775, South Carolina cast her fate with her neighbors, ousting the Royal governor and voting to raise regulars to protect the colony. Roberts initially served as the major of Colonel Christopher Gadsden's 1st South Carolina Regiment, but in November he was promoted to command a new artillery regiment, the 4th South Carolina. Jackson soon followed his guardian to the colors.

Jackson may well have donned uniform prior to his seventeenth birthday. Probably with Roberts' help, he obtained appointment as a cadet in the 1st South Carolina. Eighteenth-century cadets were young men preparing to become officers in effect through on-the-job training. Jackson apparently learned quickly, for in May 1776 he was commissioned a second lieutenant in the regiment.

The Soldier

Jackson's battlefield initiation was not long in coming. Relying on faulty information from Americans in England and outdated letters from the last Royal governors, the King's ministers had concluded that the revolt in the southern colonies was the work of an armed minority, and that a show of force in the area would rally Loyalists and restore the governors. To prove the point, an expedition under General Sir Henry Clinton, consisting of several regiments of red-coated regulars and a small naval squadron, was mounted against Charleston, the most important of the southern cities. The invading fleet appeared off the city's harbor in June, and Jackson's unit took up position to face the foe.

South Carolina did not have to meet the challenge alone. The Continental Congress had by then accepted

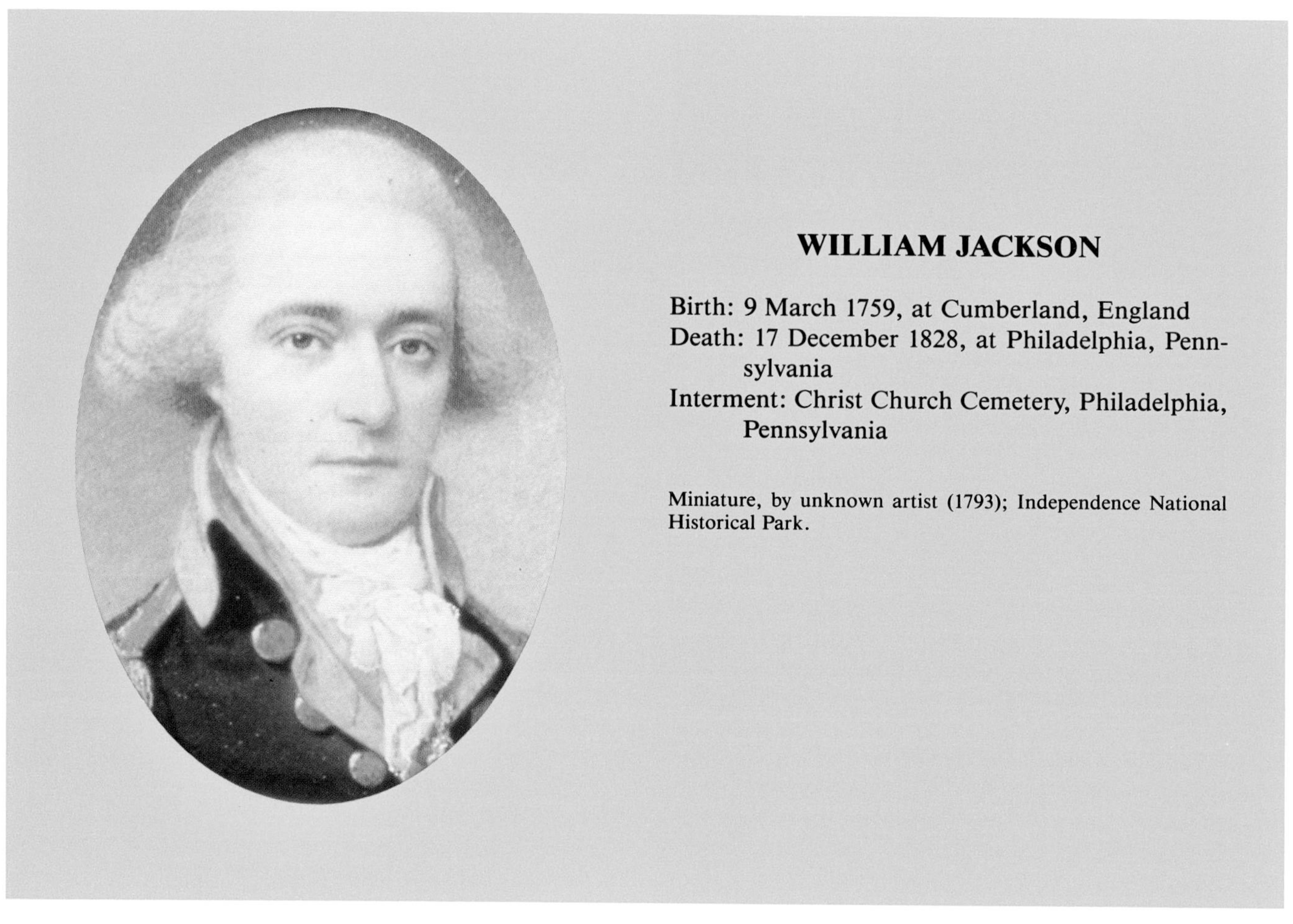

WILLIAM JACKSON

Birth: 9 March 1759, at Cumberland, England
Death: 17 December 1828, at Philadelphia, Pennsylvania
Interment: Christ Church Cemetery, Philadelphia, Pennsylvania

Miniature, by unknown artist (1793); Independence National Historical Park.

the responsibility for the war effort, and its delegates had begun drafting a Declaration of Independence. The state transferred its regular regiments to national control as part of the new Continental Army. Reinforced by other units from North Carolina and Virginia, along with a force of local militia, the Americans under Major General Charles Lee repulsed the British, ending the first significant threat to the region with relative ease.

While attention focused on events further north during the next years, the 1st South Carolina Regiment settled down to garrison duty in Charleston and the forts around the large harbor. Jackson spent his time perfecting the skills of a junior officer, winning two promotions. During the latter part of this period, Jackson first witnessed the defeat of American forces under arms. In 1778 Major General Robert Howe, who had succeeded Lee, assembled a small force of regulars and militiamen in Georgia, intending to capture the thinly settled and lightly defended Royal colony of East Florida, a rallying point for the region's Loyalists. But Howe lacked the logistical apparatus to sustain even a small force, and bickering between contingents halted operations short of St. Augustine, the objective. When an epidemic then broke out in the American force, Jackson's regiment was among the ragtag remnant forced to fall back to South Carolina.

Congress reacted to the fiasco of the Florida invasion by replacing the prickly Howe with Major General Benjamin Lincoln of Massachusetts. The delegates hoped that Lincoln's background as a militia commander would improve civil-military relations in the south and enable the Americans to withstand new threats by the British. Forced to recast their strategic objectives after France entered the war as America's ally in 1778, the British had shifted forces to Georgia. They intended to recapture the colonies one at a time, gaining momentum as they rolled north.

London's "southern strategy" led indirectly to a major change in Jackson's career. His regimental commander (and future signer of the Constitution), Charles C. Pinckney, believed that Lincoln needed a diplomatic assistant to bridge any gap between the Yankee general and his southern subordinates. He persuaded Lincoln to appoint Jackson as an aide. The assignment carried with it a temporary promotion to the rank of major and brought the twenty-year-old into contact with men from a completely different section of the nation. Jackson served with Lincoln in skirmishes that followed the

American loss of Savannah, including the bloody battle at Stono Ferry in June 1779, and later in an American counteroffensive at Savannah in conjunction with the Comte d'Estaing's French fleet and troops. During these operations, Jackson again saw the Americans defeated. At Stono Ferry he also experienced personal tragedy when his guardian was killed in action. After the unsuccessful siege of Savannah, Jackson participated in the allied retreat and watched French and American commanders blame each other for the failure.

Worse reverses were to come in 1780. Clinton reacted to the Savannah counterattack by shifting additional forces to the south and launching a new attack on Charleston. This time adequate resources enabled the British to conduct a formal siege. Lincoln refused to withdraw and valiantly prolonged the siege for forty-two days, but finally had to surrender on 12 May in the worst American defeat of the war. Jackson was among the almost 5,000 captured. Because of his status as an aide, he escaped the horrors of the disease-ridden prisoner-of-war facilities and was sent instead on parole to Philadelphia. In November he, along with Lincoln and others, was exchanged.

The fall of Charleston marked Jackson's last appearance on the battlefield. His skill as a staff officer and Lincoln's influence led shortly to his assignment as secretary to Lt. Col. John Laurens, Washington's aide. The two South Carolinians went to France to negotiate the shipment of vital war supplies. Laurens returned in the summer with materiel for the Yorktown campaign, leaving Jackson behind to coordinate with Benjamin Franklin and John Adams and the Dutch government for the shipment of more supplies. Jackson finally arrived back in Philadelphia in early 1782 and accepted Lincoln's offer to serve as Assistant Secretary at War. Lincoln had become the first Secretary a few months earlier, and he now relied heavily on his former aide to help with the day-to-day operations of the office and to act as a liaison between Congress and the Army. In October 1783, with demobilization almost complete, Jackson resigned.

The Statesman

The death of Jackson's guardian had seriously altered the young veteran's prospects. Influenced by his friends and his wartime experiences, he quit Charleston to seek new opportunities. He first decided to become a merchant and to that end traveled through Europe in the early months of peace. But life in the trading house held little appeal, and he finally settled down in Philadelphia to study law, winning admittance to the bar in the summer of 1788.

Jackson's intense interest in the political discussion of the day caused him to interrupt his legal training. When the Constitutional Convention assembled in Philadelphia in 1787, he successfully applied for the position as its secretary. His wartime contacts with many of the delegates, especially Alexander Hamilton, clearly helped him edge out Benjamin Franklin's grandson for the post. Jackson was sworn to protect the secrecy of the deliberations, and, on instruction of the delegates, he destroyed all records except for the official journal after the final draft of the Constitution was signed.

Jackson hoped to serve as a legislative secretary in the new federal government, but he failed to secure a post in the Senate. Instead, he was selected by Washington to be his secretary, thus becoming one of the original civil servants in the executive department. He performed well in that demanding assignment, drawing on his wartime skills as an aide, before resigning for financial reasons in December 1791. Jackson declined Washington's offer of the post of Adjutant General of the Army and embarked on a business career and a law practice. But his marriage to a daughter of Thomas Willing, a wealthy Philadelphia merchant, led him to look more kindly on renewed federal employment. Shortly after the wedding, he was appointed surveyor of customs for the port of Philadelphia.

Jackson was a staunch supporter of the Federalist party, and when Thomas Jefferson became President in 1801, marking the executive branch's first change in political alignment, the surveyor of customs lost his job. For a time he edited Philadelphia's *Political and Commercial Register,* a pro-Federalist newspaper. He also returned to the law. In one of his last major cases he represented a group of Continental Army veterans who were petitioning for pensions originally promised during the Revolution. He always remained faithful to his old comrades in arms, serving for more than a quarter century as the national secretary of the Society of the Cincinnati, a veterans' organization of ex-officers from the Continental Army, and toward the end of his life he officially welcomed his old friend and ally, General Lafayette, to Philadelphia during the Frenchman's tour of America in 1824.

Jackson was typical of many immigrants who contributed gladly to the defense of their new homeland. A strong nationalist, he gave unstintingly of himself both in uniform and in a quieter way within the halls of national government.

Bibliography

George Washington

Ambler, Charles H. *George Washington and the West.* Chapel Hill: University of North Carolina Press, 1936.

Bellamy, Francis R. *The Private Life of George Washington.* New York: Crowell, 1951.

Boller, Paul F. *George Washington & Religion.* Dallas: Southern Methodist University Press, 1963.

Bradley, Harold W. "The Political Thinking of George Washington." *Journal of Southern History* 11 (November 1945):469–86.

Callahan, North. *George Washington, Soldier and Man.* New York: Morrow, 1972.

Catlin, George B. "George Washington Looks Westward." *Michigan History Magazine* 16 (Spring 1932):127–42.

Chinard, Gilbert, ed. and trans. *George Washington as the French Knew Him; a Collection of Texts.* Princeton: Princeton University Press, 1940.

Coleman, Christopher B. "George Washington and the West." *Indiana Magazine of History* 28 (September 1932):151–67.

Cook, Roy B. *Washington's Western Lands.* Strasburg, Va.: Shenandoah Publishing House, 1930.

Cunliffe, Marcus. *George Washington, Man and Monument.* Boston: Little, Brown, 1958.

Da Costa, B. F. "The Traditional Washington Vindicated." *Magazine of American History* 5 (August 1880):81–104.

Fitzpatrick, John C. *George Washington Himself; A Common-Sense Biography Written from His Manuscripts.* Indianapolis: Bobbs-Merrill Co., 1933.

———. "George Washington and Religion." *Catholic Historical Review* 15 (April 1929):23–42.

Flexner, James T. *George Washington.* 4 vols. Boston: Little, Brown, 1965–1972.

Ford, Paul L. *The True George Washington.* Philadelphia: J. B. Lippincott Co., 1896.

Freeman, Douglas Southall. *George Washington: A Biography.* 7 vols. (Vol. 7 with John A. Carroll and Mary Wells Ashworth.) New York: Scribner's, 1948–1957.

Frothingham, Thomas G. *Washington: Commander in Chief.* Boston: Houghton Mifflin, 1930.

Garraghan, Gilbert J. "George Washington, Man of Character." *Mid-America* 17 (January 1935):37–59.

Hixon, Ada H. "George Washington, Land Speculator." *Illinois State Historical Society Journal* 11 (January 1919):566–75.

Irving, Washington. *Life of George Washington.* 5 vols. New York: G. P. Putnam, 1855–1859.

Jackson, Donald D. "The Papers of George Washington." *Manuscripts* 22 (Winter 1970):2–11.

Knollenberg, Bernhard. *George Washington, the Virginia Period, 1732–1775.* Durham: Duke University Press, 1964.

Knox, Dudley W. *The Naval Genius of George Washington.* Boston: Houghton Mifflin, 1932.

Knox, James H. Mason. "The Medical History of George Washington, His Physicians, Friends, and Advisers." *Bulletin of the Institute of the History of Medicine* 1 (June 1933):174–91.

Kohn, Richard H. "The Greatness of George Washington: Lessons for Today." *Assembly* 36 (March 1978): 6–7, 28–29.

Lewis, Fielding O. "Washington's Last Illness." *Annals of Medical History* new ser. 4 (May 1932):245–48.

Lodge, Henry C. *George Washington.* 2 vols. Boston: Houghton Mifflin, 1891.

Lossing, Benson J. *Life of Washington; A Biography, Personal, Military, and Political.* 3 vols. New York: Virtue, 1860.

Marshall, John, comp. *The Life of George Washington, Commander in Chief of the American Forces, During the War Which Established the Independence of His Country, and First President of the United States.* 5 vols. Philadelphia: C. P. Wayne, 1804–1807.

Mayo, Bernard. "George Washington." *Georgia Review* 13 (Summer 1959):135–50.

Morison, Samuel E. *The Young Man Washington.* Cambridge, Mass.: Harvard University Press, 1932.

Morris, Richard B. "Washington and Hamilton: A Great Collaboration." *American Philosophical Society Proceedings* 102 (April 1958):107–16.

Nettles, Curtis P. *George Washington and American Independence.* Boston: Little, Brown, 1951.

Parton, Robert. "The Changing Images of George Washington from Weems to Freeman." *Social Studies* 56 (February 1965):52–59.

Paxson, Frederick L. "Washington and the Western Fronts, 1753–1795." *Illinois State Historical Society Journal* 24 (January 1932):589–605.

Ramsay, David. *The Life of George Washington, Commander in Chief of the Armies of the United States of America, Throughout the War Which Established Their Independence; and First President of the United States.* New York: Hopkins & Seymour, 1807.

Sparks, Jared. "Was Washington a Marshal of France?" *Proceedings of the Massachusetts Historical Society* 7 (December 1863):283–91.

Washington, George. *Diaries, 1748–1799.* Edited by

John C. Fitzpatrick. 4 vols. Boston: Houghton Mifflin, 1925.

——. *General Washington's Correspondence Concerning the Society of the Cincinnati*. Edited by Edgar Erskine Hume. Baltimore: Johns Hopkins Press, 1941.

——. *The Writings of George Washington from the Original Manuscript Sources, 1745–1799*. Edited by John C. Fitzpatrick. 39 vols. Washington: Government Printing Office, 1931–1944.

Wright, Esmond. *Washington and the American Revolution*. New York: Macmillan, 1957.

Abraham Baldwin

"Abraham Baldwin." *Georgia Historical Society Quarterly* 3 (December 1919):169–73. (This is a reprint of Baldwin's obituary from the 28 March 1807 *Republican and Savannah Evening Ledger*.)

Baldwin, Abraham. "A Sermon for the mutinous troops of the Connecticut Line, 1782." Edited by Patrick J. Furlong. *New England Quarterly* 43 (December 1970):621–31.

Brooks, Robert P. "Abraham Baldwin, statesman and educator." *Georgia Historical Quarterly* 11 (June 1927):171–78.

Johnston, Henry, ed. *Record of Service of Connecticut Men in the War of the Revolution, War of 1812, Mexican War*. Hartford: Case, Lockwood & Brainard Co. for the Adjutant General's Office, 1889.

Jones, Charles C., Jr. *Biographical Sketches of the Delegates from Georgia to the Continental Congress*. Boston: Houghton Mifflin, 1891.

Northern, William J., ed. *Men of Mark in Georgia: A Complete and Elaborate History of the State from its Settlement to the Present Time, Chiefly Told in Biographies and Autobiographies of the Most Eminent Men of Each Period of Georgia's Progress and Development*. 6 vols. Atlanta: A. B. Caldwell, 1907–1912.

White, Henry Clay. *Abraham Baldwin, One of the Founders of the Republic, and Father of the University of Georgia, the First of American State Universities*. Athens: McGregor Co., 1926.

Richard Bassett

Conrad, Henry C. *History of the State of Delaware*. 3 vols. Wilmington: Privately printed, 1908.

Delaware. *Delaware Archives, Military*. 5 vols. Wilmington: Public Archives Commission of Delaware, 1911–1919.

Johnston, George. *History of Cecil County, Maryland, and the Early Settlements Around the Head of Chesapeake Bay and on the Delaware River, with Sketches of Some of the Old Families of Cecil County*. Elkton: Privately printed, 1881.

Mallery, Charles P. *Ancient Families of Bohemia Manor, Their Homes and Their Graves*. Washington Historical Society of Delaware, 1888.

Pattison, Robert E. *The Life and Character of Richard Bassett*. Wilmington: Historical Society of Delaware, 1900.

Scharf, John Thomas. *History of Delaware 1609–1888*. 2 vols. Philadelphia: L. J. Richards & Co., 1888.

William Blount

Force, Peter, ed. *American State Papers, Class II: Indian Affairs, Vol. 1*. Washington: Gales and Seaton, 1832.

Goodpasture, Albert V. "William Blount and the Old Southwest Territory." *American Historical Magazine and Tennessee Historical Society Quarterly* 8 (January 1903):1–13.

Keith, Alice B. "Three North Carolina Blount Brothers in Business and Politics, 1783–1812." Ph.D. dissertation, University of North Carolina, 1940.

——. "William Blount in North Carolina Politics." In Joseph C. Sitterson, ed., *Studies in Southern History*. Chapel Hill: University of North Carolina Press, 1957, pp. 47–61.

Masterson, William Henry. *William Blount*. Baton Rouge: Louisiana State University Press, 1954.

Turner, Frederick Jackson, ed. "Documents on the Blount Conspiracy, 1795–1797." *American Historical Review* 10 (April 1905):574–606.

Wright, Marcus Joseph. *Some Account of the Life and Services of William Blount, ...* Washington: E. J. Gray, 1884.

David Brearly

American Historical Society. *Cyclopedia of New Jersey Biography*. 3 vols. Newark: Memorial History Co., 1916.

Brearley, William. *Genealogical Chart of the American Branch of the Brearley* [sic] *Family*. Detroit: Privately printed, 1886.

Lee, Francis Bazley. *History of Trenton, New Jersey. The Record of Its Early Settlement and Corporate Progress*. Trenton: F. T. Smiley & Co., 1895.

McLaughlin, Andrew C. *The Courts, the Constitution, and Parties: Studies in Constitutional History and Politics*. Chicago: University of Chicago Press, 1912.

Schuyler, Hamilton. *A History of St. Michael's Church, Trenton . . . .* Princeton: Princeton University Press, 1926.

Scott, Austin. "Holmes vs. Walton: The New Jersey Precedent." *American Historical Review* 4 (April

1899):456–69.

Stryker, William S. *General Maxwell's Brigade of the New Jersey Continental Line in the Expedition Against the Indians, in the Year 1779.* Trenton: W. S. Sharp Printing Co., 1885.

———, comp. *Official Register of the Officers and Men of New Jersey in the Revolutionary War, Compiled under the Orders of His Excellency Theodore F. Randolph, Governor, by William S. Stryker, Adjutant General. With Added Digest and Revision for the use of the Society of the Cincinnati in the State of New Jersey (1911) Revised and Compiled by James W. S. Campbell.* 1872. Reprint ed., Baltimore: Genealogical Publishing Co., 1967.

Pierce Butler

Edgar, Walter B., et al., comps. *Biographical Directory of the South Carolina House of Representatives.* Columbia: University of South Carolina Press, 1974–.

Ford, Worthington C., comp. "British Officers Serving in America, 1754-1774." *New England Historical and Genealogical Register* 48 (1894):36–46, 157–68, 299–310, 424–36; 49 (1895):47–58, 160–71, 292–96.

Johnson, Joseph. *Traditions and Reminiscences, Chiefly of the American Revolution in the South.* Charleston: Walker & James, 1851.

McCrady, Edward. *History of South Carolina in the Revolution, 1775–1780.* New York: Macmillan, 1901.

Salley, Alexander S. *Delegates to the Continental Congress from South Carolina, 1774–1789, with Sketches of the Four Who Signed the Declaration of Independence.* Columbia: Historical Commission of South Carolina, 1927.

Shy, John. *Toward Lexington: The Role of the British Army in the Coming of the American Revolution.* Princeton: Princeton University Press, 1965.

Ulmer, S. Sidney. "The Role of Pierce Butler in the Constitutional Convention." *Review of Politics* 22 (July 1960):361–74.

Wolfe, John H. *Jeffersonian Democracy in South Carolina.* Chapel Hill: University of North Carolina Press, 1940.

Jonathan Dayton

American Historical Society. *Cyclopedia of New Jersey Biography.* 3 vols. Newark: Memorial History Co., 1916.

Clayton, W. Woodford, ed. *History of Union and Middlesex Counties, New Jersey.* Philadelphia: Everts & Peck, 1882.

Coriell, Mrs. Abner S. "Major-General Elias Dayton 1737–1807." *Union County Historical Society Proceedings* 2 (1923–34):204–11.

Dayton, Elias, "Papers of General Elias Dayton." *Proceedings of the New Jersey Historical Society* 9 (January 1864):175–94.

Elizabeth, N.J., Sesqui-centennial Committee. *Revolutionary History of Elizabeth, New Jersey.* Elizabeth: n.p., 1926.

Fleming, Thomas. *The Forgotten Victory: The Battle for New Jersey—1780.* New York: E. P. Dutton & Co., 1973.

Hatfield, Edwin Francis. *History of Elizabeth, New Jersey; including the early history of Union County.* New York: Carlton & Lanahan, 1868.

Murray, Nicholas. *Notes, Historical and Biographical, Concerning Elizabethtown, Its Eminent Men, Churches, and Ministers.* Elizabethtown: E. Sanderson, 1844.

Stryker, William S. *General Maxwell's Brigade of the New Jersey Continental Line in the Expedition Against the Indians, in the Year 1779.* Trenton: W. S. Sharp Printing Co., 1885.

———, comp. *Official Register of the Officers and Men of New Jersey in the Revolutionary War, Compiled under the Orders of His Excellency Theodore F. Randolph, Governor, by William S. Stryker, Adjutant General. With Added Digest and Revision for the use of the Society of the Cincinnati in the State of New Jersey (1911) Revised and Compiled by James W. S. Campbell.* 1872. Reprint ed., Baltimore: Genealogical Publishing Co., 1967.

Symmes, John Cleves. *The Correspondence of John Cleves Symmes, Founder of the Miami Purchase.* Edited by Beverley W. Bond, Jr. New York: Historical and Philosophical Society of Ohio, 1926.

Thayer, Theodore. *As We Were: The Story of Old Elizabethtown.* Newark: New Jersey Historical Society, 1964.

John Dickinson

Colburn, Howard T. "The Historical Perspective of John Dickinson." In Dickinson College, *Early Dickinsonia.* Carlisle: n.p., 1961, pp. 3–37.

———. "John Dickinson, Historical Revolutionary." *Pennsylvania Magazine of History and Biography* 83 (July 1959):271–92.

Conrad, Henry C. *History of the State of Delaware.* 3 vols. Wilmington: Privately printed, 1908.

Cook, Frank G. "John Dickinson." *Atlantic Monthly* 65 (January 1890):70–83.

Delaware. *Delaware Archives. Military.* 5 vols. Wilmington: Public Archives Commission of Delaware, 1911–1919.

Devine, Francis E. "The Pennsylvania Flying Camp,

July–November 1776." *Pennsylvania History* 46 (January 1979):59–78.

[Dickinson, John.] *The Letters of Fabius, in 1788, on the Federal Constitution; and in 1797 on the Present Situation of Public Affairs.* Wilmington: W. C. Smyth, 1797.

Dickinson, John. "Speech of John Dickinson Opposing the Declaration of Independence, 1 July, 1776." Edited by J. H. Powell. *Pennsylvania Magazine of History and Biography* 65 (October 1941):458–81.

Flower, Milton E. *John Dickinson: Conservative Revolutionary.* Charlottesville: University Press of Virginia, 1983.

Gummere, Richard M. "John Dickinson, the Classical Penman of the Revolution." *Classical Journal* 52 (November 1956):81–88.

Hooker, Richard J. "John Dickinson on Church and State." *American Literature* 16 (May 1944):82–98.

Jacobson, David L. *John Dickinson and the Revolution in Pennsylvania, 1764–1776.* Berkeley: University of California Press, 1965.

Knollenberg, Bernhard. "John Dickinson vs. John Adams, 1774–1776." *American Philosophical Society Proceedings* 107 (April 1963):138–44.

Moore, George Henry. *John Dickinson, The Author of the Declaration, On Taking Up Arms in 1775.* New York: Privately printed, 1890.

Powell, John H. "John Dickinson, Penman of the American Revolution." Ph.D. dissertation, State University of Iowa, 1938.

———. "John Dickinson and the Constitution." *Pennsylvania Magazine of History and Biography* 60 (January 1936):1–14.

———. "A Certain Great Fortune and Piddling Genius." In Dickinson College, *Early Dickinsonia* Carlisle: n.p., 1961, pp. 41–72.

Power, M. Susan. "John Dickinson: Freedom, Change, and Protest." *Susquehanna University Studies* 9 (June 1972):99–121.

Richards, Robert Haven. *The Life and Character of John Dickinson.* Wilmington: Historical Society of Delaware, 1901.

Stille, Charles J. *The Life and Times of John Dickinson, 1732–1808.* Philadelphia: Historical Society of Pennsylvania, 1891.

Tolles, Frederick B. "John Dickinson and the Quakers." In Dickinson College, *John and Mary's College.* Westwood, N.J.: Revell, 1956, pp. 67–88.

Wolf, Edwin. *John Dickinson, Forgotten Patriot.* Wilmington: n.p., 1967.

William Few

Jones, Charles C., Jr. *Biographical Sketches of the Delegates from Georgia to the Continental Congress.* Boston: Houghton Mifflin, 1891.

———. "William Few Lieutenant-Colonel Georgia Militia in the Revolutionary Service with Autobiography of Col. William Few of Georgia." *Magazine of American History* 7 (November 1881):339–58.

Northern, William J., ed. *Men of Mark in Georgia: A Complete and Elaborate History of the State from its Settlement to the Present Time, Chiefly Told in Biographies and Autobiographies of the Most Eminent Men of Each Period of Georgia's Progress and Development.* 6 vols. Atlanta: A. B. Caldwell, 1907-1912.

Walton, George; Howley, R.; and Few, William. *Observations upon the effects of certain late political suggestions. By the delegates of Georgia. Printed in the year 1781.* Wormsloe, Ga.: Privately printed, 1847.

Thomas Fitzsimons

Burnett, Edmund C. "The Catholic Signers of the Constitution." In *The Constitution of the United States: Addresses In Commemoration of the Sesquicentennial of Its Signing 17 September 1787,* edited by Herbert Wright. Washington: Catholic University of America, 1938, pp. 40–54.

Clarke, William P. *Official History of the Militia and the National Guard of the State of Pennsylvania From the Earliest Period to the Present Time.* Philadelphia: C. J. Hendler, 1909. (Only one of a projected three volumes published.)

Farrell, James A. "Thomas FitzSimons." *American Catholic Historical Society Records* 39 (September 1928):175–224.

Flanders, Henry. "Thomas Fitzsimmons." *Pennsylvania Magazine of History and Biography* 2 (1878):306–14.

Griffin, Martin I. J. "Thomas Fitz Simons, Pennsylvania's Catholic Signer of the Constitution of the United States." *American Catholic Historical Researches* 5 (January 1888):2–27. (Revised and expanded edition appeared in *Catholic Historical Society Records* 2 [1886/88]:45–111.)

Ireland, Owen. "Partisanship and the Constitution: Pennsylvania 1787." *Pennsylvania History* 45 (October 1978):315–32.

Nicholas Gilman

Bell, Charles Henry. *Exeter in 1776. Sketches of an old New Hampshire town as it was a hundred years ago.* Exeter: News-Letter Press, 1876.

———. *History of the Town of Exeter, New Hampshire.* Exeter: J. E. Farwell & Co., 1888.

Gilman, Arthur. *The Gilman Family Traced in the Line*

of Hon. John Gilman, of Exeter, N.H., With an Account of Many other Gilmans in England and America. Albany: Joel Munsell, 1869.

Nichols, Willard Atherton. *Ancestors of Willard Atherton Nichols Who Participated in the Civil and Military Affairs of the American Colonies and those who were Soldiers in the Continental Armies during the War of the Revolution and those who served in the War of 1812.* Redlands, Ca.: Privately printed, 1911.

Potter, Chandler Eastman. *Military History of New Hampshire, from Its Settlement, in 1623, to the Year 1861.* 2 vols. Concord: Adjutant General's Office, New Hampshire, 1866–1868.

Sterns, Ezra S.; Whitcher, William F.; and Parker, Edward E., eds. *Genealogical and Family History of the State of New Hampshire: A Record of the Achievements of Her People in the Making of a Commonwealth and the Founding of a Nation.* 4 vols. New York: Lewis Publishing Co., 1908.

Alexander Hamilton

Adair, Douglass C., and Harvey, Martin. "Was Alexander Hamilton a Christian Statesman?" *William and Mary Quarterly* 3d ser. 12 (April 1955):308–29.

Aimone, Alan C., and Manders, Eric I. "A Note on New York City's Independent Companies, 1775–1776." *New York History* 63 (January 1982):59–73.

Aly, Bower. *The Rhetoric of Alexander Hamilton.* New York: Columbia University Press, 1941.

Bernstein, Leonard H. "Alexander Hamilton and Political Factions in New York to 1787." Ph.D. dissertation, New York University, 1970.

Bramble, Max E. "Alexander Hamilton and Nineteenth Century American Historians: A Study of Selected Interpretations." Ph.D. dissertation, Michigan State University, 1968.

Cantor, Milton, comp. *Hamilton.* Englewood Cliffs: Prentice-Hall, 1971.

Cooke, Jacob Ernest. *Alexander Hamilton.* New York: Charles Scribner's Sons, 1982.

———, comp. *Alexander Hamilton: A Profile.* New York: Hill and Wang, 1967.

Davisson, Ora B. "The Early Pamphlets of Alexander Hamilton." *Quarterly Journal of Speech* 30 (April 1944):168–73.

Dietze, Gottfried. "Hamilton's Concept of Free Government." *New York History* 38 (October 1957):351–67.

Ellis, Ivan C. "A Study of the Influence of Alexander Hamilton on George Washington." Ph.D. dissertation, University of Southern California, 1956.

Flexner, James Thomas. *The Young Hamilton.* Boston: Little, Brown, 1978.

Govan, Thomas P. "The Rich, The Well-born, and Alexander Hamilton." *Mississippi Valley Historical Review* 36 (March 1950):675–80.

Hacker, Louis M. *Alexander Hamilton in the American Tradition.* New York: McGraw-Hill, 1957.

Hamilton, Alexander. *Papers.* Edited by Harold C. Syrett et al. 26 vols. New York: Columbia University Press, 1961–1979.

———. *Alexander Hamilton's Pay Book.* Edited by E. P. Panagopoulus. Detroit: Wayne State University Press, 1961.

———. *Alexander Hamilton and the Founding of the Nations.* Edited by Richard B. Morris. New York: Dial Press, 1957.

Hamilton, John C. *The Life of Alexander Hamilton.* 2 vols. New York: D. Appleton, 1840.

Hendrickson, Robert. *Hamilton I (1757–1789).* New York: Mason/Charter, 1976.

Kenyon, Cecelia M. "Alexander Hamilton: Rousseau of the Right." *Political Science Quarterly* 73 (June 1958):161–78.

Koch, Adrienne. "Hamilton, Adams and the Pursuit of Power." *Review of Politics* 16 (January 1954):37–66.

———. "Hamilton and Power." *Yale Review* 47 (Summer 1958):537–51.

Krout, John A. "Hamilton's Place in the Founding of the Nation." *American Philosophical Society Proceedings* 102 (April 1958):124–28.

Larson, Harold. "Alexander Hamilton: The Fact and Fiction of his Early Years." *William and Mary Quarterly* 3d ser. 9 (April 1952):139–51.

Lodge, Henry Cabot. *Alexander Hamilton.* Boston: Houghton Mifflin, 1898.

Lycan, Gilbert L. *Alexander Hamilton & American Foreign Policy: A Design for Greatness.* Norman: University of Oklahoma Press, 1970.

Miller, John C. *Alexander Hamilton: Portrait in Paradox.* New York: Harper & Brothers, 1959.

Mitchell, Broadus. *Alexander Hamilton.* 2 vols. New York: Macmillan, 1957–1962.

———. "Hamilton's Quarrel With Washington, 1781." *William and Mary Quarterly* 3d ser. 12 (April 1955):199–216.

Ottenberg, Louis. "Alexander Hamilton's First Court Case: Elizabeth Rutgers vs. Joshua Waddington in the Mayor's Court of New York City, 1784." *New-York Historical Society Quarterly* 41 (October 1957):423–39.

Padover, Saul K. *The Mind of Alexander Hamilton.* New York: Harper & Brothers, 1958.

Rossiter, Clinton L. *Alexander Hamilton and the Constitution.* New York: Harcourt, Brace & World, 1964.

Schachner, Nathan. "Alexander Hamilton Viewed By His Friends." *William and Mary Quarterly* 3d ser. 4 (April 1947):203–25.

Stourzh, Gerald. *Alexander Hamilton and the Idea of Republican Government*. Stanford: Stanford University Press, 1970.

Syrett, Alexander C. "Alexander Hamilton: History by Stereotype." *New-York Historical Society Quarterly* 43 (January 1959):38-50.

Rufus King

Arbena, Joseph L. "Politics or Principle? Rufus King and the Opposition to Slavery." *Essex Institute Historical Collections* 101 (January 1965):56-77.

Brush, Edward H. *Rufus King and His Times*. New York: N. L. Brown, 1926.

Ernst, Robert. *Rufus King, American Federalist*. Chapel Hill: University of North Carolina Press, 1968.

King, Rufus. *The Life and Correspondence of Rufus King; Comprising His Letters, Private and Official, His Public Documents, and His Speeches*. Edited by Charles R. King. 6 vols. New York: G. P. Putnam's Sons, 1894-1900.

———. "Letters of Rufus King." *Massachusetts Historical Society Proceedings* 49 (1915-16):81-89.

Wehtje, Myron F. "Rufus King and the Formation of the Constitution." *Studies in History and Society* 1 (April 1969):17-31.

Welch, Richard E. "Rufus King of Newburyport: The Formative Years (1767-1788)." *Essex Institute Historical Collections* 96 (October 1960):241-76.

John Langdon

Corning, Charles R. *John Langdon*. Concord: Rumford Printing Co., 1903.

Elwyn, Alfred Langdon. "Some Account of John Langdon." In New Hampshire, *Early State Papers of New Hampshire* 20 (1891):850-80.

———, ed. *Letters by Washington, Adams, Jefferson, and Others, Written During and After the Revolution, to John Langdon, New Hampshire*. Philadelphia: H. B. Ashmead, 1880.

Lacy, Harriet S. "The Langdon Papers, 1716-1841." *Historical New Hampshire* 22 (Autumn 1967):55-65.

Mayo, Lawrence S. *John Langdon of New Hampshire*. Concord: Rumford Press, 1937.

———. "John Langdon's Speech; a New Hampshire Tradition." *Colonial Society of Massachusetts Transactions* 26 (1924-1926):270-75.

Potter, Chandler Eastman. *Military History of New Hampshire, from Its Settlement, in 1623, to the Year 1861*. 2 vols. Concord: Adjutant General's Office, New Hampshire, 1866-1868.

William Livingston

American Historical Society. *Cyclopedia of New Jersey Biography*. 3 vols. Newark: Memorial History Co., 1916.

Dillon, Dorothy Rita. *The New York Triumvirate; A Study of the Legal and Political Careers of William Livingston, John Morin Scott, William Smith, Jr.* New York: Columbia University Press, 1949.

Elizabeth, N.J., Sesqui-centennial Committee. *Revolutionary History of Elizabeth, New Jersey*. Elizabeth: n.p., 1926.

Hatfield, Edwin Francis. *History of Elizabeth, New Jersey; including the early history of Union County*. New York: Carlton & Lanahan, 1868.

Klein, Milton Martin. "The American Whig: William Livingston of New York." Ph.D. dissertation, Columbia University, 1954.

———. "The Rise of the New York Bar: The Legal Career of William Livingston." *William and Mary Quarterly* 3d ser. 15 (July 1958):334-58.

Livingston, Edwin B. *The Livingstons of Livingston Manor*. New York: Knickerbocker Press, 1910.

Livingston, William. *The Papers of William Livingston*. Edited by Carl E. Prince et al. Trenton: New Jersey Historical Commission, 1979-.

———. *Selection from the Correspondence of the Executive, 1776-1786*. Newark: Daily Advertiser Office, 1848.

MacMillan, Margaret Burnham. *The War Governors in the American Revolution*. New York: Columbia University Press, 1943.

Monaghan, Frank, ed. "Unpublished Correspondence of William Livingston and John Jay." *Proceedings of the New Jersey Historical Society* 52 (July 1934):141-62.

Murray, Nicholas. *Notes, Historical and Biographical, Concerning Elizabethtown, Its Eminent Men, Churches, and Ministers*. Elizabethtown: E. Sanderson, 1844.

Prince, Carl E. *William Livingston, New Jersey's First Governor*. Trenton: New Jersey Historical Commission, 1975.

Sedgwick, Theodore, Jr. *A Memoir of the Life of William Livingston, Member of Congress in 1774, 1775, and 1776; Delegate to the Federal Convention in 1787, and Governor of the State of New-Jersey from 1776 to 1790*. New York: J.&J. Harper, 1833.

Stryker, William S., comp. *Official Register of the Officers and Men of New Jersey in the Revolutionary War, Compiled under the Orders of His Excellency Theodore F. Randolph, Governor, by William S. Stryker, Adjutant General. With Added Digest and Revi-*

sion for the use of the Society of the Cincinnati in the State of New Jersey (1911) Revised and Compiled by James W. S. Campbell. 1872. Reprint ed., Baltimore: Genealogical Publishing Co., 1967.

Thatcher, Harold Wesley. *The Social Philosophy of William Livingston.* Chicago: University of Chicago Libraries, 1938.

———. "The Political Ideas of New Jersey's First Governor." *New Jersey Historical Society Proceedings* 60 (April–July 1942):81–98, 184–99.

———. "The Social and Economic Ideas of New Jersey's First Governor." *New Jersey Historical Society Proceedings* 60 (October 1942):225–38; 61 (January 1943):31–46.

Thayer, Theodore. *As We Were: The Story of Old Elizabethtown.* Newark: New Jersey Historical Society, 1964.

James McHenry

Beall, Mary S. "The Military and Private Secretaries of George Washington." *Columbia Historical Society Records* 1 (1897):89–118.

Bell, William G. *Secretaries of War and Secretaries of the Army.* Washington: Government Printing Office, 1982.

Brown, Frederick J. *A Sketch of the Life of Dr. James McHenry.* Baltimore: J. Murphy, 1877.

Coad, Oral S., ed. "James McHenry, a Minor Poet." *Rutgers University Library Journal* 8 (June 1945):33–64.

Fernow, Berthold. "Washington's Military Family." *Magazine of American History* 7 (August 1881):81–103.

McHenry, James. *A Sidelight on History: Being the Letters of James McHenry, Aide-de-Camp of the Marquis de Lafayette to Thomas Sim Lee, Governor of Maryland, Written During the Yorktown Campaign, 1781.* Southampton, N.Y.: Privately printed, 1931.

———. *Journal of a March, a Battle, and a Waterfall, being the version elaborated by James McHenry from his diary of the year 1778, begun at Valley Forge, & containing accounts of the British, the Indians, and the Battle of Monmouth.* Greenwich, Conn.(?): Privately printed, 1945.

———. "Papers of Dr. James McHenry on the Federal Convention of 1787." Edited by J. Franklin Jameson. *American Historical Review* 11 (April 1906):595–624.

———. "Some Revolutionary Correspondence of Dr. James McHenry." Edited by Bernard C. Steiner. *Pennsylvania Magazine of History and Biography* 29 (January 1905):53–64.

———. "The Battle of Monmouth Described by Dr. James McHenry, Secretary to General Washington." Edited by Thomas H. Montgomery. *Magazine of American History* 3 (June 1879):355–63.

Steiner, Bernard C. *The Life and Correspondence of James McHenry, Secretary of War under Washington and Adams.* Cleveland: Burrows Bros. Co., 1907.

———, ed. "Dr. James McHenry's Speech Before the Maryland House of Delegates in November, 1787." *Maryland Historical Magazine* 4 (December 1909):336–44.

Thomas Mifflin

Carp, E. Wayne. *To Starve the Army at Pleasure: Continental Army Administration and American Political Culture, 1775–1783.* Chapel Hill: University of North Carolina Press, 1983.

Clarke, William P. *Official History of the Militia and the National Guard of the State of Pennsylvania From the Earliest Period to the Present Time.* Philadelphia: C. J. Hendler, 1909. (Only one of a projected three volumes published.)

Heathcote, Charles W. "General Thomas Mifflin—Colleague of Washington and Pennsylvania Leader." *Picket Post* 62 (November 1958):7–12.

Huston, James A. *The Sinews of War: Army Logistics 1775–1953.* Washington: Government Printing Office, 1966.

Rawle, William. "Sketch of the Life of Thomas Mifflin." *Pennsylvania Historical Society Memoirs* 2 (1830):105–26.

Risch, Erna. *Supplying Washington's Army.* Washington: Government Printing Office, 1981.

Rossman, Kenneth R. *Thomas Mifflin and the Politics of the American Revolution.* Chapel Hill: University of North Carolina Press, 1952.

———. "Thomas Mifflin: Revolutionary Patriot." *Pennsylvania History* 15 (January 1948):9–23.

Gouverneur Morris

Aimone, Alan C., and Manders, Eric I. "A Note on New York City Independent Companies, 1775–1776." *New York History* 63 (January 1982):59–73.

Alexander, Arthur J. "Exemptions From Militia Service in New York State During the Revolutionary War." *New York History* 27 (April 1946):204–12.

Kline, Mary-Jo. "Gouverneur Morris and the New Nation, 1775–1788." Ph.D. dissertation, Columbia University, 1970.

Mintz, Max M. *Gouverneur Morris and the American Revolution.* Norman: University of Oklahoma Press, 1970.

Morris, Gouverneur. *The Diary and Letters of Gouver-*

neur Morris. Edited by Anne Cary Morris. 2 vols. New York: C. Scribner's Sons, 1888.
Roosevelt, Theodore. *Gouverneur Morris*. Boston: Houghton Mifflin, 1888.
Sparks, Jared. *The Life of Gouverneur Morris, With Selections from His Correspondence, and Miscellaneous Papers; Detailing Events in the American Revolution, the French Revolution, and in the Political History of the United States*. Boston: Gray & Brown, 1832.
Swiggett, Howard. *The Extraordinary Mr. Morris*. Garden City: Doubleday, 1952.
Walther, Daniel. *Gouverneur Morris, Witness of Two Revolutions*. Translated by Elinore Denniston. New York: Funk & Wagnalls Co., 1934.

Charles Pinckney

Bethea, Andrew Jackson. *The Contributions of Charles Pinckney to the Formation of the American Union*. Richmond: Garrett & Massie, 1937.
Bowen, William E. *Charles Pinckney, a Forgotten Statesman*. Greenville (?): n.p., 1928.
Edgar, Walter B. et al., comps. *Biographical Directory of the South Carolina House of Representatives*. Columbia: University of South Carolina Press, 1974–.
Hennig, Helen K. *Great South Carolinians From Colonial Days to the Confederate War*. Chapel Hill: University of North Carolina Press, 1940.
Johnson, Joseph. *Traditions and Reminiscences, Chiefly of the American Revolution in the South*. Charleston: Walker & James, 1851.
McCrady, Edward. *History of South Carolina in the Revolution, 1775–1780*. New York: Macmillan, 1901.
Salley, Alexander S. *Delegates to the Continental Congress from South Carolina, 1774–1789, with Sketches of the Four Who Signed the Declaration of Independence*. Columbia: Historical Commission of South Carolina, 1927.
Ulmer, S. Sidney. "Charles Pinckney: Father of the Constitution?" *South Carolina Law Quarterly* 10 (Winter 1958):235–47.
Webber, Mabel L. "The Thomas Pinckney Family of South Carolina." *South Carolina Historical and Genealogical Magazine* 39 (January 1938):15–35.
Wolfe, John H. *Jeffersonian Democracy in South Carolina*. Chapel Hill: University of North Carolina Press, 1940.

Charles Cotesworth Pinckney

Edgar, Walter B. et al., comps. *Biographical Directory of the South Carolina House of Representatives*. Columbia: University of South Carolina Press, 1974–.
Gadsden, Christopher. *A Sermon Preached at St. Philip's Church, August 21, 1825, by Christopher E. Gadsden, on the Occasion of the Decease of Gen. Charles Cotesworth Pinckney*. Charleston: A. E. Miller, 1825.
Garden, Alexander. *Eulogy on Gen. Chas. Cotesworth Pinckney, President-General of the Society of the Cincinnati*. Charleston: A. E. Miller, 1825.
Hennig, Helen K. *Great South Carolinians From Colonial Days to the Confederate War*. Chapel Hill: University of North Carolina Press, 1940.
Johnson, Joseph. *Traditions and Reminiscences, Chiefly of the American Revolution in the South*. Charleston: Walker & James, 1851.
McCrady, Edward. *History of South Carolina in the Revolution, 1775–1780*. New York: Macmillan, 1901.
Pinckney, Charles Cotesworth. *Life of General Thomas Pinckney*. Boston: Houghton Mifflin, 1895.
Salley, Alexander S., ed. "An Order Book of the 1st Regt., S.C. Line, Continental Establishment." *South Carolina Historical and Genealogical Magazine* 7 (1906):75–80, 130–42, 194–203; 8 (1907):19–28, 69–87.
Webber, Mabel L. "The Thomas Pinckney Family of South Carolina." *South Carolina Historical and Genealogical Magazine* 39 (January 1938):15–35.
Williams, Frances Leigh. *A Founding Family: The Pinckneys of South Carolina*. New York: Harcourt, Brace, Jovanovich, 1978.
Zahniser, Marvin R. *Charles Cotesworth Pinckney, Founding Father*. Chapel Hill: University of North Carolina Press, 1967.

Richard Dobbs Spaight

Andrews, Alexander B. "Richard Dobbs Spaight." *North Carolina Historical Review* 1 (April 1924):95–120.
Ashe, Samuel A., ed. *Biographical History of North Carolina from Colonial Times to the Present*. 8 vols. Greensboro: C. L. Van Noppen, 1905–1917.
Trenholme, Louise Irby. *The Ratification of the Federal Constitution in North Carolina*. New York: Columbia University Press, 1932.
Wheeler, John H. *Sketch of the Life of Richard Dobbs Spaight of North Carolina*. Baltimore: W. K. Boyle, 1880.

Hugh Williamson

Ashe, Samuel A., ed. *Biographical History of North Carolina from Colonial Times to the Present*. 8 vols. Greensboro: C. L. Van Noppen, 1905–1917.
Gilpatrick, Delbert H. "Contemporary Opinion of

Hugh Williamson." *North Carolina Historical Review* 17 (January 1940):26–36.

Hosack, David. *A Biographical Memoir of Hugh Williamson.* New York: C. S. Van Winkle, 1820.

Neal, John W. "Life and Public Services of Hugh Williamson." *Trinity College Historical Society Papers* 13 (1919):62–115.

Trenholme, Louise Irby. *The Ratification of the Federal Constitution in North Carolina.* New York: Columbia University Press, 1932.

Williamson, Hugh. *The History of North Carolina.* Philadelphia: Thomas Dobson, 1812.

William Jackson

Beall, Mary S. "The Military and Private Secretaries of George Washington." *Columbia Historical Society Records* 1 (1897):89–118.

Grimke, John Faucheraud. "Order Book of John Faucheraud Grimke. August 1778 to May 1780." *South Carolina Historical and Genealogical Magazine* 13 (1912):42–55, 89–123, 146–53, 205–12; 14 (1913):44–57, 98–111, 160–70, 219–24; 15 (1914):51–59, 82–90, 124–32, 166–70; 16 (1915):39–48, 80–85, 123–28, 178–83; 17 (1916):26–33, 82–86, 116–20, 167–74; 18 (1917):78–84, 149–53, 175–79; 19 (1918):101–04, 181–88.

Jackson, Joseph. *Encyclopedia of Philadelphia.* 4 vols. Harrisburg: National Historical Association, 1931–1933.

Jackson, William. *Documents Relative to the Claim of the Surviving Officers of the Revolutionary Army of the United States, for an Equitable Settlement of the Half Pay for Life, as Stipulated by the Resolves of Congress.* n.p., 1818.

———. *Eulogium on the Character of George Washington . . . .* Philadelphia: John Ormrod, 1800.

———. *An Oration to Commemorate the Independence of the United States of North-America, delivered at the Reformed Calvinist Church, in Philadelphia, July 4th, 1786, and Published at the Request of the Pennsylvania Society of the Cincinnati.* Philadelphia: Eleazer Oswald, 1786.

Littell, Charles W. "Major William Jackson, Secretary of the Federal Convention." *Pennsylvania Magazine of History and Biography* 2 (1878):353–69.

Paltsits, Victor H., ed. "The Siege of Charleston. 1780." *Year Book, City of Charleston for 1897,* pp. 341–425.

Salley, Alexander S., ed. "An Order Book of the 1st Regt. S.C. Line, Continental Establishment." *South Carolina Historical and Genealogical Magazine* 7 (1906):75–80, 130–42, 194–203; 8 (1907):19–28, 69–87.

Simpson, Henry. *The Lives of Eminent Philadelphians now Deceased.* Philadelphia: W. Brotherhead, 1859.

"The Death of Warren at Bunker Hill," above, was painted shortly after the Revolution by John Trumbull to dramatize the stand of the New England troops on 14 June 1775. *(Oil, 1786; copyright Yale University Art Gallery.)* In contrast, the dark days following the loss of New York City in late 1776 are clearly evident in Howard Pyle's 19th century "Retreat Through the Jerseys." *(Oil; Howard Pyle Collection, Delaware Art Museum.)*

These two paintings by John Trumbull celebrate Washington's great victories that turned the tide during the winter of 1776–77. "The Capture of the Hessians at Trenton," above, shows the moment of the Germans' surrender on 26 December 1776; "The Death of Mercer at Princeton" reminded viewers of the sacrifices made on 3 January 1777. *(Oils, 1786–97; copyright Yale University Art Gallery.)*

Washington's loss of Philadelphia in 1777 contrasted sharply with Gates' victory in the north, triggering a review by Congress of national military policy the following winter. Top, Xavier della Gatta's "The Battle of Germantown" (1782) highlights the Chew House. "The Surrender of Burgoyne at Saratoga" was painted (1816–18) by eyewitness John Trumbull as part of a series on historic moments from the Revolution. *(Oils; the della Gatta, courtesy of Valley Forge Historical Society; the Trumbull, copyright Yale University Art Gallery.)*

A well-trained force of citizen-soldiers came of age at Valley Forge, Pennsylvania. Washington and his Inspector General, Frederick von Steuben (1730–94), left, successfully added professional discipline to the individualism and initiative central to the colonial military tradition. "The March to Valley Forge, December 19, 1777" is an 1883 rendering by William B. T. Trego. *(Oil; Valley Forge Historical Society.)* Charles Willson Peale painted Steuben in 1781–82. (*Oil; Independence National Historical Park.)*

Nathanael Greene (1742–1786), right, was painted in 1783 by Charles Willson Peale. *(Oil; Independence National Historical Park.)* Greene's masterful and successful blending of militiamen and Steuben-trained regulars is depicted here in H. Charles McBarron, Jr.'s modern watercolor of the battle of "Guilford Court House, 15 March 1781." *(Army Art Collection.)*

"The Siege of Yorktown" is an accurate 1784 depiction by Nicholas Van Blarenbergh. Francois-Joseph-Paul, comte de Grasse (1722–88) is shown in an 1842 portrait by Jean-Baptiste Mauzaisse. *(Both oils; Musees Nationaux Francais, Musee de Versailles.)* Jean-Baptiste-Donatien de Vimeur, comte de Rochambeau (1725–1807), bottom right, was painted by Charles Willson Peale. *(Oil, 1782; Independence National Historical Park.)*

Twenty-eight talented men served in the Revolution as aides or secretaries to Washington, including three future signers of the Constitution. Some, like John Laurens (1754–82), top left, died during or immediately after the war; others, like Joseph Reed (1741–1785) left the staff during the war for political office; most, like diplomat David Humphreys (1752–1818), bottom, became leaders under the Constitution. *(Laurens: miniature, by Charles Willson Peale, c. 1784; Reed: oil, by Charles Willson Peale, 1783; Humphreys: oil, by Rembrandt Peale, undated. All in Independence National Historical Park.)*

Charles Willson Peale completed "Washington and His Generals at Yorktown" soon after that important victory. John Trumbull's 1816–22 work, "The Resignation of Washington," below, captures the general's dramatic statement of the principle of military subordination to civilian authority. *(Oils; the Peale, courtesy of Maryland Historical Society; the Trumbull, copyright Yale University Art Gallery.)*

OTHER SIGNERS OF THE CONSTITUTION

Gunning Bedford, Jr.

Delaware

Gunning Bedford was the quintessential champion of the rights of the small states. His experience in local politics, along with his service in the Continental Congress, taught him much about the political and economic vulnerabilities of states like Delaware. Unlike some other small-state representatives who looked to the creation of a strong central government to protect their interests against more powerful neighbors, Bedford sought to limit the powers of the new government. But when the conflict over representation threatened to wreck the Constitutional Convention, he laid regional interests aside and, for the good of the country, sought to compromise.

CAREER BEFORE THE CONSTITUTIONAL CONVENTION. Bedford's family could trace its roots back to the settlement of Jamestown. He was a cousin of Colonel Gunning Bedford, a Revolutionary War hero and Delaware politician with whom he is often confused. Bedford attended the College of New Jersey (now Princeton) where he was a roommate of James Madison. After graduating in 1771, he studied law with Joseph Read, an influential politician with connections in both Pennsylvania and Delaware who would also sign the Constitution. Little is known about Bedford's early career until he opened a law practice in Dover, and then in Wilmington, during the later years of the Revolution. He sat briefly in the Delaware legislature during the early postwar period and represented his state in the Continental Congress (1783–85). He also served as the state's attorney general (1784–89). Although selected in 1786 to represent his state at the Annapolis Convention, Bedford was among those delegates who missed the sessions of that brief meeting. Evidence suggests that he shared the convention's concern with the political and economic problems associated with the Articles of Confederation, a concern that led the Annapolis delegates to call for what became the Constitutional Convention.

CONTRIBUTIONS TO THE CONSTITUTIONAL CONVENTION. Concerned primarily with the fate of the small states in a federal union potentially dominated by powerful, populous neighbors, the fiery Bedford warned the delegates at Philadelphia that the small states might have to seek foreign alliances for their own protection. At first he joined with those who sought merely to amend the Articles of Confederation, believing, as one delegate contended, "there is no middle way between a perfect consolidation [of the states into one nation] and a mere confederacy of the states. The first is out of the question, and in the latter they must continue if not perfectly yet equally sovereign." But when the idea of drafting a new Constitution was accepted, he supported the New Jersey Plan, a scheme that provided equal representation for the states in the national legislature, a point on which the Delaware legislature had instructed its delegates not to compromise. He called for strong limitations on the powers of the executive branch and recommended measures by which the states could maintain close control over the national legislature and judiciary, including the appointment of federal judges by the state legislatures. Bedford's speeches in support of these ideas led Georgia delegate William Pierce to describe him as a "bold" speaker, with "a very commanding and striking manner," but "warm and impetuous in his temper and precipitate in his judgement."

Realizing as the Convention sessions went on that unyielding adherence to his position would endanger the union, Bedford adopted a more flexible stance. He agreed to sit on the committee that drafted the Great Compromise, which settled the thorny question of representation and made possible the Convention's acceptance of the new plan of government.

CAREER AFTER THE CONSTITUTIONAL CONVENTION. Bedford was a delegate to Delaware's ratification convention. Thanks to his efforts, along with those of John Dickinson, William Bassett, and others, Delaware became the first state to approve the Constitution. Resigning his post as Delaware's attorney general in 1789, he served that year and again in 1793 as a presidential elector, casting ballots both times for George Washington. Widely respected for his knowledge of the law, Bedford was asked by Delaware's senators and fellow signers George Read and William Bassett to review a bill, then under consideration, on the organization of the federal judiciary system. Bedford praised the document, which would become the Judiciary Act of 1789, one of the most important pieces of legislation of the period, as a "noble work," but expressed some concerns as well. He admitted that the common law of the United States was difficult to define. "Yet," he claimed, "the dignity of America requires that it [a definition] be ascertained, and that where we refer to laws they should be laws of our own country. If the principles of the laws of any other country are good and worthy of adoption, incorporate them into your own." He believed the Constitution's ratification had been the moment of "legal emancipation," declaring that "as the foundation is laid so must the superstructure be built." In September 1789 Washington selected Bedford to be federal district judge for Delaware, a position he held until his death.

Bedford never lost interest in his local community. Believing the establishment of schools "is, on all hands, justly acknowledged to be an object of first importance," he worked for the improvement of education in Wilmington. He was president of the Board of Trustees of Wilmington Academy, and when that institution became Wilmington College, he became its first president.

PERSONAL DATA
BIRTH: 1747 (exact date unknown), in Philadelphia
DEATH: 30 March 1812, at Wilmington, Delaware
INTERMENT: Graveyard of the First Presbyterian Church, Wilmington; later reinterred at the Masonic Home, Christiana Hundred, Delaware.

John Blair
Virginia

John Blair was one of the best-trained jurists of his day. A legal scholar, he avoided the hurly-burly of state politics, preferring to work behind the scenes. But he was devoted to the idea of a permanent union of the newly independent states and loyally supported fellow Virginians James Madison and George Washington at the Constitutional Convention. His greatest contribution as a Founding Father came not in Philadelphia, but later as a judge on the Virginia court of appeals and on the U.S. Supreme Court, where he influenced the interpretation of the Constitution in a number of important decisions. Contemporaries praised Blair for such personal strengths as gentleness and benevolence, and for his ability to penetrate immediately to the heart of a legal question.

CAREER BEFORE THE CONSTITUTIONAL CONVENTION. Blair was a member of a prominent Virginia family. His father served on the Virginia Council and was for a time acting Royal governor. His grand-uncle, James Blair, was founder and first president of the College of William and Mary. Blair attended William and Mary and in 1775 went to London to study law at the Middle Temple. Returning home to practice law, he was quickly thrust into public life, beginning his public career shortly after the close of the French and Indian War with his election to the seat reserved for the College of William and Mary in the House of Burgesses (1766–70). He went on to become clerk of the Royal Governor's Council, the upper house of the colonial legislature (1770–75).

Blair originally joined the moderate wing of the Patriot cause. He opposed Patrick Henry's extremist resolutions in protest of the Stamp Act, but the dissolution of the House of Burgesses by Parliament profoundly altered his views. In response to a series of Parliamentary taxes on the colonies, Blair joined George Washington and others in 1770 and again in 1774 to draft nonimportation agreements which pledged their supporters to cease importing British goods until the taxes were repealed. In the latter year he reacted to Parliament's passage of the Intolerable Acts by joining those calling for a Continental Congress and pledging support for the people of Boston who were suffering economic hardship because of Parliament's actions.

When the Revolution began, Blair became deeply involved in the government of his state. He served as a member of the convention that drew up Virginia's constitution (1776) and held a number of important committee positions, including a seat on the Committee of 28 that framed Virginia's Declaration of Rights and plan of government. He served on the Privy Council, Governor Patrick Henry's major advisory group (1776–78). The legislature elected him to a judgeship in the general court in 1778 and soon thereafter to the post of chief justice. He was also elected to Virginia's high court of chancery (1780), where his colleague was George Wythe, later a fellow delegate to the Constitutional Convention. These judicial appointments automatically made Blair a member of Virginia's first court of appeals. In 1786, the legislature, recognizing Blair's prestige as a jurist, appointed him Thomas Jefferson's successor on a committee revising Virginia's laws.

CONTRIBUTIONS TO THE CONSTITUTIONAL CONVENTION. Although a faithful attendee, Blair never addressed the Convention nor sat on any of its committees. When the question of how the President should be elected arose, he joined George Mason and Edmund Randolph in advocating election by the Congress, thus splitting the Virginia delegation. Coming to realize that his stand was weakening his delegation in the voting process and impeding the progress of the Convention, he abandoned his position and voted with Washington and Madison, whom, as a stalwart nationalist, he supported for the remainder of the Convention.

CAREER AFTER THE CONSTITUTIONAL CONVENTION. Blair returned to Williamsburg, where he supported the new Constitution in a heated ratification struggle that pitted him and his colleagues against opponents who included some of the greatest orators of the day.

He continued to sit on the Virginia court of appeals, where he made a number of decisions important in the formation of Virginia jurisprudence. In *Commonwealth vs. Posey*, he based his decision on a 200-year-old precedent in English Common Law, thus establishing as a principle in American law that the accepted judicial understanding of a statute forms a part of the law itself and must be adhered to. More importantly, he and his colleagues on the court drafted a *Remonstrance of the Judges* that was successful in defending judges from the jurisdiction of the state legislature, thus preserving the principle of separation of powers in the state.

President George Washington, Blair's longtime

friend, chose him to be an associate justice of the U.S. Supreme Court (1789–96), where he was involved in several important constitutional cases. Well known as a strict constructionist, Blair could find no solution in the clauses of the Constitution to the question posed by *Chisolm vs. Georgia* concerning the right of an individual to sue a state. The Chisolm case led directly to the passage of the Eleventh Amendment, which declared that the states were immune from citizens' suits. Blair considered the separation of powers the basis of political liberty. When Congress passed an act in 1792 subjecting certain judicial decisions to legislative review, Blair was among the justices who, using arguments from the *Remonstrance*, attacked the act as an infringement upon the independence of the courts. From the bench he also pressed his view that the central government had precedence over the governments of the states. In *Penhallow et al. vs. Doane's Administrators*, Blair asserted this primacy by defending the power of the federal circuit courts to overturn the decisions of the state maritime courts.

PERSONAL DATA
BORN: 1732 (exact date unknown), in Williamsburg, Virginia
DEATH: 31 August 1800, in Williamsburg
INTERMENT: Graveyard of Bruton Parish Church, Williamsburg, Virginia

Jacob Broom

Delaware

Jacob Broom was a local politician whose interests remained focused throughout his career on the government of his city and state. Thrust onto the national stage, he realized the opportunities presented to the small states by a strong central government and supported the Constitution. Surrounded by wealthy planters, lawyers, and merchants at the Constitutional Convention, he quietly voiced the concerns of the down-home politician.

CAREER BEFORE THE CONSTITUTIONAL CONVENTION. Broom was the son of a blacksmith turned prosperous farmer. After receiving his primary education at Wilmington's Old Academy, he became in turn a farmer, surveyor, and finally, a prosperous local businessman. Even as a young man Broom attracted considerable attention in Wilmington's thriving business community, a prominence that propelled him into a political career. He held a variety of local offices, including borough assessor, president of the city's "street regulators," a group responsible for the care of the street, water, and sewage systems, and justice of the peace for New Castle County. He became assistant burgess (vice-mayor) of Wilmington in 1776, winning reelection to this post six times over the next few decades. He also served as chief burgess of the city four times.

Although the strong pacifist influence of his Quaker friends and relatives kept him from fighting in the Revolution, Broom was nevertheless a Patriot who contributed to the cause of independence. For example, he put his abilities as a surveyor at the disposal of the Continental Army, preparing detailed maps of the region for General Washington shortly before the battle of Brandywine. Broom's political horizons expanded after the Revolution when his community sent him as their representative to the state legislature (1784–86 and 1788), which in turn chose him to represent the state at the Annapolis Convention. Like many other delegates, Broom was unable to attend the sessions of the short meeting, but he likely sympathized with the convention's call for political reforms.

CONTRIBUTIONS TO THE CONSTITUTIONAL CONVENTION. Despite his lack of involvement in national politics prior to the Constitutional Convention, Broom was a dedicated supporter of strong central government. When George Washington visited Wilmington in 1783, Broom urged him to "contribute your advice and influence to promote that harmony and union of our infant governments which are so essential to the permanent establishment of our freedom, happiness and prosperity."

Broom carried these opinions with him to Philadelphia, where he consistently voted for measures that would assure a powerful government responsive to the needs of the states. He favored a nine-year term for members of the Senate, where the states would be equally represented. He wanted the state legislatures to pay their representatives in Congress, which, in turn, would have the power to veto state laws. He also sought to vest state legislatures with the power to select presidential electors, and he wanted the President to hold office for life. Broom faithfully attended the sessions of the Convention in Philadelphia and spoke out several times on issues that he considered crucial, but he left most of the speechmaking to more influential and experienced delegates. Georgia delegate William Pierce described him as "a plain good Man, with some abilities, but nothing to render him conspicuous, silent in public, but chearful and conversible in private."

CAREER AFTER THE CONSTITUTIONAL CONVENTION. Broom's exposure to the national political scene proved short-lived. His primary interest remained in local government, and after the Convention he returned to familiar political surroundings. In addition to continuing his service in Wilmington's government, he became the city's first postmaster (1790–92). His long-standing affiliation with the Old Academy led him to become involved in its reorganization into the College of Wilmington, and to serve on the college's first Board of Trustees. Broom was also deeply involved in his community's religious affairs as a lay leader of the Old Swedes Church.

PERSONAL DATA
BIRTH: 1752 (exact date unknown), in Wilmington, Delaware
DEATH: 1810 (exact date unknown), in Philadelphia
INTERMENT: Christ Church Burial Ground, Philadelphia, Pennsylvania

Daniel Carroll
Maryland

Daniel Carroll was a prominent member of one of America's great colonial families, a family that produced a signer of the Declaration of Independence in Charles Carroll of Carrollton, a cousin, and the first Catholic bishop in the United States, Daniel's brother John. Daniel Carroll was a patrician planter who fused family honor with the cause of American independence, willingly risking his social and economic position in the community for the Patriot cause. Later, as a friend and staunch ally of George Washington, he worked for a strong central government which could secure the achievements and fulfill the hopes of the Revolution. Ironically, for one whose name was synonymous with the colonial aristocracy, Carroll fought in the Convention for a government responsible directly to the people.

CAREER BEFORE THE CONSTITUTIONAL CONVENTION. Typical of wealthy colonial Catholics, Carroll went abroad for his education. Between 1742 and 1748 he studied under the Jesuits at St. Omer's in Flanders. After his return, he only gradually joined the Patriot cause. A large landholder, he was concerned lest the Revolution fail economically and bring about not only his family's financial ruin, but mob rule as well. Furthermore, he was initially prevented from becoming involved in Maryland politics by laws that excluded Catholics from holding public office. Once these laws were nullified by the Maryland constitution of 1776, the way was cleared for his election to the upper house of the Maryland legislature (1777–81). At the end of his term, he became a member of the Continental Congress (1781–84), where, in 1781, he signed the Articles of Confederation. His involvement in the Revolution, like that of other Patriots in this patrician's extended family, was inspired by the family's ancient motto: "Strong in Faith and War."

CONTRIBUTIONS TO THE CONSTITUTIONAL CONVENTION. Carroll was an active member of the Constitutional Convention, despite the fact that illness prevented him from attending the early sessions. Like his good friend James Madison, Carroll was convinced that a strong central government was needed to regulate commerce among the states and with other nations. He also spoke out repeatedly in opposition to the payment of members of Congress by the states, reasoning that such compensation would sabotage the strength of the new government because "the dependence of both Houses on the state Legislatures would be compleat. . . .The new government in this form is nothing more than a second edition of [the Continental] Congress in two volumes, instead of one, and perhaps with very few amendments." He wanted governmental power vested in the people, and he joined James Wilson in campaigning for popular sovereignty. When it was suggested that the President should be elected by the Congress, it was Carroll, seconded by James Wilson, who moved that the words "by the legislature" be replaced with "by the people." His signature on the Constitution made him one of two Catholics to sign the document, a further symbol of the advance of religious freedom in America during the Revolutionary period.

CAREER AFTER THE CONSTITUTIONAL CONVENTION. Following the Convention, Carroll immersed himself in state and national affairs. He was a key participant in the Maryland ratification struggle. He also defended the Constitution in the pages of the Maryland *Journal*, most notably in his response to the arguments advanced by the well-known Antifederalist Samuel Chase. After ratification was achieved in Maryland, Carroll became a representative in the First Congress, where, reflecting his concern for economic and fiscal stability, he voted for the assumption of state debts by the federal government.

He later served in the Maryland senate and as one of three commissioners appointed to survey the District of Columbia. He then became a commissioner (co-mayor) of the new capital city, but advanced age and failing health forced him to retire in 1795. Even then, interest in the good of his region kept him active. In the last year of his life he became one of George Washington's partners in the Patowmack Company, a business enterprise intended to link the middle states with the expanding west by means of a Potomac River canal.

PERSONAL DATA
BIRTH: 22 July 1730, at Upper Marlboro, Maryland
DEATH: 5 July 1796, at "Rock Creek" (Forest Glen),

Montgomery County, Maryland
INTERMENT: St. John's Catholic Cemetery, Forest Glen, Maryland

George Clymer
Pennsylvania

George Clymer was a successful businessman with an abiding interest in the welfare of the common man. He never served in uniform during the Revolutionary War, but he made a significant contribution to the cause of liberty by organizing essential congressional support for needed military reforms and by personally helping to reorganize the Continental Army. As a politician he tended to avoid the limelight, preferring to work on committees where he could bring his administrative skills to bear. He was a soft-spoken man who, as a contemporary said, "was never heard to speak ill of any one." He signed the Declaration of Independence as well as the Constitution.

CAREER BEFORE THE CONSTITUTIONAL CONVENTION. Clymer was orphaned as an infant and adopted by an uncle, William Coleman, a wealthy Philadelphia merchant and friend of Benjamin Franklin. Informally educated, he became a clerk and, later, partner in his uncle's mercantile firm, which he would inherit. In 1765 he married Elizabeth Meredith, whose socially prominent family introduced him to George Washington and other Patriot leaders. He eventually merged his business with that of his in-laws to form Meredith-Clymer, a leading Pennsylvania merchant house.

Clymer became politically active in response to British tax policies and trade restrictions on colonial business. In 1773 he led a committee of Pennsylvania Patriots that forced the resignation of Philadelphia tea consignees appointed by Parliament under the Tea Act. An ardent Patriot, he commanded a company of the Associators, Philadelphia's volunteer militia. (Clymer is not included among the Soldier-Statesmen because he never served on active duty during the Revolutionary War.) While a member of the Pennsylvania Council of Safety, the executive agency created by the legislature to govern the newly emerging state when the legislature was not in session, he became an early advocate of complete independence for the colonies.

Clymer brought his significant managerial and financial skills with him to national political service. He served as Continental treasurer (1775–76), an office organized by the Continental Congress to supervise the financing of the Revolution. He proved his faith in the new government by exchanging his own money (gold, silver, and British pounds) for the paper currency issued by the Continental Congress. He also supported the Continental Loan, a plan advanced by Congress to finance the Revolution with money borrowed from the citizenry.

He went on to represent Pennsylvania in the Continental Congress (1776–77 and 1780–82). He rarely entered into debates, but was influential in committees dealing with military, financial, and commercial matters. In a noteworthy act of personal bravery, Clymer remained with Robert Morris and George Walton in Philadelphia to manage government affairs during the winter of 1776–77 while the rest of Congress fled to Baltimore to escape capture by the advancing British. His work in helping to organize the resupply of Washington's battered main army during those crucial months made the victories at Trenton and Princeton possible. Clymer subsequently became deeply involved in Continental Army affairs, even visiting units in the field. He worked hard to improve the lot of the common soldier, supporting Washington's efforts to improve administrative efficiency, especially by reforming the Army's commissary system. His investigation of Indian uprisings at Fort Pitt (now Pittsburgh) in December 1777 led Congress to organize an abortive military expedition intended to reduce the British stronghold at Detroit. In retaliation for Clymer's role in this effort, Redcoats operating in the Philadelphia area sought out and vandalized his home.

Elected by his neighbors to serve in the Pennsylvania legislature (1784–88), he further displayed his strong humanitarian bent by advocating reform of the penal code and abolition of the death penalty.

CONTRIBUTIONS TO THE CONSTITUTIONAL CONVENTION. At the Convention, Clymer served on those committees concerned with the military, commercial, and financial powers and responsibilities of the new government. An advocate of strong central government, he supported the Federalist position taken by Washington, Hamilton, and Madison.

CAREER AFTER THE CONSTITUTIONAL CONVENTION. Clymer was a member of the House of Representatives in the First Congress (1789–91), where he supported a liberal naturalization policy and closer ties with France. His continuing interest in the concerns of the common citizen caused him, like Madison, to gravitate toward the new political party emerging around Thomas Jefferson in opposition to his old Federalist allies.

Clymer held two other federal offices, first as collector of excise taxes on alcoholic beverages in Pennsylvania and later as a member of the commission that negotiated a treaty with the Cherokee and Creek Indians in Georgia. Retiring from public life in 1796, he went on to be the first president of the Philadelphia Bank and a sponsor of the Pennsylvania Academy of Fine Arts.

PERSONAL DATA
BIRTH: 16 March 1739, in Philadelphia
DEATH: 23 January 1813, at "Sommerseat," an estate in Morrisville, New Jersey, near Philadelphia
INTERMENT: Friends Meeting House Cemetery, Trenton, New Jersey

Benjamin Franklin
Pennsylvania

Benjamin Franklin was admired on two continents for his scientific accomplishments, wit, unpretentious manners, diplomatic ability, and kindly personality. He employed these personal qualities in the service of his country as an able diplomat and as the universally respected advocate of compromise in the critical moments of the early republic.

CAREER BEFORE THE CONSTITUTIONAL CONVENTION. Franklin was the tenth son of a Massachusetts soap and candle maker. Largely self-taught, Franklin displayed an intellectual ability, readily apparent to those around him, that would earn him an international reputation in various fields. He began his career as a printer, going on to found the *New England Courant*, the fourth newspaper in the colonies. Following a serious argument with his brother in 1723, Franklin left Boston to start life anew in Philadelphia. There he quickly became an honored citizen and began his lifelong participation in political affairs. He served in Pennsylvania's colonial legislature (1736–64), both as delegate and elected clerk of the general assembly. In 1737 he also became postmaster of Philadelphia. He rose to prominence throughout the colonies when he became deputy postmaster general of British North America (1753–74).

During this period Franklin found time to publish the *Pennsylvania Gazette* and to write and publish *Poor Richard's Almanac,* which enhanced his reputation as a philosopher, scientist, and inventor. His publishing ventures brought financial independence, allowing him to become a philanthropist and to indulge his love for scientific investigation. As a philanthropist, he supported and encouraged such varied programs as the establishment of public schools and libraries and the installation of street lighting. He was elected a member of the Royal Society in recognition of his scientific achievements, especially for his study of electricity. His scientific renown earned him honorary degrees from Yale and Harvard in 1753 and from William and Mary in 1756.

In 1754 Franklin was selected to represent Pennsylvania at the Albany Congress, called to unite the colonies during the French and Indian War. At the congress, Franklin advanced his Albany Plan of Union, one of the first proposals to bring the colonies together under some form of central authority. The plan was adopted by the congress, but rejected by the colonial legislatures because they believed it encroached upon their powers.

Franklin then entered what was to be a pivotal period in his life. He went to London as an agent representing the interests of Pennsylvania, and then later as an agent for Georgia, New Jersey, and Massachusetts (1757–62 and 1764–75). Beginning as a contented Englishman who favored Royal rule and distrusted popular movements, he emerged as a leading spokesman for American rights. When the Stamp Act crisis arose, he demonstrated his new political sentiments by speaking out against the Act. He gradually adopted the theory that Parliament did not have the power to tax or to legislate in the colonies, and that the colonies and Great Britain were united "as England and Scotland were before the Union, by having one common Sovereign, the King."

Returning to America, he advanced to the forefront of the Patriot cause as a member of the Continental Congress (1775–76). He served on the committee that drafted the Declaration of Independence. (It has been said that he was not chosen to draft the document for fear that he might conceal a joke in it.) He was the eldest signer of the Declaration of Independence, and when he finished signing the document, he joked, "Gentlemen, we must now all hang together, or we shall most assuredly all hang separately." Ironically, while Franklin was working on the Declaration, his son William, a militant Loyalist and the last Royal governor of New Jersey, was being incarcerated in Connecticut. Franklin left the Continental Congress to become president of Pennsylvania's constitutional convention in 1776.

The greatest achievement of Franklin's public career occurred during his tenure as one of the fledgling nation's ambassadors. His work as minister to France (1776–85) was critical to the achievement of the nation's first foreign alliance, so essential to the success of the Revolutionary War effort. The respected and admired old statesman obtained loans, negotiated treaties of commerce and alliance, and, along with John Jay and John Adams, negotiated the Treaty of Paris that ended the War for Independence. Once independence was achieved, Franklin came home to Pennsylvania to serve as the president of the Supreme Executive Council of Philadelphia (1785–88).

CONTRIBUTIONS TO THE CONSTITUTIONAL CONVENTION. At the age of 81, Franklin was the senior statesman of the Constitutional Convention, but his advanced years only served to enhance his importance in the Convention, giving him a singular role to play. His few formal discourses were written out and read, since he was no orator, and none of his major ideas, including a single-chambered legislature, an executive board rather than a single President, and service in public office without pay, was ever adopted. Yet he remained among the most influential delegates because of his unique ability to soothe disputes and encourage compromise through his prestige, humor, and powers of diplomacy. When a deadlock developed over the question of how the states should be represented in Congress, Franklin rephrased the problem in simple yet direct terms: "If a property representation takes place, the small states contend their liberties will be in danger. If an equality of votes takes place, the large states say their money will be in danger. When a broad table is to be made, and the planks do not fit, the artist takes a little from both, and makes a good joint." In the end, Franklin was an important member of the committee that adjusted the matter of representation, thus working out the "good joint" that was to be the most important prerequisite to the adoption of the Constitution. When the time came to sign the document, Franklin encouraged his fellow delegates to take this spirit of compromise to its conclusion by lending the Constitution their unanimous support, despite the fact that he himself did not approve of every aspect of the new plan of government. He concluded: "On the whole . . . I cannot help expressing a wish that every member of the Convention . . . would with me, on this occasion, doubt a little of his own infallibility, and to make manifest our unanimity, put his name to the instrument."

CAREER AFTER THE CONSTITUTIONAL CONVENTION. Franklin's last public acts were to sign a memorial to Congress urging the abolition of slavery, a cause with which he had sympathized since the 1730s, and to become the first president of the Pennsylvania Society for the Abolition of Slavery. His funeral in 1790 became a national event attended by some 20,000 people.

PERSONAL DATA
BIRTH: 17 January 1706, in Boston, Massachusetts
DEATH: 17 April 1790, in Philadelphia
INTERMENT: Christ Church Burial Ground in Philadelphia, Pennsylvania

Nathaniel Gorham
Massachusetts

Nathaniel Gorham was a self-made businessman who contributed significantly to the success of the Revolution by assuming an important role as a civilian in the management of his state's military affairs. Gorham's practical experiences in commercial matters led him to realize that a strong central government would benefit the nation economically. Although representing one of the large states, he also argued that the new government should be granted powers sufficient to ensure that the states could not dominate it. At the same time, Gorham was a political realist who was willing to compromise on details to ensure acceptance of the new instrument of government.

CAREER BEFORE THE CONSTITUTIONAL CONVENTION. Gorham was the son of a packet-boat operator and member of an Old Bay Colony family of modest means. He received little formal education, but was apprenticed at age fifteen to Nathaniel Coffin, a merchant in New London, Connecticut. Gorham succeeded in business because of personal ability rather than family prominence. Already well known in Charlestown by 1770, he began his public career as a notary, soon winning election to the colonial legislature (1771–75) where he emerged an ardent Patriot. During the Revolution his political star continued to rise when he displayed a special talent for administration that proved crucial to the wartime government of his state. In particular he served on the Board of War, which organized Massachusetts' military logistics and manpower (1778–81). When the Continental Army left Massachusetts for the campaign in New York, the Board of War not only provided for the coastal defenses of the region, but also supported the military effort in the northeastern section of the state, where American forces were engaged in several important expeditions against British bases in Nova Scotia. Gorham also was a delegate to Massachusetts' first constitutional convention (1779–80) and represented his community in the upper (1780) and lower (1781–87) houses of the new state legislature, serving several terms as speaker of the lower house.

In recognition of Gorham's work during the war, Massachusetts appointed him a delegate to the Continental Congress (1782–83 and 1785–87) where for a period he served as president. Despite his lack of formal legal training, the state also appointed him judge of Middlesex County's court of common pleas (1785–96).

CONTRIBUTIONS TO THE CONSTITUTIONAL CONVENTION. Gorham played an influential part in the Constitutional Convention, speaking frequently, sitting on the Committee of Detail, and serving as chairman of the Committee of the Whole. Representing the commercial-cosmopolitan interests in Massachusetts, he pushed for a central government strong enough to protect interstate commerce, promote international trade, and regulate the use of paper money. To free the new government from passing fads and prejudices, he favored long presidential and senatorial terms. He also wanted to give Congress broad powers, but he urged the appointment of federal judges by the executive. Finally, he wanted a consolidation of military authority through control of the militia by the central government. Ironically, in view of his support of the new republic, Gorham was pessimistic about the future of his state and country. He believed, in the aftermath of Shays' Rebellion, that Massachusetts would divide between east and west "on the question [of the Constitution] as it has on all questions for several years past," and that the country, because of its great size, would divide into several independent nations within 150 years.

CAREER AFTER THE CONSTITUTIONAL CONVENTION. Gorham was a key participant in Massachusetts' struggle for ratification, won only when Gorham and other Federalists proposed possible amendments to the Constitution to attract the moderates who held the deciding votes. While retaining his seat on the court of common pleas, Gorham also served for a brief period (1788–89) on the Governor's Council, an advisory group to the state's chief executive. His later years were marked by a reverse in his personal fortunes. Along with a business associate, Oliver Phelps, he bought 2,600,000 acres in western New York, a transaction that ruined him financially when the value of paper money, and hence the real value of his debt, suddenly rose.

PERSONAL DATA
BIRTH: 27 May 1738, in Charlestown, Massachusetts
DEATH: 11 June 1796, at Charlestown, Massachusetts
INTERMENT: Phipps Street Cemetery, Charlestown, Massachusetts

Jared Ingersoll

Pennsylvania

Jared Ingersoll overcame the strong influence of his Loyalist father to become a supporter of the Revolutionary cause. His training as a lawyer convinced him that the problems of the newly independent states were caused by the inadequacy of the Articles of Confederation. He became an early and ardent proponent of constitutional reform, although, like a number of his colleagues at the Constitutional Convention, he believed this reform could be achieved by a simple revision of the Articles. Only after weeks of debate did he come to see that a new document was necessary. Ironically, his major contribution to the cause of constitutional government came not during the Convention, but later during a lengthy and distinguished legal career when he helped define many of the principles enunciated at Philadelphia.

CAREER BEFORE THE CONSTITUTIONAL CONVENTION. Ingersoll was the son of a prominent British official, whose strong Loyalist sentiments would lead to his being tarred and feathered at the hands of radical Patriots. Ingersoll graduated from Yale College in 1766, studied law in Philadelphia, and was admitted to the bar in 1773. Although by training and inclination a Patriot sympathizer, the young Ingersoll shied away from the cause at the outset because of a strong sense of personal loyalty to his distinguished father. On his father's advice, he sought to escape the growing political controversy at home by retiring to London to continue his study of the law at the Middle Temple (1773–76) and to tour extensively through Europe. But shortly after the colonies declared their independence, Ingersoll renounced his family's views, made his personal commitment to the cause of independence, and returned home. In 1778 he arrived in Philadelphia as a confirmed Patriot. With the help of influential friends he quickly established a flourishing law practice, and shortly thereafter he entered the fray as a delegate to the Continental Congress (1780–81). Always a supporter of strong central authority in political affairs, he became a leading agitator for reforming the national government in the postwar years, preaching the need for change to his friends in Congress and to the legal community.

CONTRIBUTIONS TO THE CONSTITUTIONAL CONVENTION. At the Convention, Ingersoll was counted among those who favored revision of the existing Articles of Confederation, but in the end he joined with the majority and supported a plan for a new federal government. Despite his national reputation as an attorney, Ingersoll seldom participated in the Convention debates, although he attended all sessions.

CAREER AFTER THE CONSTITUTIONAL CONVENTION. Once the new national government was created, Ingersoll returned to the law. Except for a few excursions into politics—he was a member of Philadelphia's Common Council (1789) and, as a stalwart Federalist who considered the election of Thomas Jefferson in 1800 a "great subversion," he ran unsuccessfully for Vice President on the Federalist ticket in 1812—his public career centered on legal affairs. He served as attorney general of Pennsylvania (1790–99 and 1811–17), as Philadelphia's city solicitor (1798–1801), and as U.S. district attorney for Pennsylvania (1800–1801). For a brief period (1821–22) he sat as presiding judge of the Philadelphia district court.

Ingersoll contributed to the constitutional process through his involvement in several key Supreme Court cases that defined basic points in constitutional law dur-

Gunning Bedford, Jr. *(Oil, by Charles Willson Peale, c. 1787; courtesy of the Architect of the Capitol.)*

John Blair. *(Pastel, by William Williams, undated; courtesy of Colonial Williamsburg Foundation.)*

Daniel Carroll. *(Oil, by John Wollaston, c. 1758; courtesy of Maryland Historical Society.)*

George Clymer. *(Oil, by Charles Willson Peale, c. 1807–10; Pennsylvania Academy of Fine Arts.)*

Clockwise from right:

George Read. *(Oil, by Thomas Sully after Robert Edge Pine, 1860; Independence National Historical Park.)*

James Wilson. *(Oil, by Philip F. Wharton, 1937, after miniature by James Peale; Independence National Historical Park.)*

John Rutledge. *(Oil on wood, by John Trumbull, 1791; copyright Yale University Art Gallery.)*

William Samuel Johnson. *(Oil, by John Wesley Jarvis, c. 1814; National Portrait Gallery, Smithsonian Institution.)*

Daniel of St. Thomas Jenifer. *(Oil, by John Hesselius, c. 1765; National Portrait Gallery, Smithsonian Institution.)*

Nathaniel Gorham. *(Oil, by Charles Willson Peale, c. 1793; courtesy of the Museum of Fine Arts, Boston, gift of Edwin H. Abbott, Jr.)*

Jared Ingersoll. *(Oil, by Charles Willson Peale, 1820; Independence National Historical Park.)*

ing the early years of the new republic. For example, he represented Georgia in *Chisolm vs. Georgia* (1793), a landmark case in states' rights. Here the court decided against him, ruling that a state might be sued by a citizen of another state. This complete reversal of the notion of state sovereignty was later rescinded by the Eleventh Amendment to the Constitution. In representing Hylton in *Hylton vs. U.S.* (1796), Ingersoll was also involved in the first legal challenge to the constitutionality of an act of Congress. In this case the Supreme Court upheld the government's right to impose a tax on carriages. Ingersoll also served as counsel in various cases that helped clarify constitutional issues concerning the jurisdiction of federal courts and U.S. relations with other sovereign nations.

PERSONAL DATA
BIRTH: 27 October 1749, at New Haven, Connecticut
DEATH: 31 October 1822, in Philadelphia
INTERMENT: First Presbyterian Church Cemetery, Philadelphia, Pennsylvania

Daniel of St. Thomas Jenifer
Maryland

Daniel of St. Thomas Jenifer was an honored and effective local leader who, when conflict arose with Great Britain, embraced the Patriot cause, willingly abandoning the ordered society of colonial Maryland for the uncertainty of revolution. One of the oldest delegates in Philadelphia, he used his prestige to work for a strong and permanent union of the states. Contemporaries noted his good humor and pleasant company, which won him many friends at the Convention. When Luther Martin, who refused to sign the document, said that he feared being hanged if the people of Maryland approved the Constitution, Jenifer told him, humorously, that Martin should stay in Philadelphia, so that he would not hang in his home state. Along with Benjamin Franklin, Jenifer used laughter to help reconcile the opposing views of the delegates and to formulate the compromises that made the Convention a success.

CAREER BEFORE THE CONSTITUTIONAL CONVENTION. Jenifer was the son of a colonial planter of Swedish and English descent. Born long before conflicts with Great Britain emerged, he was for many years a leader in Maryland's colonial government. As a young man, he acted as a receiver-general, the local financial agent for the last two proprietors of Maryland. Jenifer served as justice of the peace for Charles County and later for the western circuit of Maryland. He sat on a commission that settled a boundary dispute between Pennsylvania and Maryland (1760) and on the Governor's Council, the upper house of the Maryland legislature that also served as the colony's court of appeals and as a board of senior advisers to the governor (1773–76).

Despite his close ties with the colonial government, Jenifer strongly resented what he and most of the colonial gentry saw as Parliament's arbitrary interference with the colonies' affairs, especially its laws concerning taxation and trade regulation. Years before the struggle for independence began, he had defended the proprietors of Maryland against those who sought to make Maryland a Royal colony, and when the Revolution came he lent his considerable support as a wealthy landowner to the Patriot cause, despite the fact that many leading Patriots had been his enemies in the proprietorship struggle. He became the president of Maryland's Council of Safety, the Patriot body established to organize Maryland's military forces for the Revolution (1775–77). When, in 1776, a new constitution was framed for the state of Maryland, Jenifer commented on the document's neglect of popular sovereignty: "The Senate does not appear to me to be a Child of the people at Large, and therefore will not be Supported by them longer than there Subsists the most perfect Union between the different Legislative branches." He represented his state in the Continental Congress (1778–82) while simultaneously serving as president of the state's first senate (1777–80). As manager of the state's finances between 1782 and 1785, he drew on his experiences as a landholder to help the state survive the critical postwar economic depression.

During these years, Jenifer became increasingly concerned with national affairs. Along with James Madison, John Dickinson, and his good friend George Washington, he began to explore ways to solve the economic and political problems that had arisen under the weak Articles of Confederation. Consequently, he attended the Mount Vernon Conference, a meeting that would lead eventually to the Constitutional Convention.

CONTRIBUTIONS TO THE CONSTITUTIONAL CONVENTION. Like his old friend Benjamin Franklin, Jenifer enjoyed the status of elder statesman at the Philadelphia Convention. He took stands on several important issues, although his advanced age restricted his activity in the day-to-day proceedings. Business experience gained while managing a large plantation had convinced him that an active central government was needed to ensure financial and commercial stability. To that end, he favored a strong and permanent union of the states in which a Congress representing the people had the power to tax. Concerned with continuity in the new government, he favored a three-year term for the House of

Representatives. Too frequent elections, he concluded, might lead to indifference and would make prominent men unwilling to seek office. Jenifer was outvoted on this point, but his reaction was to marvel at the delegates' ability to come to agreement on a plan of government: "The first month we only came to grips, and the second it seemed as though we would fly apart forever, but we didn't—we jelled."

CAREER AFTER THE CONSTITUTIONAL CONVENTION. Jenifer, now in his sixty-fourth year, retired to "Stepney," his great plantation near Annapolis.

PERSONAL DATA

BIRTH: 1723 (exact date unknown), at "Coates Retirement" (now "Ellerslie"), an estate near Port Tobacco in Charles County, Maryland

DEATH: 16 November 1790, in Annapolis, Maryland

INTERMENT: Exact location of his grave, which is on the Ellerslie estate, is unknown.

William Samuel Johnson

Connecticut

William Samuel Johnson was one of the best educated of the Founding Fathers. His knowledge of the law led him to oppose taxation without representation as a violation of the colonists' rights as Englishmen, but his strong ties with Great Britain made renunciation of the King personally reprehensible. Torn by conflicting loyalties, he remained neutral during the Revolution, speaking out only against extremism on both sides. Once George III accepted American independence, however, Johnson felt released from his allegiance and readily committed his considerable intellectual abilities to the strengthening of the new nation. Fellow delegate William Pierce said of him, "Johnson possesses the manners of a Gentleman and engages the Hearts of Men by the sweetness of his temper, and that affectionate style of address with which he accosts his acquaintance. . . . eloquent and clear, always abounding with information and instruction, . . . [He is] one of the first classics in America."

CAREER BEFORE THE CONSTITUTIONAL CONVENTION. Johnson was already a prominent figure before the Revolution. The son of a well-known Anglican clergyman and later president of King's (Columbia) College, Johnson received his primary education at home. He then graduated from Yale College in 1744, going on to receive a master's degree from his alma mater in 1747 (as well as an honorary degree from Harvard the same year). Although his father urged him to enter the clergy, Johnson decided instead to pursue a legal career. Self-educated in the law, he quickly developed an important clientele and established business connections extending beyond the boundaries of his native colony. He also held a commission in the Connecticut colonial militia for over 20 years, rising to the rank of colonel, and he served in the lower house of the Connecticut legislature (1761 and 1765) and in the upper house (1766 and 1771–75). He was a member as well of the colony's supreme court (1772–74).

Johnson was first attracted to the Patriot cause by what he and his associates considered Parliament's unwarranted interference in the government of the colonies. He attended the Stamp Act Congress in 1765 and served on the committee that drafted an address to the King arguing the right of the colonies to decide tax policies for themselves. He opposed the Townshend Acts passed by Parliament in 1767 to pay for the French and Indian War and supported the nonimportation agreements devised by the colonies to protest taxation without representation.

As the Patriots became more radical in their demands for independence, Johnson found it difficult to commit himself wholeheartedly to the cause. Although he believed British policy unwise, he found it difficult to break his own connections with the mother country. A scholar of international renown, he had many friends in Britain and among the American Loyalists. As the famous English author, Samuel Johnson, said of him, "Of all those whom the various accidents of life have brought within my notice, there is scarce anyone whose acquaintance I have more desired to cultivate than yours." He was also bound to Britain by religious and professional ties. He enjoyed close associations with the Anglican Church in England and with the scholarly community at Oxford, which awarded him an honorary degree in 1766. He lived in London from 1767 to 1771, serving as Connecticut's agent in its attempt to settle the colony's title to Indian lands.

Fearing the consequences of independence for both the colonies and the mother country, Johnson sought to avoid extremism and to reach a compromise on the outstanding political differences between the protagonists. He rejected his election to the First Continental Congress, a move strongly criticized by the Patriots, who removed him from his militia command. He was also strongly criticized when, seeking an end to the fighting after Lexington and Concord, he personally visited the British commander, General Thomas Gage. The incident led to his arrest for communicating with the enemy, but the charges were eventually dropped.

Johnson's pro-peace activities apparently never seriously damaged his prestige. He served as a legal counsel for Connecticut in its dispute with Pennsylvania over western lands (1779–80) and was nominated by Joseph Reed, president of the College of Philadelphia (later the University of Pennsylvania), to succeed him as head of the college.

Once independence was achieved, Johnson felt free to participate in the government of the new nation, serving in the Continental Congress (1785–87). His influence as a delegate was recognized by his contemporaries. Jeremiah Wadsworth wrote of him to a friend, "Dr. Johnson has, I believe, much more influence than either you or myself. The Southern Delegates are vastly fond of him."

CONTRIBUTIONS TO THE CONSTITUTIONAL CONVENTION. Johnson played a major role as one of the Convention's most important and respected delegates. His eloquent speeches on the subject of representation carried great weight during the debate. He looked to a strong federal government to protect the rights of Connecticut and the other small states from encroachment by their more powerful neighbors. To that end he supported the so-called New Jersey Plan, which called for equal representation of the states in the national legislature.

In general, he favored extension of federal authority. He argued that the judicial power "ought to extend to equity as well as law" (the words "in law and equity" were adopted at his motion) or, in other words, that the inflexibility of the law had to be tempered by fairness. He denied that there could be treason against a separate state since sovereignty was "in the Union," and he opposed prohibition of any *ex post facto* law, one which made an act a criminal offense retroactively, because such prohibition implied "an improper suspicion of the National Legislature."

Johnson was influential even in the final stages of framing the Constitution. He gave his fullest support to the Connecticut Compromise, which foreshadowed the final Great Compromise that devised a national legislature with a Senate that provided equal representation for all states and a House of Representatives based on population. He also served on the Committee of Style, which framed the final form of the document.

CAREER AFTER THE CONSTITUTIONAL CONVENTION. Johnson played an active role in Connecticut's ratification process, emphasizing the advantages that would accrue to the small states under the Constitution. He was especially proud of the document's legal clauses, in which "the force, which is to be employed, is the energy of Law; and this force is to operate only on individuals, who fail in their duty to their country."

As one of Connecticut's first senators (1789–91), Johnson took an active part in shaping the Judiciary Act of 1789, a critical law that established the details of the federal judiciary system. He also supported Hamiltonian measures that sought to strengthen the role of the executive in the federal government, but voted against giving the President the power to remove cabinet officers without senatorial approval. Johnson had become president of Columbia College in 1787, and when the federal government moved from New York to Philadelphia at the end of the First Congress, he retired from public office to retain his position at the school.

As president of Columbia to 1800, Johnson recruited faculty members and established the school on a firm financial basis. While maintaining the school's strongly religious spirit, he did much to improve its prestige and reputation for scholarship. As a prominent Anglican layman, he also helped reorganize the church under a new, American episcopate.

PERSONAL DATA
BIRTH: 7 October 1727, in Stratford, Connecticut
DEATH: 14 November 1819, in Stratford, Connecticut
INTERMENT: Old Episcopal Cemetery, Stratford, Connecticut

James Madison
Virginia

James Madison's prominence and leadership at the Constitutional Convention have earned him the title "Father of the Constitution." He was an unassuming but confident statesman who, financially independent, could devote his abundant energies and exceptional intellect to public affairs. This commitment was most evident in his tireless efforts to protect individual liberty through the creation of a strong but compassionate central government. He believed "that a well-founded commonwealth may . . . be immortal." A note found among his writings entitled "Advice to my Country" concludes with the following, "The advice nearest to my heart and deepest in my convictions is, that the Union of the States be cherished and perpetuated. Let the open enemy of it be regarded as a Pandora with her box opened, and the disguised one as the serpent creeping with his deadly wiles into paradise."

CAREER BEFORE THE CONSTITUTIONAL CONVENTION. Madison was a product of the American planter aristocracy. He graduated from the College of New Jersey (later Princeton) in 1771, where he was a diligent student of history and government. He was interested in the law, but initially considered a career in the ministry. After studying theology for a year, however, he returned to "Montpelier," his estate in Orange County (near "Mon-

ticello," the home of his friend Thomas Jefferson), undecided about a profession. The Revolution quickly transformed him into a politician.

Madison was politically active throughout the Revolution. He was named commander of the Orange County militia, but his poor health precluded any active military service. Along with his father, he sat on the Orange County Committee of Safety in 1775, and was a delegate to the Virginia constitutional convention in 1776. Madison's chief contribution to the convention was a resolution that declared the free exercise of religion a right and not something merely to be tolerated in a state with an established church. He was a member of Virginia's new House of Delegates (1776–77) and sat on the Council of State, the committee of senior advisers to Governor Thomas Jefferson (1778–80).

In 1780 Madison became the youngest member of the Continental Congress. He played a major role in its deliberations, advocating tariffs as the means of raising federal revenue, criticizing the negotiators of the Treaty of Paris for working behind the backs of the French, and defending Virginia's western land claims. He served until December 1783 and again from 1786 to 1788.

Madison spent the early postwar years engaged in intellectual pursuits. He studied law in an effort, as he put it, to obtain a profession that would depend as little as possible on the labor of slaves. He also studied the natural history of Orange County, sharing his findings with his friend and fellow natural history enthusiast, Thomas Jefferson. Madison later returned to the Virginia House of Delegates (1784–86). His influence can be seen in almost every piece of legislation of the period.

Most importantly, Madison set in motion the process that would eventually lead to the Constitutional Convention of 1787. He wrote extensively about deficiencies in the Articles of Confederation, and he organized a series of meetings of delegates from different states to discuss national economic problems. The Mount Vernon Conference of 1785 was convened to settle conflicting claims of Virginia and Maryland over navigation rights on the Potomac River. This conference, as Madison had hoped, underscored the fact that the Virginia-Maryland dispute was just one instance of controversy over interstate commerce. The Annapolis Convention of 1786, which Madison attended, was arranged to address the problem of interstate commerce in general, and again as Madison had hoped, it succeeded in demonstrating that commerce was only a part of the larger problems of disunity among the states and of weakness on the part of Congress because of the deficiencies of the Articles.

CONTRIBUTIONS TO THE CONSTITUTIONAL CONVENTION. The Constitutional Convention of 1787 presented Madison with the opportunity for which he had so long prepared. Success, he believed, was imperative because failure would lead to a return to monarchy or to the dissolution of the United States into several separate governments. Basing his theories on the historical experiences of both ancient and modern confederacies, which, he charged, had failed because of the weakness of their central authorities, Madison arrived fully prepared to become the leading advocate of a strong central government.

The Virginia Plan embodied his principal proposals, including a legislature of two houses with differing terms of office and with representation favoring the large states. He wanted the national government clothed "with positive and compleat authority in all cases which require uniformity." The upper house of the legislature was to have a veto on state legislation, and he proposed a national executive. The new government would have the power to enforce its laws. Recognizing that so radical a change required popular approval, he proposed placing the new Constitution before the citizens in ratifying conventions created especially for that purpose.

Madison's outstanding preparation, sharp mind, and flexibility in changing situations made him the undisputed leader of the Convention; he rose to address his colleagues at Philadelphia more than 150 times. He was a member of numerous committees, most importantly the Committees on Postponed Matters and Style, and he authored the definitive notes of the Convention's deliberations, which to this day are one of the best references available in understanding both the Convention and the intentions of the Founding Fathers. One delegate wrote of him, "Every Person seems to acknowledge his greatness. He blends together the profound politician with the Scholar. In the management of every great question he evidently took the lead in the Convention, and tho' he cannot be called an Orator, he is a most agreeable, eloquent, and convincing Speaker. . . . The affairs of the United States, he perhaps, has the most correct knowledge of, of any Man in the Union."

CAREER AFTER THE CONSTITUTIONAL CONVENTION. Madison played a critical role in the ratification process in Virginia, where approval was essential because of the state's size and population. He defended the Constitution against the objections of such influential men as Patrick Henry and Richard Henry Lee. He also collaborated with John Jay and Alexander Hamilton in producing a series of essays later published as *The Federalist Papers* (1787–88). This work, one of the most lucid expositions of the republican ideals that underlie the Constitution, is considered a classic of political theory.

Madison was elected to the House of Representatives (1789–97), where he helped frame the Bill of Rights and assisted in organizing the executive branch. He also helped create the federal tax system. At the same time, he was a key player in the first emergence of political parties in the United States, for he led the opposition to Alexander Hamilton, his old political ally, in the new national government. Along with his friend and mentor, Thomas Jefferson, Madison was a founder of the Democratic-Republican party, which, in defining the national government's functions, emphasized different portions of the Constitution than did Hamilton and the Federalists.

When Federalist John Adams became President (1797–1801), Madison retired. During these years, his only public act was to author the Virginia Resolutions, which attacked the Federalist-sponsored Alien and Sedition Acts. With the ascent of the Democratic-Republicans in the elections of 1801, Madison returned to office, as President Jefferson's Secretary of State (1801–09). Although inexperienced in diplomacy, Madison brought to the job intelligence, insight, and charm, which earned him the respect of diplomats in Washington. He was encumbered in the performance of his duties, however, by the lingering suspicions of many of his fellow Democratic-Republicans, who remembered his earlier association with Hamilton and others who remained stalwart Federalists.

Madison succeeded Jefferson as President (1809–17). His term of office was dominated by the War of 1812, the result of many differences with the British growing out of the Napoleonic Wars. The United States especially objected to British interference with American shipping and impressment of American sailors into the King's service. The war raised much domestic controversy and ended in the virtual restoration of the status quo, although Andrew Jackson's victory at the battle of New Orleans two weeks after the peace treaty was signed left the nation with the impression that it had won the war. The resulting wave of nationalism gave Madison's Democratic-Republicans uncontested sway in national politics.

Madison retired to Montpelier after a second term, but by no means withdrew from public life. He served as the cochairman of Virginia's constitutional convention (1829–30). He wrote newspaper articles defending his friend President James Monroe and served as Monroe's foreign policy adviser. Concerned with the future of the union that he had worked so hard to help found, he spoke out against the emerging rivalries among southern, northern, and western interests. Madison also devoted time to intellectual and philanthropic pursuits. Although he had held slaves all of his life, he was active in the American Colonization Society, which sought to resettle slaves in Africa. He edited his journal of the Constitutional Convention, published by the government four years after his death, and he assisted Jefferson in founding the University of Virginia, succeeding him as rector of the university (1826–36).

PERSONAL DATA
BIRTH: 16 March 1751, in Port Conway, King George County, Virginia
DEATH: 28 June 1836, at "Montpelier," Orange County, Virginia
INTERMENT: On the grounds of "Montpelier"

Robert Morris

Pennsylvania

Robert Morris was the master financier of the Revolution and the early republic. A contemporary described him as "bold and enterprising of great mercantile knowledge, fertile in expedients and an able financier. Very popular in and out of the Congress . . . grown extremely rich." His firm profited handsomely from the sale of munitions to the Continental Army, but it did so fairly, and Morris acted within the ethical standards of the time. His labors and his willingness to secure loans with his own personal credit saved the Army and the government from bankruptcy on several occasions. Although never in uniform, he exhibited singular personal bravery when he stayed at his post in Philadelphia to continue his wartime duties after the British captured the city.

Based on his profound understanding of finances and public credit, he was a forceful proponent of a strong central government as the best course for a new nation blessed with great economic potential. Except for Roger Sherman, Morris was the only person to sign all three of the era's principal documents, the Declaration of Independence, the Articles of Confederation, and the Constitution.

CAREER BEFORE THE CONSTITUTIONAL CONVENTION. Morris was born near Liverpool, England, immigrating to Maryland in 1747 to join his father, who was engaged in the tobacco export business at Oxford. The family moved the next year to Philadelphia where Morris briefly attended local schools before entering business. At the age of twenty, he became a partner of Charles Willing. Their firm would become one of America's leading import-export houses. Morris began his public career in 1765 when he served on a local committee organized to protest the Stamp Act. Along with other businessmen, Morris considered taxes imposed by Parliament without the consent of the colonial legislatures a form of taxation without representation and an abuse of the colonists' rights as English citizens. The committee petitioned local tax collectors to ignore the new law.

When hostilities broke out in New England, Morris committed himself to the Revolutionary cause. He served in a number of political posts established in Pennsylvania to oversee the transition from colony to independent state. He was a member of Pennsylvania's Committee of Correspondence. He also sat on Pennsylvania's Council of Safety (1775–76), the body that organized the arming of the state, and he was warden of the port of Philadelphia (1776), charged with protecting that great seaport in the opening phase of the Revolution. He also began the first of several terms representing his neighbors in the state legislature (1775).

Morris represented Pennsylvania in the Continental Congress (1775–78) where he voted against independence when it was first discussed on 1 July 1776. Still hesitant the next day, he absented himself from deliberations on the subject in the Pennsylvania delegation, but by 4 July he had changed his mind and signed the Declaration when it was presented to the Congress for formal approval. In Congress he concentrated on financial affairs and military procurement, conducting much of Congress' banking and serving on its Secret Committee for the Procurement of Munitions. In August 1778 he became chairman of the Finance Committee (he also served on the Ways and Means Committee). He managed to borrow money in spite of military reverses and other political difficulties, procuring funds and supplies from often reluctant states and obtaining personal loans from wealthy businessmen. His role in obtaining provisions and supplies for the Continental Army was so important that historians have concluded that improvement in the Army's combat effectiveness was in good part due to his singular efforts.

An able and energetic delegate, he also served on a committee to consider fortification of seaports and on the Committee of Secret Correspondence which supervised negotiations leading to the alliance with France. Concerned not only with the immediate cause of independence but with the long-range stability of the country as well, he participated in the debates over the Articles of Confederation and signed them on behalf of Pennsylvania in March 1778. He was among the small group of delegates who, at considerable personal risk, remained in Philadelphia to continue committee work when Congress moved to Baltimore during the winter of 1776–77 to escape capture by the British. By 1778 his influence was so strong that Morris, along with Richard Henry Lee and the Adamses, could be said to have controlled Congress. Yet, at the height of his popularity, Morris came under attack from Thomas Paine and others who accused him of war profiteering. Although a congressional investigation exonerated him, concluding that "Robert Morris . . . has acted with fidelity and integrity and an honorable zeal for the happiness of his country," his reputation was considerably damaged by the charges.

He continued to serve in the Pennsylvania legislature after leaving Congress, but returned to national service as the Superintendent of Finance (1781–84) when the Articles of Confederation went into force. In this position, Morris was responsible for saving the country from financial ruin during the last years of the Revolution. He understood the severity of the economic crisis: "The least breach of faith must ruin us forever," he wrote, and "Congress will know that the public credit cannot be restored without method, economy, and punctual performance of contracts." He understood good faith in the dealings of a debtor, whether person or nation: "The United States may command everything I have, except my integrity [i.e., commercial credit], and the loss of that would effectually disable me from serving them more." He immediately set about restoring the nation's credit. Assisted by Gouverneur Morris, he worked with the states to levy taxes to be paid in specie, slashed military and government spending, and personally bought supplies for the Army and Navy. His crusade against waste brought about a dramatic improvement in accounting procedures and, more importantly, laid the logistical basis for the decisive Franco-American victory at Yorktown. As the war reached its final phase, he strained his personal credit by issuing notes for government expenses over his own signature. Funds he borrowed from France, along with some of his own money, became the capital of the Bank of North America, the first government-incorporated bank in the United States. "I am determined," he wrote, "that the bank shall be well supported, until it can support itself and then it can support us."

CONTRIBUTIONS TO THE CONSTITUTIONAL CONVENTION. Although well known for his strong defense of the nationalist cause, Morris had little confidence in himself as a lawmaker despite the high regard in which he was held by his contemporaries. "The science of law is entirely out of my line," he apologized. As a result, he spoke only once during the sessions at Philadelphia and did not participate in the Convention's committee work, preferring to express his views through private conversations with various delegates, including his powerful friends Alexander Hamilton, Gouverneur Morris, and George Washington. In Benjamin Franklin's absence, he enjoyed the privilege of nominating Washington as president of the Convention.

CAREER AFTER THE CONSTITUTIONAL CONVENTION. President Washington offered Morris the post of Secretary of Treasury in the new government, but he declined the honor, which went instead to Alexander Hamilton. He preferred to enter the Congress where, despite his reservations about his legislative abilities, he served as one of Pennsylvania's first senators (1789–95).

Toward the end of his career Morris speculated widely

in land in the newly incorporated District of Columbia and in the west, a move that led to financial ruin. He was cast into debtor's prison (1798–1801), and the grandiose Philadelphia mansion designed for him by L'Enfant was left unfinished, to be dubbed thereafter "Morris' Folly."

PERSONAL DATA
BIRTH: 31 January 1734, near Liverpool, England
DEATH: 8 May 1806, in Philadelphia, Pennsylvania
INTERMENT: Graveyard of Christ Church, Philadelphia

William Paterson

New Jersey

William Paterson was a rising young lawyer who applied his legal and executive skills to the service of the country during the Revolution, the Constitutional Convention, and the formative years of the new republic. Paterson particularly concerned himself with the question of representation in the national government. He was the father of what came to be called the New Jersey Plan. He argued with considerable force that the legal jurisdiction of the Convention was limited, that the delegates were assembled not to devise a pure democratic government in which each *citizen* was equally represented, but a federation of independent states in which each *state* was equally represented. In the end, he yielded on this point for the sake of compromise and union. Commenting on his influence during the proceedings, Georgia delegate William Pierce noted that Paterson was "one of those kind of Men whose powers break in upon you, and create wonder and astonishment. He is a man of great modesty whose looks bespeak talent of no great extent, but he is a Classic and a Lawyer, and an Orator—and of a disposition so favorable to his advancement that everyone seemed ready to exalt him with their praises." A grateful New Jersey named the city of Paterson in his honor.

CAREER BEFORE THE CONSTITUTIONAL CONVENTION. Paterson was born in County Antrim, Ireland. After immigrating to America, he attended local schools and the College of New Jersey (later Princeton), where he graduated in 1763. He then studied law under Richard Stockton, a future signer of the Declaration of Independence. Even as a young man, Paterson showed a strong interest in national affairs and citizens' rights. As early as 1763 he discussed the philosophy of patriotism in his commencement address to his Princeton graduating class, applying the values of the Enlightenment philosophers he had studied to the special concerns of colonial society.

When Parliament in the aftermath of the French and Indian War began to try to tax the colonies, putting aside its previous "salutary neglect," the young lawyer quickly became a leader of the Patriot cause in New Jersey. He represented Somerset County as the secretary of New Jersey's Provincial Congress, an extralegal legislature established by the Patriots to organize the transition from Royal colony to independent state (1775–76), and at New Jersey's first constitutional convention (1776). For a year he held a seat in the state senate (1776–77). He also served in an executive capacity, first as a member of the legislative council, a group organized by the legislature to run the state when it was not in session (1776–77), and on the Council of Safety, the body that developed and managed New Jersey's military forces for the war (1777). Although he received a militia commission in the Somerset County battalion of Minutemen, he never saw active service.

Paterson's major interest remained the law, and in 1776 he assumed the post of attorney general of New Jersey. The responsibilities of this position grew so great that he had to decline election to the Continental Congress in 1780. He remained in office until 1783, when, independence won, he moved to New Brunswick and resumed his law practice.

CONTRIBUTIONS TO THE CONSTITUTIONAL CONVENTION. Although Paterson missed the last month of the Convention's sessions, returning only in September to sign the Constitution, he nevertheless played an important role in the Convention's proceedings. He was coauthor of the New Jersey (or Paterson) Plan that asserted the rights of the small states by proposing a national legislature that, ignoring differences in size and population, gave equal voice to all the states. The proposal countered the Virginia Plan introduced by Edmund Randolph, which granted special recognition to differences in population and, therefore, favored the large states.

The Constitution that emerged from the deliberations was essentially a compromise incorporating elements of both of these plans (a Senate giving equal representation to the states and a House based solely on population).

Paterson also defended the concept of states' rights at the Convention, believing that it was the will of the people to protect the powers of the states from federal encroachments. Commenting on proposals favored by the large states, he noted that "the idea of a national Government as contradistinguished from a federal one, never entered into the mind of any of them [the people], and to the public mind we must accommodate ourselves. We have no power to go beyond the federal scheme, and if we had the people are not ripe for any other."

CAREER AFTER THE CONSTITUTIONAL CONVENTION.

Paterson went on to become one of New Jersey's first U.S. senators (1789–90). He was a strong nationalist who supported the Federalist party. As a member of the Senate Judiciary Committee, he played an important role in drafting the Judiciary Act of 1789 that established the federal court system. The first nine sections of this very important law are in his handwriting.

He resigned from the Senate in 1790 in order to succeed fellow signer William Livingston as governor of New Jersey. As governor, he pursued his interest in legal matters by codifying the English statutes that had been in force in New Jersey before the Revolution in *Laws of the State of New Jersey.* He also published a revision of the rules of the chancery and common law courts in *Paterson's Practice Laws,* later adopted by the New Jersey legislature.

He resigned the governorship to become an associate justice of the Supreme Court (1793–1806). There he presided over the trials of individuals indicted for treason in the Whiskey Rebellion, a revolt by farmers in western Pennsylvania over the federal excise tax on whiskey, the principal product of their cash crop. Militia sent out by President Washington successfully quelled the uprising, and for the first time the courts had to interpret the provisions of the Constitution in regard to the use of troops in civil disturbances. Here, and in fact throughout his long career, Paterson extolled the primacy of law over governments, a principle embodied in the Constitution he helped write.

PERSONAL DATA
BIRTH: 24 December 1745, in County Antrim, Ireland
DEATH: 9 September 1806, in Albany, New York
INTERMENT: Vault at the manor house of son-in-law, Stephen Van Rensselear; later reinterred in Albany Rural Cemetery, Menands, New York

George Read

Delaware

George Read was described by a contemporary as tall, slight, agreeable, austere, and sternly moral. His public career also showed him to be a man possessed of strong principles. After a lengthy search for a moderate solution to the crisis with England, he became a Patriot and supported the Revolution wholeheartedly. But he was determined that his small state should not trade the tyranny of a distant Parliament for that imposed by a combination of its powerful neighbors. He worked hard to create a strong national government that would perpetuate the freedoms won in the Revolution.

CAREER BEFORE THE CONSTITUTIONAL CONVENTION. Read was the son of an Irish immigrant, a well-to-do landowner from Dublin who eventually settled his family in New Castle, Delaware. Read attended local schools in Chester, Pennsylvania, and Reverend Francis Alison's well-known academy in New London, Pennsylvania, before reading law under John Moland of Philadelphia. He married Gertrude (Ross) Till, daughter of a future signer of the Declaration of Independence. Read established a legal practice in New Castle in 1754 and quickly developed a local reputation as an honest lawyer and a clientele that extended beyond the boundaries of his colony. He began his public career when he accepted appointment from the Royal governor as attorney general (1763–74) of the Three Lower Counties (the colonial name for Delaware). But he was soon speaking out in sympathy with those protesting Parliament's increasing interference with colonial self-government. In reference to the Stamp Act, an internal tax which Parliament sought to use to recoup the cost of the French and Indian War, he said that if it or anything like it were enforced, "the colonists will entertain an opinion that they are to become the slaves" of Great Britain and will endeavor "to live as independently of the mother country as possible."

Elected to the colonial legislature (1765–76), Read worked in union with the moderate representatives of the local merchants and landowners to press for nonimportation measures to protest Parliament's actions. Later he supported the committees established throughout the colonies to organize relief for the citizens of Boston, who were suffering from the severe economic measures imposed by Parliament in the wake of the Tea Party.

Read represented Delaware in the Continental Congress (1774–76). An irregular attendee, he moved in conservative Patriot circles with delegates such as his friend (and fellow signer of the Constitution) John Dickinson. They were willing to fight for colonial rights, but were wary of extremism. Although he voted against independence on 2 July 1776 because he thought that reconciliation with Great Britain was still possible, he came round and, on 4 July, fully supported the Declaration.

Read presided over Delaware's constitutional convention (1776), where he exercised more influence than any other member. He chaired the drafting committee, serving as a voice for moderation by balancing the revolutionary impulses of the people with the legitimate rights of property owners. His service as speaker of the Legislative Council (the upper house of the Delaware legislature) made him, in effect, the assistant governor of the state. In November 1777, after narrowly escaping capture by British troops while en route from Philadelphia to Dover, he assumed the presidency (governorship) of Delaware, a post he held until March 1778. Back in the Legislative Council in 1779, he drafted the act authorizing Delaware's ratification of the Articles of Confederation. Reflecting the views of the smaller states, Read argued that taxes levied by Congress should be based on the population of the states, rather than on the value of lands and improvements, and that the title to western lands should be held jointly with specific limits placed on the claims of individual states to them.

Following a brief retirement necessitated by ill health, he resumed his seat in the Legislative Council (1782–88) and also served as judge on the state's court of appeals and on a commission to settle land claims in disputes with Massachusetts and New York. He was primarily active in promoting measures to improve the state's commerce and finances. Ignoring popular pressure, he opposed inflationary measures that he feared would impair Delaware's long-term financial credit.

CONTRIBUTIONS TO THE CONSTITUTIONAL CONVENTION. At the Convention, Read immediately pushed for a new national government based on a new Constitution. As he put it: "to amend the Articles was simply putting old cloth on a new garment." He was a leader in the fight for a strong central government, advocating, at one time, the abolition of the states altogether and the consolidation of the country under one powerful national government. "Let no one fear the states, the people are with us," he declared to a Convention shocked by this radical proposal. With no one to support his motion, he settled for protecting the rights of the small states against the infringements of their larger, more populous neighbors who, he feared, would "probably combine to swallow up the smaller ones by addition, division or impoverishment." He warned that Delaware "would become at once a cypher in the union" if the principle of equal representation embodied in the New Jersey (small-state) Plan was not adopted and if the method of amendment in the Articles was not retained. He favored giving Congress the right to veto state laws, making the federal legislature immune to popular whims by having senators hold office for nine years or during good behavior, and granting the President broad appointive powers. Outspoken, he threatened to lead the Delaware delegation out of the Convention if the rights of the small states were not specifically guaranteed in the new Constitution.

CAREER AFTER THE CONSTITUTIONAL CONVENTION. Read was elected as one of Delaware's first U.S. senators (1789–93). In the Senate he allied himself with the Federalists, supporting assumption of state debts, establishment of a national bank, and imposition of excise laws. He resigned in 1793 to accept the post of chief justice of Delaware, which he retained until his death in 1798.

PERSONAL DATA
BIRTH: 18 September 1733, near the community of North East in Cecil County, Maryland
DEATH: 21 September 1798, in New Castle, Delaware
INTERMENT: Immanuel Episcopal Churchyard, New Castle, Delaware

John Rutledge
South Carolina

John Rutledge faithfully mirrored the beliefs and attitudes of the southern planter aristocracy. He subscribed to the idea of an ordered society that guaranteed the rights and privileges of men of property. At the same time, he was a fearless Patriot who sacrificed his own considerable wealth to the cause of independence. Well educated, Rutledge proved to be an able leader in a crucial era in the history of his state and nation. As governor of South Carolina during the Revolution and as an active delegate at the Constitutional Convention, he exhibited attractive and important qualities of leadership: tact, industry, courage, and political conviction.

CAREER BEFORE THE CONSTITUTIONAL CONVENTION. Rutledge, the son of an Irish immigrant and physician, received his education at the hands of his father and private tutors. He also studied law at London's Middle Temple and was admitted to the English bar in 1760. Shortly thereafter he returned to Charleston where, pursuing business opportunities in agriculture, he quickly amassed a fortune in plantations and slaves. Typical of rising young men of the landowner class, Rutledge gravitated toward politics, winning election to the provincial assembly in 1761, where he represented Christ Church Parish until the Revolution. (He also served during most of 1764 as the colony's attorney general.) His political philosophy was typical of his class as well. He believed that those with wealth and social standing, men with the greatest stake in society, had the duty to govern. But he also reflected the teachings of the Enlightenment philosophers that he had imbibed during his studies in London. He believed that government was a contract between the people and their sovereign and that both had inalienable rights that could not be abridged by an act of Parliament.

Rutledge represented South Carolina in the Stamp Act Congress, organized by colonial leaders in 1765 in response to Parliament's efforts to impose an internal tax on the colonies, thereby intruding into the area of local self-government. Rutledge advocated a moderate policy, one that would avoid severing ties with the mother country while insisting on colonial self-government. He chaired the committee that drafted the congress' petition to Parliament seeking a repeal of the tax.

Continuing as a leader of the moderate wing of the Patriot cause, he was elected to the First Continental Congress in 1774. Again he advocated a nonviolent course, calling for an embargo on English goods and a boycott of English markets (although he fought successfully to keep rice, a South Carolina staple, off the embargo list). He returned to Philadelphia as a member of the Second Continental Congress (1775–76), until replaced by his younger brother Edward, who signed the Declaration of Independence.

Back in South Carolina in 1776, John Rutledge also came to accept the need for independence. He joined the local Committee of Safety, the political arm of the Revolutionary cause, and helped write the state's first constitution. Elected to the state legislature (1776–78), he served as president of the lower house. He resigned in protest when the legislature insisted on making revisions to the new state constitution, including the disestablishment of the Anglican Church.

Rutledge served his state with distinction as its governor during those years of the Revolution when South Carolina was most threatened (1779–82). When Charleston was besieged by the British in 1780, the legislature granted him war powers ("to do anything necessary for the public good, except the taking away of a citizen without legal trial"). The city fell in May, the greatest defeat for American arms during the war, and Rutledge's property was seized, but he escaped to North Carolina, where he attempted to rally forces for the recapture of Charleston. His task was made especially difficult when General Gates' army of continentals and local militia, whom Rutledge had helped raise, suffered a devastating defeat at Camden, South Carolina. Despite protests that Camden heralded the death of the Revolution in the Carolinas, Rutledge worked undespairingly to raise a new force. This second army, under the command of General Nathanael Greene, regained control of most of the state in 1781 and restored civil government. Rutledge tried to unify the state by granting pardons to many Loyalists on the condition that they report for six months' militia duty within 30 days. With the end of the Revolution approaching in 1782, he resigned the governorship and reentered the lower house of the legislature where, except for brief stints in the Continental Congress (1782–83) and the state's chancery court (1784), he remained until 1790. He never recouped his personal financial losses suffered during the war.

CONTRIBUTIONS TO THE CONSTITUTIONAL CONVENTION. Believing that the weaknesses of the Articles of Confederation threatened the rights that had been won by the Revolution and guaranteed by provisions in the state constitutions, Rutledge cooperated closely with James Wilson in championing a strong central government. Rutledge was an influential delegate from the start of the Convention, when his proposal to conduct the sessions behind closed doors and submit all of the members to an oath of secrecy was accepted by all the delegates. His influence and activity continued throughout the Convention, where he served on five committees and chaired the important Committee on Detail that set the agenda of the meetings. He attended all sessions and spoke often and effectively, taking a nationalist position while supporting the social and economic interests of the southern states. He advocated wealth as a basis for representation, assumption of state debts, an unrestricted slave trade, election of the President by Congress, and election of Congress by state legislatures. Towards the end of the Convention, he was instrumental in drafting the final document, which was born out of a spirit of compromise that he, during one of the debates, had eloquently encouraged and praised, saying, "Is it not better that I should sacrifice one prized opinion than that all of us should sacrifice everything we might otherwise gain?" He returned home to play a key role in South Carolina's ratification process in 1788.

CAREER AFTER THE CONSTITUTIONAL CONVENTION. Rutledge served as a presidential elector in 1789, joining in the unanimous choice of George Washington. The final phase of his public career saw him in high judicial positions, first for one year as an associate justice of the U.S. Supreme Court and then as chief justice of the South Carolina supreme court (1791–95). He was nominated by Washington to replace Chief Justice John Jay in 1795, but the Senate refused to confirm him because of his vehement opposition to Jay's Treaty with Great Britain and because of recurring illness following the death of his wife in 1792, an illness that effectively ended his public career.

PERSONAL DATA
BIRTH: September 1739 (exact date unknown), in Christ Church Parish, South Carolina
DEATH: 18 June 1800, in Charleston, South Carolina
INTERMENT: St. Michael's Episcopal Church, Charleston, South Carolina

Roger Sherman
Connecticut

Roger Sherman's public career reflected the heritage and concerns of his native New England. He attributed his rise from humble beginnings to the twin virtues of hard work and honesty, virtues that he assiduously applied to the service of the republic. John Adams, himself an heir to the same tradition, described Sherman as "an old Puritan, as honest as an angel and as firm in the cause of American Independence as Mount Atlas." Sherman was the only Founding Father to sign the four major documents of the era: the Articles of Association (1774), a Patriot call for the boycott of British goods; the Declaration of Independence; the Articles of Confederation; and the Constitution.

CAREER BEFORE THE CONSTITUTIONAL CONVENTION. Sherman was a descendant of Captain John Sherman, who settled in Massachusetts in 1636, and the son of a Newton cobbler. Destined to follow his father's trade, Sherman received little formal education, but he read widely, especially in theology, history, mathematics, law, and politics. Tradition pictures the young Sherman at the cobbler's bench, always with a book open in front of him. Sherman moved to New Milford, Connecticut, in 1743, two years after his father's death, to live with his brother. His strong personality and dedication to the work ethic soon led to success. He purchased a store and became county surveyor, a lucrative position that enabled him in time to become a major landowner. He also assumed a variety of town offices, including juryman, town clerk, deacon, and school committeeman. He taught himself the law during this period and in 1754 was admitted to the bar, marking the beginning of a distinguished legal career.

Elected to serve his community in the colonial legislature (1755–61), Sherman was also justice of the peace for Litchfield County, county judge (1759), and commissary for Connecticut troops (1759), charged with organizing supplies for the militia during the decisive campaign of the French and Indian War. In addition to commercial and public pursuits, he found time to publish an essay on monetary theory, which, among other things, criticized the importation of luxuries as a serious drawback to the economic advancement of the colony.

In 1761 he abandoned his law practice and sold his various businesses, moving to New Haven where he operated a store that catered to Yale students. He soon became a friend and benefactor of Yale, serving as its treasurer (1765–76) and contributing to the construction of its chapel. (His commitment to the school earned him an honorary master's degree from Yale in 1768.) By 1772 he was prosperous enough to retire from business and devote himself full time to public office. He held a number of colonial and state offices throughout the Revolutionary period, sitting in the lower house (1764–66) and upper house (1766–85) of the Connecticut legislature. During most of these years he also served as an associate judge of Connecticut's superior court (1766–89).

Although he opposed extremism, Sherman resented Parliament's interference in colonial affairs and enlisted early in the Patriot cause. He supported nonimportation measures and advocated the boycott of New York merchants who did not participate in them. He was also the leader of the New Haven Committee of Correspondence, an extralegal political association that was part of a communications network among Patriot leaders in all thirteen colonies.

Sherman was an active and influential member of the Continental Congress (1774–81 and 1783–84). He was one of the first to deny the supremacy of Parliament, stating that Parliament had no right to make laws for America and, as a member of the committees that drafted the Declaration of Independence and the Articles of Confederation, he remained in the forefront of Revolutionary politics. Like Benjamin Franklin, Sherman proposed a plan of union of the North American colonies. John Adams said, "Mr. Sherman's [plan] was best liked, but very little was finally adopted from either."

Sherman served on several other congressional committees, including the Ways and Means Committee and those that dealt with Indian affairs, war and ordnance, and the Treasury Board. He advocated imposing higher taxes rather than borrowing or issuing paper money as solutions to the country's economic problems. His last important actions in Congress dealt with western lands.

This tremendous amount of activity, combined with worry about the well-being of several sons serving in the Continental Army, began to take their toll on Sherman's health. As early as 1777 he wrote, "I must leave Congress soon . . . for my constitution will not admit of so close an application to business much longer." He did not leave, however, and fellow delegate Jeremiah Wadsworth honored his effectiveness in concluding with some irony that he was "as cunning as the Devil in managing legislation." Toward the end of the war, he was the most influential figure in Congress.

Membership in the Continental Congress did not preclude other activities. He attended a convention of the New England states in 1777 to express his ideas on taxes, currency, and credit, and he was a delegate to the New Haven Convention on Prices in 1778.

CONTRIBUTIONS TO THE CONSTITUTIONAL CONVENTION. Sherman had originally favored strengthening the Articles of Confederation. While in Congress, he had gone so far as to draft a series of amendments which would have given that body the power to levy imposts, to establish a supreme court, and to make laws binding on all the people. He went to the Convention "disposed to patch up the old scheme of Government," but soon realized the need for a new one. Sherman was opposed to the democratic tendencies he saw among Convention delegates. He favored an executive dominated by the legislature, and the election of congressmen and senators in turn by the state legislatures. He also thought popular ratification of the new Constitution was unnecessary.

He played an important role at the Convention, attending almost every session and sitting on the Committee on Postponed Matters. He probably helped draft the New Jersey Plan, the proposal favored by the small states since it gave equal representation to all states in the new government. He was the prime mover behind the Connecticut Compromise, the basis for the so-called Great Compromise that finally solved the problem of representation. His plan called for the creation of a Senate that gave equal representation to all states and a lower House with representation based on population.

CAREER AFTER THE CONSTITUTIONAL CONVENTION. Sherman joined the fight for ratification of the new Constitution in Connecticut, enlisting support in a series of open letters in the New Haven *Gazette* entitled "To the People of Connecticut from A Countryman." He stepped down as a judge on Connecticut's superior court to serve as a representative in the First U.S. Congress (1789–91). There he advocated measures popular in New England: imposition of tariffs to protect local manufacturers, assumption of state debts by the federal government, and sale of western lands to finance the national debt. He also opposed amending the Constitution and locating the new national capital in the south (on the banks of the Potomac River). In 1791 he assumed fellow signer William Samuel Johnson's seat in the U.S. Senate, where he served until his death two years later.

Perhaps the most notable of Sherman's personal characteristics was his firm religiosity. He opposed appointment of fellow signer Gouverneur Morris as minister to France because he considered that high-living Patriot to be of an "irreligious nature." He even published works that demonstrated his deep interest in theology, including *A Short Sermon on the Duty of Self-Examination Preparatory to Receiving the Lord's Supper* (1789).

PERSONAL DATA
BIRTH: 19 April 1721, in Newton, Massachusetts
DEATH: 23 July 1793, in New Haven, Connecticut
INTERMENT: Grove Street Cemetery, New Haven, Connecticut

James Wilson

Pennsylvania

James Wilson was probably the leading constitutional lawyer among the Founding Fathers. Strongly committed to the cause of nationalism and possessed of an exceptional clarity of vision, he firmly believed that, from a legal perspective, both the Declaration of Independence and the Constitution required a philosophical statement justifying the national programs laid out by their authors. His well-informed leadership, especially in legal matters, played a vital role at a critical time in the nation's history.

CAREER BEFORE THE CONSTITUTIONAL CONVENTION. Wilson was born in Scotland, where he attended three universities, but failed to earn a degree. Shortly after arriving in America in 1765, he became a Latin tutor at the College of Philadelphia (now the University of Pennsylvania), and successfully petitioned that institution to grant him an honorary master's degree. He soon decided that the law, rather than the academy, was the shortest route to advancement in America. He studied under John Dickinson, a fellow signer of the Constitution, and established a practice in Reading, Pennsylvania, in 1768. Two years later, he moved westward to the Scots-Irish settlement of Carlisle, Pennsylvania, where his new practice quickly prospered. Land speculation and lecturing on English literature at the College of Philadelphia occupied his remaining time.

Wilson involved himself in Revolutionary politics early and daringly. He was chairman of the Carlisle Committee of Correspondence, the local political organ of the Patriots, in 1774. During this time he completed preparation of *Considerations on the Nature and Extent of the Legislative Authority of the British Parliament,* which, when circulated both in the Continental Congress and among the public, earned him a reputation as a Patriot leader. In this essay, he became one of the first spokesmen in the colonies to assert that Parliament had no authority within the colonies in any instance. He stated a principle similar to that upon which the later British Commonwealth of Nations would be based: "all the different members of the British empire are distinct States independent of each other but under the same sovereign." He also served as a member of Pennsylvania's provincial assembly (1775).

Wilson took his leadership abilities to the Continental Congress (1774–77), where he served on committees dealing with Indian and military affairs. He was reflecting the cautious attitudes of his constituency when, like his mentor John Dickinson, he voted to postpone, for a three-week period, consideration of Richard Henry Lee's 7 June 1776 motion for independence, an action for which he was strongly criticized, although he subsequently voted for independence and signed the Declaration. About this time Wilson was elected a colonel in the Cumberland County Associators, part of the military organization established by Pennsylvania in the absence of a militia, but he never saw active service.

Wilson's career in the Continental Congress was interrupted the next year by a controversy surrounding the Pennsylvania constitution of 1776. Wilson opposed the popular new plan of government on the grounds that its unicameral legislature and its lack of a system of checks and balances would lead to mob rule rather than to ordered government. Because of this opposition, the leaders of the state government removed Wilson from Congress and relieved him of his militia commission. Wilson now took up residence in Annapolis, Maryland (1777–78), but this move only intensified the scandal since he was now charged with abandoning his state. As news of his opposition to the Pennsylvania constitution spread, his popularity continued to wane. In 1779, after he moved back to Pennsylvania, a mob attacked Wilson and a number of conservative state legislators barricaded in Wilson's Philadelphia home. The skirmish that ensued resulted in casualties on both sides. Thereafter, the citizens of Philadelphia dubbed the old house "Fort Wilson."

Wilson's fortunes now took a turn for the better. Because of his reputation as a skillful and knowledgeable lawyer, France selected him as its Advocate General in America (1779–83), a position that required him to advise the new nation's ally on aspects of American law, especially in commercial and maritime matters. Although he was not then a delegate to the Continental Congress, that body recognized his skill as a financier when in 1781 it appointed Wilson director of the Bank of North America, recently founded by Robert Morris to help finance the war effort. With more moderate Patriots once more in power in Pennsylvania, Wilson was again elected to the Continental Congress (1782 and 1785–87). There he became one of the first to promoting strengthening the central government when he urged the states to surrender their western land claims, proposed greater revenue and taxation powers for Congress, and argued for representation in Congress based on free population. These outspoken positions marked him as one of the most farsighted leaders in the new nation.

CONTRIBUTIONS TO THE CONSTITUTIONAL CONVENTION. Wilson was among the most influential delegates at the Convention. One of eighteenth-century America's foremost political theorists and advocates of democracy, he cooperated with James Madison in promoting popular sovereignty, especially in the election of congressmen, and led the opposition against those delegates who sought to reserve special rights and privileges for the rich and well-born. He considered the election of the national legislature by the people to be "not only the cornerstone, but the foundation of the fabric." Reflecting more than any other delegate what would one day become the mainstream of American political thought, Wilson was practically alone among the Founding Fathers in advocating the direct election of the President as well. He served on the important Committee of Detail and delivered more speeches than anyone at the Convention with the exception of Gouverneur Morris. Duplicating the arguments he advanced while serving in Congress, Wilson became one of the Convention's leading advocates of a strong executive, and, in general, of a powerful federal government. Although he worked unstintingly for this goal, he also recognized the importance of compromise in constructing the new plan of government. After the Convention, he praised his colleagues, saying that "we kept steadily in our View that which appears to us the greatest Interest of every true American, the consolidation of our Union. . . . And thus the Constitution which we now present is the result of a Spirit of Amity, and of that mutual Deference and Concession which the Peculiarity of our political Situation rendered indispensible."

CAREER AFTER THE CONSTITUTIONAL CONVENTION. Wilson's life after the Convention brought both success and failure. He led the ratification struggle in Pennsylvania, which became the second state to approve the Constitution. He also worked to reform the government established under Pennsylvania's 1776 constitution by helping to draft a new constitution (1789–90), and he was chosen as the first professor of law at the College of Philadelphia. Wilson also joined the new national government, serving as an associate justice of the Supreme Court (1789–98). At the same time, however, he was speculating in lands in western New York, Pennsylvania, and Georgia and promoting a grandiose scheme to recruit European immigrants to settle there. The investments proved ruinous, and Wilson was forced to move, in the last months of his life, to Burlington, New Jersey, to escape debtor's prison.

PERSONAL DATA

BIRTH: 14 September 1742, in Carskerdo, near St. Andrews, Scotland

DEATH: 21 August 1798, in Edenton, North Carolina

INTERMENT: Buried on Hayes Plantation near Edenton, North Carolina; reinterred in graveyard of Christ Church, Philadelphia, Pennsylvania

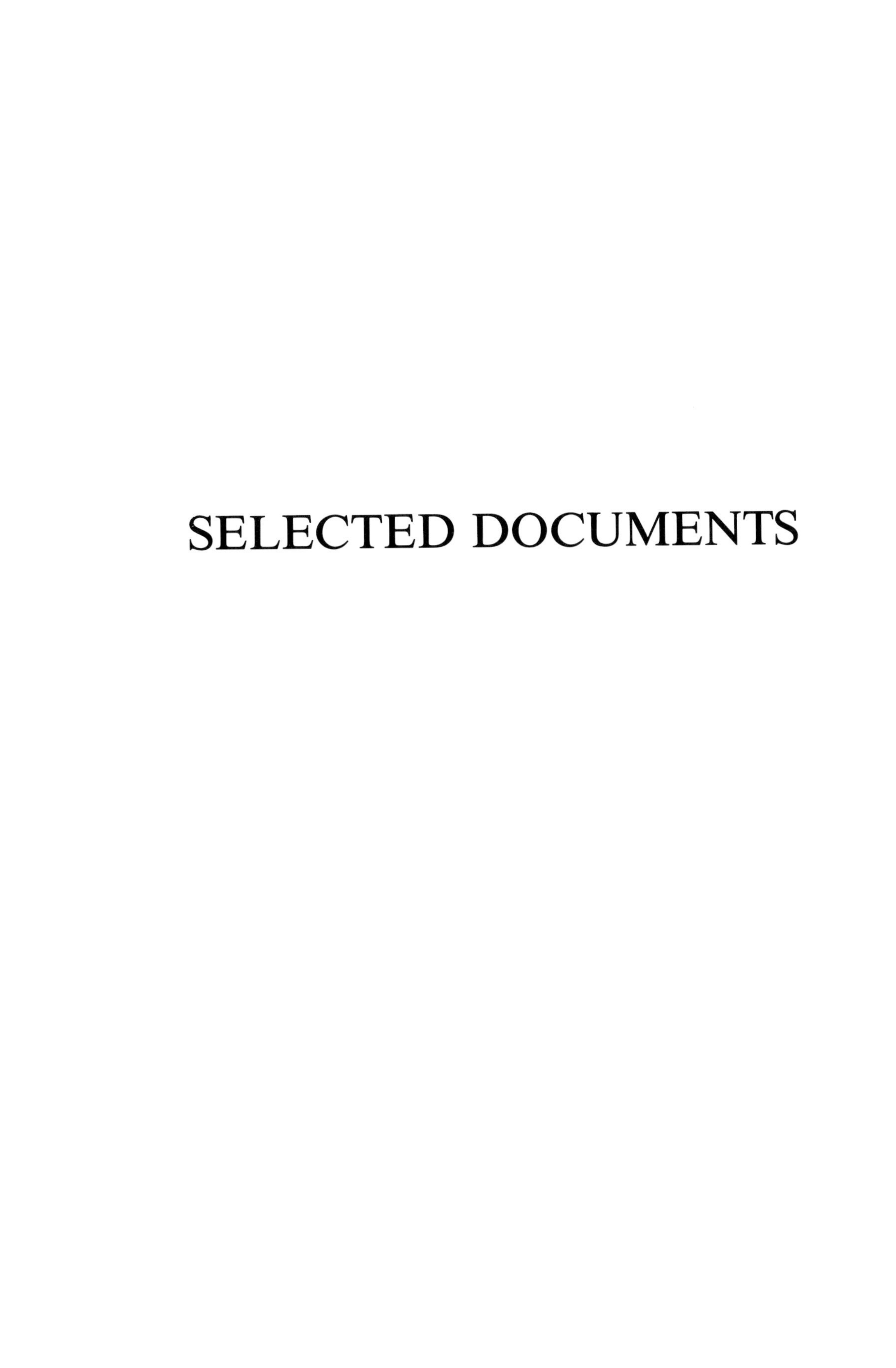

SELECTED DOCUMENTS

The formation of the American republic was a richly documented event. The Founding Fathers had emerged from a political tradition shaped in part by the treatment of the colonies by the British government. The achievement of independence continued this tradition in the form of a general suspicion of any government powers that were not specifically defined. The new nation demanded from its political leaders a careful definition of their positions and the promulgation of written constitutions and laws. In short, the Founding Fathers, reflecting the expectations of a literate public, tended to write everything down, an instinct that has since provided students with an unmatched opportunity to observe the evolution of political thought in the eighteenth century.

The Founding Fathers' consideration of the role of the armed forces in a free society was a case in point. Beginning with the resolution of the Continental Congress that established the Continental Army to defend American rights, and ending with the enactment of a law fixing the peace establishment in 1815, the record of the era is replete with debate and decisions concerning the nature and role of the military. It reveals an emerging consensus concerning the proper division of military responsibility between the regular forces and a nationally coordinated militia. The documents particularly underscore how those in authority moved from a theoretical discussion of military matters, so important in the early Revolutionary period, to the pragmatic application of resources in times of war and peace during the years following adoption of the new Constitution.

The documents presented below are meant to supplement the information provided in the preceding sections of this book. When read in this light, they amplify the account of the particular role of the Soldier-Statesmen in the formation of the country's military policies. These men were citizen-soldiers in the broadest sense of the term. They had fought in the Revolution and, with independence achieved, they returned to civilian life to take up the task of nation building. That they never lost sight of their wartime experience is evident in the practical way they addressed the perennial problems of the citizen's duty to defend his country and the government's duty to protect its citizens from unwarranted military control. In such works as Washington's "Sentiments on a Peace Establishment," Hamilton's application of constitutional theory to military matters in the *Federalist Papers,* and Henry Knox's plan for the arrangement of the militia under the new government, a common theme emerged: that the nation's experiences in the Revolution had led directly to its citizens' resolve to establish a government that provided for the common defense as part of its broader obligation to secure the blessings of liberty. The documents cited from the immediate post-Revolutionary period state precisely what the Founding Fathers believed were the nation's military needs. Those cited from the early years of the new republic show clearly that in spite of partisan rhetoric and considerable differences of opinion, both Federalists and Jeffersonians in the end closely followed this blueprint.

It should be noted that beyond minor deletions, as indicated, because of space limitations, these documents appear without any historical editing on our part. For those specialists who desire to consult complete texts with annotations, a list of the printed primary sources appears at the conclusion of this section.

The Revolutionary Years

Resolution of the Continental Congress Adopting the Continental Army, 14 June 1775.

The resolutions being read, were adopted as follows:

Resolved, That six companies of expert rifflemen, be immediately raised in Pensylvania, two in Maryland, and two in Virginia; that each company consist of a captain, three lieutenants, four serjeants, four corporals, a drummer or trumpeter, and sixty-eight privates.

That each company, as soon as compleated, shall march and join the army near Boston, to be there employed as light infantry, under the command of the chief Officer in that army.

That the pay of the Officers and privates be as follows, viz. a captain @ 20 dollars per month; a lieutenant @ 13⅓ dollars; a serjeant @ 8 dollars; a corporal @ 7⅓ dollars; drummer or [trumpeter] @ 7⅓ doll.; privates @ 6⅔ dollars; to find their own arms and cloaths.

That the form of the enlistment be in the following words:

I   have, this day, voluntarily enlisted myself, as a soldier, in the American continental army, for one year, unless sooner discharged: And I do bind myself to conform, in all instances, to such rules and regulations, as are, or shall be, established for the government of the said Army.

Upon motion, *Resolved,* That Mr. [George] Washington, Mr. [Philip] Schuyler, Mr. [Silas] Deane, Mr. [Thomas] Cushing, and Mr. [Joseph] Hewes be a committee to bring in a draft of Rules and regulations for the government of the army.

Resolution of the Continental Congress Appointing George Washington as Commander in Chief of the Continental Army, 15 June 1775.

The report of the committee being read and debated, *Resolved,* That a General be appointed to command all the continental forces, raised, or to be raised, for the defence of American liberty.

That five hundred dollars, per month, be allowed for his pay and expences.

The Congress then proceeded to the choice of a general, by ballot, when George Washington, Esq. was unanimously elected.

Washington's Commission as Commander in Chief of the Continental Army, 17 June 1775.

IN CONGRESS

The delegates of the United Colonies of New Hampshire, Massachusetts bay, Rhode Island, Connecticut, New York, New Jersey, Pensylvania, the Counties of New-Castle, Kent, and Sussex, on Delaware, Maryland, Virginia, North Carolina, and South Carolina: To George Washington, Esq.

WE, reposing special trust and confidence in your patriotism, valor, conduct, and fidelity, do, by these presents, constitute and appoint you to be General and Commander in chief, of the army of the United Colonies, and of all the forces now raised, or to be raised, by them, and of all others who shall voluntarily offer their service, and join the said Army for the Defence of American liberty, and for repelling every hostile invasion thereof: And you are hereby vested with full power and authority to act as you shall think for the good and welfare of the service.

And we do hereby strictly charge and require all Officers and Soldiers, under your command, to be obedient to your orders, and diligent in the exercise of their several duties.

And we do also enjoin and require you, to be careful in executing the great trust reposed in you, by causing strict discipline and order to be observed in the army, and that the soldiers be duly exercised, and provided with all convenient necessaries.

And you are to regulate your conduct in every respect by the rules and discipline of war, (as herewith given you,) and punctually to observe and follow such orders and directions, from time to time, as you shall receive from this, or a future Congress of these United Colonies, or committee of Congress.

This commission to continue in force, until revoked by this, or a future Congress.

By order of the Congress.

Dated, Philadelphia, June 17, 1775.

Continental Congress' Declaration on the Causes and Necessity for Taking Up Arms, 6 July 1775.

A declaration by the Representatives of the United Colonies of North America, now met in General Congress at Philadelphia, setting forth the causes and necessity of their taking up arms.

If it was possible for men, who exercise their reason, to believe, that the Divine Author of our existence intended a part of the human race to hold an absolute property in, and an unbounded power over others, marked out by his infinite goodness and wisdom, as the objects of a legal domination never rightfully resistible, however severe and oppressive, the Inhabitants of these Colonies might at least require from the Parliament of Great Britain some evidence, that this dreadful authority over them, has been granted to that body. But a reverence for our great Creator, principles of humanity, and the dictates of common sense, must convince all those who reflect upon the subject, that government was instituted to promote the welfare of mankind, and ought to be administered for the attainment of that end. The legislature of Great Britain, however, stimulated by an inordinate passion for a power, not only unjustifiable, but which they know to be peculiarly reprobated by the very constitution of that kingdom, and desperate of success in any mode of contest, where regard should be had to truth, law, or right, have at length, deserting those, attempted to effect their cruel and impolitic purpose of enslaving these Colonies by violence, and have thereby rendered it necessary for us to close with their last appeal from Reason to Arms.—Yet, however blinded that assembly may be, by their intemperate rage for unlimited domination, so to slight justice and the opinion of mankind, we esteem ourselves bound, by obligations of respect to the rest of the world, to make known the justice of our cause.

Our forefathers, inhabitants of the island of Great Britain, left their native land, to seek on these shores a residence for civil and religious freedom. At the expence of their blood, at the hazard of their fortunes, without the least charge to the country from which they removed, by unceasing labor, and an unconquerable spirit, they effected settlements in the distant and inhospitable wilds of America, then filled with numerous and warlike nations of barbarians. Societies or governments, vested with perfect legislatures, were formed under charters from the crown, and an harmonious intercourse was established between the colonies and the kingdom from which they derived their origin. The mutual benefits of this union became in a short time so extraordinary, as to excite astonishment. It is universally confessed, that the amazing increase of the wealth, strength, and navigation of the realm, arose from this source; and the minister, who so wisely and successfully directed the measures of Great Britain in the late war, publicly declared, that these colonies enabled her to triumph over her enemies.—Towards the conclusion of that war, it pleased our sovereign to make a change in his counsels.—From that fatal moment, the affairs of the British empire began to fall into confusion, and gradually sliding from the summit of glorious prosperity, to which they had been advanced by the virtues and abilities of one man, are at length distracted by the convulsions, that now shake it to its deepest foundations. The new ministry finding the brave foes of Britain, though frequently defeated, yet still contending, took up the unfortunate idea of granting them a hasty peace, and of then subduing her faithful friends.

These devoted colonies were judged to be in such a state, as to present victories without bloodshed, and all the easy emoluments of statuteable plunder.—The uninterrupted tenor of their peaceable and respectful behaviour from the beginning of colonization, their dutiful, zealous, and useful services during the war, though so recently and amply acknowledged in the most honorable manner by his majesty, by the late king, and by Parliament, could not save them from the meditated innovations.—Parliament was influenced to adopt the pernicious project, and assuming a new power over them, have, in the course of eleven years, given such decisive specimens of the spirit and consequences attending this power, as to leave no doubt concerning the effects of acquiescence under it. They have undertaken to give and grant our money without our consent, though we have ever exercised an exclusive right to dispose of our own property; statutes have been passed for extending the jurisdiction of courts of Admiralty and Vice-Admiralty beyond their ancient limits; for depriving us of the accustomed and inestimable privilege of trial by jury, in cases affecting both life and property; for suspending the legislature of one of the colonies; for interdicting all commerce to the capital of another; and for altering fundamentally the form of government established by charter, and secured by acts of its own legislature solemnly confirmed by the crown; for exempting the "murderers" of colonists from legal trial, and in effect, from punishment; for erecting in a neighboring province, acquired by the joint arms of Great Britain and America, a despotism dangerous to our very existence; and for quartering soldiers upon the colonists in time of profound peace. It has also been resolved in parliament, that colonists charged with committing certain offences, shall be transported to England to be tried.

But why should we enumerate our injuries in detail? By one statute it is declared, that parliament can "of right make laws to bind us IN ALL CASES WHATSOEVER." What is to defend us against so enormous, so unlimited a power? Not a single man of those who assume it, is chosen by us; or is subject to our controul or influence; but, on the contrary, they are all of them exempt from the operation of such laws, and an American revenue, if not diverted from the ostensible purposes for which it is raised, would actually lighten their own burdens in proportion as they increase ours. We saw the misery to which such despotism would reduce us. We for ten years incessantly and ineffectually besieged the Throne as supplicants; we reasoned, we remonstrated with parliament, in the most mild and decent language. But Administration, sensible that we should regard these oppressive measures as freemen ought to do, sent over fleets and armies to enforce them. The indignation of the Americans was roused, it is true; but it was the indignation of a virtuous, loyal, and affectionate people. A Congress of Delegates from the United Colonies was assembled at Philadelphia, on the fifth day of last September. We resolved again to offer an humble and dutiful petition to the King, and also addressed our fellow-subjects of Great Britain. We have pursued every temperate, every respectful measure: we have even proceeded to break off our commercial intercourse with our fellow-subjects, as the last peaceable admonition, that our attachment to no nation upon earth should supplant our attachment to liberty.—This, we flattered ourselves, was the ultimate step of the controversy: But subsequent events have shewn, how vain was this hope of finding moderation in our enemies.

Several threatening expressions against the colonies were inserted in his Majesty's speech; our petition, though we were told it was a decent one, and that his Majesty had been pleased to receive it graciously, and to promise laying it before his Parliament, was huddled into both houses amongst a bundle of American papers, and there neglected. The Lords and Commons in their address, in the month of February, said, that "a rebellion at that time actually existed within the province of Massachusetts bay; and that those concerned in it, had been countenanced and encouraged by unlawful combinations and engagements, entered into by his Majesty's subjects in several of the other colonies; and therefore they besought his Majesty, that he would take the most effectual measures to enforce due obedience to the laws and authority of the supreme legislature."—Soon after, the commercial intercourse of whole colonies, with foreign countries, and with each other, was cut off by an act of Parliament; by another, several of them were entirely prohibited from the fisheries in the seas near their coasts, on which they always depended for their sustenance; and large re-inforcements of ships and troops were immediately sent over to General Gage.

Fruitless were all the entreaties, arguments, and eloquence of an illustrious band of the most distinguished Peers, and Commoners, who nobly and strenuously asserted the justice of our cause, to stay, or even to mitigate the heedless fury with which these accumulated and unexampled outrages were hurried on.—Equally fruitless was the interference of the city of London, of Bristol, and many other respectable towns in our favour. Parliament adopted an insidious manoeuvre calculated to divide us, to establish a perpetual auction of taxations where colony should bid against colony, all of them uninformed what ransom would redeem their lives; and thus to extort from us, at the point of the bayonet, the unknown sums that should be sufficient to gratify, if possible to gratify, ministerial rapacity, with the miserable indulgence left to us of raising, in our own mode, the prescribed tribute. What terms more rigid and humiliating could have been dictated by remorseless victors to conquered enemies? In our circumstances to accept them, would be to deserve them.

Soon after the intelligence of these proceedings arrived on this continent, General Gage, who in the course of the last year had taken possession of the town of Boston, in the province of Massachusetts Bay, and still occupied it as a garrison, on the 19th day of April, sent out from that place a large detachment of his army, who made an unprovoked assault on the inhabitants of the said province, at the town of Lexington, as appears by the affidavits of a great number of persons, some of whom were officers and soldiers of that detachment, murdered eight of the inhabitants, and wounded many others. From thence the troops proceeded in warlike array to the town of Concord, where they set upon another party of the inhabitants of the same province, killing several and wounding more, until compelled to retreat by the country people suddenly assembled to repel this cruel aggression. Hostilities, thus commenced by the British troops, have been since prosecuted by them without regard to faith or reputation.—The inhabitants of Boston being confined within that town by the General their Governor, and having, in order to procure their dismission, entered into a treaty with him, it was stipulated that the said inhabitants having deposited their arms with their own magistrates, should have liberty to depart, taking with them their other effects. They accordingly delivered up their arms, but in open violation of honor, in defiance of the obligation of treaties, which even savage nations esteemed sacred, the Governor ordered the arms deposited as aforesaid, that they might be preserved for their owners, to be seized by a body of soldiers; detained the greatest part of the inhabitants in the town, and compelled the few who were permitted to retire, to leave their most valuable effects behind.

By this perfidy wives are separated from their husbands, children from their parents, the aged and the sick from their relations and friends, who wish to attend and comfort them; and those who have been used to live in plenty and even elegance, are reduced to deplorable distress.

The General, further emulating his ministerial masters, by a proclamation bearing date on the 12th day of June, after venting the grossest falsehoods and calumnies against the good people of these colonies, proceeds to "declare them all, either by name or description, to be rebels and traitors, to supersede the course of the common law, and instead thereof to publish and order the use and exercise of the law martial." —His troops have butchered our countrymen, have wantonly burnt Charles-Town, besides a considerable number of houses in other places; our ships and vessels are seized; the necessary supplies of provisions are intercepted, and he is exerting his utmost power to spread destruction and devastation around him.

We have received certain intelligence that General Carleton, the Governor of Canada, is instigating the people of that province and the Indians to fall upon us; and we have but too much reason to apprehend, that schemes have been formed to excite domestic enemies against us. In brief, a part of these colonies now feels, and all of them are sure of feeling, as far as the vengance of administration can inflict them, the complicated calamities of fire, sword, and famine.—We are reduced to the alternative of chusing an unconditional submission to the tyranny of irritated ministers, or resistance by force.—The latter is our choice.—We have counted the cost of this contest, and find nothing so dreadful as voluntary slavery.—Honor, justice, and humanity, forbid us tamely to surrender that freedom which we received from our gallant ancestors, and which our innocent posterity have a right to receive from us. We cannot endure the infamy and guilt of resigning succeeding generations to that wretchedness which inevitably awaits them, if we basely entail hereditary bondage upon them.

Our cause is just. Our union is perfect. Our internal resources are great, and, if necessary, foreign assistance is undoubtedly attainable.—We gratefully acknowledge, as signal instances of the Divine favour towards us, that his Providence would not permit us to be called into this severe controversy, until we were grown up to our present strength, had been previously exercised in warlike operation, and possessed of the means of defending ourselves.—With hearts fortified with these animating reflections, we most solemnly, before God and the world, declare, that, exerting the utmost energy of those powers, which our beneficent Creator hath graciously bestowed upon us, the arms we have been compelled by our enemies to assume, we will, in defiance of every hazard, with unabating firmness and perseverance, employ for the preservation of our liberties; being with our [one] mind resolved to dye Free-men rather than live Slaves.

Lest this declaration should disquiet the minds of our friends and fellow-subjects in any part of the empire, we assure them that we mean not to dissolve that Union which has so long and so happily subsisted between us, and which we sincerely wish to see restored.—Necessity has not yet driven us into that desperate measure, or induced us to excite any other nation to war against them.—We have not raised armies with ambitious designs of separating from Great Britain, and establishing independent states. We fight not for glory or for conquest. We exhibit to mankind the remarkable spectacle of a people attacked by unprovoked enemies, without any imputation or even suspicion of offence. They boast of their privileges and civilization, and yet proffer no milder conditions than servitude or death.

In our own native land, in defence of the freedom that is our birth-right, and which we ever enjoyed till the late violation of it—for the protection of our property, acquired solely by the honest industry of our fore-fathers and ourselves, against violence actually offered, we have taken up arms. We shall lay them down when hostilities shall cease on the part of the aggressors, and all danger of their being renewed shall be removed, and not before.

With an humble confidence in the mercies of the supreme and impartial Judge and Ruler of the universe, we most devoutly implore his divine goodness to protect us happily through this great conflict, to dispose our adversaries to reconciliation on reasonable terms, and thereby to relieve the empire from the calamities of civil war.

By order of Congress,

JOHN HANCOCK,

President.

Attested,

CHARLES THOMSON,

Secretary.

Philadelphia, July 6th, 1775.

The Declaration of Independence, 4 July 1776.

Agreeable to the order of the day, the Congress resolved itself into a committee of the whole, to take into their farther consideration, the declaration; and, after some time, the president resumed the chair. Mr. [Benjamin] Harrison reported, that the committee of the whole Congress have agreed to a Declaration, which he delivered in.

The Declaration being again read, was agreed to as follows:

The unanimous Declaration of the thirteen United States of America.

When, in the Course of human events, it becomes necessary for one people to dissolve the political bands which have connected them with another, and to assume, among the Powers of the earth, the separate and equal station to which the Laws of Nature and of Nature's God entitle them, a decent respect to the opinions of mankind requires that they should declare the causes which impel them to the separation.

We hold these truths to be self-evident, that all men are created equal, that they are endowed by their Creator with certain unalienable Rights, that among these, are Life, Liberty, and the pursuit of Happiness. That, to secure these rights, Governments are instituted among Men, deriving their just Powers from the consent of the governed. That, whenever any form of Government becomes destructive of these ends, it is the Right of the People to alter or to abolish it, and to institute new Government, laying its foundation on such Principles, and organizing its Powers in such form, as to them shall seem most likely to effect their Safety and Happiness. Prudence, indeed, will dictate that Governments long established should not be changed for light and transient causes; and, accordingly, all experience hath shewn, that mankind are more disposed to suffer, while evils are sufferable, than to right themselves by abolishing the forms to which they are accustomed. But, when a long train of abuses and usurpations, pursuing invariably the same Object, evinces a design to reduce them under absolute Despotism, it is their right, it is their duty, to throw off such Government, and to provide new Guards for their future Security. Such has been the patient sufferance of these Colonies; and such is now the necessity which constrains them to alter their former Systems of Government. The history of the present King of Great Britain is a history of repeated injuries and usurpations, all having in direct object the establishment of an absolute Tyranny over these States. To prove this, let Facts be submitted to a candid world.

He has refused his Assent to Laws the most wholesome and necessary for the public good.

He has forbidden his Governors to pass Laws of immediate and pressing importance, unless suspended in their operation till his Assent should be obtained; and when so suspended, he has utterly neglected to attend to them.

He has refused to pass other Laws for the accommodation of large districts of People, unless those People would relinquish the right of Representation in the legislature; a right inestimable to them and formidable to tyrants only.

He has called together legislative bodies at places unusual, uncomfortable, and distant from the depository of their Public Records, for the sole Purpose of fatiguing them into compliance with his measures.

He has dissolved Representative Houses repeatedly, for opposing, with manly firmness, his invasions on the rights of the People.

He has refused for a long time, after such dissolutions, to cause others to be elected; whereby the Legislative Powers, incapable of Annihilation, have returned to the People at large for their exercise; the State remaining in the mean time exposed to all the dangers of invasion from without, and convulsions within.

He has endeavoured to prevent the Population of these States; for that purpose obstructing the Laws for Naturalization of Foreigners; refusing to pass others to encourage their migrations hither, and raising the conditions of new Appropriations of Lands.

He has obstructed the Administration of Justice, by refusing his Assent to Laws for establishing Judiciary Powers.

He has made Judges dependent on his Will alone, for the tenure of their offices, and the amount and payment of their salaries.

He has erected a multitude of New Offices, and sent hither swarms of Officers to harrass our People, and eat out their substance.

He has kept among us, in times of Peace, Standing Armies, without the Consent of our legislatures.

He has affected to render the Military independent of and superior to the Civil Power.

He has combined with others to subject us to a jurisdiction foreign to our constitution, and unacknowledged by our laws; giving his Assent to their Acts of pretended Legislation:

For quartering large bodies of armed troops among us:

For protecting them, by a mock Trial, from Punishment for any Murders which they should commit on the Inhabitants of these States:

For cutting off our Trade with all parts of the world:

For imposing Taxes on us without our Consent:

For depriving us, in many cases, of the benefits of Trial by Jury:

For transporting us beyond Seas to be tried for pretended offences:

For abolishing the free System of English Laws in a neighbouring province, establishing therein an Arbitrary government, and enlarging its Boundaries, so as to render it at once an example and fit instrument for introducing the same absolute rule into these Colonies:

For taking away our Charters, abolishing our most valuable Laws, and altering fundamentally the Forms of our Governments:

For suspending our own Legislatures, and declaring themselves invested with Power to legislate for us in all cases whatsoever.

He has abdicated Government here, by declaring us out of his protection, and waging War against us.

He has plundered our seas, ravaged our Coasts, burnt our towns, and destroyed the Lives of our People.

He is at this time transporting large Armies of foreign Mercenaries to compleat the works of death, desolation and tyranny, already begun with circumstances of Cruelty and perfidy scarcely paralleled in the most barbarous ages, and totally unworthy the Head of a civilized nation.

He has constrained our fellow Citizens, taken Captive on the high Seas, to bear Arms against their Country, to become the executioners of their friends and Brethren, or to fall themselves by their Hands.

He has excited domestic insurrections amongst us, and has endeavoured to bring on the inhabitants of our frontiers, the merciless Indian Savages, whose known rule of warfare, is an undistinguished destruction of all ages, sexes and conditions.

In every stage of these Oppressions, We have Petitioned for Redress, in the most humble terms: Our repeated Petitions, have been answered only by repeated injury. A Prince, whose character is thus marked by every act which may define a Tyrant, is unfit to be the ruler of a free People.

Nor have We been wanting in attentions to our Brittish brethren. We have warned them from time to time of attempts by their legislature to extend an unwarrantable jurisdiction over us. We have reminded them of the circumstances of our emigration and settlement here. We have appealed to their native justice and magnanimity, and we have conjured them by the ties of our common kindred, to disavow these usurpations, which, would inevitably interrupt our connexions and correspondence. They too have been deaf to the voice of justice and of consanguinity. We must, therefore, acquiesce in the necessity, which denounces our Separation, and hold them, as we hold the rest of mankind, Enemies in War, in Peace Friends.

We, therefore, the Representatives of the united States of America, in GENERAL CONGRESS assembled, appealing to the Supreme Judge of the World for the rectitude of our intentions, DO, in the Name, and by Authority of the good People of these Colonies, solemnly PUBLISH and DECLARE, That these United Colonies are, and of Right, ought to be Free and Independent States; that they are Absolved from all Allegiance to the British Crown, and that all political connexion between them and the State of Great Britain, is and ought to be totally dissolved; and that, as FREE and INDEPENDENT STATES, they have full Power to levy War, conclude Peace, contract Alliances, establish Commerce, and to do all other Acts and Things which Independent States may of right do. And for the support of this Declaration, with a firm reliance on the protection of divine Providence, we mutually pledge to each other our Lives, our Fortunes, and our sacred Honour.

The foregoing declaration was, by order of Congress, engrossed, and signed by the following members:

John Hancock.

Josiah Bartlett.
Wm Whipple.
Saml Adams.
John Adams.
Robt Treat Paine.
Elbridge Gerry.
Steph. Hopkins.
William Ellery.
Roger Sherman.
Samel Huntington.
Wm Williams.
Oliver Wolcott.
Matthew Thornton.
Wm Floyd.
Phil Livingston.
Frans Lewis.
Lewis Morris.
Richd Stockton.
Jno Witerhspoon.
Fras Hopkinson.
John Hart.
Abra Clark.
Robt Morris.
Benjamin Rush.
Benja Franklin.
John Morton.
Geo Clymer.
Jas Smith.

Geo. Taylor.
James Wilson.
Geo. Ross.
Caesar Rodney.
Geo Read.
Thos M:Kean.
Samuel Chase.
Wm Paca.
Thos Stone.
Charles Carroll of Carrollton.
George Wythe.
Richard Henry Lee.
Th. Jefferson.
Benja Harrison.
Thos Nelson, Jr.
Francis Lightfoot Lee.
Carter Braxton.
Wm Hooper.
Joseph Hewes.
John Penn.
Edward Rutledge.
Thos Heyward, Junr
Thomas Lynch, Junr
Arthur Middleton.
Button Gwinnett.
Lyman Hall.
Geo Walton.

The Eighty-Eight Battalion Resolution of the Continental Congress Authorizing an Expanded Continental Army To Serve for the Duration of the War, 16 September 1776.

Agreeable to order, Congress resolved itself into a committee of the whole, to take into consideration the report of the Board of War; and, after some time, the president resumed the chair, and Mr. [Thomas] Nelson reported, the committee have had under consideration the report of the Board of War, and have made sundry amendments, which they ordered him to lay before Congress:

Congress then took into consideration the report of the Board of War, with the amendments offered by the committee of the whole; and, thereupon, came to the following resolutions:

That eighty eight batallions be inlisted as soon as possible, to serve during the present war, and that each state furnish their respective quotas in the following proportions, viz.

New Hampshire,	-	3 batallions.
Massachusetts bay,	-	15
Rhode Island,	-	2
Connecticut,	-	8
New York,	-	4
New Jersey,	-	4
Pensylvania,	-	12
Delaware,	-	1
Maryland,	-	8
Virginia,	-	15
North Carolina,	-	9
South Carolina,	-	6
Georgia,	-	1

That twenty dollars be given as a bounty to each noncommissioned officer and private soldier, who shall inlist to serve during the present war, unless sooner discharged by Congress:

That Congress make provision for granting lands, in the following proportions: to the officers and soldiers who shall so engage in the service, and continue therein to the close of the war, or until discharged by Congress, and to the representatives of such officers and soldiers as shall be slain by the enemy:

Such lands to be provided by the United States, and whatever expence shall be necessary to procure such land, the said expence shall be paid and borne by the states in the same proportion as the other expences of the war, viz.

To a colonel, 500 acres; to a lieutenant colonel, 450; to a major, 400; to a captain, 300; to a lieutenant, 200; to an ensign, 150; each noncommissioned officer and soldier, 100:

That the appointment of all officers, and filling up vacancies, (except general officers) be left to the governments of the several states, and that every state provide arms, cloathing, and every necessary for its quota of troops, according to the foregoing estimate: The expence of the cloathing to be deducted from the pay of the soldiers, as usual:

That all officers be commissioned by Congress:

That it be recommended to the several states, that they take the most speedy and effectual measures for inlisting their several quotas:

That the money to be given for bounties be paid by the pay master in the department where the soldier shall inlist:

That each soldier receive pay and subsistence from the

time of their inlistment.

Resolutions of the Continental Congress Expanding the Continental Army and Extending Emergency Powers to Washington, 27 December 1776.

The committee on the state of the army, brought in their report, which was taken into consideration; Whereupon;

Resolved, That a brigadier general of artillery be appointed; and, the ballots being taken,

Colonel Henry Knox was elected.

Resolved, That General Washington be empowered to use every endeavour, by giving bounties and otherwise, to prevail upon the troops, whose time of inlistment shall expire at the end of the month, to stay with the army so long after that period, as its situation shall render their stay necessary:

That the new levies in Virginia, Maryland, the Delaware state, Pensylvania, and New Jersey, be ordered to march by companies, and parts of companies, as fast as they shall be raised, and join the army under General Washington, with the utmost despatch:

That the foregoing resolution be transmitted by the president to the executive powers of the states before mentioned, who are requested to carry it into execution; to appoint commissaries to precede the troops, and procure provision for them on their march; and that they be empowered to draw money for this purpose from the nearest continental pay master:

That General Washington be empowered to appoint a commissary of prisoners, and a cloathier general for supplying the army; to fix their salaries, and return their names to Congress:

That General Washington be requested to fix upon that system of promotion in the continental army, which, in his opinion, and that of the general officers with him, will produce most general satisfaction; that it be suggested to him, whether a promotion of field officers in the colonial line, and of captains and subalterns in the regimental line, would not be the most proper:

That the Committee of Congress at Philadelphia be desired to contract with proper persons for erecting at Carlisle, in Pensylvania, a magazine sufficient to contain ten thousand stand of arms and two hundred tons of gun powder, and also for erecting an elaboratory adjacent to such magazine.

That the council of Massachusetts bay be desired to contract with proper persons for erecting in the town of Brookfield in that state, a magazine sufficient to contain ten thousand stand of arms and two hundred tons of gun powder, and also for erecting an elaboratory adjacent to such magazine.

That Congress approve of General Washington's directing the quarter master general to provide teams for each regiment, and for other necessary purposes:

That the Committee of Secret Correspondence be desired to direct the Commissioners at the Court of France to procure, if possible, from that Court an hundred thousand stand of small arms.

That the 2d and 7th Virginia regiments, with all the convalescents from the other corps left in that state, and now fit for duty, be ordered to march and join the army under General Washington, with the utmost despatch, leaving the arms that they have at present, with the governor and council of that state, as they will be provided with others at the Head of Elk:

That three of the regiments, upon the new establishment, in North Carolina, be ordered to march immediately . . . to join General Washington:

That the state of Virginia be empowered to call into service, at the continental expence, three regiments of militia, or minute men, if such a measure shall be, by that state, judged necessary.

The unjust, but determined, purpose of the British court to enslave these free states, obvious through every delusive insinuation to the contrary, having placed things in such a situation, that the very existence of civil liberty now depends on the right execution of military powers, and the vigorous, decisive conduct of these, being impossible to distant, numerous, and deliberative bodies:

This Congress, having maturely considered the present crisis; and having perfect reliance on the wisdom, vigour, and uprightness of General Washington, do, hereby,

Resolve, That General Washington shall be, and he is hereby, vested with full, ample, and complete powers to raise and collect together, in the most speedy and effectual manner, from any or all of these United States, 16 batallions of infantry, in addition to those already voted by Congress; to appoint officers for the said batallions; to raise, officer, and equip three thousand light horse; three regiments of artillery, and a corps of engineers, and to establish their pay; to apply to any of the states for such aid of the militia as he shall judge necessary; to form such magazines of provisions, and in such places, as he shall think proper; to displace and appoint all officers under the rank of brigadier general, and to fill up all vacancies in every other department in the American armies; to take, wherever he may be, whatever he may want for the use of the army, if the inhabitants will not sell it, allowing a reasonable price for the same; to arrest and confine persons who refuse to take the continental currency, or are otherwise disaffected to the American cause; and return to the states of which they are citizens, their names, and the nature of their offences, together with the witnesses to prove them:

That the foregoing powers be vested in General Washington, for and during the term of six months from the date hereof, unless sooner determined by Congress.

John Dickinson's Draft of the Articles of Confederation, 12 July 1776.

Articles of confederation and perpetual union, between the colonies of

New Hampshire,	*The counties of New Castle, Kent and Sussex on Delaware,*
Massachusetts Bay,	
Rhode Island,	*Maryland,*
Connecticut,	*Virginia,*
New York,	*North Carolina,*
New Jersey,	*South Carolina, and*
Pennsylvania,	*Georgia.*

ART. I. THE Name of this Confederacy shall be "THE UNITED STATES OF AMERICA."

ART. II. The said Colonies unite themselves so as never to be divided by any Act whatever, and hereby severally enter into a firm League of Friendship with each other, for their common Defence, the Security of their Liberties, and their mutual and general Welfare, binding the said Colonies to assist one another against all Force offered to or attacks made upon them or any of them, on Account of Religion, Sovereignty, Trade, or any other Pretence whatever.

ART. III. Each Colony shall retain and enjoy as much of its present Laws, Rights and Customs, as it may think fit, and reserves to itself the sole and exclusive Regulation and Government of its internal police, in all matters that shall not interfere with the Articles of this Confederation.

ART. IV. No Colony or Colonies, without the Consent of the United States assembled, shall send any Embassy to or receive any Embassy from, or enter into any Treaty, Convention or Conference with the King or Kingdom of Great-Britain, or any foreign Prince or State; nor shall any Colony or Colonies, nor any Servant or Servants of the United States, or of any Colony or Colonies, accept of any Present, Emolument, Office, or Title of any Kind whatever, from the King or Kingdom of Great-Britain, or any foreign Prince or State; nor shall the United States assembled, or any Colony grant any Title of Nobility.

ART. V. No two or more Colonies shall enter into any Treaty, Confederation or Alliance whatever between them, without the previous and free Consent and Allowance of the United States assembled, specifying accurately the Purposes for which the same is to be entered into, and how long it shall continue.

ART. VI. The Inhabitants of each Colony shall henceforth always have the same Rights, Liberties, Privileges, Immunities and Advantages, in the other Colonies, which the said Inhabitants now have, in all Cases whatever, except in those provided for by the next following Article.

ART. VII. The Inhabitants of each Colony shall enjoy all the Rights, Liberties, Privileges, Immunities, and Advantages, in Trade, Navigation, and Commerce, in any other Colony, and in going to and from the same from and to any Part of the World, which the Natives of such Colony . . . enjoy.

ART. VIII. Each Colony may assess or lay such Imposts or Duties as it thinks proper, on Importations or Exportations, provided such Imposts or Duties do not interfere with any Stipulations in Treaties hereafter entered into by the United States assembled, with the King or Kingdom of Great Britain, or any foreign Prince or State.

ART. IX. No standing Army or Body of Forces shall be kept up by any Colony or Colonies in Times of Peace, except such a Number only as may be requisite to garrison the Forts necessary for the Defence of such Colony or Colonies: But every Colony shall always keep up a well regulated and disciplined Militia, sufficiently armed and accoutred; and shall provide and constantly have ready for Use in public Stores, a due Number of Field Pieces and Tents, and a proper Quantity of Ammunition, and Camp Equipage.

ART. X. When Troops are raised in any of the Colonies for the common Defence, the Commission Officers proper for the Troops raised in each Colony, except the General Officers, shall be appointed by the Legislature of each Colony respectively, or in such manner as shall by them be directed.

ART. XI. All Charges of Wars and all other Expences that shall be incurred for the common Defence, or general Welfare, and allowed by the United States assembled, shall be defrayed out of a common Treasury, which shall be supplied by the several Colonies in Proportion to the Number of Inhabitants of every Age, Sex and Quality, except Indians not paying Taxes, in each Colony, a true Account of which, distinguishing the white Inhabitants, shall be triennially taken and transmitted to the Assembly of the United States. The Taxes for paying that Proportion shall be laid and levied by the Authority and Direction of the Legislatures of the several Colonies, within the Time agreed upon by United States assembled.

ART. XII. Every Colony shall abide by the Determinations of the United States assembled, concerning the Services performed and Losses or Expences incurred by every Colony for the common Defence or general Welfare, and no Colony or Colonies shall in any Case whatever endeavor by Force to procure Redress of any Injury or Injustice supposed to be done by the United States to such Colony or Colonies in not granting such Satisfactions, Indemnifications, Compensations, Retributions, Exemptions, or Benefits of any Kind, as such Colony or Colonies may think just or reasonable.

ART. XIII. No Colony or Colonies shall engage in any War without the previous Consent of the United States assembled, unless such Colony or Colonies be actually invaded by Enemies, or shall have received certain Advice of a Resolution being formed by some Nations of Indians to invade such Colony or Colonies, and the Danger is so imminent, as not to admit of a Delay, till the other Colonies can be consulted: Nor shall any Colony or Colonies grant Commissions to any Ships or Vessels of War, nor Letters of Marque or Reprisal, except it be after a Declaration of War by the United States assembled, and then only against the Kingdom or State and the Subjects thereof, against which War has been so declared, and under such Regulations as shall be established by the United States assembled.

ART. XIV. A perpetual Alliance, offensive and defensive, is to be entered into by the United States assembled as soon as may be, with the Six Nations, and all other neighbouring Nations of Indians; their Limits to be ascertained, their Lands to be secured to them, and not encroached on; no Purchases of Lands, hereafter to be made of the Indians by Colonies or private Persons before the Limits of the Colonies are ascertained, to be valid: All Purchases of Lands not included within those Limits, where ascertained, to be made by Contracts between the United States assembled, or by Persons for that Purpose authorized by them, and the great Councils of the Indians, for the general Benefit of all the United Colonies.

ART. XV. When the Boundaries of any Colony shall be ascertained by Agreement, or in the Manner herein after directed, all the other Colonies shall guarantee to such Colony the full and peaceable Possession of, and the free and entire Jurisdiction in and over the Territory included within such Boundaries.

ART. XVI. For the more convenient Management of the general Interests of the United States, Delegates should be annually appointed in such Manner as the Legislature of each Colony shall direct [or such Branche thereof as the Colony shall authorize for that purpose], to meet at the City of Philadelphia, in the Colony of Pennsylvania, until otherwise ordered by the United States assembled; which Meeting shall be on the first Monday of November in every Year, with a Power reserved to those who appointed the said Delegates, respectively to recal them or any of them at any time within the Year, and to send new Delegates in their stead for the Remainder of the Year. Each Colony shall support its own Delegates in a Meeting of the States, and while they act as Members of the Council of State, herein after mentioned.

ART. XVII. In determining Questions each Colony shall have one Vote.

ART. XVIII. The United States assembled shall have the sole and exclusive Right and Power of determining on Peace and War, except in the Cases mentioned in the thirteenth Article—Of establishing Rules for deciding in all Cases, what Captures on Land or Water shall be legal—In what Manner Prizes taken by land or naval Forces in the Service of the United States shall be divided or appropriated—Granting Letters of Marque and Reprisal in Times of Peace—Appointing Courts for the Trial of all Crimes, Frauds and Piracies committed on the High Seas, or on any navigable River, not within the Body of a County or Parish—Establishing Courts for receiving and determining finally Appeals in all Cases of Captures—Sending and receiving Ambassadors under any Character—Entering into Treaties and Alliances—Settling all Disputes and Differences now subsisting, or that hereafter may arise between two or more Colonies concerning Boundaries, Jurisdictions, or any other Cause whatever—Coining Money and regulating the Value thereof—Regulating the Trade, and managing all Affairs with the Indians—Limiting the Bounds of those Colonies, which by Charter or Proclamation, or under any Pretence, are said to extend to the South Sea, and ascertaining those Bounds of any other Colony that appear to be indeterminate—Assigning Territories for new Colonies, either in Lands to be thus separated from Colonies and heretofore purchased or obtained by the Crown of Great-Britain from the Indians, or hereafter to be purchased or obtained from them—Disposing of all such Lands for the general Benefit of all the United Colonies—Ascertaining Boundaries to such new Colonies, within which Forms of Government are to be established on the Principles of Liberty—Establishing and regulating Post-Offices throughout all the United Colonies, on the Lines of Communication from one Colony to another—Appointing General Officers of the Land Forces in the Service of the United States—Commissioning such other Officers of the said Forces as shall be appointed by Virtue of the tenth Article—Appointing all the Officers of the Naval Forces in the Service of the United States—Making Rules for the Government and Regulation of the Said Land and Naval Forces, and directing the operations—Appointing a Council of State, and such Committees and civil Officers as may be necessary for managing the general Affairs of the United States, under their Direction while assembled, and in their Recess, of the Council of State—Appointing one of their number to preside, and a suitable Person for Secretary—And adjourning to any Time within the Year.

The United States assembled shall have Authority for the Defence and Welfare of the United Colonies and every of them, to agree upon and fix the necessary Sums and Expences—To emit Bills, or to borrow Money on the Credit of the United Colonies—To raise Naval Forces—To agree upon the Number of Land Forces to be raised, and to make Requisitions from the Legislature of each Colony, or the Persons therein authoritized by the Legislature to execute such Requisitions, for the Quota of each Colony, which is to be in Proportion to the Number of white Inhabitants in the Colony, which Requisitions shall be binding, and thereupon the Legislature of each Colony or the Persons authorized as aforesaid, shall appoint the Regimental Officers, raise the Men, and arm and equip them in a soldier-like Manner; and the Officers and Men so armed and equipped, shall march to the Place appointed, and within the Time agreed on by the United States assembled.

But if the United States assembled shall on Consideration of Circumstances judge proper, that any Colony or Colonies should not raise Men, or should raise a smaller Number than the Quota or Quotas of such Colony or Colonies, and that any other Colony or Colonies should raise a greater number of men than the Quota or Quotas thereof, such extra-numbers shall be raised, officered, armed and equipped in the same Manner as the Quota or Quotas of such Colony or Colonies, unless the Legislature of such Colony or Colonies respectively, shall judge, that such extra-numbers cannot be safely spared out of the same, in which Case they shall raise, officer, arm and equip as many of such extra-numbers as they judge can be safely spared; and the Officers and Men so armed and equip[p]ed shall march to the Place appointed, and within the Time agreed on by the United States assembled.

To establish the same Weights and Measures throughout the United Colonies.

But the United States assembled shall never impose or levy any Taxes or Duties, except in managing the Post-Office, nor interfere in the internal Police of any Colony, any further than such Police may be affected by the Articles of this Confederation. The United States assembled shall never engage the United Colonies in a War, nor grant Letters of Marque and Reprisal in Time of Peace, nor enter into Treaties or Alliances, nor coin Money nor regulate the Value thereof, nor agree upon nor fix the Sums and Expences necessary for the Defence and Welfare of the United Colonies, or any of them, nor emit Bills, nor borrow Money on the Credit of the United Colonies, nor raise Naval Forces, nor agree upon the Number of Land Forces to be raised, unless the Delegates of nine Colonies freely assent to the same: Nor shall a Question on any other Point, except for adjourning, be determined, unless the Delegates of seven Colonies vote in the affirmative.

No Person shall be capable of being a Delegate for more than three Years in any Term of six Years.

No Person holding any Office under the United States, for which he, or another for his Benefit, receives any Salary, Fees, or Emolument of any Kind, shall be capable of being a Delegate.

The Assembly of the United States to publish the Journal of their Proceedings monthly, except such Parts thereof relating to Treaties, Alliances, or military Operations, as in their Judgment require Secrecy—The Yeas and Nays of the Delegates of each Colony on any Question to be entered on the Journal, where it is desired by any Delegate; and the Delegates of a Colony, or any of them, at his or their Request, to be furnished with a Transcript of the said Journal, except such Parts as are above excepted, to lay before the Legislatures of the several Colonies.

ART. XIX. The Council of State shall consist of one Delegate from each C[o]lony, to be named annually by the Delegates of each Colony, and where they cannot agree, by the United States assembled.

This Council shall have Power to receive and open all Letters directed to the United States, and to return proper Answers; but not to make any Engagements that shall be binding on the United States—To correspond with the Legislature of each Colony, and all Persons acting under the Authority of the United States, or of the said Legislatures—To apply to such Legislatures, or to the Officers in the several Colonies who are entrusted with the executive Powers of Government, for occasional Aid whenever and wherever necessary—To give Counsel to the Commanding Officers, and to direct military Operations by Sea and Land, not changing any Objects or Expeditions determined on by the United States assembled, unless an Alteration of Circumstances which shall come to the Knowledge of the Council after the Recess of the States, shall make such Change absolutely necessary—To attend to the Defence and Preservation of Forts and strong Posts, and to prevent the Enemy from acquiring new Holds—To procure Intelligence of the Condition and Designs of the Enemy—To expedite the Execution of such Measures as may be resolved on by the United States assembled, in Pursuance of the Powers hereby given to them—To draw upon the Treasurers for such Sums as may be appropriated by the United States assembled, and for the Payment of such Contracts as the said Council may make in Pursuance of the Powers hereby given to them—To superintend and controul or suspend all Officers civil and military, acting under the Authority of the United States—In Case of the Death or Removal of any Officer within the Appointment of the United States assembled, to employ a Person to fulfill the Duties of such Office until the Assembly of the States meet—To publish and disperse authentic Accounts of military Operations—To summon an Assembly of the States at an earlier Day than that appointed for their next Meeting, if any great and unexpected Emergency should render it necessary for the Safety or Welfare of the United Colonies or any of them—To prepare Matters for the Consideration of the United States, and to lay before them at their next Meeting all Letters and Advices received by the Council, with a Report of their Proceedings—To appoint a proper Person for their Clerk, who shall take an Oath of Secrecy and Fidelity, before he enters on the Exercise of his Office—Seven Members shall have Power to act—In Case of the Death of any Member, the Council shall immediately apply to his surviving Colleagues to appoint some one of themselves to be a Member thereof till the Meeting of the States, and if only one survives, they shall give him immediate Notice, that he may take his Seat as a Councilor till such Meeting.

ART. XX. Canada acceding to this Confederation, and entirely joining in the measures of the United Colonies, shall be admitted into and entitled to all the Advantages of this Union: But no other Colony shall be admitted into the same, unless such Admission be agreed to by the Delegates of nine Colonies.

These Articles shall be proposed to the Legislatures of all the United Colonies, to be by them considered, and if approved by them, they are advised to authorize their Delegates to ratify the same in the Assembly of the United States, which being done, the Articles of this Confederation shall inviolably be observed by every Colony, and the Union is to be perpetual: Nor shall any Alteration be at any Time hereafter made in these Articles or any of them, unless such Alteration be agreed to in an Assembly of the United States, and be afterwards confirmed by the Legislatures of every Colony.

The Articles of Confederation, 1 March 1781.

Articles of Confederation and perpetual Union between the states of Newhampshire, Massachusetts-bay, Rhodeisland and Providence Plantations, Connecticut, New-York, New-Jersey, Pennsylvania, Delaware, Maryland, Virginia, North-Carolina, South-Carolina and Georgia.

Article I. The Stile of this confederacy shall be "The United State of America."

Article II. Each state retains its sovereignty, freedom, and independence, and every Power, Jurisdiction and right, which is not by this confederation expressly delegated to the United States, in Congress assembled.

Article III. The said states hereby severally enter into a firm league of friendship with each other, for their common defence, the security of their Liberties, and their mutual and general welfare, binding themselves to assist each other, against all force offered to, or attacks made upon them, or any of them, on account of religion, sovereignty, trade, or any other pretence whatsoever.

Article IV. The better to secure and perpetuate mutual friendship and intercourse among the people of the different states in this union, the free inhabitants of each of these states, paupers, vagabonds and fugitives from justice excepted, shall be entitled to all privileges and immunities of free citizens in the several states; and the people of each state shall have free ingress and regress to and from any other state, and shall enjoy therein all the privileges of trade and commerce, subject to the same duties, impositions and restrictions as the inhabitants thereof respectively, provided that such restriction shall not extend so far as to prevent the removal of property imported into any state, to any other state, of which the Owner is an inhabitant; provided also that no imposition, duties or restriction shall be laid by any state, on the property of the united states, or either of them.

If any Person guilty of, or charged with treason, felony, or other high misdemeanor in any state, shall flee from Justice, and be found in any of the united states, he shall, upon demand of the Governor or executive power, of the state from which he fled, be delivered up and removed to the state having jurisdiction of his offence.

Full faith and credit shall be given in each of these states to the records, acts and judicial proceedings of the courts and magistrates of every other state.

Article V. For the more convenient management of the general interests of the united states, delegates shall be annually appointed in such manner as the legislature of each state shall direct, to meet in Congress on the first Monday in November, in every year, with a power reserved to each state, to recal its delegates, or any of them, at anytime within the year, and to send others in their stead, for the remainder of the Year.

No state shall be represented in Congress by less than two, nor by more than seven Members; and no person shall be capable of being a delegate for more than three years in any term of six years; nor shall any person, being a delegate, be capable of holding any office under the united states, for which he, or another for his benefit receives any salary, fees or emolument of any kind.

Each state shall maintain its own delegates in a meeting of the states, and while they act as members of the committee of the states.

In determining questions in the united states in Congress assembled, each state shall have one vote.

Freedom of speech and debate in Congress shall not be impeached or questioned in any Court, or place out of Congress, and the members of congress shall be protected in their persons from arrests and imprisonments, during the time of their going to and from, and attendance on congress, except for treason, felony, or breach of the peace.

Article VI. No state, without the Consent of the united states in congress assembled, shall send any embassy to, or receive any embassy from, or enter into any conference, agreement, alliance or treaty with any King prince or state; nor shall any person holding any office of profit or trust under the united states, or any of them, accept of any present, emolument, office or title of any kind whatever from any king, prince or foreign state; nor shall the united states in congress assembled, or any of them, grant any title of nobility.

No two or more states shall enter into any treaty, confederation or alliance whatever between them, without the consent of the united states in congress assembled, specifying accurately the purposes for which the same is to be entered into, and how long it shall continue.

No state shall lay any imposts or duties, which may interfere with any stipulations in treaties, entered into by the united states in congress assembled, with any king, prince or state, in pursuance of any treaties already proposed by congress, to the courts of France and Spain.

No vessels of war shall be kept up in time of peace by any state, except such number only, as shall be deemed necessary by the united states in congress assembled, for the defence of such state, or its trade; nor shall any body of forces be kept up by any state, in time of peace, except such number only, as in the judgment of the united states, in congress assembled, shall be deemed requisite to garrison the forts necessary for the defence of such state; but every state shall always keep up a well regulated and disciplined militia, sufficiently armed and accoutred, and shall provide and constantly have ready for use, in public stores, a due number of field pieces and tents, and a proper quantity of arms, ammunition and camp equipage.

No state shall engage in any war without the consent of the united states in congress assembled, unless such state be actually invaded by enemies, or shall have received certain advice of a resolution being formed by some nation of Indians to invade such state, and the danger is so imminent as not to admit of a delay till the united states in congress assembled can be consulted: nor shall any state grant commissions to any ships or vessels of war, nor letters of marque or reprisal, except it be after a declaration of war by the united states in congress assembled, and then only against the kingdom or state and the subjects thereof, against which war has been so declared, and under such regulations as shall be established by the united states in congress assembled, unless such state be infested by pirates, in which case vessels of war may be fitted out for that occasion, and kept so long as the danger shall continue, or until the united states in congress assembled, shall determine otherwise.

Article VII. When land-forces are raised by any state for the common defence, all officers of or under the rank of colonel, shall be appointed by the legislature of each state respectively, by whom such forces shall be raised, or in such manner as such state shall direct, and all vacancies shall be filled up by the State which first made the appointment.

Article VIII. All charges of war, and all other expences that shall be incurred for the common defence or general welfare, and allowed by the united states in congress assembled, shall be defrayed out of a common treasury, which shall be supplied by the several states in proportion to the value of all land within each state, granted to or surveyed for any Person, as such land and the buildings and improvements thereon shall be estimated according to such mode as the united states in congress assembled, shall from time to time direct and appoint. The taxes for paying that proportion shall be laid and levied by the authority and direction of the legislatures of the several states within the time agreed upon by the united states in congress assembled.

Article IX. The united states in congress assembled, shall have the sole and exclusive right and power of determining on peace and war, except in the cases mentioned in the sixth article—of sending and receiving ambassadors—entering into treaties and alliances, provided that no treaty of commerce shall be made whereby the legislative power of the respective states shall be restrained from imposing such imposts and duties on foreigners, as their own people are subjected to, or from prohibiting the exportation or importation of any species of goods or commodities whatsoever—of establishing rules for deciding in all cases, what captures on land or water shall be legal, and in what manner prizes taken by land or naval forces in the service of the united states shall be divided or appropriated—of granting letters of marque and reprisal in times of peace—appointing courts for the trial of piracies and felonies committed on the high seas and establishing courts for receiving and determining finally appcals in all cases of captures, provided that no member of congress shall be appointed a judge of any of the said courts.

The united states in congress assembled shall also be the last resort on appeal in all disputes and differences now subsisting or that hereafter may arise between two or more states concerning boundary, jurisdiction or any other cause whatever; which authority shall always be exercised in the manner following. Whenever the legislative or executive authority or lawful agent of any state in controversy with another shall present a petition to congress stating the matter in question and praying for a hearing, notice thereof shall be given by order of congress to the legislative or executive authority of the other state in controversy, and a day assigned for the appearance of the parties by their lawful agents, who shall then be directed to appoint by joint consent, commissioners or judges to constitute a court for hearing and determining the matter in question: but if they cannot agree, congress shall name three persons out of each of the united states, and from the list of such persons each party shall alternately strike out one, the petitioners beginning, until the number shall be reduced to thirteen; and from that number not less than seven, nor more than nine names as congress shall direct, shall in the presence of congress be drawn out by lot, and the persons whose names shall be so drawn or any five of them, shall be commissioners or judges, to hear and finally determine the controversy, so always as a major part of the judges who shall hear the cause shall agree in the determination: and if either party shall neglect to attend at the day appointed, without showing reasons, which congress shall judge sufficient, or being present shall refuse to strike, the congress shall proceed to nominate three persons out of each state, and the secretary of congress shall strike in behalf of such party absent or refusing; and the judgment and sentence of the court to be appointed, in the manner before prescribed, shall be final and conclusive; and if any of the parties shall refuse to submit to the authority of such court, or to appear or defend their claim or cause, the court shall nevertheless proceed to pronounce sentence, or judgment, which shall in like manner be final and decisive, the judgment or sentence and other proceedings being in either case transmitted to congress, and lodged among the acts of congress for the security of the parties concerned: provided that every commissioner, before he sits in judgment, shall take an oath to be administred by one of the judges of the supreme or superior court of the state, where the cause shall be tried, "well and truly to hear and determine the matter in question, according to the best of his judgment, without favour, affection or hope of reward:" provided also, that no state shall be deprived of territory for the benefit of the united states.

All controversies concerning the private right of soil claimed under different grants of two or more states, whose jurisdictions as they may respect such lands, and the states which passed such grants are adjusted, the said grants or either of them being at the same time claimed to have originated antecedent to such settlement of jurisdiction, shall on the petition of either party to the congress of the united states, be finally determined as near as may be in the same manner as is before prescribed for deciding disputes respecting territorial jurisdiction between different states.

The united states in congress assembled shall also have the sole and exclusive right and power of regulating the alloy and value of coin struck by their own authority, or by that of the respective states—fixing the standard of weights and measures throughout the united states—regulating the trade and managing all affairs with the Indians, not members of any of the states, provided that the legislative right of any state within its own limits be not infringed or violated—establishing or regulating post-offices from one state to another, throughout all the united states, and exacting such postage on the papers passing thro' the same as may be requisite to defray the expences of the said office—appointing all officers of the land forces, in the service of the united states, excepting regimental officers—appointing all the officers of the naval forces, and commissioning all officers whatever in the service of the united states—making rules for the government and regulation of the said land and naval forces, and directing their operations.

The united states in congress assembled shall have authority to appoint a committee, to sit in the recess of congress, to be denominated "A Committee of the States," and to consist of one delegate from each state; and to appoint such other committees and civil officers as may be necessary for managing the general affairs of the united states under their direction—to appoint one of their number to preside, provided that no person be allowed to serve in the office of president more than one year in any term of three years; to ascertain the necessary sums of Money to be raised for the service of the united states, and to appropriate and apply the same for defraying the public expences—to borrow money, or emit bills on the credit of the united states, transmitting every half year to the respective states an account of the sums of money so borrowed or emitted,—to build and equip a navy—to agree upon the number of land forces, and to make requisitions from each state for its quota, in proportion to the number of white inhabitants in such state; which requisition shall be binding, and thereupon the legislature of each state shall appoint the regimental officers, raise the men and cloath, arm and equip them in a soldier like manner, at the expence of the united states; and the officers and men so cloathed, armed and equipped shall march to the place appointed, and within the time agreed on by the united states in congress assembled: But if the united states in congress assembled shall, on consideration of circumstances judge proper that any state should not raise men, or should raise a smaller number than its quota, and that any other state should raise a greater number of men than the quota thereof, such extra number shall be raised, officered, cloathed, armed and equipped in the same manner as the quota of such state, unless the legislature of such state shall judge that such extra number cannot be safely spared out of the same, in which case they shall raise officer, cloath, arm and equip as many of such extra number as they judge can be safely spared. And the officers and men so cloathed, armed and equipped, shall march to the place appointed, and within the time agreed on by the united states in congress assembled.

The united states in congress assembled shall never engage in a war, nor grant letters of marque and reprisal in time of peace, nor enter into any treaties or alliances, nor coin money, nor regulate the value thereof, nor ascertain the sums and expences necessary for the defence and welfare of the united states, or any of them, nor emit bills, nor borrow money on the credit of the united states, nor appropriate money, nor agree upon the number of vessels of war, to be built or purchased, or the number of land or sea forces to be raised, nor appoint a commander in chief of the army or navy, unless nine states assent to the same: nor shall a question on any other point, except for adjourning from day to day be determined, unless by the votes of a majority of the united states in congress assembled.

The congress of the united states shall have power to adjourn to any time within the year, and to any place within the united states, so that no period of adjournment be for a longer duration than the space of six Months, and shall publish the Journal of their proceedings monthly, except such parts thereof relating to treaties, alliances or military operations, as in their judgment require secrecy; and the yeas and nays of the delegates of each state on any question shall be entered on the Journal, when it is desired by any delegate; and the delegates of a state, or any of them, as his or their request shall be furnished with a transcript of the said Journal, except such parts as are above excepted, to lay before the legislatures of the several states.

Article X. The committee of the states, or any nine of them, shall be authorized to execute, in the recess of congress, such of the powers of congress as the united states in congress assembled, by the consent of nine states, shall from time to time think expedient to vest them with; provided that no power be delegated to the said committee, for the exercise of which, by the articles of confederation, the voice of nine states in the congress of the united states assembled is requisite.

Article XI. Canada acceding to this confederation, and joining in the measures of the united states, shall be admitted into, and entitled to all the advantages of this union: but no other colony shall be admitted into the same, unless such admission be agreed to by nine states.

Article XII. All bills of credit emitted, monies borrowed and debts contracted by, or under the authority of congress, before the assembling of the united states, in pursuance of the present confederation, shall be deemed and considered as a charge against the united states, for payment and satisfaction whereof the said united states, and the public faith are hereby solemnly pledged.

Article XIII. Every state shall abide by the determinations of the united states in congress assembled, on all questions which by this confederation are submitted to them. And the Articles of this confederation shall be inviolably observed by every state, and the union shall be perpetual; nor shall any alteration at any time hereafter be made in any of them; unless such alteration be agreed to in a congress of the united states, and be afterwards confirmed by the legislatures of every state.

And Whereas it hath pleased the Great Governor of the World to incline the hearts of the legislatures we respectively represent in congress, to approve of, and to authorize us to ratify the said articles of confederation and perpetual union. Know Ye that we the undersigned delegates, by virtue of the power and authority to us given for that purpose, do by these presents, in the name and in behalf of our respective constituents, fully and entirely ratify and confirm each and every of the said articles of confederation and perpetual union, and all and singular the matters and things therein contained: And we do further solemnly plight and engage the faith of our respective constituents, that they shall abide by the determinations of the united states in congress assembled, on all questions, which by the said confederation are submitted to them. And that the articles thereof shall be inviolably observed by the states we respectively represent, and that the union shall be perpetual. In Witness whereof we have hereunto set our hands in Congress. Done at Philadelphia in the state of Pennsylvania the ninth day of July, in the Year of our Lord one Thousand seven Hundred and Seventy-eight, and in the third year of the independence of America.

Washington's Speech to the Officers of the Continental Army, Newburgh, New York, 15 March 1783.

Gentlemen: By an anonymous summons, an attempt has been made to convene you together; how inconsistent with the rules of propriety! how unmilitary! and how subversive of all order and discipline, let the good sense of the Army decide.

In the moment of this Summons, another anonymous production was sent into circulation, addressed more to the feelings and passions, than to the reason and judgment of the Army. The author of the piece, is entitled to much credit for the goodness of his Pen and I could wish he had as much credit for the rectitude of his Heart, for, as Men see thro' different Optics, and are induced by the reflecting faculties of the Mind, to use different means, to attain the same end, the Author of the Address, should have had more charity, than to mark for Suspicion, the Man who should recommend moderation and longer forbearance, or, in other words, who should not think as he thinks, and act as he advises. But he had another plan in view, in which candor and liberality of Sentiment, regard to justice, and love of Country, have no part; and he was right, to insinuate the darkest suspicion, to effect the blackest designs.

That the Address is drawn with great Art, and is designed to answer the most insidious purposes. That it is calculated to impress the Mind, with an idea of premeditated injustice in the Sovereign power of the United States, and rouse all those resentments which must unavoidably flow from such a belief. That the secret mover of this Scheme (whoever he may be) intended to take advantage of the passions, while they were warmed by the recollection of past distresses, without giving time for cool, deliberative thinking, and that composure of Mind which is so necessary to give dignity and stability to measures is rendered too obvious, by the mode of conducting the business, to need other proof than a reference to the proceeding.

Thus much, Gentlemen, I have thought it incumbent on me to observe to you, to shew upon what principles I opposed the irregular and hasty meeting which was proposed to have been held on Tuesday last: and not because I wanted a disposition to give you every oppertunity consistent with your own honor, and the dignity of the Army, to make known your grievances. If my conduct heretofore, has not evinced to you, that I have been a faithful friend to the Army, my declaration of it at this time wd. be equally unavailing and improper. But as I was among the first who embarked in the cause of our common Country. As I have never left your side one moment, but when called from you on public duty. As I have been the constant companion and witness of your Distresses, and not among the last to feel, and acknowledge your Merits. As I have ever considered my own Military reputation as inseperably connected with that of the Army. As my Heart has ever expanded with joy, when I have heard its praises, and my indignation has arisen, when the mouth of detraction has been opened against it, it can *scarcely be supposed,* at this late stage of the War, that I am indifferent to its interests. But, how are they to be promoted? The way is plain, says the anonymous Addresser. If War continues, remove into the unsettled Country; there establish yourselves, and leave an ungrateful Country to defend itself. But who are they to defend? Our Wives, our Children, our Farms, and other property which we leave behind us. or, in this state of hostile seperation, are we to take the two first (the latter cannot be removed), to perish in a Wilderness, with hunger, cold and nakedness? If Peace takes place, never sheath your Swords Says he untill you have obtained full and ample justice; this dreadful alternative, of either deserting our Country in the extremest hour of her distress, or turning our Arms against it, (which is the apparent object, unless Congress can be compelled into instant compliance) has something so shocking in it, that humanity revolts at the idea. My God! what can this writer have in view, by recommending such measures? Can he be a friend to the Army? Can he be a friend to this Country? Rather, is he not an insidious Foe? Some Emissary, perhaps, from New York, plotting the ruin of both, by sowing the seeds of discord and seperation between the Civil and Military powers of the Continent? And what a Compliment does he pay to our Understandings, when he recommends measures in either alternative, impracticable in their Nature?

But here, Gentlemen, I will drop the curtain, because it wd. be as imprudent in me to assign my reasons for this opinion, as it would be insulting to your conception, to suppose you stood in need of them. A moment's reflection will convince every dispassionate Mind of the physical impossibility of carrying either proposal into execution.

There might, Gentlemen, be an impropriety in my taking notice, in this Address to you, of an anonymous production, but the manner in which that performance has been introduced to the Army, the effect it was intended to have, together with some other circumstances, will amply justify my observations on the tendency of that Writing. With respect to the advice given by the Author, to suspect the Man, who shall recommend moderate measures and longer forbearance, I spurn it, as every Man, who regards that liberty, and reveres that justice for which we contend, undoubtedly must; for if Men are to be precluded from offering their Sentiments on a matter, which may involve the most serious and alarming consequences, that can invite the consideration of Mankind, reason is of no use to us; the freedom of Speech may be taken away, and, dumb and silent we may be led, like sheep, to the Slaughter.

I cannot, in justice to my own belief, and what I have great reason to conceive is the intention of Congress, conclude this Address, without giving it as my decided opinion, that that Honble Body, entertain exalted sentiments of the Services of the Army; and, from a full conviction of its merits and sufferings, will do it compleat justice. That their endeavors, to discover and establish funds for this purpose, have been unwearied, and will not cease, till they have succeeded, I have not a doubt. But, like all other large Bodies, where there is a variety of different Interests to reconcile, their deliberations are slow. Why then should we distrust them? and, in consequence of that distrust, adopt measures, which may cast a shade over that glory which, has been so justly acquired; and tarnish the reputation of an Army which is celebrated thro' all Europe, for its fortitude and Patriotism? and for what is this done? to bring the object we seek nearer? No! most certainly, in my opinion, it will cast it at a greater distance.

For myself (and I take no merit in giving the assurance, being induced to it from principles of gratitude, veracity and justice), a grateful sence of the confidence you have ever placed in me, a recollection of the chearful assistance, and prompt obedience I have experienced from you, under every vicissitude of Fortune, and the sincere affection I feel for an Army, I have so long had the honor to Command, will oblige me to declare, in this public and solemn manner, that, in the attainment of compleat justice for all your toils and dangers, and in the gratification of every wish, so far as may be done consistently with the great duty I owe my Country, and those powers we are bound to respect, you may freely command my Services to the utmost of my abilities.

While I give you these assurances, and pledge myself in the most unequivocal manner, to exert whatever ability I am possessed of, in your favor, let me entreat you, Gentlemen, on your part, not to take any measures, which, viewed in the calm light of reason, will lessen the dignity, and sully the glory you have hitherto maintained; let me request you to rely on the plighted faith of your Country, and place a full confidence in the purity of the intentions of Congress; that, previous to your dissolution as an Army they will cause all your Accts. to be fairly liquidated, as directed in their resolutions, which were published to you two days ago, and that they will adopt the most effectual measures in their power, to render ample justice to you, for your faithful and meritorious Services. And let me conjure you, in the name of our common Country, as you value your own sacred honor, as you respect the rights of humanity, and as you regard the Military and National character of America, to express your utmost horror and detestation of the Man who wishes, under any specious pretences, to overturn the liberties of our Country, and who wickedly attempts to open the flood Gates of Civil discord, and deluge our rising Empire in Blood. By thus determining, and thus acting, you will pursue the plain and direct road to the attainment of your wishes. You will defeat the insidious designs of our Enemies, who are compelled to resort from open force to secret Artifice. You will give one more distinguished proof of unexampled patriotism and patient virtue, rising superior to the pressure of the most complicated sufferings; And you will, by the dignity of your Conduct, afford occasion for Posterity to say, when speaking of the glorious example you have exhibited to Mankind, "had this day been wanting, the World had never seen the last stage of perfection to which human nature is capable of attaining."

Washington's Farewell Orders to the Armies of the United States, 2 November 1783.

Rock Hill, near Princeton.

The United States in Congress assembled after giving the most honorable testimony to the merits of the foederal Armies, and presenting them with the thanks of their Country for their long, eminent, and faithful services, having thought proper by their proclamation bearing date the 18th. day of October last. to discharge such part of the Troops as were engaged for the war, and to permit the Officers on furlough to retire from service from and after to-morrow; which proclamation having been communicated in the publick papers for the information and government of all concerned; it only remains for the Comdr in Chief to address himself once more, and that for the last time, to the Armies of the U States (however widely dispersed the individuals who compose them may be) and to bid them an affectionate, a long farewell.

But before the Comdr in Chief takes his final leave of those he holds most dear, he wishes to indulge himself a few moments in calling to mind a slight review of the past. He will then take the liberty of exploring, with his military friends, their future prospects, of advising the general line of conduct, which in his opinion, ought to be pursued, and he will conclude the Address by expressing the obligations he feels himself under for the spirited and able assistance he has experienced from them in the performance of an arduous Office.

A contemplation of the compleat attainment (at a period earlier than could have been expected) of the object for which we contended against so formidable a power cannot but inspire us with astonishment and gratitude. The disadvantageous circumstances on our part, under which the war was undertaken, can never be forgotten. The singular interpositions of Providence in our feeble condition were such, as could scarcely escape the attention of the most unobserving; while the unparalleled perseverence of the Armies of the U States, through almost every possible suffering and discouragement for the space of eight long years, was little short of a standing miracle.

It is not the meaning nor within the compass of this address to detail the hardships peculiarly incident to our service, or to describe the distresses, which in several instances have resulted from the extremes of hunger and nakedness, combined with the rigours of an inclement season; nor is it necessary to dwell on the dark side of our past affairs. Every American Officer and Soldier must now console himself for any unpleasant circumstances which may have occurred by a recollection of the uncommon scenes in which he has been called to Act no inglorious part, and the astonishing events of which he has been a witneses, events which have seldom if ever before taken place on the stage of human action, nor can they probably ever happen again. For who has before seen a disciplined Army form'd at once from such raw materials? Who, that was not a witness, could imagine that the most violent local prejudices would cease so soon, and that Men who came from the different parts of the Continent, strongly disposed, by the habits of education, to despise and quarrel with each other, would instantly become but one patriotic band of Brothers, or who, that was not on the spot, can trace the steps by which such a wonderful revolution has been effected, and such a glorious period put to all our warlike toils?

It is universally acknowledged, that the enlarged prospects of happiness, opened by the confirmation of our independance and sovereignty, almost exceeds the power of description. And shall not the brave men, who have contributed so essentially to these inestimable acquisitions, retiring victorious from the field of War to the field of agriculture, participate in all the blessings which have been obtained; in such a republic, who will exclude them from the rights of Citizens and the fruits of their labour. In such a Country, so happily circumstanced, the pursuits of Commerce and the cultivation of the soil will unfold to industry the certain road to competence. To those hardy Soldiers, who are actuated by the spirit of adventure the Fisheries will afford ample and profitable employment, and the extensive and fertile regions of the West will yield a most happy asylum to those, who, fond of domestic enjoyments are seeking for personal independence. Nor is it possible to conceive, that any one of the U States will prefer a national bankruptcy and a dissolution of the union, to a compliance with the requisitions of Congress and the payment of its just debts; so that the Officers and Soldiers may expect considerable assistance in recommencing their civil occupations from the sums due to them from the public, which must and will most inevitably be paid.

In order to effect this desirable purpose and to remove the prejudices which may have taken possession of the minds of any of the good people of the States, it is earnestly recommended to all the Troops that with strong attachments to the Union, they should carry with them into civil society the most conciliating dispositions; and that they should prove themselves not less virtuous and useful as Citizens, than they have been persevering and victorious as Soldiers. What tho, there should be some envious individuals who are unwilling to pay the debt the public has contracted, or to yield the tribute due to merit; yet, let such unworthy treatment produce no invective or any instance of intemperate conduct; let it be remembered that the unbiassed voice of the few Citizens of the United States has promised the just reward, and given the merited applause; let it be known and remembered, that the reputation of the foederal Armies is established beyond the reach of malevolence; and let a conscientiousness of their achievements and fame still unite the men, who composed them to honourable actions; under the persuasion that the private virtues of oeconomy, prudence, and industry, will not be less amiable in civil life, than the more splendid qualities of valour, perseverance, and enterprise were in the Field. Every one may rest assured that much, very much of the future happiness of the Officers and Men will depend upon the wise and manly conduct which shall be adopted by them when they are mingled with the great body of the community. And, altho the General has so frequently given it as his opinion, in the most public and explicit manner, that, unless the principles of the federal government were properly supported and the powers of the union increased, the honour, dignity, and justice of the nation would be lost forever. Yet he cannot help repeating, on this occasion, so interesting a sentiment, and leaving it as his last injunction to every Officer and every Soldier, who may view the subject in the same serious point of light, to add his best endeavours to those of his worthy fellow Citizens towards effecting these great and valuable purposes on which our very existence as a nation so materially depends.

The Commander in chief conceives little is now wanting to enable the Soldiers to change the military character into that of the Citizen, but that steady and decent tenor of behaviour which has generally distinguished, not only the Army under his immediate command, but the different detachments and seperate Armies through the course of the war. From their good sense and prudence he anticipates the happiest consequences; and while he congratulates them on the glorious occasion, which renders their services in the field no longer necessary, he wishes to express the strong obligations he feels himself under for the assistance he has received from every Class, and in every instance. He presents his thanks in the most serious and affectionate manner to the General Officers, as well for their counsel on many interesting occasions, as for their Order in promoting the success of the plans he had adopted. To the Commandants of Regiments and Corps, and to the other Officers for their great zeal and attention, in carrying his orders promptly into execution. To the Staff, for their alacrity and exactness in performing the Duties of their several Departments. And to the Non Commissioned Officers and private Soldiers, for their extraordinary patience in suffering, as well as their invincible fortitude in Action. To the various branches of the Army the General takes this last and solemn opportunity of professing his inviolable attachment and friendship. He wishes more than bare professions were in his power, that he were really able to be useful to them all in future life. He flatters himself however, they will do him the justice to believe, that whatever could with propriety be attempted by him has been done, and being now to conclude these his last public Orders, to take his ultimate leave in a short time of the military character, and to bid a final adieu to the Armies he has so long had the honor to Command, he can only again offer in their behalf his recommendations to their grateful country, and his prayers to the God of Armies. May ample justice be done them here, and may the choicest of heaven's favours, both here and hereafter, attend those who, under the devine auspices, have secured innumerable blessings for others; with these wishes, and this benediction, the Commander in Chief is about to retire from Service. The Curtain of seperation will soon be drawn, and the military scene to him will be closed for ever.

Washington's Address to the Continental Congress Resigning His Commission as Commander in Chief of the Continental Army, 23 December 1783.

Mr. President: The great events on which my resignation depended having at length taken place; I have now the honor of offering my sincere Congratulations to Congress and of presenting myself before them to surrender into their hands the trust committed to me, and to claim the indulgence of retiring from the Service of my Country.

Happy in the confirmation of our Independence and Sovereignty, and pleased with the oppertunity afforded the United States of becoming a respectable Nation, I resign with satisfaction the Appointment I accepted with diffidence. A diffidence in my abilities to accomplish so arduous a task, which however was superseded by a confidence in the rectitude of our Cause, the support of the Supreme Power of the Union, and the patronage of Heaven.

The Successful termination of the War has verified the most sanguine expectations, and my gratitude for the interposition of Providence, and the assistance I have received from my Countrymen, encreases with every review of the momentous Contest.

While I repeat my obligations to the Army in general, I should do injustice to my own feelings not to acknowledge in this place the peculiar Services and distinguished merits of the Gentlemen who have been attached to my person during the War. It was impossible the choice of confidential Officers to compose my family should have been more fortunate. Permit me Sir, to recommend in particular those, who have continued in Service to the present moment, as worthy of the favorable notice and patronage of Congress.

I consider it an indispensable duty to close this last solemn act of my Official life, by commending the Interests of our dearest Country to the protection of Almighty God, and those who have the superintendence of them, to his holy keeping.

Having now finished the work assigned me, I retire from the great theatre of Action; and bidding an Affectionate farewell to this August body under whose orders I have so long acted, I here offer my Commission, and take my leave of all the employments of public life.

Resolution of the Continental Congress Disbanding the Continental Army, 2 June 1784.

So it was *Resolved*, That the commanding officer be, and he is hereby directed to discharge the troops now in the service of the United States, except 25 privates, to guard the stores at Fort Pitt, and 55 to guard the stores at West Point and other magazines, with a proportionate number of officers; no officer to remain in service above the rank of a captain, and those privates to be retained who were inlisted on the best terms: Provided Congress, before its recess, shall not take other measures respecting the disposition of those troops. That the arrearages of their pay and rations after the 3d of November last, be settled in the same manner as the accounts of the troops lately discharged; and that the Superintendant of Finance take order for furnishing them two months pay.

The Peace Establishment

George Washington, Sentiments on a Peace Establishment, 2 May 1783.

A Peace Establishment for the United States of America may in my opinion be classed under four different heads Vizt:

First. A regular and standing force, for Garrisoning West Point and such other Posts upon our Northern, Western, and Southern Frontiers, as shall be deemed necessary to awe the Indians, protect our Trade, prevent the encroachment of our Neighbours of Canada and the Florida's, and guard us at least from surprizes; Also for security of our Magazines.

Secondly. A well organized Militia; upon a Plan that will pervade all the States, and introduce similarity in their Establishment Manoeuvres, Exercise and Arms.

Thirdly. Establishing Arsenals of all kinds of Military Stores.

Fourthly. Accademies, one or more for the Instruction of the Art Military; particularly those Branches of it which respect Engineering and Artillery, which are highly essential, and the knowledge of which, is most difficult to obtain. Also Manufactories of some kinds of Military Stores.

Upon each of these, and in the order in which they stand, I shall give my sentiments as concisely as I can, and with that freedom which the Committee have authorized.

Altho' a *large* standing Army in time of Peace hath ever been considered dangerous to the liberties of a Country, yet a few Troops, under certain circumstances, are not only safe, but indispensably necessary. Fortunately for us our relative situation requires but few. The same circumstances which so effectually retarded, and in the end conspired to defeat the attempts of Britain to subdue us, will now powerfully tend to render us secure. Our *distance* from the European States in a great degree frees us of apprehension, from their numerous regular forces and the Insults and dangers which are to be dreaded from their Ambition.

But, if our danger from those powers was more imminent, yet we are too poor to maintain a standing Army adequate to our defence, and was our Country more populous and rich, still it could not be done without great oppression of the people. Besides, as soon as we are able to raise funds more than adequate to the discharge of the Debts incurred by the Revolution, it may become a Question worthy of consideration, whether the surplus should not be applied in preparations for building and equipping a Navy, without which, in case of War we could neither protect our Commerce, nor yield that Assistance to each other, which, on such an extent of Sea-Coast, our mutual Safety would require.

Fortifications on the Sea Board may be considered in two points of view, first as part of the general defence, and next, as securities to Dock Yards, and Arsenals for Ship Building, neither of which shall I take into this plan; because the first would be difficult, if not, under our circumstances, impracticable; at any rate amazingly expensive. The other, because it is a matter out of my line, and to which I am by no means competent, as it requires a consideration of many circumstances, to which I have never paid attention.

The Troops requisite for the Post of West Point, for the Magazines, and for our Northern, Western and Southern Frontiers, ought, in my opinion, to amount to 2631 Officers of all denominations included; besides the Corps of Invalids. If this number should be thought large, I would only observe; that the British Force in Canada is now powerful, and, by report, will be increased; that the frontier is very extensive; that the Tribes of Indians within our Territory are numerous, soured and jealous; that Communications must be established with the exterior Posts; And, that it may be policy and oeconomy, to appear respectable in the Eyes of the Indians, at the Commencement of our National Intercourse and Traffic with them. In a word, that it is better to reduce our force hereafter, by degrees, than to have it to increase after some unfortunate disasters may have happened to the Garrisons; discouraging to us, and an inducement to the Enemy to attempt a repetition of them.

Besides these Considerations, we are not to forget, that altho' by the Treaty, half the Waters, and the free Navigation of the Lakes appertain to us, yet, in Case of a rupture with Great Britain we should in all probability, find little benefits from the Communications with our upper Posts, by the Lakes Erie and Ontario; as it is to be presumed, that the Naval superiority which they now have on those Waters, will be maintained. It follows as a Consequence then, that we should open new or improve the present half explored Communications with Detroit and other Posts on the Lakes, by the Waters of the Susquehannah Potowmack or James River, to the Ohio, from whence, with short Portages several Communications by Water may be opened with Lake Erie. To do which, posts should be established at the most convenient places on the Ohio. This would open several doors for the supply of the Garrisons on the Lakes; and is absolutely necessary for such others as may be tho't advisable to establish upon the Mississippi. The Ohio affording the easiest, as well as the safest Route to the Illinois settlements, and the whole Country below on the Mississippi, quite to our Southern boundary.

To protect the Peltry and Fur Trade, to keep a watch upon our Neighbours, and to prevent their encroaching upon our Territory undiscovered, are all the purposes that can be answered by an extension of our Posts, at this time, beyond Detroit, to the Northward or Westward: but, a strong Post on the Scioto, at the carrying place between it and the River Sandusky, which empties into Lake Erie, mentioned in Hutchins's Description of that Country Page 24, and more plainly pointed out by Evans's Map, is indispensably necessary for the security of the present Settlers, and such as probably, will *immediately* settle within those Limits. And by giving security to the Country and covering its Inhabitants, will enable them to furnish supplies to the Garrisons Westward and Northward of these settlements, upon moderate and easy Terms.

The 2,631 Men beforementioned, I would have considered to all Intents and purposes as Continental Troops; looking up to Congress for their Orders, their pay, and supplies of every kind.

Not having that *particular* knowledge of the situation of the Southern and Western Boundaries of the Carolinas and Georgia, which is necessary to decide on the Posts to be established in that District, the allotment of only one Regiment thereto, may be judged inadequate; should that be the case, a greater force may be established and a sufficient allowance made them.

The above establishment differs from our present one, in the following instances Vizt: The exclusion of the light Company and reducing a sergeant and 18 Privates from each of the Poattalion Companies, and giving a Chaplain to each Regiment instead of a Brigade. If it should be asked why the Reduction of Non Commisd. Officers and Privates is made, while the Commissioned Officers remain the same? It may be answered, that the number of Men which compose the Infantry, will be sufficient for my Calculation, and that the situation of our Frontiers renders it convenient to divide them into so many Corps as have been mentioned, for the ease and propriety of Command. I may also say, that in my Opinion, the number of our Commissioned Officers, has always been disproportionate to the Men. And that in the detached State in which these Regiments must be employed, they cannot consistently with the good of Service be reduced.

It may also be observed, that in case of War and a necessity of assembling their Regiments in the Field, nothing more will be necessary, than to recruit 18 Men to each Compy. and give the Regiment its flank Company. Or if we should have occasion to add strength to the Garrisons, or increase the number of our Posts, we may augment 900 Men including Serjeants, without requiring more than the Officers of 4 Companies, or exceeding our present Establishment. In short, it will give us a Number of Officers well skilled in the Theory and Art of War, who will be ready on any occasion, to mix and diffuse their knowledge of Discipline to other Corps, without that lapse of Time, which, without such Provision, would be necessary to bring intire new Corps acquainted with the principles of it.

Besides the 4 Regiments of Infantry, one of Artillery will be indispensably necessary. The Invalid Corps should also be retained. Motives of humanity, Policy and justice will all combine to prevent their being disbanded. The numbers of the last will, from the nature of their composition, be fluctuating and uncertain. . . .

To this Regiment of Artillery should be annexed 50 or 60 Artificers, of the various kinds which will be necessary, who may be distributed in equal numbers into the different Companies and being part of the Regiment, will be under the direction and Command of the Commanding Officer, to be disposed into different services as Circumstances shall require. By thus blending Artificers with Artillery, the expence of Additional Officers will be saved; and they will Answer all the purposes which are to be expected from them, as well as if formed into a distinct Corps.

The Regiment of Artillery, with the Artificers, will furnish all the Posts in which Artillery is placed, in proportionate numbers to the Strength and importance of them. The residue, with the Corps of Invalids, will furnish Guards for the Magazines, and Garrison West Point. The importance of this last mentioned Post, is so great, as justly to have been considered, the key of America; It has been so pre-eminently advantageous to the defence of the United States, and is still so necessary in that view, as well as for the preservation of the Union, that the loss of it might be productive of the most ruinous Consequences. A Naval superiority at Sea and on Lake Champlain, connected by a Chain of Posts on the Hudson River, would effect an entire separation of the States on each side, and render it difficult, if not impracticable for them to co-operate.

Altho' the total of the Troops herein enumerated does not amount to a large number, yet when we consider their detached situation, and the extent of Country they are spread over: the variety of objects that are to be attended to, and the close inspection that will be necessary to prevent abuses or to correct them before they become habitual; not less than two General Officers in my opinion will be competent to the Duties to be required of them. They will take their Instructions from the Secretary at War, or Person acting at the Head of the Military Department, who will also assign them their respective and distinct Districts. Each should twice a Year visit the Posts of his particular District, and notice the Condition they are in, Inspect the Troops, their discipline and Police, Examine into their Wants, and see that strict justice is rendered them and to the Public, they should also direct the Colonels, at what intermediate Times they shall perform the like duties at the Posts occupied by the Detachments of their respective Regiments. The visiting General ought frequently, if not always, to be accompanied by a Skillful Engineer, who should point out such alterations and improvements as he may think necessary from time to time, for the defence of any of the Posts; which, if approved by the General, should be ordered to be carried into execution.

Each Colonel should be responsible for the Administration of his Regiment; and when present, being Commanding Officer of any Post, which is occupied by a Detachment from his Regt., he may give such directions as he may think proper, not inconsistent with the Orders of his Superior Officer, under whose general superintendence the Troops are. He will carefully exact Monthly Returns from all detachments of his Regiment; and be prepared to make a faithful report of all occurrences, when called upon by the General Officer in whose Department he may be placed and whose instructions he is at all times to receive and obey. These Returns and Reports, drawn into a General one, are to be transmitted to the Secretary at War, by the visiting General, with the detail of his own proceedings, remarks and Orders.

The three Years Men now in service will furnish the proposed Establishment, and from these, it is presumed, the Corps must in the first Instance be composed. But as the pay of an American Soldier is much greater than any other we are acquainted with; and as there can be little doubt of our being able to obtain them in time of Peace, upon as good Terms as other Nations, I would suggest the propriety of inlisting those who may come after the present three years Men, upon Terms of similarity with those of the British, or any other the most liberal Nations.

When the Soldiers for the War have frolicked a while among their friends, and find they must have recourse to hard labour for a livelyhood, I am persuaded numbers of them will reinlist upon almost any Terms. Whatever may be adopted with respect to Pay, Clothing and Emoluments, they should be clearly and unequivocally expressed and promulgated, that there may be no deception or mistake. Discontent, Desertion and frequently Mutiny, are the natural consequences of these; and it is not more difficult to know how to punish, than to prevent these inconveniencies, when it is known, that there has been delusion on the part of the Recruiting Officer, or a breach of Compact on the part of the public. The pay of the Battalion Officer's is full low, but those of the Chaplain, Surgeon and Mate are too high; and a proper difference should be made between the Non-Commissioned Officers (serjeants particularly) and Privates, to give them that pride and consequence which is necessary to Command.

At, or before the Time of discharging the Soldiers for the War, the Officers of the Army may signify their wishes either to retire, upon the Half pay, or to continue in the service; from among those who make the latter choice, the number wanted for a Peace Establishment may be selected; and it were to be wished, that they might be so blended together from the Several Lines, as to remove, as much as possible, all Ideas of State distinctions.

No Forage should be allowed in time of Peace to Troops in Garrison, nor in any circumstances, but when actually on a March.

Soldiers should not be inlisted for *less* than three Years, to commence from the date of their attestations; and the more difference there is in the commencement of their terms of Service, the better; this Circumstance will be the means of avoiding the danger and inconvenience of entrusting any important Posts to raw Recruits unacquainted with service.

Rum should compose no part of a Soldier's Ration; but Vinegar in large quantities should be issued. Flour or Bread, and a stipulated quantity of the different kinds of fresh or Salted Meat, with Salt, when the former is Issued, is all that should be contracted for.

Vegetables they can, and ought to be compelled to raise. If spruce, or any other kind of small Beer, could be provided, it ought to be given gratis, but not made part of the Compact with them. It might be provided also, that they should receive one or two days fish in a Week, when to be had; this would be a saving to the public, (the Lakes and most of the Waters of the Ohio and Mississippi abounding with Fish) and would be no disservice to the Soldier.

A proper recruiting fund should be established; from which the Regiment may always be kept complete.

The Garrisons should be changed as often as it can be done with convenience; long continuance in the same place is injurious. Acquaintances are made, Connections formed, and habits acquired, which often prove very detrimental to the service. By this means, public duty is made to yield to interested pursuits, and real abuses are the Result. To avoid these Evils, I would propose, that there should be a change made in every Regiment once a Year, and one Regiment with another every two Years.

An Ordinance for the service of Troops in Garrison, should be annexed to our present Regulations for the order and discipline of the Army. The latter should be revised, corrected and enlarged so as to form a Basis of Discipline under all circumstances for Continental Troops, and, as far as they will apply, to the Militia also: that one uniform system may pervade all the States.

As a peace establishment may be considered as a change in, if not the Commencement of our Military system it will be the proper time, to introduce new and beneficial regulations, and to expunge all customs, which from experience have been found unproductive of general good. Among the latter I would ask, if promotion by Seniority is not one? That it is a good general rule admits of no doubt, but that it should be an invariable one, is in my opinion wrong. It cools, if it does not destroy, the incentives to Military Pride and Heroic Actions. On the one hand, the sluggard, who keeps within the verge of his duty, has nothing to fear. On the other hand, the enterprising Spirit has nothing to expect. Whereas, if promotion was the *sure* reward of Merit, *all* would contend for Rank and the service would be benefited by their Struggles for Promotion. In establishing a mode by which this is to be done, and from which nothing is to be expected, or apprehended, either from favour or prejudice, lies the difficulty. Perhaps, reserving to Congress the right inherent in Sovereignties, of making all Promotions. A Board of superior Officers, appointed to receive and examine the claims to promotions out of common course, of any Officer, whether founded on particular merit, or extra service, and to report their opinion thereon to Congress; might prove a likely means of doing justice. It would certainly give a Spur to Emulation, without endangering the rights, or just pretentions of the Officers.

Before I close my observations under this head, of a regular force, and the Establishment of Posts, it is necessary for me to observe, that, in fixing a Post at the North End of Lake Champlain I had three things in view. The Absolute Command of the entrance into the Lake from Canada. A cover to the Settlements on the New Hampshire Grants and the prevention of any illicit intercourse thro' that Channel. But, if it is known, or should be found, that the 45th Degree crosses the Lake South of any spot which will command the entrance into it, the primary object fails; And it then becomes a question of whether any place beyond Ticonderoga or Crown Point is eligible.

Altho' it may be somewhat foreign to, and yet not altogether unconnected with the present subject, I must beg leave, from the importance of the object, as it appears to my mind, and for the advantages which I think would result from it to the United States, to hint, the propriety of Congress taking some early steps, by a liberal treatment, to gain the affections of the French settlements of Detroit, those of the Illinois and other back Countries. Such a measure would not only hold out great encouragement to the Inhabitants already on those lands, who will doubtless make very useful and valuable subjects of the United States; but would probably make deep and conciliatory impressions on their friends in the British settlements, and prove a means of drawing thither great numbers of Canadian Emigrants, who, under proper Regulations and establishments of Civil Government, would make a hardy and industruous race of Settlers on that Frontier; and who, by forming a barrier against the Indians, would give great security to the Infant settlement, which, soon after the close of the War, will probably be forming in the back Country.

I come next in the order I have prescribed myself, to treat of the Arrangements necessary for placing the Militia of the Continent on a respectable footing for the defence of the Empire and in speaking of this great Bulwark of our Liberties and independence, I shall claim the indulgence of suggesting whatever general observations may occur from experience and reflection with the greater freedom, from a conviction of the importance of the subject; being persuaded, that the immediate safety and future tranquility of this extensive Continent depend in a great measure upon the peace Establishment now in contemplation; and being convinced at the same time, that the only probable means of preventing insult or hostility for any length of time and from being exempted from the consequent calamities of War, is to put the National Militia in such a condition as that they may appear truly respectable in the Eyes of our Friends and formidable to those who would otherwise become our enemies.

Were it not totally unnecessary and superfluous to adduce arguments to prove what is conceded on all hands the Policy and expediency of resting the protection of the Country on a respectable and well established Militia, we might not only shew the propriety of the measure from our peculiar local situation, but we might have recourse to the Histories of Greece and Rome in their most virtuous and Patriotic ages to demonstrate the Utility of such Establishments. Then passing by the Mercinary Armies, which have at one time or another subverted the liberties of allmost all the Countries they have been raised to defend, we might see, with admiration, the Freedom and Independence of Switzerland supported for Centuries, in the midst of powerful and jealous neighbours, by means of a hardy and well organized Militia. We might also derive useful lessons of a similar kind from other Nations of Europe, but I believe it will be found, the *People of this Continent* are too well acquainted with the Merits of the subject to require information or example. I shall therefore proceed to point out some general outlines of their duty, and conclude this head with a few particular observations on the regulations which I conceive ought to be immediately adopted by the States at the instance and recommendation of Congress.

It may be laid down as a primary position, and the basis of our system, that every Citizen who enjoys the protection of a free Government, owes not only a proportion of his property, but even of his personal services to the defence of it, and consequently that the Citizens of America (with a few legal and official exceptions) from 18 to 50 Years of Age should be borne on the Militia Rolls, provided with uniform Arms, and so far accustomed to the use of them, that the Total strength of the Country might be called forth at a Short Notice on any very interesting Emergency, for these purposes they ought to be duly organized into Commands of the same formation; (it is not of *very* great importance, whether the Regiments are large or small, provided a sameness prevails in the strength and composition of them and I do not know that a better establishment, than that under which the Continental Troops now are, can be adopted. They ought to be regularly Mustered and trained, and to have their Arms and Accoutrements inspected at certain appointed times, not less than once or twice in the course of every [year] but as it is obvious, amongst such a Multitude of People (who may indeed be useful for temporary service) there must be a great number, who from domestic Circumstances, bodily defects, natural awkwardness or disinclination, can never acquire the habits of Soldiers; but on the contrary will injure the appearance of any body of Troops to which they are attached, and as there are a sufficient proportion of able bodied young Men, between the Age of 18 and 25, who, from a natural fondness for Military parade (which passion is almost ever prevalent at that period of life) might easily be enlisted or drafted to form a Corps in every State, capable of resisting any sudden impression which might be attempted by a foreign Enemy, while the remainder of the National forces would have time to Assemble and make preparations for the Field. I would wish therefore, that the former, being considered as a *denier resort,* reserved for some great occasion, a judicious system might be adopted for forming and placing the latter on the best possible Establishment. And that while the Men of this description shall be viewed as the Van and flower of the American Forces, ever ready for Action and zealous to be employed whenever it may become necessary in the service of their Country; they should meet with such exemptions, privileges or distinctions, as might tend to keep alive a true Military pride, a nice sense of honour, and a patriotic regard for the public. Such sentiments, indeed, ought to be instilled into our Youth, with their earliest years, to be cherished and inculcated as frequently and forcibly as possible.

It is not for me to decide positively, whether it will be ultimately most interesting to the happiness and safety of the United States, to form this Class of Soldiers into a kind of Continental Militia, selecting every 10th 15th or 20th. Man from the Rolls of each State for the purpose; Organizing, Officering and Commissioning those Corps upon the same principle as is now practiced in the Continental Army. Whether it will be best to comprehend in this body, all the Men fit for service between some given Age and no others, for example between 18 and 25 or some similar description, or whether it will be preferable in every Regiment of the proposed Establishment to have one additional Company inlisted or drafted from the best Men for 3, 5, or 7 years and distinguished by the name of the additional or light Infantry Company, always to be kept complete. These Companies might then be drawn together occasionally and formed into particular Battalions or Regiments under Field Officers appointed for that Service. One or other of these plans I think will be found indispensably necessary, if we are in earnest to have an efficient force ready for Action at a moments Warning. And I cannot conceal my private sentiment, that the formation of additional, or light Companies will be most consistent with the genius of our Countrymen and perhaps in their opinion most consonant to the spirit of our Constitution.

I shall not contend for names or forms, it will be altogether essential, and it will be sufficient that perfect Uniformity should be established throughout the Continent, and pervade, as far as possible, every Corps, whether of standing Troops or Militia, and of whatever denomination they may be. To avoid the confusion of a contrary practice, and to produce the happy consequences which will attend a uniform system of Service, in case Troops from the different parts of the Continent shall ever be brought to Act together again, I would beg leave to propose, that Congress should employ some able hand, to digest a Code of Military Rules and regulations, calculated immediately for the Militia and other Troops of the United States; And as it should seem the present system, by being a little simplified, altered, and improved, might be very well adopted to the purpose; I would take the liberty of recommending, that measures should be immediately taken for the accomplishment of this interesting business, and that an Inspector General should be appointed to superintend the execution of the proposed regulations in the several States.

Congress having fixed upon a proper plan to be established, having caused the Regulations to be compiled, having approved, Printed and distributed them to every General Field Officer, Captain and Adjutant of Militia, will doubtless have taken care, that whenever the system shall be adopted by the States the encouragement on the one hand, and the fines and penalties on the other will occasion an universal and punctual compliance therewith.

Before I close my remarks on the establishment of our National Militia, which is to be the future guardian of those rights and that Independence, which have been maintain'd so gloriously, by the fortitude and perseverance of our Countrymen, I shall descend a little more minutely to the interior arrangements, and sum up what I have to say on this head with the following Positions.

1st. That it appears to me extremely necessary there should be an Adjutant General appointed in each State, with such Assistants as may be necessary for communicating the Orders of the Commander in Chief of the State, making the details, collecting the Returns and performing every other duty incident to that Office. A duplicate of the Annual Returns should always be lodged in the War Office by the 25th of Decr. in every year, for the information of Congress; with any other reports that may be judged expedient. The Adjutant Generals and Assistants to be considered as the deputies of the Inspector General, and to assist him in carrying the system of Discipline into effect.

2d. That every Militia Officer should make himself acquainted with the plan of Discipline, within a limited time, or forfeit his Commission, for it is in vain to expect the improvement of the Men, while the Officers remain ignorant, which many of them will do, unless Government will make and enforce such a Regulation.

3dly. That the formation of the Troops ought to be perfectly simple and entirely uniform, for example each

Regiment should be composed of two Battalions, each Battalion to consist of 4 Companies and each Company as at present of 1 Captain, 1 Lieutenant, 1 Ensign, 5 Sergeants, 3 Corporals, 2 Music, 65 Privates.

Two Battalions should form a Regiment four Regts a Brigade and two Brigades a Division. This might be the general formation; but as I before observed, I conceive it will be eligible to select from the district forming a Regiment, the flower of the young Men to compose an additional or light Company to every Regiment, for the purposes before specified, which undoubtedly ought to be the case unless something like a Continental Militia shall be instituted. To each Division two Troops of Cavalry and two Companies of Artillery might also be annexed, but no Independent or Volunteer Companies foreign to the Establishment should be tolerated.

4thly. It is also indispensable that such a proportion of the Militia (under whatever discription they are comprehended) as are always to be held in readiness for service, nearly in the same manner the Minute Men formerly were, should be excercised at least from 12 to 25 days in a year, part of the time in Company, part in Battalion and part in Brigade, in the latter case, by forming a Camp, their Discipline would be greatly promoted, and their Ideas raised, as near as possible, to real service; Twenty five days might be divided thus, ten days for training in squads, half Companies and Companies, ten in Battalion and five in Brigade.

5thly. While in the Field or on actual duty, there should not only be a Compensation for the time thus spent, but a full allowance of Provisions Straw, Camp Equipage &c; it is also of so great consequence that there should be, a perfect similarity in the Arms and Accoutrements, that they ought to be furnished, in the first instance by the public, if they cannot be obtained in any other way, some kind of Regimentals or Uniform Clothing (however cheap or course they may be) are also highly requisite and should be provided for such occasions. Nor is it unimportant that every Article should be stamped with the appearance of regularity; and especially that all the Articles of public property should be numbered, marked or branded with the name of the Regiment or Corps that they may be properly accounted for.

6thly. In addition to the Continental Arsenals, which will be treated of under the next head. Every State ought to Establish Magazines of its own, containing Arms, Accoutrements, Ammunitions, all kinds of Camp Equipage and Warlike Stores, and from which the Militia or any part of them should be supplied whenever they are call'd into the Field.

7thly. It is likewise much to be wished, that it might be made agreeable to Officers who have served in the Army, to accept Commands in the Militia; that they might be appointed to them so far as can be done without creating uneasiness and jealousy, and that the principle Characters in the Community would give a countenance to Military improvements, by being present at public reviews and Exhibitions, and by bringing into estimation amongst their fellow Citizens, those who appear fond of cultivating Military knowledge and who excel in the Exercise of Arms. By giving such a tone to our Establishment; by making it universally reputable to bear Arms and disgraceful to decline having a share in the performance of Military duties; in fine, by keeping up in Peace "a well regulated, and disciplined Militia," we shall take the fairest and best method to preserve, for a long time to come, the happiness, dignity and Independence of our Country.

With regard to the third Head in Contemplation, to wit the "Establishment of Arsenals of all kinds of Military Stores." I will only observe, that having some time since seen a plan of the Secretary of War, which went fully into the discussion of this branch of Arrangement, and appeared (as well as I can, at this time recollect) to be in general perfectly well founded, little more need be said on the subject, especially as I have been given to understand the plan has been lately considerably improved and laid before Congress for their approbation; and indeed there is only one or two points in which I could wish to suggest any Alteration.

According to my recollection, five grand Magazines are proposed by the Secretary at War, one of which to be fixed at West Point. Now, as West Point is considered not only by our selves, but by all who have the least knowledge of the Country, as a post of the greatest importance, as it may in time of Peace, from its situation on the Water be somewhat obnoxious to surprise or *Coup de Main* and as it would doubtless be a first object with any Nation which might commence a War against the United States, to seize that Post and occupy or destroy the Stores, it appears to me, that we ought particularly to guard against such an event, so far as may be practicable, and to remove some part of the Allurements to enterprise, by establishing the grand Arsenals in the Interior part of the Country, leaving only to West Point an adequate supply for its defence in almost any extremity.

I take the liberty also to submit to the consideration of the Committee, whether, instead of five great Arsenals, it would not be less expensive and equally convenient and advantageous to fix three general Deposits, one for the Southern, one for the Middle and one for the Eastern States, including New York, in each of which there might be deposited, Arms, Ammunition, Field Artillery, and Camp Equipage for thirty thousand Men, Also one hundred heavy Cannon and Mortars, and all the Apparatus of a Seige, with a sufficiency of Ammunition.

Under the fourth General Division of the subject, it was proposed to consider the Establishment of Military Academies and Manufacturies, as the means of preserving that knowledge and being possessed of those Warlike Stores, which are essential to the support of the Sovereignty and Independence of the United States. But as the Baron Steuben has thrown together his Ideas very largely on these Articles, which he had communicated to me previous to their being sent to the secretary at War, and which being now lodged at the War Office, I imagine have also been submitted to the inspection of the Committee, I shall therefore have the less occasion for entering into the detail, and may, without impropriety, be the more concise in my own observations.

That an Institution calculated to keep alive and diffuse the knowledge of the Military Art would be highly expedient, and that some kinds of Military Manufactories and Elaboratories may and ought to be established, will not admit a doubt; but how far we are able at this time to go into great and expensive Arrangements and whether the greater part of the Military Apparatus and Stores which will be wanted can be imported or Manufactured, in the cheapest and best manner: I leave those to whom the observations are to be submitted, to determine, as being more competent, to the decision than I can pretend to be. I must however mention some things, which I think cannot be dispensed with under the present or any other circumstances; Until a more perfect system of Education can be adopted, I would propose that Provision should be made at some Post or Posts where the principle Engineers and Artillerists shall be stationed, for instructing a certain number of young Gentlemen in the Theory of the Art of War, particularly in all those branches of service which belong to the Artillery and Engineering Departments. Which, from the affinity they bear to each other, and the advantages which I think would result from the measure, I would have blended together; And as this species of knowledge will render them much more accomplished and capable of performing the duties of Officers, even in the Infantry or any other Corps whatsoever, I conceive that appointments to vacancies in the Established Regiments, ought to be made from the candidates who shall have completed their course of Military Studies and Exercises. As it does in an essential manner qualify them for the duties of Garrisons, which will be the principal, if not only service in which our Troops can be employed in time of Peace and besides the Regiments of Infantry by this means will become in time a nursery from whence a number of Officers for Artillery and Engineering may be drawn on any great or sudden occasion.

Of so great importance is it to preserve the knowledge which has been acquired thro' the various Stages of a long and arduous service, that I cannot conclude without repeating the necessity of the proposed Institution, unless we intend to let the Science become extinct, and to depend entirely upon the Foreigners for their friendly aid, if ever we should again be involved in Hostility. For it must be understood, that a Corps of able Engineers and expert Artillerists cannot be raised in a day, nor made such by any exertions, in the same time, which it would take to form an excellent body of Infantry from a well regulated Militia.

And as to Manufactories and Elaboratories it is my opinion that if we should not be able to go largely into the business at present, we should nevertheless have a reference to such establishments hereafter, and in the means time that we ought to have such works carried on, wherever our principal Arsenals may be fixed, as will not only be sufficient to repair and keep in good order the Arms, Artillery, Stores &c of the Post, but shall also extend to Founderies and some other essential matters.

Thus have I given my sentiments without reserve on the four different heads into which the subject seemed naturally to divide itself, as amply as my numerous avocations and various duties would permit. Happy shall I be, if any thing I have suggested may be found of use in forming an Establishment which will maintain the lasting Peace, Happiness and Independence of the United States.

Alexander Hamilton, Report of a Committee to the Continental Congress on a Military Peace Establishment, 18 June 1783.

The Committee observe with respect to a military peace establishment, that before any plan can with propriety be adopted, it is necessary to inquire what powers exist for that purpose in the confederation.

By the 4th. clause of the 6th article it is declared that "no vessels of war shall be kept up by any state in time of peace, except such number only as shall be deemed necessary by the United States in Congress assembled, for the defence of such state or its trade; nor shall any body of forces be kept up by any state in time of peace, except such number only, as in the judgment of the United States in Congress assembled shall be deemed requisite to garrison the forts necessary for the defence of such state."

By the 5th. clause of the 9th article, The United States in Congress assembled are empowered generally (and without mention of peace or war) "to build and equip a navy, to agree upon the number of land forces, and to make requisitions from each state for its quota, in proportion to the number of white inhabitants in each state, which requisition shall be binding, and thereupon the legislature of each state, shall appoint the Regimental officers, raise the men and clothe arm and equip them in a soldier-like manner at the expence of the United States and the officers and men so cloathed armed and equipped shall march to the place appointed and within the time agreed on by the United States in Congress assembled."

By the 4th. clause of the same article the United States are empowered "to appoint all officers of the land forces except regimental officers, to appoint all officers of the naval forces, and to commission all officers whatever in the service of the United States, making rules for the government and regulation of the said land and naval forces and directing their operations."

It appears to the Committee that the terms of the first clause are rather restrictive on the particular states than directory to the United States, intended to prevent any state from keeping up forces land or naval without the approbation and sanction of the Union, which might endanger its tranquillity and harmony, and not to contravene the positive power vested in the United States by the subsequent clauses, or to deprive them of the right of taking such precautions as should appear to them essential to the general security. A distinction that this is to be provided for in time of war, by the forces of the Union, in time of peace, by those of each state would involve, besides other inconveniences, this capital one, that when the forces of the Union should become necessary to defend its rights and repel any attacks upon them, the United States would be obliged to *begin to create* at the very moment they would have occasion *to employ* a fleet and army. They must wait for an actual commencement of hostilities before they would be authorised to prepare for defence, to raise a single regiment or to build a single ship. When it is considered what a length of time is requisite to levy and form an army and still more to build and equip a navy, which is evidently a work of leisure and of peace requiring a gradual preparation of the means—there cannot be presumed so improvident an intention in the Confederation as that of obliging the United States to suspend all provision for the common defence 'till a declaration of war or an invasion. If this is admitted it will follow that they are at liberty to make such establishments in time of peace as they shall judge requisite to the common safety. This is a principle of so much importance in the apprehension of the Committee to the welfare of the union, that if any doubt should exist as to the true meaning of the first-mentioned clause, it will in their opinion be proper to admit such a construction as will leave the general power, vested in the United States by the other clauses, in full force; unless the states respectively or a Majority of them shall declare a different interpretation. The Committee however submit to Congress, (in conformity to that spirit of Candour and to that respect for the sense of their constituents, which ought ever to characterize their proceedings) the propriety of transmitting the plan which they may adopt to the several states to afford an opportunity of signifying their sentiments previous to its final execution.

The Committee, are of opinion, if there is a contitutional power in the United States for that purpose, that there are conclusive reasons in favour of foederal in preference to state establishments.

First there are objects for which separate provision cannot conveniently be made; posts within certain districts, the jurisdiction and property of which are not yet constitutionally ascertained—territory appertaining to the United States not within the original claim of any of the states—the navigation of the Missippi and of the lakes—the rights of the fisheries and of foreign commerce; all which belonging to the United States depending on the laws of nations and on treaty, demand the joint protection of the Union, and cannot with propriety be trusted to separate establishments.

Secondly, the fortifications proper to be established ought to be constructed with relation to each other on a general and well-digested system and their defence should be calculated on the same principles. This is equally important in the double view of safety and oeconomy. If this is not done under the direction of the United States, each state following a partial and disjointed plan, it will be found that the posts will have no mutual dependence or support—that they will be improperly distributed, and more numerous than is necessary as well as less efficacious—of course more easily reduced and more expensive both in the construction and defence.

3dly. It happens, that from local circumstances particular states, if left to take care of themselves, would be in possession of the chief part of the standing forces and of the principal fortified places of the union; a circumstance inconvenient to them and to the United States—to them, because it would impose a heavy exclusive burthen in a matter the benefit of which will be immediately shared by their neighbours and ultimately by the states at large—to the United States, because it confides the care of the safety of the *whole* to a *part,* which will naturally be unwilling as well as unable to make such effectual provision at its particular expence, as the common welfare requires—because a single state from the peculiarity of its situation, will in a manner keep the keys of the United States—because in fiine a considerable force in the hands of a few states may have an unfriendly aspect on the confidence and harmony which ought carefully to be maintained between the whole.

4thly. It is probable that a provision by the [Congress] of the forces necessary to be kept up will [be based] upon a more systematic and oeconomical plan than a provision by the states separately; especially as it will be of importance as soon as the situation of affairs will permit, to establish founderies, manufactaries of arms, powder &c; by means of which the labour of a part of the troops applied to this purpose will furnish the United States with those essential articles on easy terms, and contribute to their own support.

5thly. There must be a corps of Artillery and Engineers kept on foot in time of peace, as the officers of this corps require science and long preliminary study, and cannot be formed on an emergency; and as the neglect of this institution would always oblige the United States to have recourse to foreigners in time of war for a supply of officers in this essential branch—an inconvenience which it ought to be the object of every nation to avoid. Nor indeed is it possible to dispense with the service of such a corps in time of peace, as it will be indispensable not only to have posts on the frontier; but to have fortified harbours for the reception and protection of the fleet of the United States. This corps requiring particular institutions for the instruction and formation of the officers cannot exist upon separate establishments without a great increase of expence.

6thly. It appears from the annexed papers No. 1 to 4, to be the concurrent opinion of the Commander in Chief, the Secretary at War, the Inspector General and the Chief Engineer, not only that some militia establishment is indispensable but that it ought in all respects to be under the authority of the United States as well for military as political reasons. The plan hereafter submitted on considerations of oeconomy is less extensive that proposed by either of them.

The Committee upon these principles submit the following plan.

The Military peace establishment of the United States to consist of four regiments of infantry, and, one of Artillery incorporated in a corps of Engineers, with the denomination of the corps of Engineers.

Each Regiment of infantry to consist of two batalions, each batalion of four companies, each company of 64 rank and file, with the following, commissioned and Non commissioned officers, pay, rations and cloathing; to be however recruited to one hundred & twenty eight rank & file in time of war, preserving the proportion of corporals to privates.

Frederick Steuben, A Letter on the Subject of an Established Militia, and Military Arrangements, Addressed to the Inhabitants of the United States, 1784.

Friends and Fellow Citizens,

It is the duty of every member of the community, particularly in a Republic, to be attentive to its welfare, and to exert himself to contribute to its prosperity. Under the influence of this idea permit me to engage your attention, on a subject of the utmost importance to every country, but more particularly to one having so recently emerged from the waves of despotism, and now taking her station amongst the Nations, on the broad basis of Liberty and Independence. I have risqued my fortune in the general feale, and hazarded my life for the attainment of the inestimable blessings of Liberty, for which you have bravely fought, bled, and conquered. I acknowledge myself interested for your happiness and cannot be silent.

Having spent the greatest part of my life in military pursuits, I feel a confidence in my subject, and thinking it by no means probable that I shall ever engage on the busy theatre of life again, having no personal views to answer by the operation of the system, I shall write with freedom, confident that if any idea not immediately connected with the subject should fall from my pen, it will be ascribed not to the vanity or assurance of a political projector, but to that honest anxiety which I have ever felt for the dignity and happiness of this rising empire.

The immediate object of my address is to hold up to your calm consideration what I conceive to be the best possible Military Establishment for the United States. Be not alarmed Fellow Citizens at the expression; for no country ever risqued their political existence without one that did not fall a prey to the avarice or ambition of her neighbours. Though America has hitherto been successful, and though no immediate cloud seems to threaten the sunshine of her tranquility, yet it would be idle indeed were we to conclude from thence that she was always to stand exempted from the fortunes and fate of other nations.

The local situation of America, happily removed from Europe and her wranglings, must long continue to make a large army unnecessary—it is not however without its difficulties and its dangers.

On the East an unguarded coast, and a dangerous and formidable Colony planted. On the West a defenceless frontier. Neighbours on the one side who may never be friends; and Savages on the other who are unalterably your enemies. This is your local situation. The security of the former must necessarily be committed in a great measure to a Navy; but a Navy can only grow out of dock-yards and arsenals, and the well regulated commerce of your country; and until they begin to operate, for they are the products of industry and time. Your principal ports at least should be raised superior to the fear of injury, or the dishonour of insult.

The latter, *vis.* the protection of your Western frontier, is a subject of perhaps more immediate importance; for upon this rests not only your share of a most lucrative commerce, but closely connects with it the peace, prosperity, and extensions of your Western settlements. These objects are not to be secured but by a chain of well chosen ports, strongly fortified and respectably garrisoned. Hence arises the necessity of an established Continental Corps; and as their services will be lasting and national, their establishment ought to be federal and permanent.

To draught a Militia for such duty, so distant from their homes, and so much more trying to patience than to valour, would be extremely embarrassing and expensive, and fall infinitely short of both the wishes and expectations of Government. But independent of arguments resulting from the nature of the service or general expence, individual embarrassments or eventual disappointments, which must avail every plan for performing it by Militia draughts, there are other and very powerful motives for a small regular establishment.

A Spirit of Providence is one of the strongest assurances of national wisdom, and it may not be improper to lay out your accounts for foreign war or domestic struggle. Where, in an exigency of this kind, without an establishment, would government look up for military talents and experience? Would she call upon her servants who have been engaged in the late controversy? If she did she should find many, if not all of those to whom she could most safely have committed the interest of the Republic, old or disabled—busy or dissatisfied—diffident of themselves—superior to the necessity of hazarding either life, reputation, or care; and totally lost to every military idea and remembrance, except the hardships and the cares. If we examine mankind under the impressions of property and interest, we will find that to make any art a study it should not only be a passion but a business. The Merchant may read Marshal Saxe, the Mathematician Monsieur Vauban, but it is the Soldier alone who regards their lessons and takes up the sword; not as the hasty avenger of a sudden wrong, but as his companion for life, that will study and digest them.

I am conscious in the opinion of many I am undertaking a difficult task in attempting to convince a free people, who have established their liberties by the unparalleled exercise of their virtue, that a permanent Military Establishment is necessary to their happiness, absolutely so to their federal existence. I shall not in this essay address your passions, but I appeal forcibly to your reason. I shall convince you by the statement of a regular and exact calculation, that your present system of Militia draughts recommended by Congress, is not only impracticable in itself, and replete with every inconvenience that can shackle military movements, but it takes a double proportion of every necessary to collect and station them, and more than double the sum to support your frontier in this mode, than by a small regular establishment. Every objection to this system the operations of simple reasoning will fully obviate, by attending to the numbers and materials that shall compose your establishment, and the arrangement that may be made concerning enlistment, reception and muster, sources but too often of much unneccessary expenditure, and of the most flagrant abuse.

Upon a review of all the military of Europe, there does not appear to be a single form which could be safely adopted by the United States; they are unexceptionably different from each other, and like all other human institutions, seem to have started as much out of accident as design. The local situation of the country; the spirit of the government; the character of the nation, and in many instances the character of the Prince, have all had their influence in settling the foundation and discipline of their respective troops, and render it impossible that we should take either as a model. The Legion alone has not been adopted by any, and yet I am confident in asserting, that whether it be examined as applicable to all countries, or as it may more immediately apply to the existing or probable necessity of this, it will be found strikingly superior to any other—1st. Being a compleat and little army of itself, it is ready to begin its operations on the shortest notice or slightest alarm. 2d. Having all the component parts of the largest army of any possible description, it is prepared to meet every species of war that may present itself. And, 3d. As in every case of detachment the first constitutional principle will be preserved, and the embarassments of draughting and detail, which in armies differently framed too often distract the commanding officer, will be avoided.

It may easily suggest itself from this sketch that in forming a Legion the most difficult task is to determine the necessary proportion of each species of soldiers which is to compose it; this must obviously depend upon what will be the theatre, and what the style of the war. On the plains of Poland, whole brigades of cavalry would be necessary against every enemy, but in the forest and among the hills of America, a single regiment would be more than sufficient against any, and as there are but two kinds of war to which we are much exposed, *viz.* an attack from the sea side by an European Power, aided by our sworn enemies settled on our extreme left, and an invasion of our back settlements by an Indian enemy, it follows of course that Musketteers and Light Infantry should make the greatest part of your army; on these principles I should propose the following draught. That a Legion consist, 1st. Of a Legionary Brigade and Regimental Staff. 2d. Of two Brigades of Musketteers, each Brigade of two Regiments, each Regiment of eight Companies forming two Battalions, each Company of a Captain, Lieutenant, Ensign, six Sergeants, one Drum, one Fife, sixty Privates, and four Supernumeraries. 3d. Of a Battalion of Rifle-men of four Companies, each Company to have a Captain, three Lieutenants, six Sergeants, a Bugle-horn and Drum, sixty Privates, and four Supernumeraries. 4th. A Division of Field Artillery consisting of two Companies, each to have a Captain, Captain-Lieutenant, three Lieutenants, six Sergeants, twenty Artificers, forty Matrosses, Drum, Fife, and four Supernumeraries. 5th. A Squadron of Cavalry consisting of two Troops, each Troop to have a Captain, two Lieutenants, a Cornet, six Sergeants, one Farrier, one Saddler, one Trumpeter, sixty Dragoons, and four Supernumeraries. 6th. Of a Train of Artillery and Equipage, to consist of one Quarter-Master, one Clothing and Pay-Master, five Conductors, twenty Artificers, and seventy Waggoners and Drivers.

The principal Staff and Regimental Staff Officers, will be named by Congress—the subordinate Staff by Head of Departments—both to be commissioned by Congress, and subject to their orders alone. The men will be enlisted for eight years, and supported at the common expence of the United States, who after the expiration of their enlistment will accommodate each man with a given quantity of land. The most exact uniformity should be established throughout the component parts of this Corps. The distinction of States should be carefully avoided, and their service as well as their recompense be entirely dependent upon Congress. The Corps of Artillery, though not a part of the Legion (excepting the Field Artillery), bears an immediate relation to it, and it cannot be more properly considered than at this moment. It is not necessary to say more upon it, than, that it shall be under the immediate command of its own General, and that the subordinate Officers shall be composed of field Engineers, Geographers, and Artillerists, men who have and will make military mathematics their study. Their obvious employment will be designing and constructing magazines and dock-yards, superintending military manufactures, surveying high-ways, bays, harbours, etc., etc., while the Soldiers will be employed in garrisoning the forts, and guarding the naval and military stores and places of deposit, and Artificers in such manufactures and works as shall be added to them. The Corps of Horse may be of much service; divided into detachments it may be usefully engaged in keeping up a ready communication between the different posts, and with proper arrangements will be much less expensive than expresses. But as the whole Corps will not exceed one hundred and twenty, rank and file, they may with great propriety be employed in guarding the residence of Congress, the public offices, papers, etc. Congress and their executive officers should never be exposed to the mad proceedings of a mob. Guards are necessary, and always proper at the seat of government.

In looking back upon what I have written, I am so happy as to find that much of what I have proposed to say on the uses of this Establishment, has been anticipated in the course of my Introduction; I will close the sketch however with this summary view of them. The American army at present should consist of neither more nor less than one compleat Legion of 3000 men permanent and Continental; a Corps of Artillery, Sappers, Miners, Artificers, etc., of 1000, permanent and Continental also; and seven Legions of well disciplined Militia of 3000 men each, subject to the call of their country, and ready to act on the shortest notice. Agreeable to this your standing force in time of peace will be but 4000 men, and your effective force in case of invasion 25,000 well disciplined troops.

To your established Corps you will commit the security of your docks and arsenals, the defence of those forts which already exist, and such others as may hereafter be constructed. From them you will derive all necessary assurance relative to your dependent settlements, and effectually preserve that important water communication which has fallen to you by treaty. In times of peace they will operate as a principle of discipline and formation to your established Militia, and in those of war become a ready barrier against the designs of avarice and the assaults of ambition; and finally, they will serve as a nursery to those talents which it must ever be your wisdom to encourage, and which in the course of fortune it may become your interest to employ.

In treating the latter part of this subject, *viz.* the established Militia, it may be previously necessary, to take a view of your present system. It is a flattering but I believe a mistaken idea that every Citizen should be a soldier. It would be as sensible and consistent to say every Citizen should be a Sailor. An apprenticeship must necessarily precede the acquisition of any trade, and the use of arms is as really a trade as shoe or boot making. Were courage the only qualification requisite in a Soldier, it would be otherwise, but galantry alone leaves the character very incomplete; to this must be added youth, size, temperance and inclination, docility of temper, and adroitness in the exercise of the field, and a patience under every vicissitude of fortune. Some of these are no easy lesson to a mind filled with ideas of equality and freedom; and in many instances are only to be learned with industry and pains. I have but one inference to draw from these remarks, *i.e.* that however gallant your Militia may be (and I know them to be brave) they must necessarily want much of the true military character. It may now be asked what are the sources of this defect? I will venture to suggest them: a want of uniformity in their discipline and in their arms—the inadequacy of the several laws under which they exist—the imperfect execution of those laws, such as they are—and the indifference with which every man must regard a business not in some degree pleasing or professional. Hence has arisen that uncertainty of temper—that want of confidence in themselves, that reluctancy to come out, that impatience to get home, and that waste of public and destruction of private property—which has ever marked an operation merely Militia.

These are characteristics that cannot be denied, and which must be as lasting as your belief and declaration, "That every Citizen without exception, must be a Soldier." But when we add the expence of such establishment to the probable disappointment which must follow its operations, it will appear ruinous indeed.

Pennsylvania, it is said, enrols by its Militia Law, about sixty thousand men—and I suppose, that in the article of expence it does not differ widely from those of the other States; these men are obliged to assemble six times in a year at some given place of rendezvous; four days of the six are employed in exercise and two in reviews.

For non-attendence on reviews, each delinquent pays ten shillings per day, and for non-attendance upon exercise five shillings per day; therefore the man who absents himself from all will pay forty shillings per annum, and he who attends all must necessarily lose six days labour, while some, from their distance from the place of rendezvous, will lose ten or twelve. But taking eight as an average, and calculating the expence of each man at six shillings per day, it will amount to forty-eight shillings per man per annum; it then follows, that if the whole Militia should assemble six days in the year, the aggregate expence will amount to 386,666 dollars per annum—if on the other hand they neglect this service and pay the fines, they will amount to 320,000 dollars per annum. View it in any point of light, how imposing and vexatious must this be to the people. For by attendance do they promote the interest of the State? Or does the individual return to his home satisfied, that the information and instruction he has received is any compensation for the loss he sustains? And what is the obvious consequence of non-attendance? Are the fines a revenue to the State, a serviceable one I mean; or can the good wishes or confidence of a people be increased by the operation of a law, whose penalty they prefer to its obligation? I am convinced that under another name these impositions would not be tolerated, and that an insurrection would follow the exercise of them.

If the annual expence of Pennsylvania for training her Militia be 386,666 dollars, and if we consider her as an eighth part of the United States, the aggregate expence of the United States in times of perfect peace, for the instruction of men to whom she cannot risque her fate in war, will be annually 3,113,328 dollars; what it would be in war is beyond all calculation, but it may not be amiss to take a view of the obviously additional sources which must then take place. It is I believe an acknowledged fact, that the expence of any corps will depend upon its discipline. An old soldier will live upon half the allowance of a new levy—not because he has less appetite, but because he has more care and more management. The one will regard his arms and accoutrements with all the solicitude of friendship; the other with all the indifference of contempt. The veteran, taught by the diseases he has felt or the observations he has made, is attentive to his health, and though attentive to his duty avoids everything which would most probably expose it; the militiaman, or new levy, fatigued and disheartened perhaps by the march of a single day, and measuring the tedious hours of his enlistment, throws himself down without any regard to the place or situation; rises in the morning reluctant and languid, and perhaps for want of attention to himself incapable of performing his duty. These are facts which cannot be contradicted, and which hold up to your view some articles of expence, which should be considered, though they cannot be ascertained.

There are many other of the same description; such for instance is the loss sustained by the inefficiency of convoys and the inattention of guards, and such the loss in calling forth a Farmer, a Mechanic, or a Merchant at a shilling a day; the Farmer it is true loses less than either, but still there is no proportion between the profits of his farm and the wages of his sword. Under these considerations trade and agriculture cannot remain unhurt, they must feel some unkind influence foreign to their habits, and unfriendly to their genius. But there is still another more pressing and calamitous: I mean the Rotation Service. For example: A State whose Militia consists of 100,000 men is invaded, the whole cannot be called forth—10,000 may be equal to the contest—but unless the war be almost instantly closed, and that is not to be expected, the principle of rotation must be adopted, and the first detachment is relieved by a second, the second by a third, and the third by a fourth, so that in reality the State must a very large proportion of the time pay and feed 20,000 men, to have 10,000 in the field. How then are these defects to be supplied? I answer by changing their constitution, and lessening their numbers. The Militia of the United States may be calculated at 400,000 men; on what occasion, or for what purpose, shall we ever want this number? The difficulty of bringing a twentieth part of them together has been sufficiently evinced; the impossibility of instructing, and what is still more of feeding them if collected, wants no proof. Giving up therefore the chimerical idea of having 400,000 Militia, and that every Citizen is a Soldier, let us look for a number that will be less expensive, sooner collected, and more easily taught, those lessons necessary for a Soldier to know.

At one period of the late war, Great-Britain attacked us with an army of more than 40,000 effectives; where is the European Power that can do more? We cannot therefore want 400,000 men, nor do we want 50,000; for as we cannot be surprised, an army of 25,000 will be equal to any foreign attack, or internal convulsion, that may happen to exist. I would therefore repeat my proposal, that in addition to the established Continental Legion, that Seven Legions be formed from the whole militia force of the United States; call them the Established Militia, and let their composition and construction be exactly the same with your Continental Legion.

To determine what proportion of the corps will fall to each State, an exact register of the numbers in each should be previously obtained; but not to stop at what is very immaterial in mere proportion, I would hazard the following: North Department, to New Hampshire, Massachusetts, Rhode Island, and Connecticut, Two Legions. Middle Department, to New York, Jersey, Pennsylvania, and Maryland, Three Legions. Southern Department, to Virginia, North Carolina, South Carolina, and Georgia, Two Legions.

It is to simplify the system, and to render its operations easy, that I make this division into departments; the proportion of the States composing each may be easily determined—the smaller will give companies, the larger Battalions, until the several Legions are compleat. In the appointment of Officers for the established Militia, I think the following method should be pursued. Each State appoints the Officers necessary for its own contingent of troops. If either send a Company only, they send no Officer higher than a Captain; if a Battalion, a Lieutenant-Colonel and Major; if a Regiment, a Colonel; if two Regiments, a Brigadier; and if two Brigades, a Major-General. In instances where neither State sends a sufficient number to give these higher ranks, the superior Officers are called from the district which has furnished the largest contingent.

These Officers remain absolutely subject to the State which has sent them, and are dismissed with the same formality with which they have been appointed. For instance: If a Court-Martial should sentence to disgrace a Major, who belongs to a state which only furnishes a Company, the approbation or disapprobation belongs to the Supreme of that State which furnishes the largest part of the Regiment. If a Colonel or Brigadier belonging to a State which has furnished only a Battalion or Regiment, should be tried by a Court-Martial, the sentence is invalid without the approbation of the Grand Convention of the Empire.

Officers or whatever rank will receive pay only for those days which they actually spend in the service of the Public; they will have a right to resign their places after each yearly review, but while they hold their commissions, they will be subject to whatever ordinance may be issued by Government. This ordinance will regulate the pay and emoluments of each grade; determine the uniformity of the discipline, arms, and accoutrements, and the duties of the service in general. With regard to the men the following regulations should take place.

I. That the first class be engaged for three different periods; one third for two years, one third for three, and one third for four; that is, in a company of seventy-two men, twenty-four will be engaged for two years, twenty-four for three years, and twenty-four for four years.

II. That after the expiration of the time of the two years men, their places shall be supplied by another enlistment of the same number of men for three years, and that all subsequent engagements shall be for no less time than this. By this arrangement when the times of one third of a corps expire, a like number will be enlisted; this will prevent a total expiration, and there will be always two-thirds disciplined troops to one-third recruits.

III. That none but Citizens be received.

IV. That their age be not less than eighteen, nor more than twenty-four.

V. That each man be well formed and at least five feet six inches high.

VI. That both Negroes and Mulattoes be excluded.

The best method of engaging men in service is by bounty; the expence will not be great, and the inconveniency and ill humour which attends draughting be avoided. The bounty need not exceed ten dollars per man; to this must be added for the whole term of service, a hat, coat, vest, pair of overalls, pair of shoes, and a stock; and at the expiration of his service, provided he has not been capitally censured, his arms and accoutrements should be given to him. In the operation of this system, at the expiration of every third year 7000 well disciplined men, with their arms and accoutrements, will be added to the effective force of the United States, and the best possible magazine for a Republic firmly established, (*viz.*) arms and accoutrements in the course of a few years be put into the hands of every member of the community, and a perfect knowledge of the duties of a soldier engraved on the mind of every citizen. This will secure you a respectable station amongst the Powers of Europe; and if not ensure you a perfect peace, at least furnish you with the ability of checking the ardour of any Power that may be hardy enough to attack you.

The whole annual expence of this establishment will not exceed fifteen dollars per man per annum, and for this he subjects himself to military discipline thirty-one days in a year, twelve of which he will be employed in exercise, in detail, and twelve in learning the evolutions and maneuvres, and seven in reviews.

The time for these exercises must depend upon the season of year and the place, upon the population of the State, etc., etc., but it were to be wished that at each rendezvous of inspection, one Legion compleat might be assembled, and that on every third year all the troops of the department would encamp together.

The Soldier and the State must come under this farther obligation to each other, that each months service (exclusive of the time taken up in repairing to the rendezvous for which he will receive a certain stipulated allowance) shall count for a year; but should an invasion or any other cause make it necessary for Government to call him out, he shall be obliged to repair to the place appointed on the shortest notice, and to serve any length of time not exceeding one year, which Government may deem expedient. For this time he shall receive that pay and emoluments annexed to a war establishment. By such an arrangement, I dare assure to the United States, an army as useful and as respectable as that of any Republic in Europe; and as to its expence, I will venture again to advance, that it will not cost more than one third of the sum which is now expended; and this may be levied upon every man who falls under the present system, and will not demand from him but twelve shillings and sixpence per annum, in lieu of forty, which simply considered is evidently more eligible; but when viewed as a discharge from the irksome routine of militia duty, I cannot but suppose but it must be embraced with ardour by every individual at present enrolled in the Militia.

As I have in a former instance made the Militia establishment of Pennsylvania a subject of calculation, it may not be improper to say what would be the expence of that Commonwealth, under the operation of the system proposed. For the support of her share of a board of war and inspection, the Continental Legion, Corps of Artillerists and others, her share of the expence will be 65,000 dollars, and for her proportion of the seven Militia Legions 35,000 dollars, the whole annual expence then will amount to 10,000 dollars, and consequently she must have yearly 286,666 dollars—how striking is this difference.

Should it be objected that the scale upon which I have gone is too small, the proportion of each State may be increased without breaking in upon the principles of formation, or should the finances of any State permit, or her politics require another corps, it may be raised upon the same plan.

Much of what has been said on the uses of the federal Legion may be applied to the Militia Corps, like that in peace they will be a most excellent school for the instruction of the young, and in war present an immediate guard or barrier, behind which Government may take its further measures of defence with confidence and ease; and if necessary in war, the rank and file of your army may be doubled, and the list of your officers remain the same; for being perfectly trained in the military schools, which the operation of this plan will establish, I should without hesitation pledge myself for their abilities in their professions.

Having now filled up the limits which I had prescribed for myself upon this occasion, I cannot but hope a plan so clearly efficient, as well as economical will not fail to secure the attention of the United States.

I foresee, however, it will be subject to one very popular objection, "It is in fact a Standing Army." Yes Fellow Citizens I admit it—it is a Standing Army, but composed of your brothers and your sons. Can you require or conceive a better security—are they not your natural guardians? And shall it be supposed a cockade and feather, the *Vox et preteria nihil* of the military character, can alienate either their affections or their interests: Be assured you reflect upon yourselves by nourishing the suspicion, and wound the feelings of men who at least are entitled to your gratitude and esteem.

Letter, George Washington to Frederick Steuben, 15 March 1784.

My Dear Baron: I have perused with attention the plan which you have formed for establishing a Continental Legion, and for training a certain part of the Arms bearing men of the Union as a Militia in times of peace; and with the small alterations which have been suggested and made, I very much approve of it.

It was no unpleasing, and flattering circumstance to me, to find such a coincidence of ideas as appear to run thro' your plan, and the one I had the honor to lay before a Committee of Congress in May last. Mine however, was a hasty production, the consequence of a sudden call, and little time for arrangement. Yours of maturer thought and better digestion, I, at the same time that I hinted the *propriety* of a Continental Militia; glided almost insensibly into what I thought *would*, rather than what I conceived *ought* to be a proper peace Establishment for this Country.

A peace establishment ought always to have two objects in view. The one present security of Posts, of Stores and the public tranquillity. The other, to be prepared, if the latter is impracticable, to resist with efficacy, the sudden attempts of a foreign or domestic enemy. If we have no occasion of Troops for the first purposes, and were certain of not wanting any for the second; then all expence of every nature and kind whatsoever on this score, would be equally nugatory and unjustifiable; but while men have a disposition to wrangle, and to disturb the peace of Society, either from ambitious, political or interested motives, common prudence and foresight requires such an establishment as is likely to ensure to us the blessings of Peace, altho' the undertaking should be attended with difficulty and expence; and I can think of no plan more likely to answer the purpose, than the one you have suggested; which (the principle being established) may be enlarged, or diminished at pleasure, according to circumstances; it therefore meets my approbation and has my best wishes for its success. I have the honor etc.

Resolution of the Continental Congress Creating the Peace Establishment, 3 June 1784.

Whereas a body of troops, to consist of seven hundred non-commissioned officers and privates, properly officered, are immediately and indispensably necessary for taking possession of the western posts, as soon as evacuated by the troops of his britannic Majesty, for the protection of the northwestern frontiers, and for guarding the public stores;

Resolved, That it be, and it is hereby recommended to the states hereafter named, as most conveniently situated, to furnish forthwith from their militia, seven hundred men, to serve for twelve months, unless sooner discharged, in the following proportions, viz.

Connecticut,	165	New Jersey,	110
New York,	165	Pensylvania,	260
			—700

Resolved, That the Secretary in the War Office take order for forming the said troops when assembled, into one regiment, to consist of eight companies of infantry, and two of artillery, arming and equipping them in a soldier-like manner; and that he be authorised to direct their destination and operations, subject to the order of Congress, and of the Committee of the states in the recess of Congress.

Resolved, That the pay, subsistance and rations of the officers and men shall be the same as has been heretofore allowed to the troops of the United States; and that each officer and soldier shall receive one month's pay after they are embodied, before their march.

Resolved, That the staff and commissioned officers of the said troops, consist of the following, and be furnished by the several states hereinafter mentioned; that is to say, one lieutenant colonel commandant from Pensylvania; two majors, one from Connecticut, and one from New York, each major to command a company; eight captains from the several states furnishing the troops in the nearest proportion to the number of the men furnished; ten lieutenants, one to act as adjutant; ten ensigns; one regimental chaplain; one surgeon; four mates.

Resolved, That the secretary in the War office give the necessary order for the inferior arrangements and organization of the said troops, and make the apportionment of the officers to be furnished by the several states, not herein particularly directed.

Resolved, That the said troops when embodied, on their march, on duty, and in garrison, shall be liable to all the rules and regulations formed for the government of the late army of the United States, or such rules and regulations as Congress or a committee of the states may form.

Resolved, That the Superintendant of the finances of the United States, take order for furnishing, on the warrant of the secretary in the war office, the sums requisite for carrying the foregoing resolutions into effect.

On the question to agree to the report as amended, the yeas and nays being required by Mr. [Ephraim] Paine, . . . So it was resolved in the affirmative.

Resolution of the Continental Congress Ascertaining the Powers and Duties of the Secretary at War, 27 January 1785.

The ordinance for ascertaining the powers and duties of the Secretary at War, was taken up and being read a third time, was passed as follows:

An Ordinance for ascertaining the powers and duties of the Secretary at War.

Be it ordained by the United States in Congress Assembled, that the powers and duty of the Secretary at War shall be as follows, to wit: To examine into the present state of the war department, the returns and present state of the troops, ordnance, arms, ammunition, cloathing and supplies of the Troops of these states, and report the same to Congress: To keep exact and regular returns of all the forces of these states, and of all the military stores, equipments and supplies in the Magazines of the United States, or in other places for their use; and to receive into his care, from the officers in whose possession they may be, all such as are not in actual service; to form estimates of all such stores, equipments and supplies as may be requisite for the military service, and for keeping up competent magazines, and to report the same to the Commissioners of the treasury of the United States, that measures may be taken in due time, for procuring the same; to prepare estimates for paying and recruiting the troops of these United States; to carry into effect all ordinances and resolves of Congress for raising and equipping troops for the service of the United States, and for inspecting the said troops; and to direct the arrangement, destination and operation of such troops as are or may be in service, subject to the Orders of Congress or of the Committee of the States in the recess of Congress; to make out, seal and countersign the commissions of all such military officers as shall be employed in the service of the United States; to take order for the transportation, safe keeping and distributing the necessary supplies for such troops and garrisons as may be kept up by the United States. He shall appoint and remove at pleasure all persons employed under him, and shall be responsible for their conduct in office; all which appointments shall be immediately certified to Congress, and such certificate, or the substance thereof, registered in a book to be kept for that purpose in the office of the Secretary of Congress. He shall keep a public and convenient Office in the place where Congress shall reside. He shall, at least once a year, visit all the magazines and deposits of public stores, and report the state of them with proper arrangements to Congress; and shall twice a year, or oftner if thereto required, settle the accounts of his department. That as well the Secretary at war, as his assistants or clerks, before they shall enter on the duties of their Office, shall respectively take and subscribe an Oath or affirmation of fidelity to the United States, and for the faithful execution of the trust reposed in them; and which oaths or affirmations shall be administered by the Secretary of Congress, and a certificate thereof filed in his Office. The Oath of fidelity shall be in the words following: "I A. B. appointed to the office of do acknowledge that I do owe faith and true allegiance to the United States of America, and I do swear (or affirm) that I will, to the utmost of my power, support, maintain and defend the said United States in their freedom, sovereignty and independence, against all opposition whatsoever." And the Oath of Office shall be in the words following: "I, A. B. appointed to the office of do swear (or affirm) that I will faithfully, truly, and impartially execute the office of to which I am so appointed, according to the best of my skill and judgment; and that I will not disclose or reveal any thing, that shall come to my knowledge in the execution of the said office, or from the confidence I may thereby acquire, which, in my own judgment, or by the injunction of my superiors, ought to be kept secret." That the form of the oath of fidelity heretofore prescribed by Congress, and all former resolutions of Congress, relative to the department of war, be, and they are hereby repealed. Done by the United States in Congress assembled, &c.

Resolutions of the Continental Congress Renewing the Peace Establishment, 1, 7, and 12 April 1785.

Friday, April 1, 1785

Congress took into consideration the report of a committee, to whom were referred sundry motions relative to the western frontiers, and a paragraph thereof relative to the raising of troops being under debate, a motion was made by Mr. [David] Howell, seconded by Mr. [John] Beatty, that the same be postponed, in order to take up the following: "That it is necessary, that a body of troops, consisting of non-commissioned officers and privates, be raised to serve for the term of three years, unless sooner discharged, for the protection of the north western frontiers, and for guarding public stores; to be raised by the States in the following proportions, viz. N. H. &c.

It is the opinion of the Committee that the United States in Congress assembled should proceed . . . to make requisitions on the states for men and money in order to establish such garrisons.

On the question, the paragraphs of the report being postponed, and the motion taken up and amended, a division was called for, and on the question to agree to the first clause as amended,

Resolved, That it is necessary that a body of troops consisting of 700 noncommissioned officers and privates, be raised to serve for the term of three years, unless sooner discharged, for the protection of the northwestern frontiers, to defend the settlers on the land belonging to the United States, from the depredations of the Indians, and to prevent unwarrantable intrusions thereon, and for guarding the public stores.

After debate on the latter clause of the motion,

Ordered, That the further consideration thereof be postponed.

Thursday, April 7, 1785

Congress resumed the Consideration of the report on the motions relative to the western frontiers, and a motion being made by Mr. [David] Howell, seconded by Mr. [John] Beatty,

That the 700 non commissioned officers and privates determined to be necessary, by the act of 1 April, be raised by the following states, in the following proportions:

A motion was made by Mr. [William] Ellery, seconded by Mr. [Rufus] King, to postpone that motion, in order to take up the following:

That it be recommended to the states hereafter named, as most conveniently situated, to furnish forthwith, from their militia, the seven hundred non commissioned officers and men, agreed to be raised by the resolution of 1 April, in the following proportions, viz.

And on the question to postpone for the purpose aforesaid, the yeas and nays being required by Mr. [Rufus] King, . . . So the question was lost.

After further debate the original motion was withdrawn, and thereupon,

On motion of Mr. [William] Ellery, seconded by Mr. [Rufus] King,

Resolved, That it be recommended to the states hereafter named, as most conveniently situated, to furnish forthwith, the seven hundred non commissioned officers and men, agreed to be raised by the resolution of 1 April, in the following proportions:

Ordered, That the remainder of the report be committed, and that the committee be instructed to report the states to be called upon, and the proportions to be furnished by them respectively.

Tuesday, April 12, 1785

On the report of a committee, consisting of Mr. [James] Monroe, Mr. [William Samuel] Johnson, Mr. R. R. Livingston, Mr. [Rufus] King, Mr. [John] Beatty, Mr. [John] Henry and Mr. [Gunning] Bedford,

Resolved, That the non commissioned Officers and privates to be raised by the resolution of the seventh day of the present month April, be furnished by the states hereinafter mentioned, in the following proportions:

Connecticut,	165	New Jersey,	110
New York,	165	Pennsylvania,	260
			—— 700

That the following commissioned Officers be furnished by the said States, for the said troops, in the following proportions:

One lieutenant colonel from Pennsylvania.

Two majors, one from Connecticut, and one from New York, each to command a company.

Eight captains, ten lieutenants, one to act as adjutant, one as quarter master, and one as pay master. Ten ensigns, one surgeon and four mates, to be furnished by the said States in proportion to the number of privates which they respectively furnish.

That the pay of the lieutenant colonel be 50 dollars per month; that of the Major, 45; Captain, 35; lieutenant, 26; Ensign, 20; Serjeant, 6; Corporal, 5; Drum, 5; Fife, 5; private, 4; Surgeon, 45; Mate, 30.

That the lieutenants acting as adjutant, quarter master and pay master, shall receive, in consideration of the said extra duty, each 10 dollars per month.

That each Officer and soldier shall receive one month's pay after they are embodied, before their march.

That the Secretary at War be directed to form the said troops when raised into one regiment, consisting of eight companies of infantry, and two of artillery, to appoint their places of rendezvous, direct their subsequent operations, and make all other inferior necessary arrangements not herein particularly mentioned, subject to the Order of Congress, and of the Committee of the States in the recess of Congress; and That the Commissioners of the treasury be instructed to furnish on his warrant, the sums necessary for carrying the same into effect.

That the said troops when embodied, on their march, on duty, or in garrison, shall be subject to all the rules and regulations formed for the government of the late army, or such other rules as Congress or a Committee of the States may form.

That the Secretary at War ascertain the necessary clothing and rations proper for the troops, and report the same to Congress.

That the Commissioners of the treasury contract for the supply of rations at such places and in such quantities as the Secretary at War shall judge necessary.

Resolution of the Continental Congress Expanding the Peace Establishment, 20 October 1786.

The committee, consisting of Mr. [Charles] Pettit, Mr. [Henry] Lee, Mr. [Charles] Pinckney, Mr. [John] Henry and Mr. [Melancton] Smith, to whom was referred the letter from the war Office, with the papers enclosed, containing intelligence of the hostile intentions of the Indians in the Western country, having reported,

That the uniform tenor of the intelligence from the western country plainly indicates the hostile disposition of a number of Indian Nations, particularly the Shawanese, Puteotamies, Chippawas, Tawas and Twightwees: That these nations are now assembling in the Shawanese towns, and are joined by a banditti of desperadoes, under the name of Mingoes and Cherokees, who are outcasts from other nations, and who have associated and settled in that country for the purpose of war and plunder: That they are labouring to draw in other nations to unite with them in a war with the Americans: That it is expected one thousand warriors will soon be collected in the Shawanese towns, from whence they have already despatched parties to commence hostilities: That from the motions of the Indians to the southward as well as the northward, and the exertions made in different quarters to stimulate the various nations against the Americans, there is the strongest reason to believe that, unless the speediest measures are taken effectually to counteract and defeat their plan, the war will become general, and will be attended with the most dangerous and lasting Consequences: That the committee, therefore, deem it highly necessary that the troops in the service of the United States be immediately augmented, not only for the protection and support of the frontiers of the states, bordering on the western territory and the valuable settlements on and near the margin of the Mississippi, but to establish the possession and facilitate the surveying and selling of those intermediate lands which have been so much relied on for the reduction of the debts of the United States: Whereupon,

Resolved unanimously, That the number of one thousand three hundred and forty noncommissioned Officers and privates be raised for the term of three years, unless sooner discharged, and that they, together with the troops now in service, be formed into a legionary corps, to consist of 2040 noncommissioned Officers and privates: That the additional troops be raised by the following states in the following proportions, to wit:

New Hampshire, 260, Massachusetts, 660, Rhode Island, 120, and Connecticut, 180, Infantry and Artillery. Maryland and Virginia each 60 cavalry, making 120.

That the Secretary at War inform the executive authorities of the respective states, in which the troops are to be raised, the number and rank of commissioned Officers to be furnished by each State, in proportion to the men.

That the pay and allowances to the troops, to be raised by this resolve, be the same as established by the Act of Congress of the 12 of April, 1785.

That the said troops shall be subject to the existing articles of war, or such as may hereafter be formed by Congress or a committee of the States.

That the board of treasury contract for a supply of Cloathing and rations, at such places and in such quantities as the Secretary at war shall judge necessary.

Resolved unanimously, That the states above-mentioned be, and they are hereby requested to use their utmost exertions, to raise the quotas of troops respectively assigned them, with all possible expedition, and that the executive of the said states be, and hereby are requested, in case any of their legislatures should not be in session, immediately to convene them for this purpose, as a delay may be attended with the most fatal Consequences.

Ordered, That the board of treasury, without delay, devise ways and means for the pay and support of the troops of the United States upon the present establishment, and report the same to Congress.

Resolution of the Continental Congress Renewing the Peace Establishment, 3 October 1787.

Whereas the time for which the greater part of the troops on the frontiers are engaged will expire in the course of the ensuing year

Resolved That the interests of the United States require that a corps of seven hundred troops should be stationed on the frontiers to protect the settlers on the public lands from the depredations of the Indians, to facilitate the surveying and selling of the said lands in Order to reduce the public debt and to prevent all unwarrantable intrusions thereon.

Resolved That in Order to save the great expence of transporting new levies to the distant frontiers of the United States and also to avail the public of the discipline and knowledge of the country acquired by the troops on the frontiers it is highly expedient to retain as many of them as shall voluntarily reengage in the service.

Resolved That seven hundred non commissioned Officers and privates be raised for the term of three years unless sooner discharged and that the same be furnished in the proportion herein specified by the states which raised the troops agreeably to the requisitions of Congress of April 1785

Connecticut	one hundred and sixty five
New York	one hundred and sixty five
New Jersey	one hundred and ten
Pensylvania	two hundred and sixty

That the commissioned Officers for the said troops be furnished by the said States agreeably to the present proportions.

That the Organization of the said troops together with the two companies of Artillery raised by virtue of the resolves of Congress of the 20th of October 1786 be according to the present establishment; to wit, One regiment of infantry of eight companies, each company four sergeants, four corporals two musicians and sixty privates. And one battalion of Artillery of four companies each company four sergeants four corporals two musicians and sixty privates.

That the secretary at war make the necessary arrangements from time to time to replace the men on the frontiers whose engagements shall expire.

That the said troops shall be governed by such rules and Articles of War as are or shall be established by Congress or a committee of the States.

That the pay and allowances of the said troops be the same as directed by the resolve of Congress of April 12th 1785.

That the board of treasury make the necessary provisions of Clothing and rations from time to time at such places as the secretary at war shall judge necessary.

The Constitutional Convention

The Virginia Plan, 29–30 May 1787.

1. Resolved that the articles of Confederation ought to be so corrected and enlarged as to accomplish the objects proposed by their institution; namely, "common defence, security of liberty and general welfare."

2. Resolved therefore that the rights of suffrage in the National Legislature ought to be proportioned to the Quotas of contribution, or to the number of free inhabitants, as the one or the other rule may seem best in different cases.

3. Resolved that the National Legislature ought to consist of two branches.

4. Resolved that the members of the first branch of the National Legislature ought to be elected by the people of the several States every   for the term of   ; to be of the age of   years at least, to receive liberal stipends by which they may be compensated for the devotion of their time to public service; to be ineligible to any office established by a particular State, or under the authority of the United States, except those peculiarly belonging to the functions of the first branch, during the term of service, and for the space of   after its expiration; to be incapable of re-election for the space of   after the expiration of their term of service, and to be subject to recall.

5. Resolved that the members of the second branch of the National Legislature ought to be elected by those of the first, out of a proper number of persons nominated by the individual Legislatures, to be of the age of   years at least; to hold their offices for a term sufficient to ensure their independency, to receive liberal stipends, by which they may be compensated for the devotion of their time to public service; and to be ineligible to any office established by a particular State, or under the authority of the United States, except those peculiarly belonging to the functions of the second branch, during the term of service, and for the space of   after the expiration thereof.

6. Resolved that each branch ought to possess the right of originating Acts; that the National Legislature ought to be impowered to enjoy the Legislative Rights vested in Congress by the Confederation and moreover to legislate in all cases to which the separate States are incompetent, or in which the harmony of the United States may be interrupted by the exercise of individual Legislation; to negative all laws passed by the several States, contravening in the opinion of the National Legislature the articles of Union; and to call forth the force of the Union against any member of the Union failing to fulfill its duty under the articles thereof.

7. Resolved that a National Executive be instituted; to be chosen by the National Legislature for the term of   years, to receive punctually at stated times a fixed compensation for the services rendered, in which no increase or diminution shall be made so as to affect the Magistracy, existing at the time of increase or diminution, and to be ineligible a second time; and that besides a general authority to execute the National Laws, it ought to enjoy the Executive rights vested in Congress by the Confederation.

8. Resolved that the Executive and a convenient number of the National Judiciary, ought to compose a council of revision with authority to examine every act of the National Legislature before it shall operate, and every act of a particular Legislature before a Negative thereon shall be final; and that the dissent of the said Council shall amount to a rejection, unless the Act of the National Legislature be again passed, or that of a particular Legislature be again negatived by   of the members of each branch.

9. Resolved that a National Judiciary be established to consist of one or more supreme tribunals, and of inferior tribunals to be chosen by the National Legislature, to hold their offices during good behaviour; and to receive punctually at stated times fixed compensation for their services, in which no increase or diminution shall be made so as to affect the persons actually in office at the time of such increase or diminution, that the jurisdiction of the inferior tribunals shall be to hear and determine in the first instance, and of the supreme tribunal to hear and determine in the dernier resort, all piracies and felonies on the high seas, captures from an enemy; cases in which foreigners or citizens of other States applying to such jurisdictions may be interested, or which respect the collection of the National revenue; impeachments of any National officers, and questions which may involve the national peace and harmony.

10. Resolved that provision ought to be made for the admission of States lawfully arising within the limits of the United States, whether from a voluntary junction of Government and Territory or otherwise, with the consent of a number of voices in the National legislature less than the whole.

11. Resolved that a Republican Government and the territory of each State, except in the instance of a voluntary junction of Government and territory, ought to be guaranteed by the United States to each state.

12. Resolved that provision ought to be made for the continuance of Congress and their authorities and privileges, until a given day after the reform of the articles of

Union shall be adopted, and for the completion of all their engagements.

13. Resolved that provision ought to be made for the amendment of the Articles of Union whensoever it shall seem necessary, and that the assent of the National Legislature ought not to be required thereto.

14. Resolved that the Legislative Executive and Judiciary powers within the several States ought to be bound by oath to support the articles of Union.

15. Resolved that the amendments which shall be offered to the Confederation, by the Convention ought at a proper time, or times, after the approbation of Congress to be submitted to an assembly or assemblies of Representatives, recommended by the several Legislatures to be expressly chosen by the people, to consider and decide thereon.

The New Jersey Plan, 15 June 1787

1. Resolved that the articles of Confederation ought to be so revised, corrected and enlarged, as to render the federal Constitution adequate to the exigencies of Government, and the preservation of the Union.

2. Resolved that in addition to the powers vested in the United States in Congress, by the present existing articles of Confederation, they be authorized to pass acts for raising a revenue, by levying a duty or duties on all goods or merchandizes of foreign growth or manufacture, imported into any part of the United States, by Stamps on paper, vellum or parchment, and by a postage on all letters or packages passing through the general post-Office, to be applied to such federal purposes as they shall deem proper and expedient; to make rules and regulations for the collection thereof; and the same from time to time, to alter and amend in such manner as they shall think proper: to pass Acts for the regulation of trade and commerce as well with foreign nations as with each other: provided that all punishments, fines, forfeitures and penalties to be incurred for contravening such acts rules and regulations shall be adjudged by the Common law Judiciarys of the State in which any offence contrary to the true intent and meaning of such Acts rules and regulations shall have been committed or perpetrated, with liberty of commencing in the first instance all suits and prosecutions for that purpose in the superior Common law Judiciary in such State, subject nevertheless, for the correction of all errors, both in law and fact in rendering judgment, to an appeal to the Judiciary of the United States.

3. Resolved that whenever requisitions shall be necessary, instead of the rule for making requisitions mentioned in the articles of Confederation, the United States in Congress be authorized to make such requisitions in proportion to the whole number of white and other free citizens and inhabitants of every age sex and condition including those bound to servitude for a term of years and three fifths of all other persons not comprehended in the foregoing description, except Indians not paying taxes; that if such requisitions be not complied with, in the time specified therein, to direct the collection thereof in the non complying States and for that purpose to devise and pass acts directing and authorizing the same; provided that none of the powers hereby vested in the United States in Congress shall be exercised without the consent of at least   States, and in that proportion if the number of Confederated States should hereafter be increased or diminished.

4. Resolved that the United States in Congress be authorized to elect a federal Executive to consist of   persons, to continue in office for the term of   years, to receive punctually at stated times a fixed compensation for their services, in which no increase or diminution shall be made so as to affect the persons composing the Executive at the time of such increase or diminution, to be paid out of the federal treasury; to be incapable of holding any other office or appointment during their time of service and for   years thereafter; to be ineligible a second time, and removeable by Congress on application by a majority of the Executives of the several States; that the Executives besides their general authority to execute the federal acts ought to appoint all federal officers not otherwise provided for, and to direct all military operations; provided that none of the persons composing the federal Executive shall on any occasion take command of any troops, so as personally to conduct any enterprise as General, or in other capacity.

5. Resolved that a federal Judiciary be established to consist of a supreme Tribunal the Judges of which to be appointed by the Executive, and to hold their offices during good behaviour, to receive punctually at stated times a fixed compensation for their services in which no increase or diminution shall be made, so as to affect the persons actually in office at the time of such increase or diminution; that the Judiciary so established shall have authority to hear and determine in the first instance on all impeachments of federal officers, and by way of appeal in the dernier resort in all cases touching the rights of Ambassadors, in all cases of captures from an enemy, in all cases of piracies and felonies on the high seas, in all cases in which foreigners may be interested, in the construction of any treaty or treaties, or which may arise on any of the Acts for regulation of trade, or the collection of the federal Revenue: that none of the Judiciary shall during the time they remain in Office be capable of receiving or holding any other office or appointment during their time of servie, or for   thereafter.

6. Resolved that all Acts of the United States in Congress made by virtue and in pursuance of the powers hereby and by the articles of confederation vested in them, and all Treaties made and ratified under the authority of the United States shall be the supreme law of the respective States so far forth as those Acts or Treaties shall relate to the said States or their Citizens, and that the Judiciary of the several States shall be bound thereby in their decisions, any thing in the respective laws of the Individual States to the contrary notwithstanding; and that if any State, or any body of men in any State shall oppose or prevent the carrying into execution such acts or treaties, the federal Executive shall be authorized to call forth the power of the Confederated States, or so much thereof as may be necessary to enforce and compel an obedience to such Acts, or an Observance of such Treaties.

7. Resolved that provision be made for the admission of new States into the Union.

8. Resolved the rule for naturalization ought to be the same in every State.

9. Resolved that a Citizen of one State committing an offence in another State of the Union, shall be deemed guilty of the same offence as if it had been committed by a Citizen of the State in which the Offence was committed.

Constitution of the United States, 17 September 1787.

We the People of the United States, in Order to form a more perfect Union, establish Justice, insure domestic Tranquility, provide for the common defence, promote the general Welfare, and secure the Blessings of Liberty to ourselves and our Posterity, do ordain and establish this Constitution for the United States of America.

Article. I.

Section. 1. All legislative Powers herein granted shall be vested in a Congress of the United States, which shall consist of a Senate and House of Representatives.

Section. 2. The House of Representatives shall be composed of Members chosen every second Year by the People of the several States, and the Electors in each State have the Qualifications requisite for Electors of the most numerous Branch of the State Legislature.

No Person shall be a Representative who shall not have attained to the Age of twenty five Years, and been seven Years a Citizen of the United States, and who shall not, when elected, be an Inhabitant of that State in which he shall be chosen.

Representatives and direct Taxes shall be apportioned among the several States which may be included within this Union, according to their respective Numbers, which shall be determined by adding to the whole Number of free Persons, including those bound to Service for a Term of Years, and excluding Indians not taxed, three fifths of all other Persons. The actual Enumeration shall be made within three Years after the first Meeting of the Congress of the United States, and within every subsequent Term of ten Years, in such Manner as they shall by Law direct. The number of Representatives shall not exceed one for every thirty Thousand, but each State shall have at Least one Representative; and until such enumeration shall be made, the State of New Hampshire shall be entitled to chuse three, Massachusetts eight, Rhode-Island and Providence Plantations one, Connecticut five, New-York six, New Jersey four, Pennsylvania eight, Delaware one, Maryland six, Virginia ten, North Carolina five, South Carolina five, and Georgia three.

When vacancies happen in the Representation from any State, the Executive Authority thereof shall issue Writs of Election to fill such Vacancies.

The House of Representatives shall chuse their Speaker and other Officers; and shall have the sole Power of Impeachment.

Section. 3. The Senate of the United States shall be composed of two Senators from each State, chosen by the Legislature thereof, for six Years; and each Senator shall have one Vote.

Immediately after they shall be assembled in Consequence of the first Election, they shall be divided as equally as may be into three Classes. The Seats of the Senators of the first Class shall be vacated at the Expiration of the second Year, of the second Class at the Expiration of the fourth Year, and of the third Class at the Expiration of the sixth Year, so that one third may be chosen every second year; and if Vacancies happen by Resignation, or otherwise, during the Recess of the Legislature of any State, the Executive thereof may make temporary Appointments until the next Meeting of the Legislature, which shall then fill such Vacancies.

No Person shall be a Senator who shall not have attained to the Age of thirty Years, and been nine Years a Citizen of the United States, and who shall not, when elected, be an Inhabitant of that State for which he shall be chosen.

The Vice President of the United States shall be President of the Senate, but shall have no Vote, unless they be equally divided.

The Senate shall chuse their other Officers, and also a President pro tempore, in the Absence of the Vice President, or when he shall exercise the Office of President of the United States.

The Senate shall have the sole Power to try all Impeachments. When sitting for that Purpose, they shall be on Oath or Affirmation. When the President of the

United States is tried, the Chief Justice shall preside: And no Person shall be convicted without the Concurrence of two thirds of the Members present.

Judgment in Cases of Impeachment shall not extend further than to removal from Office, and disqualification to hold and enjoy any Office of honor, Trust or Profit under the United States: but the Party convicted shall nevertheless be liable and subject to Indictment, Trial, Judgment and Punishment, according to Law.

Section. 4. The Times, Places and Manner of holding Elections for Senators and Representatives, shall be prescribed in each State by the Legislature thereof; but the Congress may at any time by Law make or alter such Regulations, except as to the Places of chusing Senators.

The Congress shall assemble at least once in every Year, and such Meeting shall be on the first Monday in December, unless they shall by Law appoint a different Day.

Section. 5. Each House shall be the Judge of the Elections, Returns and Qualifications of its own Members, and a Majority of each shall constitute a Quorum to do Business; but a smaller Number may adjourn from day to day, and may be authorized to compel the Attendance of absent Members, in such Manner, and under such Penalties as each House may provide.

Each House may determine the Rules of its Proceedings, punish its Members for disorderly Behaviour, and, with the Concurrence of two thirds, expel a Member.

Each House shall keep a Journal of its Proceedings, and from time to time publish the same, excepting such Parts as may in their Judgment require Secrecy; and the Yeas and Nays of the Members of either House on any question shall, at the Desire of one fifth of those Present, be entered on the Journal.

Neither House, during the Session of Congress, shall, without the Consent of the other, adjourn for more than three days, nor to any other Place than that in which the two Houses shall be sitting.

Section. 6. The Senators and Representatives shall receive a Compensation for their Services, to be ascertained by Law, and paid out of the Treasury of the United States. They shall in all Cases, except Treason, Felony and Breach of the Peace, be privileged from Arrest during their Attendance at the Session of their respective Houses, and in going to and returning from the same; and for any Speech or Debate in either House, they shall not be questioned in any other Place.

No Senator or Representative shall, during the Time for which he was elected, be appointed to any civil Office under the Authority of the United States, which shall have been created, or the Emoluments whereof shall have been encreased during such time; and no Person holding any Office under the United States, shall be a Member of either House during his Continuance in Office.

Section. 7. All Bills for raising Revenue shall originate in the House of Representatives; but the Senate may propose or concur with Amendments as on other Bills.

Every Bill which shall have passed the House of Representatives and the Senate, shall, before it becomes a Law, be presented to the President of the United States; If he approve he shall sign it, but if not he shall return it, with his Objections to that House in which it shall have originated, who shall enter the Objections at large on their Journal, and proceed to reconsider it. If after such Reconsideration two thirds of that House shall agree to pass the Bill, it shall be sent, together with the Objections, to the other House, by which it shall likewise be reconsidered, and if approved by two thirds of that House, it shall become a Law. But in all such Cases the Votes of both Houses shall be determined by yeas and Nays, and the Names of the Persons voting for and against the Bill shall be entered on the Journal of each House respectively. If any Bill shall not be returned by the President within ten Days (Sundays excepted) after it shall have been presented to him, the Same shall be a Law, in like Manner as if he had signed it, unless the Congress by their Adjournment prevent its Return, in which Case it shall not be a Law.

Every Order, Resolution, or Vote to which the Concurrence of the Senate and House of Representatives may be necessary (except on a question of Adjournment) shall be presented to the President of the United States; and before the Same shall take Effect, shall be approved by him, or being disapproved by him, shall be repassed by two thirds of the Senate and House of Representatives, according to the Rules and Limitations prescribed in the Case of a Bill.

Section. 8. The Congress shall have Power To lay and collect Taxes, Duties, Imposts and Excises, to pay the Debts and provide for the common Defence and general Welfare of the United States; but all Duties, Imposts and Excises shall be uniform throughout the United States;

To borrow Money on the credit of the United States;

To regulate Commerce with foreign Nations, and among the several States, and with the Indian Tribes;

To establish an uniform Rule of Naturalization, and uniform Laws on the subject of Bankruptcies throughout the United States;

To coin Money, regulate the Value thereof, and of foreign Coin, and fix the Standard of Weights and Measures;

To provide for the Punishment of counterfeiting the Securities and current Coin of the United States;

To establish Post Offices and post Roads;

To promote the Progress of Science and useful Arts, by securing for limited Times to Authors and Inventors the exclusive Right to their respective Writings and Discoveries;

To constitute Tribunals inferior to the supreme Court;

To define and punish Piracies and Felonies committed on the high Seas, and Offenses against the Law of Nations;

To declare War, grant Letters of Marque and Reprisal, and make Rules concerning Captures on Land and Water;

To raise and support Armies, but no Appropriation of Money to that Use shall be for a longer Term than two Years;

To provide and maintain a Navy;

To make Rules for the Government and Regulation of the land and naval Forces;

To provide for calling forth the Militia to execute the Laws of the Union, suppress Insurrections and repel Invasions;

To provide for organizing, arming, and disciplining, the Militia, and for governing such Part of them as may be employed in the Service of the United States, reserving to the States respectively, the Appointment of the Officers, and the Authority of training the Militia according to the discipline prescribed by Congress;

To exercise exclusive Legislation in all Cases whatsoever, over such District (not exceeding ten Miles square) as may, by Cession of particular States, and the Acceptance of Congress, become the Seat of the Government of the United States, and to exercise like Authority over all Places purchased by the Consent of the Legislature of the State in which the Same shall be, for the Erection of Forts, Magazines, Arsenals, dock-Yards and other needful Buildings;—And

To make all Laws which shall be necessary and proper for carrying into Execution the foregoing Powers, and all other Powers vested by this Constitution in the Government of the United States, or in any Department or Officer thereof.

Section. 9. The Migration or Importation of such Persons as any of the States now existing shall think proper to admit, shall not be prohibited by the Congress prior to the Year one thousand eight hundred and eight, but a Tax or duty may be imposed on such Importation, not exceeding ten dollars for each Person.

The Privilege of the Writ of Habeas Corpus shall not be suspended, unless when in Cases of Rebellion or Invasion the public Safety may require it.

No Bill of Attainder or ex post facto Law shall be passed.

No Capitation, or other direct, Tax shall be laid, unless in Proportion to the Census or Enumeration herein before directed to be taken.

No Tax or Duty shall be laid on Articles exported from any State.

No Preference shall be given by any Regulation of Commerce or Revenue to the Ports of one State over those of another: nor shall Vessels bound to, or from, one State, be obliged to enter, clear, or pay Duties in another.

No Money shall be drawn from the Treasury, but in Consequence of Appropriations made by Law; and a regular Statement and Account of the Receipts and Expenditures of all public Money shall be published from time to time.

No Title of Nobility shall be granted by the United States: And no Person holding any Office of Profit or Trust under them, shall, without the Consent of the Congress, accept of any present, Emolument, Office, or Title, of any kind whatever, from any King, Prince, or foreign State.

Section. 10. No State shall enter into any Treaty, Alliance, or Confederation; grant Letters of Marque and Reprisal; coin Money; emit Bills of Credit; make any Thing but gold and silver Coin a Tender in Payment of Debts; pass any Bill of Attainder, ex post facto Law, or Law impairing the Obligation of Contracts, or grant any Title of Nobility.

No State shall, without the Consent of the Congress, lay any Imposts or Duties on Imports or Exports, except what may be absolutely necessary for executing it's inspection Laws: and the net Produce of all Duties and Imposts, laid by any State on Imports or Exports, shall be for the Use of the Treasury of the United States; and all such Laws shall be subject to the Revision and Controul of the Congress.

No State shall, without the Consent of Congress, lay any Duty of Tonnage, keep Troops, or Ships of War in time of Peace, enter into any Agreement or Compact with another State, or with a foreign Power, or engage in War, unless actually invaded, or in such imminent Danger as will not admit of delay.

Article. II.

Section. 1. The executive Power shall be vested in a President of the United States of America. He shall hold his Office during the Term of four Years, and, together with the Vice President, chosen for the same Term, be elected, as follows

Each State shall appoint, in such Manner as the Legislature thereof may direct, a Number of Electors, equal to the whole Number of Senators and Representatives to which the State may be entitled in the Congress: but no Senator or Representative, or Person holding an Office of Trust or Profit under the United States, shall be appointed an Elector.

The Electors shall meet in their respective States, and vote by Ballot for two Persons, of whom one at least shall not be Inhabitant of the same State with themselves. And they shall make a List of all the Persons voted for, and of the Number of Votes for each; which List they shall sign and certify, and transmit sealed to the Seat of the Government of the United States, directed to the President of the Senate. The President of the Senate shall, in the Presence of the Senate and House of Representatives, open all the Certificates, and the Votes shall then be counted. The Person having the greatest Number of Votes shall be the President, if such Number be a Majority of the whole Number of Electors appointed; and if there be more than one who have such Majority, and have an equal Number of Votes, then the House of Representatives shall immediately chuse by Ballot one of them for President; and if no Person have a Majority, then from the five highest on the List the said House shall in like Manner chuse the President. But in chusing the President, the Votes shall be taken by States, the Representation from each State having one Vote; A quorum for this Purpose shall consist of a Member or Members from two thirds of the States, and a Majority of all the States shall be necessary to a Choice. In every Case, after the Choice of the President, the Person having the greatest Number of Votes of the Electors shall be the Vice President. But if there should remain two or more who have equal Votes, the Senate shall chuse from them by Ballot the Vice President.

The Congress may determine the Time of chusing the Electors, and the Day on which they shall give their Votes; which Day shall be the same throughout the United States.

No Person except a natural born Citizen, or a Citizen of the United States, at the time of the Adoption of this Constitution, shall be eligible to the Office of the President; neither shall any person be eligible to that Office who shall not have attained to the Age of thirty five Years, and been fourteen Years a Resident within the United States.

In Case of the Removal of the President from Office, or of his Death, Resignation, or Inability to discharge the Powers and Duties of the said Office, the Same shall devolve on the Vice President, and the Congress may by Law provide for the Case of Removal, Death, Resignation or Inability, both of the President and Vice President, declaring what Officer shall then act as President, and such Officer shall act accordingly, until the Disability be removed, or a President shall be elected.

The President shall, at stated Times, receive for his Services, a Compensation, which shall neither be increased nor diminished during the Period for which he shall have been elected, and he shall not receive within that Period any other Emolument from the United States, or any of them.

Before he enter on the Execution of his Office, he shall take the following Oath or Affirmation:—"I do solemnly swear (or affirm) that I will faithfully execute the Office of President of the United States, and will to the best of my Ability, preserve, protect and defend the Constitution of the United States."

Section. 2. The President shall be Commander in Chief of the Army and Navy of the United States, and of the Militia of the several States, when called into the actual Service of the United States; he may require the Opinion, in writing, of the principal Officer in each of the executive Departments, upon any Subject relating to the Duties of their respective Offices, and he shall have Power to grant Reprieves and Pardons for Offenses against the United States, except in Cases of Impeachment.

He shall have Power, by and with the Advice and Consent of the Senate, to make Treaties, provided two thirds of the Senators present concur; and he shall nominate, and by and with the Advice and Consent of the Senate, shall appoint Ambassadors, other public Ministers and Consuls, Judges of the supreme Court, and all other Officers of the United States, whose Appointments are not herein otherwise provided for, and which shall be established by Law: but the Congress may by Law vest the Appointment of such inferior Officers, as they think proper, in the President alone, in the Courts of Law, or in the Heads of Departments.

The President shall have Power to fill up all Vacancies that may happen during the Recess of the Senate, by granting Commissions which shall expire at the End of their next Session.

Section. 3. He shall from time to time give to the Congress Information of the State of the Union, and recommend to their Consideration such Measures as he shall judge necessary and expedient; he may, on extraordinary Occasions, convene both Houses, or either of them, and in Case of Disagreement between them, with Respect to the Time of Adjournment, he may adjourn them to such Time as he shall think proper; he shall receive Ambassadors and other public Ministers; he shall take Care that the Laws be faithfully executed, and shall Commission all the Officers of the United States.

Section. 4. The President, Vice President and all civil Officers of the United States, shall be removed from Office on Impeachment for, and Conviction of, Treason, Bribery, or other high Crimes and Misdemeanors.

Article. III.

Section. 1. The judicial Power of the United States, shall be vested in one supreme Court, and in such inferior Courts as the Congress may from time to time ordain and establish. The Judges, both of the supreme and inferior Courts, shall hold their Offices during good Behaviour, and shall, at stated Times, receive for their Services, a Compensation, which shall not be diminished during their Continuance in Office.

Section. 2. The judicial Power shall extend to all Cases, in Law and Equity, arising under this Constitution, the Laws of the United States, and Treaties made, or which shall be made, under their Authority;—to all Cases affecting Ambassadors, other public Ministers and Consuls;—to all Cases of admiralty and maritime Jurisdiction;—to Controversies to which the United States shall be a Party;—to Controversies between two or more States; between a State and Citizens of another State;—between Citizens of different States—between Citizens of the same State claiming Lands under Grants of different States, and between a State, or the Citizens thereof, and foreign States, Citizens or Subjects.

In all Cases affecting Ambassadors, other public Ministers and Consuls, and those in which a State shall be Party, the supreme Court shall have original Jurisdiction. In all the other Cases before mentioned, the supreme Court shall have appellate Jurisdiction, both as to Law and Fact, with such Exceptions, and under such Regulations as the Congress shall make.

The Trial of all Crimes, except in Cases of Impeachment; shall be by Jury; and such Trial shall be held in the State where the said Crimes shall have been committed; but when not committed within any State, the Trial shall be at such Place or Places as the Congress may by Law have directed.

Section. 3. Treason against the United States, shall consist only in levying War against them, or in adhering to their Enemies, giving them Aid and Comfort. No Person shall be convicted of Treason unless on the Testimony of two Witnesses to the same overt Act, or on Confession in open Court.

The Congress shall have Power to declare the Punishment of Treason, but no Attainder of Treason shall work Corruption of Blood, or Forfeiture except during the Life of the Person attainted.

Article. IV.

Section. 1. Full Faith and Credit shall be given in each State to the public Acts, Records, and judicial Proceedings of every other State; And the Congress may by general Laws prescribe the Manner in which such Acts, Records and Proceedings shall be proved, and the Effect thereof.

Section. 2. The Citizens of each State shall be entitled to all Privileges and Immunities of Citizens in the several States.

A Person charged in any State with Treason, Felony, or other Crime, who shall flee from Justice, and be found in another State, shall on Demand of the executive Authority of the State from which he fled, be delivered up, to be removed to the State having Jurisdiction of the Crime.

No Person held to Service or Labour in one State, under the Laws thereof, escaping into another, shall, in Consequence of any Law or Regulation therein, be discharged from such Service or Labour, but shall be delivered up on Claim of the Party to whom such Service or Labour may be due.

Section. 3. New States may be admitted by the Congress into this Union; but no new State shall be formed or erected within the Jurisdiction of any other State; nor any State be formed by the Junction of two or more States, or Parts of States, without the Consent of the Legislatures of the States concerned as well as of the Congress.

The Congress shall have Power to dispose of and make all needful Rules and Regulations respecting the Territory or other Property belonging to the United States; and nothing in this Constitution shall be so construed as to Prejudice any Claims of the United States, or of any particular State.

Section. 4. The United States shall guarantee to every State in this Union a Republican Form of Government, and shall protect each of them against Invasion; and on Application of the Legislature, or of the Executive (when the Legislature cannot be convened) against domestic Violence.

Article. V.

The Congress, whenever two thirds of both Houses shall deem it necessary, shall propose Amendments to this Constitution, or, on the Application of the Legislatures of two thirds of the several States, shall call a Convention for proposing Amendments, which, in either Case, shall be valid to all Intents and Purposes, as Part of this Constitution, when ratified by the Legislatures of three fourths of the several States, or by Conventions in three fourths thereof, as the one or the other Mode of Ratification may be proposed by the Congress; Provided that no Amendment which may be made prior to the Year One thousand eight hundred and eight shall in any Manner affect the first and fourth Clauses in the Ninth Section of the first Article; and that no State, without its Consent, shall be deprived of it's equal Suffrage in the Senate.

Article. VI.

All Debts contracted and Engagements entered into, before the Adoption of this Constitution, shall be as valid against the United States under this Constitution, as under the Confederation.

This Constitution, and the Laws of the United States which shall be made in Pursuance thereof; and all Treaties made, or which shall be made, under the Authority of the United States, shall be the supreme Law of the Land; and the Judges in every State shall be bound thereby, any Thing in the Constitution or Laws of any

State to the Contrary notwithstanding.

The Senators and Representatives before mentioned, and the Members of the several State Legislatures, and all executive and judicial Officers, both of the United States and of the several States, shall be bound by Oath or Affirmation, to support this Constitution; but no religious Test shall ever be required as a Qualification to any Office or public Trust under the United States.

Article. VII.

The Ratification of the Conventions of nine States, shall be sufficient for the Establishment of this Constitution between the States so ratifying the Same.

done in Convention by the Unanimous Consent of the States present the Seventeenth Day of September in the Year of our Lord one thousand seven hundred and Eighty seven and of the Independence of the United States of America the Twelfth In Witness whereof We have hereunto subscribed our Names,

The Word, "the," being interlined between the seventh and eighth Lines of the first Page, The Word "Thirty" being partly written on an Erazure in the fifteenth Line of the first Page, The Words "is tried" being interlined between the thirty second and thirty third Lines of the first Page and the Word "the" being interlined between the forty third and forty fourth Lines of the second Page.

Attest William Jackson Secretary

G° Washington—Presid.t
and deputy from Virginia

New Hampshire	John Langdon Nicholas Gilman
Massachusetts	Nathaniel Gorham Rufus King
Connecticut	Wm. Saml. Johnson Roger Sherman
New York	Alexander Hamilton
New Jersey	Wil: Livingston David Brearley Wm. Paterson Jona: Dayton
Pennsylvania	B Franklin Thomas Mifflin Robt Morris Geo. Clymer Thos. FitzSimons Jared Ingersoll James Wilson Gouv Morris
Delaware	Geo: Read Gunning Bedford jun John Dickinson Richard Bassett Jaco: Broom
Maryland	James McHenry Dan of St Thos. Jenifer Danl Carroll
Virginia	John Blair— James Madison Jr.
North Carolina	Wm. Blount Richd. Dobbs Spaight Hu Williamson
South Carolina	J. Rutledge Charles Cotesworth Pinckney Charles Pinckney Pierce Butler
Georgia	William Few Abr Baldwin

Ratification

The fight for ratification stimulated a widespread public debate on constitutional issues. The following extracts from that discussion concentrate on the question of the proper control of military power in a republic. Representing the opposition to the new Constitution are the preeminent publicists Elbridge Gerry ("a Columbian Patriot") and Richard Henry Lee ("the Federal Farmer"). Representing the federal position are John Jay and Alexander Hamilton in extracts from the celebrated Federalist Papers.

Extract from Richard Henry Lee, "Observations leading to a fair examination of the system of government, proposed by the late Convention; and to several essential and necessary alterations in it. In a manner of Letters from the Federal Farmer to the Republican," 1787.

By the constitution it is proposed that congress shall have power "to raise and support armies, but no appropriation of money to that use shall be for a longer term than two years; to provide and maintain a navy; to provide for calling forth the militia to execute the laws of the union; suppress insurrections, and repel invasions: to provide for organizing, arming, and disciplining the militia;" reserving to the states the right to appoint the officers, and to train the militia according to the discipline prescribed by congress; congress will have unlimited power to raise armies, and to engage officers and men for any number of years; but a legislative act applying money for their support can have operation for no longer term than two years, and if a subsequent congress do not within the two years renew the appropriation, or further appropriate monies for the use of the army, the army will be left to take care of itself. When an army shall once be raised for a number of years, it is not probable that it will find much difficulty in getting congress to pass laws for applying monies to its support. I see so many men in America fond of a standing army, and especially among those who probably will have a large share in administering the federal system; it is very evident to me, that we shall have a large standing army as soon as the monies to support them can be possibly found. An army is not a very agreeable place of employment for the young gentlemen of many families. A power to raise armies must be lodged some where; still this will not justify the lodging this power in a bare majority of so few men without any checks; or in the government in which the great body of the people, in the nature of things, will be only nominally represented. In the state governments the great body of the people, the yeomanry, &c. of the country, are represented: It is true they will chuse the members of congress, and may now and then chuse a man of their own way of thinking; but it is not impossible for forty, or thirty thousand people in this country, one time in ten to find a man who can possess similar feelings, views, and interests with themselves: Powers to lay and collect taxes and to raise armies are of the greatest moment; for carrying them into effect, laws need not be frequently made, and the yeomanry, &c. of the country ought substantially to have a check upon the passing of these laws; this check ought to be placed in the legislatures, or at least, in the few men the common people of the country, will, probably, have in congress, in the true sense of the word, "from among themselves." It is true, the yeomanry of the country possess the lands, the weight of property, possess arms, and are too strong a body of men to be openly offended—and, therefore, it is urged, they will take care of themselves, that men who shall govern will not dare pay any disrespect to their opinions. It is easily perceived, that if they have not their proper negative upon passing laws in congress, or on the passage of laws relative to taxes and armies, they may in twenty or thirty years be by means imperceptible to them, totally deprived of that boasted weight and strength: This may be done in a great measure by congress, if disposed to do it, by modelling the militia, Should one fifth or one eighth part of the men capable of bearing arms, be made a select militia, as has been proposed, and those the young and ardent part of the community, possessed of but little or no property, and all the others put upon a plan that will render them of no importance, the former will answer all the purposes of an army, while the latter will be defenceless. The state must train the militia in such form and according to such systems and rules as congress shall prescribe: and the only actual influence the respective states will have respecting the militia will be in appointing the officers. I see no provision made for calling out the *posse comitatus* for executing the laws of the union, but provision is made for congress to call forth the militia for the execution of them—and the militia in general, or any select part of it, may be called out under military officers, instead of the sheriff to enforce an execution of federal laws, in the first instance, and thereby introduce an entire military execution of the laws. I know that powers to raise taxes, to regulate the military strength of the community on some uniform plan. To provide for its defence and internal order, and for duly executing the laws, must be lodged somewhere; but still we ought not so to lodge them, as evidently to give one order of men in the community, undue advantages over others; or commit the many to the mercy, prudence, and moderation of the few. And so far as it may be necessary to lodge any of the peculiar powers in the general government, a more safe exercise of them ought to be secured, by requiring the consent of two-thirds or three-fourths of congress thereto—until the federal representation can be increased, so that the democratic members in congress may stand some tolerable chance of a reasonable negative, in behalf of the numerous, important, and democratic part of the community.

Extract from Elbridge Gerry, "Observations on the new Constitution and on the Federal and State Conventions By a Columbian Patriot," 1788.

Though it has been said by Mr. *Wilson* and many others, that a Standing-Army is necessary for the dignity and safety of America, yet freedom revolts at the idea, when the Divan, or the Despot, may draw out his dragoons to suppress the murmurs of a few, who may yet cherish those sublime principles which call forth the exertions, and lead to the best improvements of the human mind. It is hoped this country may yet be governed by milder methods than are usually displayed beneath the bannerets of military law.—Standing armies have been the nursery of vice and the bane of liberty from the Roman legions to the establishment of the artful Ximenes, and from the ruin of the Cortes of Spain, to the planting of the British cohorts in the capitals of America:—By the edicts of an authority vested in the sovereign power by the proposed constitution, the militia of the country, the bulwark of defence, and the security of national liberty if no longer under the controul of civil authority; but at the rescript of the Monarch, or the aristocracy, they may either be employed to extort the enormous sums that will be necessary to support the civil list—to maintain the regalia of power—and the splendour of the most useless part of the community, or they may be sent into foreign countries for the fulfilment of treaties, stipulated by the President and two-thirds of the Senate. . . .

We were then told by him [Royal Governor Thomas Hutchinson], in all the soft language of insinuation, that no form of government, of human construction can be perfect—that we had nothing to fear—that we had no reason to complain—that we had only to acquiesce in their illegal claims, and to submit to the requisition of parliament, and doubtless the lenient hand of government would redress all grievances, and remove the oppressions of the people:—Yet we soon saw armies of mercenaries encamped on our plains—our commerce ruined—our harbours blockaded—and our cities burnt. It may be replied that this was in consequence of an obstinate defence of our privileges; this may be true; and when the "*ultima ratio*" is called to aid, the weakest must fall. But let the best informed historian produce an instance when bodies of men were entrusted with power, and the proper checks relinquished, if they were ever found destitute of ingenuity sufficient to furnish pretences to abuse it. And the people at large are already sensible, that the liberties which America has claimed, which reason has justified, and which have been so gloriously defended by the swords of the brave; are not about to fall before the tyranny of foreign conquest: it is native usurpation that is shaking the foundations of peace, and spreading the sable curtain of despotism over the United States. The banners of freedom were erected in the wilds of America by our ancestors, while the wolf prowled for his prey on the one hand, and more savage man on the other; they have been since rescued from the invading hand of foreign power, by the valor and blood of their posterity; and there was reason to hope they would continue for ages to illumine a quarter of the globe, by nature kindly separated from the proud monarchies of Europe, and the infernal darkness of Asiatic slavery.—And it is to be feared we shall soon see this country rushing into the extremes of confusion and violence, in consequence of the proceeding of a set of gentlemen, who disregarding the purposes of their appointment, have assumed powers unauthorized by any commission, have unnecessarily rejected the confederation of the United States, and annihilated the sovereignty and independence of the individual governments.—The causes which have inspired a few men to assemble for very different purposes with such a degree of temerity as to break with a single stroke the union of America, and disseminate the seeds of discord through the land may be easily investigated, when we survey the partizans of monarchy in the state conventions, urging the adoption of a mode of government that militates with the former professions and exertions of this country, and with all ideas of republicanism, and the equal rights of men.

Passion, prejudice, and error, are characteristics of human nature; and as it cannot be accounted for on any principles of philosophy, religion, or good policy; to these shades in the human character must be attributed the mad zeal of some, to precipitate to a blind adoption of the measures of the late federal convention, without giving opportunity for better information to those who are misled by influence or ignorance into erroneous opinions.—Litterary talents may be prostituted, and the powers of genius debased to subserve the purposes of ambition or avarice; but the feelings of the heart will dictate the language of truth, and the simplicity of her accents will proclaim the infamy of those, who betray the rights of the people, under the specious, and popular pretence of *justice, consolidation,* and *dignity*.

It is presumed the great body of the people unite in sentiment with the writer of these observations, who most devoutly prays that public credit may rear her declining head, and remunerative justice pervade the land; nor is there a doubt if a free government is continued, that time and industry will enable both the public and private debtor to liquidate their arrearages in the most equitable manner. They wish to see the Confederated States bound together by the most indissoluble union, but without renouncing their separate sovereignties and independence, and becoming tributaries to a consolidated fabrick of aristocratick tyranny.—They wish to see government established, and peaceably holding the reins with honour, energy, and dignity; but they wish for no *federal city* whose "*cloud cap't towers*" may screen the state culprit from the hand of justice; while its exclusive jurisdiction may protect the riot of armies encamped within its limits.—They deprecate discord and civil convulsions, but they are not yet generally prepared with the ungrateful Israelites to ask a King, nor are their spirits sufficiently broken to yield the best of their olive grounds to his servants, and to see their sons appointed to run before his chariots—It has been observed by a zealous advocate for the new system, that most governments are the result of fraud or violence, and this with design to recommend its acceptance—but has not almost every step toward its fabrication been fraudulent in the extreme? Did not the prohibition strictly enjoined by the general Convention, that no member should make any communication to his Constituents, or to gentlemen of consideration and abilities in the other States, bear evident marks of fraudulent designs?—This circumstance is regretted in strong terms by Mr. Martin, a member from Maryland, who acknowledges "He had no idea that all the wisdom, integrity, and virtue of the States was contained in that Convention, and that he wished to have corresponded with gentlemen of eminent political characters abroad, and to give their sentiments due weight"—he adds, "so extremely solicitous were they, that their proceedings should not transpire, that the members were prohibited from taking copies of their resolutions, or extracts from the Journals, without express permission, by vote."—And the hurry with which it has been urged to the acceptance of the people, without giving time, by adjournments, for better information, and more unanimity has a deceptive appearance; and if finally driven to resistance, as the only alternative between that and servitude, till in the confusion of discord, the reins should be seized by the violence of some enterprizing genius, that may sweep down the last barrier of liberty, it must be added to the score of criminality with which the fraudulent usurpation at Philadelphia, may be chargeable.—Heaven avert such a tremendous scence! and let us still hope a more happy termination of the present ferment:—may the people be calm and wait a legal redress; may the mad transport of some of our infatuated capitals subside; and every influential character through the States, make the most prudent exertions for a new general Convention, who may vest adequate powers in Congress, for all national purposes, without annihilating the individual governments, and drawing blood from every pore by taxes, impositions and illegal restrictions.—This step might again reestablish the Union. . . .

The happiness of mankind depends much on the modes of government, and the virtues of the governors; and America may yet produce characters who have genius and capacity sufficient to form the manners and correct the morals of the people, and virtue enough to lead their country to freedom, Since their dismemberment from the British empire, America has, in many instances, resembled the conduct of a restless, vigorous, luxurious youth, prematurely emancipated from the authority of a parent, but without the experience necessary to direct him to act with dignity or discretion. Thus we have seen her break the shackles of foreign dominion, and all the blessings of peace restored on the most honourable terms: She acquired the liberty of framing her own laws, choosing her own magistrates, and adopting manners and modes of government the most favourable to the freedom and happiness of society. But how little have we availed ourselves of these superior advantages: The glorious fabric of liberty successfully reared with so much labor and assiduity totters to the foundation, and may be blown away as the bubble of fancy by the rude breath of military combinations, and politicians of yesterday.

It is true this country lately armed in opposition to regal despotism—impoverished by the expences of a long war, and unable immediately to fulfil their public or private engagements that appeared in some instances, with a boldness of spirit that seemed to set at defiance all authority, government, or order, on the one hand; while on the other, there has been, not only a secret wish, but an open avowal of the necessity of drawing the reins of government much too taught, not only for a republicanism, but for a wise and limited monarchy.—But the character of this people is not averse to a degree of subordination, the truth of this appears from the easy restoration of tranquility, after a dangerous insurrection in one of the states; this also evinces a little necessity of a complete revolution of government throughout the union. But it is a republican principle that the majority should rule; and if a spirit of moderation should be cultivated on both sides, till the voice of the people at large could be fairly heard it should be held sacred.—And if, on such a scrutiny, the proposed constitution should appear repugnant to their character and wishes; if they, in the language of a late elegant pen, should acknowledge that "no confusion in my mind, is more terrible to them than the stern disciplined regularity and vaunted police of arbitrary governments, where every heart is depraved by fear, where mankind dare not assume their natural characters, where the free spirit must crouch to the slave in office, where genius must repress her effusions, or like the Egyptian worshippers, offer them in sacrifice to the calves in power, and where the human mind, always in shackles, shrinks from every generous effort." Who would then have the effrontery to say, it ought not to be thrown out with indignation, however some respectable names have appeared to support it.—But if after all, on a dispassionate and fair discussion, the people generally give their voices for a voluntary dereliction of their privileges, let every individual who chooses the active scenes of life strive to support the peace and unanimity of his country, though every other blessing may expire—And while the statesman is plodding for power, and the courtier practising the arts of dissimulation without check—while the rapacious are growing rich by oppression, and fortune throwing her gifts into the lap of fools, let the sublimer characters, the philosophic lovers of freedom who have wept over her exit, retire to the calm shades of contemplation, there they may look down with pity on the inconsistency of human nature, the revolution of states, the rise of kingdoms, and the fall of empires.

Extract from John Jay, The Federalist Papers.

Number 3

Among the many objects to which a wise and free people find it necessary to direct their attention, that of providing for their *safety* seems to be the first. The *safety* of the people doubtless has relation to a great variety of circumstances and considerations, and consequently affords great latitude to those who wish to define it precisely and comprehensively.

At present I mean only to consider it as it respects security for the preservation of peace and tranquility, as well as against dangers from *foreign arms and influence*, as from dangers of the *like kind* arising from domestic causes. As the former of these comes first in order, it is proper it should be the first discussed. Let us therefore proceed to examine whether the people are not right in their opinion that a cordial Union, under an efficient national government, affords them the best security that can be devised against *hostilities* from abroad.

The number of wars which have happened or will happen in the world will always be found to be in proportion to the number and weight of the causes, whether *real* or *pretended*, which *provoke* or *invite* them. If this remark be just, it becomes useful to inquire whether so many *just* causes of war are likely to be given by *united America* as by *disunited* America; for if it should turn out that united America will probably give the fewest, then it will follow that in this respect the Union tends most to preserve the people in a state of peace with other nations.

The *just* causes of war, for the most part, arise either from violations of treaties or from direct violence. America has already formed treaties with no less than six foreign national, and all of them, except Prussia, are maritime, and therefore able to annoy and injure us. She has also extensive commerce with Portugal, Spain, and Britain, and, with respect to the two latter, has, in addition, the circumstance of neighborhood to attend to.

It is of high importance to the peace of America that she observe the laws of nations towards all these powers, and to me it appears evident that this will be more perfectly and punctually done by one national government than it could be either by thirteen separate States or by three or four distinct confederacies. For this opinion various reasons may be assigned.

When once an efficient national government is established, the best men in the country will not only consent to serve, but also will generally be appointed to manage it; for, although town or country, or other contracted influence, may place men in State assemblies, or senates, or courts of justice or executive departments, yet more general and extensive reputation for talents and other qualifications will be necessary to recommend men to offices under the national government—especially as it will have the widest field for choice, and never experience that want of proper persons which is not uncommon in some of the States. Hence, it will result that the administration, the political counsels, and the judicial decisions of the national government will be more wise, systematical, and judicious than those of individual States, and consequently more satisfactory with respect to other nations, as well as more safe with respect to us.

So far, therefore, as either designed or accidental violations of treaties and of the laws of nations afford *just* causes of war, they are less to be apprehended under one general government than under several lesser ones, and in that respect the former most favors the *safety* of the people.

As to those just causes of war which proceed from direct and unlawful violence, it appears equally clear to me that one good national government affords vastly more security against dangers of that sort than can be derived from any other quarter.

Such violences are more frequently occasioned by the passions and interests of a part than of the whole, of one or two States than of the Union. Not a single Indian war has yet been produced by aggressions of the present federal government, feeble as it is; but there are several instances of Indian hostilities having been provoked by the improper conduct of individual States, who, either unable or unwilling to restrain or punish offenses, have given occasion to the slaughter of many innocent inhabitants.

The neighborhood of Spanish and British territories, bordering on some States and not on others, naturally confines the causes of quarrel more immediately to the borderers. The bordering States, if any, will be those who, under the impulse of sudden irritation, and a quick sense of apparent interest or injury, will be most likely, by direct violence, to excite war with those nations; and nothing can so effectually obviate that danger as a national government, whose wisdom and prudence will not be diminished by the passions which actuate the parties immediately interested.

But not only fewer just causes of war will be given by the national government, but it will also be more in their power to accommodate and settle them amicably. They will be more temperate and cool, and in that respect, as well as in others, will be more in capacity to act with circumspection than the offending State. The pride of states, as well as of men, naturally disposes them to justify all their actions, and opposes their acknowledging, correcting, or repairing their errors and offenses. The national government, in such cases, will not be affected by this pride, but will proceed with moderation and candor to consider and decide on the means most proper to extricate them from the difficulties which threaten them.

Besides, it is well known that acknowledgments, explanations, and compensations are often accepted as satisfactory from a strong united nation, which would be rejected as unsatisfactory if offered by a State or confederacy of little consideration or power.

Extracts from Alexander Hamilton, The Federalist Papers.

Number 24

To the powers proposed to be conferred upon the federal government, in respect to the creation and direction of the national forces, I have met with but one specific objection, which, if I understand it rightly, is this—that proper provision has not been made against the existence of standing armies in time of peace; an objection which I shall now endeavor to show rests on weak and unsubstantial foundations.

It has indeed been brought forward in the most vague and general form, supported only by bold assertions without the appearance of argument; without even the sanction of theoretical opinions; in contradiction to the practice of other free nations, and to the general sense of America, as expressed in most of the existing constitution. The propriety of this remark will appear the moment it is recollected that the objection under consideration turns upon a supposed necessity of restraining the LEGISLATIVE authority of the nation in the article of military establishments; a principle unheard of, except in one or two of our State constitutions, and rejected in all the rest.

A stranger to our politics, who was to read our newspapers at the present juncture without having previously inspected the plan reported by the convention, would be naturally led to one of two conclusions: either that it contained a positive injunction and standing armies should be kept up in time of peace; or that it vested in the EXECUTIVE the whole power of levying troops without subjecting his discretion, in any shape, to the control of the legislature.

If he came afterwards to peruse the plan itself, he would be surprised to discover that neither the one nor the other was the case; that the whole power of raising armies was lodged in the *legislature,* not in the *executive;* that this legislature was to be a popular body, consisting of the representatives of the people periodically elected; and that instead of the provision he had supposed in favor of standing armies, there was to be found in respect to this object an important qualification even of the legislative discretion in that clause which forbids the appropriation of money for the support of an army for any longer period than two years—a precaution which upon a nearer view of it will appear to be a great and real security against military establishments without evident necessity.

Disappointed in his first surmise, the person I have supposed would be apt to pursue his conjectures a little further. He would naturally say to himself, it is impossible that all this vehement and pathetic declamation can be without some colorable pretect. It must needs be that this people, so jealous of their liberties, have, in all the preceding models of the constitutions which they have established, inserted the most precise and rigid precautions on this point, the omission of which in the new-plan has given birth to all this apprehension and clamor.

If under this impression he proceeded to pass in review the several State constitutions, how great would be his disappointment to find that *two* only of them contained an interdiction of standing armies in time of peace; that the other eleven had either observed a profound silence on the subject, or had in express terms admitted the right of the legislature to authorize their existence.

Still, however, he would be persuaded that there must be some plausible foundation for the cry raised on this head. He would never be able to imagine, while any source of information remained unexplored, that it was nothing more than an experiment upon the public credulity, dictated either by a deliberate intention to deceive, or by the overflowings of a zeal too intemperate to be ingenous. It would probably occur to him that he would be likely to find the precautions he was in search of in the primitive compact between the States. Here, at length, he would expect to meet with a solution of the enigma. No doubt he would observe to himself the existing Confederation must contain the most explicit provisions against military establishments in time of peace; and a departure from this model in a favorite point has occasioned the discontent which appears to influence these political champions.

If he should now apply himself to a careful and critical survey of the articles of Confederation, his astonishment would not only be increased, but would acquire a mixture of indignation at the unexpected discovery that these articles, instead of containing the prohibition he looked for, and though they had with a jealous circumspection restricted the authority of the State legislatures in this particular, had not imposed a single restraint on that of the United States. If he happened to be a man of quick sensibility, or ardent temper, he could now no longer refrain from pronouncing these clamors to be the dishonest artifices of a sinister and unprincipled opposition to a plan which ought at least to receive a fair and candid examination from all sincere lovers of their country! How else, he would say, could the authors of them have been tempted to vent such loud censures upon that plan about a point in which it seems to have conformed itself to the general sense of America as declared in its different forms of government, and in which it has even superadded a new and powerful guard unknown to any of them? If, on the contrary, he happened to be a man of calm and dispassionate feelings, he would indulge a sigh for the frailty of human nature, and would lament that in a matter so interesting to the happiness of millions the true merits of the question should be perplexed and obscured by expedients so unfriendly to an impartial and right determination. Even such a man could hardly forbear remarking that a conduct of this kind has too much the appearance of an intention to mislead the people by alarming their passions, rather than to convince them by arguments addressed to their understandings.

But however little this objection may be countenanced, even by precedents among ourselves, it may be satisfactory to take a nearer view of its intrinsic merits. From a close examination it will appear that restraints upon the discretion of the legislature in respect to military establishments would be improper to be imposed, and if imposed, from the necessities of society, would be unlikely to be observed.

Though a wide ocean separates the United States from Europe, yet there are various considerations that warn us against an excess of confidence or security. On one side of us, and stretching far into our rear, are growing settlements subject to the dominion of Britain. On the other side, and extending to meet the British settlements, are colonies and establishments subject to the dominion of Spain. This situation and the vicinity of the West India Islands, belonging to these two powers, create between them, in respect to their American possessions and in relation to us, a common interest. The savage tribes on our Western frontier ought to be regarded as our natural enemies, their natural allies, because they have most to fear from us, and most to hope from them. The improvements in the art of navigation have, as to the facility of communication, rendered distant nations, in a great measure, neighbors. Britain and Spain are among the principal maritime powers of Europe. A future concert of views between these nations ought not to be regarded as improbable. The increasing remoteness of consanguinity is every day diminishing the force of the family compact between France and Spain. And politicians have ever with great reason considered the ties of blood as feeble and precarious links of political connection. These circumstances combined admonish us not to be too sanguine in considering ourselves as entirely out of the reach of danger.

Previous to the Revolution, and ever since the peace, there has been a constant necessity for keeping small garrisons on our Western frontier. No person can doubt that these will continue to be indispensable, if it should only be against the ravages and depredations of the Indians. These garrisons must either be furnished by occasional detachments from the militia, or by permanent corps in the pay of the government. The first is impracticable; and if practicable, would be pernicious. The militia would not long, if at all, submit to be dragged from their occupations and families to perform that most disagreeable duty in times of profound peace. And if they could be prevailed upon or compelled to do it, the increased expense of a frequent rotation of service, and the loss of labor and disconcertion of the industrious pursuits of individuals, would form conclusive objections to the scheme. It would be as burdensome and injurious to the public as ruinous to private citizens. The latter resource of permanent corps in the pay of the government amounts to a standing army in time of peace; a small one, indeed, but not the less real for being small. Here is a simple view of the subject that shows us at once the impropriety of a constitutional interdiction of such establishments, and the necessity of leaving the matter to the discretion and prudence of the legislature.

In proportion to our increase in strength, it is probable, nay, it may be said certain, that Britain and Spain would augment their military establishments in our neighborhood. If we should not be willing to be exposed in a naked and defenseless condition to their insults and encroachments, we should find it expedient to increase our frontier garrisons in some ratio to the force by which our Western settlements might be annoyed. There are, and will be, particular posts, the possession of which will include the command of large districts of territory, and facilitate future invasions of the remainder. It may be added that some of those posts will be keys to the trade with the Indian nations. Can any man think it would be wise to leave such posts in a situation to be at any instant seized by one of the other of two neighboring and formidable powers? To act this part would be to desert all the usual maxims of prudence and policy.

If we mean to be a commercial people, or even to be secure on our Atlantic side, we must endeavor, as soon as possible, to have a navy. To this purpose there must be dockyards and arsenals; and for the defense of these, fortifications, and probably garrisons. When a nation has become so powerful by sea that it can protect its dockyards by its fleets, this supersedes the necessity of garrisons for that purpose; but where naval establishments are in their infancy, moderate garrisons will, in all likelihood, be found an indispensable security against descents for the destruction of the arsenals and dockyards, and sometimes of the fleet itself.

Number 25

It may perhaps be urged that the objects enumerated in the preceding number ought to be provided for by the State governments, under the direction of the Union. But this would be in reality an inversion of the primary principle of our political association, as it would in practice transfer the care of the common defense from the federal head to the individual members: a project oppressive to some States, dangerous to all, and baneful to the Confederacy.

The territories of Britain, Spain, and of the Indian nations in our neighborhood do not border on particular States, but encircle the Union from Maine to Georgia. The danger, though in different degrees, is therefore common. And the means of guarding against it ought in like manner to be the objects of common councils, and of a common treasury. It happens that some States, from local situation, are more directly exposed. New York is of this class. Upon the plan of separate provisions, New York would have to sustain the whole weight of the establishments requisite to her immediate safety, and to the mediate or ultimate protection of her neighbors. This would neither be equitable as it respected New York, nor safe as it respected the other States. Various inconveniences would attend such a system. The States, to whose lot it might fall to support the necessary establishments, would be as little able as willing for a considerable time to come to bear the burden of competent provisions. The security of all would thus be subjected to the parsimony, improvidence, or inability of a part. If the resources of such part becoming more abundant and extensive, its provisions should be proportionally enlarged, the other States would quickly take the alarm at seeing the whole military force of the Union in the hands of two or three of its members, and those probably amongst the most powerful. They would each choose to have some counterpoise, and pretenses could easily be contrived. In this situation, military establishments, nourished by mutual jealousy, would be apt to swell beyond their natural or proper size; and being at the separate disposal of the members, they would be engines for the abridgment or demolition of the national authority.

Reasons have been already given to induce a supposition that the State governments will too naturally be prone to a rivalship with that of the Union, the foundation of which will be the love of power; and that in any contest between the federal head and one of its members, the people will be most apt to unite with their local government. If, in addition to this immense advantage, the ambition of the members should be stimulated by the separate and independent possession of military forces, it would afford too strong a temptation and too great facility to them to make enterprises upon, and finally to subvert, the constitutional authority of the Union. On the other hand, the liberty of the people would be less safe in this state of things than in that which left the national forces in the hands of the national government. As far as an army may be considered as a dangerous weapon of power, it had better be in those hands of which the people are most likely to be jealous than in those of which they are least likely to be jealous. For it is a truth, which the experience of all ages has attested, that the people are commonly most in danger when the means of injuring their rights are in the possession of those of whom they entertain the least suspicion.

The framers of the existing Confederation, fully aware of the dangers to the Union from the separate possession of military forces by the States, have in express terms prohibited them from having either ships or troops, unless with the consent of Congress. The truth is, that the existence of a federal government and military establishments under State authority are not less at variance with each other than a due supply of the federal treasury and the system of quotas and requisitions.

There are other lights besides those already presented in which the impropriety of restraints on the discretion of the national legislature will be equally manifest. The design of the objection which has been mentioned is to preclude standing armies in time of peace, though we have never been informed how far it is desired the prohibition should extend: whether to raising armies as well as to *keeping them up* in a season of tranquillity or not. If it be confined to the latter it will have no precise signification, and it will be ineffectual for the purpose intended. When armies are once raised what shall be denominated "keeping them up," contrary to the sense of the Constitution? What time shall be requisite to ascertain the violation? Shall it be a week, a month, or a year? Or shall we say they may be continued as long as the danger which occasioned their being raised continues? This would be to admit that they might be kept up *in time of peace,* against threatening or impending danger, which would be at once to deviate from the literal meaning of the prohibition and to introduce an extensive latitude of construction. Who shall judge of the continuance of the danger? This must undoubtedly be submitted to the national government, and the matter would then be brought to this issue, that the national government to provide against apprehended danger might in the first instance raise troops, and might afterwards keep them on foot as long as they supposed the peace or safety of the community was in any degree of jeopardy. It is easy to perceive that a discretion so latitudinary as this would afford ample room for eluding the force of the provision.

The supposed utility of a provision of this kind must be founded upon a supposed probability, or at least possibility, of a combination between the executive and legislative in some scheme of usurpation. Should this at any time happen, how easy would it be to fabricate pretenses of approaching danger? Indian hostilities, instigated by Spain or Britain, would always be at hand. Provocations to produce the desired appearances might even be given to some foreign power, and appeased again by timely concessions. If we can reasonably presume such a combination to have been formed, and that the enterprise is warranted by a sufficient prospect of success, the army, when once raised from whatever cause, or on whatever pretext, may be applied to the execution of the project.

If, to obviate this consequence, it should be resolved to extend the prohibition to the *raising* of armies in time of peace, the United States would then exhibit the most extraordinary spectacle which the world has yet seen—that of a nation incapacitated by its Constitution to prepare for the defense before it was actually invaded. As the ceremony of a formal denunciation of war has of late fallen into disuse, the presence of an enemy within our territories must be waited for as the legal warrant to the government to begin its levies of men for the protection of the State. We must receive the blow before we could even prepare to return it. All that kind of policy by which nations anticipate distant danger and meet the gathering storm must be abstained from, as contrary to the genuine maxims of a free government. We must expose our property and liberty to the mercy of foreign invaders and invite them, by our weakness, to seize the naked and defenseless prey, because we are afraid that rulers, created by our choice, dependent on our will, might endanger that liberty, by an abuse of the means necessary to its preservation.

Here, I expect we shall be told that the militia of the country is its natural bulwark, and would be at all times equal to the national defense. This doctrine, in substance, had like to have lost us our independence. It cost millions to the United States that might have been saved. The facts which from our own experience forbid a reliance of this kind are too recent to permit us to be the dupes of such a suggestion. The steady operations of war against a regular and disciplined army can only be successfully conducted by a force of the same kind. Considerations of economy, not less than of stability and vigor, confirm this position. The American militia, in the course of the late war, have, by their valor on numerous occasions, erected eternal monuments to their fame; but the bravest of them feel and know that the liberty of their country could not have been established by their efforts alone, however great and valuable they were. War, like most other things, is a science to be acquired and perfected by diligence, by perseverance, by time, and by practice.

All violent policy, contrary to the natural and experienced course of human affairs, defeats itself. Pennsylvania at this instant affords an example of the truth of this remark. The Bill of Rights of that State declares that standing armies are dangerous to liberty, and ought not to be kept up in time of peace. Pennsylvania, nevertheless, in a time of profound peace from the existence of partial disorders in one or two of her counties, has resolved to raise a body of troops; and in all probability will keep them up as long as there is an appearance of danger to the public peace. The conduct of Massachusetts affords a lesson on the same subject, though on different ground. That State (without waiting for the sanction of Congress, as the articles of the Confederation require) was compelled to raise troops to quell a domestic insurrection, and still keeps a corps in pay to prevent a revival of the spirit of revolt. The particular constitution of Massachusetts opposed no obstacle to the measure; but the instance is still of use to instruct us that cases are likely to occur under our government, as well as under those of other nations, which will sometimes render a military force in time of peace essential to the security of the society, and that it is therefore improper in this respect to control the legislative discretion. It also teaches us, in its application to the United States, how little the rights of a feeble government are likely to be respected, even by its own constituents. And it teaches us, in addition to the rest, how unequal parchment provisions are to a struggle with public necessity.

It was a fundamental maxim of the Lacedemonian commonwealth that the post of admiral should not be conferred twice on the same person. The Peloponnesian confederates, having suffered a severe defeat at sea from the Athenians, demanded Lysander, who had before served with success in that capacity, to command the combined fleets. The Lacedemonians, to gratify their allies and yet preserve the semblance of an adherence to their ancient institutions, had recourse to the flimsy subterfuge of investing Lysander with the real power of admiral under the nominal title of vice-admiral. This instance is selected from among a multitude that might be cited to confirm the truth already advanced and illustrated by domestic examples; which is, that nations pay little regard to rules and maxims calculated in their very nature to run counter to the necessities of society. Wise politicians will be cautious about fettering the government with restrictions that cannot be observed, because they know that every breach of the fundamental laws, though dictated by necessity, impairs that sacred reverence which ought to be maintained in the breast of rulers towards the constitution of a country, and forms a precedent for other breaches where the same plea of necessity does not exist at all, or is less urgent and palpable.

Number 26

It was a thing hardly to be expected that in a popular revolution the minds of men should stop at that happy mean which marks the salutary boundary between POWER and PRIVILEGE, and combines the energy of government with the security of private rights. A failure in this delicate and important point is the great source of the inconveniences we experience, and if we are not cautious to avoid a repetition of the error in our future attempts to rectify and ameliorate our system we may travel from one chimerical project to another; we may try change after change; but we shall never be likely to make any material change for the better.

The idea of restraining the legislative authority in the means of providing for the national defense is one of those refinements which owe their origin to a zeal for liberty more ardent than enlightened. We have seen, however, that it has not had thus far an extensive prevalency; that even in this country, where it made its first appearance, Pennsylvania and North Carolina are the only two States by which it has been in any degree patronized; and that all the others have refused to give it the least countenance; wisely judging that confidence must be placed somewhere; that the necessity of doing it is implied in the very act of delegating power; and that it is better to hazard the abuse of that confidence than to embarrass the government and endanger the public safety by impolitic restrictions on the legislative authority. The opponents of the proposed Constitution combat, in this respect, the general decision of America; and instead of being taught by experience the propriety of correcting any extremes into which we may have heretofore run, they appear disposed to conduct us into others still more dangerous and more extravagant. As if the tone of government had been found too high, or too rigid, the doctrines they teach are calculated to induce us to depress or to relax it by expedients which, upon other occasions, have been condemned or forborne. It may be affirmed without the imputation of invective that if the principles they inculcate on various points could so far obtain as to become the popular creed, they would utterly unfit the people of this country for any species of government whatever. But a danger of this kind is not to be apprehended. The citizens of America have too much discernment to be argued into anarchy. And I am much mistaken if experience has not wrought a deep and solemn conviction in the public mind that greater energy of government is essential to the welfare and prosperity of the community.

It may not be amiss in this place concisely to remark the origin and progress of the idea, which aims at the exclusion of military establishments in time of peace. Though in speculative minds it may arise from a contemplation of the nature and tendency of such institutions, fortified by the events that have happened in other ages and countries, yet as a national sentiment it must be traced to those habits of thinking which we derive from the nation from whom the inhabitants of these States have in general sprung.

In England, for a long time after the Norman Conquest, the authority of the monarch was almost unlimited. Inroads were gradually made upon the prerogative in favor of liberty, first by the barons and afterwards by the people, till the greatest part of its most formidable pretensions became extinct. But it was not till the revolution in 1688, which elevated the Prince of Orange to the throne of Great Britain, that English liberty was completely triumphant. As incident to the undefined power of making war an acknowledged prerogative of the crown, Charles II had, by his own authority, kept on foot in time of peace a body of 5,000 regular troops. And this number James II increased to 30,000, which were paid out of his civil list. At the revolution, to abolish the exercise of so dangerous an authority, it became an article of the Bill of Rights then framed that "the raising or keeping a standing army within the kingdom in time of peace, *unless with the consent of Parliament,* was against law."

In that kingdom, when the pulse of liberty was at its highest pitch, no security against the danger of standing armies was thought requisite, beyond a prohibition of their being raised or kept up by the mere authority of the executive magistrate. The patriots who effected that memorable revolution were too temperate, too well-informed, to think of any restraint on the legislative discretion. They were aware that a certain number of troops for guards and garrisons were indispendable; that no precise bounds could be set to the national exigencies; that a power equal to every possible contingency must exist somewhere in the government: and that when they referred the exercise of that power to the judgment of the legislature, they had arrived at the ultimate point of precaution which was reconcilable with the safety of the community.

From the same source, the people of America may be said to have derived an hereditary impression of danger to liberty from standing armies in time of peace. The circumstances of a revolution quickened the public sensibility on every point connected with the security of popular rights, and in some instances raised the warmth of our zeal beyond the degree which consisted with the due temperature of the body politic. The attempts of two of the States to restrict the authority of the legislature in the article of military establishments are of the number of these instances. The principles which had taught us to be jealous of the power of an hereditary monarch were by an injudicious excess extended to the representatives of the people in their popular assemblies. Even in some of the States, where this error was not adopted, we find unnecessary declarations that standing armies ought not to be kept up in time of peace WITHOUT THE CONSENT OF THE LEGISLATURE. I call them unnecessary, because the reason which had introduced a similar provision into the English Bill of Rights is not applicable to any of the State constitutions. The power of raising armies at all under those constitutions can by no construction be deemed to reside anywhere else than in the legislatures themselves; and it was superfluous, if not absurd, to declare that a matter should not be done without the consent of a body, which alone had the power of doing it. Accordingly, in some of those constitutions, and among others, in that of the State of New York, which has been justly celebrated both in Europe and America as one of the best of the forms of government established in this country, there is a total silence upon the subject.

It is remarkable that even in the two States which seem to have meditated an interdiction of military establishments in time of peace, the mode of expression made use of is rather monitory than prohibitory. It is not said that standing armies *shall not be* kept up, but that they *ought not* to be kept up, in time of peace. This ambiguity of terms appears to have been the result of a conflict between jealousy and conviction; between the desire of excluding such establishments at all events and the persuasion that an absolute exclusions would be unwise and unsafe.

Can it be doubted that such a provision, whenever the situation of public affairs was understood to require a departure from it, would be interpreted by the legislature into a mere admonition, and would be made to yield to the necessities or supposed necessities of the State? Let the fact already mentioned with respect to Pennsylvania decide. What then (it may be asked) is the use of such a provision, if it cease to operate the moment there is an inclination to disregard it?

Let us examine whether there be any comparison in point of efficacy between the provision alluded to and that which is contained in the new Constitution for restraining the appropriations of money for military purposes to the period of two years. The former, by aiming at too much, is calculated to effect nothing; the latter, by steering clear of an imprudent extreme, and by being perfectly compatible with a proper provision for the exigencies of the nation, will have a salutary and powerful operation.

The legislature of the United States will be *obliged* by this provision, once at least in every two years, to deliberate upon the propriety of keeping a military force on foot; to come to a new resolution on the point; and to declare their sense of the matter by a formal vote in the face of their constituents. They are not *at liberty* to vest in the executive department permanent funds for the support of an army, if they were even incautious enough to be willing to repose in it so improper a confidence. As the spirit of party in different degrees must be expected to infect all political bodies, there will be, no doubt, persons in the national legislature willing enough to arraign the measures and criminate the views of the majority. The provision for the support of a military force will always be a favorable topic for declamation. As often as the question comes forward, the public attention will be roused and attracted to the subject by the party in opposition; and if the majority should be really disposed to exceed the proper limits, the community will be warned of the danger, and will have an opportunity of taking measures to guard against it. Independent of parties in the national legislature itself, as often as the period of discussion arrived, the State legislatures, who will always be not only vigilant but suspicious and jealous guardians of the rights of the citizens against encroachments from the federal government, will constantly have their attention awake to the conduct of the national rulers, and will be ready enough, if anything improper appears, to sound the alarm to the people, and not only to be the VOICE, but, if necessary, the ARM of their discontent.

Schemes to subvert the liberties of a great community *require time* to mature them for execution. An army, so large as seriously to menace those liberties, could only be formed by progressive augmentations; which would suppose not merely a temporary combination between the legislature and executive, but a continued conspiracy for a series of time. Is it probable that such a combination would exist at all? Is it probable that it would be persevered in, and transmitted along through all the successive variations in a representative body, which biennial elections would naturally produce in both houses? Is it presumable that every man the instant he took his seat in the national Senate or House of Representatives would commence a traitor to his constituents and to his country? Can it be supposed that there would not be found one man discerning enough to detect so atrocious a conspiracy, or bold or honest enough to apprise his constituents of their danger? If such presumptions can fairly be made, there ought to be at once an end of all delegated authority. The people should resolve to recall all the powers they have heretofore parted with out of their own hands, and to divide themselves into as many States as there are counties in order that they may be able to manage their own concerns in person.

If such suppositions could even be reasonably made, still the concealment of the design for any duration would be impracticable. It would be announced by the very circumstance of augmenting the army to so great an extent in time of profound peace. What colorable reason could be assigned in a country so situated for such vast augmentations of the military force? It is impossible that the people could be long deceived; and the destruction of the project and of the projectors would quickly follow the discovery.

It has been said that the provision which limits the appropriation of money for the support of an army to the period of two years would be unavailing, because the executive, when once possessed of a force large enough to awe the people into submission, would find resources in that very force sufficient to enable him to dispense with supplies from the acts of the legislature. But the question again recurs, upon what pretense could he be put in possession of a force of that magnitude in time of peace? If we suppose it to have been created in consequence of some domestic insurrection or foreign war, then it becomes a case not within the principle of the objection; for this is leveled against the power of keeping up troops in time of peace. Few persons will be so visionary as seriously to contend that military forces ought not to be raised to quell a rebellion or resist an invasion; and if the defense of the community under such circumstances should make it necessary to have any army so numerous as to hazard its liberty, this is one of those calamities for which there is neither preventative nor cure. It cannot be provided against by any possible form of government; it might even result from a simple league offensive and defensive, if it should ever be necessary for the confederates or allies to form an army for common defense.

But it is an evil infinitely less likely to attend us in a united than in a disunited state; nay, it may be safely asserted that it is an evil altogether unlikely to attend us in the former situation. It is not easy to conceive a possibility that dangers so formidable can assail the whole Union as to demand a force considerable enough to place our liberties in the least jeopardy, especially if we take into our view the aid to be derived from the militia, which ought to be always counted upon as a valuable and powerful auxiliary. But in a state of disunion (as has been fully shown in another place), the contrary of this supposition would become not only probable, but almost unavoidable.

Number 28

That there may happen cases in which the national government may be necessitated to resort to force cannot be denied. Our own experience has corroborated the lessons taught by the examples of other nations; that emergencies of this sort will sometimes exist in all societies, however constituted; that seditions and insurrections are, unhappily, maladies as inseparable from the body politic as tumors and eruptions from the natural body; that the idea of governing at all times by the simple force of law (which we have been told is the only admissible principle of republican government) has no place but in the reveries of those political doctors whose sagacity disdains the admonitions of experimental instruction.

Should such emergencies at any time happen under the national government, there could be no remedy but force. The means to be employed must be proportioned to the extent of the mischief. If it should be a slight commotion in a small part of a State, the militia of the residue would be adequate to its suppression; and the natural presumption is that they would be ready to do their duty. An insurrection, whatever may be its immediate cause, eventually endangers all government. Regard to the public peace, if not to the rights of the Union, would engage the citizens to whom the contagion had not communicated itself to oppose the insurgents; and if the general government should be found in practice conducive to the prosperity and felicity of the people, it were irrational to believe that they would be disinclined to its support.

If, on the contrary, the insurrection should pervade a whole State, or a principal part of it, the employment of a different kind of force might become unavoidable. It appears that Massachusetts found it necessary to raise troops for suppressing the disorders within that State; that Pennsylvania, from the mere apprehension of commotions among a part of her citizens, has thought proper to have recourse to the same measure. . . .

If the representatives of the people betray their constituents, there is then no resource left but in the exertion of that original right of self-defense which is paramount to all positive forms of government, and which against the usurpations of the national rulers may be exerted with infinitely better prospect of success than against those of the rulers of an individual State. In a single State, if the persons intrusted with supreme power become usurpers, the different parcels, subdivisions, or districts of which it consists, having no distinct government in each, can take no regular measures for defense. The citizens must rush tumultuously to arms, without concert, without system, without resource; except in their courage and despair. The usurpers, clothed with the forms of legal authority, can too often crush the opposition in embryo. The smaller the extent of the territory, the more difficult will it be for the people to form a regular or systematic plan of opposition, and the more easy will it be to defeat their early efforts. Intelligence can be more speedily obtained of their preparations and movements, and the military force in the possessions of the usurpers can be more rapidly directed against the part where the opposition has begun. In this situation there must be a peculiar coincidence of circumstances to insure success to the popular resistance.

The obstacles to usurpation and the facilities of resistance increase with the increased extent of the state, provided the citizens understand their rights and are disposed to defend them. The natural strength of the people in a large community, in proportion to the artificial strength of the government, is greater than in a small, and of course more competent to a struggle with the attempts of the government to establish a tyranny. But in a confederacy the people, without exaggeration, may be said to be entirely the masters of their own fate. Power being almost always the rival of power, the general government will at all times stand ready to check the usurpations of the state governments, and these will have the same disposition towards the general government. The people, by throwing themselves into either scale, will infallibly make it preponderate. If their rights are invaded by either, they can make use of the other as the instrument of redress. How wise will it be in them by cherishing the union to preserve to themselves an advantage which can never be too highly prized!

It may safely be received as an axiom in our political system that the State governments will, in all possible contingencies, afford complete security against invasions of the public liberty by the national authority. Projects of usurpation cannot be masked under pretenses so likely to escape the penetration of select bodies of men, as of the people at large. The legislatures will have better means of information. They can discover the danger at a distance; and possessing all the organs of civil power and the confidence of the people, they can at once adopt a regular plan of opposition, in which they can combine all the resources of the community. They can readily communicate with each other in the different States, and unite their common forces for the protection of their common liberty.

The great extent of the country is a further security. We have already experienced its utility against the attacks of a foreign power. And it would have precisely the same effect against the enterprises of ambitious rulers in the national councils. If the federal army should be able to quell the resistance of one State, the distant States would be able to make head with fresh forces. The advantages obtained in one place must be abandoned to subdue the opposition in others; and the moment the part which had been reduced to submission was left to itself, its efforts would be renewed, and its resistance revive.

We should recollect that the extent of the military force must, at all events, be regulated by the resources of the country. For a long time to come it will not be possible to maintain a large army; and as the means of doing this increase, the population and natural strength of the community will proportionably increase. When will the time arrive that the federal government can raise and maintain an army capable of erecting a despotism over the great body of the people of an immense empire, who are in a situation, through the medium of their State governments, to take measures for their own defense, with all the celerity, regularity, and system of independent nations? The apprehension may be considered as a disease, for which there can be found no cure in the resources of argument and reasoning.

Number 29

The power of regulating the militia and of commanding its services in times of insurrection and invasion are natural incidents to the duties of superintending the common defense, and of watching over the internal peace of the Confederacy.

It requires no skill in the science of war to discern that uniformity in the organization and discipline of the militia would be attended with the most beneficial effects, whenever they were called into service for the public defense. It would enable them to discharge the duties of the camp and of the field with mutual intelligence and concert—an advantage of peculiar moment in the operations of an army; and it would fit them much sooner to acquire the degree of proficiency in military functions which would be essential to their usefulness. This desirable uniformity can only be accomplished by confiding the regulation of the militia to the direction of the national authority. It is, therefore, with the most evident propriety that the plan of the convention proposes to empower the Union "to provide for organizing, arming, and disciplining the militia, and for governing such part of them as may be employed in the service of the United States, *reserving to the States respectively the appointment of the officers, and the authority of training the militia according to the discipline prescribed by Congress.*"

Of the different grounds which have been taken in opposition to this plan there is none that was so little to have been expected, or is so untenable in itself, as the one from which this particular provision has been attacked. If a well-regulated militia be the most natural defense of a free country, it ought certainly to be under the regulation and at the disposal of that body which is constituted the guardian of the national security. If standing armies are dangerous to liberty, an efficacious power over the militia in the same body ought, as far as possible, to take away the inducement and the pretext to such unfriendly institutions. If the federal government can command the aid of the militia in those emergencies which call for the military arm in support of the civil magistrate it can the better dispense with the employment of a different kind of force. If it cannot avail itself of the former, it will be obliged to recur to the latter. To render an army unnecessary will be a more certain method of preventing its existence than a thousand prohibitions upon paper.

In order to cast an odium upon the power of calling forth the militia to execute the laws of the Union, it has been remarked that there is nowhere any provision in the proposed Constitution for requiring the aid of the POSSE COMITATUS to assist the magistrate in the execution of his duty; whence it has been inferred that military force was intended to be his only auxiliary. There is a striking incoherence in the objections which have appeared, and sometimes even from the same quarter, not much calculated to inspire a very favorable opinion of the sincerity or fair dealing of their authors. The same persons who tell us in one breath that the powers of the federal government will be despotic and unlimited inform us in the next that it has not authority sufficient even to call out the POSSE COMITATUS. The latter, fortunately, is as much short of the truth as the former exceeds it. It would be absurd to doubt that a right to pass all laws *necessary* and *proper* to execute its declared powers would include that of requiring the assistance of the citizens to the officers who may be intrusted with the execution of those laws as it would be to believe that a right to enact laws necessary and proper for the imposition and collection of taxes would involve that of varying the rules of descent and of the alienation of landed property, or of abolishing the trial by jury in cases relating to it. It being therefore evident that the supposition of a want of power to require the aid of the POSSE COMITATUS is entirely destitute of color, it will follow that the conclusion which has been drawn from it, in its application to the authority of the federal government over the militia, is as uncandid as it is illogical. What reason could there be to infer that force was intended to be the sole instrument of authority, merely because there is a power to make use of it when necessary? What shall we think of the motives which could induce men of sense to reason in this extraordinary manner? How shall we prevent a conflict between charity and conviction?

By a curious refinement upon the spirit of republican jealousy, we are even taught to apprehend danger from the militia itself in the hands of the federal government. It is observed that select corps may be formed, composed of the young and the ardent, who may be rendered subservient to the views of arbitrary power. What plan for the regulation of the militia may be pursued by the national government is impossible to be foreseen. But so far from viewing the matter in the same light with those who object to select corps as dangerous, were the Constitution ratified and were I to deliver my sentiments to a member of the federal legislature on the subject of a militia establishment, I should hold to him, in the substance, the following discourse:

"The project of disciplining all the militia of the United States is as futile as it would be injurious if it were capable of being carried into execution. A tolerable expertness in military movements is a business that requires time and practice. It is not a day, nor a week nor even a month, that will suffice for the attainment of it. To oblige the great body of the yeomanry and of the other classes of the citizens to be under arms for the purpose of going through military exercises and evolutions, as often as might be necessary to acquire the degree of perfection which would entitle them to the character of a well regulated militia, would be a real grievance to the people and a serious public inconvenience and loss. It would form an annual deduction from the productive labor of the country to an amount which, calculating upon the present numbers of the people, would not fall far short of a million pounds. To attempt a thing which would abridge the mass of labor and industry to so considerable an extent would be unwise: and the experiment, if made, could not succeed, because it would not long be endured. Little more can reasonably be aimed at with respect to the people at large than to have them properly armed and equipped; and in order to see that this be not neglected, it will be necessary to assemble them once or twice in the course of a year.

"But though the scheme of disciplining the whole nation must be abandoned as mischievous or impracticable; yet it is a matter of the utmost importance that a well digested plan should, as soon as possible, be adopted for the proper establishment of the militia. The attention of the government ought particularly to be directed to the formation of a select corps of moderate size, upon such principles as will really fit it for service in case of need. By thus circumscribing the plan, it will be possible to have an excellent body of well-trained militia ready to take the field whenever the defense of the State shall require it. This will not only lessen the call for military establishments, but if circumstances should at any time oblige the government to form an army of any magnitude that army can never be formidable to the liberties of the people while there is a large body of citizens, little if at all inferior to them in discipline and the use of arms, who stand ready to defend their own rights and those of their fellow-citizens. This appears to me the only substitute that can be devised for a standing army, and the best possible security against it, if it should exist."

Thus differently from the adversaries of the proposed Constitution should I reason on the same subject, deducing arguments of safety from the very sources which they represent as fraught with danger and perdition. But how the national legislature may reason on the point is a thing which neither they nor I can foresee.

There is something so far-fetched and so extravagant in the idea of danger to liberty from the militia that one is at a loss whether to treat it with gravity or with raillery; whether to consider it as a mere trial of skill, like the paradoxes of rhetoricians; as a disingenuous artifice to instil prejudices at any price; or as the serious offspring of political fanaticism. Where in the name of common sense are our fears to end if we may not trust our sons, our brothers, our neighbors, our fellow-citizens? What shadow of danger can there be from men who are daily mingling with the rest of their countrymen and who participate with them in the same feelings, sentiments, habits, and interests? What reasonable cause of apprehension can be inferred from a power in the Union to prescribe regulations for the militia and to command its services when necessary, while the particular States are to have the *sole and exclusive appointment of the officers?* If it were possible seriously to indulge a jealousy of the militia upon any conceivable establishment under the federal government, the circumstance of the officers being in the appointment of the States ought at once to extinguish it. There can be no doubt that this circumstance will always secure to them a preponderating influence over the militia.

In reading many of the publications against the Constitution, a man is apt to imagine that he is perusing some ill-written tale or romance, which, instead of natural and agreeable images, exhibits to the mind nothing but frightful and distorted shapes—

> "Gorgons, Hydras, and Chimeras dire;"

discoloring and disfiguring whatever it represents, and transforming everything it touches into a monster.

A sample of this is to be observed in the exaggerated and improbable suggestions which have taken place respecting the power of calling for the services of the militia. That of New Hampshire is to be marched to Georgia, of Georgia to New Hampshire, of New York to Kentucky, and of Kentucky to Lake Champlain. Nay, the debts due to the French and Dutch are to be paid in militiamen instead of Louis d'ors and ducats. At one moment there is to be a large army to lay prostrate the liberties of the people; at another moment the militia of Virginia are to be dragged from their homes five or six hundred miles to tame the republican contumacy of Massachusetts; and that of Massachusetts is to be transported an equal distance to subdue the refractory haughtiness of the aristocratic Virginians. Do the persons who rave at this rate imagine that their art or their eloquence can impose any conceits or absurdities upon the people of America for infallible truths?

If there should be an army to be made use of as the engine of despotism, what need of the militia? If there should be no army, whither would the militia, irritated at being required to undertake a distant and distressing expedition for the purpose of riveting the chains of slavery upon a part of their countrymen, direct their course, but to the seat of the tyrants, who had meditated so foolish as well as so wicked a project to crush them in their imagined intrenchments of power, and to make them an example of the just vengeance of an abused and incensed people? Is this the way in which usurpers stride to dominion over a numerous and enlightened nation? Do they begin by exciting the detestation of the very instruments of their intended usurpations? Do they usually commence their career by wanton and disgustful acts of power, calculated to answer no end, but to draw upon themselves universal hatred and execration? Are suppositions of this sort the sober admonitions of discerning patriots to a discerning people? Or are they the inflamatory ravings of chagrined incendiaries or distempered enthusiasts? If we were even to suppose the national rulers actuated by the most ungovernable ambition, it is impossible to believe that they would employ such preposterous means to accomplish their designs.

In times of insurrection, or invasion, it would be natural and proper that the militia of a neighboring State should be marched into another, to resist a common enemy, or to guard the republic against the violence of faction or sedition. This was frequently the case in respect to the first object in the course of the late war; and this mutual succor is, indeed, a principal end of our political association. If the power of affording it be placed under the direction of the Union, there will be no danger of a supine and listless inattention to the dangers of a neighbor till its near approach had superadded the incitements of self-preservation to the too feeble impulses of duty and sympathy.

The Early Republic

An Act to establish an Executive Department to be denominated the Department of War, 7 August 1789.

That there shall be an Executive Department to be denominated the Department of War; and that there shall be a principal officer therein, to be called the Secretary for the Department of War, who shall perform and execute such duties as shall, from time to time, be enjoined on, or entrusted to him, by the President of the United States, agreeable to the constitution, relative to military commissions, or to the land or naval forces, ships or warlike stores, of the United States, or to such other matters respecting military or naval affairs, as the President of the United States shall assign to the said department, or relative to the granting of lands to persons entitled thereto, for military services rendered to the United States, or relative to Indian affairs: and furthermore, that the said principal officer shall conduct the business of the said department in such manner as the President of the United States shall, from time to time, order or instruct.

SEC. 2. That there shall be in the said department, an inferior officer, to be appointed by the said principal officer, to be employed therein as he shall deem proper, and to be called the chief clerk in the department of war, and who, whenever the said principal officer shall be removed from office by the President of the United States, or in any other case of vacancy, shall, during such vacancy, have the charge and custody of all records, books and papers, appertaining to the said department.

SEC. 3. That the said principal officer, and every other person to be appointed or employed in the said department, shall, before he enters on the execution of his office, or employment, take an oath or affirmation *well and faithfully to execute the trust committed to him.*

SEC. 4. That the Secretary for the department of war, to be appointed in consequence of this act, shall, forthwith after his appointment, be entitled to have the custody and charge of all records, books and papers, in the office of secretary for the department of war, heretofore established by the United States in Congress assembled. *[Approved, August* 7, 1789.]

An Act to recognize and adapt to the constitution of the United States, the establishment of the troops raised under the resolves of the United States in Congress assembled and for other purposes, 29 September 1789.

That the establishment contained in the resolve of the late Congress, of the 3d of October, 1787, except as to the mode of appointing the officers, and also as is hereinafter provided, be, and the same is hereby recognized to be the establishment for the troops in the service of the United States.

SEC. 2. That the pay and allowances of the said troops, be the same as have been established by the United States in Congress assembled, by their resolution of the 12th of April, 1785.

SEC. 3. That all commissioned and non-commissioned officers, and privates, who are, or shall be, in the service of the United States, shall take the following oaths or affirmations, to wit: "I, A. B., do solemnly swear or affirm (as the case may be) that I will support the constitution of the United States." "I, A. B., do solemnly swear or affirm (as the case may be) to bear true allegiance to the United States of America, and to serve them honestly and faithfully, against all their enemies or opposers whatsoever, and to observe and obey the orders of the President of the United States of America, and the orders of the officers appointed over me."

SEC. 4. That the said troops shall be governed by the rules and articles of war, which have been established by the United States in Congress assembled, or by such rules and articles of war as may hereafter by law be established.

SEC. 5. That, for the purpose of protecting the inhabitants of the frontiers of the United States from the hostile incursions of the Indians, the President is hereby authorized to call into service, from time to time, such part of the militia of the states, respectively, as he may judge necessary for the purpose aforesaid; and that their pay and subsistence, while in service, be the same as the pay and subsistence of the troops above mentioned.

SEC. 6. That this act shall continue, and be in force, until the end of the next session of Congress, and no longer.

Henry Knox, **Plan for the General Arrangement of the Militia of the United States, 18 January 1790.**

The Introduction

That a well-constituted republic is more favorable to the liberties of society, and that its principles give an higher elevation to the human mind than any other form of government, has generally been acknowledged by the unprejudiced and enlightened part of mankind.

But it is at the same time acknowledged that unless a republic prepares itself by proper arrangements to meet those exigencies to which all states are in a degree liable, that its peace and existence are more precarious than the forms of government in which the will of one directs the conduct of the whole, for the defense of the nation.

A government whose measures must be the result of multiplied deliberations, is seldom in a situation to produce instantly those exertions which the occasion may demand; therefore it ought to possess such energetic establishments as should enable it, by the vigor of its own citizens, to control events as they arise, instead of being convulsed or subverted by them.

It is the misfortune of modern ages, that governments have been formed by chance and events, instead of system—that without fixed principles, they are braced or relaxed, from time to time, according to the predominating power of the rulers or the ruled—the rulers possessing separate interests from the people, excepting in some of the high-toned monarchies, in which all opposition to the will of the princes seems annihilated.

Hence we look round Europe in vain for an extensive government, rising on the power inherent in the people, and performing its operations entirely for their benefit. But we find artificial force governing every where, and the people generally made subservient to the elevation and caprice of the few. Almost every nation appearing to be busily employed in conducting some external war; grappling with internal commotion; or endeavoring to extricate itself from impending debts which threaten to overwhelm it with ruin. Princes and ministers seem neither to have leisure nor inclination to bring forward institutions for diffusing general strength, knowledge and happiness; But they seem to understand well the Machivalian maxim of politics—divide and govern.

May the United States avoid the errors and crimes of other governments; and possess the wisdom to embrace the present invaluable opportunity of establishing such institutions as shall invigorate, exalt and perpetuate the great principles of freedom. An opportunity pregnant with the fate of millions—but rapidly borne on the wings of time, any may never again return.

The public mind, unbaffled by superstition or prejudice, seems happily prepared to receive the impressions of wisdom. The latent springs of human action, ascertained by the standard of experience, may be regulated and made subservient to the noble purpose of forming a dignified national character.

The causes by which nations have ascended and declined, through the various ages of the world, may be calmly and accurately determined; and the United States may be placed in the singularly fortunate condition of commencing their career of empire, with the accumulated knowledge of all the known societies and governments of the globe.

The strength of the government, like the strength of any other vast and complicated machine, will depend on a due adjustment of its several parts. Its agriculture—its commerce—its laws—its finance—its system of defense, and its manners and habits, all require consideration, and the highest exercise of political wisdom.

It is the intention of the present attempt to suggest the most efficient system of defence which may be compatible with the interests of a free people. A system which shall not only produce the expected effect, but which in its operations shall also produce those habits and manners which will impart strength and durability to the whole government.

The modern practice of Europe, with respect to the employment of standing armies, has created such a mass of opinion in their favor, that even philosophers, and the advocates for liberty, have frequently confessed their use, and necessity, in certain cases.

But whoever seriously and candidly estimates the power of discipline, and the tendency of military habits, will be constrained to confess, that whatever may be the efficacy of a standing army in war, it cannot in peace be considered as friendly to the rights of human nature. The recent instance in France cannot with propriety be brought to overturn the general principle, built upon the uniform experience of mankind. It may be found, on examining the causes that appear to have influenced the military of France, that while the springs of power were wound up in the nation to the highest pitch, that the discipline of the army was proportionably relaxed. But any argument on this head, may be considered as unnecessary to the enlightened citizens of the United States.

A small corps of well-disciplined and well-informed artillerists and engineers, and a legion for the protection of the frontiers, and the magazines and arsenals, are all the military establishment which may be required for the present use of the United States. The privates of the corps to be enlisted for a certain period, and after the expiration of which to return to the mass of the citizens.

An energetic National Militia is to be regarded as the CAPITAL SECURITY of a free republic; and not a standing army, forming a distinct class in the community.

It is the introduction and diffusion of vice and corruption of manners into the mass of the people, that renders a standing army necessary. It is when public spirit is despised, and avarice, indolence and effeminacy of manners predominate, and prevent the establishment of institutions which would elevate the minds of the youth in the paths of virtue and honor, that a standing army is formed and rivetted forever.

While the human character remains unchanged, and societies and governments of considerable extent are formed; a principle ever ready to execute the laws and defend the state, must constantly exist. Without this vital principle, the government would be invaded or overturned, and trampled upon by the bold and ambitious. No community can be long held together, unless its arrangements are adequate to its probable exigencies.

If it should be decided to reject a standing army for the military branch of the government of the United States, as possessing too fierce an aspect, and being hostile to the principles of liberty, it will follow that a well-constituted militia ought to be established.

A consideration of the subject will show the impracticability of disciplining at once the mass of the people. All discussions on the subject of a powerful militia, will result in one or other of the following principles.

First. Either efficient institutions must be established for the military education of the youth; and that the knowledge acquired therein shall be diffused throughout the community, by the mean of rotation. Or,

Secondly. That the militia must be formed of substitutes, after the manner of the militia of Great Britain.

If the United States possess the vigor of mind to establish the first institution, it may reasonably be expected to produce the most unequivocal advantages. A glorious national spirit will be introduced, with its extensive train of political consequences. The youth will imbibe a love of their country; reverence and obedience to its laws; courage and elevation of mind; openness and liberality of character; accompanied by a just spirit of honor. In addition to which their bodies will acquire a robustness, greatly conducive to their personal happiness, as well as the defense of their country. While habit, with its silent, but efficacious operations, will durably cement the system.

Habit, that powerful and universal law, incessantly acting on the human race, well deserves the attention of legislators. Formed at first in individuals, by separate and almost imperceptible impulses, until at length it acquires a force which controls with irresistible sway. The effects of salutary or pernicious habits, operating on a whole nation are immense, and decides its rank and character in the world.

Hence the science of legislation teaches to scrutinize every national institution, as it may introduce proper or improper habits; to adopt with religious zeal the former, and reject with horror the latter.

A republic, constructed on the principles herein stated, would be uninjured by events, sufficient to overturn a government supported solely by the uncertain power of a standing army.

The well-informed members of the community, actuated by the highest motives of self-love, would form the real defense of the country. Rebellions would be prevented, or suppressed with ease. Invasions of such a government would be undertaken only by madmen; and the virtues and knowledge of the people would effectually oppose the introduction of tyranny.

But the second principle—a militia of substitutes, is pregnant, in a degree, with the mischiefs of a standing army; as it is highly probably the substitutes from time to time, will be nearly the same men, and the most idle and worthless part of the community. Wealthy families, proud of distinctions which riches may confer, will prevent their sons from serving in the militia of substitutes; the plan will degenerate into hubitual contempt; a standing army will be introduced, and the liberties of the people subjected to all the contingencies of events.

The expense attending an energetic establishment of militia may be strongly urged as an objection to the institution. But it is to be remembered, that this objection is levelled at both systems, whether by rotation or by substitutes. For if the numbers are equal, the expense will also be equal. The estimate of the expense will show its unimportance, when compared with the magnitude and beneficial effects of the institution.

Every intelligent mind would rejoice in the establishment of an institution, under whose auspices the youth and vigor of the constitution would be renewed with each successive generation, and which would appear to secure the great principles of freedom and happiness against the injuries of time and events.

The following Plan is formed on these general principles.

First. That it is the indispensible duty of every nation, to establish all necessary institutions for its own perfection and defence.

Secondly. That it is a capital security to a free state, for the great body of the people to possess a competent knowledge of the military art.

Thirdly. That this knowledge cannot be attained in the present state of society, but by establishing adequate institutions for the military education of youth; and that the knowledge acquired therein should be diffused throughout the community, by the principles of rotation.

Fourthly. That every man of the proper age and ability of body, is firmly bound by the social compact, to perform, personnally, his proportion of military duty for the defence of the state.

Fifthly. That all men of the legal military age, should be armed, enrolled, and held responsible for different degrees of military service.

And, sixthly. That, agreeably to the Constitution, the United States are to provide for organizing, arming and disciplining the militia; and for governing such part of them as may be employed in the service of the United States; reserving to the States, respectively, the appointment of the officers, and the authority of training the militia according to the discipline prescribed by Congress.

The Plan

The period of life in which military service shall be required of the citizens of the United States, to commence at eighteen, and terminate at the age of sixty years.

The men comprehended by this description, exclusive of such exceptions as the legislatures of the respective States may think proper to make, and ALL ACTUAL MARINERS, shall be enrolled for different degrees of military duty, and divided into three distinct classes.

The first class shall comprehend the youth of eighteen, nineteen, and twenty years of age; to be denominated the ADVANCED CORPS.

The second class shall include the men from twenty-one to forty-five years of age; to be denominated the MAIN CORPS.

The third class shall comprehend, inclusively, the men from forty-six to sixty years of age, to be denominated the RESERVED CORPS.

All the militia of the United States shall assume the form of the legion, which shall be the permanent establishment thereof.

A legion shall consist of one hundred and fifty-three commissioned officers, and two thousand eight hundred and eighty non-commissioned officers and privates, formed in the following manner.

First. The Legionary Staff.

One legionary, or major-general.

Two aids-de-camp, of the rank of major; one of whom to be the legionary quarter-master.

One inspector and deputy adjutant-general, of the rank of lieutenant-colonel.

One chaplain.

Second. The Brigade Staff.

One brigadier-general.

One brigade inspector, to serve as an aid-de-camp.

Third. The Regimental Staff.

One lieutenant-colonel, commandant.

Two majors.

One adjutant.

One pay-master, or agent.

One quarter-master.

Fourth. Two Brigades of Infantry.

Each brigade of two regiments; each regiment of eight companies, forming two battalions; each company of a captain, lieutenant, ensign, six serjeants, one drum, one fife, and sixty-four rank and file.

Fifth. Two Companies of Riflemen.

Each company to have a captain, lieutenant, ensign, six serjeants, a bugle-horn, one drum, and sixty-four rank and file.

Sixth. A Battalion of Artillery.

Consisting of four companies; each to have a captain, a captain-lieutenant, one lieutenant, six serjeants, twelve artificers, and fifty-two rank and file.

Seventh. A Squadron of Cavalry.

Consisting of two troops; each troop to have a captain, two lieutenants, a cornet, six serjeants, one farrier, one saddler, one trumpeter, and sixty-four dragoons.

In case the whole number of the advanced corps in any State, should be insufficient to form a legion of this extent, yet the component parts must be preserved, and the reduction proportioned, as nearly as may be, to each part.

The companies of all the corps shall be divided into SECTIONS of twelve each. It is proposed by this division, to establish one uniform vital principle, which in peace and war shall pervade the militia of the United States.

All requisitions for men to FORM AN ARMY, either for State or federal purposes, shall be furnished by the advanced and main corps, by means of the sections.

The executive government, or commander in chief of the militia of each State, will assess the numbers required, on the respective legions of these corps.

The legionary general will direct the proportions to be furnished by each part of his command. Should the demand be so great as to require one man from each section, then the operation hereby directed shall be performed by single sections. But if a less number should be required, they will be furnished by an association of sections, or companies, according to the demand. In any case, it is probable that mutual convenience may dictate an agreement with an individual, to perform the service required. If however, no agreement can be made, one must be detached by an indiscriminate draught; and the others shall pay him a sum of money, equal to the averaged sum which shall be paid in the same legion for the voluntary performance of the service required.

In case any sections, or companies of a legion, after having furnished its own quota, should have more men, willing to engage for the service required, other companies of the same legion shall have permission to engage them. The same role to extend to the different legions in the State.

The legionary general must be responsible to the commander in chief of the militia of the State, that the men furnished are according to the description, and that they are equipped in the manner, and marched to the rendezvous, conformably to the orders for that purpose.

The men who may be draughted, shall not serve more than three years at one time.

The reserved corps being destined for the domestic defense of the State, shall not be obliged to furnish men, excepting in cases of actual invasion, or rebellion—and then the men required shall be furnished by means of the sections.

The actual commissioned officers of the respective corps, shall not be included in the sections, nor in any of the operations thereof.

The respective States shall be divided into portions or districts; each of which to contain, as nearly as may be, some complete part of a legion.

Every citizen of the United States, who shall serve his country in the field, for the space of one year, either as an officer or soldier, shall, if under the age of twenty-one years, be exempted from the service required in the advanced corps. If he shall be above the age of twenty-one years, then every year he shall so serve in the field, shall be estimated as equal to six years service in the main or reserved corps, and shall accordingly exempt him from every service therein for the said term of six years, except in cases of actual invasion of, or rebellion within the State in which he resides. And it shall also be a permanent establishment, that six years actual service in the field, shall entirely free every citizen from any further demands of service, either in the militia, or in the field, unless in cases of invasion or rebellion.

ALL ACTUAL MARINERS or seamen, in the respective States, shall be registered in districts, and divided into two classes. The first class to consist of all the seamen, from the age of sixteen to thirty years, inclusively. The second class to consist of all those of the age of thirty-one to forty-five, inclusively.

The first class shall be responsible to serve three years on board of some public armed vessel or ship of war, as a commissioned officer, warrant officer, or private mariner, for which service they shall receive the customary wages and emoluments.

But should the State not demand the said three years service during the above period, from the age of sixteen to thirty years, then the party to be exempted entirely therefrom. . . .

Of the Advanced Corps.

The advanced corps are designed not only as a school in which the youth of the United States are to be instructed in the art of war, but they are, in all cases of exigence, to serve as an actual defence to the community.

The whole of the armed corps shall be clothed according to the manner hereafter directed, armed and subsisted at the expense of the United States; and all the youth of the said corps, in each State, shall be encamped together if practicable, or by legions, which encampments shall be denominated THE ANNUAL CAMPS OF DISCIPLINE.

The youth of *eighteen* and *nineteen* years, shall be disciplined for THIRTY days successively in each year; and those of *twenty* years shall be disciplined only for ten days in each year, which shall be the last ten days of the annual encampments.

The non-commissioned officers and privates are not to receive any pay during the said time. But the commissioned officers will receive the pay of their relative ranks, agreeable to the federal establishment for the time being. . . .

The advanced legions, in all cases of invasion, or rebellion, shall, on requisition of lawful authority, be obliged to march to any place within the United States, to remain embodied for such time as shall be directed, not to exceed one year, to be computed from the time of marching from the regimental parades; during the period of their being on such service, to be placed on the continental establishment, of pay, subsistence, cloathing, forage, tents, camp-equipage, and all such other allowances, as are made to the federal troops at the same time, and under the same circumstances. . . .

In case the legions of the advanced corps should march to any place, in consequences of a requisition of the general government, all legal and proper expenses of such march, shall be paid by the United States. But should they be embodied, and march in consequence of an order, derived from the authority of the State to which they belong, and for State purposes, then the expenses will be borne by the State.

The advanced corps shall be constituted on such principles, that when completed, it will receive one third part, and discharge one third part of its numbers annually. By this arrangement, two thirds of the corps will at all times be considerably disciplined; but as it will only receive those of eighteen years of age, it will not be completed until the third year afters its institution. Those who have already attained the ages of nineteen and twenty years, will, in the first instance, be enrolled in the main corps. . . .

Of the Main Corps.

As the main and reserved corps are to be replenished by the principle of rotation, from the advanced corps, and ultimately to consist of men, who have received their military education therein, it is proper that one uniform arrangement should pervade the several classes.

It is for this reason the legion is established as the common form of all the corps of the militia.

The main legions, consisting of the great majority of the men of the military age, will form the principal defence of the country.

They are to be responsible for their proportion of men, to form an army whenever necessity shall dictate the measure; and on every sudden occasion to which the advanced corps shall be incompetent, an adequate number of non-commissioned officers and privates shall be added thereto, from the main corps, by means of the sections.

The main corps will be perfectly armed in the first instance, and will practice the exercise and maneuvres, four days in each year, and will assemble in their respective districts, by companies, battalions, regiments, or legions, as shall be directed by the legionary general; but it must be a fixed rule, that in the populous parts of the States, the regiments must assemble once annually, and the legions once in three years.

Although the main corps cannot acquire a great degree of military knowledge in the few days prescribed for its annual exercise, yet by the constant accession of the youth from the advanced corps, it will soon command respect for its discipline, as well as its numbers.

When the youth are transferred from the advanced corps, they shall invariably join the flank companies, the cavalry, or artillery of the main corps, according to the nature of their former services.

The reserved corps will assemble only twice annually, for the inspection of arms, by companies, battalions, or regiments, as shall be directed by each State. It will assemble by legions, whenever the defence of the State may render the measure necessary.

SUCH are the propositions of the plan: To which it may be necessary to add some explanations.

Although the substantial political maxim, which requires personal services of all the members of the community for the defense of the State, is obligatory under all forms of society, and is the main pillar of a free government, yet the degrees thereof may vary at the different periods of life, consistently with the general welfare. The public convenience may also dictate a relaxation of the general obligation as it respects the principal magistrates and the ministers of justice and of religion, and perhaps some religious sects. But it ought to be remembered, that measures of national importance, never should be frustrated by the accommodation of individuals.

The military age has generally commenced at sixteen, and terminated at the age of sixty years; but the youth of sixteen do not commonly attain such a degree of robust strength, as to enable them to sustain without injury, the hardships incident to the field; therefore the commencement of military service, is herein fixed at eighteen, and the termination, as usual, at sixty years of age.

As the plan proposes, that the militia shall be divided into three capital classes, and that each class shall be formed into legions, the reasons for which shall be given in succession.

The advanced corps, and annual camps of discipline, are instituted in order to introduce an operative military spirit in the community. To establish a course of honorable military service, which will at the same time, mould the minds of the young men, to a due obedience of the laws; instruct them in the art of war, and by the manly exercises of the field, form a race of hardy citizens, equal to the dignified task of defending their country.

An examination into the employments and obligations of the individuals composing the society, will evince the impossibility of diffusing an adequate knowledge of the art of war, by any other means than a course of discipline, during the period of nonage. The time necessary to acquire this important knowledge, cannot be afforded at any other period of life, with so little injury to the public or private interests.

Without descending to minute distinctions, the body of the people of the United States, may be divided into two parts. The yeomanry of the country, and the men of various employments, resident in towns and cities. In both parts, it is usual for the male children, from the age of fourteen to twenty-one years, to learn some trade or employment, under the direction of a parent or master. In general, the labour or service of the youth during this period, besides amply repaying the trouble of tuition, leaves a large profit to the tutor. This circumstance is stated to shew, that no great hardships will arise in the first operations of the proposed plan; a little practice will render the measure perfectly equal, and remove every difficulty.

Youth is the time for the State to avail itself of those service which it has a right to demand, and by which it is to be invigorated and preserved; in this season, the passions and affections are stongly influenced by the splendor of military parade. The impressions the mind receives will be retained through life. The young man will repair with pride and pleasure to the field of exercise; while the head of a family, anxious for its general welfare, and perhaps its immediate subsistence, will reluctantly quit his domestic duties for any length of time.

The habits of industry will be rather strengthened than relaxed, by the establishment of the annual camps of discipline, as all the time will be occupied by the various military duties. Idleness and dissipation will be regarded as disgraceful, and punished accordingly. As soon as the youth attain the age of manhood, a natural solicitude to establish themselves in the society, will occur in its full force. The public claims for military service, will be too inconsiderable to injure their industry. It will be sufficiently stimulated to proper exertions, by the prospects of opulence attending on the cultivation of a fertile soil, or the pursuits of a productive commerce.

It is presumed that thirty days annually during the eighteenth and nineteenth, and ten days during the twentieth year, is the least time that ought to be appropriated by the youth to the acquisition of military art. The same number of days might be added during the twentieth as during the two preceding years, were not the expense an objection.

Every means will be provided by the public to facilitate the military education of the youth, which it is proposed shall be an indispensible qualification of a free citizen, therefore they will not be entitled to any pay. But the officers being of the main corps, are in a different predicament; they are supposed to have passed through the course of discipline required by the law, and to be competent to instruct others in the military art. As the public will have but small claims for personal services on them, and as they must incur considerable expenses to prepare themselves, to execute properly their respective offices, they ought to be paid while on actual duty.

As soon as the service of the youth expires in the advanced corps, they are to be enrolled in the main corps. On this occasion, the republic receives disciplined and free citizens, who understand their public rights, and are prepared to defend them.

The main corps is instituted, to preserve and circulate throughout the community, the military discipline, acquired in the advanced corps; to arm the people, and fix firmly, by practice and habit, those forms and maxims, which are essential to the life and energy of a free government.

The reserved corps is instituted to prevent men being sent to the field, whose strength is unequal to sustain the severities of an active campaign. But by organizing and rendering them eligible for domestic service, a greater proportion of the younger and robust part of the community, may be enabled in cases of necessity, to encounter the more urgent duties of war.

It would be difficult, previously to the actual formation of the annual camps of discipline, to ascertain the number in each State, of which it would be composed. The frontier counties of several States are thinly inhabited, and require all their internal force for their immediate defence. There are other infant settlements, from which it might be injurious to draw away their youth annually for the purpose of discipline. . . .

Three hundred and twenty-five thousand therefore may be affirmed, as the number of operative, sensible men, to compose the militia. The proportion of the several classes of which would be nearly as follows—

Firstly—The advanced corps, one tenth composed of the youth of the ages of 18, 19, and 20 years, 32,500.

Secondly—The main corps, six tenths and one twentieth, 211,250.

Thirdly—The reserved corps, two tenths and one twentieth, 31,250. . .

The institution of the section is intended to interest the patriotism and pride of every individual in the militia, to support the legal measures of a free government; to render every man active in the public cause, by introducing the spirit of emulation, and a degree of personal responsibility.

The common mode of recruiting is attended with too great destruction of morals to be tolerated; and is too uncertain to be the principal resource of a wise nation in time of danger. The public faith is frequently wounded by unworthy individuals, who hold out delusive promises, which can never be realized. By such means, an unprincipled banditti are often collected for the purpose of defending every thing that should be dear to freemen. The consequences are natural; such men either desert in time of danger, or are ever ready on the slightest disgust to turn their arms against their country.

By the establishment of the section, an ample and permanent source is opened, whence the state, in every exigence, may be supplied with men, whose all depend upon the prosperity of their country.

In cases of necessity, an army may be formed of citizens, whose previous knowledge of discipline will enable it to proceed to an immediate accomplishment of the designs of the State, instead of exhausting the public resources, by wasting whole years in preparing to face the enemy.

The previous arrangements, necessary to form and maintain the annual encampments, as well as the discipline acquired therein, will be an excellent preparation for war. The artillery and its numerous appendages, arms and accoutrements of every kind, and all species of ammunition, ought to be manufactured within the United States. It is of high importance that the present period should be embraced to establish adequate institutions to produce the necessary apparatus of war.

It is unworthy of the dignity of a rising and free empire, to depend on foreign and fortuitous supplies of the essential means of defense. . . .

The constitutions of the respective States, and of the United States, having directed the modes in which the officers of the militia shall be appointed, no alteration can be made therein. Although it may be supposed that some modes of appointment are better calculated than others to inspire the highest propriety of conduct, yet there are none so defective to serve as a sufficient reason for rejecting an efficient system for the militia. It is certain that the choice of officers, is the point on which the reputation and importance of a corps must depend. Therefore every person who may be concerned in the appointment, should consider himself as responsible to his country for a proper choice. . . .

It is conceded, that people, solicitous to be exonerated from their proportion of public duty, may exclaim against the proposed arrangement as an intolerable hardship: But it ought to be strongly impressed, that while society has its charms, it also has its indispensible obligations. That to attempt such a degree of refinement, as to exonerate the members of the community from all personal service, is to render them incapable of the exercise, and unworthy of the characters of freeman.

Every State possesses, not only the right of personal service from its members, but the right to regulate the service on principles of equality for the general defense. All being bound, none can complain of injustice, on being obliged to perform his equal proportion. Therefore it ought to be a permanent rule, that those who in youth decline, or refuse to subject themselves to the course of military education, established by the laws, should be considered as unworthy of public trust, or public honors, and be excluded therefrom accordingly.

If the majesty of the laws should be preserved inviolate in this respect, the operations of the proposed plan would foster a glorious public spirit; infuse the principles of energy and stability into the body politic; and give an high degree of political splendor to the national character.

An Act for regulating the Military Establishment of the United States, 30 April 1790.

That the commissioned officers hereinafter mentioned, and the number of one thousand two hundred and sixteen non-commissioned officers, privates, and musicians, shall be raised for the service of the United States, for the period of three years, unless they should previously by law be discharged.

SEC. 2. That the non-commissioned officers and privates aforesaid, shall, at the time of their enlistments, respectively, be able-bodied men, not under five feet six inches in height, without shoes; nor under the age of eighteen, nor above the age of forty-six years.

SEC. 3. That the commissioned officers hereinafter mentioned, and the said non-commissioned officers, privates, and musicians, shall be formed into one regiment of infantry, to consist of three battalions, and one battalion of artillery. The regiment of infantry to be composed of one lieutenant-colonel commandant, three majors, three adjutants, three quartermasters, one paymaster, one surgeon, two surgeon's mates, and twelve companies, each of which shall consist of one captain, one lieutenant, one ensign, four sergeants, four corporals, sixty-six privates, and two musicians. The battalion of artillery shall be composed of one major commandant, one adjutant, one quartermaster, one paymaster, one surgeon's mate, and four companies; each of which shall consist of one captain, two lieutenants, four sergeants, four corporals, sixty-six privates, and two musicians: *Provided always,* That the adjutants, quartermasters, and paymasters, shall be appointed from the line, of subalterns of the aforesaid corps, respectively. . . .

SEC. 11. That if any commissioned officer, non-commissioned officer, private, or musician, aforesaid, shall be wounded or disabled, while in the line of his duty in public service, he shall be placed on the list of the invalids of the United States, at such rate of pay and under such regulations as shall be directed by the President of the United States, for the time being: *Provided always,* That the rate of compensation for such wounds or disabilities shall never exceed, for the highest disability, half the monthly pay received by any commissioned officer, at the time of being so wounded or disabled; and that the rate of compensation to non-commissioned officers, privates, and musicians, shall never exceed $5 per month: *And provided also,* That all inferior disabilities shall entitle the person so disabled to receive only a sum in proportion to the highest disability.

SEC. 12. That every commissioned officer, non-commissioned officer, private, and musician, aforesaid, shall take and subscribe the following oath or affirmation, to wit: "I, A. B., do solemnly swear or affirm (as the case may be) to bear true allegiance to the United States of America, and to serve them honestly and faithfully, against all their enemies or opposers whomsoever, and to observe and obey the orders of the President of the United States of America, and the orders of the officers appointed over me, according to the articles of war."

SEC. 13. That the commissioned officers, non-commissioned officers, privates, and musicians, aforesaid, shall be governed by the rules and articles of war, which have been established by the United States in Congress assembled, as far as the same may be applicable to the constitution of the United States, or by such rules and articles as may hereafter by law be established.

SEC. 14. That the "act for recognizing, and adapting to the constitution of the United States, the establishment of the troops raised under the resolves of the United States in Congress assembled, and for other purposes therein mentioned," passed the 29th September, 1789, be, and the same is hereby, repealed: *Provided, always,* That the non-commissioned officers and privates, continued and engaged under the aforesaid act of the 29th September, 1789, and who shall decline to reenlist under the establishment made by this act, shall be discharged whenever the President of the United States shall direct the same: *Provided further,* That the whole number of non-commissioned officers, privates, and musicians, in the service of the United States at any one time, either by virtue of this act, or by virtue of the aforesaid act, passed the 29th September, 1789, shall not exceed the number of one thousand two hundred and sixteen.

SEC. 15. That for the purpose of aiding the troops now in service, or to be raised by this act, in protecting the inhabitants of the frontiers of the United States, the President is hereby authorized to call into service, from time to time, such part of the militia of the states, respectively, as he may judge necessary for the purpose aforesaid; and that their pay and subsistence, while in service, be the same as the pay and subsistence of the troops above mentioned, and they shall be subject to the rules and articles of war.

[Approved, April 30, 1790.*]*

An Act for raising and adding another regiment to the military establishment of the United States, and for making farther provision for the protection of the frontiers, 3 March 1791.

That there shall be raised an additional regiment of infantry, which, exclusive of the commissioned officers, shall consist of nine hundred and twelve non-commissioned officers, privates, and musicians.

SEC. 2. That the said regiment shall be organized in the same manner as the regiment of infantry described in the act, entitled "An act for regulating the military establishment of the United States.". . .

SEC. 5. That in case the President of the United States should deem the employment of major-general, brigadier-general, a quartermaster, and chaplain, or either of them, essential to the public interest, that he be, and he hereby is, empowered, by and with the advice and consent of the Senate, to appoint the same accordingly. And a major-general so appointed, may choose his aid-de-camp, and a brigadier-general his brigade-major, from the captains, or subalterns, of the line: *Provided always,* That the major-general and brigadier-general, so to be appointed, shall, respectively, continue in pay during such term only, as the President of the United States, in his discretion, shall deem it requisite for the public service. . . .

SEC. 7. That if, in the opinion of the President, it shall be conducive to the good of the service, to engage a body of militia to serve as cavalry, they furnishing their own horses, arms, and provisions, it shall be lawful for him to offer such allowances, to encourage their engaging in the service, for such time, and on such terms, as he shall deem it expedient to prescribe.

SEC. 8. That if the President should be of opinion that it will be conducive to the public service, to employ troops enlisted under the denomination of levies, in addition to, or in place of, the militia which, in virtue of the powers vested in him by law, he is authorized to call into the service of the United States, it shall be lawful for him to raise, for a term not exceeding six months, (to be discharged sooner, if the public service will permit,) a corps, not exceeding two thousand non-commissioned officers, privates, and musicians, with a suitable number of commissioned officers. And in case it shall appear probable to the President, that the regiment directed to be raised by the aforesaid act, and by this act, will not be completed in time to prosecute such military operations as exigencies may require, it shall be lawful for the President to make a substitute for the deficiency, by raising such farther number of levies, or by calling into the service of the United States, such a body of militia as shall be equal thereto.

SEC. 9. That the President be, and he hereby is, empowered to organize the said levies, and alone to appoint the commissioned officers thereof, in the manner he may judge proper.

SEC. 10. That the commissioned and non-commissioned officers, privates, and musicians, of the militia, or said corps of levies, shall, during the time of their service, be subject to the rules and articles of war; and they shall be entitled to the same pay, rations, and forage, and in case of wounds or disability in the line of their duty, to the same compensation as the troops of the United States. . . .

[Approved, March 3, 1791.]

An Act for making farther and more effectual provision for the protection of the frontiers of the United States, 5 March 1792.

That the battalion of artillery now in service, be completed according to the establishment, and that the two regiments of infantry now in service, be completed to the number of nine hundred and sixty non-commissioned officers, privates, and musicians, each.

SEC. 2. That there shall be raised, for a term not exceeding three years, three additional regiments, each of which, exclusively of the commissioned officers, shall consist of nine hundred and sixty non-commissioned officers, privates, and musicians; and that one of the said regiments be organized in the following manner, that is to say: two battalions of infantry, each of which, exclusively of the commissioned officers, shall consist of three hundred and twenty non-commissioned officers, privates, and musicians; and one squadron of light dragoons, which, exclusively of the commissioned officers, shall consist of three hundred and twenty non-commissioned officers, privates, and musicians: and that it shall be a condition in the enlistment of the said dragoons, to serve as dismounted dragoons, whenever they shall be ordered thereto: That the organization of the said squadron of light dragoons shall be as follows, to wit: one major, one adjutant, one quartermaster, one surgeon's mate; and four troops, each of which shall consist of one captain, one lieutenant, one cornet, four sergeants, four corporals, one farrier, one saddler, one trumpeter, and sixty-nine dragoons; and the President may arm the said troops, as he shall think proper.

SEC. 3. *Provided always*, That it shall be lawful for the President of the United States to organize the said five regiments of infantry, and the said corps of horse and artillery, as he shall judge expedient, diminishing the number of corps, or taking from one corps and adding to another, as shall appear to him proper, so that the whole number of officers and men shall not exceed the limits above prescribed: *Provided,* That the said three regiments shall be discharged as soon as the United States shall be at peace with the Indian tribes.

SEC. 4. That the non-commissioned officers, privates, and musicians, of the said three regiments, shall be enlisted for the term of three years, unless previously discharged. . . .

SEC. 11. That all the commissioned and non-commissioned officers, privates, and musicians, of the said three regiments, shall take the same oaths, shall be governed by the same rules and regulations, and, in cases of disabilities, shall receive the same compensations as are described in the before-mentioned act, entitled "An act for regulating the military establishment of the United States."

SEC. 12. That it shall be lawful for the President of the United States to forbear to raise, or to discharge after they shall be raised, the whole, or any part, of the said three additional regiments, in case events shall, in his judgment, render his so doing consistent with the public safety.

SEC. 13. That the President be, and he hereby is, authorized, from time to time, to call into service, and for such periods as he may deem requisite, such number of cavalry as, in his judgment, may be necessary for the protection of the frontiers. . . .

SEC. 14. That the President alone be, and he hereby is, authorized to appoint, for the cavalry so to be engaged, the proper commissioned officers, who shall not exceed, in number and rank, the proportions assigned to the said three regiments, and whose pay and other allowances shall not, exclusively of 50 cents per day for the use and risk of their horses, exceed those of officers of corresponding rank in the said regiments.

SEC. 15. That the President of the United States be authorized, in case he shall deem the measure expedient, to employ such number of the Indians, and for such compensations, as he may think proper: *Provided,* The said compensations do not, in the whole, exceed $20,000.

[Approved, March 5, 1792.]

An Act supplemental to the act for making further and more effectual provision for the protection of the frontiers of the United States, 28 March 1792.

That it shall be lawful for the President of the United States, by and with the advice and consent of the Senate, to appoint such number of brigadier-generals as may be conducive to the good of the public service. Provided the whole number appointed, or to be appointed, shall not exceed four.

An Act to provide for calling forth the militia to execute the laws of the Union, to suppress insurrections and repel invasions, 2 May 1792.

SEC. 1. [Same as sec. 1 of chap. 36, February 28, 1795, *post.*]

SEC. 2. That whenever the laws of the United States shall be opposed, or the execution thereof obstructed, in any state, by combinations too powerful to be suppressed by ordinary course of judicial proceedings, or by the powers vested in the marshals by this act, the same being notified to the President of the United States by an associate justice, or the district judge, it shall be lawful for the President of the United States to call forth the militia of such state to suppress such combinations, and to cause the laws to be duly executed. And if the militia of the state, where such combinations may happen, shall refuse or be insufficient to suppress the same, it shall be lawful for the President, if the legislature of the United States be not in session, to call forth and employ such numbers of the militia of any other state or states most convenient thereto, as may be necessary, and the use of the militia, so to be called forth, may be continued, if necessary, until the expiration of thirty days after the commencement of the ensuing session.

SEC. 3. That whenever it may be necessary in the judgment of the President to use the militia force hereby directed to be called forth, the President shall forthwith, and previous thereto, by proclamation, command such insurgents to disperse and retire peaceably to their respective homes, within a limited time.

SEC. 4. That the militia employed in the service of the United States shall receive the same pay and allowances as troops of the United States, who may be in service at the same time, or who were last in service, and shall be subject to the same rules and articles of war: And that no officer, non-commissioned officer, or private of the militia shall be compelled to serve more than three months in any one year, nor more than in due rotation with every other able-bodied man of the same rank in the battalion to which he belongs.

SEC. 5. [Same as 5th sec. of chap. 36, February 28, 1795, except that, besides being cashiered by court-martial, offenders may be, by act of 1795, incapacitated from holding commissions in the militia for twelve months at the discretion of the said court.]

Sections 6, 7, 8, and 9 are same as corresponding section of act of 1795; and section 10 limits the existence of the act for two years, and from thence to the end of the next session of Congress thereafter, and no longer.

[Approved, May 2, 1792.]

An Act more effectually to provide for the national defence, by establishing an uniform militia throughout the United States, 8 May 1792.

That each and every free able-bodied white male citizen of the respective states, resident therein, who is or shall be of the age of eighteen years, and under the age of forty-five years, (except as hereinafter excepted,) shall, severally and respectively, be enrolled in the militia by the captain or commanding officer of the company, within whose bounds such citizen shall reside, and that within twelve months after the passing of this act. And it shall, at all times hereafter, be the duty of every such captain or commanding officer of a company, to enrol every such citizen, as aforesaid, and also those who shall, from time to time, arrive at the age of eighteen years, or being of the age of eighteen years, and under the age of forty-five years, (except as before excepted,) shall come to reside within his bounds; and shall, without delay, notify such citizen of the said enrolment, by a proper non-commissioned officer of the company, by whom such notice may be proved. That every citizen so enrolled and notified, shall, within six months thereafter, provide himself with a good musket, or firelock, a sufficient bayonet and belt, two spare flints, and a knapsack, a pouch, with a box therein to contain not less than twenty-four cartridges, suited to the bore of his musket or firelock, each cartridge to contain a proper quantity of powder and ball; or, with a good rifle, knapsack, shot pouch and powder horn, twenty balls, suited to the bore of his rifle, and a quarter of a pound of powder; and shall appear, so armed, accoutred, and provided, when called out to exercise, or into service; except, that when called out on company days exercise only, he may appear without a knapsack. That the commissioned officers shall, severally, be armed with a sword or hanger, and espontoon; and that, from and after five years from the passing of this act, all muskets for arming the militia, as herein required, shall be of bores sufficient for balls of the eighteenth part of a pound. And every citizen so enrolled, and providing himself with the arms, ammunition, and accoutrements, required as aforesaid, shall hold the same exempted from all suits, distresses, executions, or sales, for debt, or for the payment of taxes.

SEC. 2. That the Vice-President of the United States; the officers, judicial and executive, of the government of the United States; the members of both houses of Congress, and their respective officers; all custom-house officers, with their clerks; all post-officers, and stage-drivers, who are employed in the care and conveyance of the mail of the post-office of the United States; all ferrymen employed at any ferry on the postroad; all inspectors of exports; all pilots; all mariners, actually employed in the sea-service of any citizen or merchant within the United States; and all persons who now are, or may hereafter be, exempted by the laws of the respective States, shall be, and are hereby, exempted from militia duty, notwithstanding their being above the age of eighteen, and under the age of forty-five years.

SEC. 3. That within one year after the passing of this act, the militia of the respective states shall be arranged into divisions, brigades, regiments, battalions, and companies, as the legislature of each state shall direct; and each division, brigade, and regiment, shall be numbered at the formation thereof, and a record made of such numbers in the adjutant-general's office in the state; and when in the field, or in service in the state, each division, brigade, and regiment shall, respectively, take rank according to their numbers, reckoning the first or lowest number highest in rank. That, if the same be convenient, each brigade shall consist of four regiments; each regiment of two battalions; each battalion of five companies; each company of sixty-four privates. That the said militia shall be officered by the respective states, as follows: To each division, one major-general and two aids-de-camp, with the rank of major; to each brigade, one brigadier-general, with one brigade-inspector, to serve also as brigade-major, with the rank of a major; to each regiment, *one lieutenant-colonel commandant;* and to each battalion, one major; to each company, one captain, one lieutenant, one ensign, four sergeants, four corporals, one drummer, and one fifer or bugler. That there shall be a regimental staff, to consist of one adjutant and one quartermaster, to rank as lieutenants; one paymaster; one surgeon, and one surgeon's mate; one sergeant-major; one drum-major, and one fife-major.

SEC. 4. That out of the militia enrolled, as is herein directed, there shall be formed, for each battalion, at least one company of grenadiers, light infantry, or riflemen; and that, to each division, there shall be at least one company of artillery, and one troop of horse: there shall be to each company of artillery, one captain, two lieutenants, four sergeants, four corporals, six gunners, six bombardiers, one drummer, and one fifer. The officers to be armed with a sword, or hanger, a fusee, bayonet and belt, with a cartridge box, to contain twelve cartridges; and each private, or matross, shall furnish himself with all the equipments of a private in the infantry, until proper ordnance and field artillery is provided. There shall be, to each troop of horse, one captain, two lieutenants, one cornet, four sergeants, four corporals, one saddler, one farrier, and one trumpeter. The commissioned officers to furnish themselves with good horses, of at least fourteen hands and a half high, and to be armed with a sword, and pair of pistols, the holsters of which to be covered with bearskin caps. Each dragoon to furnish himself with a serviceable horse, at least fourteen hands and a half high, a good saddle, bridle, mail pillion, and valise, holsters, and a breastplate and crupper, a pair of boots and spurs, a pair of pistols, a sabre and a cartouch box, to contain twelve cartridges for pistols. That each company of artillery and troop of horse shall be formed of volunteers from the brigade, at the discretion of the commander-in-chief of the state, not exceeding one company of each to a regiment, nor more in number than one-eleventh part of the infantry, and shall be uniformly clothed in regimentals, to be furnished at their own expense; the color and fashion to be determined by the brigadier commanding the brigade to which they belong.

SEC. 5. That each battalion and regiment shall be provided with the state and regimental colors, by the field officers, and each company with a drum, and fife or bugle horn, by the commissioned officers of the company, in such manner as the legislature of the respective states shall direct.

SEC. 6. That there shall be an adjutant-general appointed in each state, whose duty it shall be to distribute all orders from the commander-in-chief of the state to the several corps; to attend all public reviews, when the commander-in-chief of the state shall review the militia, or any part thereof; to obey all orders from him, relative to carrying into execution and perfecting the system of military discipline established by this act; to furnish blank forms of different returns, that may be required, and to explain the principles on which they should be made; to receive from the several officers of the different corps, throughout the state, returns of the militia under their command, reporting the actual situation of their arms, accoutrements, and ammunition, their delinquencies, and every other thing which relates to the general advancement of good order and discipline: All which, the several officers of the divisions, brigades, regiments, and battalions are hereby required to make, in the usual manner, so that the said adjutant-general may be furnished therewith: from which all returns he shall make proper abstracts, and lay the same annually before the commander-in-chief of the state.

SEC. 7. That the rules of discipline, approved and established by Congress, in their resolution of the 29th of March, 1779, shall be the rules of discipline to be observed by the militia throughout the United States; except such deviations from the said rules as may be rendered necessary by the requisitions of this act, or by some other unavoidable circumstances. It shall be the duty of the commanding officer, at every muster, whether by battalion, regiment, or single company, to cause the militia to be exercised and trained agreeably to the said rules of discipline.

SEC. 8. That all commissioned officers shall take rank according to the date of their commissions; and when two of the same grade bear an equal date, then their rank to be determined by lot, to be drawn, by them, before the commanding officer of the brigade, regiment, battalion, company, or detachment.

SEC. 9. That if any person, whether officer or soldier, belonging to the militia of any state, and called out into the service of the United States, be wounded or disabled while in actual service, he shall be taken care of and provided for at the public expense.

SEC. 10. That it shall be the duty of the brigade-inspector, to attend the regimental and battalion meetings of the militia composing their several brigades, during the time of their being under arms, to inspect their arms, ammunition, and accoutrements; superintend their exercise and manoeuvres, and introduce the system of military discipline, before described, throughout the brigade, agreeable to law, and such orders as they shall, from time to time, receive from the commander-in-chief of the state; to make returns to the adjutant-general of the state, at least once in every year, of the militia of the brigade to which be belongs, reporting therein the actual situation of the arms, accoutrements, and ammunition, of the several corps, and every other thing which, in his judgment, may relate to their government and the general advancement of good order and military discipline; and the adjutant-general shall make a return of all the militia of the state, to the commander-in-chief of the said state, and a duplicate of the same to the President of the United States.

And whereas sundry corps of artillery, cavalry, and infantry, now exist in several of the said states, which, by the laws, customs, or usages thereof, have not been incorporated with, or subject to, the general regulations of the militia:

SEC. 11. That such corps retain their accustomed privileges, subject, nevertheless, to all other duties required by this act in like manner with the other militia.
[Approved, May 8, 1792.]

An Act for raising and organizing a Corps of Artillerists and Engineers, 9 May 1794.

That the number of seven hundred and sixty-four non-commissioned officers, privates, and artificers, to serve as privates, and musicians, shall be engaged for the term of three years, by voluntary enlistments; and that the proper proportion of commissioned officers shall be appointed to command the same.

SEC. 2. That the aforesaid commissioned and non-commissioned officers, privates, artificers, and musicians, shall be incorporated with the corps of artillery now in the service of the United States, and denominated the corps of artillerists and engineers; and that the entire number of the said corps, exclusively of the commissioned officers, shall be nine hundred and ninety-two.

SEC. 3. That the organization of the said corps be as herein mentioned, to wit: one lieutenant-colonel commandant, one adjutant, one surgeon; four battalions, each to consist of one major, one adjutant and paymaster, and one surgeon's mate; and four companies, each to consist of one captain, two lieutenants, two cadets, with the pay, clothing, and rations of a sergeant, four sergeants, four corporals, forty-two privates, sappers, and miners, and ten artificers to serve as privates, and two musicians.

SEC. 4. That the additional commissioned officers, non-commissioned officers, privates, artificers, and musicians, by this act directed to be raised, shall receive the same pay and allowances, in all respects, as the troops already in the service of the United States; and they shall also be governed by the same rules and articles of war, which have been, or may be, by law established.

SEC. 5. That it shall be the duty of the secretary of war to provide, at the public expense, under such regulations as shall be directed by the President of the United States, the necessary books, instruments, and apparatus, for the use and benefit of the said corps.

SEC. 6. That the President of the United States shall cause such proportions of the said corps to serve in the field, on the frontiers, or in the fortifications on the seacoast, as he shall deem consistent with the public service.

An Act to provide for calling forth the militia to execute the laws of the Union, suppress insurrections, and repel invasions; and to repeal the act now in force for those purposes, 28 February 1795.

That whenever the United States shall be invaded, or be in imminent danger of invasion, from any foreign nation or Indian tribe, it shall be lawful for the President of the United States to call forth such number of the militia of the state or states, most convenient to the place of danger, or scene of action, as he may judge necessary to repel such invasion, and to issue his orders, for that purpose, to such officer or officers of the militia as he shall think proper. And in case of an insurrection in any state, against the government thereof, it shall be lawful for the President of the United States, on application of the legislature of such state, or of the Executive, (when the legislature cannot be convened,) to call forth such number of the militia of any other state or states, as may be applied for, as he may judge sufficient to suppress such insurrection.

SEC. 2. That whenever the laws of the United States shall be opposed, or the execution thereof obstructed, in any state, by combinations too powerful to be suppressed by the ordinary course of judicial proceedings, or by the powers vested in the marshals by this act, it shall be lawful for the President of the United States to call forth the militia of such state, or of any other state or states, as may be necessary to suppress such combinations, and to cause the laws to be duly executed; and the use of militia so to be called forth may be continued, if necessary, until the expiration of thirty days after the commencement of the then next session of Congress.

SEC. 3. That whenever it may be necessary, in the judgment of the President, to use the military force hereby directed to be called forth, the President shall forthwith, by proclamation, command such insurgents to disperse, and retire peaceably to their respective abode, within a limited time.

SEC. 4. That the militia employed in the service of the United States shall be subject to the same rules and articles of war as the troops of the United States: and that no officer, non-commissioned officer, or private, of the militia, shall be compelled to serve more than three months after his arrival at the place of rendezvous, in any one year, nor more than in due rotation with every other able-bodied man of the same rank in the battalion to which he belongs.

SEC. 5. That every officer, non-commissioned officer, or private, of the militia, who shall fail to obey the orders of the President of the United States, in any of the cases before recited, shall forfeit a sum not exceeding one year's pay, and not less than one month's pay, to be determined and adjudged by a court-martial; and such officer shall, moreover, be liable to be cashiered by sentence of a court-martial, and be incapacitated from holding a commission in the militia, for a term not exceeding twelve months, at the discretion of the said court: and such non-commissioned officers and privates shall be liable to be imprisoned, by a like sentence, on failure of the payment of fines adjudged against them, for one calendar month, for every five dollars of such fine.

SEC. 6. That courts-martial for the trial of militia, shall be composed of militia officers only.

SEC. 7. That all fines to be assessed, as aforesaid, shall be certified by the presiding officer of the court-martial before whom the same shall be assessed, to the marshal of the district in which the delinquent shall reside, or to one of his deputies and also to the supervisor of the revenue of the same district, who shall record the said certificate in a book to be kept for that purpose. The said marshal, or his deputy, shall forthwith proceed to levy the said fines, with costs, by distress and sale of the goods and chattels of the delinquent; which costs, and the manner of proceeding, with respect to the sale of the goods distrained, shall be agreeable to the laws of the state in which the same shall be, in other cases of distress. And where any non-commissioned officer or private shall be adjudged to suffer imprisonment, there being no goods or chattels to be found whereof to levy the said fines, the marshal of the district, or his deputy, may commit such delinquent to jail, during the term for which he shall be so adjudged to imprisonment, or until the fine shall be paid, in the same manner as other persons condemned to fine and imprisonment at the suit of the United States may be committed.

SEC. 8. That the marshals and their deputies shall pay all such fines by them levied, to the supervisor of the revenue in the district in which they are collected, within two months after they shall have received the same, deducting therefrom five per centum as a compensation for their trouble; and in case of failure, the same shall be recoverable by action of debt or information, in any court of the United States, of the district in which such fines shall be levied, having cognizance thereof, to be sued for, prosecuted, and recovered, in the name of the supervisor of the district, with interest and costs.

SEC. 9. That the marshals of the several districts, and their deputies, shall have the same powers, in executing the laws of the United States, as sheriffs, and their deputies, in the several states, have by law in executing the laws of the respective states.

SEC. 10. That the act entitled "An act to provide for calling forth the militia to execute the laws of the Union, suppress insurrections, and repel invasions," passed the 2d day of May, 1792, shall be, and the same is hereby, repealed.

[*Approved, February* 28, 1795.]

An Act to ascertain and fix the military establishment of the United States, 30 May 1796.

That the military establishment of the United States, from and after the last day of October next, be composed of the corps of artillerists and engineers, as established by the act entitled "An act providing for raising and organizing a corps of artillerists and engineers;" two companies of light dragoons, who shall do duty on horse or foot, at the discretion of the President of the United States; and four regiments of infantry, of eight companies each; the company of dragoons shall consist of one captain, two lieutenants, one cornet, four sergeants, four corporals, one farrier, one saddler, one trumpeter, and fifty-two privates; and shall be armed and accoutred in such manner as the President of the United States may direct.

SEC. 2. That each regiment of infantry shall consist of one lieutenant-colonel commandant, two majors, one adjutant, one paymaster, one quartermaster, one surgeon, two surgeon's mates, eight captains, eight lieutenants, eight ensigns, two sergeant-majors, two quartermaster sergeants, two senior musicians, thirty-two sergeants, thirty-two corporals, sixteen musicians, and four hundred and sixteen privates: *Provided always,* That the President of the United States may, in his discretion, appoint an additional number of surgeon's mates, not exceeding ten, and distribute the same, according to the necessity of the service.

SEC. 3. That there shall be one major-general, with two aids-de-camps; one brigadier-general, who may choose his brigade-major from the captains or subalterns of the line . . . one quartermaster-general; one inspector, who shall do the duty of adjutant-general; and one paymaster-general: and that the adjutants, quartermasters, and paymasters of regiments, shall be appointed from the subalterns of their respective regiments.

SEC. 4. That the President of the United States cause to be arranged, the officers, non-commissioned officers, privates, and musicians, of the legion of the United States, and light dragoons, in such manner as to form and complete out of the same the four regiments aforesaid, and two companies of light dragoons: And the supernumerary officers, privates, and musicians, shall be considered, from and after the last day of October next, discharged from the service of the United States.

SEC. 5. That the corps of artillerists and engineers be completed, conformably to the act of the 8th day of May, 1794, establishing the same, and prescribing the number and term of enlistments, and the method of organization. . . .

SEC. 15. That every person who shall procure or entice a soldier, in the service of the United States, to desert, or who shall purchase from any soldier, his arms, uniform clothing, or any part thereof; and every captain or commanding officer of any ship or vessel, who shall enter on board such ship or vessel, as one of his crew, knowing him to have deserted, or otherwise carry away any such soldier, or shall refuse to deliver him up to the orders of his commanding officer, shall, upon legal conviction, be fined, at the discretion of the court, in any sum not exceeding $300, or be imprisoned, for any term not exceeding one year.

SEC. 16. That no non-commissioned officer, or private, shall be arrested, or subject to arrest, for any debt under the sum of $20.

SEC. 17. That if any non-commissioned officer, musicians, or private, shall desert from the service of the United States, he shall, in addition to the penalties mentioned in the Rules and Articles of War, be liable to serve for and during such a period as shall, with the time he may have served previous to his desertion, amount to the full term of his enlistment, and such soldier shall and may be tried and sentenced by a regimental or garrison court-martial, although the term of his enlistment may have elapsed previous to his being apprehended or tried.

SEC. 18. That the sentences of general courts-martial, in time of peace, extending to the loss of life, the dismission of a commissioned officer; or which shall, either in time of peace or war, respect a general officer, shall, with the whole of the proceedings in such cases, respectively, be laid before the President of the United States; who is hereby authorized to direct the same to be carried into execution, or otherwise, as he shall judge proper.

SEC. 19. That if any officer, non-commissioned officer, private, or musician, aforesaid, shall be wounded or disabled, while in the line of his duty, in public service, he shall be placed on the list of the invalids of the United States, at such rate of pay, and under such regulations, as shall be directed by the President of the United States, for the time being; *Provided always,* That the rate of compensation to be allowed for such wounds or disabilities, to a commissioned officer, shall never exceed, for the highest disability, half the monthly pay of such officer, at the time of his being so disabled or wounded; and that the rate of compensation to non-commissioned officers, privates, and musician, shall never exceed $5 per month: *And provided also,* That all inferior disabilities shall entitle the person so disabled, to receive an allowance proportionate to the highest disability.

SEC. 20. That the officers, non-commissioned officers, privates, and musicians, aforesaid, shall be governed by the rules and articles of war which have been established by the United States, in Congress assembled, (except so much of the same as is by this act altered or amended,) as far as the same may be applicable to the constitution of the United States; or by such rules and articles as may hereafter be by law established.

SEC. 21. That every officer, non-commissioned officer, private, and musician, aforesaid, shall take and subscribe the following oath or affirmation, to wit: "I, A. B., do solemnly swear, or affirm, (as the case may be,) to bear true allegiance to the United States of America, and to serve them honestly and faithfully, against their enemies or opposers whomsoever, and to observe and obey the orders of the President of the United States, and the orders of the officers appointed over him, according to the rules and articles of war."

SEC. 22. That so much of any act or acts, now in force, as comes within the purview of this act, shall be, and the same is hereby, repealed: saving, nevertheless, such parts thereof as relate to the enlistments or term of service of any of the troops, which, by this act, are continued on the present military establishment of the United States.

SEC. 23. That the general staff, as authorized by this act, shall continue in service until the 4th day of next March, and no longer.

[*Approved, May* 30, 1796.]

An Act authorizing the President of the United States to raise a provisional army, 28 May 1798.

That the President of the United States be, and he is hereby, authorized, in the event of a declaration of war against the United States, or of actual invasion of their territory, by a foreign power; or of imminent danger of such invasion discovered, in his opinion, to exist, before the next session of Congress, to cause to be enlisted, and to call into actual service, a number of troops, not exceeding ten thousand non-commissioned officers, musicians, and privates, to be enlisted for a term not exceeding three years; each of whom shall be entitled to receive a bounty of $10, one half on enlisting, and the other half on joining the corps to which he may belong.

SEC. 2. That the President be, and he is hereby, authorized to organize, with a suitable number of major-generals, and conformably to the military establishment of the United States, the said troops into corps of artillery, cavalry, and infantry, as the exigencies of the service may require; and, in the recess of the Senate, alone, to appoint the commissioned officers. The appointment of the field officers to be submitted to the advice and consent of the Senate at their next subsequent meeting. The commissioned and non-commissioned officers, musicians, and privates, raised in pursuance of this act, shall be subject to the rules and articles of war, and regulations for the government of the army, and be entitled to the same pay, clothing, rations, forage, and all other emoluments, bounty excepted, and in case of wounds or disability, received in service, to the same compensation, as the troops of the United States are by law entitled.

SEC. 3. That, in addition to the aforesaid number of troops, the President is hereby empowered, at any time within three years after the passing of this act, if, in his opinion, the public interest shall require, to accept of any company or companies of volunteers, either of artillery, cavalry, or infantry, who may associate and offer themselves for the service, who shall be armed, clothed, and equipped at their own expense, and whose commissioned officers the President is hereby authorized to appoint; who shall be liable to be called upon to do military duty, at any time the President shall judge proper, within two years after he shall accept the same; and when called into actual service, and while remaining in the same, shall be under the same rules and regulations, and shall be entitled to the same pay, rations, forage, and emoluments of every kind, excepting bounty and clothing, as the other troops to be raised by this act.

SEC. 4. That in case any such volunteer, while in actual service, and in the line of his duty, sustains any damage, by injury done to his horse, arms, or equipage, or by loss of the same, without any fault or negligence on his part, a reasonable sum, to be ascertained in such manner as the President shall direct, shall be allowed for each and every such damage or loss.

SEC. 5. That whenever the President shall deem it expedient, he is hereby empowered to appoint, by and with the advice and consent of the Senate, a commander of the army which may be raised by virtue of this act, and who, being commissioned as lieutenant-general, may be authorized to command the armies of the United States . . . who shall have authority to appoint from time to time, such number of aids, not exceeding four, and secretaries, not exceeding two, as he may judge proper, each to have the rank, pay, and emoluments of a lieutenant-colonel.

SEC. 6. That, whenever the President shall deem it expedient, he is hereby empowered, by and with the advice and consent of the Senate, to appoint an inspector-general, with the rank of major-general; . . . And at the time aforesaid, the President is further empowered, by and with the advice and consent of the Senate, to appoint an adjutant-general, who shall have the rank, pay, and emoluments of a brigadier-general. And the President is hereby authorized, alone, to appoint, from time to time, when he shall judge proper, assistant inspectors, to every separate portion of the army, consisting of one or more divisions, who shall be deputy adjutant-generals thereof, respectively, and who shall be taken from the line of the army, . . . and, likewise, to appoint inspectors and sub-inspectors to each brigade and corps, of every description, at his discretion, taking them from the line of the army, . . .

SEC. 7. That in case the President shall judge the employment of a quartermaster-general, physician-general, and paymaster-general, or either of them, essential to the public interest, he is hereby authorized, by and with the advice and consent of the Senate, to appoint the same accordingly, who shall be entitled to the rank, pay, and emoluments which follow, viz.: quartermaster-general, the rank, pay, and emoluments of a lieutenant-colonel; physician-general, and paymaster-general, each, the pay and emoluments of a lieutenant-colonel; *Provided,* That in case the President shall judge it expedient to appoint a commander of the army, an inspector-general, adjutant-general, quartermaster-general, physician-general, and paymaster-general, or either of them, in the recess of the Senate, he is hereby authorized to make any or all of said appointments, and grant commissions thereon, which shall expire at the end of the next session of the Senate thereafter. . . .

SEC. 9. That the commander of the army, inspector-general, adjutant-general, quartermaster-general, physician-general, and paymaster-general, and the general, field, and commissioned officers, who may be appointed by virtue of this act, shall, respectively, continue in commission during such term only as the President shall judge requisite for the public service; and that it shall be lawful for the President to discharge the whole, or any part, of the troops, which may be raised, or accepted, under the authority of this act, whenever he shall judge the measure consistent with the public safety.

SEC. 10. That no commissioned or staff officer, who shall be appointed by virtue of this act, shall be entitled to receive pay or emoluments until he shall be called in actual service, nor for any longer time than he shall continue therein: *Provided,* nothing in this section shall be construed to prevent captains and subalterns from receiving pay and emoluments while employed in the recruiting service: *And provided also,* That no enlistment shall take place by virtue of this act, after three years from the passing thereof.

SEC. 11. That it shall be lawful for the President of the United States, at his discretion, upon the request of any militia corps, established by law, in any state, disposed to inform themselves in the use of artillery, or of the executive of any state, in behalf of such corps, to suffer to be loaned to them such pieces, not exceeding two to any one corps, of the field artillery of the United States, as may be most convenient spared, to be taken, removed, and returned, at the expense of the party requesting; who are to be accountable for the same, and to give receipts accordingly.

SEC. 12. That the President of the United States shall be, and he is hereby, authorized, when, under his orders, any portion of the militia, or any volunteer corps, shall be called forth and engaged in the actual service of the United States, to suffer to be loaned, at the request of the executive of the state from which such militia shall be called forth, or of such volunteer corps, appearing to be unavoidably deficient, a supply of field artillery, arms, and accoutrements, from the arsenals of the United States, as the case may require; proper receipts and security being given to be accountable to return the same, the accidents of the service excepted. . . .

SEC. 14. That the private soldiers who are, and who shall be enlisted and employed in the service of the United States, shall be, and they are hereby, exempted, during their term of service, from all personal arrests, for any debt or contract. And whenever any soldier shall be arrested, whether by mesne process, or in execution, contrary to the intent hereof, it shall be the duty of the judge of the district court of the district in which the arrest shall happen, and of any justice of the supreme court of the United States, and of any court or judge of a state, who, by the laws of such state, are authorized to

issue writs of habeas corpus, respectively, on application, by any officer of the corps in which such soldier shall be engaged, to grant a writ of habeas corpus, returnable before himself; and, upon due hearing and examination, in a summary manner, to discharge the soldier from such arrest, taking common bail, if required, in any case upon mesne process, and commit him to the applicant, or some other officer of the same corps.
[Approved, May 28, 1798.]

An Act supplementary to, and to amend, the Act entitled "An Act authorizing the President of the United States to raise a provisional army," 22 June 1798.

That the companies of volunteers, and the members of each company, who shall be duly engaged and accepted by the President of the United States, and organized with proper officers commissioned by him, pursuant to the third section of the act, entitled "An act authorizing the President of the United States to raise a provisional army," shall submit to and observe such rules of training and discipline, as shall be thought necessary to prepare them for actual service; and which rules the President of the United States is hereby authorized to make and establish; and all such companies and volunteers are hereby exempted, until their discharge, or during the time of their engagement, as aforesaid, from all militia duty which is or shall be required by the laws of the United States, or of any state, and from every fine, penalty, or disability, which is or shall be provided to enforce the performance of any duty or service in the militia.

SEC. 2. That the President of the United States shall be, and he is hereby, authorized, by and with the consent of the Senate, or by himself, in the recess of Congress, pursuant to the said act, to appoint and commission, as soon as he shall think it expedient, such and so many field officers as shall be necessary for the organizing and embodying in legions, regiments, or battalions, any volunteer companies who shall engage, and shall be accepted, as aforesaid; and such field officers shall have authority, accordingly, to train and discipline such volunteer companies, pursuant to the rules therefor, which shall be established, as aforesaid: *Provided,* That no officer or volunteer, who shall be appointed, engaged, or employed in any training or discipline, as aforesaid, shall be considered as in the pay of the United States, until called into actual service. . . .

SEC. 4. That the President of the United States may proceed to appoint and commission, in the manner prescribed by the said act, such and so many of the officers authorized thereby, for the raising, organizing, and commanding, the provisional army of ten thousand men, as, in his opinion, the public service shall more immediately require; any thing which may be supposed in the said act, to the contrary hereof notwithstanding: *Provided,* That the officers who shall be so appointed, shall not be entitled to any pay, subsistence, or other emolument, by reason of such commission, until they shall be, respectively, employed in the actual service of the United States: *And provided,* That the further raising of the said army shall not be authorized otherwise than as by the said act is provided.
[Approved, June 22, 1798.]

An Act to augment the army of the United States, and for other purposes, 16 July 1798.

That from and after the passage of this act, each regiment of infantry in the army of the United States, shall consist of one lieutenant-colonel commandant, two majors, one adjutant, one paymaster, one quartermaster, one surgeon, two surgeon's mates, ten captains, ten lieutenants, ten ensigns, one sergeant-major, one quartermaster-sergeant, two senior musicians, forty sergeants, forty corporals, twenty musicians, and six hundred privates; and that the several regiments of infantry now in the service of the United States, be augmented accordingly: *Provided always,* That the President of the United States may, in his discretion, appoint and distribute such additional number of surgeon's mates, and for such length of time, as the exigencies of the service may require.

SEC. 2. That the President of the United States be, and he hereby is, authorized to raise, in addition to the present military establishment, twelve regiments of infantry, and six troops of light dragoons, to be enlisted for and during the continuance of the existing differences between the United States and the French Republic, unless sooner discharged; and the said six troops, together with the two troops of dragoons now in service, shall be formed into a regiment, and there shall be appointed thereto one lieutenant-colonel commandant, two majors, one adjutant, one paymaster, one quartermaster, one sergeant-major, and one quartermaster-sergeant, whose pay and emoluments, as well as those of the cornets, respectively, shall be the same as are by law allowed to officers of the same grades in the infantry.

SEC. 3. That there shall be two major-generals, with two aids-de-camp each; one inspector-general, with the rank, pay, and emoluments of a major-general, and two aids-de-camp; three brigadier-generals, in addition to the present establishment; two assistant inspectors, (who shall be taken from the line of the army,) one adjutant-general, with one or more assistant or assistants, (to be taken from the line of the army,) and four chaplains. . . .

SEC. 7. That the President of the United States be, and he hereby is authorized to appoint a number, not exceeding four, teachers of the arts and sciences, necessary for the instruction of the artillerists and engineers, . . .

SEC. 8. That the officers, non-commissioned officers, musicians, and privates, raised by virtue of this act, shall take and subscribe the oath or affirmation prescribed by the law, entitled "An act to ascertain and fix the military establishment of the United States," and that they shall be governed by the rules and articles of war which have been, or may be, established by law, and shall be entitled to the legal emoluments in case of wounds or disabilities, received while in actual service, and in the line of duty. And in recess of Senate, the President of the United States is hereby authorized to appoint all the regimental officers proper to be appointed under this act, and likewise to make appointments to fill any vacancies in the army, which may have happened during the present session of the Senate.

SEC. 9. That there shall be appointed an inspector of the artillery, taken from the line of artillerists and engineers, . . .

[Approved, July 16, 1798.]

An Act giving eventual authority to the President of the United States to augment the army, 2 March 1799.

That it shall be lawful for the President of the United States, in case war shall break out between the United States and a foreign European power, or in case imminent danger of invasion of their territory by any such power, shall, in his opinion, be discovered to exist, to organize and cause to be raised, in addition to the other military force of the United States, twenty-four regiments of infantry, a regiment and a battalion of riflemen, a battalion of artillerists and engineers, and three regiments of cavalry, or such part thereof as he shall judge necessary; the non-commissioned officers and privates of which to be enlisted for a term not exceeding three years, and to be entitled each to a bounty of $10; one-half to be paid at the time of enlistment, and the remainder at the time of joining the regiment to which they may belong.

SEC. 2. That the President of the United States be authorized, whenever it shall appear to him expedient, if during the session of the Senate, with their advice and consent, if in their recess, alone, to appoint and commission all officers for the said troops, agreeably to the rules and regulations prescribed by law for the military establishment: *Provided,* That the general and field officers who may be appointed in the recess of the Senate, shall, at the next meeting thereof, be nominated and submitted to them for their advice and consent.

SEC. 3. That the officers, non-commissioned officers, and privates, of the troops, which may be organized and raised pursuant to this act, shall be entitled to the like pay, clothing, rations, forage, and other emoluments, and to the like compensation in case of disability by wounds, or otherwise, incurred in the service, as the officers, non-commissioned officers, and privates of other troops of correspondent denominations, composing the army of the United States; and, with them, shall be subject to the rules and articles of war, and to all other regulations for the discipline and government of the army. *Provided,* That no officer, except captains and subalterns who may be employed in the recruiting service, shall be entitled to any pay or other emolument until he shall be called into actual service.

SEC. 4. That the laws of the United States respecting the regulations and emoluments of recruiting officers, punishment of persons who shall procure or entice a soldier to desert, or shall purchase his arms, uniform, clothing, or any part thereof, and the punishment of every commanding officer of every ship or vessel, who shall receive on board his ship or vessel, as one of his crew, knowing him to have deserted, or otherwise carry away any soldier, or refuse to deliver him up to the orders of his commanding officer; and the law respecting the oath or affirmation to be taken by officers, non-commissioned officers, musicians, and privates; and respecting the inserting of conditions in the enlistments; and all other laws respecting the military establishment of the United States, excepting in such cases where different and specific regulations are made by this act, shall be in force, and apply to all persons, matters, and things, within the intent and meaning of this act, in the same manner as they would were they inserted at large in the same.

SEC. 5. That it shall be lawful for the President of the United States, at his discretion, to discharge the whole, or any part of the troops which may be raised by virtue of this act, whensoever he shall think fit.

SEC. 6. That the President of the United States be authorized to organize all such companies of volunteers, as have been, or shall be, accepted by him pursuant to the act entitled "An act authorizing the President of the United States to raise a provisional army," into regiments, brigades, and divisions, and to appoint all officers thereof, agreeably to the organization prescribed by law for the army of the United States: and the said volunteers shall not be compelled to serve out of the state in which they reside, a longer time than three months after their arrival at the place of rendezvous.

SEC. 7. That it shall not be lawful for the President of the United States to call forth and employ the said volunteers in all the cases, and to effect all the purposes, for which he is authorized to call forth and employ the militia, by the act entitled "An act to provide for calling forth the militia to execute the laws of the Union, suppress insurrections, and repel invasions, and to repeal the act now in force for these purposes."

SEC. 8. That it shall not be lawful for the President of the United States to accept a greater number of the said volunteers, in any of the states or territories of the United States, than is hereinafter apportioned to them, respectively; that is to say: To New Hampshire, three thousand; to Massachusetts, ten thousand; to Rhode Island, one thousand; to Vermont, two thousand; to Connecticut, five thousand; to New York, seven thousand; to New Jersey, five thousand; to Pennsylvania, ten thousand; to Delaware, one thousand; to Maryland, five thousand; to Virginia, ten thousand; to Kentucky, one thousand; to North Carolina, seven thousand; to Tennessee, one thousand; to South Carolina, four thousand; to Georgia, fifteen hundred; to North-Western Territory, one thousand; and to Mississippi Territory, five hundred. . . .

SEC. 11. That the powers, by the first and second sections of this act vested in the President of the United States, shall cease at the expiration of the session of Congress next ensuing the present, unless they shall be, by some future law, continued in force for a longer time. *[Approved, March* 2, 1799.]

An Act to suspend, in part, an Act, entitled "An Act to augment the army of the United States, and for other purposes," 20 February 1800.

That all further enlistments under the second section of an act, entitled "An act to augment the army of the United States, and for other purposes," shall be suspended until the further order of Congress, unless, in the recess of Congress, and during the continuance of the existing differences between the United States and the French Republic, war shall break out between the United States and the French Republic, or imminent danger of invasion of their territory, by the said republic, shall, in the opinion of the President of the United States, be discovered to exist.

An Act supplementary to the Act to suspend part of an Act, entitled "An Act to augment the army of the United States, and for other purposes," 14 May 1800.

That it shall be lawful for the President of the United States to suspend any further military appointments under the act to augment the army of the United States, and for other purposes, and under the ninth section of the act for the better organization of the troops of the United States, and for other purposes, according to his discretion, having reference to economy and the good of the service.

SEC. 2. That the President of the United States shall be, and hereby is, authorized and empowered to discharge, on or before the 15th day of June next, all such officers, non-commissioned officers, and privates, as have heretofore been appointed, commissioned, or raised, under and by virtue of the said acts, or either of them, except the engineers, inspector of artillery, and inspector of fortifications: *Provided always,* That nothing in this act contained shall be construed to authorize any reduction of the first four regiments of infantry, the two regiments of artillerists and engineers, the two troops of light dragoons, or of the general and other staff, authorized by the several laws for the establishing and organizing of the aforesaid corps. . . .

An Act fixing the Military Peace Establishment of the United States, 16 March 1802.

That the military peace establishment of the United States, from and after the 1st of June next, shall be composed of one regiment of artillerists, and two regiments of infantry, with such officers, military agents, and engineers, as are hereinafter mentioned.

SEC. 2. That the regiment of artillerists shall consist of one colonel, one lieutenant-colonel, four majors, one adjutant, and twenty companies, each company to consist of one captain, one first lieutenant, one second lieutenant, two cadets, four sergeants, four corporals, four musicians, eight artificers, and fifty-six privates: to be formed into five battalions: *Provided always,* That it shall be lawful for the President of the United States to retain, with their present grade, as many of the first lieutenants, now in service, as shall amount to the whole number of lieutenants required; but that, in proportion as vacancies happen therein, new appointments be made to the grade of second lieutenants, until their number amount to twenty; and each regiment of infantry shall consist of one colonel, one lieutenant-colonel, one major, one adjutant, one sergeant-major, two teachers of music, and ten companies; each company to consist of one captain, one first and one second lieutenant, one ensign, four sergeants, four corporals, four musicians, and sixty-four privates.

SEC. 3. That there shall be one brigadier-general, with one aid-de-camp, who shall be taken from the captains or subalterns of the line; one adjutant and inspector of the army, to be taken from the line of field officers; one paymaster of the army, seven paymasters, and two assistants, to be attached to such districts as the President of the United States shall direct, to be taken from the line of commissioned officers, who, in addition to their other duties, shall have charge of the clothing of the troops; three military agents, and such number of assistant military agents, as the President of the United States shall deem expedient, not exceeding one to each military post; which assistants shall be taken from the line; two surgeons, twenty-five surgeon's mates, to be attached to the garrisons or posts, and not to corps. . . .

SEC. 9. That the President of the United States cause to be arranged the officers, non-commissioned officers, musicians, and privates of the several corps of troops now in the service of the United States, in such manner as to form and complete, out of the same, the corps aforesaid: and cause the supernumerary officers, non-commissioned officers, musicians, and privates, to be discharged from the service of the United States, from and after the 1st day of April next, or as soon thereafter as circumstances may permit.

SEC. 10. That the officers, non-commissioned officers, musicians, and privates, of the said corps, shall be governed by the rules and articles of war, which have been established by the United States in Congress assembled, or by such rules and articles as may be hereafter by law established: *Provided, nevertheless,* That the sentence of general courts-martial, extending to the loss of life, the dismission of a commissioned officer, or which shall respect the general officer, shall, with the whole of the proceedings of such cases, respectively, be laid before the President of the United States, who is hereby authorized to direct the same to be carried into execution, or otherwise, as he shall judge proper.

SEC. 11. That the commissioned officers who shall be employed in the recruiting service, to keep up, by voluntary enlistments, the corps as aforesaid, shall be entitled to receive, for every effective, able-bodied citizen of the United States, who shall be duly enlisted by him, for the term of five years, and mustered, of at least five feet six inches high, and between the ages of eighteen and thirty-five years, the sum of $2: *Provided, nevertheless,* That this regulation, so far as respects the height and age of the recruit, shall not extend to musicians, or to those soldiers who may re-enlist into the service: *And provided, also,* That no person under the age of twenty-one years shall be enlisted by any officer, or held in the service of the United States, without the consent of his parent, or guardian, or master, first had and obtained, if any he have; and if any officer shall enlist any person contrary to the true intent and meaning of this act, for every such offence he shall forfeit and pay the amount of the bounty and clothing which the person so recruited may have received from the public, to be deducted out of the pay and emoluments of such officer. . . .

SEC. 18. That if any non-commissioned officer, musician, or private, shall desert the service of the United States, he shall, in addition to the penalties mentioned in the rules and articles of war, be liable to serve, for and during such a period, as shall, with the time he may have served previous to his desertion, amount to the full term of his enlistment; and such soldier shall and may be tried by a court-martial, and punished, although the term of his enlistment may have elapsed previous to his being apprehended or tried.

SEC. 19. That every person who shall procure, or entice, a soldier in the service of the United States to desert, or who shall purchase from any soldier his arms, uniform clothing, or any part thereof; and every captain or commanding officer of any ship or vessel, who shall enter on board such ship or vessel, as one of his crew, knowing him to have deserted, or otherwise carry away any such soldier, or shall refuse to deliver him up to the orders of his commanding officer, shall, upon legal conviction, be fined, at the discretion of any court having cognizance of the same, in any sum not exceeding $300, or be imprisoned, any term not exceeding one year.

SEC. 20. That every officer, non-commissioned officer, musician, and private, shall take and subscribe the following oath or affirmation. to wit: "I, A. B., do solemnly swear, or affirm, (as the case may be,) that I will bear true faith and allegiance to the United States of America, and that I will serve them honestly and faithfully, against their enemies or opposers whomsoever; and that I will observe and obey the orders of the President of the United States, and the orders of the officers appointed over me, according to the rules and articles of war." . . .

SEC. 22. That where any commissioned officer shall be obliged to incur any extra expense in travelling, and sitting on general courts-martial, he shall be allowed a reasonable compensation for such extra expense, actually incurred, not exceeding $1.25 per day to officers who are not entitled to forage, and not exceeding $1 per day to such as shall be entitled to forage.

SEC. 23. That no non-commissioned officer, musician, or private, shall be arrested, or subject to arrest, or to be taken in execution, for any debt under the sum of $20, contracted before enlistment, nor for any debt contracted after enlistment.

SEC. 24. That, whenever any officer or soldier shall be discharged from the service, except by way of punishment for any offence, he shall be allowed his pay and rations, or an equivalent in money, for such term of time as shall be sufficient for him to travel from the place of discharge to the place of his residence, computing at the rate of twenty miles to a day.

SEC. 25. That to each commissioned officer, who shall be deranged by virtue of this act, there shall be allowed and paid, in addition to the pay and emoluments to which they will be entitled by law at the time of their discharge, to each officer whose term of service in any military corps of the United States shall not have exceeded three years, three months' pay; to all other officers, so deranged, one month's pay of their grades, respectively, for each year of past service in the army of the United States, or in any regiment or corps now or formerly in the service thereof.

SEC. 26. That the President of the United States is hereby authorized and empowered, when he shall deem it expedient, to organize and establish a corps of engineers, to consist of one engineer, with the pay, rank, and emoluments of a major; two assistant engineers, with the pay, rank, and emoluments of captains; two other assistant engineers, with the pay, rank, and emoluments of first lieutenants: two other assistant engineers, with the pay, rank, and emoluments of second lieutenants; and ten cadets, with the pay of sixteen dollars per month, and two rations per day: and the President of the United States is, in like manner, authorized, when he shall deem it proper, to make such promotions in the said corps, with a view to particular merit, and without regard to rank, so as not to exceed one colonel, one lieutenant-colonel, two majors, four captains, four first lieutenants, four second lieutenants, and so as that the number of the whole corps shall, at no time, exceed twenty officers and cadets.

SEC. 27. That the said corps, when so organized, shall be stationed at West Point, in the State of New York, and shall constitute a military academy; and the engineers, assistant engineers, and cadets of the said corps, shall be subject, at all times, to do duty in such places, and on such service, as the President of the United States shall direct.

SEC. 28. That the principal engineer, and in his absence the next in rank, shall have the superintendence of the said military academy, under the direction of the President of the United States; and the secretary of war is hereby authorized, at the public expense, under such regulations as shall be directed by the President of the United States, to procure the necessary books, implements, and apparatus for the use and benefit of the said institution.

SEC. 29. That so much of any act or acts now in force, as comes within the purview of this act, shall be, and the same is hereby, repealed; saving, nevertheless, such parts thereof as relate to the enlistments, or term of service, of any of the troops which by this act are continued on the present military establishment of the United States.

[Approved, March 16, 1802.]

An Act making provision for arming and equipping the whole body of the Militia of the United States, 23 April 1808.

That the annual sum of two hundred thousand dollars be, and the same hereby is appropriated for the purpose of providing arms and military equipments for the whole body of the militia of the United States, either by purchase or manufacture, by and on account of the United States.

SEC. 2. That the President of the United States be, and he hereby is, authorized to purchase sites for, and erect, such additional arsenals and manufactories of arms as he may deem expedient, under the limitations and restrictions now provided by law: *Provided, also,* That so much of any law as restricts the number of workmen in the armories of the United States to one hundred men, be, and the same hereby is, repealed.

SEC. 3. That all the arms procured in virtue of this act shall be transmitted to the several states composing this union, and territories thereof, to each state and territory, respectively, in proportion to the number of the effective militia in each state and territory, and by each state and territory to be distributed to the militia in such state and territory, under such rules and regulations as shall be by law prescribed by the legislature of each state and territory.

[Approved, April 23, 1808.]

An Act declaring war between the United Kingdom of Great Britain and Ireland and the dependencies thereof, and the United States of America and their Territories, 18 June 1812.

That war be, and the same is hereby, declared to exist between the United Kingdom of Great Britain and Ireland and the dependencies thereof, and the United States of America and their Territories; and that the President of the United States is hereby authorized to use the whole land and naval force of the United States to carry the same into effect, and to issue to private armed vessels of the United States, commissions, or letters of marque and general reprisal, in such form as he shall think proper, under the seal of the United States, against the vessels, goods, and effects of the government of the said United Kingdom of Great Britain and Ireland, and the subjects thereof.

An Act fixing the Military Peace Establishment of the United States, 3 March 1815.

That the military peace establishment of the United

States shall consist of such proportions of artillery, infantry, and riflemen, not exceeding, in the whole, ten thousand men, as the President of the United States shall judge proper, and that the corps of engineers, as at present established, be retained.

SEC. 2. That the corps of artillery shall have the same organization as is prescribed by the act passed the 30th of March, 1814, and the regiment of light artillery the same organization as is prescribed by the act passed the 12th day of April, 1808; and that each regiment of infantry and riflemen shall consist of one colonel, one lieutenant-colonel, one major, one adjutant, one quartermaster, one paymaster, one surgeon, and two surgeon's mates, one sergeant-major, one quartermaster-sergeant, two principal musicians, and ten companies; each company to consist of one captain, one first lieutenant, and one second lieutenant, four sergeants, four corporals, two musicians, and sixty-eight privates.

SEC. 3. That there shall be two major-generals, and four brigadier-generals; the major-generals to be entitled to two aids-de-camp, and the brigadier-generals to one aid-de-camp, each, to be taken from the subalterns of the line; four brigade-inspectors, and four brigade-quartermasters, and such number of hospital surgeons and surgeon's mates as the service may require, not exceeding five surgeons and fifteen mates, with *one steward and one ward-master to each hospital.* The brigade-inspectors, appointed under this act, shall be taken from the line, and the brigade quartermasters, the adjutants, regimental quartermasters, and paymasters, from the subalterns of the line.

SEC. 4. That the compensation, subsistence, and the clothing of the officers, cadets, non-commissioned officers, musicians, artificers, and privates, composing the military peace establishment, shall be the same as are prescribed by the act entitled "An act fixing the military peace establishment of the United States," passed 16th March, 1802, and the act entitled "An act to raise, for a limited time, an additional military force," passed 12th of April, 1808; and that the major-generals shall be entitled to the same compensation as is provided by an act entitled "An act to raise an additional military force," passed 11th January, 1812.

SEC. 5. That the President of the United States cause to be arranged the officers, non-commissioned officers, musicians, and privates, of the several corps of troops now in the service of the United States, in such a manner as to form and complete out of the same the corps authorized by this act, and cause the supernumerary officers, non-commissioned officers, musicians, and privates, to be discharged from the service of the United States, from and after the 1st day of May next, or as soon as circumstances may permit.

SEC. 6. That to each commissioned officer, who shall be deranged by virtue of this act, there shall be allowed and paid, in addition to the pay and emoluments to which they will be entitled by law at the time of his discharge, three months' pay.

SEC. 7. That the several corps authorized by this act shall be subject to the rules and articles of war, be recruited in the same manner, and with the same limitations, and that officers, non-commissioned officers, musicians, and privates, shall be entitled to the same provision for wounds and disabilities, the same provision for widows and children, and the same benefits and allowances in every respect, not inconsistent with the provisions of this act, as are authorized by the act of 16th March, 1802, entitled "An act fixing the military peace establishment of the United States," and the act of the 12th April, 1808, entitled "An act to raise, for a limited time, an additional military force;" and that the bounty to the recruit, and compensation to the recruiting officer, shall be the same as are allowed by the aforesaid act of the 12th of April, 1808.

[Approved, March 3, 1815.]

The following editions of the primary sources were used in the above reproductions:

Callan, John F. *The Military Laws of the United States, Relating to the Army, Volunteers, Militia, and to Bounty Lands and Pensions, from the Foundation of the Government to the Year 1863*. Philadelphia: George W. Childs, 1863.

Farrand, Max, ed. *The Records of the Federal Convention of 1787.* Rev. ed. 4 vols. New Haven: Yale University Press, 1937.

Fitzpatrick, John C., ed. *The Writings of George Washington from the Original Manuscript Sources, 1745–1799.* Washington: Government Printing Office, 1931–44.

Ford, Paul L., ed. *Pamphlets on the Constitution of the United States Published During its Discussion by the People, 1787–1788.* Brooklyn: n.p., 1888.

Ford, Worthington C., ed. *Journals of the Continental Congress, 1774–1789.* 34 vols. Washington: Government Printing Office, 1904–1937.

Rossiter, Clinton, ed. *The Federalist Papers.* New York: New American Library, 1961.

Syrett, Harold C., ed. *The Papers of Alexander Hamilton.* New York: Columbia University Press, 1962.

The documents by Steuben and Knox were published in 1784 and 1790 respectively. Copies of these rare volumes are on deposit at the Library of Congress. The version of the Constitution printed above is from the version prepared by the Commission on the Bicentennial of the United States Constitution in 1986.

GALLERY OF SOLDIER-STATESMEN OF THE EARLY REPUBLIC

The men who served in uniform during the Revolution contributed in numerous ways to the new republic. Some sat in the Constitutional Convention of 1787, and many held a wide array of national and state offices. Veteran soldier-statesmen included two Presidents, influential members of the Supreme Court, and an impressive group of cabinet members and senior diplomats. Former continentals and militiamen appeared among the leaders of the Federalist and Democratic-Republican parties in both houses of Congress, and in the governor's chair in every one of the original thirteen states.

The influence exercised by Revolutionary veterans also extended far beyond the political realm. The emerging artistic culture of early America drew heavily on veterans for its painters and poets, and on Revolutionary scenes and figures for subjects. Former militiamen and continentals joined the flow of westward movement, expanded the economy as inventors and developers, and opened new routes of oceanic commerce. Another group, the European volunteers, returned to play vital roles in the Old World, particularly in the French Revolution.

President James Monroe (1758–1831). *(Oil, by John Vanderlyn, 1816; National Portrait Gallery, Smithsonian Institution.)*

Chief Justice John Marshall (1755–1835). *(Oil, by William James Hubard, c. 1832; National Portrait Gallery, Smithsonian Institution.)*

Executive Branch

Clockwise from right:

William Richardson Davie (1756–1820). *(Pastel, by James Sharples, Sr., c. 1795; Independence National Historical Park.)*

Timothy Pickering (1745–1829). *(Oil, by Charles Willson Peale, 1792; Independence National Historical Park.)*

John Armstrong, Jr., (1758–1843). *(Oil, attributed to John Wesley Jarvis, undated; National Portrait Gallery, Smithsonian Institution.)*

United States Senate
Clockwise from right:

William North (1755–1836). *(Oil, by Charles Willson Peale, 1785; Detroit Institute of Fine Arts.)*

Thomas Sumter (1734–1832). *(Oil, by Rembrandt Peale, undated; Independence National Historical Park.)*

Samuel Smith (1752–1839). *(Oil, by Gilbert Stuart, c. 1800; National Portrait Gallery, Smithsonian Institution.)*

House of Representatives

William Findley (c. 1741–1821). *(Oil, by Rembrandt Peale, undated; Independence National Historical Park.)*

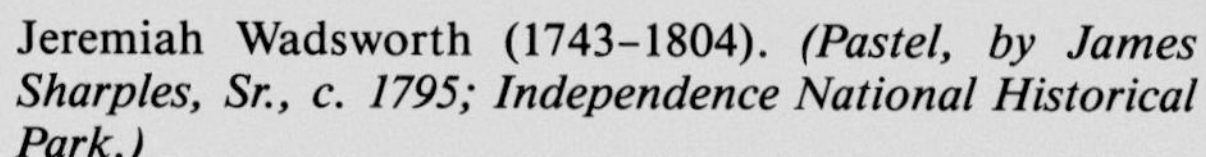

Jeremiah Wadsworth (1743–1804). *(Pastel, by James Sharples, Sr., c. 1795; Independence National Historical Park.)*

Benjamin Tallmadge (1754–1835). *(Oil, by Ralph Earl, 1790; courtesy of the Litchfield Historical Society.)*

Elias Boudinot (1740–1821). *(Oil, by Charles Willson Peale, c. 1782; Independence National Historical Park.)*

Governors

Morgan Lewis (1754–1844). *(Miniature, by unknown artist, undated; courtesy of Anderson House Museum, Society of the Cincinnati; photograph by Sgt. Jim Moore.)*

William Moultrie (1730–1805). *(Oil, by Charles Willson Peale, 1782; National Portrait Gallery, Smithsonian Institution; transfer from the National Gallery of Art; gift of Andrew W. Mellon.)*

William Smallwood (1732–1792). *(Oil, by Charles Willson Peale, c. 1781; Independence National Historical Park.)*

Henry Lee (1756–1818). *(Oil, by Charles Willson Peale, 1782; Independence National Historical Park.)*

Self-portrait of Charles Willson Peale (1741–1827), one of America's leading artists and a militia veteran. *(Oil, 1777/78; courtesy of the American Philosophical Society.)*

Militia veteran Enoch Crosby (1750–1835) provided the model for James Fenimore Cooper's *The Spy. (Oil, by Samuel Lovett Waldo and William Jewett, 1830; National Portrait Gallery, Smithsonian Institution.)*

Rufus Putnam (1738–1824) encouraged the settlement of Revolutionary veterans in the northwest. *(Pastel, attributed to James Sharples, Sr., c. 1795; Independence National Historical Park.)*

Louis Le Begue de Presle Duportail (1743–1802), Continental Army Chief of Engineers, returned to France and rose to be Minister of War. *(Oil, by Charles Willson Peale, c. 1782; Independence National Historical Park.)*

APPENDIXES

APPENDIX A

The Annapolis Convention

It took several decades to turn thirteen separate colonies into the United States of America. The process began as early as the French and Indian War and led colonists from various regions to assert American rights to self-government through Committees of Correspondence and other informal, extralegal means. The practical result of these first steps was the creation of the Continental Congress, an assembly of delegates sent to Philadelphia by the provisional governments of the thirteen colonies. It was this "states in congress assembled" that proclaimed Independence on July 4, 1776. During the Revolutionary War the Continental Congress assumed the functions of a national government, financing the Continental Army and directing the war effort. It sought allies for the Patriot cause and in the end its representatives signed the Treaty of Paris in which Britain recognized the United States. This event, however, only ended the combat—the task of producing a unified nation remained.

Congress tried to establish a basic governmental framework with the Articles of Confederation, ratified by the states in 1781. But the central government remained little more than a loose wartime alliance of independent states, and Congress, under the Articles, experienced serious difficulty in restoring a war-torn economy, regulating foreign trade, and protecting and developing the frontier between the Appalachian Mountains and the Mississippi River. Congress did accept the notion that security was a national responsibility, and in June 1784 it authorized, on a temporary basis, a small peacetime Regular Army to occupy frontier forts. Competing state territorial claims, however, blocked plans for extending national government to the region.

George Washington, who emerged as a leading nationalist, was particularly concerned with the future of the west. He understood the region's vast potential and urged the development of rivers and roads as the means of keeping the frontier settlers tied to the union. In 1784 his colleague, James Madison, took a positive step toward realizing the general's goal by setting up a meeting at Annapolis in December between Maryland and Virginia (represented by Washington) to discuss the development of the Potomac River as a route to the west. There the states formed a corporation, the Patowmack Company, to improve the waterway and settled disputes over the upper reaches of the river.

Madison succeeded in arranging another conference between the two states in March 1785 at Alexandria, Virginia. Washington encouraged the commissioners, hosting some of the sessions at his plantation, and the "Mount Vernon Compact," signed on 28 March, settled the outstanding issues regarding the use of the Chesapeake Bay and its tributaries. Before departing, the commissioners recommended that yet another meeting with an expanded agenda be called, this time to include representatives from other nearby states. In January 1786, Virginia invited all the states to a special meeting at Annapolis in September to discuss commercial issues.

Madison, who had been a key figure in Virginia's initiative, arrived in Annapolis on 4 September and took up lodging at George Mann's Tavern, which became the site of the Annapolis Convention. He was soon joined by eleven other elected representatives from five states. Their informal discussions preceded the opening session on 11 September, when Delaware's John Dickinson, the elder statesman of the group and author of the Articles of Confederation, was chosen chairman. The delegates agreed that the absence of so many states and the differing instructions given to the delegates would prevent the meeting from accomplishing its stated purpose. But the strong nationalism of the dozen men, seven of whom had served under arms during the Revolution, led them to decide to use the opportunity to express their views in a report to the individual state legislatures and Congress.

Virtually everyone agreed that the question of trade regulation could not be divorced from larger political issues, an area that the delegates had no authority to discuss. One delegate, apparently Abraham Clark of New Jersey, therefore suggested that the report recommend another meeting explicitly empowered to frame measures to strengthen the Articles. When the others agreed, Alexander Hamilton prepared a draft with the assistance of Madison and Edmund Jennings Randolph. The full convention then polished the text before adjourning on the afternoon of the 14th. Each delegation carried a copy of the report back to its own legislature, while Dickinson delivered a copy to Congress. On 21 February that body endorsed the call for a convention to meet in Philadelphia on the second Monday in May of 1787—the convention that would write the Constitution.

On 19 September 1786 the *Maryland Journal* printed the first public notice about the Annapolis Convention. Its author commented, "Should this Address have its Effect, we may hope to see the Federal Union of these States established upon Principles, which will secure the

CONVENTION DELEGATES

NAME/STATE	*BIRTH/DEATH* (All dates are "New Style")
*DICKINSON, John (Delaware) (Chairman)	19 November 1732–14 February 1808 BIRTH: "Croisiadore," Talbot County, Md. DEATH: Wilmington, Del.
*BASSETT, Richard (Delaware)	2 April 1745–15 August 1815 BIRTH: "Bohemia Manor," Cecil County, Md. DEATH: Kent County, Del.
BENSON, Egbert (New York)	21 June 1746–24 August 1833 BIRTH: New York, N.Y. DEATH: Jamaica, N.Y.
CLARK, Abraham (New Jersey)	15 February 1726–15 September 1794 BIRTH: Near Elizabethtown, N.J. DEATH: Rahway, N.J.
COXE, Tench (Pennsylvania)	22 May 1755–16 July 1824 BIRTH: Philadelphia, Pa. DEATH: Philadelphia, Pa.
*HAMILTON, Alexander (New York)	11 January 1757–12 July 1804 BIRTH: Nevis, British West Indies DEATH: New York, N.Y.
**HOUSTOUN, William Churchill (New Jersey)	c. 1746–12 August 1788 BIRTH: Cabarrus County(?), N.C. DEATH: Frankford, Pa.
*MADISON, James, Jr. (Virginia)	16 March 1751–28 June 1836 BIRTH: Port Conway, King George County, Va. DEATH: "Montpelier," Orange County, Va.
**RANDOLPH, Edmund Jennings (Virginia)	10 August 1753–12 September 1813 BIRTH: "Tazewell Hall," Williamsburg, Va. DEATH: Clarke County, Va.
*READ, George (Delaware)	18 September 1733–21 September 1798 BIRTH: North East, Cecil County, Md. DEATH: Newcastle, Del.
SCHUREMAN, James (New Jersey)	12 February 1756–22 January 1824 BIRTH: New Brunswick, N.J. DEATH: New Brunswick, N.J.
TUCKER, St. George (Virginia)	10 July 1752–10 November 1827 BIRTH: Port Royal, Bermuda DEATH: "Edgewood," Nelson County, Va.

*Signer of the Constitution

**Member of the Constitutional Convention who did not sign

OCCUPATION/EDUCATION	*ACTIVE MILITARY DUTY IN THE REVOLUTION*	*PUBLIC OFFICES*
Lawyer Middle Temple, London, England	Militia, 4 years Highest rank: Brigadier General	Colonial legislature, 9 years; Continental Congress, 4 years; Governor of Pennsylvania, 4 years; Governor of Delaware, 1 year
Lawyer/planter No formal education	Militia, 3 years Highest rank: Captain	State legislature, 4 years; Governor of Delaware, 2 years; Senate, 4 years
Lawyer King's College (Columbia University)	None	Colonial legislature, 2 years; Continental Congress, 4 years; state legislature, 6 years; House of Representatives, 5 years
Farmer/surveyor No formal education	None	Colonial legislature, 1 year; Continental Congress, 7 years; Signer of the Declaration of Independence; House of Representatives, 4 years; state legislature, 4 years
Merchant College of Philadelphia (University of Pennsylvania) but did not graduate	None (Militia officer)	Continental Congress, 1 year; Assistant Secretary of the Treasury, 3 years; Commissioner of Revenue, 5 years
Lawyer King's College but did not graduate	Continental Army, 6 years Highest rank: Lieutenant Colonel	Continental Congress, 4 years; Secretary of the Treasury, 6 years; Inspector General, United States Army, 2 years
Teacher/lawyer College of New Jersey (Princeton University)	Militia, 2 years Highest rank: Captain	Colonial legislature, 1 year; Continental Congress, 5 years; Receiver of Continental Taxes, 3 years; state legislature, 3 years
Lawyer/planter College of New Jersey	None (Militia officer)	Continental Congress, 8 years; state legislature, 4 years; House of Representatives, 8 years; Secretary of State, 8 years; President of the United States, 8 years
Lawyer College of William and Mary but did not graduate	Continental Army, 1 year Highest rank: Lieutenant Colonel	Colonial legislature, 1 year; Continental Congress, 4 years; state legislature, 2 years; Governor of Virginia, 2 years; Attorney General, 4 years; Secretary of State, 2 years
Lawyer No formal education	None	Colonial legislature, 10 years; Continental Congress, 4 years; Signer of the Declaration of Independence; state legislature, 9 years; Senate, 5 years
Merchant Queen's College (Rutgers University)	Militia, 1 year Highest rank: Lieutenant (Prisoner of War)	Continental Congress, 2 years; state legislature, 7 years; House of Representatives, 6 years; Senate, 2 years
Lawyer/planter College of William and Mary	Militia, 3 years Highest rank: Lieutenant Colonel	Federal District Judge, 14 years

Mann's Tavern, Annapolis, Maryland. *(Drawing, by Polli Rodriguez; courtesy of Maryland Office for the Bicentennial of the U.S. Constitution, Maryland State Archives.)*

Dignity, Harmony and Felicity of these confederated Republics; and not only rescue them from their present Difficulties, but from that insolent Hauteur and contemptuous Neglect, which they have experienced as a Nation."

Like the delegates at Annapolis, a majority of the men who would sign the Constitution had seen active military service during the Revolutionary War. Undoubtedly this experience had taught them much about the dangers of a weak central government and had helped shape their ideas of a national union that would take precedence over the competing demands of states and sections. The foresight of these soldier-statesmen of the Constitution would more than answer the hopes raised for that long-ago Maryland journalist by the Annapolis Convention.

APPENDIX B

Committee Membership of the Constitutional Convention

Name	State	Committee(s) Served On
*Baldwin, Abraham	Georgia	Representation (2 July); Postponed Matters
*Bassett, Richard	Delaware	—
Bedford, Gunning, Jr.	Delaware	Representation (2 July)
Blair, John	Virginia	—
*Blount, William	North Carolina	—
*Brearly, David	New Jersey	Postponed Matters
Broom, Jacob	Delaware	—
*Butler, Pierce	South Carolina	Postponed Matters
Carroll, Daniel	Maryland	Postponed Matters
Clymer, George	Pennsylvania	—
*Davie, William Richardson	North Carolina	Representation (2 July)
*Dayton, Jonathan	New Jersey	—
*Dickinson, John	Delaware	Postponed Matters
Ellsworth, Oliver	Connecticut	Representation (2 July); Detail
*Few, William	Georgia	—
*Fitzsimons, Thomas	Pennsylvania	—
Franklin, Benjamin	Pennsylvania	Representation (2 July)
Gerry, Elbridge	Massachusetts	Representation (2 July)
*Gilman, Nicholas	New Hampshire	Postponed Matters
Gorham, Nathaniel	Massachusetts	Detail
*Hamilton, Alexander	New York	Rules and Procedures; Style
Houstoun, William	Georgia	—
Houstoun, William Churchill	New Jersey	—
Ingersoll, Jared	Pennsylvania	—
Jenifer, Daniel of St. Thomas	Maryland	—
Johnson, William Samuel	Connecticut	Style
*King, Rufus	Massachusetts	Postponed Matters; Style
*Langdon, John	New Hampshire	—
*Lansing, John	New York	—
*Livingston, William	New Jersey	—
*McClurg, James	Virginia	—
*McHenry, James	Maryland	—
Madison, James, Jr.	Virginia	Postponed Matters; Style
*Martin, Alexander	North Carolina	Representation (2 July)
Martin, Luther	Maryland	—
Mason, George	Virginia	Representation (2 July)
*Mercer, John Francis	Maryland	—
*Mifflin, Thomas	Pennsylvania	—
*Morris, Gouverneur	Pennsylvania	Postponed Matters; Style
Morris, Robert	Pennsylvania	—
Paterson, William	New Jersey	Representation (2 July)
*Pierce, William	Georgia	—
*Pinckney, Charles	South Carolina	Rules and Procedures
*Pinckney, Charles Cotesworth	South Carolina	—
*Randolph, Edmund Jennings	Virginia	Detail
Read, George	Delaware	—
Rutledge, John	South Carolina	Representation (2 July); Detail
Sherman, Roger	Connecticut	Postponed Matters
*Spaight, Richard Dobbs	North Carolina	—
Strong, Caleb	Massachusetts	—
*Washington, George	Virginia	—
*Williamson, Hugh	North Carolina	Postponed Matters
Wilson, James	Pennsylvania	Detail
Wythe, George	Virginia	Rules and Procedures
Yates, Robert	New York	Representation (2 July)

*Veterans of active military service in the Revolutionary War.

APPENDIX C

Delegates to the Constitutional Convention Who Did Not Sign

NAME/STATE	*BIRTH/DEATH* (All dates are "New Style")	*OCCUPATION/EDUCATION*	*ACTIVE MILITARY DUTY IN THE REVOLUTION*	*PUBLIC OFFICES*
DAVIE, William Richardson (North Carolina)	20 June 1756–29 November 1820 BIRTH: Egremont, Cumberlandshire, England DEATH: Lancaster Co., S.C.	Lawyer Queen's Museum College (Charlotte, North Carolina) and College of New Jersey*	Continentals, 1 year Highest rank: Captain State troops, 2 years Highest rank: Colonel	Brigadier General, U.S. Army, 2 years; Minister to France, 1 year; Governor of North Carolina, 2 years; state legislature, 12 years
ELLSWORTH, Oliver (Connecticut)	29 April 1745–26 November 1807 BIRTH: Windsor, Conn. DEATH: Windsor, Conn.	Lawyer Yale College and College of New Jersey*	None	Continental Congress, 7 years; U.S. Supreme Court, 3 years; U.S. Senate, 7 years; state legislature, 14 years; Connecticut Superior Court, 4 years
GERRY, Elbridge (Massachusetts)	17 July 1744–23 November 1814 BIRTH: Marblehead, Mass. DEATH: Washington, D.C.	Merchant and land speculator Harvard College	None	Colonial legislature, 4 years; Continental Congress, 11 years; U.S. Vice President, 2 years (died in office); House of Representatives, 4 years; Minister to France, 1 year; Governor of Massachusetts, 2 years; Massachusetts legislature, 4 years
HOUSTOUN, William (Georgia)	c. 1755–c. 1833 (Exact dates unknown) BIRTH: Savannah, Ga. DEATH: Savannah, Ga.	Lawyer Inner Temple (London)	None	Continental Congress, 2 years
HOUSTOUN, William Churchill (New Jersey)	c. 1746–12 August 1788 BIRTH: Cabarrus County(?), N.C. DEATH: Frankford, Pa.	Teacher/lawyer College of New Jersey*	Militia, 2 years Highest rank: Captain	Colonial legislature, 1 year; Continental Congress, 5 years; Receiver of Continental Taxes, 3 years; state legislature, 3 years
LANSING, John (New York)	30 January 1754–12 December 1829 (?) BIRTH: Albany, N.Y. DEATH: New York, N.Y. (Disappearance under mysterious circumstances; presumed to have been murdered.)	Lawyer	Continentals, 2 years Highest rank: Major	Continental Congress, 2 years; state legislature, 6 years; Chancellor of New York, 13 years; New York Superior Court, 11 years; Mayor of Albany, 4 years
McCLURG, James (Virginia)	c. 1746–9 July 1823 BIRTH: Elizabeth City Co., Va. DEATH: Williamsburg, Va.	Physician College of William and Mary and University of Edinburgh	State troops, 6 years Highest rank: Surgeon	State Executive Council, 10 years

MARTIN, Alexander (North Carolina)	c. 1740–2 November 1807 BIRTH: Hunterdon Co., N.J. DEATH: Rockingham Co., N.C.	Merchant and lawyer College of New Jersey*	Continentals, 2 years Highest rank: Colonel	Colonial legislature, 1 year; Continental Congress, 1 year; U.S. Senate, 6 years; Governor of North Carolina, 6 years; state legislature, 11 years
MARTIN, Luther (Maryland)	c. 1748–10 July 1826 BIRTH: near New Brunswick, N.J. DEATH: New York, N.Y.	Teacher and lawyer College of New Jersey*	None	Continental Congress, 1 year; Attorney General of Maryland, 31 years
MASON, George (Virginia)	c. 1725–7 October 1792 BIRTH: Doeg's (now Mason's) Neck, Stafford Co., Va. DEATH: "Gunston Hall," Fairfax Co., Va.	Planter	None	Colonial legislature, 1 year; state legislature, 1 year
MERCER, John Francis (Maryland)	17 May 1759–30 August 1821 BIRTH: "Marlborough," Stafford Co., Va. DEATH: Philadelphia, Pa.	Lawyer and businessman College of William and Mary	Continental Army, 4 years Highest rank: Major Militia, 2 years Highest rank: Lieutenant Colonel	Virginia state legislature, 2 years; Continental Congress, 3 years; U.S. House of Representatives, 2 years; Governor of Maryland, 2 years; Maryland assembly, 6 years
PIERCE, William (Georgia)	c. 1740–10 December 1789 BIRTH: Probably Georgia (exact location unknown) DEATH: Savannah, Ga.	Businessman	Continental Army, 7 years Highest rank: Major	Continental Congress, 1 year
RANDOLPH, Edmund Jennings (Virginia)	10 August 1753–12 September 1813 BIRTH: "Tazewell Hall," Williamsburg, Va. DEATH: Clarke County, Va.	Lawyer College of William and Mary but did not graduate	Continental Army, 1 year Highest rank: Lieutenant Colonel	Colonial legislature, 1 year; Continental Congress, 4 years; state legislature, 2 years; Governor of Virginia, 2 years; Attorney General, 4 years; Secretary of State, 2 years
STRONG, Caleb (Massachusetts)	9 January 1745–7 November 1819 BIRTH: Northampton, Mass. DEATH: Northampton, Mass.	Lawyer Harvard College	None	State legislature, 12 years; U.S. Senate, 7 years; Governor of Massachusetts, 12 years
WYTHE, George (Virginia)	c. 1726–8 June 1806 BIRTH: Elizabeth City Co., Va. DEATH: Richmond, Va.	Lawyer College of William and Mary but did not graduate	None	Colonial legislature, 12 years; Continental Congress, 1 year; state legislature, 1 year; Chancellor of Virginia, 22 years
YATES, Robert (New York)	27 June 1738–9 September 1801 BIRTH: Schenectady, N.Y. DEATH: Albany, N.Y.	Lawyer	None	New York Superior Court, 22 years

*Note: The College of New Jersey is now Princeton University.

APPENDIX D

The Ratification of the Constitution

On the afternoon of 17 September 1787, the delegates who had spent the summer in Philadelphia fashioning a new document to replace the Articles of Confederation assembled one last time. Meeting as before in the Pennsylvania State House (later called Independence Hall), they joined in a simple but formal ceremony to affix their signatures to the Constitution.

Many long debates were behind them. The final document contained a number of key provisions that reflected critical compromises between the two opposing sides: those who argued that survival depended on increasing the efficiency and strength of the central government and those, concerned most about potential abuses of power, who sought to reserve as much authority as possible to the states, where government was closer to the people. The Constitution had resolved these opposing emphases in a pragmatic and uniquely American way. It devised a federal system of checks and balances that divided responsibility between the states and the national government, separating the latter's powers into executive, legislative, and judicial branches and subordinating the military to elected civilian government.

When the final session of the Constitutional Convention opened, Secretary William Jackson probably read the finished document one more time, and Benjamin Franklin urged the doubters to make approval unanimous. In the end 38 of the 41 delegates present signed. Only Edmund Randolph and George Mason of Virginia and Elbridge Gerry of Massachusetts, who each had reservations over specific provisions and omissions, refused. John Dickinson of Delaware, who was absent because of illness, had his name affixed by fellow delegate George Read. About four in the afternoon Secretary Jackson also signed, certifying the other signatures, and the Convention adjourned. Jackson then set out for New York where, on 20 September, he delivered the Constitution with a covering letter from Washington to Charles Thomson, the secretary of the Continental Congress.

Transmittal did not turn the Constitution into the law of the land. The earlier Articles of Confederation went into force only after they had been ratified by the state legislatures. The delegates deliberately chose a different path this time, even though they knew that it would extend their own labors. Under Article VII, the Constitution had to be approved not by the legislatures but by citizens meeting in special conventions elected solely for that purpose. Only when a clear majority, nine, gave their assent, could the new government begin, although everyone understood that the Framers intended all thirteen states to be part of the Union. This procedure gave substance to the Preamble's claim that the United States derived its authority from the people, not simply the states. It also set the stage for a political fight of unprecedented dimensions reflecting many of the debates heard first in the Convention. Once more the Soldier-Statesmen of the Constitution, those hundreds of veterans of the Revolutionary War who now served in key political posts throughout the thirteen states, would lend the weight of their experience to the ongoing process of nation-building.

The Opposing Sides

Attention quickly focused on the struggle between those in favor of the Constitution (the Federalists) and those opposed to it (who came to be called the Antifederalists). Although the proponents of the new federal system had little assurance that their work would be well received at home, they held the initiative. Realistic politicians, they had shied away from abstract philosophy during the Convention, and the Constitution they devised, built upon a century and a half of colonial experience and the lessons learned since 1775, sought to create an effective central government without putting personal liberties at risk.

The Antifederalists were more loosely organized and suffered the natural disadvantage of being an opposition with no comprehensive alternative to offer to meet the existing political and economic crisis. They could count on the leadership of just a handful of Convention delegates. Along with Mason and Gerry, these included Luther Martin and John Francis Mercer of Maryland and Robert Yates and John Lansing of New York and only a few other figures of national stature: Patrick Henry and Richard Henry Lee in Virginia, Samuel Chase in Maryland, and George Clinton in New York. These men called on the voters to reject the Constitution because of vaguely specified "defects." Actually, they tended to be inherently suspicious of any concentration of power, fearing a strong national government because it was further removed from the people than the state governments and therefore, in their view, more susceptible to abuse of power. Called by one historian "Men of Little Faith," they clung to older traditions and argued that a republic could survive only if it was kept small; their solution was to preserve a confederation of thirteen separate republics under a modified set of Articles of Confederation. Following the same logic, the Antifederalists also opposed the creation of a peacetime army and sought to limit the nation's military to state-controlled militias. Their arguments were couched in terms used a century earlier in England's "Glorious Revolution" and more recently against Parliament. Still, these were men of exceptional eloquence, many with names intimately associated with the cause of independence, figures of importance in many key states. In sum, though the Federalists held the initiative provided by the Convention, they certainly had their work cut out for them.

The Federalists realized that the central issues raised by the Constitution touched many deeply held personal convictions about government and that the new debates would also inevitably become entangled in local politics. Led by the signers, the Federalists quickly established a nationwide network to coordinate the ratification effort. George Washington was the key to their hopes. Hero of the Revolution to a grateful public and beloved commander to a host of Continental veterans, Washington was the obvious choice to lead the new government if the Constitution went into effect. This fact alone was a major advantage for the Federalists, but beyond that, Washington, the consummate role model of the Soldier-Statesmen, lent his enormous prestige to the political fight. With assistance from such able lieutenants as signers James Madison and Alexander Hamilton and Secretary at War Henry Knox, he played a vital behind-the-scenes role in the enterprise. Not to be overlooked in this national alliance of Federalist strength were the Soldier-Statesmen themselves. These men had become convinced by their wartime experiences in the Army that a strong central government was essential if the promises of the Declaration of Independence were to be fulfilled. From their ranks had come the core support for the Constitution in Philadelphia; now they would join with their old commander to fight for its ratification in the separate state conventions.

The Federalists devised a two-part strategy. First, as a response to the charge that the Constitution might endanger the liberties won during the Revolutionary War, they embarked on an unprecedented campaign to bring their arguments to the public. In countless speeches, newspaper articles, and pamphlets, Federalist spokesmen focused on those issues where consensus was possible and ignored those that were potentially divisive. Three themes with broad popular appeal quickly emerged: the very real economic problems under the Articles, national security, and national pride. Secondly, as experienced politicians, the Federalist leaders also knew that timing had great tactical significance. By taking advantage of the fact that supporters of the Constitution already formed a majority in some states, they planned to create a sense of momentum calculated to swing undecided voters. At the same time, they decided to concentrate their efforts in Pennsylvania, Virginia, Massachusetts, and New York, the four states whose approval was deemed essential to the viability of the new nation because of their size, population, and wealth.

Antifederalists tended to avoid the national perspective. Instead, they focused on individual rights and local issues—areas, they believed, where potential abuse of power under the Constitution was most threatening. At the heart of their argument, also put forward in speeches, pamphlets, and articles, were two specific objections to the new Constitution. They deeply feared its omission of a bill of rights to protect individual liberties, an item included in every state constitution adopted since the Revolution. They also considered the Constitution's supremacy clause (Paragraph 2 of Article VI) dangerous because, they charged, it could allow the central government to override rights and prerogatives of the individual states.

Vanguard of Victory

After signing the Constitution, most of the Framers returned to their homes to begin the arduous task of convincing their neighbors to support the new government. About a dozen others went to New York City where they resumed their seats in Congress and fought the first of the ratification battles. These Federalists quickly came under attack by Virginia's Richard Henry Lee and a handful of supporters. On 26 September 1787, Lee proposed a long list of changes to the Constitution, changes that in effect would have nullified the Framers' handiwork. But the Federalists had the votes. With only New York opposing, Congress agreed to send the Constitution without change to the state governments with a request that they call the required ratification conventions. On 28 September, to win over New York and make the congressional action unanimous, the Federalists agreed to a resolution in which Congress specifically took no stand on the Convention's work. The ratification struggle now passed to the states and entered the first of three distinct phases.

Pennsylvania's William Bingham had been nervously awaiting this news, for his state's legislature, now strongly pro-Federalist, would be adjourning on 29 September. The Federalists were looking for a quick call for a ratification convention in Pennsylvania before the Antifederalists could organize an opposition in the October state elections. As soon as Congress voted, Bingham paid a special courier to race across New Jersey with the news.

Actually, Pennsylvania's Federalists had already begun to act on their own initiative. Without waiting for the vote in New York, George Clymer introduced a call for a Pennsylvania convention. When a test vote indicated that this measure would pass easily, the outnumbered Antifederalists decided that their only hope of frustrating passage was to absent themselves, thus (by a lone vote) preventing a quorum. But the Federalists were not to be denied. When Bingham's messenger arrived with the news on the twenty-ninth, they sent the sergeant at arms to hunt down the missing delegates. A mob found two of them first and literally dragged them to the State House, where they were seated against their will. The Federalists then quickly passed the necessary legislation and adjourned.

Outraged Antifederalists, charging that such strong-arm tactics proved that the Constitution itself was a threat to liberties, mustered their strength for the coming elections. With the publication of a series of letters signed by "Centinel" (probably Samuel Bryan), they began what would be the first of many press wars for popular support. They also sent news of their plight to sympathetic allies in other states, triggering similar campaigns elsewhere, although seldom with the personal vitriol common in the Pennsylvania press.

If the battle for the Constitution began in Pennsylvania, the first victory was registered in tiny Delaware. That state's recently elected legislature opened its annual session on 24 October 1787 and received Congress' resolution the same day. Because of pressing state issues, the legislators did not get around to approving a call for a ratification convention until 10 November. The subsequent election of delegates for the special convention revolved around personalities rather than issues, but the convention, despite the election's rowdiness, demonstrated a strong consensus when it assembled in Dover on 3 December. The Federalists carefully cultivated this consensus. Led by signers John Dickinson and George Read, they emphasized the natural advantages of a strong protective national government for the small states. After only three days of debate, all thirty delegates voted for adoption, formally signing the document on 7 December. Delaware's unanimous decision gave the state the honor of being the first to ratify. It also allowed its Federalists to turn their energies to the national stage. Dickinson took the lead, preparing a masterful set of articles under the name "Fabius" that appeared in papers across the country in the spring.

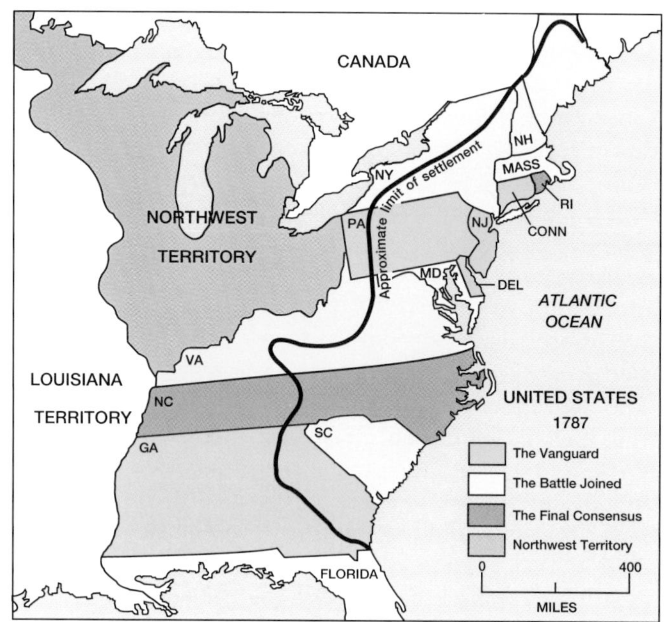

Meanwhile, the Pennsylvania convention had assembled in Philadelphia on 21 November. Its sixty-nine members knew that the outcome was a foregone conclusion, for the Federalists had rolled up a two-to-one majority. Under the leadership of James Wilson (the only convention delegate who had signed the Constitution), Thomas McKean, and Benjamin Rush, they attempted to push for speedy approval. The Antifederalist leaders, men of deep commitment but relatively limited political experience, sought to stall in the hope that something would emerge to reverse public sentiment. Although they mustered enough votes to drag matters out for three weeks, they failed to force an adjournment so that the voters could consider fifteen Antifederalist amendments. At the end of a session marked by flaring tempers and debates that nearly degenerated into fisticuffs, the Federalists won approval for unconditional ratification on 12 December by a vote of 46 to 23.

On 13 December the majority paraded to the city court house, accompanied by various public officials and the Philadelphia militia, to proclaim the news to the people. Their convention marked an important Federalist triumph, bringing one of the four key states into the fold at the outset, but it was a bruising experience. The losing side refused to concede victory and left determined to galvanize opposition in other states.

Three small states rapidly fell into line behind Delaware and Pennsylvania as the Federalists' plan to establish a sense of momentum took hold. New Jersey was clearly predisposed to the new government. Along with Connecticut and New York it had borne much of the burden of supporting George Washington's troops during the Revolution, and thereafter it had upheld the principle that only a strong central government could effectively provide for national defense. It was also popularly assumed in New Jersey that the new Constitution would bar the discriminatory tariffs being imposed by the ports of Philadelphia and New York. Beyond these important considerations, a quick Federalist victory seemed likely because the Antifederalists were poorly organized, while two signers, the immensely popular Governor William Livingston and state Chief Justice David Brearly, led the fight for approval. In the end it took just nine days in Trenton for the 38-member convention to complete its business. Only four of them were consumed in actual debate before ratification passed unanimously on 18 December.

Georgia followed suit with a unanimous vote (26–0) on 31 December. Like New Jersey, the state was greatly concerned with fairly apportioned and effective national defense. It too had undergone invasion by British forces during the Revolution, and in succeeding years population growth along its frontier had raised the specter of conflict with the Indians. Local leaders knew that they could not hope to cope with that eventuality alone. Their legislature received the official news of the Constitution on 18 October and eight days later approved a convention, whose members were to be elected at the same time as the regular state officials. Unlike any other state, Georgia specified that no person sitting in the ratification convention could hold any state "position of honor or pay," thereby excluding most of the state's experienced politicians.

This decision had little impact on the outcome, but it did create problems in organizing the convention. Scheduled to begin on Christmas Day in Augusta, the convention could not raise a quorum until 28 December. But once seated, the delegates worked with considerable speed. After a day and a half consumed with procedural matters and an equal time for discussion of the Constitution, they voted approval on 31 December. After another delay while the delegates debated the wording of their assenting resolution, Georgia formally ratified the Constitution on 2 January 1788.

After one serious, if lopsided, contest and three easy votes, the Federalists turned their attention to Connecticut. Here the issues were somewhat confused. The state had compiled an excellent reputation for supporting the Continental Army throughout the Revolution, but it was part of New England, where tradition and sentiment ran strongly in favor of direct participatory democracy as exercised through the town meeting—a sentiment that might have predisposed voters to the Antifederalist side. Fortunately for the Federalists, they enjoyed the support of most of the experienced leaders in the state, headed by the wartime governor, Jonathan Trumbull, now in retirement, and Samuel Huntington, once president of Congress and now governor. All ten of the state's newspapers supported ratification, and signers Roger Sherman (under the pen names "A Farmer" and "A Countryman") and Oliver Ellsworth ("The Land-Holder") came home to lead the campaign in the press.

Connecticut's ratification convention—with nearly 200 members, by far the largest to date—assembled on 3 January in the capitol building in Hartford, but it moved the next day to the First Congregational Church, which enjoyed a heating system. Six days of debate followed, with the overwhelming Federalist majority giving full consideration to the objections of the minority and answering them with reasoned speeches, a marked departure from events in Pennsylvania the previous fall. On 9 January the convention voted its approval, and the yeas signed the ratification instrument. Although forty Antifederalists refused to sign, they left the convention feeling far more reconciled to the outcome than their brethren in the Keystone State. This fact was not lost on George Washington and the other Federalist leaders. Avoiding strong-arm tactics immediately became a cardinal tenet of their strategy as the campaign for ratification entered its second, critical phase.

The Battle Joined

The Federalists had enjoyed commanding advantages in each of the first five states to consider ratification. Widespread popular support for the new instrument of government already existed in each, and their state governments provided for the speedy election of the special ratification conventions. None of the remaining eight states promised such easy victory. In these states the sense of political momentum in favor of the Constitution that had served so well in the initial battles would mean little since the opposition was strong and prepared. For the ensuing contests, the Federalists had to rely heavily on their efforts to convince individual voters to support Federalist candidates for seats in the ratification conventions.

At the heart of these efforts were many articles and broadsides that offered a host of reasons why the Constitution deserved popular support. In particular, Alexander Hamilton, James Madison, and John Jay published eighty-five essays under the collective pen name "Publius." Intended merely as a point-by-point rebuttal of the main Antifederalist arguments and offered in the heat of a partisan political campaign, they endure as *The Federalist Papers*, one of the most important works of political theory in the western world.

After delegates were elected to each ratification convention, the Federalists tried to apply superior organization, parliamentary skills, and the leadership of prominent political veterans to offset any remaining numerical disadvantages. They also employed their nationwide network of allies to exert their influence across state lines.

Massachusetts, the second of the Federalists' four key states to vote on ratification, provided the first true test of the Constitution's popularity. Not only did it share the traditional New England suspicion of central authority, but many of its voters harbored reservations about the manner in which the leaders of the emerging Federalist party had dealt with Shays' Rebellion, an uprising by the state's debtor farmers frustrated with the indifference to their plight shown by the mercantile interests who dominated the state government. Antifederalist forces took heart both from the fact that John Hancock, the popular governor, carefully refrained from taking sides on the ratification issue and from Elbridge Gerry's skillful denunciations of what he saw as the Constitution's defects. As a member of the Constitutional Convention, Gerry carried special weight with the state's voters. Heated arguments in the town meetings used for the election of ratification delegates seemed to indicate a trend against the Constitution. The fact that the convention would be the largest in any state—with roughly one delegate for every 1,000 eligible voters, the election would be the most representative in the state's history—also seemed to work in favor of the Antifederalists.

But when the 364 delegates assembled in Boston on 9 January, the outcome began to favor the Federalists. They were encouraged by the fact that 46 of the 318 towns entitled to representation chose not to participate in the convention. They were also heartened by the greater political experience of the Federalist leaders. Neither Samuel Adams nor John Hancock, the only two men of stature who could have organized an opposition, chose to take an active part. On the other hand, the Federalists boasted two signers, Nathaniel Gorham and Rufus King; two Revolutionary War generals, William Heath and Benjamin Lincoln; a former governor, James Bowdoin; and three rising politicians, Theodore Sedgwick, Theophilus Parsons, and Fisher Ames. After assessing the situation, the Federalist leaders quickly acquiesced in Hancock's election as presiding officer and state Chief Justice William Cushing's selection as vice president. They then set out to argue dispassionately the merits of the Constitution, using the tactics that had proved so successful in Connecticut.

STATE CONVENTIONS FOR THE RATIFICATION OF THE CONSTITUTION

State	*Dates of Convention*	*Site of Convention*	*Presiding Officer*	*Date of Vote*	*For/Against*
Delaware	2–7 December 1787	Dover	James Latimer	6 December 1787	30–0
Pennsylvania	21 November–14 December 1787	Philadelphia	Frederick A. C. Muhlenberg	12 December 1787	46–23
New Jersey	11–18 December 1787	Trenton	John Stevens	18 December 1787	38–0
Georgia	25 December 1787–5 January 1788	Augusta	John Wereat	31 December 1787	26–0
Connecticut	3–9 January 1788	Hartford	Matthew Griswold	9 January 1788	128–40
Massachusetts	9 January–7 February 1788	Boston	John Hancock	6 February 1788	187–168
Maryland	21–29 April 1788	Annapolis	George Plater	26 April 1788	63–11
South Carolina	12–24 May 1788	Charleston	Thomas Pinckney	23 May 1788	149–73
New Hampshire	13–22 February 1788	Exeter	John Sullivan	22 February 1788	(56–51 [a])
	18–21 June 1788	Concord	John Sullivan	21 June 1788	57–47
Virginia	2–27 June 1788	Richmond	Edmund Pendleton	26 June 1788	89–79
New York	17 June–26 July 1788	Poughkeepsie	George Clinton	26 July 1788	30–27
North Carolina	21 July–2 August 1788	Hillsboro	Samuel Johnston	2 August 1788	(84–184 [b])
	16–23 November 1789	Fayetteville	Samuel Johnston	21 November 1789	194–77
Rhode Island	1–6 March 1790	South Kingstown	Daniel Owen	6 March 1790	(28–41 [c])
	24–29 May 1790	South Kingstown	Daniel Owen	29 May 1790	34–32

[a] Vote taken on motion to adjourn (Federalist position).
[b] Vote taken on motion to neither ratify nor reject (Antifederalist position).
[c] Vote taken on motion to adjourn (Antifederalist position).

The Federalists won an important parliamentary victory on the first day, turning back an Antifederalist motion to adjourn and passing rules requiring a detailed, clause-by-clause discussion before any ratification vote could take place. In six-day work weeks, the Federalists responded to each and every objection with respectful and erudite arguments. Cushing presided in place of an ailing Hancock, who continued to avoid taking a stand on the ratification issue.

The Federalists came to the conclusion that a crucial block of delegates might swing their way if the issue of the absence of a bill of rights could be resolved. Convinced that none of the remaining state conventions would give unconditional approval to the Constitution, they turned to the idea of a ratification instrument that included amendments *recommended* for implementation after the new government went into effect. It was a tricky point, for the instrument of approval had to be phrased in a way that would not make the adoption of the changes a *condition* of approval, since such a conditional ratification would violate the spirit of the Framers' intent. They had another problem: a motion to include recommendations for a bill of rights would be more effective as the basis for compromise if it emanated from a neutral party. Hancock was an obvious choice, and the Federalists successfully convinced him now to take his seat as presiding officer and to introduce nine amendments drawn up by the Federalists.

It took another week for this plan to succeed, but finally on 6 February, after a round of conciliatory speeches, the ratification instrument, with Hancock's nine amendments, passed by a vote of 187 to 168. The wisdom of the Federalists' nonconfrontational approach was immediately apparent when, in marked contrast to the experience in Pennsylvania, most of the Antifederalist leaders in Massachusetts agreed that the democratic process had been followed in the convention and that they would now support the will of the majority.

Supporters of the Constitution also faced an uncertain outcome in New Hampshire. Its ratification convention assembled in Exeter on 13 February. The Antifederalists had outpolled the Federalists in the selection of delegates, but both signer John Langdon and Revolutionary War general John Sullivan, the leaders of the state's two major political factions, supported ratification, and their combined experience and the discipline of their followers easily offset the Antifederalist edge in delegates. Sullivan was elected presiding officer, and under his watchful eye the convention spent a week in a clause-by-clause discussion of the Constitution, a delaying tactic that worked to the Federalists' advantage. Finally, on 22 February, the Federalists were able to swing enough votes to push through an adjournment. This apparent first setback for the nationalist cause in the ratification process actually marked an important victory for the Federalists. They had come to realize that a number of key delegates, convinced by the arguments they had heard, now wanted to change their positions. In keeping with New England's venerable political customs, however, these men felt honor bound to vote according to their towns' initial instructions. The Federalists determined that a recess would allow time for these men to return home and persuade their town meetings to alter those orders.

Before New Hampshire's convention could reconvene, the fight passed to two southern states. The Antifederalists were confident of quick victory in Maryland because so many of the state's political leaders, including Luther Martin and John F. Mercer, both delegates to Philadelphia, had publicly come out against the Constitution. But their confidence cost them dearly. In the first place they failed to organize an effective campaign during the election for convention delegates and consequently were soundly beaten by the Federalists. Then to compound their error, their leaders delayed their arrival in Annapolis until after the convention had opened on 21 April, only to find themselves outmaneuvered by the Federalists in the first parliamentary rounds.

The Antifederalists had assumed that by delaying the opening session and taking advantage of the Federalists' habit of discussing the issues at length, they might drag things out until neighboring Virginia began its convention. News of the widely anticipated defeat of the Constitution in Virginia, they calculated, would offset their minority strength in the Maryland convention. Instead, the Federalists took advantage of their majority to push through rules of procedure that limited discussion and forced an early vote. On 26 April a belated attempt by the Antifederalists to introduce a list of twenty-eight amendments failed, and, by a lopsided margin of 63 to 11, the Constitution was approved without qualification. Two more days were spent completing convention business, during which time the Federalists easily quashed a second attempt to introduce crippling amendments.

Maryland's convention marked the last time the Federalists mustered the strength to win a straight yes or no vote. In the remaining contests a more even balance between the political sides forced the Constitution's supporters to compromise, employing the tactic introduced in Massachusetts whereby approval would include a series of amendments recommended by the state to the new government.

South Carolina's Federalists were the first to follow the Massachusetts example. Its convention met in solidly Federalist Charleston on 12 May, but strong Antifederalist forces from the western counties were well represented and promised a good fight. Three days were consumed with procedural matters, including the election of Governor Thomas Pinckney, a Continental Army veteran, as presiding officer, before a detailed debate of each article of the Constitution began.

For nine days the Federalists discussed the articles in reasoned tones, concentrating on the specific objections voiced by their western opponents. But here the tactic failed to move the western delegates, who remained deeply suspicious of any political arguments coming from representatives of the Tidewater region. Charles Pinckney and his cousin, Charles Cotesworth Pinckney, both signers of the Constitution, and the other Federalist leaders then began to offer a series of recommended amendments to try to swing western votes to the yea column. An attempt by the Antifederalists to defeat the Constitution by adjournment failed on 21 May, and two days later a committee reported out four proposed amendments that were designed to strengthen the rights of states in dealing with the central government. After the Federalists mustered sufficient strength to reject additional amendments offered from the floor, including a bill of rights, a motion to ratify the Constitution that included a recommendation that the four amendments be added later to the document then passed by the comfortable margin of 149 to 73.

South Carolina's vote increased the total of states that had approved the Constitution to eight; one more would put the document into effect. The drama mounted as June 1788 began, for both Virginia and New York (the remaining two key states) were scheduled to consider ratification during that month, and New Hampshire was due to meet again. The Antifederalists, unbowed by their string of defeats, were still determined to seize the day. Secure in the knowledge that both Virginia and New York were governed by popular men who had openly attacked the Constitution, they redoubled their efforts in those states. For their part, the Federalists used a network of politicians and veterans to establish a courier service to link the three conventions in order to coordinate the efforts of their forces.

The New Hampshire delegates assembled last, but acted first. Thanks to the Federalists' skillful maneuver in February to adjourn the convention so that delegates could report to their town meetings for new instructions, Langdon and Sullivan arrived at the new convention site in Concord on 19 June with enough votes in hand to render ratification a foregone conclusion. On the third day of debate a bipartisan committee crafted a list of twelve amendments. At this point the only real question left was whether the Antifederalists would try to make them a binding condition for ratification. After the Federalists carried that point, ratification was approved by a final vote of 57 to 47 at 1 P.M. on 21 June 1788. The hour was carefully noted in the convention's journal to establish New Hampshire's claim to being the state that turned the Constitution into a reality. Langdon and Sullivan immediately sent messengers hurrying south to try to influence the outcome in New York and Virginia.

Ironically, other factors proved more important. The results of the New York and Virginia conventions would hinge instead on debates between teams of highly articulate spokesmen for the respective sides. The contests in both states demonstrated just how flexible and creative the Federalists had become in carrying through their program, especially when the opposition not only enjoyed an enormous numerical advantage, but could finally boast leaders to match the Federalists in experience and talent.

Virginia's convention assembled in Richmond with evenly matched galaxies of leaders. The Antifederalists rallied behind the popular ex-governor Patrick Henry and George Mason, while the Federalists included James Madison, Henry Lee, Edmund Pendleton, and George Wythe. Offstage, the commanding figure of General George Washington lent further credibility to the nationalist cause. At issue were the votes of the uncommitted delegates who would spell the margin of victory. After electing Pendleton as presiding officer and Wythe as chairman of the committee of the whole, where most of the actual debate would occur, the two sides agreed to a lengthy line-by-line discussion of the merits and defects of the document. They also quickly chose more expansive quarters in the new Academy building on Shockoe Hill, in part to provide room for the crowds of spectators.

Serious debate began on 4 June with the unexpected announcement by Governor Randolph, who had refused to sign the Constitution in Philadelphia, that he had experienced a change of heart. This statement infuriated Mason, who later compared the governor to Benedict Arnold. For three weeks the crowded galleries were treated to ringing rhetorical exchanges. Henry's famed oratory appeared to be winning over the undecided. But the long days of debate began to wear on the delegates, especially those who served simultaneously in the Virginia legislature, which began to sit on 23 June. This widespread weariness, plus the Federalist assessment that they did not have the votes to win outright, caused them to shift tactics. Applying what had worked before, Madison and his companions turned to developing another series of recommended amendments to achieve compromise.

This move changed the focus of the debate. Ratification if accompanied by amendments was now conceded by all. At issue again was whether these amendments would be in the form of *recommendations* as proposed by the Federalists or binding *conditions* of ratification as demanded by the Antifederalists. The issue was joined on 24 June during a session that began routinely enough. Pendleton gaveled the body to order and turned the chair over to the committee of the whole. But in a departure from normal procedure, he called upon Thomas Mathews rather than Wythe to preside. This tactic allowed the widely respected Wythe to participate in the actual debating, and Mathews immediately recognized him. Wythe introduced a motion to consider a list of recommended amendments. A furious Henry countered with a proposal to consider a series of conditional amendments. Randolph then asked whether Henry was prepared for the consequences if the new federal government chose not to honor conditional amendments—would the Antifederalists then want Virginia to secede from the Union? Further discussion was drowned out by the noise of a violent thunderstorm, and the convention was forced to adjourn.

The postponement proved advantageous to the Federalists, for Virginia Attorney General James Innes, their best public speaker, finally arrived the next day in time to deliver a major summation of the Federalist position. He eloquently pressed the notion that the convention had nothing further to gain from prolonging debate, and that the Constitution's supporters were willing to back any amendments that did not violate the basic intent of the Framers. In a move that stunned the convention and promptly removed any Antifederalist chance of victory, Patrick Henry rose to concede that Innes made a great deal of sense and that perhaps it would be best to amend the Constitution later by using the methods devised by its Framers.

After some further discussion, the committee of the whole transformed itself into a formal session. The motion to make ratification conditional on acceptance of the amendments was defeated 80 to 88, and the Wythe motion for merely recommending amendments passed 89 to 79. The convention finally adjourned on 27 June after delegates made a number of conciliatory speeches and approved the Constitution without a roll call but with a covering letter that included a 27-part bill of rights and twenty other amendments. It was not until the following day that news of New Hampshire's decision reached Richmond.

If in Virginia the Constitution won through the skill of its defenders and the weight of their arguments, in New York timing was all. By the day New York's convention assembled in Poughkeepsie's court house, seven long months of intense public discussion of the issues had taken place. Voters had been able to weigh the arguments advanced by Antifederalist writers such as "Cato," and, in particular, by signer Alexander Hamilton on the other side. The citizens had registered their decision by electing 46 Antifederalists, led by Governor George Clinton, a former Continental Army general, and only 19 Federalists, headed by Hamilton.

The delegates spent two days, 17 and 18 June, on procedural matters, including selection of Clinton as presiding officer. The Federalists were surprised when Clinton agreed to allow a lengthy debate of each article of the Constitution before taking a vote. Actually, Clinton, sure of victory, was reluctant to have New York be the first state to vote down the Constitution. He was willing to delay the final vote in the hope that either Virginia or New Hampshire would record the first rejection. For the next month the opponents engaged in a great verbal sparring match (primarily pitting Hamilton against Melancthon Smith) that apparently changed few if any opinions. Not even the news of New Hampshire's ratification, which arrived on 25 June, shook the Antifederalist ranks. On the other hand, it did subtly alter the essence of the debate, for now the key issue revolved around the question of whether New York would join the Union, not whether the Union would come into being.

The news from Virginia put the issue in starker terms. About noon on 2 July William S. Livingston, a Federalist and former Continental Army officer, arrived in Poughkeepsie after riding the 82 miles from New York City in seven and a half hours. He brought word that Virginia had ratified. Now only North Carolina and tiny Rhode Island remained with New York outside the fold. Such isolation was an unexpected development. Two days later, on the anniversary of Independence, the Federalists, in a move designed to take advantage of the new situation, abruptly altered their tactics and refused to participate in further debate.

The Antifederalists had little room left in which to maneuver. The only real issue for them to consider was what form of ratification they could accept, for they had no intention of keeping the state out of the Union. On 23 July Antifederalist Smith took the floor and said he had never wanted outright rejection of the Constitution, but rather had sought to remedy its defects. Now, he added, he had come to accept the Federalists' sincerity in promising to push for amendments after the document went into effect. A number of other Antifederalist leaders followed suit, and a hasty test vote indicated that the compromise position held a slim 31 to 29 advantage. On 25 July the committee of the whole voted for ratification 31 to 28, and the full convention gave its consent the next day by a vote of 30 to 27. The Federalists then joined in a unanimous vote to send a circular letter to every state suggesting a second national convention to deal with the amendment process and to adjourn the convention.

Final Consensus

The votes of the last two key states, Virginia and New York, ended the second, critical phase of the ratification struggle. At this point only two states remained outside the fold, but to the Federalists unanimity now became the objective. Both North Carolina and Rhode Island had particular local political situations that contributed to a lack of popular support for the Constitution. Neither would ratify before the new government opened for business, and both would take several tries to complete action. North Carolina had a very strong traditional antagonism between its sections and was fragmented into a multitude of ethnic, cultural, and religious groups, all busily contending for a share of power. Shortly after the vote to send delegates to Philadelphia in 1787, the balance of power swung to a new alliance of politicians, heavily influenced by western counties. They were far less interested in national issues, and felt no compelling reason to change the existing structure of government. Therefore, when the state legislature voted on 6 December 1787 to call a ratification convention, it deliberately put off its opening until 21 July 1788.

North Carolina's convention assembled in Hillsboro in the full knowledge that the Constitution had already won approval. In effect, participation in the Union, not ratification of the Constitution, was the issue to be decided by the delegates. Although Governor Samuel Johnston was accorded the honor of presiding, the dominant figure was Antifederalist Willie Jones, who controlled a majority of votes. Badly outnumbered, the Federalists relied heavily on William R. Davie, the only delegate who had been in Philadelphia, to present the case for the Constitution. The basis of the Federalist argument was that the Antifederalists were trying to declare independence for North Carolina. The Antifederalists countered by citing Thomas Jefferson's view that if only a minimum number of states ratified, a second convention would be needed to accommodate the minority through a discussion of amendments. After winning approval for a long series of amendments by a vote of 184 to 84, the Antifederalists forced adjournment without further action on the Constitution. After considering minor state matters, including a resolution to move the state capital to Raleigh, the convention dissolved on 4 August.

North Carolina did not have the luxury of acting in isolation. The First Congress under the Constitution convened in New York City on 4 March 1789, with the House of Representatives achieving a quorum on 1 April and the Senate five days later. As soon as formalities were completed, Congress met in joint session as specified in Section 1, Article II, to open and count the ballots of the Electoral College, which had voted on 4 February. To no one's surprise, they discovered that George Washington had been unanimously elected as the first President. He took his oath of office on 30 April and in partnership with the Congress proceeded to organize the executive and judicial branches.

In his opening day address to the newly elected state legislature on 3 November 1789, Governor Johnston warned that Congress was in the process of passing legislation that affected North Carolina without having North Carolinians present in either chamber. The Antifederalists failed to block the Federalists' effort to call an election for a new ratification convention, and the convention was called to order in Fayetteville on 16 November.

The Federalists had considerably improved their fortunes in the interval between conventions. This time they fielded better candidates, gathering considerable support in the western counties because of the need for military protection against the Indians. Most North Carolinians found George Washington's administration quite acceptable and were well aware that Madison was already at work in the House of Representatives drafting a bill of rights to be added to the Constitution. Only three days of debate were needed before North Carolina voted 194 to 77 in favor of ratification on 21 November.

Rhode Island, the last of the original thirteen states to come into the fold, had traditionally put particular emphasis on local government and, like North Carolina, harbored strong suspicions of the power of a distant national government. Overriding other considerations was the issue of paper currency. A majority of Rhode Islanders objected to the Constitution's prohibitions concerning state currency. Accordingly, the state legislature, based on instructions its members received from their local town meetings voted eleven times between February 1788 and January 1790 *not* to call a ratification convention. Finally, pressures exerted by the federal government persuaded Governor John Collins to cast a tie-breaking vote (a move that would cost him renomination) in favor of a ratification convention.

The convention assembled in South Kingstown on 1 March 1790 and spent six days discussing the Constitution and Madison's twelve-part Bill of Rights, which Congress had approved and had sent to the states. The delegates added another eighteen potential amendments. On 6 March, over vigorous objections from the Federalist minority, they decided to adjourn until May to allow the annual April town meetings to consider the issues. On 24 May the same delegates reassembled and faced an immediate crisis. Providence, the largest economic center in the state, had voted in its town meeting to secede from Rhode Island if the Constitution was not ratified. Newport, the state's other major port, probably would do the same. For five days the members argued back and forth. Finally, on Saturday, 29 May 1790, by the narrowest of margins (34 to 32, with three known Antifederalists deliberately absenting themselves) the last of the states gave its assent. The convention also approved eleven of Madison's amendments and recommended a further twenty-one.

It was probably inevitable that the ratification process—the vital task of persuading representatives of the American people to adopt the Constitution in 1788—has been overshadowed historically by the events surrounding the writing of the Constitution. The work of the Founding Fathers at Philadelphia in the summer of 1787 has rightly been celebrated as a paramount achievement in American history and as a crowning step in the development of applied political philosophy. Without question, the Constitution was a singular work of political genius, one that has allowed the nation to prosper for two hundred years, and one that reflected the particular experience and perspective of the Soldier-Statesmen of the Constitution, those veterans who energetically supported the concept of strong central government. But popular neglect of the thirteen separate ratification conventions should not mask the fact that winning approval of the Constitution was also a key event in the history of the nation. If many people assume today that ratification was a given once the Constitution was signed, it certainly did not appear that way to the dedicated men who had to defend the articles of the new document before concerned locally elected delegates. As this account demonstrates, ratification was accomplished with the aid of some luck, but also with a great deal of skill, perseverance, and carefully considered arguments.

It can be convincingly shown that the ratification process was in its own right an important step in creating a sense of nationhood. Through the issues raised in the town and county elections for convention delegates, in town meetings held to discuss the Constitution, in the state convention debates, and in the great outpouring of articles, printed speeches, and broadsides for and against the new document, the people at large were made aware as never before of just what a federal republic was, and what their rights and responsibilities were under such a novel form of government. Those who defended the Constitution at the special ratification conventions had to convince their fellow citizens that it was all right to divide their loyalty and trust between their state, which still represented the ideal of independence, and the first strong central government since England's defeat. Prominent among these defenders were such Soldier-Statesmen as Hamilton, Dickinson, Livingston, Brearly, King, Langdon, and the two Pinckneys, as well as such Revolutionary War generals as Heath, Lincoln, and Sullivan.

It was no mean feat that the Federalists were able to convince the American people that central government could be checked in a democratic way and that the powers of that government would therefore be harnessed for the greater public good. In a very real sense the ratification process brought to the people a clearer understanding of the concept of a government of the people and gave birth to the Bill of Rights.

Newspapers used visual images to depict the course of the ratification struggle. A favorite Federalist device showed a Temple of Liberty, Justice, and Peace, with voters adding a pillar to the "federal edifice" as each state ratified. The design shown above is based on that used by the *Massachusetts Centinel.*

APPENDIX E

Statistics

This study of the Soldier-Statesmen of the Constitution grew out of a mass of biographical data gathered on more than a thousand men who served in various prominent positions in the federal and state governments between 1775 and 1815. This data provided the statistical evidence undergirding the thesis of the book: that a significant percentage of the nation's political leadership during the first generation of the new republic were veterans of the Revolutionary War. It also provided the raw material for a statistical comparison of veteran and nonveteran strength in government. The tables and charts that follow are based on this material and are meant to illustrate for the general reader the changes and trends in the percentage of veterans in government throughout the Constitutional generation with special emphasis on those who signed the Constitution. They are followed by a roster of some 400 veterans who served in senior positions in the federal executive, legislative, and judicial branches and as state governors before 1815. It should be noted that this roster lists only service in the Revolution. In fact many of these veterans also saw service in the French and Indian War or in later military action on the frontier or against the British in the War of 1812.

EXECUTIVE BRANCH MEMBERS
WITH ACTIVE MILITARY SERVICE IN THE REVOLUTION

	Percentage of Veterans		
Administration	*Presidents and Vice Presidents*	*Cabinet Officers*	*Diplomats of Ambassadorial Rank*
1st Washington	50	83.5	100
2d Washington	50	80	75
Adams	0	75	50
1st Jefferson	50	57	75
2d Jefferson	50	43	33
1st Madison	50	60	20
2d Madison	0	31	11

SUPREME COURT JUSTICES
WITH ACTIVE MILITARY SERVICE IN THE REVOLUTION

	Percentage of Veterans	
President By Whom Appointed	*Chief Justice*	*Associate Justice*
Washington	0	22
Adams	100	100
Jefferson		67
Madison		0

STATE GOVERNORS
WITH ACTIVE MILITARY SERVICE IN THE REVOLUTION

	Percentage of Veterans			
State	1775–1782	1783–1788	1789–1800	1801–1815
Connecticut	0	0	67	25
Delaware	100	50	100	40
Georgia	67	67	80	67
Kentucky			100	100
Louisiana				0
Maryland	67	67	67	67
Massachusetts	100	50	25	25
New Hampshire	0	67	100	80
New Jersey	100	100	67	75
New York	100	100	50	67
North Carolina	50	67	100	57
Ohio				0
Pennsylvania	40	67	100	50
Rhode Island	0	50	100	67
South Carolina	33	100	80	28.5
Tennessee			100	50
Vermont			67	75
Virginia	75	100	100	57

U.S. CONGRESS MEMBERS WITH ACTIVE MILITARY SERVICE IN THE REVOLUTION (Arranged by Congress)

Congress	Percentage of Veterans		
	Senate	House	Total
1st (1789–91)	51.5	63.5[d]	60[d]
2d (1791–93)	53	62[d]	59[d]
3d (1793–95)	51.5	69[e]	65[e]
4th (1795–97)	67.5	66[d]	63.5[d]
5th (1797–99)	67	54[d]	57.5[d]
6th (1799–1801)	71	54[d]	58.5[d]
7th (1801–03)	61	53.5	56.5
8th (1803–05)	61	52	54
9th (1805–07)	60	37	47
10th (1807–09)	58.5	36[c]	41[c]
11th (1809–11)	49	31[cdf]	35[cdf]
12th (1811–13)	38.5	30[cdf]	31.5[cdf]
13th (1813–15)	22.5	24.5[f]	24.5[f]

[c] Includes one individual who saw active duty in a regular Loyalist Regiment of the British Army.
[d] Includes one individual who served at sea on a privateer.
[e] Includes two individuals who served at sea on privateers.
[f] Includes one individual who served at sea in the Continental Navy.

U.S. CONGRESS MEMBERS WITH ACTIVE MILITARY SERVICE IN THE REVOLUTION (Arranged by State)

State	Percentage of Veterans in Each Congress												
	1st	2d	3d	4th	5th	6th	7th	8th	9th	10th	11th	12th	13th
Connecticut	28.5	37.5	40	45.5	27	40	33	33	40	50	54.5	44	40
Delaware	33	33	60	67	40	33	0	0	0	0	0	0	0
Georgia	100	100	75	100	100	75	83	67	40	28.5	14	28.5	18
Kentucky[a]		50	50	75	75	75	75	75	60	12.5	10	12.5	6
Louisiana[b]												25	0
Maryland	37.5	18	50	54	36	36	50	58	46	45.5[c]	54[c]	54.5[c]	45.5
Massachusetts	50[d]	55.5[d]	62.5[e]	55[d]	53[d]	57[d]	59	52.5	26	24	13.5	31.5[d]	20
New Hampshire	40	60	67	67	43	43	33	28.5	28.5	57	37.5[d]	14	10
New Jersey	67	67	75	75	75	100	100	87.5	75	55.5	70	50	33
New York	75	75	75	69	53.5	71.5	61.5	62.5	37	55	31.5[f]	25[f]	19[f]
North Carolina	57	57	75	77	69	33	23	43	40	43	28.5	26.5	26.5
Ohio[g]								0	0	0	20	0	0
Pennsylvania	50	55.5	62.5	37.5	44.5	50	52.5	52.5	45.5	41	43	35	38.5
Rhode Island	67	67	50	60	33	0	40	40	25	0	40	20	25
South Carolina	71.5	71.5	77.5	89	80	62.5	72.5	72.5	50	50	41.5	30	9
Tennessee[h]				67	67	67	67	60	60	60	33	50	30
Vermont[i]		100	100	100	100	100	100	67	67	62.5	50	67	50
Virginia	80	69	65	67	68	72.5	57	51.5	40	48	34.5	32	29.5

[a] Admitted to the Union 1 June 1792 from territory ceded by Virginia.
[b] Admitted to the Union 30 April 1812; formed from part of the Territory of Orleans.
[c] Includes one individual who saw active duty in a regular Loyalist Regiment of the British Army.
[d] Includes one individual who served at sea on a privateer.
[e] Includes two individuals who served at sea on privateers.
[f] Includes one individual who served at sea in the Continental Navy.
[g] Admitted to the Union 29 November 1802 from part of the territory northwest of the Ohio River; did not send a delegation to the 7th Congress.
[h] Admitted to the Union 1 June 1796 from the territory south of the Ohio River.
[i] Admitted to the Union 4 March 1791.

SOLDIER-STATESMEN OF THE EARLY REPUBLIC

Name	*State*	*Birth/ Death*	*National Office*	*Military Service*
Adair, John	Kentucky	1757–1840	Senate 1805–1806 Governor 1820–1824 House 1831–1833	Militia
Alexander, Nathaniel	North Carolina	1756–1808	House 1803–1805 Governor 1805–1807	Continental
Ames, Fisher	Massachusetts	1758–1808	House 1789–1797	Militia
Anderson, Isaac	Pennsylvania	1760–1838	House 1803–1807	Militia
Anderson, Joseph	Tennessee	1757–1837	Senate 1797–1815 (President Pro Tem 1805)	Continental
Anderson, William	Pennsylvania	1762–1829	House 1809–1815; 1817–1819	Continental
Archer, John	Maryland	1741–1810	House 1801–1807	Continental
Armstrong, James	Pennsylvania	1748–1828	House 1793–1795	Continental
Armstrong, John	Pennsylvania New York	1758–1843	Continental Congress 1787 Senate 1800–1802; 1803–1804 Minister to France 1804–1810 Secretary of War 1813–1814	Continental
Ashe, John Baptista	North Carolina	1748–1802	Continental Congress 1787 House 1789–1793	Continental
Ashe, Samuel	North Carolina	1725–1813	Governor 1795–1797	Militia
Avery, Daniel	New York	1766–1842	House 1811–1815; 1816–1817	Militia
Bailey, Theodorus	New York	1758–1828	House 1793–1797; 1799–1803 Senate 1803–1804	Militia
*Baldwin, Abraham	Georgia	1754–1807	Continental Congress 1786–1789 House 1789–1799 Senate 1799–1807 (President Pro Tem 1801–1802)	Continental
Barker, Joseph	Massachusetts	1751–1815	House 1805–1809	None
Barlow, Joel	Connecticut	1754–1812	Minister to France 1811–1812	Continental
Barnett, William	Georgia	1761–1832	House 1812–1815	Militia
Barnwell, Robert	South Carolina	1761–1814	Continental Congress 1788–1789 House 1791–1793	Militia
Bartlett, Josiah	New Hampshire	1729–1795	Continental Congress 1775–1776; 1778–1779 Governor 1790–1795	Militia
*Bassett, Richard	Delaware	1745–1815	Senate 1789–1793 Governor 1799–1801	Militia
Beatty, John	New Jersey	1749–1826	Continental Congress 1784–1785 House 1793–1795	Continental
Bedford, Gunning	Delaware	1742–1797	Governor 1796–1797	Continental
Bedinger, George Michael	Kentucky	1756–1843	House 1803–1807	Militia
Benton, Lemuel	South Carolina	1754–1818	House 1793–1799	Militia
Bishop, Phanuel	Massachusetts	1739–1812	House 1799–1807	Militia
Blake, John, Jr.	New York	1762–1826	House 1805–1809	Militia
Bland, Theodoric	Virginia	1742–1790	Continental Congress 1780–1783 House 1789–1790	Continental
Bloom, Isaac	New York	c. 1716–1803	House 1803	Militia
Bloomfield, Joseph	New Jersey	1753–1823	Governor 1801–1812 House 1817–1821	Continental
Blount, Thomas	North Carolina	1759–1812	House 1793–1799; 1805–1809; 1811–1812	Continental
*Blount, William	North Carolina Tennessee	1749–1800	Continental Congress 1782–1783; 1786–1787 Governor of Territory South of Ohio 1790–1796 Senate 1796–1797	Continental
Boude, Thomas	Pennsylvania	1752–1822	House 1801–1803	Continental
Boudinot, Elias	New Jersey	1740–1821	Continental Congress 1777–1778; 1781–1782 (President 1782–1783) House 1789–1795	Continental
Bourne, Benjamin	Rhode Island	1755–1808	House 1790–1796	Continental
Bowie, Robert	Maryland	1750–1818	Governor 1803–1807; 1811–1812	Militia
Bowie, Walter	Maryland	1748–1810	House 1802–1805	Militia
Bradford, William	Pennsylvania	1755–1795	Attorney General 1794–1795	Continental
Bradley, Stephen Row	Vermont	1754–1830	Senate 1791–1795; 1801–1813 (President Pro Tem 1802–1803; 1808–1809)	Militia
Breckinridge, James	Virginia	1763–1833	House 1809–1817	Militia
Breckinridge, John	Kentucky	1760–1806	Senate 1801–1805 Attorney General 1805–1806	Militia
Brigham, Elijah	Massachusetts	1751–1816	House 1811–1816	Militia
Brigham, Paul	Vermont	1746–1824	Governor 1797	Continental

*Signer of the Constitution.

Name	State	Birth/ Death	National Office	Military Service
Brooke, Robert	Virginia	c. 1761–1800	Governor 1794–1796	Militia
Brooks, David	New York	1756–1838	House 1797–1799	Militia
Brown, John	Virginia	1757–1837	Continental Congress 1787–1788	Militia
			House 1789–1792	
	Kentucky		Senate 1792–1805	
			(President Pro Tem 1803–1805)	
Brown, Robert	Pennsylvania	1744–1823	House 1798–1815	Militia
Bryan, Nathan	North Carolina	1748–1798	House 1795–1798	Militia
Buck, Daniel	Vermont	1753–1816	House 1795–1797	Militia
Bulloch, Archibald	Georgia	c. 1730–1777	Continental Congress 1775–1776	Militia
			Governor 1776–1777	
Bullock, Stephen	Massachusetts	1735–1816	House 1797–1799	Militia
Burges, Dempsey	North Carolina	1751–1800	House 1795–1799	Militia
Burke, Aedanus	South Carolina	1743–1802	House 1789–1791	Continental
Burr, Aaron	New York	1756–1836	Senate 1791–1797	Continental
			Vice President 1801–1805	
Butler, Ezra	Vermont	1763–1838	House 1813–1815	Militia
			Governor 1826–1828	
*Butler, Pierce	South Carolina	1744–1822	Continental Congress 1787	Militia
			Senate 1789–1796; 1802–1804	
Butler, William	South Carolina	1759–1821	House 1801–1813	Militia
Cabell, Samuel Jordan	Virginia	1756–1818	House 1795–1803	Continental
Cadwalader, Lambert	New Jersey	1742–1823	Continental Congress 1784–1787	Continental
			House 1789–1791; 1793–1795	
Calhoun, Joseph	South Carolina	1750–1817	House 1807–1811	Militia
Carleton, Peter	New Hampshire	1755–1828	House 1807–1809	Continental
Carr, Francis	Massachusetts	1751–1821	House 1812–1813	Militia
Casey, Levi	South Carolina	1749–1807	House 1803–1807	Militia
Caswell, Richard	North Carolina	1729–1789	Continental Congress 1774–1776	Militia
			Governor 1776–1780; 1785–1788	
Chamberlain, William	Vermont	1755–1828	House 1803–1805; 1809–1811	Militia
Champion, Epaphroditus	Connecticut	1756–1834	House 1807–1817	Continental
Chandler, John	Massachusetts	1762–1841	House 1805–1809	Militia
	Maine		Senate 1820–1829	
Chipman, Nathaniel	Vermont	1752–1843	Senate 1797–1803	Continental
Claiborne, Thomas	Virginia	1749–1812	House 1793–1799; 1801–1805	Militia
Clay, Matthew	Virginia	1754–1815	House 1797–1813; 1815	Continental
Clayton, Joshua	Delaware	1744–1798	Governor 1789–1796	Militia
			Senate 1798	
Clinton, George	New York	1739–1812	Continental Congress 1775–1776	Continental
			Governor 1777–1795; 1801–1804	
			Vice President 1805–1812	
Clopton, John	Virginia	1756–1816	House 1795–1799; 1801–1816	Militia
Cobb, David	Massachusetts	1748–1830	House 1793–1795	Continental
Cocke, William	Tennessee	1747–1828	Senate 1796–1797; 1799–1805	Militia
Coffin, Peleg, Jr.	Massachusetts	1756–1805	House 1793–1795	Privateer
Coles, Isaac	Virginia	1747–1813	House 1789–1791; 1793–1797	Militia
Colhoun, John Ewing	South Carolina	1749–1802	Senate 1801–1802	Militia
Collins, John	Rhode Island	1717–1795	Continental Congress 1778–1783	Continental
			Governor 1786–1790	
Collins, Thomas	Delaware	?–1789	Governor 1786–1789	Militia
Condit, John	New Jersey	1755–1834	House 1799–1803; 1819	Militia
			Senate 1803–1817	
Contee, Benjamin	Maryland	1755–1815	Continental Congress 1787–1788	Militia
			House 1789–1791	
Cooper, William	New York	1754–1809	House 1795–1797; 1799–1801	Continental
Cox, James	New Jersey	1753–1810	House 1809–1810	Militia
Crabb, Jeremiah	Maryland	1760–1800	House 1795–1796	Continental
Crouch, Edward	Pennsylvania	1764–1827	House 1813–1815	Militia
Culpepper, John	North Carolina	1764–1841	House 1807–1809; 1813–1817; 1819–1821;	Militia
			1823–1825; 1827–1829	
Cushing, William	Massachusetts	1732–1810	Supreme Court 1789–1810	Continental
Cutler, Manasseh	Massachusetts	1742–1823	House 1801–1805	Continental
Davenport, Franklin	New Jersey	1755–1832	Senate 1798–1799	Militia
			House 1799–1801	
Davenport, James	Connecticut	1758–1797	House 1796–1797	Continental

SOLDIER-STATESMEN OF THE EARLY REPUBLIC—CONTINUED

Name	*State*	*Birth/ Death*	*National Office*	*Military Service*
Davenport, John	Connecticut	1752–1830	House 1799–1817	Continental
Davie, William Richardson	North Carolina	1756–1820	Governor 1798–1799	Continental
			Minister to France 1799–1800	
*Dayton, Jonathan	New Jersey	1760–1824	Continental Congress 1787–1789	Continental
			House 1791–1799	
			(Speaker 1795–1799)	
			Senate 1799–1805	
Dean, Josiah	Massachusetts	1748–1818	House 1807–1809	Militia
Dearborn, Henry	Massachusetts	1751–1829	House 1793–1797	Continental
			Secretary of War 1801–1809	
			Minister to Portugal 1822–1824	
Dent, George	Maryland	1756–1813	House 1793–1801	Militia
*Dickinson, John	Pennsylvania	1732–1808	Continental Congress 1774–1776	Militia
			Governor 1782–1785	
	Delaware		Continental Congress 1779–1781	
			Governor 1781	
Dickinson, Philemon	Delaware	1739–1809	Continental Congress 1782–1783	Militia
	New Jersey		Senate 1790–1793	
Dickson, Joseph	North Carolina	1745–1825	House 1799–1801	Militia
Dwight, Thomas	Massachusetts	1758–1819	House 1803–1805	Militia
Earle, John Baylis	South Carolina	1766–1863	House 1803–1805	Militia
Earle, Samuel	South Carolina	1760–1833	House 1795–1797	Continental
Edmund, William	Connecticut	1755–1838	House 1797–1801	Continental
Eggleston, Joseph	Virginia	1754–1811	House 1798–1801	Continental
Elbert, Samuel	Georgia	1740–1788	Governor 1785–1786	Continental
Elmer, Ebenezer	New Jersey	1752–1843	House 1801–1807	Continental
Emanuel, David	Georgia	1744–1810	Governor 1801	Militia
Eustis, William	Massachusetts	1753–1825	House 1801–1805; 1820–1823	Continental
			Secretary of War 1809–1812	
			Minister to Holland 1814–1818	
			Governor 1823–1824	
Evans, Thomas	Virginia	?-?	House 1797–1801	Continental
Farrow, Samuel	South Carolina	1759–1824	House 1813–1815	Militia
Fenner, Arthur	Rhode Island	1745–1805	Governor 1790–1805	Continental
*Few, William	Georgia	1748–1828	Continental Congress 1780–1788	Militia
			Senate 1789–1793	
Findley, William	Pennsylvania	c. 1741–1821	House 1791–1799; 1803–1817	Militia
Fisk, James	Vermont	1763–1844	House 1805–1809; 1811–1815	Continental
			Senate 1817–1818	
*Fitzsimons, Thomas	Pennsylvania	1741–1811	Continental Congress 1782–1783	Militia
			House 1789–1795	
Floyd, William	New York	1734–1821	Continental Congress 1774–1783	Militia
			House 1789–1791	
Forney, Peter	North Carolina	1756–1834	House 1813–1815	Militia
Forrest, Uriah	Maryland	1756–1805	Continental Congress 1786–1787	Continental
			House 1793–1794	
Fowler, John	Kentucky	1755–1840	House 1797–1807	Militia
Franklin, Jesse	North Carolina	1760–1823	House 1795–1797	Militia
			Senate 1799–1805; 1807–1813	
			(President Pro Tem 1804–1805)	
			Governor 1820–1821	
Freeman, Jonathan	New Hampshire	1745–1808	House 1797–1801	Militia
Freylinghuysen, Frederick	New Jersey	1753–1804	Continental Congress 1778–1779;1782–1783	Militia
			Senate 1793–1796	
Gale, George	Maryland	1756–1815	House 1789–1791	Militia
Galusha, Jonas	Vermont	1753–1834	Governor 1809–1813; 1815–1820	Militia
Garrard, James	Kentucky	1749–1822	Governor 1796–1804	Militia
Giles, William Branch	Virginia	1762–1830	House 1790–1798; 1801–1803	Militia
			Senate 1803–1815	
			Governor 1827–1830	
Gillespie, James	North Carolina	1747–1805	House 1793–1799; 1803–1805	Militia
Gillon, Alexander	South Carolina	1741–1794	House 1793–1794	Militia
Gilman, John Taylor	New Hampshire	1753–1828	Continental Congress 1782–1783	Militia
			Governor 1794–1805; 1813–1816	
*Gilman, Nicholas	New Hampshire	1755–1814	Continental Congress 1786–1788	Continental
			House 1789–1797	
			Senate 1805–1814	

Name	*State*	*Birth/ Death*	*National Office*	*Military Service*
Glen, Henry	New York	1739–1814	House 1793–1801	Continental
Gloninger, John	Pennsylvania	1758–1836	House 1813	Militia
Goode, Samuel	Virginia	1756–1822	House 1799–1801	Militia
Goodhue, Benjamin	Massachusetts	1748–1814	House 1789–1796 Senate 1796–1800	Militia
Goodrich, Elizur	Connecticut	1761–1849	House 1799–1801	Militia
Goodwyn, Peterson	Virginia	1745–1818	House 1803–1818	Militia
Gordon, James	New York	1739–1810	House 1791–1795	Militia
Gore, Christopher	Massachusetts	1758–1827	Minister to Great Britain 1796–1803 Governor 1809–1810 Senate 1813–1816	Militia
Grayson, William	Virginia	1742–1790	Continental Congress 1785–1787 Senate 1789–1790	Continental
Greenup, Christopher	Kentucky	1750–1818	House 1792–1797 Governor 1804–1808	Continental
Gregg, Andrew	Pennsylvania	1755–1835	House 1791–1807 Senate 1807–1813 (President Pro Tem 1809–1810)	Militia
Griffin, Isaac	Pennsylvania	1756–1827	House 1813–1817	Militia
Griffin, Samuel	Virginia	?–1810	House 1789–1795	Continental
Griswold, Stanley	Ohio	1763–1815	Senate 1809	Militia
Grout, Jonathan	Massachusetts	1737–1807	House 1789–1791	Militia
Guerrard, Benjamin	South Carolina	1740–1788	Governor 1783–1785	Militia
Gunn, James	Georgia	1753–1801	Senate 1789–1801	Continental
Habersham, Joseph	Georgia	1751–1815	Continental Congress 1783–1784 Postmaster General 1795–1801	Continental
Hall, Bolling	Georgia	1767–1836	House 1811–1817	Militia
Hall, David	Delaware	1752–1817	Governor 1802–1805	Continental
Halsey, Silas	New York	1743–1832	House 1805–1807	Militia
*Hamilton, Alexander	New York	1757–1804	Continental Congress 1782–1783; 1787–1788 Secretary of the Treasury 1789–1795	Continental
Hamilton, John	Pennsylvania	1754–1837	House 1805–1807	Militia
Hamilton, Paul	South Carolina	1762–1816	Governor 1804–1806 Secretary of Navy 1809–1812	Militia
Hammond, Samuel	Georgia	1757–1842	House 1803–1805	Militia
Hampton, Wade	South Carolina	1752–1835	House 1795–1797; 1803–1805	Continental
Hancock, George	Virginia	1754–1820	House 1793–1797	Continental
Hancock, John	Massachusetts	1737–1793	Continental Congress 1775–1780 (President 1775–1777) Governor 1780–1785; 1787–1793	Militia
Handley, George	Georgia	1752–1793	Governor 1788–1789	Continental
Hanna, John Andre	Pennsylvania	c. 1761–1805	House 1797–1805	Militia
Harper, Robert Goodloe	South Carolina Maryland	1765–1825	House 1795–1801 Senate 1816	Militia
Harris, John	New York	1760–1824	House 1807–1809	Continental
Harrison, Benjamin	Virginia	1726–1791	Continental Congress 1774–1778 Governor 1782–1784	Continental
Harrison, Robert Hanson	Maryland	1745–1790	Supreme Court 1789–1790	Continental
Hartley, Thomas	Pennsylvania	1748–1800	House 1789–1800	Continental
Hasbrouck, Josiah	New York	1755–1821	House 1803–1805; 1817–1819	Militia
Hathorn, John	New York	1749–1825	House 1789–1791; 1795–1797	Militia
Haven, Nathaniel Appleton	New Hampshire	1762–1831	House 1809–1811	Privateer
Hawkins, Benjamin	North Carolina	1754–1818	Continental Congress 1781–1784; 1786–1787 Senate 1790–1795	Continental
Heath, John	Virginia	1758–1810	House 1793–1797	Militia
Helms, William	New Jersey	?–1813	House 1801–1811	Continental
Henderson, Thomas	New Jersey	1743–1824	House 1795–1797	Continental
Henry, Patrick	Virginia	1736–1799	Continental Congress 1774–1776 Governor 1776–1779; 1784–1786	Militia
Hiester, Daniel	Maryland	1747–1804	House 1801–1804	Militia
Hiester, John	Pennsylvania	1745–1821	House 1807–1809	Militia
Hiester, Joseph	Pennsylvania	1752–1832	House 1797–1805; 1815–1820 Governor 1820–1824	Militia
Hillhouse, James	Connecticut	1754–1832	House 1791–1796 Senate 1796–1810 (President Pro Tem 1801)	Militia
Hoge, John	Pennsylvania	1760–1824	House 1804–1805	Continental

SOLDIER-STATESMEN OF THE EARLY REPUBLIC—CONTINUED

Name	*State*	*Birth/ Death*	*National Office*	*Military Service*
Holland, James	North Carolina	1754–1823	House 1795–1797; 1801–1811	Militia
Holten, Samuel	Massachusetts	1738–1816	Continental Congress 1778–1780; 1782–1787 House 1793–1795	Militia
Hopkins, Samuel	Kentucky	1753–1819	House 1813–1815	Continental
Houston, John	Georgia	1744–1796	Continental Congress 1775 Governor 1778–1779; 1784–1785	Militia
Howard, John Eager	Maryland	1752–1827	Continental Congress 1784–1788 Governor 1788–1791 Senate 1796–1803 (President Pro Tem 1800–1801)	Continental
Howell, Richard	New Jersey	1754–1802	Governor 1793–1801	Continental
Hubbard, Levi	Massachusetts	1762–1836	House 1813–1815	Militia
Hufty, Jacob	New Jersey	?–1814	House 1809–1814	Militia
Huger, Daniel	South Carolina	1742–1799	Continental Congress 1786–1788 House 1789–1793	Militia
Humphrey, Reuben	New York	1757–1831	House 1807–1809	Militia
Humphreys, David	Connecticut	1752–1818	Minister to Portugal 1791–1796 Minister to Spain 1796–1801	Continental
Hungerford, John Pratt	Virginia	1761–1833	House 1811; 1813–1817	Militia
Hunt, Samuel	New Hampshire	1765–1807	House 1802–1805	Militia
Hunter, John	South Carolina	1732–1802	House 1793–1795 Senate 1796–1798	Militia
Huntington, Ebenezer	Connecticut	1754–1834	House 1810–1811; 1817–1819	Continental
Ilsley, Daniel	Massachusetts	1740–1813	House 1807–1809	Militia
Imlay, James Henderson	New Jersey	1764–1823	House 1797–1801	Militia
Irvine, William	Pennsylvania	1741–1804	Continental Congress 1786–1788 House 1793–1795	Continental
Irwin, Jared	Georgia	1751–1818	Governor 1796–1798; 1806–1809	Continental
Jackson, George	Virginia	1757–1831	House 1795–1797; 1799–1803	Militia
Jackson, James	Georgia	1757–1806	House 1789–1792 Senate 1793–1795; 1801–1806 Governor 1798–1801	Continental
Johnson, James	Virginia	?–1825	House 1813–1820	Militia
Johnson, Thomas	Maryland	1732–1819	Continental Congress 1774–1777 Governor 1777–1779 Supreme Court 1792–1793	Militia
Jones, George	Georgia	1766–1838	Senate 1807	Militia
Jones, Walter	Virginia	1745–1815	House 1797–1799; 1803–1811	Continental
Jones, William	Rhode Island	1753–1822	Governor 1811–1817	Continental
Jones, William	Pennsylvania	1760–1831	House 1801–1803 Secretary of Navy 1813–1814	Militia
Key, Philip Barton	Maryland	1757–1815	House 1807–1813	Loyalist Unit
*King, Rufus	Massachusetts New York	1755–1827	Continental Congress 1784–1786 Senate 1789–1796; 1813–1825 Minister to Great Britain 1796–1803; 1825–1826	Militia
Kitchell, Aaron	New Jersey	1744–1820	House 1791–1793; 1795–1797; 1799–1801 Senate 1805–1809	Militia
Knox, Henry	Massachusetts	1750–1806	Secretary at War 1785–1789 Secretary of War 1789–1794	Continental
*Langdon, John	New Hampshire	1741–1819	Continental Congress 1775, 1787 Governor 1785–1786; 1788–1789; 1805–1809; 1810–1812 Senate 1789–1801 (President Pro Tem 1789–1791; 1792–1793)	Militia
Larned, Simon	Massachusetts	1753–1817	House 1804–1805	Continental
Latimer, Henry	Delaware	1752–1819	House 1794–1795 Senate 1795–1801	Continental
Laurance, John	New York	1750–1810	Continental Congress 1785–1787 House 1789–1793 Senate 1796–1800 (President Pro Tem 1798–1799)	Continental
Lee, Henry	Virginia	1756–1818	Continental Congress 1785–1788 Governor 1791–1794 House 1799–1801	Continental
Lee, Richard Henry	Virginia	1732–1794	Continental Congress 1774–1780; 1784–1787 (President 1784) Senate 1789–1792	Militia

Name	State	Birth/Death	National Office	Military Service
			(President Pro Tem 1792)	
Lee, Thomas Sim	Maryland	1745–1819	Governor 1779–1783; 1792–1794	Militia
			Continental Congress 1783–1784	
Leib, Michael	Pennsylvania	1760–1822	House 1799–1806	Militia
			Senate 1809–1814	
Lewis, Morgan	New York	1754–1844	Governor 1804–1807	Continental
Lewis, Thomas	Virginia	?–?	House 1803–1804	Militia
Lincoln, Levi	Massachusetts	1749–1820	House 1800–1801	Militia
			Attorney General 1801–1804	
			Governor 1808–1809	
Linn, James	New Jersey	1749–1821	House 1799–1801	Militia
Livingston, Henry Brockholst	New York	1757–1823	Supreme Court 1806–1823	Continental
*Livingston, William	New Jersey	1723–1790	Continental Congress 1774–1776	Militia
			Governor 1776–1790	
Lloyd, James	Maryland	1745–1820	Senate 1798–1800	Militia
Lloyd, James	Massachusetts	1769–1831	Senate 1808–1813; 1822–1826	Militia
Locke, Matthew	North Carolina	1730–1801	House 1793–1799	Militia
Love, John	Virginia	?–1822	House 1807–1811	Militia
Lower, Christian	Pennsylvania	1740–1806	House 1805–1806	Militia
Lyle, Aaron	Pennsylvania	1759–1825	House 1809–1817	Militia
Lyman, Samuel	Massachusetts	1749–1802	House 1795–1800	Militia
Lyon, Matthew	Vermont	1746–1822	House 1797–1801	Continental
	Kentucky		House 1803–1811	
McClenachan, Blair	Pennsylvania	?–1812	House 1797–1799	Militia
McCord, Andrew	New York	c. 1754–1808	House 1803–1805	Militia
McCoy, William	Virginia	?–1864	House 1811–1833	Militia
McDowell, Joseph	North Carolina	1756–1801	House 1797–1799	Militia
McDowell, Joseph (P. G.)	North Carolina	1758–1799	House 1793–1795	Militia
*McHenry, James	Maryland	1753–1816	Continental Congress 1783–1786	Continental
			Secretary of War 1796–1800	
McKean, Thomas	Delaware	1774–1783	Continental Congress 1774–1783	Militia
			(President 1781)	
	Pennsylvania		Governor 1799–1808	
McKim, Alexander	Maryland	1748–1832	House 1809–1815	Militia
McKinley, John	Delaware	1721–1796	Governor 1777	Militia
Maclay, Samuel	Pennsylvania	1741–1811	House 1795–1797	Militia
			Senate 1803–1809	
Maclay, William	Pennsylvania	1734–1804	Senate 1789–1791	Continental
McMinn, Joseph	Tennessee	1758–1824	Governor 1815–1821	Militia
Macon, Nathaniel	North Carolina	1758–1837	House 1791–1815	Militia
			(Speaker 1801–1807)	
			Senate 1815–1828	
			(President Pro Tem 1826–1827)	
Malbone, Francis	Rhode Island	1759–1809	House 1793–1797	Militia
			Senate 1809	
Marshall, Humphrey	Kentucky	1760–1841	Senate 1795–1801	Militia
Marshall, John	Virginia	1755–1835	House 1799–1800	Continental
			Minister to France 1797–1798	
			Secretary of State 1800–1801	
			Supreme Court 1801–1835	
			(Chief Justice 1801–1835)	
Martin, Alexander	North Carolina	1740–1807	Governor 1782–1784; 1789–1792	Continental
			Continental Congress 1786–1787	
			Senate 1793–1799	
Martin, John	Georgia	c. 1730–1786	Governor 1782–1783	Continental
Mason, Jonathan	Massachusetts	1756–1831	Senate 1800–1803	Militia
			House 1817–1820	
Mason, Stevens Thomson	Virginia	1760–1803	Senate 1794–1803	Militia
Mathews, George	Georgia	1739–1812	Governor 1787–1788; 1793–1796	Continental
			House 1789–1791	
Mathews, John	South Carolina	1744–1802	Continental Congress 1778–1782	Militia
			Governor 1782–1783	
Mattoon, Ebenezer	Massachusetts	1755–1843	House 1801–1803	Militia
Mercer, John Francis	Virginia	1759–1821	Continental Congress 1782–1785	Continental
	Maryland		House 1792–1794	
			Governor 1801–1803	
Meriwether, David	Georgia	1755–1822	House 1802–1807	Militia

Name	*State*	*Birth/ Death*	*National Office*	*Military Service*
*Mifflin, Thomas	Pennsylvania	1744–1800	Continental Congress 1774; 1780–1784 (President 1783–1784) Governor 1789–1799	Continental
Milledge, John	Georgia	1757–1818	House 1792–1793; 1795–1799; 1801–1802 Governor 1802–1806 Senate 1806–1809 (President Pro Tem 1809)	Militia
Mitchell, Nathaniel	Delaware	1753–1814	Continental Congress 1787–1788 Governor 1805–1808	Continental
Moffitt, Hosea	New York	1757–1825	House 1813–1817	Militia
Monroe, James	Virginia	1758–1831	Continental Congress 1783–1786 Senate 1790–1794 Minister to France 1794–1796; 1803 Governor 1799–1802; 1811 Minister to Great Britain 1803–1807 Secretary of State 1811–1817 Secretary of War 1814–1815 President 1817–1825	Continental
Montgomery, William	Pennsylvania	1736–1816	Continental Congress 1785 House 1793–1795	
Moore, Alfred	North Carolina	1755–1810	Supreme Court 1799–1804	Continental
Moore, Andrew	Virginia	1752–1821	House 1789–1797; 1804 Senate 1804–1809	Continental
Moore, Nicholas Ruxton	Maryland	1756–1816	House 1803–1811; 1813–1815	Continental
Moore, Thomas	South Carolina	1759–1822	House 1801–1813; 1815–1817	Continental
Morgan, Daniel	Virginia	1736–1802	House 1797–1799	Continental
Morgan, James	New Jersey	1756–1822	House 1811–1813	Militia
*Morris, Gouverneur	New York	1752–1816	Continental Congress 1778–1779 Minister to Great Britain 1790 Minister to France 1792–1794 Senate 1800–1803	Militia
Morris, Lewis Richard	Vermont	1760–1825	House 1797–1803	Continental
Morrow, John	Virginia	?–?	House 1805–1809	Militia
Mott, James	New Jersey	1739–1823	House 1801–1805	Militia
Moultrie, William	South Carolina	1730–1805	Governor 1785–1787; 1793–1795	Continental
Muhlenberg, John Peter Gabriel	Pennsylvania	1746–1807	House 1789–1791; 1793–1795; 1799–1801 Senate 1801	Continental
Nelson, Roger	Maryland	1759–1815	House 1804–1810	Continental
Nelson, Thomas, Jr.	Virginia	1738–1789	Continental Congress 1775–1777; 1779–1780 Governor 1781–1782	Militia
Neville, Joseph	Virginia	1730–1819	House 1793–1795	Militia
New, Anthony	Virginia Kentucky	1747–1833	House 1793–1805 House 1811–1813; 1821–1823	Militia
Nicholas, Wilson Cary	Virginia	1761–1820	Senate 1799–1804 House 1807–1809 Governor 1814–1817	Continental
Nicholson, John	New York	1765–1820	House 1809–1811	Continental
Niles, Nathaniel	Vermont	1741–1828	House 1791–1795	Militia
North, William	New York	1755–1836	Senate 1798	Continental
Ogden, Aaron	New Jersey	1756–1839	Senate 1801–1803 Governor 1812–1813	Continental
Ogle, Benjamin	Maryland	1749–1809	Governor 1798–1801	Militia
Olin, Gideon	Vermont	1743–1823	House 1803–1807	Militia
Osgood, Samuel	Massachusetts	1748–1813	Postmaster General 1789–1791	Continental
Page, John	Virginia	1743–1808	House 1789–1797 Governor 1802–1805	Militia
Page, Robert	Virginia	1765–1840	House 1799–1801	Militia
Paine, Elijah	Vermont	1757–1842	Senate 1795–1801	Militia
Palmer, Beriah	New York	1740–1812	House 1803–1805	Militia
Parker, Josiah	Virginia	1751–1810	House 1789–1801	Continental
Parker, Nahum	New Hampshire	1760–1839	Senate 1807–1810	Continental
Paterson, John	New York	1744–1808	House 1803–1805	Continental
Patten, John	Delaware	1746–1800	Continental Congress 1785–1786 House 1793–1794; 1795–1797	Continental
Peirce, Joseph	New Hampshire	1748–1812	House 1801–1802	Continental
Pennington, William Sandford	New Jersey	1757–1826	Governor 1813–1815	Continental
Phelps, Oliver	New York	1749–1809	House 1803–1805	Militia

SOLDIER-STATESMEN OF THE EARLY REPUBLIC—CONTINUED

Name	*State*	*Birth/ Death*	*National Office*	*Military Service*
Pickens, Andrew	South Carolina	1739–1817	House 1793–1795	Militia
Pickering, Timothy	Massachusetts	1745–1829	Senate 1803–1811	Continental
			House 1813–1817	
	Pennsylvania		Postmaster General 1791–1795	
			Secretary of War 1795–1796	
			Secretary of State 1795–1800	
*Pinckney, Charles	South Carolina	1757–1824	Continental Congress 1784–1787	Militia
			Governor 1789–1792; 1796–1798; 1806–1808	
			Senate 1799–1801	
			Minister to Spain 1801–1804	
			House 1819–1821	
*Pinckney, Charles Cotesworth	South Carolina	1746–1825	Minister to France 1796–1797	Continental
Pinckney, Thomas	South Carolina	1750–1828	Governor 1787–1789	Continental
			Minister to Great Britain 1792–1796	
			Minister to Spain 1794–1795	
			House 1797–1801	
Posey, Thomas	Louisiana	1750–1818	Senate 1812–1813	Continental
			Governor of Indiana Territory 1813–1816	
Potter, Elisha Reynolds	Rhode Island	1764–1835	House 1796–1797; 1809–1815	Militia
Potter, Samuel John	Rhode Island	1753–1804	Senate 1803–1804	Militia
Potts, Richard	Maryland	1753–1808	Continental Congress 1781–1782	Militia
			Senate 1793–1796	
Powell, Levin	Virginia	1737–1810	House 1799–1801	Continental
Pugh, John	Pennsylvania	1761–1842	House 1805–1809	Continental
Randolph, Beverly	Virginia	1753–1797	Governor 1788–1791	Militia
Randolph, Edmund Jennings	Virginia	1753–1813	Continental Congress 1779–1782	Continental
			Governor 1786–1788	
			Attorney General 1790–1794	
			Secretary of State 1794–1795	
Rea, John	Pennsylvania	1755–1829	House 1803–1811; 1813–1815	Militia
Read, Jacob	South Carolina	1751–1816	Continental Congress 1783–1786	Militia
			Senate 1795–1801	
			(President Pro Tem 1797–1798)	
Reed, Joseph	Pennsylvania	1741–1785	Continental Congress 1777–1778	Continental
			Governor 1778–1781	
Reed, Philip	Maryland	1760–1829	Senate 1806–1813	Militia
			House 1817–1819; 1822–1823	
Rhea, John	Tennessee	1753–1832	House 1803–1815; 1817–1823	Continental
Richards, Matthias	Pennsylvania	1758–1830	House 1807–1811	Militia
Riker, Samuel	New York	1743–1823	House 1804–1805; 1807–1809	Militia
Robinson, Jonathan	Vermont	1756–1819	Senate 1807–1815	Militia
Robinson, Moses	Vermont	1742–1813	Senate 1791–1796	Militia
Rodney, Caesar	Delaware	1728–1784	Continental Congress 1774–1778; 1782–1783	Militia
			Governor 1778–1782	
Rutledge, Edward	South Carolina	1749–1800	Continental Congress 1774–1777	Militia
			Governor 1798–1800	
Sage, Ebenezer	New York	1755–1834	House 1809–1815	Continental Navy
Sammons, Thomas	New York	1762–1838	House 1803–1807; 1809–1813	Militia
Sands, Joshua	New York	1757–1835	House 1803–1805; 1825–1827	Militia
Schoonmaker, Cornelius Corneliusen	New York	1745–1796	House 1791–1793	Militia
Schureman, James	New Jersey	1756–1824	Continental Congress 1786–1787	Militia
			House 1789–1791; 1797–1799; 1813–1815	
			Senate 1799–1801	
Schuyler, Philip John	New York	1733–1804	Continental Congress 1775; 1779–1780	Continental
			Senate 1789–1791; 1797–1798	
Scott, Charles	Kentucky	c. 1739–1813	Governor 1808–1812	Continental
Scudder, John Anderson	New Jersey	1759–1836	House 1810–1811	Militia
Sedgwick, Theodore	Massachusetts	1746–1813	Continental Congress 1785–1788	Continental
			House 1789–1796; 1799–1801	
			(Speaker 1799–1801)	
			Senate 1796–1799	
			(President Pro Tem 1798)	
Sevier, John	North Carolina	1745–1815	House 1790–1791	Militia
	Tennessee		Governor 1796–1801; 1803–1809	
			House 1811–1815	

SOLDIER-STATESMEN OF THE EARLY REPUBLIC—CONTINUED

Name	State	Birth/ Death	National Office	Military Service
Shelby, Isaac	Kentucky	1750–1826	Governor 1792–1796; 1812–1816	Militia
Shepard, William	Massachusetts	1737–1817	House 1797–1803	Continental
Sherburne, John Samuel	New Hampshire	1757–1830	House 1793–1797	Militia
Short, William	Virginia	1759–1849	Minister to Netherlands 1792–1794 Minister to Spain 1794–1795 Minister to Portugal 1797–1801	Militia
Sinnickson, Thomas	New Jersey	1744–1817	House 1789–1791; 1797–1799	Militia
Skinner, Thomson Joseph	Massachusetts	1752–1809	House 1797–1799; 1803–1804	Militia
Slaymaker, Amos	Pennsylvania	1755–1837	House 1814–1815	Militia
Sloan, James	New Jersey	?–1811	House 1803–1809	Continental
Smallwood, William	Maryland	1732–1792	Governor 1785–1788	Continental
Smith, Benjamin	North Carolina	?–1829	Governor 1810	Militia
Smith, Daniel	Tennessee	1748–1818	Senate 1798–1799; 1805–1809	Continental
Smith, George	Pennsylvania	?–?	House 1809–1813	Militia
Smith, Isaac	New Jersey	1740–1807	House 1795–1797	Militia
Smith, Israel	Vermont	1759–1810	House 1791–1797; 1801–1803 Senate 1803–1807 Governor 1807–1808	Militia
Smith, Jeremiah	New Hampshire	1759–1842	House 1791–1797 Governor 1809–1810	Militia
Smith, John	New York	1752–1816	House 1800–1804 Senate 1804–1813	Continental
Smith, John	Virginia	1750–1836	House 1801–1815	Militia
Smith, Josiah	Massachusetts	1738–1803	House 1801–1803	Continental
Smith, Robert	Maryland	1757–1842	Secretary of the Navy 1801–1809 Secretary of State 1809–1811	Privateer
Smith, Samuel	Maryland	1752–1839	House 1793–1803; 1816–1822 Senate 1803–1815; 1822–1823 (President Pro Tem 1805–1808)	Continental
Smith, William	South Carolina	1751–1837	House 1797–1799	Militia
Smith, William Stephens	New York	1755–1816	House 1813–1815	Continental
Southard, Henry	New Jersey	1747–1842	House 1801–1811; 1815–1821	Militia
*Spaight, Richard Dobbs	North Carolina	1758–1802	Continental Congress 1783–1785 Governor 1792–1795 House 1798–1800	Militia
Sprigg, Thomas	Maryland	1747–1809	House 1793–1797	Militia
Stanton, Joseph, Jr.	Rhode Island	1739–1807	Senate 1790–1793 House 1801–1807	Militia
Stoddert, Benjamin	Maryland	1751–1813	Secretary of the Navy 1798–1801	Continental
Stone, John Hoskins	Maryland	1745–1804	Governor 1794–1797	Continental
Stone, Michael Jenifer	Maryland	1747–1812	House 1789–1791	Militia
Storer, Clement	New Hampshire	1760–1830	House 1807–1809 Senate 1817–1819	Militia
Strong, William	Vermont	1763–1840	House 1811–1815; 1819–1821	Militia
Stuart, Philip	Maryland	1760–1830	House 1811–1819	Continental
Sturges, Lewis Burr	Connecticut	1763–1844	House 1805–1817	Continental
Sullivan, John	New Hampshire	1740–1795	Continental Congress 1774–1775; 1780–1781 Governor 1786–1788; 1789–1790	Continental
Sumter, Thomas	South Carolina	1734–1832	House 1789–1793; 1797–1801 Senate 1801–1810	Continental
Swart, Peter	New York	1752–1829	House 1807–1809	Militia
Swift, Zephaniah	Connecticut	1759–1823	House 1793–1797	Continental
Talbot, Silas	New York	1751–1813	House 1793–1795	Continental
Taliaferro, Benjamin	Georgia	1750–1821	House 1799–1802	Continental
Tallmadge, Benjamin	Connecticut	1754–1835	House 1801–1817	Continental
Tallman, Peleg	Massachusetts	1764–1840	House 1811–1813	Privateer
Tannehill, Adamson	Pennsylvania	1750–1820	House 1813–1815	Continental
Tatom, Absalom	North Carolina	1742–1802	House 1795–1796	Continental
Tattnall, Josiah	Georgia	1764–1803	Senate 1796–1799 Governor 1801–1802	Militia
Taylor, John ("of Caroline")	Virginia	1754–1824	Senate 1792–1794; 1803; 1822–1824	Continental
Tazewell, Henry	Virginia	1753–1799	Senate 1794–1799 (President Pro Tem 1795–1796)	Militia
Tenney, Samuel	New Hampshire	1748–1816	House 1800–1807	Continental
Thacher, George	Massachusetts	1754–1824	Continental Congress 1787 House 1789–1801	Privateer
Thomas, David	New York	1762–1831	House 1801–1808	Continental

Name	*State*	*Birth/ Death*	*National Office*	*Military Service*
Thomas, Richard	Pennsylvania	1744-1832	House 1795-1801	Militia
Thompson, Joel	New York	1760-1843	House 1813-1815	Militia
Thompson, John	New York	1749-1823	House 1799-1801; 1807-1811	Militia
Thomson, Mark	New Jersey	1739-1803	House 1795-1799	Militia
Tichenor, Isaac	Vermont	1754-1838	Senate 1796-1797;1815-1821 Governor 1797-1807; 1808-1809	Continental
Tillinghast, Thomas	Rhode Island	1742-1821	House 1797-1799; 1801-1803	Militia
Todd, Thomas	Kentucky	1765-1826	Supreme Court 1807-1826	Militia
Tredwell, Thomas	New York	1743-1831	House 1791-1795	Militia
Trigg, Abram	Virginia	1750-?	House 1797-1809	Militia
Trigg, John Johns	Virginia	1748-1804	House 1797-1804	Militia
Trumbull, Jonathan (Younger)	Connecticut	1740-1809	House 1789-1795 (Speaker 1791-1793) Senate 1795-1796 Governor 1797-1809	Continental
Tucker, Thomas Tudor	South Carolina	1745-1828	Continental Congress 1787-1788 House 1789-1793	Continental
Turner, Charles, Jr.	Massachusetts	1760-1839	House 1809-1813	Militia
Turner, James	North Carolina	1766-1824	Governor 1802-1805 Senate 1805-1816	Militia
Tyler, John	Virginia	1747-1813	Governor 1808-1811	Militia
Udree, Daniel	Pennsylvania	1751-1828	House 1813-1815; 1820-1821; 1822-1825	Militia
Van Cortlandt, Philip	New York	1749-1831	House 1793-1809	Continental
Van Cortlandt, Pierre, Jr.	New York	1762-1848	House 1811-1813	Militia
Vanderhorst, Arnoldus	South Carolina	1748-1815	Governor 1794-1796	Militia
Van Gaasbeck, Peter	New York	1754-1797	House 1793-1795	Militia
Van Horne, Isaac	Pennsylvania	1754-1834	House 1801-1805	Continental
Van Rensselaer, Jeremiah	New York	1738-1810	House 1789-1791	Continental
Van Rensselaer, Killian Killian	New York	1763-1845	House 1801-1811	Continental
Varnum, Joseph Bradley	Massachusetts	1751-1821	House 1795-1811 (Speaker 1809-1811) Senate 1811-1817 (President Pro Tem 1813-1814)	Militia
Wadsworth, Jeremiah	Connecticut	1743-1804	Continental Congress 1788 House 1789-1795	Continental
Wadsworth, Peleg	Massachusetts	1748-1829	House 1793-1807	Continental
Walker, Benjamin	New York	1753-1818	House 1801-1803	Continental
Walker, John	Virginia	1744-1809	Continental Congress 1780 Senate 1790	Continental
Walton, George	Georgia	1741-1804	Continental Congress 1776-1778; 1780-1781; 1787-1788 Governor 1779-1780; 1789 Senate 1795-1796	Militia
Walton, Matthew	Kentucky	?-1819	House 1803-1807	Militia
Ward, Artemas	Massachusetts	1727-1800	Continental Congress 1780-1782 House 1791-1795	Continental
Washington, Bushrod	Virginia	1762-1829	Supreme Court 1798-1829	Militia
*Washington, George	Virginia	1732-1799	Continental Congress 1774-1775 President 1789-1797	Continental
Watson, James	New York	1750-1806	Senate 1798-1800	Continental
Wayne, Anthony	Georgia	1745-1796	House 1791-1792	Continental
Widgery, William	Massachusetts	c. 1753-1822	House 1811-1813	Continental
Williams, Benjamin	North Carolina	1751-1814	House 1793-1795 Governor 1799-1802; 1807-1808	Continental
Williams, John	New York	1752-1806	House 1795-1799	
Williams, Lemuel	Massachusetts	1747-1828	House 1799-1805	Continental
*Williamson, Hugh	North Carolina	1735-1819	Continental Congress 1782-1785; 1787-1788 House 1790-1793	Militia
Willis, Francis	Georgia	1745-1829	House 1791-1793	Continental
Wilson, Nathan	New York	1758-1834	House 1808-1809	Continental
Winder, Levin	Maryland	1757-1819	Governor 1812-1815	Continental
Winn, Richard	South Carolina	1750-1818	House 1793-1797; 1803-1813	Continental
Winston, Joseph	North Carolina	1746-1815	House 1793-1795; 1803-1807	Militia
Witherell, James	Vermont	1759-1838	House 1807-1808	Continental
Wolcott, Oliver	Connecticut	1726-1797	Governor 1796-1797	Militia
Wolcott, Oliver, Jr.	Connecticut	1760-1833	Secretary of Treasury 1795-1800 Governor 1817-1826	Continental
Wood, James	Virginia	1741-1813	Governor 1796-1799	Continental

SOLDIER-STATESMEN OF THE EARLY REPUBLIC—CONTINUED

Name	*State*	*Birth/ Death*	*National Office*	*Military Service*
Wright, Robert	Maryland	1752–1826	Senate 1801–1806 Governor 1806–1809 House 1810–1817; 1821–1823	Militia

APPENDIX F

The Presidents

Of America's 41 Presidents, 30 have served their country under arms. Military service is thus one common denominator, one common bond of experience and knowledge, linking a majority of Presidents over time. Beginning with George Washington, these Presidents have been able to draw upon the lessons of their own military service. At critical times in American history, the knowledge these men gained in uniform helped guide them in defining new missions in response to new challenges as national conditions changed. Most of these Presidents had served in the tradition of the citizen-soldier, taking up arms to meet a particular emergency. For them, the concept of civilian supremacy over the military was a natural assumption, one reaffirmed by their presidential oath to support and defend the Constitution of the United States. In a very real sense, the link between military service and presidential leadership directly reflects the Founding Fathers' vision of a sufficient military establishment drawn from, and accountable to, the people.

"Provide for the Common Defence"

George Washington, the commanding general of the Continental Army during the Revolutionary War, is the nation's preeminent military hero. Nevertheless, it was a civilian Washington who presided over the Constitutional Convention in Philadelphia in 1787 and who, on the last day of April 1789, took the oath of office as the first President of the United States of America. In making this transition from military service to civilian leadership, Washington very much provided later Presidents with a model for the proper role of the Commander in Chief under the Constitution. In many ways his two terms in office established essential precedents that have ensured success and stability in providing for the common defense.

During Washington's administration, men who had served under arms during the Revolution played decisive roles in all three branches of the new federal government. Many had been instrumental in writing the Constitution and in campaigning for its ratification. They now shared responsibility for giving detailed shape to the balanced political structure outlined by that document. From the outset Washington and his fellow veterans were determined to implement the intent of the Framers to create a strong central authority to deal with national affairs. One lesson of the Revolutionary period was particularly clear to them: no longer could a weak government be allowed to impede the nation's ability to defend itself and ensure order under the law.

In military affairs, President Washington cooperated closely with Congress in giving practical meaning to the Constitution's military clauses. Under the constitutional principle of checks and balances, this partnership was essential, for although the President is Commander in Chief, only Congress can authorize and fund military forces. Washington's administration had inherited a Regular Army consisting of a single regiment serving on the frontier. To manage the federal government's control over this regular force, Washington in August 1789 obtained congressional approval, as provided by the Constitution, for a War Department. The new department was led by a civilian Secretary of War, who embodied the constitutional principle that military forces would always be subordinate to civilian control. Seeking to reinforce this principle throughout the military establishment, Congress, with Washington's support, passed a law in September requiring the members of the Army to take an oath to "support the Constitution of the United States."

During his first term, Washington and congressional leaders identified three potential sources of military conflict facing the new nation: British-supported Indians on the frontier, domestic insurrection against the laws of the new government, and invasion by the warring European powers. They made the Regular Army responsible for the threat posed by the Indians, a danger considerably alleviated in 1794 when Maj. Gen. Anthony Wayne's victory at Fallen Timbers brought a new measure of security for settlers moving west. They also agreed that the militia, the citizen-soldiers called up from the separate states, would be responsible for putting down any insurrection. Here Washington, reflecting his experience in the Continental Army, reasoned that regional defense was best

Andrew Jackson, 7th President, shown as a major general at the conclusion of the War of 1812 *(oils on canvas, c. 1815, by Ralph Earl; National Portrait Gallery, Smithsonian Institution).*

left to local military authorities whenever possible. The Constitution divided responsibility for the militia between the states and the federal government, and the Militia Act of 1792 provided the President with an effective means to use the militia in such emergencies. Washington successfully used the new law in the summer of 1794 when farmers in western Pennsylvania openly rebelled over a federal excise tax on liquor, their only cash crop. Washington promptly called up some 25,000 militiamen in an overwhelming show of force that ended the "Whiskey Rebellion" without bloodshed.

In regard to the threat of foreign invasion, Washington again applied the experience of the Revolution: only a military force composed of well-trained regulars supplemented by state forces and directed by a strong central authority could effectively respond to attacks by a modern military power. Although few Americans were concerned about foreign invasion, many feared the possibility of blockades or trans-Atlantic raids. In 1794 Washington persuaded Congress to authorize forts at selected harbors and to create a small Navy, complete with marines. The former would be manned by regular troops supported by a well-trained militia, the latter would consist of a modest sized squadron to be supplemented by a fleet of privateers (the naval equivalent of the militia) in time of war.

President Washington's foreign policy also clearly reflected his military experience. During the Revolution he had seen England finally sue for peace not just because of the victories of the Continental Army, but also because of America's successful alliance with France and the economic hardships imposed on British merchants through the loss of American trade. As President, he then shaped his foreign policy specifically to rely on diplomacy backed by growing economic power and a military strength expandable to meet emergencies.

In many ways the first half of the nineteenth century reflected Washington's pragmatic understanding of the security needs of a nation still in its formative stages—an understanding shared by most of the veterans who served in government with him. As the chart that follows shows, most of the Presidents before the Civil War had seen military service. For these veterans of the War of 1812, the Indian wars, and the Mexican War, the precedents set by President Washington and the Soldier-Statesmen of the early Republic were directly reinforced by their own experiences. They all supported the idea that the role of the central government was to raise sufficient troops, militia and regulars, when necessary to defend the country and to promote national interests such as westward expansion. At least two of them, Andrew Jackson and Zachary Taylor, owed their elections to their great military successes, but, like Washington, each as President deliberately emphasized his civilian status, leaving the trappings and honors of his military career behind.

The fact that this era of national development was in good part shaped by Presidents with military experience was significant. In taking their oath of office, they in effect were simply repeating the oath of loyalty to the Constitution that they had first sworn as soldiers. For these men, service to the nation, whether military or civilian, thus called for an unwavering commitment to a single set of binding constitutional principles. For the nation, the result was prosperity, growth, expansion, and security. In the end, it was a problem that the Constitution did not resolve—the slavery issue—that eroded a sense of united national purpose and plunged the country into a constitutional crisis that took a civil war to resolve.

"The Peace Makers" by G. P. A. Healy; Abraham Lincoln, 16th President and former militia captain, and senior commanders off City Point, Virginia, in 1865. From left to right, Maj. Gen. William Sherman, Lt. Gen. Ulysses Grant (18th President), Lincoln, and Adm. David Porter *(oil on canvas, c. 1868; The White House).*

"Insure Domestic Tranquility"

The Civil War, like the Revolution, influenced national policies for decades. Service during that conflict became a formative experience in the lives of a whole new generation of leaders, including seven Presidents. Not only did the war finally and permanently define the nature of the Union, it also changed national attitudes about the role of the Commander in Chief in providing for the common defense and ensuring domestic tranquility. During the administrations of these seven veterans, the nation reassessed its assumption that the first line of defense was the trained and ready citizen-soldier. It also reaffirmed the proper use of the military in the face of civil insurrection. Finally, and with some reluctance, it faced the need to expand and modernize its military forces.

With the Confederate surrender at Appomattox, the public demanded a rapid demobilization of the Union Army. Exhausted taxpayers insisted on giving priority to resuming settlement of the West, rebuilding the devastated South, seeking new markets, and participating in the rapid technological changes of the industrial revolution. Funds for defense were scarce, and Presidents Andrew Johnson and Ulysses Grant, the latter the victorious Union commander, faced a series of difficult choices as they attempted to balance the voters' demands with the Constitution's requirement to provide for defense. They won congressional approval for a small Army of 25,000 regulars, scattered in small garrisons in the old South to ensure order during Reconstruction and in the western territories where Indian tribes were resisting the rapid settlement of the continent. Reorganization of the militia fell to the individual state governments, who abandoned the idea of large militia calls and opted instead for

PRESIDENTS OF THE UNITED STATES WHO SERVED IN THE MILITARY

Name and State of Residence	*Birth*	*Death*	*Term of Office and Party Affiliation*	*Highest Rank/Active Service**
George Washington Virginia	2 February 1732 "Wakefield," Westmoreland Co., Va.	14 December 1799 "Mount Vernon," Fairfax Co., Va.	30 April 1789–3 March 1797 Federalist	General and Commander in Chief, Continental Army French and Indian War; Revolutionary War
Thomas Jefferson Virginia	14 April 1743 "Shadewell," Goochland Co., Va.	26 October 1819 "Monticello," Albemarle Co., Va.	4 March 1801–3 March 1809 Democratic-Republican	Colonel, Virginia Militia
James Madison Virginia	16 March 1751 Port Conway, King George Co., Va.	28 June 1836 "Montpelier," Orange Co., Va.	4 March 1809–3 March 1817 Democratic-Republican	Colonel, Virginia Militia
James Monroe Virginia	28 April 1758 Westmoreland Co., Va.	4 July 1831 New York, N.Y.	4 March 1817–3 March 1825 Democratic-Republican	Major, Continental Army Revolutionary War
Andrew Jackson Tennessee	15 March 1767 Waxhaw Settlement, S.C.	8 June 1845 Nashville, Tenn.	4 March 1829–3 March 1837 Democratic	Major General, U.S. Army Indian Wars; War of 1812
William H. Harrison Ohio	9 February 1773 "Berkeley," Charles City Co., Va.	4 April 1841 Washington, D.C.	4 March 1841–4 April 1841 Whig	Major General, Kentucky Militia Indian Wars; War of 1812
John Tyler Virginia	29 March 1790 Charles City Co., Va.	18 January 1862 Richmond, Va.	6 April 1841–3 March 1845 Whig	Captain, Virginia Militia War of 1812
James K. Polk Tennessee	2 November 1795 Mecklenburg Co., N.C.	15 June 1849 Nashville, Tenn.	4 March 1845–3 March 1849 Democratic	Major, Tennessee Militia
Zachary Taylor Kentucky	24 November 1784 Montebello Orange Co., Va.	5 July 1850 Washington, D.C.	4 March 1849–9 July 1850 Whig	Major General, U.S. Army Black Hawk War; Mexican War
Millard Fillmore New York	7 January 1800 Locke, N.Y.	8 March 1874 Buffalo, N.Y.	10 July 1850–3 March 1853 Whig	Major, New York Home Guard
Franklin Pierce New Hampshire	23 November 1804 Hillsborough, N.H.	8 October 1869 Concord, N.H.	4 March 1853–3 March 1857 Democratic	Brigadier General, New Hampshire Militia Mexican War
James Buchanan Pennsylvania	23 April 1791 Coce Gap, Pa.	1 June 1868 Near Lancaster, Pa.	4 March 1857–3 March 1861 Democratic	Private, Pennsylvania Militia War of 1812
Abraham Lincoln Illinois	12 February 1809 Hardin (now Larue) Co., Ky.	15 April 1865 Washington, D.C.	4 March 1861–15 April 1865 National Union (Republican)	Captain, Illinois Militia Black Hawk War
Andrew Johnson Tennessee	29 December 1808 Raleigh, N.C.	31 July 1875 Carter Station, Tenn.	15 April 1865–3 March 1869 Republican	Brigadier General, Volunteers Civil War
Ulysses S. Grant Illinois	27 April 1822 Point Pleasant, Ohio	23 July 1885 Mt. McGregor, N.Y.	4 March 1869–3 March 1877 Republican	General, U.S. Army Mexican War; Civil War

Name and State of Residence	*Birth*	*Death*	*Term of Office and Party Affiliation*	*Highest Rank/Active Service**
Rutherford Hayes Ohio	4 October 1822 Delaware, Ohio	17 January 1893 Spiegel Grove, Fremont, Ohio	4 March 1877–3 March 1881 Republican	Brevet Major General, Volunteers Civil War
James A. Garfield Ohio	19 November 1831 Orange, Cuyahoga Co., Ohio	19 September 1881 Elberton, N.J.	4 March 1881–19 September 1881 Republican	Major General, Volunteers Civil War
Chester A. Arthur New York	5 October 1830 Fairfield, Vt.	18 November 1886 New York, N.Y.	20 September 1881–3 March 1885 Republican	Brigadier General, New York Militia Civil War
Benjamin Harrison Indiana	20 August 1833 North Bend, Ohio	13 March 1901 Indianapolis, Ind.	4 March 1889–3 March 1893 Republican	Brevet Brigadier General, Volunteers Civil War
William McKinley Ohio	29 January 1843 Niles, Ohio	14 September 1901 Buffalo, N.Y.	4 March 1897–14 September 1901 Republican	Brevet Major, Volunteers Civil War
Theodore Roosevelt New York	27 October 1858 New York, N.Y.	6 January 1919 Oyster Bay, N.Y.	14 September 1901–3 March 1909 Republican	Colonel, Volunteers Spanish-American War
Harry S. Truman Missouri	8 May 1884 Lamar, Mo.	26 December 1972 Kansas City, Mo.	12 April 1945–20 January 1953 Democratic	Colonel, Organized Reserve Corps World War I
Dwight D. Eisenhower New York	14 October 1890 Dennison, Tex.	28 March 1969 Washington, D.C.	20 January 1953–20 January 1961 Republican	General of the Army, U.S. Army World War II
John F. Kennedy Massachusetts	29 May 1917 Brookline, Mass.	22 November 1963 Dallas, Tex.	20 January 1961–22 November 1963 Democratic	Lieutenant, U.S. Naval Reserve World War II
Lyndon B. Johnson Texas	27 August 1908 Stonewall, Tex.	22 January 1973 Near Johnson City, Tex.	22 November 1963–20 January 1969 Democratic	Commander, U.S. Naval Reserve World War II
Richard M. Nixon New York	9 January 1913 Yorba Linda, Calif.	n/a	20 January 1969–9 August 1974 Republican	Commander, U.S. Naval Reserve World War II
Gerald R. Ford Michigan	14 July 1913 Omaha, Nebr.	n/a	9 August 1974–20 January 1977 Republican	Lieutenant Commander, U.S. Naval Reserve World War II
James E. Carter Georgia	1 October 1924 Plains, Ga.	n/a	20 January 1977–20 January 1981 Democratic	Lieutenant, U.S. Navy
Ronald W. Reagan California	6 February 1911 Tampico, Ill.	n/a	20 January 1981–20 January 1989 Republican	Captain, Army Air Forces World War II
George H. W. Bush Texas	12 June 1924 Milton, Mass.	n/a	20 January 1989– Republican	Lieutenant, U.S. Naval Reserve World War II

*The rank indicated is that held at the conclusion of the term of service.

smaller but better trained volunteer contingents. In every case, military expenses were held to a minimum through recycled equipment and low pay for soldiers.

In effect, the Civil War produced a new military doctrine easily appreciated by any veteran who had fought in that conflict. The Presidents of this period understood that, in the long term, national defense required the ability to raise a large Army professionally trained and equipped with technically advanced weapons. In the generations after the war, the idea that citizens could quickly become soldiers and thereby serve as the first line of defense faded as the nation—led by veterans of that conflict—refined the military strategies of earlier generations. The new concept recognized that the country needed a permanent regular force to serve as a cadre of well-trained professionals capable of leavening the massive draft-produced Army that would characterize warfare in the century to come.

Of particular concern to these post–Civil War Presidents was the proper use of the Army in civil disturbances. With the example of President Washington's use of troops in the Whiskey Rebellion before them, succeeding Presidents had used military force against groups of citizens with great reluctance and scrupulous respect for constitutional restrictions. But during the Civil War and the Reconstruction era, these constitutional niceties were sometimes overlooked. Local civilian authorities, lacking sufficient police forces to keep the peace and otherwise operate local government, increasingly turned to the Army for help. Allowed to go on unchecked in some states and territories, officials involved nearby military units in such nebulous activities as enforcing local ordinances, guarding prisoners, and guaranteeing the peace while ignoring the Constitution's legal safeguards that required the direct involvement of the governors, state legislatures, and the President. It fell to the Presidents who were Civil War veterans to reaffirm the protection of citizen liberties and the continued subordination of military force to proper civil authority. The Posse Comitatus Act, passed during the administration of Civil War veteran Rutherford Hayes, clarified the proper role of the Army in quelling domestic violence. Succeeding Presidents, who had all participated in the war against civil insurrection, carefully used the Army, with renewed regard for the limits set in the Constitution, in responding to the massive industrial strikes and domestic upheavals that preoccupied the nation.

During the postwar period, the Army and Navy began to emerge as modern military forces. Although funds were scarce, military reform drew strong support from Civil War veterans including Presidents Hayes, James Garfield, and Chester Arthur. They took the preliminary steps to acquire advanced weapons for the Army and Navy and to consider the operational lessons identified during the Civil War. The Navy began to acquire modern warships capable of defeating an enemy beyond the horizon. New coastal forts began mounting long-range guns to form a second layer of defense in a coordinated program. Since invasion remained at most a remote possibility, only a small force was necessary, provided that it was mobile, well armed, and well trained.

These new capabilities were first tested in 1898 when the nation fought with Spain over the latter's Caribbean possessions. William McKinley, the last of the Civil War Presidents, had sought to avoid conflict, but as Commander in Chief he later ordered elements of the Regular Army augmented by volunteer militia units to Cuba. He also sent squadrons of the fleet to fight in the Caribbean and the Pacific. The "splendid little war" led to a speedy American victory, but it also provided some sobering lessons when a host of problems emerged during the mobilization that could easily have led to defeat at the hands of a more efficient opponent.

These lessons were not lost on President Theodore Roosevelt, who, as a volunteer, led the Rough Riders in combat in Cuba. Like many of the soldiers who preceded him to the White House, Roosevelt recognized that the efficient use of men and resources was often the key to victory, and he constantly sought as President to strengthen the efficiency of the nation's military forces. On the eve of America's emergence as a world power, he presided over the modernization of the militia system that began the transformation of the National Guard into a well-trained and reliable first line of reinforcement for the regulars. He also directed the reorganization of the Army, providing it with a general staff to match those of the great armies of Europe.

"Secure the Blessings of Liberty"

The two great wars of the twentieth century had a profound effect on a United States that had so recently emerged as an international power. Influenced by its role in these wars, the nation finally came to shake off its isolationism and by mid-century assumed the mantle of international leadership. Nowhere was the transforming influence of these wars more clearly demonstrated than in the presidential careers of those nine men who had served under arms. Ranging in rank from an obscure National Guard captain on the Western Front in World War I to the Supreme Allied Commander in Europe during World War II, these men drew on their firsthand

Dwight Eisenhower (left) and John Kennedy, World War II veterans who served as 34th and 35th Presidents. Eisenhower held the rank of General of the Army; Kennedy, lieutenant in the Naval Reserve *(Eisenhower, oil on canvas by Thomas Edgar Stephens, 1947, National Portrait Gallery, Smithsonian Institution; Kennedy, photograph, c. 1944, Naval Historical Center).*

experiences and came to accept the need for the United States to change its military policies. In so doing, they recognized that the formation of a large and permanent peacetime military establishment represented a major evolution in the traditional interpretation of the Constitution's military clauses.

The change to a permanent military establishment reflected the impact of technologies that had dramatically shrunk the globe, the increasing economic and social interdependence of nations, and the passions of ideology. The process of adjusting to these changes caused the country's leaders, while remaining true to the fundamental constitutional ideals identified by Washington, to redefine the nation's military missions. The emergence of large modern police forces at the local level allowed them to limit the military's constabulary functions to occasional riot duty and, increasingly, to disaster relief. The new global perspective that emerged after the World Wars, on the other hand, allowed them to merge Washington's concerns over frontier defense and foreign aggression into a single overarching mission—national security.

The Presidents who served in the World Wars recognized that traditional foreign and military policies were now inadequate, and under their leadership the country set a new military course. President Harry Truman, a veteran of World War I, and his Secretary of State, George Marshall, the Army's Chief of Staff during World War II, understood that American interests could no longer be served by a continental defense. International responsibilities now imposed a global mission on the country's military forces. In a world shrunk by technology, the United States found itself leading an alliance of Free World nations in competition with the Soviet Union. Truman led the way by strongly supporting America's role in the United Nations and by organizing a series of military commitments and related economic assistance programs.

As the postwar period unfolded, Truman and his successor, Dwight Eisenhower, came to conclude that the threat of military conflict would remain a constant for the foreseeable future. They determined that the United States could no longer rely on the luxury of a lengthy period of mobilization, a conclusion underscored by the shock of an unexpected conventional war in Korea. Reversing a policy in force since Washington's time, they organized a large Army, manned by draftees and volunteers and enhanced by a strengthened National Guard and Reserves.

Both Truman and Eisenhower, influenced by their overseas experience in the World Wars, emphasized the threat of a Soviet attack on western Europe. Their strategy called for a deterrence based on a counterthreat of massive nuclear retaliation. By the end of the 1950s, however, political and technological developments exposed gaps in this strategy, and increasingly the Presidents who followed, all military veterans who had witnessed firsthand the effects of changing military technology, emphasized a military posture that allowed the President to respond with flexibility to any aggression. Beginning with President John Kennedy—who served as a junior naval officer in World War II—and continuing under his successors, the nation added a new array of conventional forces to its nuclear arsenal. Over the next two decades these men deployed American forces to many parts of the globe, most notably to Vietnam, where the United States fought a major war on the Asian mainland thousands of miles from the frontier contemplated by George Washington.

If America's military strategy and military might in the late twentieth century differ profoundly from their origins two hundred years ago, the political principles that guide its Commanders in Chief do not. Presidents continue to take an oath to defend and protect the Constitution against all enemies foreign and domestic; they continue to subscribe to the belief that in all matters the military is the servant of the citizenry through its elected leaders.

This fundamental continuity has particular meaning to those Commanders in Chief who themselves have served in uniform. For them, their military experience not only foreshadowed their presidential oath but also in many cases provided a firsthand knowledge of the human price of military action and of the need for effective organization, authority, and personal leadership for any effective action.

An awareness of this continuity has taken many forms in American history, but Presidents themselves have clearly given much thought to their military responsibilities. President Eisenhower, the paramount soldier-statesman of the twentieth century, wrote: "New military developments . . . brought about important changes in the duties that absorbed the urgent and continuous attention of the President. The title of Commander-in-Chief of the Armed Forces had become something real and critical even in peace."

His observations concerning the remorseless influence of time and change on human institutions echo an observation of his most illustrious predecessor. "While men have a disposition to wrangle," Washington wrote to the well-known Continental Army veteran, Baron von Steuben, in 1784, "and to disturb the peace of society, either from ambitious, political or interested motives, common prudence and foresight requires such an Establishment as is likely to ensure to us the blessings of Peace, altho' the undertaking should be attended with difficulty and expense." Despite their obviously different terms of reference, both men clearly shared a fundamental understanding of the military responsibilities of the President.

APPENDIX G

The Judiciary and Military Justice

Article III of the Constitution established the judicial branch of the federal government but gave little guidance as to its operation and structure. It provided for a Supreme Court with justices protected from retaliation for their judgments and authorized the organization of inferior courts with judges enjoying the same protection, leaving the rest of the judicial structure to Congress. Congress made the creation of the federal judicial system its first matter of business. The Judiciary Act of 1789 established the number of Supreme Court justices at six and went on to create a federal judiciary. It organized thirteen inferior, or trial, courts called United States District Courts and three intermediate courts, the United States Circuit Courts. The law provided the right to appeal all District Court decisions to the Circuit Courts and, in specific instances, Circuit Court decisions to the Supreme Court.

Two hundred years later the federal court system continues to reflect the basic provisions of the 1789 statute, although subsequent and frequent legislation has brought many changes. The initial establishment of the federal courts alongside state courts produced, in effect, a dual system of justice, with each level possessing special responsibilities and privileges. The judiciary system that resulted, unique at that time, clearly carried out the federal pattern of government instituted during the Constitutional Convention in Philadelphia in 1787. It also reflected the experiences of men who had developed a clear concept of the need for a strong national government during their military service in the Revolutionary War.

The development of the federal courts, and in particular the emergence of the Supreme Court as the final interpreter of the Constitution over all other federal and state courts, ensured that the United States developed into a nation where the rule of law is paramount. As Chief Justice John Marshall noted, "this system comes home in its effect to every man's fireside; it passes on his property, his reputation, his life, his all."

The Early Supreme Court

By the end of its first quarter-century, the Supreme Court had experienced a spectacular growth in importance. In the beginning, however, the Court's calendar was extremely light, and the judiciary exhibited signs of disorganization and disunity. The authority of the Court to pass judgment on the constitutionality of actions by the other branches of the federal government and the state legislatures also remained unclear.

Chief Justice John Jay, who had served as a colonel in the New York militia during the Revolution, opened the first session of the Supreme Court on 1 February 1790. Only three of the six justices had reached New York for the opening session. Subsequent meetings of the Court, which sat only twice a year, were brief. In its first three years, the Court heard only five cases; in its first decade, only fifty-five. Meanwhile, the justices occupied much of their time serving as Circuit Court judges, an unpopular duty that forced them to spend many months of the year in arduous travel around the federal circuits, in some instances to distant parts of the Republic. Riding the circuit, as it was called, bore little resemblance to the dignified and central position a Circuit Court judge would come to enjoy in later decades.

The appointment of John Marshall as Chief Justice in 1801 transformed the Supreme Court. Marshall, like Jay, was an Army veteran. At the age of nineteen he had volunteered for the Virginia militia shortly after the skirmish between the colonials and Redcoats at Lexington and Concord had opened the American Revolution. Marshall served as a lieutenant in the early days of the war and quickly demonstrated his leadership abilities. He eventually joined the Continental Army and fought as a captain in the battles of Germantown, Brandywine, and Monmouth.

As a company commander, Marshall shared the deprivations of his men in the winter quarters at Valley Forge, where he came to know General George Washington personally. Selected junior officers would periodically be invited to dine with the commanding general, and Marshall and his fellow captains would borrow uniform items from each other to ensure they were in complete uniform while in the presence of the Commander in Chief.

It was with the Army at Valley Forge that Marshall had his first legal experiences. He was assigned as "judge advocate" to a number of courts-martial, with the responsibility for seeing that the proceedings were con-

The Supreme Court of the United States. *(DA photograph.)*

ducted lawfully and fairly. Marshall himself attributed much of his later success in life to his military experiences and to the people with whom he came in contact in the Continental Army. Marshall was particularly influenced by Washington's strong sense of nationalism, a sense reinforced by his own Continental Army service. He firmly believed that the former colonies had, in the course of the Revolution, become in fact one nation, not a confederation of states. As Chief Justice he was destined to infuse this strong nationalist sentiment into the nation's legal system.

Marshall's greatest contribution to the American court system was his definition of the Supreme Court's most striking power, the right to declare federal and state laws unconstitutional. This has come to be known as the power of judicial review and remains today as the American legal system's most famous precedent: the Supreme Court is the final interpreter of the Constitution regarding issues brought before it.

Marshall's first great decision concerning judicial review occurred in 1803 in the case of *Marbury* v. *Madison.* The case came about when President John Adams, defeated in the 1800 election, appointed William Marbury a justice of the peace late on the last night of his presidency. Other so-called midnight judges were appointed at the same time and Adams' action set off a major controversy in an era of emerging national political parties. When denied his new position by the Jefferson administration, Marbury filed suit in a case that eventually came before Marshall and the Supreme Court. The Marshall Court found that Marbury was entitled to his commission and recognized his right to petition the courts to endorse the appointment, but it also found that the Supreme Court itself could not issue such an order because, despite a provision of the Judiciary Act that permitted it, the Constitution's definition of the Court's power did not include such jurisdiction. Marshall's decision established the precedent and scope of judicial review that remains at the heart of the federal judicial system.

Although many of Marshall's opinions were important in constitutional law, one other in particular is worth noting because of its sweeping impact on the federal system of government, especially when the rights of the states conflict with the interests of the central government. In 1816 Congress charted the second Bank of the United States in an effort to provide a sound currency system. Maryland, leading the opposition among the states to the idea of central banking, sought to force the bank's closure in the state by imposing a tax on the new national bank's Baltimore branch. At that point James McCulloch, a cashier in the federal bank, sought to test the Maryland law by refusing to pay the tax, and Maryland brought suit. When the case reached the Supreme Court, Marshall ruled that even though the Constitution did not specifically provide for the establishment of a federal bank, it did empower Congress to make all laws "necessary and proper" to carry out its specific powers. His ruling established the precedent of "implied powers," which recognized Congress' power to enact law "on which the welfare of the nation essentially depends," and in turn the supremacy of the federal government over the states when their interests conflict. In one of the judiciary's most memorable phrases, Marshall declared:

> Let the end be legitimate, let it be within the scope of the Constitution, and all means which are appropriate, which are plainly adapted to that end are not prohibited, but consist with the letter and spirit of the Constitution, are constitutional.

Since 1819 every generation of the Supreme Court has used Marshall's opinion in *McCulloch* v. *Maryland* to expand or limit federal legislative power and resolve issues of states' rights versus federalism.

The Great Dissenters Harlan and Holmes

As the nation grew, so did the federal judiciary. The nineteenth century brought more business to the Supreme Court as the slavery issue developed and industrialization and commerce came of age. Although the Bill of Rights was ratified in 1791, it was only after the Civil War that the Supreme Court was called upon to deal with civil rights as a result of new legislation passed by Congress to protect the former slaves. The twentieth century was marked by the growing complexity of the nation's economic and social experiences, and it witnessed as a consequence the passage of new regulatory laws and the creation of new administrative agencies to apply them. The Supreme Court, as well as the lower federal courts, suddenly found their dockets filled with new and complicated issues evolving out of these historical developments.

John Marshall Harlan, who had fought for the Union during the Civil War, found himself in the thick of the civil rights questions that developed in the post–Civil War period. Appointed to the Court by President Rutherford B. Hayes, Harlan is most notably remembered for his constant advocacy of judicial restraint. From his service in the Civil War, Harlan gained a deep respect for the rights of individuals. Although a onetime slave owner from Kentucky, he dissented from the prevailing view of the Court in the 1896 case of *Plessy* v. *Ferguson*. That case involved the attempt of many states to enforce segregation on the basis of color, the so-called Jim Crow laws. Homer Plessy had challenged a Louisiana law in 1892 which required equal but separate passenger cars on the railroad. The Supreme Court ruled that such laws were "reasonable," but Justice Harlan dissented in his famous opinion that "our Constitution is color-blind." Despite his powerful argument that "in view of the Constitution, in the eye of the law, there is in this country no superior, dominant, ruling class of citizens. . . . The humblest is the peer of the most powerful," the Court's separate-but-equal doctrine would prevail for more than half a century.

There has been no more eminent jurist on the Supreme Court than Oliver Wendell Holmes, whose works have inspired generations of lawyers to be skeptical of traditional views and to recognize that the law must change as the needs of the country change. Selected by President Theodore Roosevelt in 1902, Holmes was a Civil War veteran, wounded three times while serving in the Union infantry. As one commentator put it, "much of his thought had a military cast. Courage and hardihood he valued. He had a definition of a gentleman not now often encountered—one who for a point of honor would gladly risk his life."

Holmes once compared the law to a "magic mirror," in which "we see reflected not only our own lives, but the lives of all men that have been." During a public career so lengthy that it allowed him to deal personally with both Presidents Abraham Lincoln and Franklin Roosevelt, he witnessed the industrialization of the nation and the great impact those economic changes had on the nation's judiciary. In particular, industrialization forced the country to face complicated problems involving the safety and health of workers in the marketplace. Some states attempted to aid the workers by limiting the num-

JUSTICES OF THE SUPREME COURT WHO SERVED IN THE MILITARY

Name and State of Residence	*Birth*	*Death*	*Term of Office*	*Military Service*
John Jay New York	12 December 1745 New York, N.Y.	17 May 1829 Bedford, N.Y.	19 October 1789–29 June 1795	Colonel, New York Militia, 1775
Thomas Johnson Maryland	4 November 1732 Calvert Co., Md.	26 October 1819 Frederick, Md.	6 August 1792–16 January 1793	Brigadier General, Maryland Militia, 1776–1777; service in the Revolution
Bushrod Washington Virginia	5 June 1762 Westmoreland Co., Va.	26 November 1829 Philadelphia, Pa.	4 February 1799–26 November 1829	Private, Continental Army, 1778–1781; service in the Revolution
Alfred Moore North Carolina	21 May 1755 New Hanover Co., N.C.	15 October 1810 "Belfont," Bladen Co., N.C.	21 April 1800–26 January 1804	Captain, Continental Army, 1775–1777; Colonel, North Carolina Militia, 1777–1781; service in the Revolution
John Marshall Virginia	24 September 1755 Germantown, Va.	6 July 1835 Philadelphia, Pa.	4 February 1801–6 July 1835	Captain, Militia, 1775–1776; Continental Army, 1776–1781; service in the Revolution
Henry Brockholst Livingston New York	25 November 1757 New York, N.Y.	18 March 1823 Washington, D.C.	20 January 1807–18 March 1823	Lieutenant Colonel, Continental Army, 1775–1779; service in the Revolution
Thomas Todd Kentucky	23 January 1765 Near Dunkirk, King and Queen Co., Va.	7 February 1826 Frankfort, Ky.	4 May 1807–7 February 1826	Private, Continental Army, 1781; service in the Revolution
Gabriel Duvall Maryland	6 December 1752 "Marietta," Prince George's Co., Md.	6 March 1844 Near Glenn Dale, Prince George's Co., Md.	23 November 1811–14 January 1835	Private, Maryland Militia, 1776–1777; service in the Revolution
James Moore Wayne Georgia	c. 1790 Savannah, Ga.	5 July 1867 Washington, D.C.	14 January 1835–5 July 1867	Captain, Georgia Hussars, 1812–1815; service in the War of 1812
John Catron Tennessee	c. 1786 Pennsylvania	30 May 1865 Nashville, Tenn.	1 May 1837–30 May 1865	Sergeant Major, U.S. Volunteers, 1813–1815; service in the War of 1812
John Archibald Campbell Alabama	24 June 1811 Washington, Ga.	12 March 1889 Baltimore, Md.	11 April 1853–30 April 1861	Cadet, U.S. Military Academy, 1825–1828; left West Point to care for ailing father
John Marshall Harlan Kentucky	1 June 1833 Boyle Co., Ky.	14 October 1911 Washington, D.C.	10 December 1877–14 October 1911	Colonel, U.S. Volunteers, 1861–1863; service in the Civil War
William Burnham Woods Georgia	3 August 1824 Newark, Ohio	14 May 1887 Washington, D.C.	5 January 1881–14 May 1887	Brigadier General (Bvt. Major General), U.S. Volunteers, 1862–1866; service in the Civil War
Stanley Matthews Ohio	21 July 1824 Cincinnati, Ohio	22 March 1889 Washington, D.C.	17 May 1881–22 March 1889	Colonel, U.S. Volunteers, 1861–1863; service in the Civil War
Lucius Quintus C. Lamar Mississippi	17 September 1825 Eatontown, Putnam Co., Ga.	23 January 1893 Vineville, Ga.	18 January 1888–23 January 1893	Lieutenant Colonel, C.S.A., 1861–1862; service in the Civil War
Edward Douglass White Louisiana	3 November 1845 Parish Lafourche, La.	19 May 1921 Washington, D.C.	12 March 1894–18 December 1910	Private, C.S.A., 1861–1863; service in the Civil War

Name and State of Residence	*Birth*	*Death*	*Term of Office*	*Military Service*
Oliver Wendell Holmes Massachusetts	8 March 1841 Boston, Mass.	6 March 1935 Washington, D.C.	8 December 1902–12 January 1932	Captain, U.S. Volunteers, 1861–1864; service in the Civil War
Horace Harmon Lurton Tennessee	26 February 1844 Newport, Ky.	12 July 1914 Atlantic City, N.J.	3 January 1910–12 July 1914	Sergeant Major, C.S.A., 1861–1865; service in the Civil War
Hugo Lafayette Black Alabama	27 February 1886 Harlan, Clay Co., Ala.	25 September 1971 Bethesda, Md.	19 August 1937–17 September 1971	Captain, U.S. Army, 1917–1918
Stanley Forman Reed Kentucky	31 December 1884 Minerva, Mason Co., Ky.	2 April 1980 Huntington, N.Y.	31 January 1938–25 February 1957	First Lieutenant, U.S. Army, 1918; service in World War I
William Orville Douglas Connecticut	16 October 1898 Maine, Minn.	19 January 1980 Washington, D.C.	17 April 1939–12 November 1975	Private, U.S. Army, 1917–1919
Frank Murphy Michigan	13 April 1890 Harbor Beach, Mich.	19 July 1949 Detroit, Mich.	5 February 1940–19 July 1949	First Lieutenant, U.S. Army, 1919; service in World War I; Lieutenant Colonel, U.S. Army Reserve, 1942
Harold Hitz Burton Ohio	22 June 1888 Jamaica Plain, Mass.	28 October 1964 Washington, D.C.	1 October 1945–13 October 1958	Captain, U.S. Army, 1918–1919; service in World War I
Thomas Campbell Clark Texas	23 September 1899 Dallas, Tex.	13 June 1977 New York, N.Y.	24 August 1949–12 June 1967	Sergeant, U.S. Army, 1918–1919
Sherman Minton Indiana	20 October 1890 Georgetown, Ind.	9 April 1965 New Albany, Ind.	12 October 1949–15 October 1956	Captain, U.S. Army, 1917–1919; service in World War I
William J. Brennan, Jr. New Jersey	25 April 1906 Newark, N.J.	n/a	16 October 1956–20 July 1990	Colonel, U.S. Army, 1942–1945; service in World War II
Potter Stewart Ohio	23 January 1915 Jackson, Mich.	7 December 1985	14 October 1958–3 July 1981	Lieutenant (junior grade), U.S. Navy, 1941–1946; service in World War II
Byron Raymond White Colorado	8 June 1917 Fort Collins, Colo.	n/a	16 April 1962–present	Lieutenant, U.S. Navy Reserve, 1942–1946; service in World War II
Arthur Joseph Goldberg Illinois	8 August 1908 Chicago, Ill.	19 January 1990 Washington, D.C.	1 October 1962–25 July 1965	Major, U.S. Army, 1942–1944; service in World War II; Colonel, U.S. Air Force Reserve, 1976
Lewis F. Powell, Jr. Virginia	19 September 1907 Suffolk, Va.	n/a	7 January 1972–26 June 1987	Colonel, U.S. Army Air Forces, 1942–1946; service in World War II
William H. Rehnquist Arizona	1 October 1924 Milwaukee, Wisc.	n/a	7 January 1972–present	Sergeant, U.S. Army Air Forces, 1943–1946; service in World War II
John Paul Stevens Illinois	20 April 1920 Chicago, Ill.	n/a	19 December 1975–present	Lieutenant Commander, U.S. Navy Reserve, 1942–1945; service in World War II
Anthony M. Kennedy California	23 July 1936 Sacramento, Calif.	n/a	18 February 1988–present	Private, First Class, California Army National Guard, 1961

ber of hours worked and the conditions under which they toiled. These state laws ran up against the Court's traditional view of freedom of contract. A traditionalist Supreme Court sided with the employers and, animated by a determination to restrain government's interference with business, declared much of the new social legislation unconstitutional. In one noteworthy case, Joseph Lochner, owner of a bakery in Utica, New York, challenged a New York maximum-hour statute. The Supreme Court ruled that the Fourteenth Amendment protected "liberty of contract" between workers and employers. Justice Holmes in *Lochner* v. *New York* wrote one of the most famous dissents in the Court's history when he stated "a constitution is not intended to embody a particular economic theory. It is made for people of fundamentally differing views." Throughout his long tenure on the Court, his opinions helped shape the social and economic changes of twentieth-century America. He left as great an impact on the Constitution as any jurist in the history of the Court.

To cite Chief Justice Marshall's precedent of judicial review and the opinions of Harlan and Holmes serves to highlight the contributions of the many Soldier-Statesmen jurists who have helped form the basic structure of a judicial system that the nation so proudly cherishes. But these are just three examples of judges taken from hundreds of others throughout the federal judiciary who spent formative periods of their lives in the uniform of their country. Through the years, the Soldier-Statesmen of the judiciary have helped develop important legal principles, establish major precedents, and set standards for the direction of social and economic change in the United States. Tempered by military service, they brought to their respective courts values and experiences which have been reflected in judicial opinions from the beginning of the Republic until the present day.

The Establishment of Military Justice

Military justice in the armed forces of the United States is firmly based in the Constitution. Article I, Section 8, of the Constitution grants Congress the power "to make Rules for the Government and Regulation of the land and naval Forces." For two hundred years, initially through the Articles of War and later through the Uniform Code of Military Justice (UCMJ), Congress has provided the framework for the nation's unique system of military justice.

Actually, the first truly national courts were the courts-martial conducted by the Continental Army. Although strictly limited to military cases, these courts were established by the Continental Congress prior to the Declaration of Independence, well before the adoption of the Constitution and passage of the federal Judiciary Act. From the beginning all concerned accepted the fact that the military must have a system of what is now called "military justice." In 1775 the Continental Congress enacted separate sets of regulations, known as Articles of War, to govern the Army and the Navy, both based on the British system. The Army's first Articles of War were the work of a five-man committee, which included George Washington. Revised a year later, the Articles were expressly recognized by Congress and continued in effect with only minor changes until 1806, and with further revisions into modern times. All of these many versions of the Articles of War provided for trial by courts-martial, although the jurisdiction and composition of these courts were modified from time to time.

The huge citizen-soldier Army that fought World War II was subject to the discipline of those same Articles of War that had met the test of over two centuries of American legal and military history. Over two million courts-martial were convened during the war, more than eighty thousand of them the most serious type, the general court-martial. This amounted to over sixty general courts-martial a day during the war. Although legal scholars generally agreed that the justice system created under the Articles of War was noteworthy for its respect for precedent and consistency in judgment and, judged by the standards of the time, was predictable and fair, it became clear that given the amount and complexity of legal business in the armed forces, a thorough overhaul was needed.

After the war, Congress turned to a reform of the military justice system. Under the direction of Edmund Morgan, a noted professor of law from Harvard University, the Uniform Code of Military Justice Committee revised the Articles of War. Morgan was no stranger to the subject. He had served as a judge advocate in the Office of the Judge Advocate General during World War I and was intimately involved in earlier disputes over the serviceman's rights of appeal. As a result of his research and subsequent deliberations in Congress, President Harry S. Truman signed into law in May 1950 the Uniform Code of Military Justice.

Since 1950 the UCMJ has served as the source of authority for the military justice system. Consisting of fewer than 150 statutory sections called Articles, the UCMJ provides the jurisdiction or power of the court-martial system; pretrial, trial, and posttrial procedures; the authority and composition of courts-martial; and review of courts-martial. At the same time, the UCMJ provides for and protects the substantive rights of soldiers, such as the right to counsel; privilege against self-incrimination; right to a speedy trial of the facts; right to compulsory process; and protection against double jeopardy.

One of the most significant aspects of the Uniform Code of Military Justice was the establishment of the United States Court of Military Appeals. The court, which sits in the nation's capital, is composed of five civilian judges. It is the highest appellate court in the military justice system, charged with reviewing the decisions of the service courts of review. Congress, convinced of the need to assure direct civilian review over military justice, deliberately chose to confer this power on a specialized court so that its civilian judges might gain over time a fully developed understanding of the distinctive problems and legal traditions of the services. Appeals from decisions of the U.S. Court of Military Appeals go directly to the United States Supreme Court.

Since Congress deemed it impossible to provide every detail of the military justice system, the new law conferred certain specific authority in the matter upon the President. Article 36 of the UCMJ, for example, specifically empowers the President as Commander in Chief to prescribe procedures for courts-martial and to set maximum punishments for offenses under the law. This delegated authority has been exercised by designated military officials under the provisions of the Manual for Courts-Martial. The courts have subsequently recognized the manual as a valid exercise of the President's rule-making authority.

The hierarchy of authority for the military justice system was further delegated when the President conferred on the Secretary of the Army the authority to prescribe rules not inconsistent with the UCMJ or the Manual for Courts-Martial. In Army Regulation 27–10, the Secretary of the Army prescribed policies and procedures pertaining to the administration of military justice within the Army. For example, the regulation contains detailed guidance for proceedings under Article 15, UCMJ, pertaining to nonjudicial punishment; creates the United States Army Trial Defense Service as an independent organization to provide the service of a defense counsel; and establishes an independent United States Army Trial Judiciary.

Through the pretrial, trial, and posttrial stages of a court-martial, the military justice system protects the rights of service members as well as ensuring fairness in the administration of justice. These rights are derived from the United States Constitution, especially the Bill of Rights (the first ten amendments to the Constitution), the Uniform Code of Military Justice, federal case law, the Manual for Courts-Martial, and regulations issued by the Department of Defense and secretaries of the various services. Under the American system of government, each member of the armed forces is ensured the following rights:

- Right to privacy
- Right against self-incrimination
- Right to military or civilian counsel
- Right to Article 32 investigation if charged with a General Court-Martial offense
- Right to review all papers, evidence, and statements held by the prosecution pertinent to the case
- Right to a speedy and public trial
- Right to not be tried twice for the same offense
- Right to trial by military judge or with court members
- Right to appeal with counsel.

Just as America's military strength and strategy today differ profoundly from their origins two hundred years ago, so too do the federal judiciary system and the military justice system of the armed forces. Upon close examination, however, it is clear that the fundamental principles underlying both have not differed since the establishment of the Republic: members of the armed forces do not forfeit their rights as citizens when they join the military; and military authority, in our Republic, is accountable to elected civilian leaders who are not beyond the law of the land, law which the Supreme Court defines for us.

APPENDIX H

The Bill of Rights

After many weeks of debate in Philadelphia during the hot summer of 1787, the Founding Fathers fashioned a new form of government to replace the Articles of Confederation. In effect, the Constitution they produced represented a victory for those who argued that survival as a nation depended on a strong and efficient central government. Their opponents, worried more about potential abuses of governmental power, had sought to reserve as much power as possible to the states, where they felt government was closer to the people.

Now the winners' handiwork was to be submitted to the citizens of the individual states for ratification. But the losers had not yet given up the fight. When the Continental Congress agreed on 20 September to transmit the newly signed Constitution to the states for ratification, everyone realized that a second great debate on constitutional government was about to begin.

National attention quickly focused on the state-by-state struggle between proponents (the Federalists) and opponents (who came to be called the Antifederalists) of the new Constitution. The better-organized Federalists appeared to have the upper hand. Skillful managers like James Madison, Alexander Hamilton, and George Washington, who played a key behind-the-scenes role, orchestrated a careful campaign to win the approval of the necessary nine states. The Antifederalists could count on the leadership of only a handful of the delegates who had been at the Philadelphia Convention and just a few figures of national stature: Patrick Henry, George Mason, and Richard Henry Lee in Virginia; Samuel Chase in Maryland; and Governor George Clinton in New York. These men called on the voters to reject the Constitution because of several specific "defects," although their arguments actually focused on what they believed was an excessive and dangerous concentration of power in the hands of the national government. Their fear had only been increased by the fact that the new Constitution failed to enumerate specifically the basic rights of citizens and of individual states.

The eminent statesman George Mason, for example, made much of the fact that the Constitution lacked a declaration of rights. Mason was the primary author of Virginia's celebrated Declaration of Rights of 1776, which had served as a model for similar declarations in the other states. To those who argued that these state declarations were sufficient protection for the rights of the people, Mason responded that the new Constitution made the laws of the central government paramount over the laws and constitutions of the states, and, therefore, could nullify the state declarations. Among his specific objections to the new Constitution he included its failure to enumerate certain liberties, including freedom of the press, trial by jury, and protection against standing armies. Despite these objections, the majority agreed with Benjamin Franklin when he said, "I agree to this Constitution with all its faults, if they are such; because I think a general Government necessary for us, and there is no form of Government but what may be a blessing to the people if well administered." On 17 September 1787, thirty-eight delegates signed the Constitution, and the presiding officer, George Washington, forwarded the document to the Continental Congress for transmission to the states.

The Federalists quickly won approval for the new Constitution in Delaware, New Jersey, Georgia, Pennsylvania, and Connecticut, but the remaining states

George Mason. *(Oil, by Dominic W. Boudet; courtesy of the Virginia Museum of Fine Arts, Richmond, Va., gift of David K. E. Bruce.)*

Chaplain conducts services for infantrymen and artillerymen in a field near Pleiku, Vietnam, in 1969. *(DA photograph.)*

promised to test their political skills to the limit. In Massachusetts, the scene of the next ratification contest, the Federalists adopted a strategy that would prove successful there and in the remaining states. They induced local political celebrities such as John Hancock and Samuel Adams to spearhead the defense of the Constitution. But more importantly, to ensure that the debate would remain focused on the need for a strong and effective central government, they sought to defuse the opposition's objections to the absence of any enumeration of specific rights in the document by agreeing that Massachusetts' approval could include a proviso that a bill of rights would be added to the Constitution after its adoption. The knowledge that the new Constitution would include amendments laying out fundamental liberties softened the opposition. Robbed of their most popular argument, the Antifederalists found their cause fatally weakened. All the remaining states except Maryland attached a similar demand for amendments to their ratification. In an exceptionally tough fight in the New York convention, the Federalists actually agreed to support the addition of thirty-two amendments to the Constitution in order to win the day.

When the first Congress under the new government assembled in 1789, the winners, in keeping with promises made during the ratification process, set about adding a bill of rights to the Constitution. As leader of the House of Representatives, James Monroe initiated the legislation for amending the Constitution as specified in Article V. Even the doughty Antifederalist, George Mason, was moved to declare: "I have received much Satisfaction from Amendments to the Federal Constitution which have lately passed the House of Representatives; I hope they will also pass the Senate. With two or three further Amts . . . I cou'd cheerfully put my Hand & Heart to the new Govt." In September both houses of Congress approved by the required two-thirds majority twelve amendments for consideration by the states. Ten survived the ratification process, and on 15 December 1791 the Bill of Rights was added to the Constitution.

Protection of the Citizen's Basic Freedoms

The Bill of Rights defines specific liberties—such as freedom of religion, speech, and assembly—and other traditional Anglo-American legal concepts widely proclaimed by eighteenth-century political philosophers. By enumerating these liberties and other freedoms, such as the right to a speedy trial, it puts the national government and the state governments on notice that these liberties and freedoms must be respected.* The protections guaranteed by the Bill of Rights also apply to every member of the armed forces, flowing down from the Constitution through federal laws, including the Uniform Code of Military Justice, through executive orders, including the Manual for Courts-Martial, and through departmental directives, service regulations, and command regulations and orders.

In effect, the Bill of Rights defines the minimum rights of all citizens. The vast panoply of laws and regulations that govern the daily lives of Americans must be in harmony with those basic liberties and freedoms guaranteed in the Constitution and the Bill of Rights and must always remain subordinate to them. At the same time, the freedoms guaranteed under the Bill of Rights are not absolute. As Justice Oliver Wendell Holmes once explained, freedom of speech does not guarantee the citizen the right to yell "fire" in a crowded theater. During the last two hundred years the courts, especially the Supreme Court, have sought to balance the legitimate needs of government, including those of the armed services, against the individual rights of citizens. This delicate balance, as the constitutional scholars call it, applies especially to the armed forces where the need for a common defense must be reconciled with the rights of the citizen in uniform.

The Amendments

The individual amendments are carefully worded statements that reflected the debates of the ratification process. They have been interpreted and applied by the courts with equal care over the years.

Amendment 1

Congress shall make no law respecting an establishment of religion, or prohibiting the free exercise thereof; or abridging the freedom of speech, or of the press, or the right of the people peaceably to assemble, and to petition the Government for a redress of grievances.

The First Amendment, probably the most familiar words in the Constitution, enumerates a series of basic personal liberties. Its guarantee of religious liberty is presented in two parts, or clauses. The establishment clause bars the government from setting up a state religion, favoring one religion over another, or entangling itself in religious affairs; the free exercise clause prevents the government from interfering with or intruding upon the religious beliefs of the citizen except where a state interest of the highest order can be demonstrated.

A practical application of the religious establishment clause in the armed forces occurred when the Supreme Court ruled that the Army could not make chapel attendance compulsory for cadets at the U.S. Military Academy because such a requirement violated a cadet's freedom under the First Amendment. The amendment's free exercise clause has also been applied to military matters. It guarantees a citizen's right to exemption from military service on the basis of religious conscience or ethical objections. In addition, the courts have used the free exercise clause of the First Amendment to uphold the right of Congress to appoint chaplains. The presence of military chaplains, the Court decreed, does not—as some charged—imply that Congress was establishing religion. Rather it ensures that members of the armed forces are given the means to exercise their religious rights.

At the same time the courts have sought to maintain the delicate balance between rights and obligations. They have ruled that the services can restrict the religious practices of servicemen and women when accommodation to an individual's religious beliefs would have an adverse impact upon military readiness, unit cohesion, safety, or discipline. Thus, the Army can prohibit its soldiers from wearing certain types of religious apparel while in uniform without violating the soldier's First Amendment rights.

The First Amendment's guarantee of freedom of speech represents, as a famous Supreme Court case once put it, "a profound national commitment to the principle that debate on public issues should be uninhibited, robust, and wide-open." But there are limits. A citizen can-

*The adoption of the Fourteenth Amendment's equal protection clause in 1868 extended the guarantees of the Bill of Rights to the states as well.

not, for example, defame another, make fraudulent misrepresentations, or incite misconduct. Nor can a soldier incite disobedience or participate in demonstrations and political activities while serving in foreign countries.

The Supreme Court has interpreted liberty of the press as a constitutional protection from previous restraints or censorship. This potent guarantee is extended to soldiers, and Army commanders have been ordered to encourage the availability of printed materials presenting wide-ranging viewpoints on public issues, including views critical of the government and the services. But again addressing the delicate balance between the government's needs and individual rights, the Supreme Court has ruled that the First Amendment does not restrict the services from banning on-post distribution of publications deemed a clear and present danger to the loyalty, discipline, or morale of the troops.

The rights of peaceable assembly and petition, and their implied derivative, the right of association, serve as a corollary to the effective exercise of free speech. Under the First Amendment, soldiers enjoy the right to petition for a redress of grievances, but again, because of the unique mission of soldiers, the courts have recognized some restraints on the exercise of this right. Thus, membership in extremist organizations, participation in military unions, and involvement in partisan political activity are prohibited, and circulation of petitions on military posts may be subject to prior review.

Amendment 2

A well regulated Militia being necessary to the security of a free State, the right of the people to keep and bear Arms, shall not be infringed.

Eighteenth-century Americans understood precisely the impact of this amendment on their lives. The Framers had a lively fear of permanent armies as a threat to representative government. Creating a "well regulated" militia—that is, one with adequate organization, weapons, and training in every state of the Union—ensured that, when mobilized, the militiamen could effectively provide for the nation's defense. George Mason and other advocates of the Second Amendment knew that during the last years of the Revolution many militia units had virtually disintegrated because they lacked sufficient arms. The amendment reinforces the militia clause in Article I of the Constitution and the concept of the citizen-soldier as the defender of the nation's liberties by explicitly providing for the right to bear arms.

Amendment 3

No Soldier shall, in time of peace be quartered in any house, without the consent of the Owner, nor in time of war, but in a manner to be prescribed by law.

One of the grievances that induced the colonists to rebel against King George was the habit of his commanders to lodge British troops in private homes contrary to their owners' wishes. Determined that such invasions of privacy in peacetime would not be countenanced under the new federal government, the Framers wanted the consent of the citizen to be an explicit requirement. At the same time they recognized the nation's possible military needs. Thus, the amendment also provides that, in time of war, the government can demand use of a citizen's property, but only by an act of Congress. Although seldom invoked, the amendment underscores both the importance the Founders placed on the sanctity of the home and the influence that the colonial military experience had on the formation of our constitutional freedoms.

Amendment 4

The right of the people to be secure in their persons, houses, papers, and effects, against unreasonable searches and seizures, shall not be violated, and no Warrants shall issue, but upon probable cause, supported by Oath or affirmation, and particularly describing the place to be searched, and the persons or things to be seized.

Protection against unreasonable search and seizure, which applies equally to civilians and soldiers, is an explicit expression of the right to privacy. Before law enforcement agencies can search a person or property or seize property for evidence to be used in a court, they must obtain explicit permission from competent authority in the form of a search warrant (or in the case of military personnel, a search authorization). The Supreme Court ruled that such warrants can be granted only upon a finding of probable cause and must specifically describe the place to be searched and the things to be seized. It also requires that the issuing authority must be "neutral and impartial." As a result, civilian and military law enforcement officials do not have authority to issue search warrants. In the civilian community, that authority rests in the judiciary. The courts, recognizing the special needs of the military, have decreed that in the case of searches and seizures on military installations, commanders and military judges and magistrates are empowered to issue an authorization to search.

One indication of the paramount constitutional importance of the citizen's right to privacy is the exclusionary rule adopted by the Supreme Court to reinforce the protection against unreasonable search or seizure. Under this rule, any evidence discovered or seized as a result of an unlawful search is excluded, that is, considered inadmissible as evidence during a trial. This rule fully applies to trials by courts-martial as well.

The courts have indicated, however, that the right of privacy is not absolute. Law enforcement officials, for example, retain the right to search when making an arrest and to stop and frisk a suspect, and immigration officials may conduct searches without warrants at ports of entry. Military commanders retain the right to search persons on entry or exit from posts. They also can inspect their troops, buildings, and equipment, much the same way certain regulated businesses in the civilian community are permitted to inspect employees without warrants.

Amendment 5

No person shall be held to answer for a capital, or otherwise infamous crime, unless on presentment or indictment of a Grand Jury, except in cases arising in the land or naval forces, or in the Militia, when in actual service in time of War or public danger; nor shall any person be subject for the same offense to be twice put in jeopardy of life or limb, nor shall be compelled in any criminal case to be a witness against himself, nor be deprived of life, liberty, or property, without due process of law; nor shall private property be taken for public use without just compensation.

The Fifth Amendment limits the government's powers in matters before the courts. The grand jury safeguards the citizen from being charged with a crime without sufficient evidence. This jury, charged with investigating serious crimes, must be composed of citizens selected from the jurisdiction where the crime occurred. Prosecutors present their cases to the grand jury. The accused is not normally present, nor is any counsel for the accused. After hearing the evidence the grand jury decides whether probable cause exists that the accused committed the crime and whether a trial is warranted. When the grand jury agrees with the prosecutor, it returns an indictment. An indictment is not a finding of guilt, but merely a declaration that sufficient evidence exists to indicate that the accused could have committed the act.

Servicemen and women, including members of the National Guard and Reserves when called to active duty during war or times of public danger, are excluded from being subject to grand jury proceedings. This does not mean that they are without pretrial protections against improper prosecutions. Unless waived by the soldier, an investigation under Article 32, Uniform Code of Military Justice, is required before charges may be referred to trial by general court-martial. During such an investigation the soldier has the right to be present, be assisted by counsel, confront and cross-examine witnesses, and present evidence in his or her defense, including extenuating and mitigating evidence. Although the recommendations of the investigating officer are not binding, they must be carefully weighed by the convening authority. This system is meant to protect soldiers from baseless charges, provide reliable information and insights as to the proper disposition of the charges to the convening authority, and serve as a discovery tool for both the prosecutor and defense.

Always fascinating to fiction writers and Hollywood, the concept of double jeopardy involves one of a citizen's most basic rights. Being placed on trial for a criminal offense exposes the accused to a danger which is legally called jeopardy. The Fifth Amendment guarantees that a citizen cannot be placed in such jeopardy more than once for the same offense by the same authority. Such a guarantee does not apply when two separate authorities hold jurisdiction. Although, for example, soldiers may not be prosecuted for an offense in both a federal civilian court and a court-martial, they may be tried in both a state court and a court-martial because two separate authorities (or sovereigns) are involved. The Fifth Amendment's double jeopardy clause also figures in a special rule found in the Manual for Courts-Martial. Under this rule a soldier involved in multiple trials cannot have the facts ruled on in one trial retried by his prosecutor in a subsequent trial.

The Fifth Amendment guarantees that a witness in any proceeding where legal testimony is given has the right to refuse to testify on the grounds that the answers given may be used against him in a subsequent prosecution. The Supreme Court provided guidelines for applying this protection in its famous Miranda decision. Miranda requires that before criminal suspects can be interrogated, they must be advised of their right to remain silent and to consult with an attorney, appointed by the court if they cannot afford one. The Fifth Amendment also prohibits prosecutors and judges from commenting when the accused declines to testify during a criminal trial. Indeed, judges must inform juries that the failure of an accused to testify may not be used as a basis to infer guilt or a motive to hide information.

Soldiers enjoy similar protections under Article 31 of the Uniform Code of Military Justice. Before a soldier is questioned in a criminal investigation, he must be advised of the nature of the offense under investigation, the right to remain silent, and the consequences of waiving that right. Soldiers in military custody also have the right to appointed counsel or may retain civilian counsel at their own expense before questioning is permitted.

Due process can be loosely defined as "fair play." The Constitution, through the due process clause, ensures that the government cannot act arbitrarily or capriciously against its citizens. The Fifth Amendment guarantees fairness in the rules and procedures by which trials and hearings are conducted; it also guarantees the right of the accused to be informed, to be heard, and to appeal. Further, it guarantees that laws do not unfairly abridge civil liberties. Life, liberty, and property cannot be taken by the government without just and fair procedures and laws. Although there are ways for the government to take private property to promote the public welfare, appropriate procedures must be followed and proper compensation must be paid to the property owner.

Soldiers are protected under the due process clause, but again the Supreme Court, recognizing the unique nature of military service, allows variations from the civilian model. For example, a soldier is not free to leave the Army prior to expiration of the enlistment contract. Likewise, a soldier's enlistment contract can be involuntarily extended by the government during a national emergency. Due process for soldiers is spelled out in the Uniform Code of Military Justice, the *Manual for Courts-Martial,* and the myriad of regulations published by the services.

Amendment 6

In all criminal prosecutions, the accused shall enjoy the right to a speedy and public trial, by an impartial jury of the State and district wherein the crime shall have been committed; which district shall have been previously ascertained by law, and to be informed of the nature and cause of accusation; to be confronted with the witnesses against him; to have compulsory process for obtaining witnesses in his favor, and to have the assistance of counsel for his defense.

The Sixth Amendment, the so-called fair trial amendment, guarantees important procedural rights before, during, and after trial. The trial must take place soon after arrest so as not to leave the accused burdened with pending charges, but with sufficient time allowed for both the prosecution and the defense to prepare their cases. The trial must be public. The jury must be impartial, excluding both those biased by acquaintance either with the accused or the case and those with any preconceptions. No particular class or group of citizens can be precluded (for example, a jury cannot systematically preclude black citizens). The accused must be informed of the charges so that a proper defense can be prepared and must be allowed to confront those testifying against him and to call witnesses on his behalf. Recent Supreme Court decisions have extended these rights to trials for all sorts of crimes, not just felonies, the legal term describing serious crimes, as was the practice in the past.

These same procedural guarantees are extended to servicemen and women accused of crimes. Members of a court-martial constitute a military jury. The Uniform Code of Military Justice requires that special courts-martial be composed of at least three members and general courts-martial of at least five members. The Sixth Amendment does not require the verdict of a courts-martial to be unanimous. In all major aspects but two, military courts follow the same procedures as a civilian court. The accused in a military court can reject a jury trial in favor of trial by a military judge. Parties to a military trial may also ask the judge for a closed trial in the interest of national security when, for example, classified information could be compromised.

Amendment 7

In Suits at common law, where the value in controversy shall exceed twenty dollars, the right of trial by jury shall be preserved, and no fact tried by a jury shall be otherwise re-examined in any Court of the United States, than according to the rules of the common law.

The purpose of the Seventh Amendment is to extend the right to trial guaranteed in criminal matters by Article III of the Constitution to civil suits that involve damages of more than twenty dollars ($1,000 in today's values). The parties to a civil lawsuit, unlike the accused in a criminal trial, may waive trial by jury and elect to have their case tried by the judge.

Amendment 8

Excessive bail shall not be required, nor excessive fines imposed, nor cruel and unusual punishment inflicted.

The constitutional guarantee against excessive bail (assurance that the accused will appear at trial by the posting of a bond) ensures that the accused is not in effect punished before conviction. In the military system Congress (through the Uniform Code of Military Justice) and the President (through the *Manual for Courts-*

Martial) replaced the bail system with one of graduated restraint. A commander is authorized to employ a wide variety of pretrial restraints on a soldier accused of a crime. He can set conditions on the soldier's liberty, place the individual on restriction, or impose pretrial confinement. Such restraints can be imposed only if there is a reasonable belief that a court-martial offense has been committed, that there is probable cause, and that circumstances require restraint. A soldier so restrained must be given notice of the terms of restraint and informed of the charges.

Pretrial confinement, the most severe restraint, is carefully controlled by law. The trial of any soldier placed in pretrial confinement must begin within 90 days after the charges are made. Within 72 hours of confinement the soldier's commander must decide whether such conditions should continue. Within 7 days a military judge or magistrate must determine whether a valid basis for such confinement exists. Unlike their counterparts in civilian courts, military authorities cannot appeal the decision of a military judge to release a soldier from pretrial confinement. But decisions to continue such confinement may be appealed by the soldier. In all cases, such confinement counts toward fulfilling the punishment, if the soldier is found guilty.

What constitutes excessive or cruel and unusual punishment is usually defined by the courts in each case. In general the courts have decided that punishments that are "degrading" or "wantonly imposed" are cruel and unusual and are therefore prohibited. Servicemen and women are carefully protected under the Uniform Code of Military Justice against such punishments. The President has prescribed the maximum punishments for all offenses, and no court-martial may impose a punishment, or combination of punishments, that exceeds these limits. The code also specifically prohibits flogging, branding, marking or tattooing the body, and other similar punishments used in the past. It authorizes the death penalty for the most serious violations, but as in the civilian courts many restrictions are placed on its imposition.

Amendment 9

The enumeration in the Constitution of certain rights shall not be construed to deny or disparage others retained by the people.

One of the Founders' fears was that by enumerating a specific list of inalienable rights, the Constitution might imply that such a list constituted the sum total of the citizen's rights. The Ninth Amendment addresses that fear by explicitly referring to the natural rights of the people and guaranteeing that government may not interfere with those rights. These unspecified natural rights, which eighteenth-century philosophers taught were derived from the natural law that governs the universe, are difficult to define. But they had a real intuitive meaning for the Founders, and over the years justices have argued that the Supreme Court should consider natural law in its decisions and, to the contrary, that it should not attempt to create new rights.

Amendment 10

The powers not delegated to the United States by the Constitution, nor prohibited by it to the States, are reserved to the States respectively, or to the people.

The distinction between reserved and delegated powers is at the heart of the federal form of government. The Tenth Amendment reiterates the philosophy of the Founders: the federal government has only those powers expressly delegated to it by the Constitution. All other powers remain with the individual states, or, where the state has not expressed its right in its own constitution, with the people. This noble concept has been the subject of continuous debate in the United States. Irreconcilable differences over federal-versus-states rights led to the Civil War. Still a source of considerable political rhetoric, the question of reserved and delegated powers has for more than a century been left to the Supreme Court to decide.

The Legacy of the Bill of Rights

The Bill of Rights has served for two hundred years as a beacon to the oppressed of the world and as a model for government in many nations. It remains the bulwark of our free society and the basis of our civil rights. As we commemorate this anniversary of the Bill of Rights, it is appropriate that we consider the familiar phrase "with rights comes responsibility." The magnificent liberties enumerated in the first ten amendments did not come free. The Soldier-Statesmen of the Constitution demonstrated in their own lives that the pursuit of liberty could require sacrifices both under arms and in the exacting work of governance. To remain effective, the Bill of Rights has required that citizens in every generation support the concept of a government of law. Through their oath to defend the Constitution, members of the armed services uphold that commitment in a particularly visible way. In doing so, they help to nurture and protect both their own and all of our liberties.

APPENDIX I

Other Amendments to the Constitution

(The first 10 Amendments were ratified December 15, 1791, and form what is known as the Bill of Rights. For the text of these Amendments, see Appendix H.)

Amendment 11

(Ratified February 7, 1795)

The Judicial power of the United States shall not be construed to extend to any suit in law or equity, commenced or prosecuted against one of the United States by Citizens of another State, or by Citizens or Subjects of any Foreign State.

Amendment 12

(Ratified July 27, 1804)

The Electors shall meet in their respective states and vote by ballot for President and Vice-President, one of whom, at least, shall not be an inhabitant of the same state with themselves; they shall name in their ballots the person voted for as President, and in distinct ballots the person voted for as Vice-President, and they shall make distinct lists of all persons voted for as President, and of all persons voted for as Vice-President, and of the number of votes for each, which lists they shall sign and certify, and transmit sealed to the seat of the government of the United States, directed to the President of the Senate;—The President of the Senate shall, in the presence of the Senate and House of Representatives, open all the certificates and the votes shall then be counted;—The person having the greatest number of votes for President, shall be the President, if such number be a majority of the whole number of Electors appointed; and if no person have such majority, then from the persons having the highest numbers not exceeding three on the list of those voted for as President, the House of Representatives shall choose immediately, by ballot, the President. But in choosing the President, the votes shall be taken by states, the representation from each state having one vote; a quorum for this purpose shall consist of a member or members from two-thirds of the states, and a majority of all the states shall be necessary to a choice. And if the House of Representatives shall not choose a President whenever the right of choice shall devolve upon them, before the fourth day of March next following, then the Vice-President shall act as President, as in the case of the death or other constitutional disability of the President.—The person having the greatest number of votes as Vice-President, shall be the Vice-President, if such number be a majority of the whole number of Electors appointed, and if no person have a majority, then from the two highest numbers on the list, the Senate shall choose the Vice-President; a quorum for the purpose shall consist of two-thirds of the whole number of Senators, and a majority of the whole number shall be necessary to a choice. But no person constitutionally ineligible to the office of President shall be eligible to that of Vice-President of the United States.

Amendment 13

(Ratified December 6, 1865)

Section 1. Neither slavery nor involuntary servitude, except as a punishment for crime whereof the party shall have been duly convicted, shall exist within the United States, or any place subject to their jurisdiction.

Section 2. Congress shall have power to enforce this article by appropriate legislation.

Amendment 14

(Ratified July 9, 1868)

Section 1. All persons born or naturalized in the United States, and subject to the jurisdiction thereof, are citizens of the United States and of the State wherein they reside. No State shall make or enforce any law which shall abridge the privileges or immunities of citizens of the United States; nor shall any State deprive any person of life, liberty, or property, without due process of law; nor deny to any person within its jurisdiction the equal protection of the laws.

Section 2. Representatives shall be apportioned among the several States according to their respective numbers, counting the whole number of persons in each State, excluding Indians not taxed. But when the right to vote at any election for the choice of electors for President and Vice President of the United States, Representatives in Congress, the Executive and Judicial officers of a State, or the members of the Legislature thereof, is denied to any of the male inhabitants of such State, being twenty-one years of age, and citizens of the United States, or in any way abridged, except for participation in rebellion, or other crime, the basis of representation therein shall be reduced in the proportion which the number of such male citizens shall bear to the whole number of male citizens twenty-one years of age in such State.

Section 3. No person shall be a Senator or Representative in Congress, or elector of President and Vice President, or hold any office, civil or military, under the United States, or under any State, who, having previously taken an oath, as a member of Congress, or as an officer of the United States, or as a member of any State legislature, or as an executive or judicial officer of any State, to support the Constitution of the United States, shall have engaged in insurrection or rebellion against the same, or given aid or comfort to the enemies thereof. But Congress may by a vote of two-thirds of each House, remove such disability.

Section 4. The validity of the public debt of the United States, authorized by law, including debts incurred for payment of pensions and bounties for services in suppressing insurrection or rebellion, shall not be questioned. But neither the United States nor any State shall assume or pay any debt or obligation incurred in aid of insurrection or rebellion against the United States, or any claim for the loss or emancipation of any slave; but all such debts, obligations and claims shall be held illegal and void.

Section 5. The Congress shall have power to enforce, by appropriate legislation, the provisions of this article.

Amendment 15

(Ratified February 3, 1870)

Section 1. The right of citizens of the United States to vote shall not be denied or abridged by the United States or by any State on account of race, color, or previous condition of servitude.

Section 2. The Congress shall have power to enforce this article by appropriate legislation.

Amendment 16

(Ratified February 3, 1913)

The Congress shall have power to lay and collect taxes on incomes, from whatever source derived, without apportionment among the several States, and without regard to any census or enumeration.

Amendment 17

(Ratified April 8, 1913)

The Senate of the United States shall be composed of two Senators from each State, elected by the people thereof for six years; and each Senator shall have one vote. The electors in each State shall have the qualifications requisite for electors of the most numerous branch of the State legislatures.

When vacancies happen in the representation of any State in the Senate, the executive authority of such State shall issue writs of election to fill such vacancies: *Provided,* That the legislature of any State may empower the executive thereof to make temporary appointments until the people fill the vacancies by election as the legislature may direct.

This amendment shall not be so construed as to affect the election or term of any Senator chosen before it becomes valid as part of the Constitution.

Amendment 18

(Ratified January 16, 1919.
Repealed December 5, 1933 by Amendment 21)

Section 1. After one year from the ratification of this article the manufacture, sale, or transportation of intoxicating liquors within, the importation thereof into, or the exportation thereof from the United States and all territory subject to the jurisdiction thereof for beverage purposes is hereby prohibited.

Section 2. The Congress and the several States shall have concurrent power to enforce this article by appropriate legislation.

Section 3. This article shall be inoperative unless it shall have been ratified as an amendment to the Constitution by the legislatures of the several States as provided in the Constitution, within seven years from the date of the submission hereof to the States by the Congress.

Amendment 19

(Ratified August 18, 1920)

The right of citizens of the United States to vote shall not be denied or abridged by the United States or by any State on account of sex.

Congress shall have power to enforce this article by appropriate legislation.

Amendment 20

(Ratified January 23, 1933)

Section 1. The terms of the President and Vice President shall end at noon on the 20th day of January, and the terms of Senators and Representatives at noon on the 3d day of January, of the years in which such terms would have ended if this article had not been ratified; and the terms of their successors shall then begin.

Section 2. The Congress shall assemble at least once in every year, and such meeting shall begin at noon on the 3d day of January, unless they shall by law appoint a different day.

Section 3. If, at the time fixed for the beginning of the term of the President, the President elect shall have died, the Vice President elect shall become President. If a President shall not have been chosen before the time fixed for the beginning of his term, or if the President elect shall have failed to qualify, then the Vice President elect shall act as President until a President shall have qualified; and the Congress may by law provide for the case wherein neither a President elect nor a Vice President elect shall have qualified, declaring who shall then act as President, or the manner in which one who is to act shall be selected, and such person shall act accordingly until a President or Vice President shall have qualified.

Section 4. The Congress may by law provide for the case of the death of any of the persons from whom the House of Representatives may choose a President whenever the right of choice shall have devolved upon them, and for the case of the death of any of the persons from whom the Senate may choose a Vice President whenever the right of choice shall have devolved upon them.

Section 5. Sections I and 2 shall take effect on the 15th day of October following the ratification of this article.

Section 6. This article shall be inoperative unless it shall have been ratified as an amendment to the Constitution by the legislatures of three-fourths of the several States within seven years from the date of its submission.

Amendment 21

(Ratified December 5, 1933)

Section 1. The eighteenth article of amendment to the Constitution of the United States is hereby repealed.

Section 2. The transportation or importation into any State, Territory, or possession of the United States for delivery or use therein of intoxicating liquors, in violation of the laws thereof, is hereby prohibited.

Section 3. This article shall be inoperative unless it shall have been ratified as an amendment to the Constitution by conventions in the several States, as provided in the Constitution, within seven years from the date of the submission hereof to the States by the Congress.

Amendment 22

(Ratified February 27, 1951)

Section 1. No person shall be elected to the office of the President more than twice, and no person who has held the office of President, or acted as President, for more than two years of a term to which some other person was elected President shall be elected to the office of the President more than once. But this Article shall not apply to any person holding the office of President when this Article was proposed by the Congress, and shall not prevent any person who may be holding the office of President, or acting as President, during the term within which this Article becomes operative from holding the office of President or acting as President during the remainder of such term.

Section 2. This article shall be inoperative unless it shall have been ratified as an amendment to the Constitution by the legislatures of three-fourths of the several States within seven years from the date of its submission to the States by the Congress.

Amendment 23

(Ratified March 29, 1961)

Section 1. The District constituting the seat of Government of the United States shall appoint in such manner as the Congress may direct:

A number of electors of President and Vice President equal to the whole number of Senators and Representatives in Congress to which the District would be entitled if it were a State, but in no event more than the least populous State; they shall be in addition to those appointed by the States, but they shall be considered, for the purposes of the election of President and Vice President, to be electors appointed by a State; and they shall meet in the District and perform such duties as provided by the twelfth article of amendment.

Section 2. The Congress shall have power to enforce this article by appropriate legislation.

Amendment 24

(Ratified January 23, 1964)

Section 1. The right of citizens of the United States to vote in any primary or other election for President or Vice President, for electors for President or Vice President, or for Senator or Representative in Congress, shall not be denied or abridged by the United States or any State by reason of failure to pay any poll tax or other tax.

Section 2. The Congress shall have power to enforce this article by appropriate legislation.

Amendment 25

(Ratified February 10, 1967)

Section 1. In case of the removal of the President from office or of his death or resignation, the Vice President shall become President.

Section 2. Whenever there is a vacancy in the office of the Vice President, the President shall nominate a Vice President who shall take office upon confirmation by a majority vote of both Houses of Congress.

Section 3. Whenever the President transmits to the President pro tempore of the Senate and the Speaker of the House of Representatives his written declaration that he is unable to discharge the powers and duties of his office, and until he transmits to them a written declaration to the contrary, such powers and duties shall be discharged by the Vice President as Acting President.

Section 4. Whenever the Vice President and a majority of either the principal officers of the executive departments or of such other body as Congress may by law provide, transmit to the President pro tempore of the Senate and the Speaker of the House of Representatives their written declaration that the President is unable to discharge the powers and duties of his office, the Vice President shall immediately assume the powers and duties of the office as Acting President.

Thereafter, when the President transmits to the President pro tempore of the Senate and the Speaker of the House of Representatives his written declaration that no inability exists, he shall resume the powers and duties of his office unless the Vice President and a majority of either the principal officers of the executive department or of such other body as Congress may by law provide, transmit within four days to the President pro tempore of the Senate and the Speaker of the House of Representatives their written declaration that the President is unable to discharge the powers and duties of his office. Thereupon Congress shall decide the issue, assembling within forty-eight hours for that purpose if not in session. If the Congress, within twenty-one days after receipt of the latter written declaration, or, if Congress is not in session, within twenty-one days after Congress is required to assemble, determines by two-thirds vote of both Houses that the President is unable to discharge the powers and duties of his office, the Vice President shall continue to discharge the same as Acting President; otherwise, the President shall resume the powers and duties of his office.

Amendment 26

(Ratified July 1, 1971)

Section 1. The right of citizens of the United States, who are eighteen years of age or older, to vote shall not be denied or abridged by the United States or by any State on account of age.

Section 2. The Congress shall have power to enforce this article by appropriate legislation.

SELECTED FURTHER READINGS

Alden, John R. *The American Revolution, 1775–1783.* New York: Harper, 1954.

Ammerman, David. *In the Common Cause: American Response to the Coercive Acts of 1774.* Charlottesville: University Press of Virginia, 1974.

Anderson, Fred. *A People's Army: Massachusetts Soldiers and Society in the Seven Years' War.* Chapel Hill: University of North Carolina Press, 1984.

Andrews, Charles M. *The Colonial Background of the American Revolution.* rev. ed. New Haven: Yale University Press, 1931.

Bailyn, Bernard. *Ideological Origins of the American Revolution.* Cambridge, Mass.: Harvard University Press, 1967.

———. *The Origin of American Politics.* New York: Knopf, 1968.

Bakeless, John, and Bakeless, Katherine. *Signers of the Declaration.* Boston: Houghton Mifflin, 1969.

Bancroft, George. *History of the Formation of the Constitution of the United States of America.* New York: D. Appleton, 1885.

Beard, Charles A. *An Economic Interpretation of the Constitution of the United States.* New York: Macmillan, 1913.

Becker, Carl L. *The Declaration of Independence, A Study in the History of Political Ideas.* New York: Harcourt, Brace, 1922.

Bell, Whitfield J. "The Federal Processions of 1788." *New-York Historical Society Quarterly* 46 (January 1962): 5–39.

Benton, William A. *Whig-Loyalism: An Aspect of Political Ideology in the American Revolutionary Era.* Rutherford, N.J.: Fairleigh Dickinson University Press, 1969.

Bernath, Stuart L. "George Washington and the Genesis of American Military Discipline." *Mid-America* 49 (April 1967): 83–100.

Billias, George A., ed. *George Washington's Generals.* New York: W. Morrow, 1964.

Billington, R. A., ed. *The Reinterpretation of Early American History.* San Marino, Calif.: Huntington Library, 1966.

Bloom, Sol. *The Story of the Constitution.* Washington: United States Constitution Sesquicentennial Commission, 1937.

Bowen, Catherine D. *Miracle at Philadelphia: The Story of the Constitutional Convention, May to September, 1787.* Boston: Little, Brown, 1966.

Boyd, Julian P. "The Disputed Authorship of the *Declaration on the Causes and Necessity of Taking up Arms, 1775.*" *Pennsylvania Magazine of History and Biography* 74 (January 1950): 51–73.

Bradsher, James Gregory. "Preserving the Revolution: Civil-Military Relations during the American War for Independence 1775–1783." Ph.D. dissertation, University of Massachusetts, 1984.

Brant, Irving. *James Madison.* 6 vols. Indianapolis: Bobbs-Merrill, 1941–1961.

———. *The Bill of Rights; Its Origin and Meaning.* Indianapolis: Bobbs-Merrill, 1965.

Bridenbaugh, Carl B. *The Spirit of '76: The Growth of American Patriotism Before Independence.* New York: Oxford University Press, 1975.

Brown, Alan S. "The Role of the Army in Western Settlement: Josiah Harmar's Command, 1785–1790." *Pennsylvania Magazine of History and Biography* 93 (April 1969): 161–78.

Brown, Robert E. *Middle-Class Democracy and the Revolution in Massachusetts, 1691–1780.* Ithaca: Cornell University Press, 1955.

———. *Reinterpretation of the Formation of the American Constitution.* Boston: Boston University Press, 1963.

Brundage, Lyle D. "The Organization, Administration and Training of the United States Ordinary and Volunteer Militia 1792–1861." Ph.D. dissertation, University of Michigan, 1959.

Buckley, John E. "The Role of Rhetoric in the Ratification of the Federal Constitution, 1787–88." Ph.D dissertation, Northwestern University, 1972.

Buel, Richard, Jr. *Securing the Revolution: Ideology in American Politics, 1789–1815.* Ithaca: Cornell University Press, 1972.

Burnett, Edmund C. *The Continental Congress.* New York: Macmillan, 1941.

———, ed. *Letters of Members of the Continental Congress.* 8 vols. Washington: Carnegie Institution of Washington, 1921–1936.

Carp, E. Wayne. "The Origins of the Nationalist Movement of 1780–1783: Congressional Administration and the Continental Army." *Pennsylvania Magazine of History and Biography* 107 (July 1983): 263–82.

———. *To Starve the Army, at Pleasure: Continental Army Administration and American Political Culture, 1775–1783.* Chapel Hill: University of North Carolina Press, 1984.

Champagne, Roger. "The Military Association of the Sons of Liberty." *New-York Historical Society Quarterly* 41 (July 1955):338–50.

Chidsey, Donald B. *The Birth of the Constitution, An Informal History.* New York: Crown Publishers, 1964.

Clarfield, Gerard. "Protecting the Frontiers: Defense Policy and the Tariff Question in the First Washington Administration." *William and Mary Quarterly* 3d ser. 32 (July 1975):433–64.

Colburn, H. Trevor. *The Lamp of Experience: Whig History and the Intellectual Origins of the American*

Revolution. Chapel Hill: University of North Carolina Press, 1965.

Collier, James L., and Collier, Christopher. *Decision in Philadelphia: The Constitutional Convention of 1787.* New York: Random House, 1986.

Cometti, Elizabeth. "The Civil Servants of the Revolutionary Period." *Pennsylvania Magazine of History and Biography* 75 (April 1951): 159–69.

Crackel, Theodore J. "The Founding of West Point: Jefferson and the Politics of Security." *Armed Forces and Society* 7 (Summer 1981):529–43.

———. "Jefferson, Politics, and the Army: An Examination of the Military Peace Establishment Act of 1802." Journal of the Early Republic 2 (April 1982):21–37.

Cress, Lawrence Delbert. *Citizens in Arms: The Army and the Militia in American Society to the War of 1812.* Chapel Hill: University of North Carolina Press, 1982.

———. "Republican Liberty and National Security: American Military Policy as an Ideological Problem, 1783 to 1789." *William and Mary Quarterly* 3d ser. 33 (January 1980):73–96.

———. "Radical Whiggery on the Role of the Military: Ideological Roots of the American Revolutionary Militia." *Journal of the History of Ideas* 40 (January–March 1979):43–60.

———. "An Armed Community: The Origins and Meaning of the Right to Bear Arms." *Journal of American History* 71 (June 1984): 22–42.

Cunliffe, Marcus. *Soldiers and Civilians: The Martial Spirit in America, 1775–1865.* Boston: Little, Brown, 1968.

Davies, Wallace E. "The Society of the Cincinnati in New England, 1783–1800." *William and Mary Quarterly* 3d ser. 5 (January 1948):3–25.

Davis, Joseph L. "Sections, Factions, and Political Centralism in the Confederation Period, 1774–1787." Ph.D. dissertation, University of Wisconsin, 1972.

DeConde, Alexander. *The Quasi-War: The Politics and Diplomacy of the Undeclared War with France, 1797–1801.* New York: Charles Scribner's Sons, 1966.

Dickerson, Oliver M. *The Navigation Acts and the American Revolution.* Philadelphia: University of Pennsylvania Press, 1951.

Donahoe, Bernard, and Smelser, Marshall. "The Congressional Power to Raise Armies: The Constitutional and Ratifying Conventions, 1787–1788." *Review of Politics* 33 (April 1971): 202–11.

Douglass, Elisha P. *Rebels and Democrats: The Struggle for Equal Political Rights and Majority Rule During the American Revolution.* Chapel Hill: University of North Carolina Press, 1955.

Dull, Jonathan R. *The French Navy & American Independence: A Study of Arms & Diplomacy.* Princeton: Princeton University Press, 1975.

———. *A Diplomatic History of the American Revolution.* New Haven: Yale University Press, 1985.

Farrand, Max. *The Framing of the Constitution of the United States.* New Haven: Yale University Press, 1936. (First published in 1913.)

———, ed. *The Records of the Federal Convention of 1787.* rev. ed. 4 vols. New Haven: Yale University Press, 1937.

Feer, Robert A. "Shays's Rebellion and the Constitution: A Study in Causation." *New England Quarterly* 42 (September 1969):388–410.

Ferguson, E. James. "The Nationalists of 1781–1783 and the Economic Interpretation of the Constitution." *Journal of American History* 56 (September 1969):241–61.

———. "Business, Government, and Congressional Investigation in the Revolution." *William and Mary Quarterly* 3d ser. 16 (July 1959):293–318.

Ferling, John E. "The New England Soldier: A Study in Changing Perceptions." *American Quarterly* 33 (Spring 1981):26–45.

———. *A Wilderness of Miseries: War & Warriors in Early America.* Westport: Greenwood Press, 1980.

Fernow, Berthold. "Washington's Military Family." *Magazine of American History* 7 (August 1881):81–103.

Ferris, Robert G., ed. *Signers of the Declaration: Historic Places Commemorating the Signing of the Declaration of Independence.* Washington: National Park Service, 1973.

Ford, Paul L., ed. *Essays on the Constitution of the United States, Published During its Discussion by the People, 1787–1788.* Brooklyn: Historical Printing Club, 1892.

———, ed. *Pamphlets on the Constitution of the United States, Published During its Discussion by the People, 1787–1788.* Brooklyn: n.p., 1888.

Ford, Worthington C., ed. *Journals of the Continental Congress, 1774–1789.* 34 vols. Washington: Government Printing Office, 1904–1937.

Fowler, James Henry II. "The Breakdown of Congressional Authority: A Study of the Relations Between the Continental Congress and the States, 1780–1783." Ph.D. dissertation, Ohio State University, 1977.

Fraser, Richard Hobbs. "The Foundations of American Military Policy (1783–1800)." Ph.D. dissertation, University of Oklahoma, 1959.

Furlong, Patrick J. "The Investigation of General Arthur St. Clair, 1792–1793." *Capitol Studies* 5 (Fall 1977): 65–86.

Gaines, William H. J. "The Forgotten Army: Recruiting for a National Emergency." *Virginia Magazine of*

History and Biography 56 (July 1948):267–79.

Gerlach, Don R. "A Note on the Quartering Act of 1774." *New England Quarterly* 39 (March 1966):80–88.

Gerlach, Larry R. "A Delegation of Steady Habits: The Connecticut Representatives to the Continental Congress, 1774–1789." *Connecticut Historical Society Bulletin* 32 (April 1967):33–39.

———. "Soldiers and Citizens: The British Army in New Jersey on the Eve of the Revolution." *New Jersey History* 93 (Spring–Summer 1975): 5–36.

Gipson, Lawrence Henry. *The Coming of the Revolution, 1763–1775*. New York: Harper & Row, 1954.

Godfrey, Carlos E. "Organization of the Provisional Army of the United States in the Anticipated War With France, 1798–1800." *Pennsylvania Magazine of History and Biography* 38 (1914):129–82.

Graham, Gerald S. "Considerations on the War of American Independence." *Institute of Historical Research Bulletin* 22 (May 1949): 22–34.

Greene, Francis Vinton. *The Revolutionary War and the Military Policy of the United States*. New York: Charles Scribner's Sons, 1911.

Greene, Jack P. "The Social Origins of the American Revolution: An Evaluation and an Interpretation." *Political Science Quarterly* 88 (March 1973):1–22.

———. "The Role of the Lower Houses of Assembly in Eighteenth-Century Politics." *Journal of Southern History* 27 (November 1961):451–74.

———. "Political Mimesis: A Consideration of the Historical and Cultural Roots of Legislative Behavior in the British Colonies in the Eighteenth Century." *American Historical Review* 75 (December 1969):337–60.

Hamilton, Alexander. "Some Notes by Alexander Hamilton of Debates in the Federal Convention of 1787." *Massachusetts Historical Society Proceedings* 2d ser. 18 (1903–04): 348–62.

———, Madison, James, and Jay, John. *The Federalist*. Edited by Jacob E. Cooke. Middletown, Conn.: Wesleyan University Press, 1961.

Hawke, David Freeman. *Honorable Treason: The Declaration of Independence and the Men Who Signed It*. New York: Viking Press, 1976.

———. *A Transaction of Free Men: the Birth & Course of the Declaration of Independence*. New York: Scribner's, 1964.

———. *In the Midst of a Revolution*. Philadelphia: University of Pennsylvania Press, 1961.

Henderson, H. James. *Party Politics in the Continental Congress*. New York: McGraw-Hill Book Co., 1974.

Higginbotham, Don R. *The War of American Independence: Military Attitudes, Policies, and Practice, 1763–1789*. New York: Macmillan, 1971.

———. "American Historians and the Military History of the American Revolution." *American Historical Review* 70 (October 1964):18–34.

———, ed. *Reconsiderations on the Revolutionary War: Selected Essays*. Westport: Greenwood Press, 1978.

Hoffman, Ronald, and Albert, Peter J., eds. *Arms and Independence: The Military Character of the American Revolution*. Charlottesville: University Press of Virginia, 1984.

Holcombe, Arthur N. "The Role of Washington in the Framing of the Constitution." *Huntington Library Quarterly* 19 (August 1956):317–34.

Horsman, Reginald. *The Frontier in the Formative Years, 1783–1815*. New York: Holt, Rinehart and Winston, 1970.

———. *Expansion and American Indian Policy, 1783–1812*. East Lansing: Michigan State University Press, 1967.

Hume, Edgar E. "The Role of the Society of the Cincinnati in the Birth of the Constitution of the United States." *Pennsylvania History* 5 (April 1938): 101–07.

Hunt, Agnes. *Provincial Committees of Safety of the American Revolution*. Cleveland: Western Reserve University, 1904.

Jacobs, James R. *The Beginning of the U.S. Army, 1783–1812*. Princeton: Princeton University Press, 1947.

Jameson, John Franklin. "Studies in the History of the Federal Convention of 1787." *American Historical Association Annual Report for 1902*, pp. 87–167.

Jensen, Merrill. *The New Nation: A History of the United States During the Confederation, 1781–1789*. New York: Knopf, 1950.

———. *The Articles of Confederation: An Interpretation of the Social-Constitutional History of the American Revolution, 1774–1781*. Madison: University of Wisconsin Press, 1948.

———. *The Founding of a Nation: A History of the American Revolution, 1763–1776*. New York: Oxford University Press, 1968.

———. *The Making of the American Constitution*. Huntington, N.Y.: R. E. Krieger Co., 1979.

Kammen, Michael. *Empire and Interest: The American Colonies and the Politics of Mercantilism*. Philadelphia: Lippincott, 1970.

Kaplan, Sidney. "Pay, Pensions and Power: Economic Grievances of the Massachusetts Officers of the Revolution." *Boston Public Library Quarterly* 3 (January–April 1951): 15–34, 127–42.

———. "Rank and Status Among Massachusetts Continental Officers." *American Historical Review* 56 (January 1951):318–26.

———. "Veteran Officers and Politics in Massachusetts, 1783–1787." *William and Mary Quarterly* 3d ser. 9

(January 1952):29–57.

Keller, Charles R., and Pierson, George W. "A New Madison Manuscript Relating to the Federal Convention of 1787." *American Historical Review* 36 (October 1930):17–30.

Kenyon, Cecelia M. "Men of Little Faith: The Antifederalists on the Nature of Representative Government." *William and Mary Quarterly* 3d ser. 12 (January 1955):3–43.

———. "Republicanism and Radicalism in the American Revolution: An Old Fashioned Interpretation." *William and Mary Quarterly* 3d ser. 19 (April 1962):153–82.

———, ed. *The Antifederalists*. Indianapolis: Bobbs-Merrill, 1966.

Knollenberg, Bernhard. *Origin of the American Revolution, 1759–1766*. New York: Macmillan, 1960.

Kohn, Richard H. *The Eagle and the Sword: The Federalists and the Creation of the Military Establishment in America 1783–1802*. New York: Free Press, 1975.

Kurtz, Stephen G., comp. *The Federalists—Creators and Critics of the Union, 1780–1801*. New York: Wiley, 1972.

———, and Hutson, James H., eds. *Essays on the American Revolution*. Chapel Hill: University of North Carolina Press, 1973.

Labaree, Benjamin Woods. *The Boston Tea Party*. New York: Oxford University Press, 1964.

Lancaster, Bruce. *From Lexington to Liberty: The Story of the American Revolution*. Garden City: Doubleday, 1955.

Lander, Ernest M. "The South Carolinians at the Philadelphia Convention, 1787." *South Carolina Historical Magazine* 57 (July 1956):134–55.

Lansing, John. *The Delegate from New York; or, Proceedings of the Federal Convention of 1787, from the Notes of John Lansing, Jr.* Edited by Joseph R. Strayer. Princeton: Princeton University Press, 1939.

Leach, Douglas E. *Arms For Empire: A Military History of the British Colonies in North America, 1607–1763*. New York: Macmillan, 1973.

Leder, Lawrence H. *Liberty and Authority: Early American Political Ideology, 1689–1763*. Chicago: Quadrangle Books, 1968.

Lettieri, Ronald, and Wetherell, Charles. "The New Hampshire Committees of Safety and Revolutionary Republicanism, 1775–1784." *Historical New Hampshire* 35 (Fall 1980):241–83.

Libby, Orin G. *The Geographical Distribution of the Vote of the Thirteen States on the Federal Constitution, 1787–8*. Madison: University of Wisconsin, 1894.

Lofgren, Charles A. "Compulsory Military Service Under the Constitution: The Original Understanding." *William and Mary Quarterly* 3d ser. 33 (January 1976):61–88.

Lynd, Staughton. "The Compromise of 1787." *Political Science Quarterly* 81 (June 1966): 225–50.

McDonald, Forrest. *E Pluribus Unum: The Formation of the American Republic 1776–1790*. Boston: Houghton Mifflin, 1965.

———. *We The People: The Economic Origins of the Constitution*. Chicago: University of Chicago Press, 1958.

———. *Novus ordo seclorum: The Intellectual Origins of the Constitution*. Lawrence: University Press of Kansas, 1985.

Mackesy, Piers. *The War for America, 1775–1783*. Cambridge, Mass.: Harvard University Press, 1964.

McLaughlin, Andrew C. *The Confederation and the Constitution, 1783–1789*. New York: Harper, 1905.

———, ed. "Sketch of Charles Pinckney's Plan for a Constitution, 1787." *American Historical Review* 9 (July 1904):735–47.

MacMillan, Margaret Burnham. *The War Governors in the American Revolution*. New York: Columbia University Press, 1943.

Madison, James. *Notes of Debates in the Federal Convention of 1787, Reported by James Madison*. Edited by Adrienne Koch. Athens: Ohio University Press, 1966.

Mahon, John K. *The American Militia: Decade of Decision, 1789–1800*. Gainesville: University of Florida Press, 1960.

———. "Anglo-American Methods of Indian Warfare, 1676–1794." *Mississippi Valley Historical Review* 45 (September 1958):254–75.

Maier, Pauline. *From Resistance to Revolution: Colonial Radicals and the Development of An Opposition to Britain, 1765–1776*. New York: Alfred A. Knopf, 1972.

Main, Jackson T. *Political Parties before the Constitution*. Chapel Hill: University of North Carolina Press, 1973.

———. *The Antifederalists: Critics of the Constitution, 1781–1788*. Chapel Hill: University of North Carolina Press, 1961.

———. *The Social Structure of Revolutionary America*. Princeton: Princeton University Press, 1965.

———. *The Upper House in Revolutionary America, 1763–1788*. Madison: University of Wisconsin Press, 1967.

Marks, Frederick W. "Foreign Affairs: A Winning Issue in the Campaign for the Ratification of the United States Constitution." *Political Science Quarterly* 86 (September 1971):444–69.

Marston, Jerrilyn Greene. "King and Congress: The Transfer of Political Legitimacy from the King to the

Continental Congress, 1774–1776." Ph.D. dissertation, Boston University, 1975.

Martin, James Kirby. *Men in Rebellion: Higher Governmental Leaders and the Coming of the American Revolution.* New Brunswick: Rutgers University Press, 1973.

——, and Lender, Mark Edward. *A Respectable Army: The Military Origins of the Republic, 1763–1789.* Arlington Heights: Harlan Davidson, 1982.

Middlekauff, Robert. *The Glorious Cause: The American Revolution 1763–1789.* New York: Oxford University Press, 1982.

Miller, John C. *Origins of the American Revolution.* Boston: Little, Brown, 1943.

Mitchell, Broadus, and Mitchell, Louise P. *A Biography of the Constitution of the United States: Its Origin, Formation, Adoption, Interpretation.* New York: Oxford University Press, 1964.

Montross, Lynn. *The Reluctant Rebels: the Story of the Continental Congress, 1774–1789.* New York: Harper, 1950.

Morgan, Edmund S. *The Birth of the Republic, 1763–1789.* Chicago: University of Chicago Press, 1956.

——. "The American Revolution: Revisionists in Need of Revising." *William and Mary Quarterly* 3d ser. 14 (January 1957):3–15.

——, and Morgan, Helen M. *The Stamp Act Crisis: Prologue to Revolution.* Chapel Hill: University of North Carolina Press, 1953.

Morison, Samuel Eliot. *The Conservative American Revolution.* Washington: Society of the Cincinnati, 1976.

Morris, Richard B. *The American Revolution Reconsidered.* New York: Harper & Row, 1967.

——. "The Confederation Period and the American Historian." *William and Mary Quarterly* 3d ser. 13 (April 1956):139–56.

——. *Witnesses at the Creation: Hamilton, Madison, Jay, the Constitution.* New York: Holt, Rinehart and Winston, 1985.

Nash, Gary B. *Class and Society in Early America.* Englewood Cliffs: Prentice-Hall, 1970.

Nelson, Paul David. "Citizen Soldiers or Regulars: The Views of American General Officers on the Military Establishment, 1775–1781." *Military Affairs* 43 (October 1979): 126–32.

Nelson, William H. "The Revolutionary Character of the American Revolution." *American Historical Review* 70 (July 1965):998–1014.

Nevins, Allen. *The American States During and After the Revolution, 1775–1789.* New York: Macmillan, 1924.

Olson, Gary D. "Between Independence and Constitution: The Articles of Confederation, 1783–1787." Ph.D. dissertation, University of Nebraska, 1968.

Paterson, William. "Papers of William Paterson on the Federal Convention, 1787." *American Historical Review* 9 (January 1904):310–40.

Pavlovsky, Arnold M. "'Between Hawk and Buzzard': Congress as Perceived by Its Members, 1775–1783." *Pennsylvania Magazine of History and Biography* 101 (July 1977): 349–64.

Peckham, Howard H. *The Colonial Wars, 1689–1762.* Chicago: University of Chicago Press, 1964.

——. *The War for Independence: A Military History.* Chicago: University of Chicago Press, 1958.

——. "Speculations on the Colonial Wars." *William and Mary Quarterly* 3d ser. 17 (October 1960):463–72.

Pierce, William. "Notes of Major William Pierce on the Federal Convention of 1787." *American Historical Review* 3 (January 1898):310–34.

Pole, Jack R. "Historians and the Problem of Early American Democracy." *American Historical Review* 67 (April 1962):626–46.

Proctor, Donald John. "From Insurrection to Independence: The Continental Congress and the Military Launching of the American Revolution." Ph.D. dissertation, University of Southern California, 1965.

Pugh, Robert C. "The Revolutionary Militia in the Southern Campaign, 1780–1781." *William and Mary Quarterly* 3d ser. 14 (April 1957):154–75.

Rakove, Jack N. *The Beginnings of National Politics: An Interpretive History of the Continental Congress.* New York: Alfred A. Knopf, 1979.

Robbins, Caroline. "Decision in '76: Reflections on the 56 Signers." *Proceedings of the Massachusetts Historical Society* 89 (1977):72–87.

Robson, Eric. *The American Revolution in Its Political and Military Aspects, 1763–1783.* New York: Oxford University Press, 1955.

Roche, John P. "The Founding Fathers: A Reform Caucus in Action." *American Political Science Review* 55 (December 1961):799–816.

Rogers, Alan. *Empire and Liberty: American Resistance to British Authority 1755–1763.* Berkeley: University of California Press, 1974.

Rogow, Arnold A. "The Federal Convention: Madison and Yates." *American Historical Review* 60 (January 1955):323–35.

Rolater, Frederick S. "The Continental Congress: A Study in the Origin of American Public Administration, 1774–1781." Ph.D. dissertation, University of Southern California, 1970.

Rossie, Jonathan Gregory. *The Politics of Command in the American Revolution.* Syracuse: Syracuse University Press, 1975.

Rossiter, Clinton L. *Seedtime of the Republic: The Origin of the American Tradition of Political Liberty.*

New York: Harcourt, Brace, 1953.
———. *1787: The Grand Convention.* New York: Macmillan, 1966.
Rowland, John K. "Origins of the Second Amendment: The Creation of the Constitutional Rights of Militia and of Keeping and Bearing Arms." Ph.D. dissertation, Ohio State University, 1978.
Rowland, Kate M. "The Mount Vernon Convention." *Pennsylvania Magazine of History and Biography* 11 (January 1888):410–25.
Royster, Charles W. *A Revolutionary People at War: The Continental Army & American Character, 1775–1783.* Chapel Hill: University of North Carolina Press, 1980.
Rutland, Robert A. *The Ordeal of the Constitution: The Antifederalists and the Ratification Struggle of 1787–1788.* Norman: University of Oklahoma Press, 1966.
———. *The Birth of the Bill of Rights, 1776–1791.* Chapel Hill: University of North Carolina Press, 1955.
Sanders, Jennings B. *The Presidency of the Continental Congress, 1774–1789; a Study in American Institutional History.* Decatur, Ga.: Lindsey Printing Co., 1930.
———. *Evolution of Executive Departments of the Continental Congress, 1774–1789.* Chapel Hill: University of North Carolina Press, 1935.
Saunders, Richard F. "The Origin and Early History of the Society of the Cincinnati: The Oldest Hereditary and Patriotic Association in the United States." Ph.D. dissertation, University of Georgia, 1970.
Schaffel, Kenneth. "The American Board of War 1776–1781." Ph.D. dissertation, City University of New York, 1983.
Schlesinger, Arthur M. "Political Mobs and the American Revolution, 1765–1776." *American Philosophical Society Proceedings* 99 (August 1955):244–50.
Shy, John. *Toward Lexington: The Role of the British Army in the Coming of the American Revolution.* Princeton: Princeton University Press, 1965.
———. *A People Numerous and Armed: Reflections on the Military Struggle for American Independence.* New York: Oxford University Press, 1976.
———. "A New Look at Colonial Militia." *William and Mary Quarterly* 3d ser. 20 (April 1963):175–85.
Smith, Paul H. et al., eds. *Letters of Delegates to Congress, 1774–1789.* Washington: Library of Congress, 1976–.
Sosin, Jack M. *The Revolutionary Frontier, 1763–1783.* New York: Holt, Rinehart and Winston, 1967.
Stagg, J. C. *Mr. Madison's War: Politics, Diplomacy & Warfare in the Early American Republic, 1783–1830.* Princeton: Princeton University Press, 1983.
Stamp Act Congress. *Proceedings of the Congress at New-York (October 7-25, 1765).* Annapolis: J. Green, 1766.
Stout, Neil R. *The Royal Navy in America, 1760–1775: A Study of Enforcement of British Colonial Policy in the Era of the American Revolution.* Annapolis: Naval Institute Press, 1973.
Stuart, Reginald C. *War and American Thought: From the Revolution to the Monroe Doctrine.* Kent: Kent State University Press, 1982.
Taylor, Robert J. "Trial at Trenton." *William and Mary Quarterly* 3d ser. 26 (October 1969):521–47.
Underdal, Stanley J., ed. *Military History of the American Revolution: The Proceedings of the 6th Military History Symposium United States Air Force Academy 10–11 October 1974.* Washington: Office of Air Force History, 1976.
United States National Park Service. *Signers of the Constitution.* Washington: Government Printing Office, 1979.
Van Doren, Carl C. *The Great Rehearsal: The Story of the Making and Ratifying of the Constitution of the United States.* New York: Viking Press, 1948.
Wallace, Willard M. *Appeal to Arms: A Military History of the American Revolution.* New York: Harper and Brothers, 1951.
Ward, Christopher. *The War of the Revolution.* Edited by John R. Alden. 2 vols. New York: Macmillan, 1952.
Ward, Harry M. *The Department of War, 1781–1795.* Pittsburgh: University of Pittsburgh Press, 1962.
White, Leonard D. *The Federalists: A Study in Administrative History.* New York: Macmillan, 1948.
———. *The Jeffersonians: A Study in Administrative History.* New York: Macmillan, 1951.
Wood, Gordon S. *The Creation of the American Republic, 1776–1787.* Chapel Hill: University of North Carolina Press, 1969.
———. "Rhetoric and Reality in the American Revolution." *William and Mary Quarterly* 3d ser. 23 (January 1966): 3–32.
Wright, Robert K., Jr. *The Continental Army.* Washington: Government Printing Office, 1983.
Yates, Abraham. "Abraham Yates's History of the Movement for the United States Constitution." Edited by Staughton Lynd. *William and Mary Quarterly* 3d ser. 20 (April 1963):223–45.
Young, Alfred F. *The Democratic Republicans of New York: The Origins, 1763–1797.* Chapel Hill: University of North Carolina Press, 1967.
Zobel, Hiller B. *The Boston Massacre.* New York: W.W. Norton Co., 1970.
Zuckerman, Michael. *Peaceable Kingdoms: New England Towns in the Eighteenth Century.* New York: Knopf, 1970.

PIN : 061580-000

☆ U. S. GOVERNMENT PRINTING OFFICE : 1992 O - 304-301 QL 3